road
atlas

USA | CANADA | MEXICO

ROAD MAPS are organized geographically. United States, Canada, and Mexico road maps are organized in a grid layout, starting in the northwest of each country. To find your way, use either the **Key to Map Pages** inside the front cover, the **Listing of State and City Maps** on page 3, or the **index** in the back of the atlas.

COUNTRY COLORS
Colors represent countries throughout the atlas.
Red → Canada
Green → Mexico
Blue → United States
Purple → United States (Northeast Corridor)

MAP SCALES
Scale bars are shown at a constant length throughout the atlas for quick and easy scale comparison between regions.

DRIVING DISTANCES
Use this chart to check driving distances between major cities within each map. Refer to distance and driving time information at the back of the atlas for travel over greater distances.

LOCATOR MAPS
A quick glance at this miniature map lets you check which states and/or provinces are shown on each page.

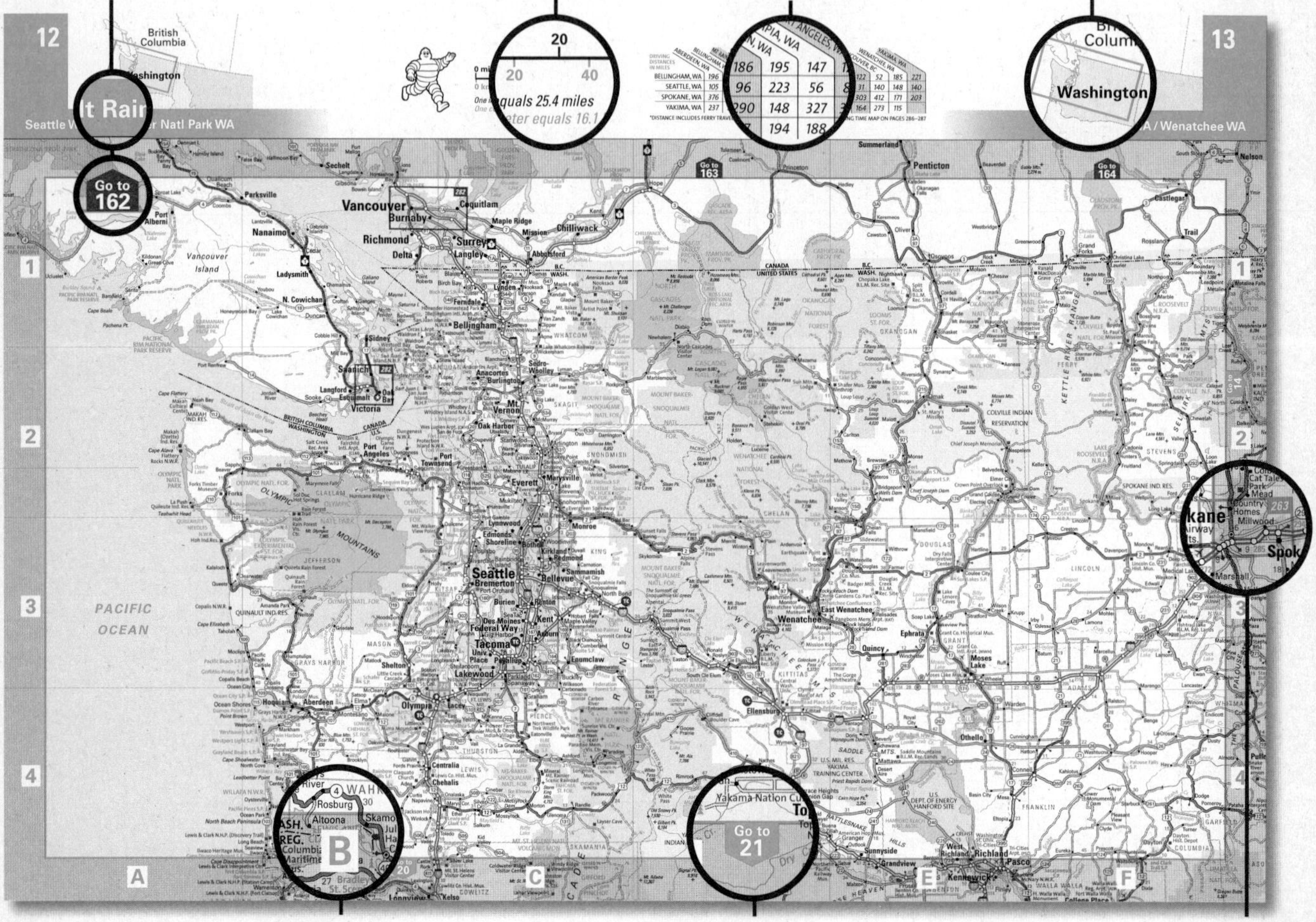

GRID REFERENCES
Use grid references to locate places listed in the index. For instance, Rosburg WA is listed in the index with "12" and "B4", indicating that the town may be found on page 12 in grid square B4.

"GO TO" POINTERS
Handy page tabs point the way to the next map, making navigation a breeze.

INSET MAP BOXES
These color-coded boxes outline areas that are featured in greater detail in the index section. The tab with "263" (above) indicates that a detailed map of Spokane may be found on page 263 (below).

HOW THE INDEX WORKS
Cities and towns are listed alphabetically, with separate indexes for the United States, Canada, and Mexico. Figures after entries indicate population, page number, and grid reference. Entries in bold color indicate cities with detailed inset maps. The U.S. index also includes counties and parishes, which are shown in bold black type.

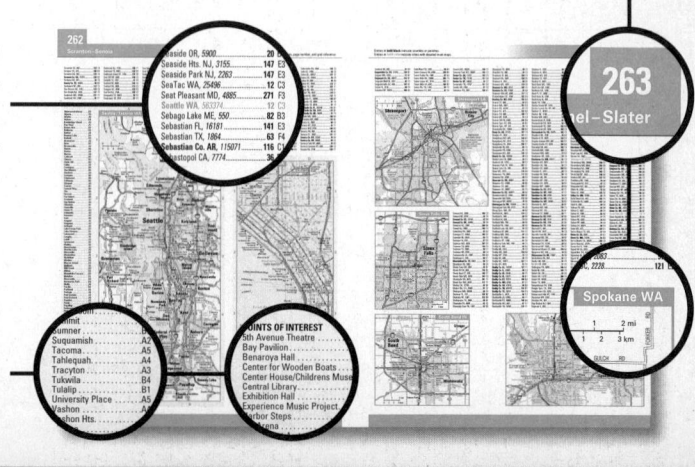

INSET MAP INDEXES
Many inset maps have their own indexes. Metro area inset map indexes list cities and towns; downtown inset map indexes list points of interest.

One inch equals 217 miles
One centimeter equals 138 kilometers

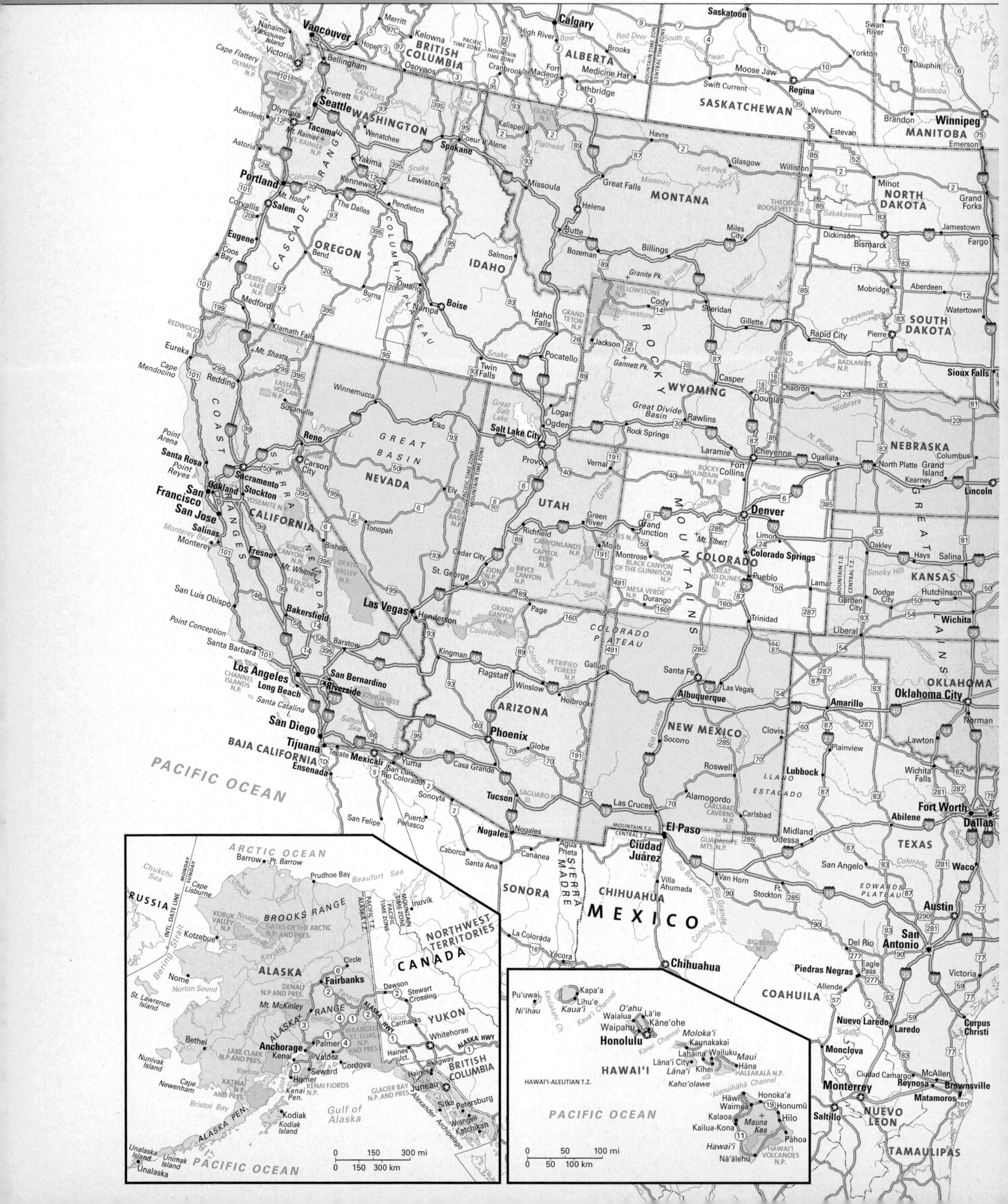

United States Interstate Map

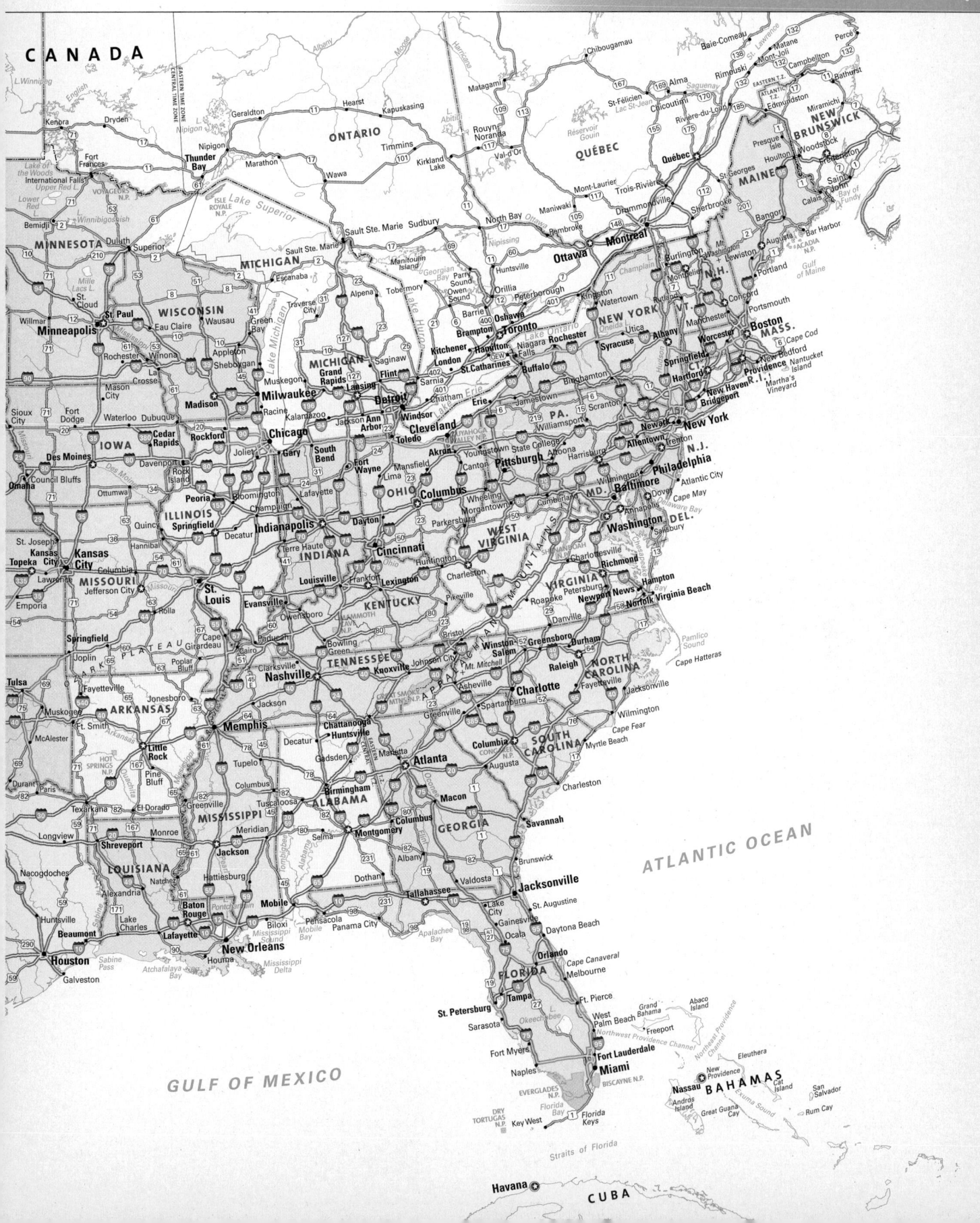

Canada Highway Map

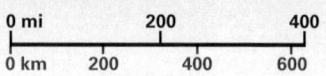

0 mi   200   400

0 km   200   400   600

One inch equals 250 miles/Un pouce équivaut à 250 milles
One cm equals 159 km/Un cm équivaut à 159 km

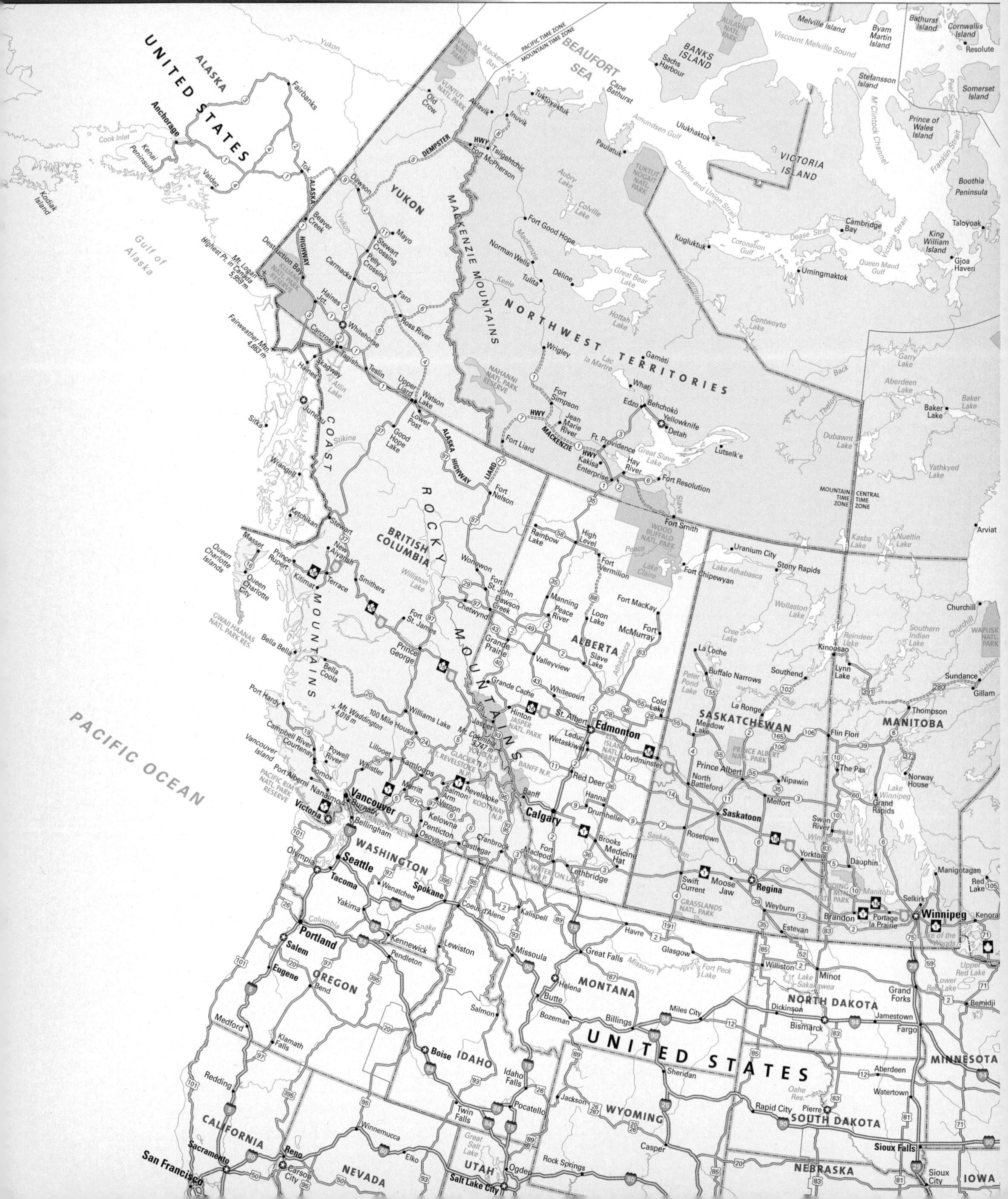

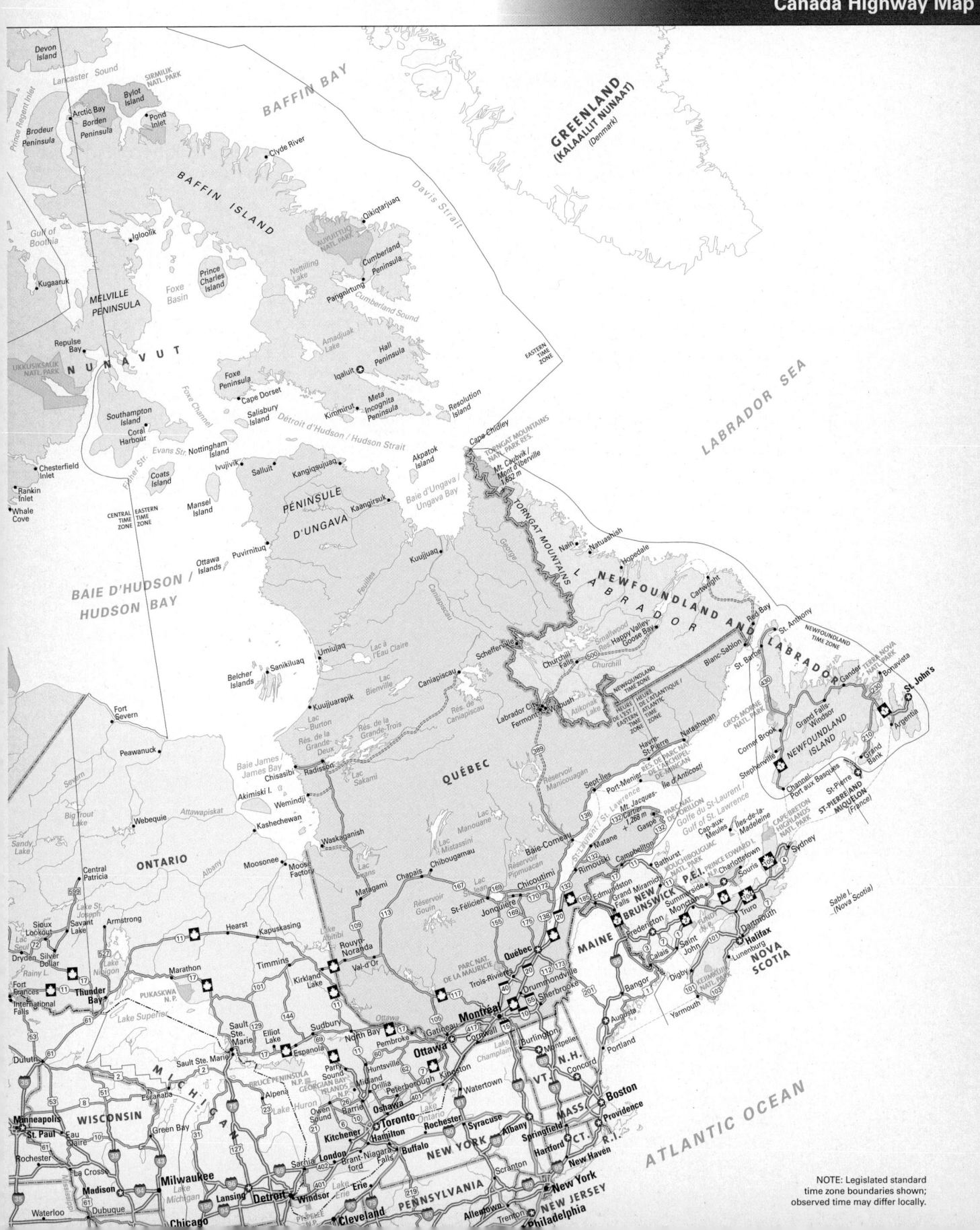

Experience the thrill of the open roads of North America with these great Scenic Drives from Michelin. The famous star ratings highlight natural and cultural attractions along the way.

★★★ **Highly recommended**
★★ **Recommended**
★ **Interesting**

Michelin Scenic Drives are indicated by a green and yellow dashed line (▬▬▬▬) on corresponding atlas maps for easy reference. The following 17 drives are also plotted for your use.

Note that sections of the routes described, particularly those through high elevations or wilderness areas, may be closed in winter.

ABBREVIATIONS			
N	North	NHS	National Historic Site
E	East	NL	National Lakeshore
S	South	NM	National Memorial/
W	West		National Monument
NE	Northeast	NMP	National Military Park
NW	Northwest	NP	National Park
SE	Southeast	NPR	National Park Reserve
SW	Southwest	NRA	National Recreation Area
Hwy.	Highway	NWR	National Wildlife Refuge
Pkwy.	Parkway	PP	Provincial Park
Rte.	Route	SHP	State Historical Park
Mi	Miles	SHS	State Historic Site
Km	Kilometers	SP	State Park
Sq Ft	Square Feet	SR	State Reserve
		VC	Visitor Center

For detailed coverage of the attractions, and for suggestions of places to dine and stay overnight, see the Michelin **Green Guide Collection**, the ultimate guidebooks for the independent traveler.

NORTHWEST

Anchorage/Fairbanks/Denali★★★
892 miles/1,436 kilometers   Maps 189, 154, 155

From **Anchorage★**, Alaska's largest city, take Rte. 1 (Glenn Hwy. and Tok Cutoff) N and then E through the broad Matanuska Valley to the small town of **Tok**. The route passes agricultural communities, the **Matanuska Glacier** and the Wrangell Mountains before heading up the Copper River Basin. From Tok, take the Alaska Hwy. (Rte. 2) NW to **Fairbanks★**, a friendly town with a frontier feel. The road passes the **Trans-Alaska Pipeline** and **Big Delta SHP** then parallels the Tanana River. From Fairbanks, opt for Rte. 3 W that crosses the river at Nenana, then veers S to **Denali NP★★★**, home of spruce forests, grassy tundra, grizzlies, moose and North America's highest peak, **Mount McKinley** (20,320ft). Return S to Anchorage via Rtes. 3 and 1.

Badlands NP

Badlands★★
164 miles/264 kilometers   Maps 253, 26

From **Rapid City★**, South Dakota, drive SE on Rte. 44 through Farmingdale and Scenic, then east to Interior. To enter **Badlands NP★★**, take Rte. 377 NE 2mi to Cedar Pass and stop at the park's **Ben Reifel VC**. From there, **Cliff Shelf Nature Trail★★** (.5mi) is popular for its shady juniper trees and **Castle Trail★★★** (5mi) is spectacular in early morning when the moonscape valley and pointed spires get first light. Turn left onto Rte. 240, **Badlands Loop Road★★★**, along the northern rim, where prairie grasslands give way to buttes and hoodoos. **Pinnacles Overlook★★** is a sweeping viewpoint to the south. Drive N to I-90, and cross the interstate N to the town of Wall. On Main St. visit **Wall Drug★**, a "drug store" tourist attraction with over 20 shops filled with historical photos, cowboy regalia, wildlife exhibits and Western art displayed in five dining rooms. In the backyard a roaring, 80ft **Tyrannosaurus** sends toddlers running. Leave Wall on I-90, driving W. Take Exit 67 to Ellsworth Air Force Base, where the **South Dakota Air and Space Museum** displays a B-1 bomber and other aircraft. Continue W on I-90 back to Rapid City to conclude the tour.

Black Hills★★
244 miles/393 kilometers   Maps 253, 26, 25

From **Rapid City★**, drive S on US-16 then US-16A S past Keystone. Take Rte. 244 W to **Mount Rushmore NM★★**. Continue W on Rte. 244 to the junction of US-16/385. En route S to Custer, **Crazy Horse Memorial★★** honors the famous Sioux chief. From Custer, head S on US-385 through Pringle to the junction of Rte. 87. Take Rte. 87 N through **Wind Cave NP★★** and into **Custer SP★★**. Follow **Wildlife Loop Road★★** (access S of Blue Bell, across from Rte. 342 junction) E and N to US-16A. Then travel W to join scenic **Needles Highway★★** (Rte. 87) NW to US-16/385 N. Where US-16 separates, continue N on US-385 to **Deadwood★★**, a former gold camp. Turn left onto US-14A, driving SW through **Lead★**, site of the former **Homestake Gold Mine★★**, to Cheyenne Crossing. Drive N on US-14A to I-90, turning SE back to Rapid City.

Columbia River Gorge★★
83 miles/134 kilometers   Maps 251, 20, 21

From **Portland★★**, Oregon's largest city, take I-84 E to Exit 17 in Troutdale. There, head E on the winding **Historic Columbia River Highway★★** (US-30), which skirts the steep cliffs above the river. For great **views★★**, stop at **Vista House at Crown Point★**. You'll pass the 620ft **Multnomah Falls★★** and moss-draped **Oneonta Gorge**. At Ainsworth State Park (Exit 35), rejoin I-84 and travel E to Mosier (Exit 69), where US-30, with its hairpin turns, begins again. Continue E on US-30, stopping at **Rowena Crest Viewpoint★★** for grand vistas—and wildflowers. Just past the Western-style town called **The Dalles**, take US-197 N to conclude the tour at **The Dalles Lock and Dam VC★**.

Grand Tetons/Yellowstone★★★
224 miles/361 kilometers   Map 24

Note: parts of this tour are closed in winter.

From **Jackson★★**, drive N on US-26 to Moose. Turn left onto Teton Park Rd. to access **Grand Teton NP★★★** and **Jenny Lake Scenic Drive★★★**. From Teton Park Rd., drive N to the junction of US-89/191/287 (**John D. Rockefeller Jr. Memorial Pkwy.**) and follow the parkway N into **Yellowstone NP★★★** to **West Thumb**. Take Grand Loop Rd. W to **Old Faithful★★★**, the world's most famous geyser. Continue N on the Grand Loop Rd., passing **Norris Geyser Basin★★** en route to **Mammoth Hot Springs★★★**. Turn E on Grand Loop Rd. to Tower Junction, then S into the **Grand Canyon of the Yellowstone★★★**. Continue S from Canyon Village through **Hayden Valley★★** to Lake Junction. Head SW, back to West Thumb, to conclude the tour.

Pacific Coast/Olympic Peninsula★★★
419 miles/675 kilometers   Maps 245, 12

From the Washington state capital of **Olympia**, drive N on US-101 (Pacific Coast Scenic Byway) to Discovery Bay. Detour on Rte. 20 NE to **Port Townsend★★**, a Victorian seaport. From Discovery Bay, head W on US-101 through **Port Angeles** to the **Heart O' the Hills** park entrance for **Olympic NP★★★** to see **Hurricane Ridge★★**. Back on US-101, head E then S to the park entrance leading to **Hoh Rain Forest★★★**. Follow US-101 S, then E after Queets to **Lake Quinault★**, home to bald eagles, trumpeter swans and loons. Continue S on US-101 to Aberdeen, taking Rte. 105 to the coast. At Raymond, return to US-101 S to **Long Beach**. Follow Rte. 103 N past the former cannery town of **Oysterville** to **Leadbetter Point★** on Willapa Bay, where oysters are still harvested. Return S to **Ilwaco** and drive E and S on US-101 to **Astoria★**, Oregon to end the tour.

The Oregon Coast★★
368 miles/592 kilometers   Maps 20, 28

Leave **Astoria★**, Oregon's first settlement, via US-101, heading SW. **Fort Clatsop National Memorial★★** recalls Lewis and Clark's historic stay. **Cannon Beach★** boasts a sandy **beach★** and tall coastal rock. At the farm community of **Tillamook★**, go west on 3rd St. to **Cape Meares** to begin **Three Capes Scenic Drive★★**. Continue S, rejoining US-101 just beyond Pacific City. Drive S on US-101 through **Newport★**, then **Yachats★**, which neighbors **Cape Perpetua Scenic Area★★**. From **Florence** to **Coos Bay★** stretches **Oregon Dunes National Recreation Area★★**. At Coos Bay, take Cape Arago Hwy. W to see the gardens of **Shore Acres State Park★**. Drive S on Seven Devils Hwy. and Beaver Hill Rd. to rejoin US-101. Pass **Bandon★**, known for its cheese factory, and **Port Orford**, with its fishing fleet. Farther S, **Boardman State Park★** shelters Sitka spruce, Douglas fir and **Natural Bridge Cove**. End the tour at **Brookings**.

Oregon Coast at Bandon

SOUTHWEST

Big Bend Area★★
581 miles/935 kilometers   Maps 211, 56, 57, 62, 60

Head S from **El Paso**★ via I-10, then E to Kent. Take Rte. 118 S to Alpine, passing **McDonald Observatory**★★ (telescope tours) and **Fort Davis NHS**★★. Continue S to Study Butte to enter **Big Bend NP**★★★, edged by the Rio Grande River and spanning 1,252sq mi of spectacular canyons, lush bottomlands, sprawling desert and mountain woodlands. The park has more species of migratory and resident birds than any other national park. Travel E on Maverick Dr. to the main VC at **Panther Junction** in the heart of the park (US-385 and Rio Grande Village Dr.). Then take US-385 N to Marathon. Turn E on US-90 to Langtry, site of **Judge Roy Bean VC**★. Continue E to **Seminole Canyon SP**★★, with its 4,000-year-old pictographs. Farther E, **Amistad NRA**★★ is popular for water sports. Continue on US-90 to conclude the tour in Del Rio.

Canyonlands of Utah★★★
481 miles/774 kilometers   Maps 39, 40

From **St. George**★, drive NE on I-15 to Exit 16. Take Rte. 9 E to Springdale, gateway to **Zion NP**★★★, with its sandstone canyon, waterfalls and hanging gardens. Continue E on Rte. 9 to Mt. Carmel Junction, turn left onto US-89 and head N to the junction with Rte. 12. Take Rte. 12 SE to **Bryce Canyon NP**★★★, with its colored rock formations. Continue SE on Rte. 12 to Cannonville, then S on Kodachrome Dr. to **Kodachrome Basin SP**★★, where sandstone chimneys rise from the desert floor. Return to Cannonville, and drive NE on Rte. 12 through Boulder to Torrey. Take Rte. 24 E through **Capitol Reef NP**★★—with its unpaved roads and trails—then N to I-70. Travel E on I-70 to Exit 182, then S on US-191 to Rte. 313 into **Canyonlands NP**★★★ to **Grand View Point Overlook**. Return to US-191, turning S to access **Arches NP**★★★— the greatest concentration of natural stone arches in the country. Continue S on US-191 to **Moab** to end the tour.

Arches NP

Central Coast/Big Sur★★★
118 miles/190 kilometers   Maps 236, 44

From **Cannery Row**★ in **Monterey**★★, take Prescott Ave. to Rte. 68. Turn right and continue to Pacific Grove Gate (on your left) to begin scenic **17-Mile Drive**★★, a private toll road. Exit at Carmel Gate to reach the upscale artists' colony of **Carmel**★★, site of Carmel **mission**★★★. The town's **Scenic Road** winds S along the beachfront. Leave Carmel by Hwy. 1 S. Short, easy trails at **Point Lobos SR**★★ line the shore. Enjoy the wild beauty of the **Big Sur**★★★ coastline en route to San Simeon, where **Hearst Castle**★★★, the magnificent estate of a former newspaper magnate, overlooks the Pacific Ocean. Continue S on Hwy. 1 to **Morro Bay**, where the tour ends.

Colorado Rockies★★★
499 miles/803 kilometers   Maps 209, 41, 33, 40
Note: US-34 (Trail Ridge Rd.) and Rte. 82 S of Leadville to Aspen are closed mid-Oct to Memorial Day due to snow.

From **Golden**★, W of **Denver**★★★, drive W on US-6 along Clear Creek to Rte. 119, heading N on the **Peak to Peak Highway**★★ to **Nederland**★. Continue N on Rte. 72, then follow Rte. 7 N to the town of **Estes Park**★. Take US-36 to enter **Rocky Mountain NP**★★★. Drive **Trail Ridge Road**★★★ (US-34) W and S to the town of **Grand Lake**★. Continue S to Granby, turn left on US-40 to I-70 at Empire. Head W on I-70 past **Georgetown**★★ and through **Eisenhower Tunnel**. You'll pass ski areas **Arapahoe Basin**, **Keystone Resort**★ and **Breckenridge**★★. At Exit 195 for **Copper Mountain Resort**★, take Rte. 91 S to **Leadville**★★, Colorado's former silver capital. Then travel S on US-24 to Rte. 82 W over **Independence Pass**★★ to **Aspen**★★★. Head NW to I-70, passing **Glenwood Springs**★★ with its **Hot Springs Pool**★★. Drive E on I-70 along **Glenwood Canyon**★★ and the Colorado River to **Vail**★★. Continue E on I-70 to the old mining town of **Idaho Springs** to return to Golden via Rte. 119.

Lake Tahoe

Lake Tahoe Loop★★
71 miles/114 kilometers   Map 37

Begin in **Tahoe City** at the intersection of Rtes. 89 and 28. Drive S on Rte. 89. **Ed Z'berg-Sugar Pine Point State Park**★ encompasses a promontory topped by the **Hellman-Ehrman Mansion**★ and other historic buildings. Farther S, **Emerald Bay State Park**★★ surrounds beautiful **Emerald Bay**★★. At the bay's tip stands **Vikingsholm**★★, a mansion that resembles an ancient Nordic castle. At **Tallac Historic Site**★, preserved summer estates recall Tahoe's turn-of-the-19C opulence. From Tahoe Valley, take Rte. 50 NE. **South Lake Tahoe**, the lake's largest town, offers lodging, dining and shopping. High-rise hotel-casinos characterize neighboring **Stateline** in Nevada. Continue N to Spooner Junction. Then follow Nevada Rte. 28 N to **Sand Harbor** (7mi), where picnic tables and a sandy beach fringe a sheltered cove. Continue through Kings Beach to end the tour at Tahoe City.

Maui's Hana Highway★★
62 miles/100 kilometers   Map 153

Leave **Kahului** on Rte. 36 E toward **Paia**, an old sugar-plantation town. Continue E on Rte. 36, which becomes Rte. 360, the **Hana Highway**★★. The road passes **Ho'okipa Beach Park**, famous for windsurfing, and **Puohokamoa Falls**, a good picnic stop, before arriving in **Hana**, a little village on an attractive bay. If adventurous, continue S on the Hana Highway to **Ohe'o Gulch**★★ in **Haleakala NP**★★★, where small waterfalls tumble from the SE flank of the dormant volcano Haleakala. Past the gulch, the grave of aviator **Charles Lindbergh** can be found in the churchyard at Palapala Hoomau Hawaiian Church. End the tour at Kipahulu.

Redwood Empire★★
182 miles/293 kilometers   Maps 36, 28

In **Leggett**, S of the junction of Hwy. 1 and US-101, go N on US-101 to pass through a massive redwood trunk at **Chandelier Drive-Thru Tree Park**. To the N, see breathtaking groves along 31mi **Avenue of the Giants**★★★. **Humboldt Redwoods SP**★★ contains **Rockefeller Forest**★★★, the world's largest virgin redwood forest. From US-101, detour W on Rte. 211 to **Ferndale**★, a quaint Victorian village. N. along US-101, **Eureka**★ preserves a logging camp cookhouse and other historic sites. The sleepy fishing town of **Trinidad**★ is home to a marine research lab. **Patrick's Point SP**★★ offers dense forests, agate-strewn beaches and clifftop **views**★★. At **Orick**, enter the **Redwood National and State Parks**★★, which protect a 379ft-high **tree**★. The tour ends in **Crescent City**.

Santa Fe Area★★★
267 miles/430 kilometers   Maps 189, 48, 260, 49

From **Albuquerque**★, drive E on I-40 to Exit 175 and take Rte. 14, the **Turquoise Trail**★★, N to **Santa Fe**★★★. This 52mi back road runs along the scenic Sandia Mountains and passes dry washes, arroyos and a series of revived "ghost towns." Continue N on US-84/285, turning NE onto Rte. 76, the **High Road to Taos**★★. East of Vadito, take Rte. 518 N to Rte. 68 N into the rustic Spanish colonial town of **Taos**★★, a center for the arts. Head N on US-64 to the junction of Rte. 522. Continue W on US-64 for an 18mi round-trip detour to see the 1,200ft-long, three-span **Rio Grande Gorge Bridge** over the river. Return to Rte. 522 and take this route, part of the **Enchanted Circle**★★ Scenic Byway, N to **Questa**, starting point for rafting trips on the Rio Grande. Turn onto Rte. 38, heading E to the mining town of **Eagle Nest**. There, detour 23mi E on US-64 to **Cimarron**, a Wild West haunt. Back at Eagle Nest, travel SW on US-64, detouring on Rte. 434 S to the resort town of **Angel Fire**. Return to Taos on US-64 W to end the tour.

Sedona/Grand Canyon NP★★★
482 miles/776 kilometers   Maps 249, 54, 47, 213

Drive N from **Phoenix**★ on I-17 to Exit 298 and take Rte. 179 N toward **Sedona**★★ in the heart of **Red Rock Country**★★★. The red-rock formations are best accessed by four-wheel-drive vehicle via 12mi **Schnebly Hill Road**★ (off Rte. 179, across Oak Creek bridge from US-89A "Y" junction), which offers splendid **views**★★★. Then head N on Rte. 89A through Sedona to begin the 14mi drive of **Oak Creek Canyon**★★. Continue N on Rte. 89A and I-17 to **Flagstaff**★, commercial hub for the region. Take US-180 NW to Rte. 64, which leads N to the **South Rim**★★★ of **Grand Canyon NP**★★★. Take the shuttle (or drive, if permitted) along **West Rim Drive**★★ to **Hermits Rest**★. Then travel **East Rim Drive**★★★ (Rte. 64 E) to **Desert View Watchtower**★ for **views**★★★ of the canyon. Continue to the junction with US-89 at Cameron. Return S to Flagstaff, then S to Phoenix via I-17.

Grand Canyon NP

The Berkshires★★★

57 miles/92 kilometers   Map 94

From **Great Barrington** take US-23 E to Monterey, turning left onto Tyringham Rd., which becomes Monterey Rd., to experience scenic **Tyringham Valley★**. Continue N on Main Rd. to Tyringham Rd., leading to **Lee**, famous for its marble. Then go NW on US-20 to **Lenox★**, with its inviting inns and restaurants. Detour on Rte. 183 W to **Tanglewood★**, site of a popular summer music festival. Return to Lenox and drive N on US-7 to **Pittsfield**, the commercial capital of the region. Head W on US-20 to enjoy **Hancock Shaker Village★★★**, a museum village relating the history of a Shaker community established here in 1790. Rte. 41 S passes West Stockbridge, then take Rte. 102 SE to **Stockbridge★★** and its picturesque **Main Street★**. Follow US-7 S to the junction with Rte. 23, passing **Monument Mountain★** en route. Return to Great Barrington.

Cape Cod★★★

164 miles/264 kilometers   Maps 151, 95

At US-6 and Rte. 3, cross **Cape Cod Canal** via Sagamore Bridge and turn onto Rte. 6A to tour the Cape's **North Shore★★**. Bear right onto Rte. 130 to reach **Sandwich★**, famous for glass manufacture. Continue on Rte. 6A E to **Orleans**. Take US-6 N along **Cape Cod National Seashore★★★**, with its wooded and marshland trails, to reach **Provincetown★★**, a resort town offering **dune tours★★** and summer theater. Return to Orleans and take Rte. 28 S through **Chatham★**, then W to **Hyannis**, where ferries depart for **Nantucket★★★**. Continue to quaint **Falmouth★**. Take Surf Rd., which becomes Oyster Pond Rd. to nearby **Woods Hole**, a world center for marine research and departure point for ferries to **Martha's Vineyard★★**. Take Woods Hole Rd. N to Rte. 28. Cross the canal via Bourne Bridge and head E on US-6 to end the tour at Rte. 3.

Maine Coast★★

238 miles/383 kilometers   Maps 82, 251, 83

From **Kittery**, drive N on US-1 to **York★**, then along US-1A to see the 18C buildings of **Colonial York★★**. Continue N on coastal US-1A; rejoin US-1 at Cape Neddick and continue N through **Ogunquit★**. Turn right at Rte. 9 and drive to **Kennebunkport★**, with its colorful shops. Take Rte. 9A/35 to **Kennebunk**. Then travel N on US-1 to **Portland★★**, Maine's largest city, where the **Old Port★★** brims with galleries and boutiques. Take US-1 N through the outlet town of **Freeport**, then on to **Brunswick**, home of Bowdoin College. Turn NE through **Bath★**, **Wiscasset**, **Rockland**, **Camden★★**, **Searsport** and **Bucksport**. At Ellsworth, take Rte. 3 S to enter **Acadia NP★★★** on **Mount Desert Island★★★**, where **Park Loop Road★★★** *(closed in winter)* parallels open coast. From the top of **Cadillac Mountain**, the **views★★★** are breathtaking. The tour ends at **Bar Harbor★**, a popular resort village.

Bar Harbor from Cadillac Mountain

Mohawk Valley★

114 miles/184 kilometers   Maps 188, 94, 80

From the state capital of **Albany★**, take I-90 NW to Exit 25 for I-890 into **Schenectady**, founded by Dutch settlers in 1661. Then follow Rte. 5 W along the Mohawk River. In Fort Hunter, **Schoharie Crossing SHS★** stretches along the Erie Canal towpath. Near Little Falls, **Herkimer Home SHS** (Rte. 169 at Thruway Exit 29A) interprets colonial farm life. Rte. 5 continues W along the Erie Canal to **Utica**. From Utica, drive W on Rte. 49 to **Rome**, where the river turns N and peters out. The tour ends in Rome, site of **Fort Stanwix NM★**.

South Shore Lake Superior★

530 miles/853 kilometers   Maps 211, 64, 65, 69

Sections of County Road H-58 through Pictured Rocks NL will close for paving through 2010. Detours will be in effect. From **Duluth★**, drive SE on I-535/US-53 to the junction of Rte. 13 at Parkland. Follow Rte. 13 E to quaint **Bayfield**, gateway to **Apostle Islands NL★★**, accessible by boat. Head S to the junction of US-2, and E through Ashland, Ironwood and Wakefield. There, turn left onto Rte. 28, heading NE to Bergland, and turning left onto Rte. 64. Drive N to Silver City and take Rte. M-107 W into **Porcupine Mountains Wilderness SP★**. Return to Rte. 64 and go E to Ontonagon. Take Rte. 38 SE to Greenland, then follow Rte. 26 NE to Houghton. Cross to Hancock on US-41 and continue NE to Phoenix. Turn left onto Rte. 26 to Eagle River and on to Copper Harbor via **Brockway Mountain Drive★★**. Return S to Houghton via US-41, then travel S and E past Marquette, turning left onto Rte. 28. Head E to Munising, then take County Road H-58 E and N through **Pictured Rocks NL★**. End the tour at Grand Marais.

Villages of Southern Vermont★★

118 miles/190 kilometers   Map 81

Head N from the resort town of **Manchester★** by Rte. 7A. At Manchester Center, take Rte. 11 E past **Bromley Mountain** ski area, to Londonderry. Detour N on Rte. 100 to **Weston★**. Continue on Rte. 11 to **Chester**, turning right onto Rte. 35 S to reach **Grafton★**, with its **Old Tavern**. Farther S, Rte. 30 S from Townshend leads to **Newfane** and its lovely village **green★**. Return to Townshend, then travel W, following Rte. 30 through West Townshend, passing **Stratton Mountain** en route to Manchester. S of Manchester by Rte. 7A, the crest of Mt. Equinox is accessible via **Equinox Skyline Drive** (fee). Then continue S on Rte. 7A to end the tour at **Arlington**, known for its trout fishing.

The White Mountains★★★

127 miles/204 kilometers   Map 81

From the all-season resort of **Conway**, drive N on Rte. 16 to **North Conway★**. Continue N on US-302/Rte. 16 through **Glen**, passing **Glen Ellis Falls★** and **Pinkham Notch★★** en route to Glen House. There, drive the **Auto Road** to the top of **Mount Washington★★★** (or take a guided van tour). Head N on Rte. 16 to Gorham, near the Androscoggin River, then W on US-2 to Jefferson Highlands. Travel SW on Rte. 115 to Carroll, then S on US-3 to Twin Mountain. Go SW on US-3 to join I-93. Head S on I-93/Rte. 3, passing scenic **Franconia Notch★★★** and **Profile Lake★★**. Bear E on Rte. 3 where it separates from the interstate to visit **The Flume★★**, a natural gorge 90ft deep. Rejoin I-93S to the intersection with Rte. 112. Head E on Rte. 112 through **Lincoln** on the **Kancamagus Highway★★★** until it joins Rte. 16 back to Conway.

Blue Ridge Parkway★★

574 miles/924 kilometers   Maps 102, 112, 111, 190, 121

Note: Sections of Skyline Drive and the Blue Ridge Parkway may be closed in winter due to weather conditions. The Parkway will be closed for repairs between Mount Mitchell SP and Asheville through 2008; a detour via Rte. 80 and I-40 will be in effect.

From **Front Royal**, take US-340 S to begin **Skyline Drive★★**, the best-known feature of **Shenandoah NP★★**. The drive follows former Indian trails along the **Blue Ridge Parkway★★**. **Marys Rock Tunnel to Rockfish Gap Entrance Station★★** passes the oldest rock in the park and **Big Meadows★**. The Drive ends at **Rockfish Gap** at I-64, but continue S on the **Blue Ridge Parkway★★**. From Terrapin Hill Overlook, detour 16mi W on Rte. 130 to see **Natural Bridge★★**. Enter NC at **Cumberland Knob**, then pass **Blowing Rock★**, **Grandfather Mountain★★** and **Linville Falls★**. Detour 4.8mi to **Mount Mitchell SP★** to drive to the top of the tallest mountain (6,684ft) E of the Mississippi. At mile 382, the **Folk Art Center** stocks high-quality regional crafts. Popular **Biltmore Estate★★** in **Asheville★** (North Exit of US-25, then 4mi N) includes formal **gardens★★**. The stretch from **French Broad River to Cherokee** courses 17 tunnels within two national forests. **Looking Glass Rock★★** is breathtaking. The Parkway ends at **Cherokee**, gateway to **Great Smoky Mountains NP★★★**.

Central Kentucky★★

379 miles/610 kilometers   Maps 230, 100, 214, 227, 110

From **Louisville★★**, home of the **Kentucky Derby★★★**, take I-64 E to **Frankfort★★**, the state capital. Continue E to **Lexington★★**, heart of **Bluegrass Country★★** with its rolling meadows and white-fenced horse farms. Stop at the **Kentucky Horse Park★★★** (4089 Iron Works Pkwy.) for the twice-daily **Parade of Breeds**. Then head S on I-75 through Richmond to the craft center/college town of **Berea★**. Return to Lexington and from US-60 follow the Blue Grass Parkway SW to Exit 25. There, US-150 W leads to Bardstown, site of **My Old Kentucky Home SP★★**, immortalized by **Stephen Foster** in what is now the state song. Drive S from Bardstown on US-31E past **Abraham Lincoln Birthplace NHS★**. Turn right onto Rte. 70 to Cave City, then take US-31W to Park City, gateway to **Mammoth Cave NP★★★**, which features the world's longest cave system. Return to Louisville via I-65 to end the tour.

Florida's Northeast Coast★★

174 miles/280 kilometers   Maps 222, 139, 141, 232

From **Jacksonville★**, drive E on Rte. 10 to **Atlantic Beach**, the most affluent of Jacksonville's beach towns. Head S on Rte. A1A through residential **Neptune Beach**, blue-collar **Jacksonville Beach** and upscale **Ponte Vedra Beach** to reach **St. Augustine★★★**, the oldest city in the US and former capital of Spanish Florida. Farther S, car-racing mecca **Daytona Beach** is known for its **international speedway**. Take US-92 across the Intracoastal Waterway to US-1, heading S to **Titusville**. Take Rte. 402 across the Indian River to **Merritt Island NWR★★** to begin **Black Point Wildlife Drive★**. Return to Titusville and follow Rte. 405 to **Kennedy Space Center★★★**, one of Florida's top attractions, to end the tour.

Florida Keys★★

168 miles/270 kilometers   Maps 143, 142

Note: Green mile-marker (MM) posts, sometimes difficult to see, line US-1 (Overseas Hwy.), showing distances from Key West (MM 0). Much of the route is two-lane, and traffic can be heavy from December to April and on weekends. Allow 3hrs for the drive. Crossing 43 bridges and causeways (only one over land), the highway offers fine views of the Atlantic Ocean (E) and Florida Bay (W). Drive S from **Miami★★★** on US-1. Near **Key Largo★**, **John Pennekamp Coral Reef SP★★** harbors tropical fish, coral and fine snorkeling waters. To the SW, **Islamorada** is known for **charter fishing**. At **Marathon** (MM 50), **Sombrero Beach** is a good swimming spot, but **Bahia Honda SP** (MM 36.8) is considered the best **beach★★** in the Keys. Pass **National Key Deer Refuge★** (MM 30.5), haven to the 2ft-tall deer unique to the lower Keys. End at **Key West★★★**, joining the gathering at **Mallory Square Dock** to view the **sunset★★**.

Florida Keys

The Ozarks★

343 miles/552 kilometers   Maps 227, 117, 219, 107, 106

From the state capital of **Little Rock**, take I-30 SW to Exit 111, then US-70 W to Hot Springs. Drive N on Rte. 7/Central Ave. to **Hot Springs NP★★** to enjoy the therapeutic waters. Travel N on Rte. 7 across the Arkansas River to Russellville. Continue on **Scenic Highway 7★** N through **Ozark National Forest** and across the **Buffalo National River** to Harrison. Take US-62/65 NW to Bear Creek Springs, continuing W on US-62 through **Eureka Springs★**, with its **historic district**, to **Pea Ridge NMP★**, a Civil War site. Return E on US-62 to the junction of Rte. 21 at Berryville. Travel N on Rte. 21 to Blue Eye, taking Rte. 86 E to US-65, which leads N to the entertainment hub of **Branson**, Missouri, to end the tour.

River Road Plantations★★

200 miles/323 kilometers   Maps 239, 134, 194

From **New Orleans★★★**, take US-90 W to Rte. 48 to the Mississippi River to Destrehan. At no. 13034, **Destrehan★★** is considered the oldest plantation house in the lower Mississippi Valley. Continue NW on Rte. 48 to US-61 to Laplace to connect to Rte. 44. Head N past **San Francisco Plantation★**, built in 1856. At Burnside, take Rte. 75 N to St. Gabriel. En route, watch for **Houmas House★** (40136 Hwy. 942). Take Rte. 30 to **Baton Rouge★**, the state capital. Cross the Mississippi River bridge (I-10) and take Rte. 1 S along the **West Bank★★** to White Castle, site of **Nottoway★**, the largest plantation home in the South. Continue to Donaldsonville, then turn onto Rte. 18. Travel E to Gretna, passing **Oak Alley★** (no. 3645) and **Laura Plantation★★** (no. 2247) along the way. From Gretna, take US-90 to New Orleans, where the tour ends.

Gaspésie, Québec★★★

933 kilometers/578 miles   Maps 178, 179

Leave **Sainte-Flavie** via Rte. 132 NE, stopping to visit **Reford Gardens★★** en route to **Matane**. After **Cap-Chat**, take Rte. 299 S to **Gaspésie Park★** for expansive **views★★**. Back on Rte. 132, follow the **Scenic Route from La Martre to Rivière-au-Renard★★**. Continue to **Cap-des-Rosiers**, entrance to majestic **Forillon NP★★**. Follow Rte. 132 along the coast through **Gaspé★**, the administrative center of the peninsula, to **Percé★★★**, a coastal village known for **Percé Rock★★**, a mammoth offshore rock wall. Drive SW on Rt. 132 through **Paspébiac** to **Carleton**, which offers a **panorama★★** from the summit of **Mont Saint-Joseph**. Farther SW, detour 6km/4mi S to see an array of fossils at **Parc National de Miguasha★**. Back on Rte. 132, travel W to Matapédia, then follow Rte. 132 N, passing **Causapscal**—a departure point for salmon fishing expeditions—to end the tour at Sainte-Flavie.

North Shore Lake Superior★★

275 kilometers/171 miles   Map 169

From the port city of **Thunder Bay★★**—and nearby **Old Fort William★★**—drive the Trans-Canada Hwy. (Rte. 11/17) E to Rte. 587. Detour to **Sleeping Giant PP★**, which offers fine **views★** of the lake. Back along the Trans-Canada Hwy., **Amethyst Mine** (take E. Loon Rd.) is a rock hound's delight (fee). Farther NE, located 12km/8mi off the highway, **Ouimet Canyon★★** is a startling environment for the area. Just after the highway's Red Rock turnoff, watch for **Red Rock Cuesta**, a natural formation 210m/690ft high. Cross the Nipigon River and continue along **Nipigon Bay★★**, enjoying **views★★** of the rocky, conifer-covered islands. The **view★★** of Kama Bay through Kama Rock Cut is striking. Continue to Schreiber to end the tour.

Nova Scotia's Cabot Trail★★

338 kilometers/210 miles   Map 181

From **Baddeck★**, follow Hwy. 105 S to the junction with Rte. 19 to **North East Margaree** in salmon-fishing country. Take this road NW to Margaree Harbour, then N to **Chéticamp**, an enclave of Acadian culture. Heading inland, the route enters **Cape Breton Highlands NP★★**, combining seashore and mountains. At Cape North, detour N around Aspy Bay to **Bay St. Lawrence**. Then head W to tiny **Capstick** for shoreline **views★**. Return S to Cape North, then drive E to South Harbour. Take White Pointe Rd. along the coast, traveling S through the fishing villages of **New Haven** and **Neils Harbour★**. Rejoin Cabot Trail S, passing the resort area of the **Ingonishs**. Take the right fork after Indian Brook to reach St. Ann's, home of **Gaelic College★**, specializing in bagpipe and Highland dance classes. Rejoin Hwy. 105 to return to Baddeck.

Capstick

Lake Louise

Canadian Rockies★★★

467 kilometers/290 miles   Map 164

Leave **Banff★★** by Hwy. 1, traveling W. After 5.5km/3.5mi, take **Bow Valley Parkway★** (Hwy. 1A) NW within **Banff NP★★★**. At Lake Louise Village, detour W to find **Lake Louise★★★**. Back on Hwy. 1, head N to the junction of Hwy. 93, turn W and follow Hwy. 1 past **Kicking Horse Pass** into **Yoho NP★★**. Continue through **Field**, and turn right onto the road N to **Emerald Lake★★★**. Return to the junction of Rte. 93 and Hwy. 1, heading N on Rte. 93 along the **Icefields Parkway★★★**. Pass **Crowfoot Glacier★★** and **Bow Lake★★** on the left. **Peyto Lake★★★** is reached by spur road. After **Parker Ridge★★**, massive **Athabasca Glacier★★★** looms on the left. Continue to **Jasper★** and **Jasper NP★★★**. From Jasper, turn left onto Hwy. 16 and head into **Mount Robson PP★★**, home to **Mount Robson★★★** (3,954m/12,972ft.). End the tour at Tête Jaune Cache.

Vancouver Island★★★

337 kilometers/209 miles   Maps 282, 163, 162

To enjoy a scenic drive that begins 11mi N of **Victoria★★★**, take Douglas St. N from Victoria to the Trans-Canada Highway (Hwy. 1) and follow **Malahat Drive★** (between Goldstream PP and Mill Bay Rd.) for 12mi. Continue N on Hwy. 1 past Duncan, **Chemainus**—known for its murals—and Nanaimo. From there take Hwy. 19A then Hwy. 19 NW to Parksville. Take winding Rte. 4 W (Pacific Rim Hwy.) passing **Englishman River Falls PP★** and **Cameron Lake**. Just beyond the lake, **Cathedral Grove★★** holds 800-year-old Douglas firs. The road descends to **Port Alberni**, departure point for cruises on Barkley Sound, and follows Sproat Lake before climbing Klitsa Mountain. The route leads to the Pacific along the Kennedy River. At the coast, turn left and drive SE to Ucluelet. Then head N to enter **Pacific Rim NPR★★★**. Continue to the road's end at **Tofino★** to end the tour.

Yukon Circuit★★

1,485 kilometers/921 miles   Map 155

Note: Rte. 9 and Rte. 5 are unpaved in places; proceed with caution. Both roads are closed in winter.

From **Whitehorse★**, capital of Yukon Territory, drive N on the **Klondike Hwy.** (Rte. 2), crossing the Yukon River at **Carmacks**. After 196km/122mi, small islands divide the river into fast-flowing channels at **Five Finger Rapids★**. From Stewart Crossing, continue NW on Rte. 2 to **Dawson City★★**, a historic frontier town. Ferry across the river and drive the **Top of the World Hwy.★★** (Rte. 9), with extensive **views★★★**, to the Alaska border. Rte. 9 joins Rte. 5, passing tiny **Chicken**, Alaska. At Tetlin Junction, head SE on Rte. 2, paralleling **Tetlin NWR**. Enter Canada and follow the **Alaska Highway★★** (Rte. 1) SE along **Kluane Lake★★** to **Haines Junction**, gateway to **Kluane NPR★★**, home of **Mount Logan**, Canada's highest peak (5,959m/19,550ft). Continue E to Rte. 2 to return to Whitehorse.

British Columbia

Washington

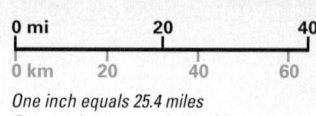

One inch equals 25.4 miles
One centimeter equals 16.1 kilometers

Seattle WA / Mt Rainier Natl Park WA

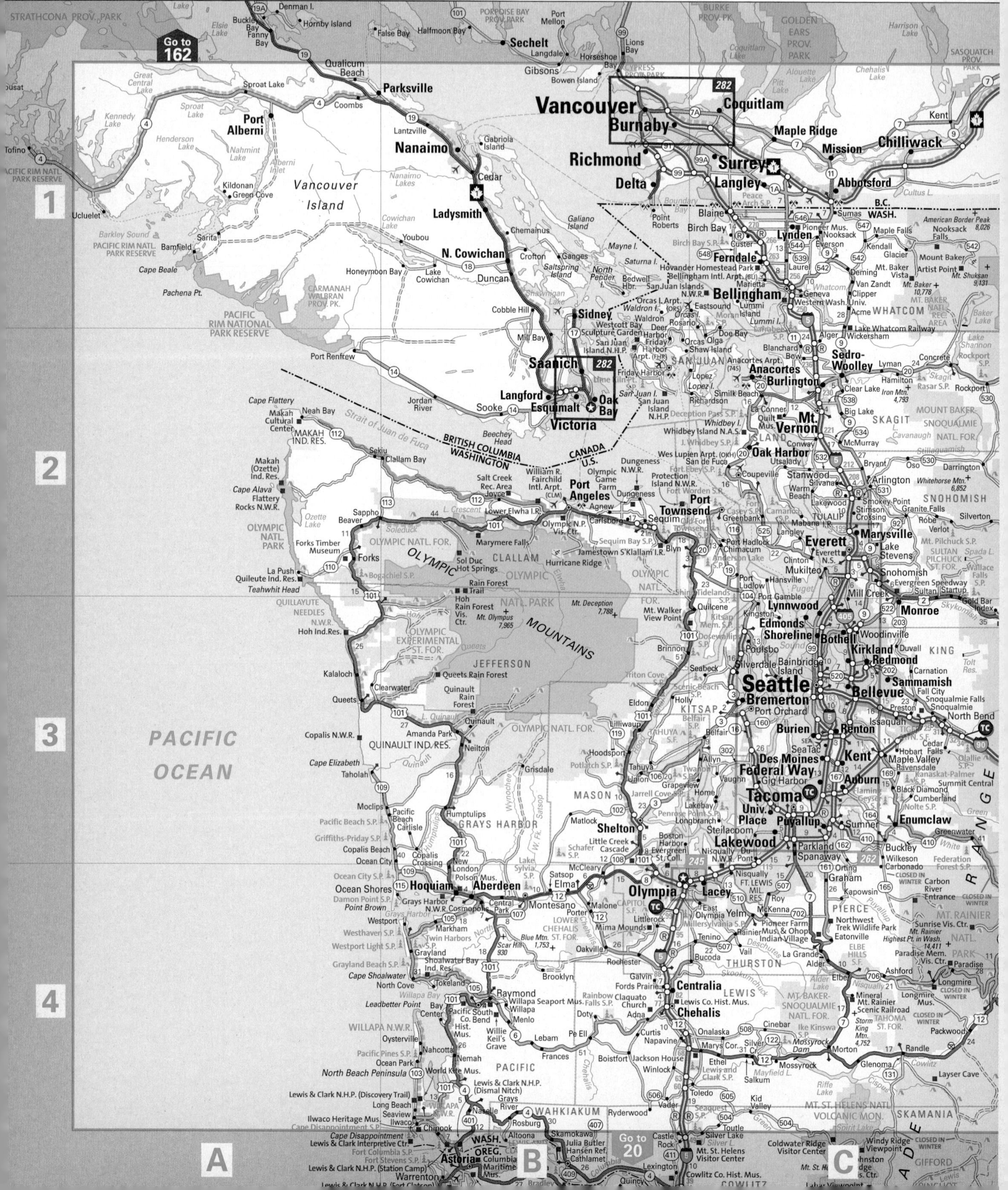

British Columbia

Washington

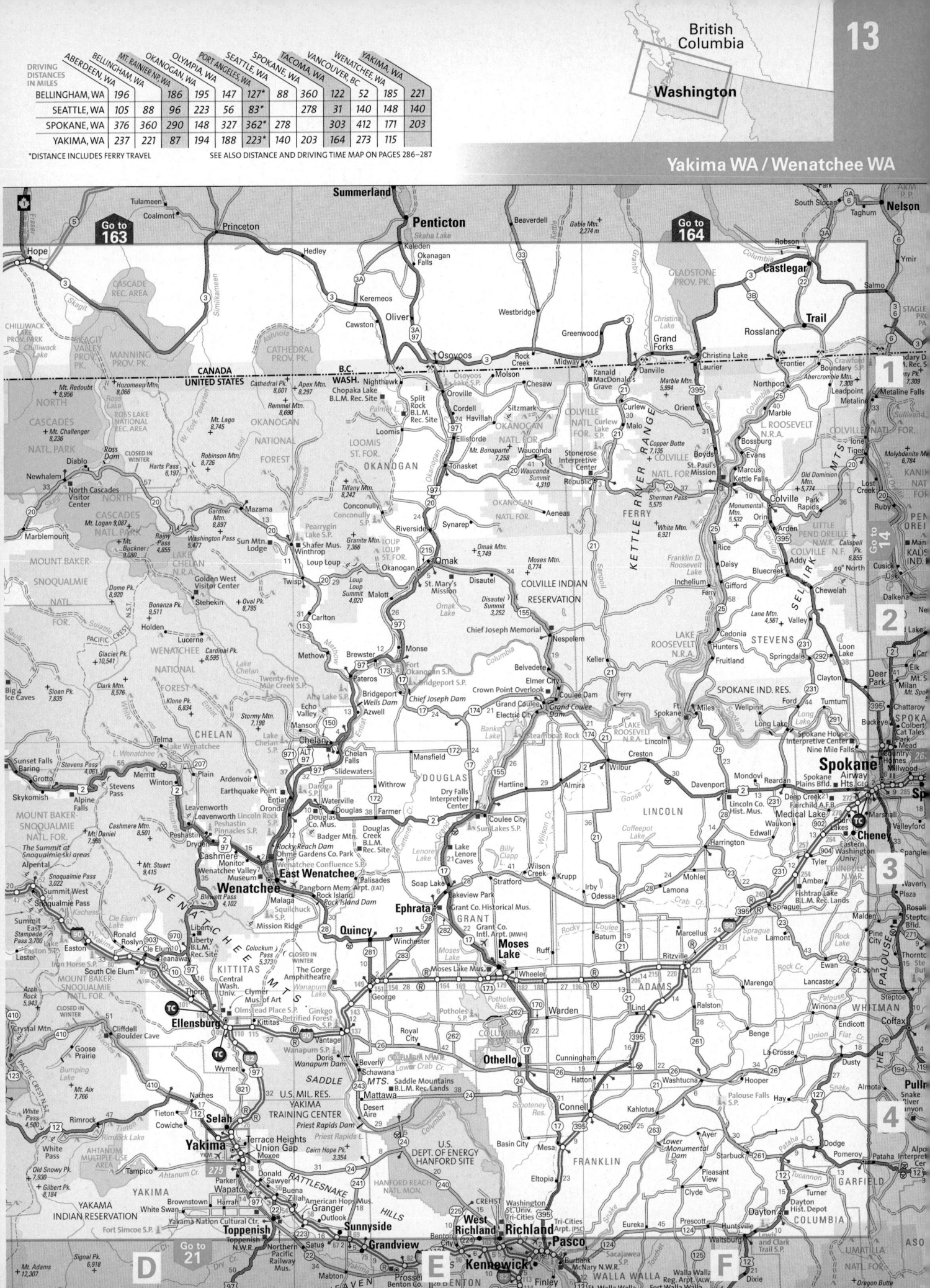

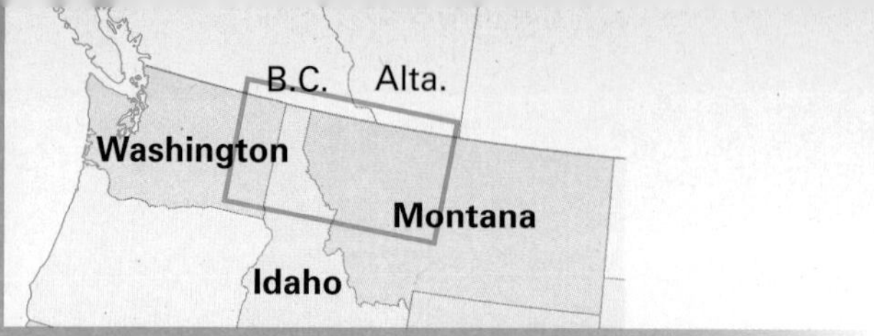

B.C. Alta.

Washington

Montana

Idaho

Spokane WA / Coeur d'Alene ID

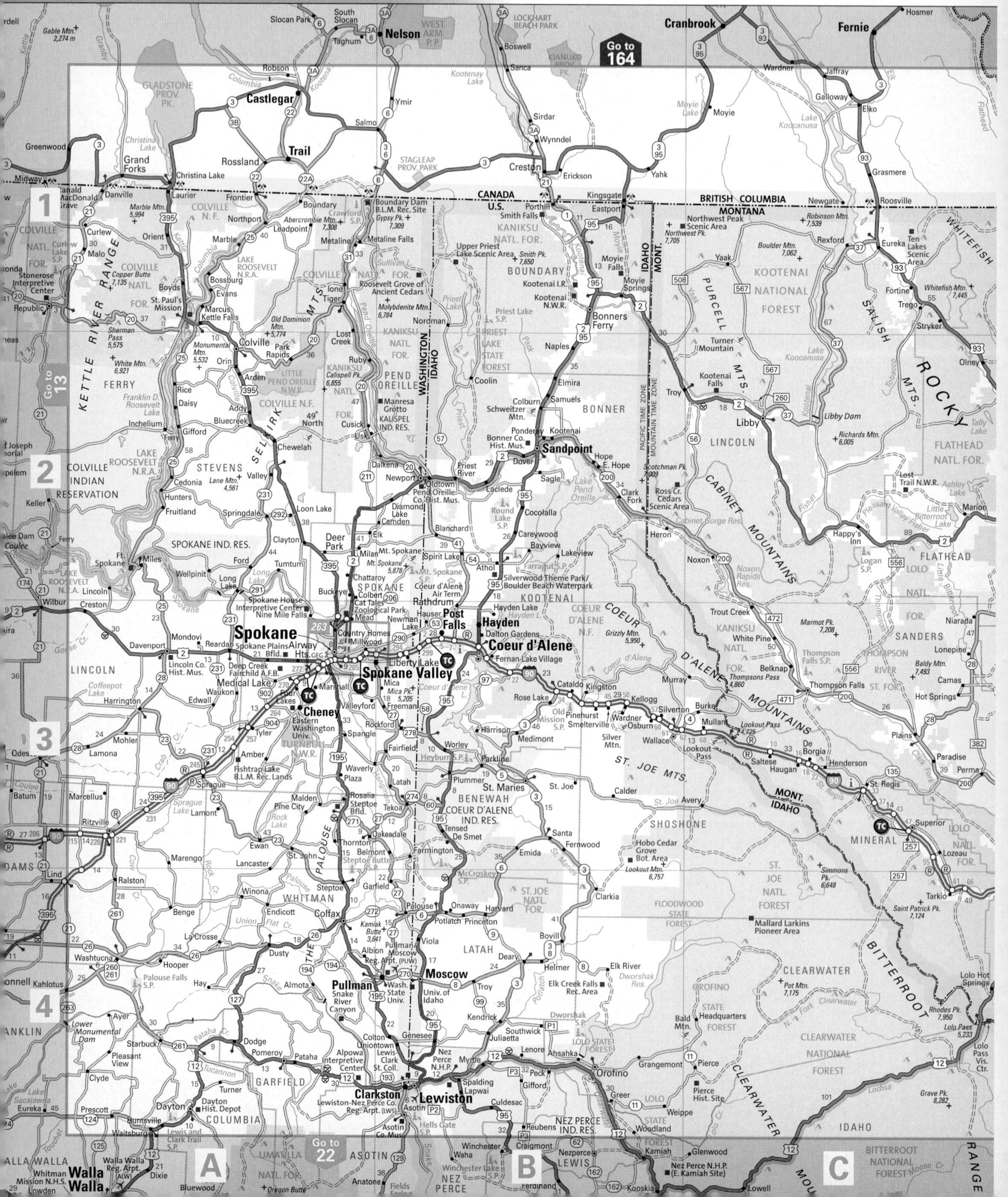

One inch equals 25.4 miles
One centimeter equals 16.1 kilometers

0 mi 20 40
0 km 20 40 60

Go to 164

Go to 13

Go to 22

Go to 164

CANADA
U.S.

BRITISH COLUMBIA
MONTANA

IDAHO
MONT.

PACIFIC TIME ZONE
MOUNTAIN TIME ZONE

MONT.
IDAHO

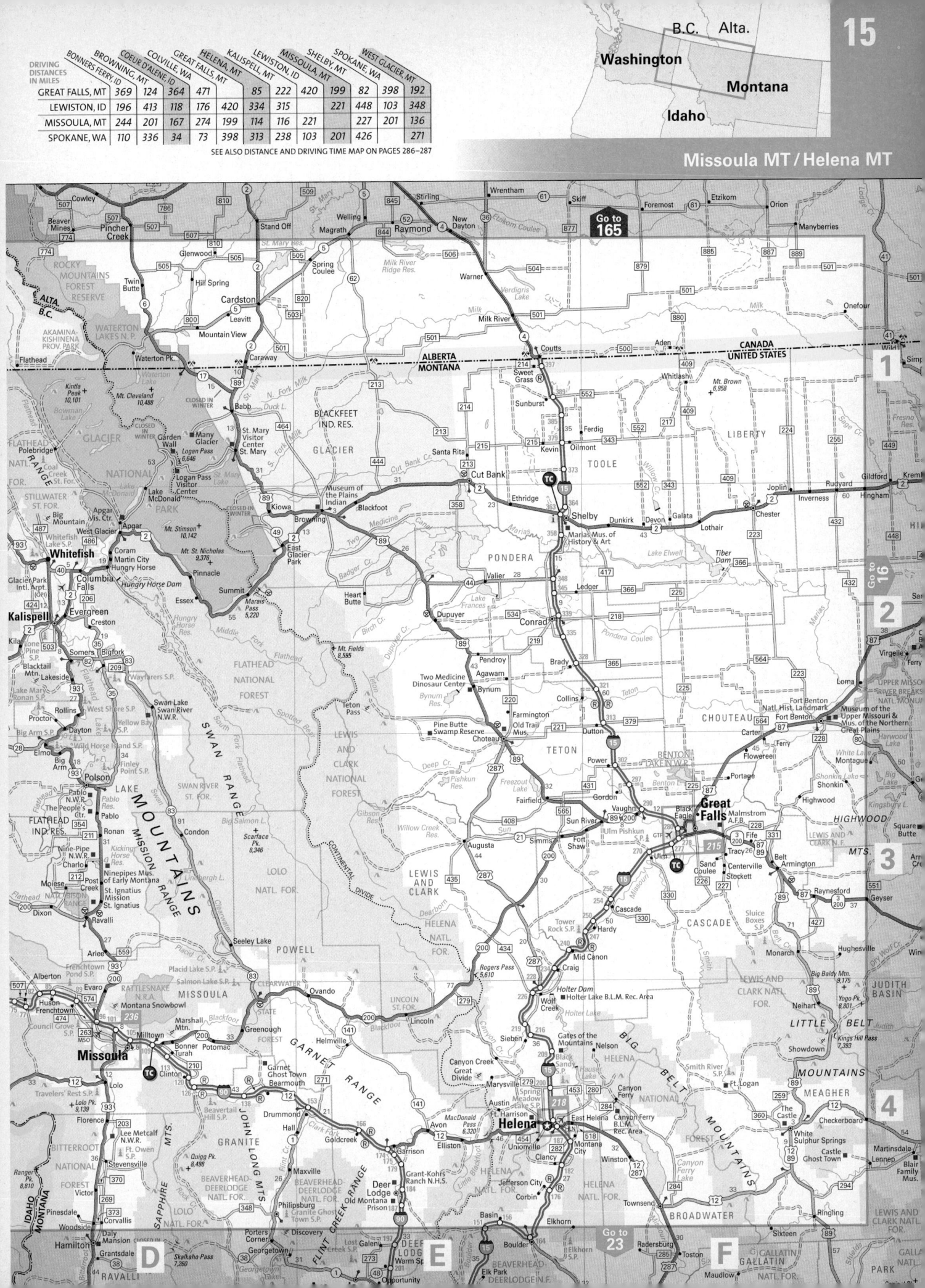

Alta. Sask.

Montana North Dakota

One inch equals 25.4 miles
One centimeter equals 16.1 kilometers

0 mi 20 40
0 km 20 40 60

Go to 165

Go to 15

Go to 24

A B C

1 2 3 4

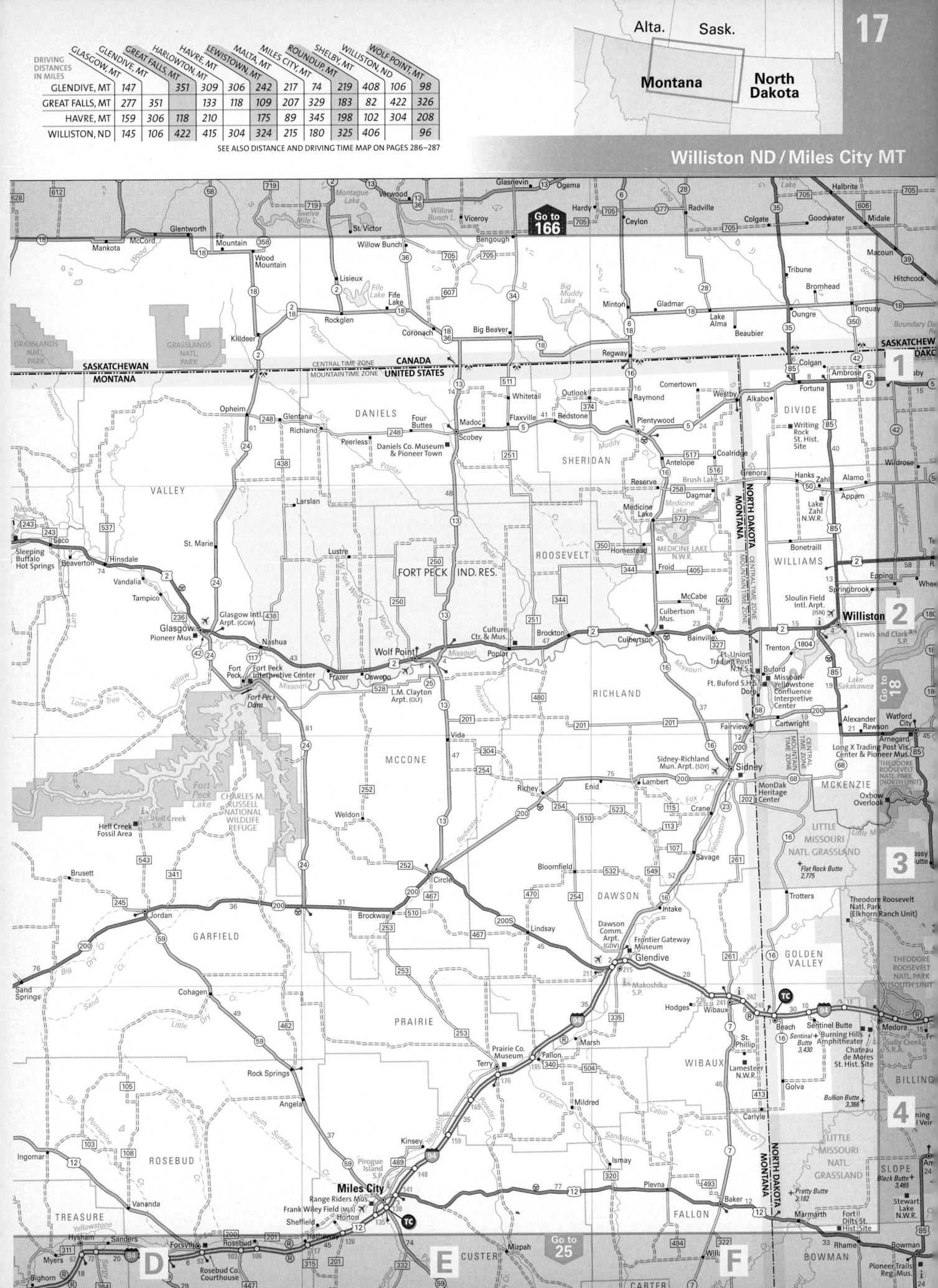

DRIVING DISTANCES IN MILES	GLASGOW, MT	GLENDIVE, MT	GREAT FALLS, MT	HARLOWTON, MT	HAVRE, MT	LEWISTOWN, MT	MALTA, MT	MILES CITY, MT	ROUNDUP, MT	SHELBY, MT	WILLISTON, ND	WOLF POINT, MT
GLENDIVE, MT	147		351	309	306	242	217	74	219	408	106	98
GREAT FALLS, MT	277	351		133	118	109	207	329	183	82	422	326
HAVRE, MT	159	306	118	210		175	89	345	198	102	304	208
WILLISTON, ND	145	106	422	415	304	324	215	180	325	406		96

SEE ALSO DISTANCE AND DRIVING TIME MAP ON PAGES 286–287

18

Sask.   Manitoba

North
Dakota   Minnesota

One inch equals 25.4 miles
One centimeter equals 16.1 kilometers

Bismarck ND / Minot ND

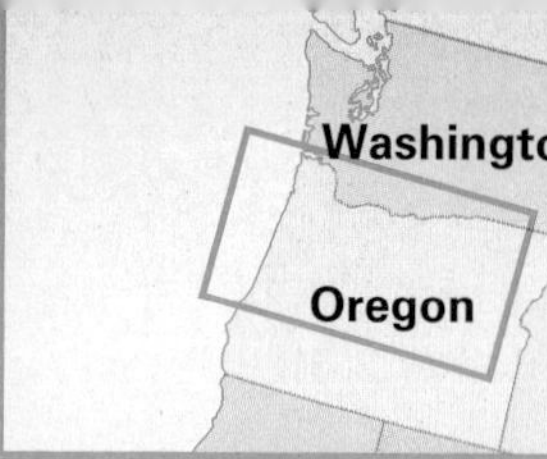

Washington

Oregon

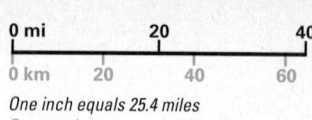

One inch equals 25.4 miles
One centimeter equals 16.1 kilometers

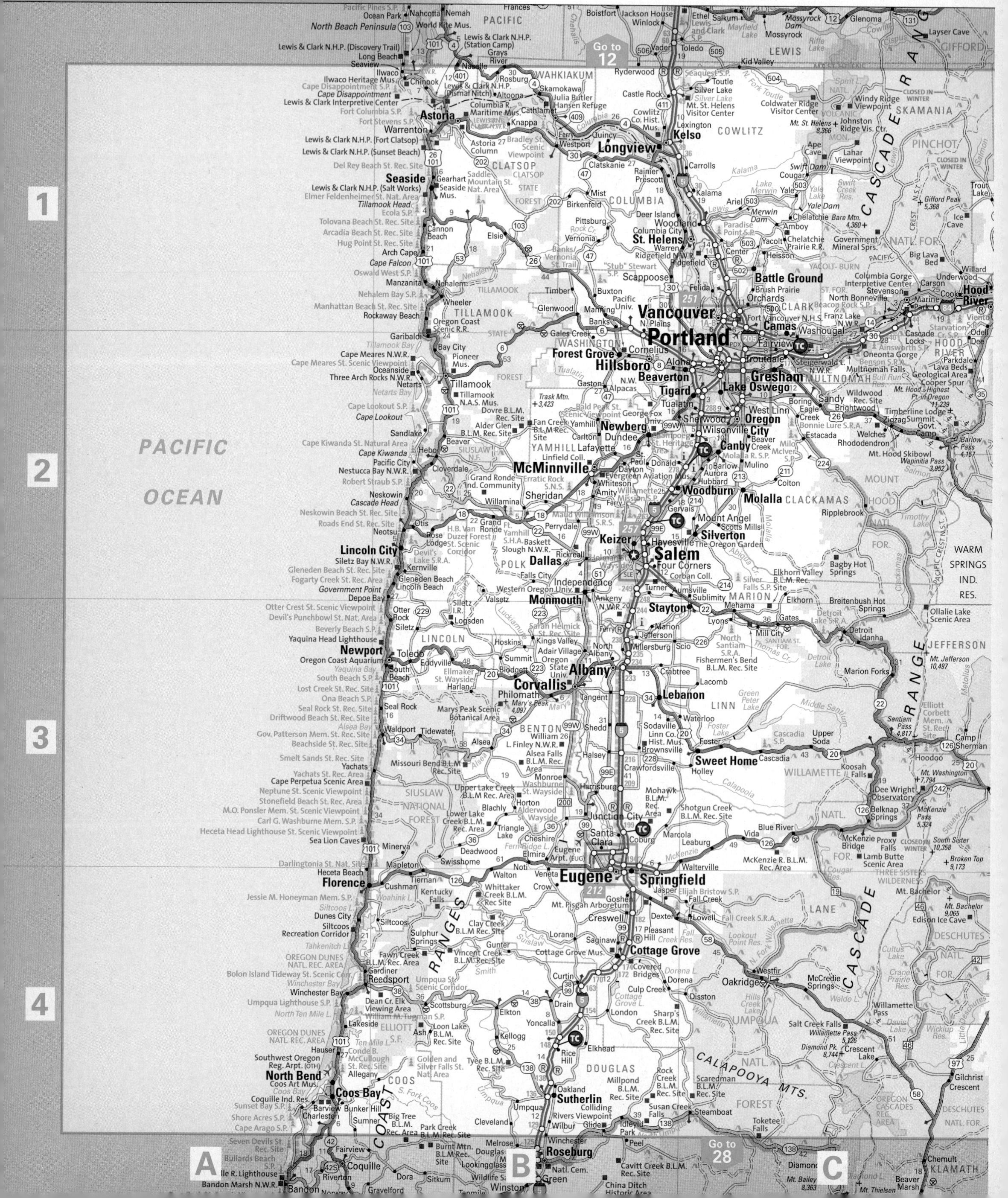

DRIVING DISTANCES IN MILES

	ASTORIA, OR	BEND, OR	BURNS, OR	COOS BAY, OR	EUGENE, OR	KENNEWICK, WA	LA GRANDE, OR	NEWPORT, OR	PORTLAND, OR	SALEM, OR	THE DALLES, OR	WALLA WALLA, WA
BEND, OR	252		142	227	115	245	295	183	158	134	137	276
EUGENE, OR	216	115	257	105		328	377	101	112	65	198	359
KENNEWICK, WA	306	245	256	440	328		111	328	212	264	131	49
PORTLAND, OR	97	158	299	224	112	212	261	116		48	82	243

SEE ALSO DISTANCE AND DRIVING TIME MAP ON PAGES 286–287

Washington
Montana
Oregon
Idaho
Wyoming

One inch equals 25.4 miles
One centimeter equals 16.1 kilometers

0 mi　20　40
0 km　20　40　60

Boise ID / La Grande OR

Go to 14
Go to 21
Go to 30

Major places: Lewiston, Clarkston, Walla Walla, Freewater, La Grande, Baker City, Weiser, Ontario, Payette, Fruitland, Nyssa, Caldwell, Nampa, Meridian, Eagle, Garden City, Boise, Kuna, Emmett, Mountain Home, Hailey, Bellevue, Ketchum, Sun Valley, Stanley, Clayton, Sunbeam, Grangeville, White Bird, Riggins, McCall, Cascade, Donnelly, New Meadows, Council, Cambridge, Midvale, Orofino, Kamiah, Kooskia, Stites, Cottonwood, Craigmont, Nezperce, Ferdinand

National Forests/Areas: Bitterroot National Forest, Clearwater National Forest, Nez Perce Natl. For., Payette National Forest, Wallowa-Whitman Natl. For., Umatilla Natl. For., Salmon-Challis Natl. For., Boise National Forest, Sawtooth National Recreation Area, Sawtooth Natl. For., Malheur N.F., Hells Canyon National Recreation Area

Peaks: Ranger Pk. 8,810, Grave Pk. 8,282, Vance Mtn. 8,742, Nez Perce Pass 6,587, Horse Creek Pass 7,305, Oregon Butte 8,463, Waugh Mtn. 8,882, Dixie, Mosquito Pk. 8,732, Mt. McGuire 10,082, Mormon Mtn. 9,545, Boston Mtn. 7,660, Sacajawea Pk. 9,839, Eagle Cap 9,595, Smith Mtn. 8,005, Council Mtn. 8,126, Big Lookout Mtn. 7,120, Pinyon Pk. 9,942, Pistol Rock 9,169, Rice Pk. 8,696, Twin Pks. 10,340, Bald Mtn. 10,313, Castle Pk. 11,815, Snowyside Pk. 10,651, Norton Pk. 10,285, Smoky Dome 10,095, Snowslide Pk. 10,551, Soldier Mountain

Oregon Butte 8,387, Ski Bluewood

Points of interest: Nez Perce N.H.P., Lewis and Clark Trail S.P., Oregon Trail Interpretive Center, National Historic Oregon Trail Interpretive Center, Wallowa Lake Tramway, Eagle Cap Excursion Train, World Center for Birds of Prey, Snake River Birds of Prey Natl. Cons. Area, City of Rocks, Shoshone Ice Caves, Redfish Lake Visitor Center, Four Rivers Cultural Center, Hells Canyon Seven Devils Scenic Area, Custer Ghost Town, Bonanza Ghost Town, Jordan Craters Geologic Area

PACIFIC TIME ZONE / MOUNTAIN TIME ZONE

WASHINGTON / OREGON
OREGON / IDAHO
IDAHO / MONTANA

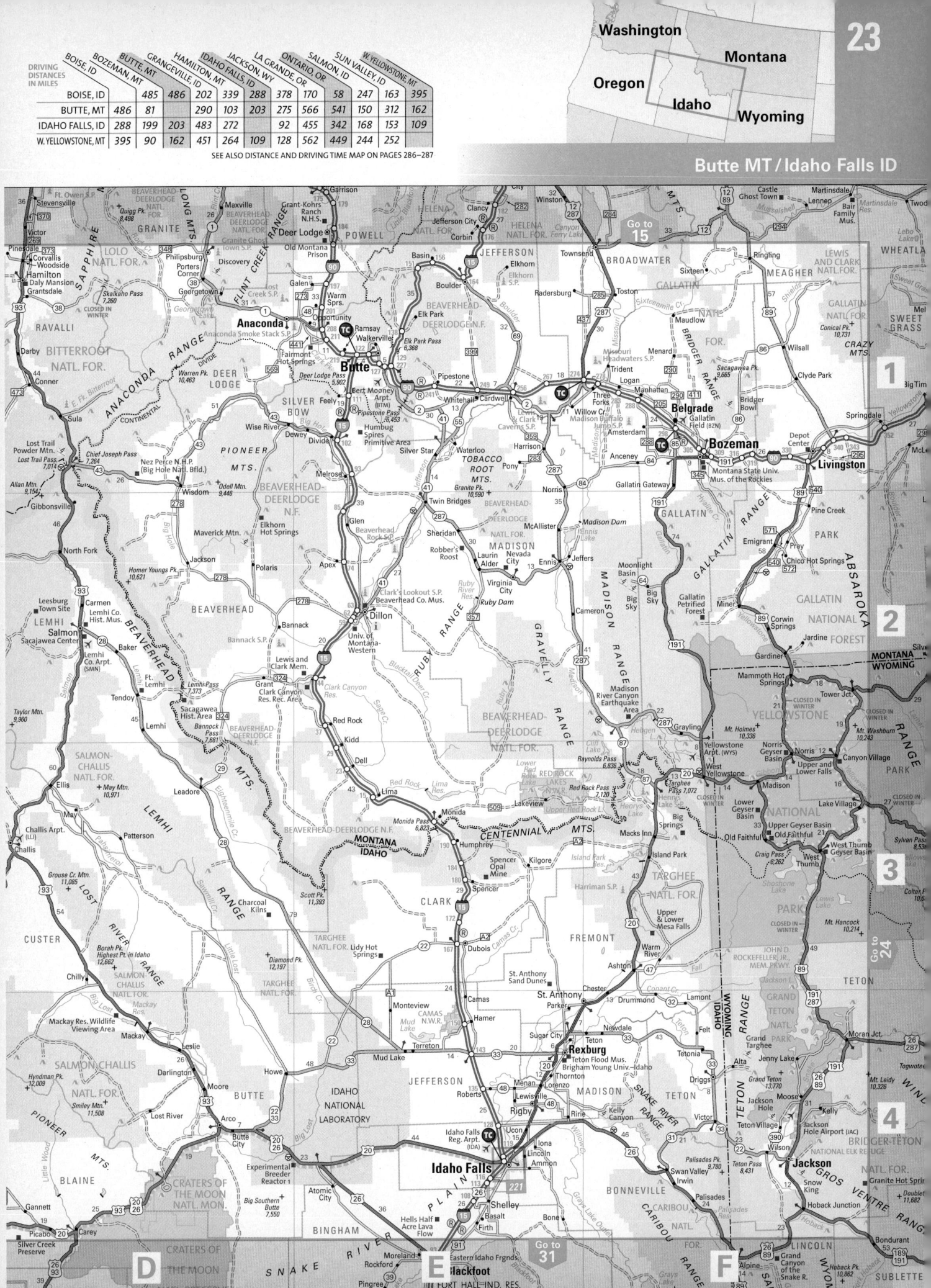

Montana | North Dakota
Idaho | South Dakota
Wyoming

0 mi   20   40
0 km   20   40   60
One inch equals 25.4 miles
One centimeter equals 16.1 kilometers

Go to 16

Go to 23

Go to 32

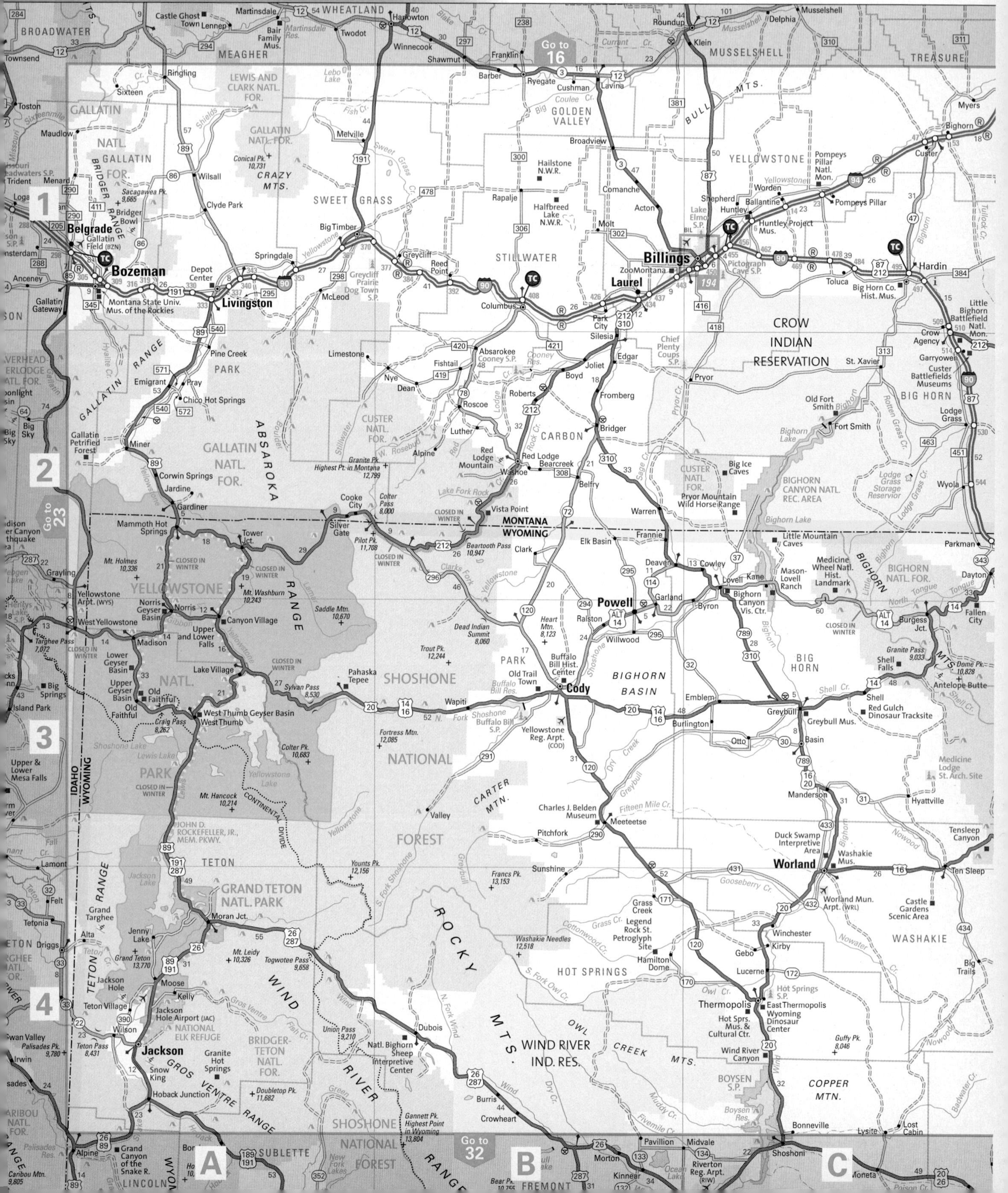

Montana   North Dakota

Idaho   South Dakota

Wyoming

DRIVING DISTANCES IN MILES	BILLINGS, MT	BOZEMAN, MT	BUFFALO, WY	CODY, WY	GILLETTE, WY	JACKSON, WY	MILES CITY, MT	RAPID CITY, SD	SHERIDAN, WY	SPEARFISH, SD	W. YELLOWSTONE, MT	WORLAND, WY
BILLINGS, MT		141	165	111	233	287	144	379	131	333	232	161
BUFFALO, WY	165	306		180	70	342	237	216	34	170	396	91
SPEARFISH, SD	333	474	170	350	100	512	186	53	202		564	261
W. YELLOWSTONE, MT	232	90	396	147	464	128	376	610	363	564		236

SEE ALSO DISTANCE AND DRIVING TIME MAP ON PAGES 286–287

North Dakota
Minnesota
South Dakota
Iowa

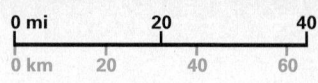

0 mi ___ 20 ___ 40
0 km __ 20 __ 40 __ 60
One inch equals 25.4 miles
One centimeter equals 16.1 kilometers

Rapid City SD / Pierre SD

DRIVING DISTANCES IN MILES	ABERDEEN, SD	BROOKINGS, SD	HOT SPRINGS, SD	HURON, SD	MITCHELL, SD	MOBRIDGE, SD	PIERRE, SD	RAPID CITY, SD	SIOUX FALLS, SD	WAHPETON, SD	WALL, SD	WATERTOWN, SD
ABERDEEN, SD		150	412	90	146	99	160	357	204	154	303	98
PIERRE, SD	160	188	247	115	155	107		193	226	301	138	189
RAPID CITY, SD	357	390	56	313	275	243	193		346	543	55	436
SIOUX FALLS, SD	204	57	401	127	73	303	226	346		210	292	103

SEE ALSO DISTANCE AND DRIVING TIME MAP ON PAGES 286–287

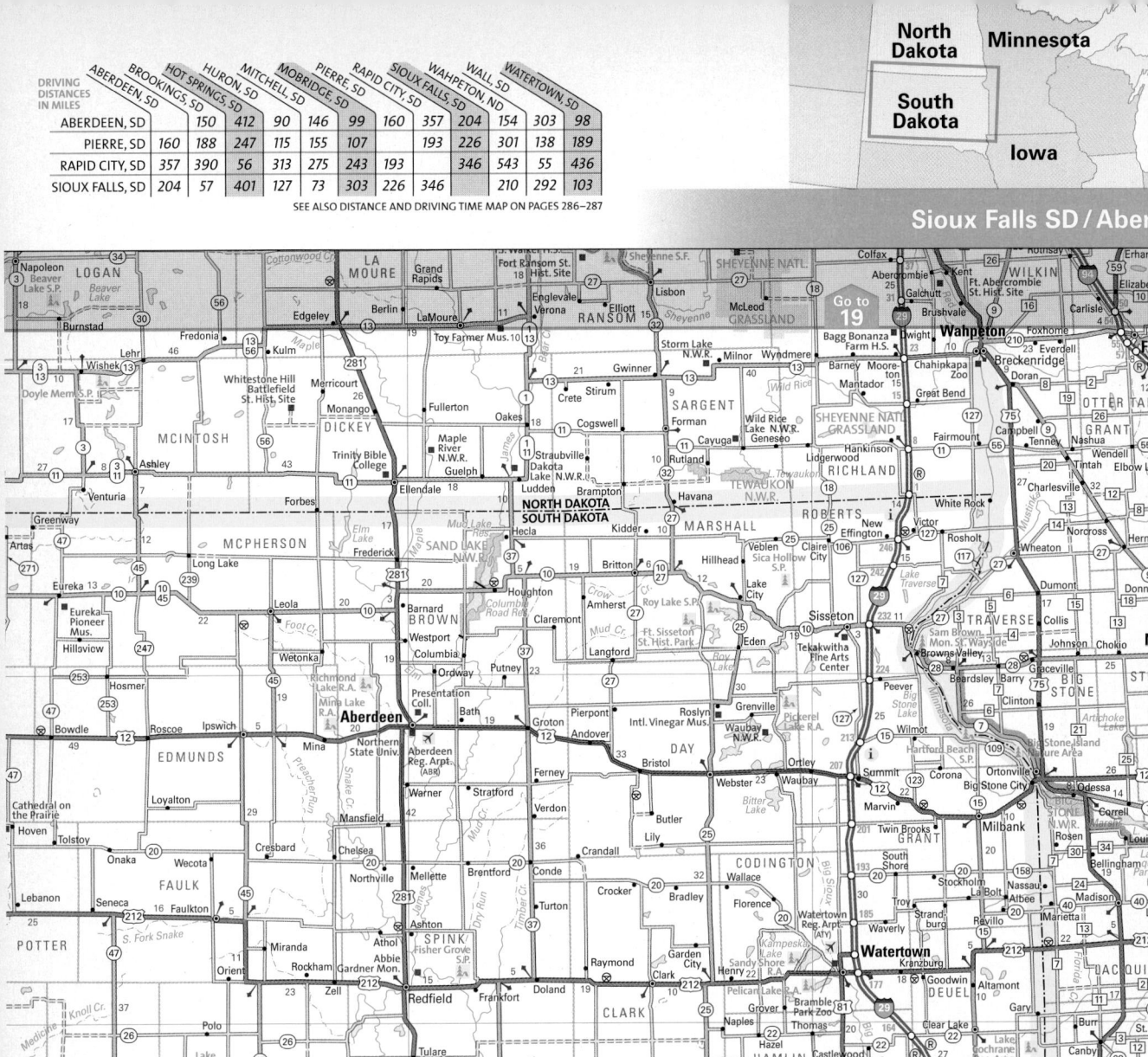

Oregon

California **Nevada**

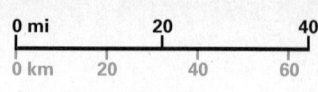

One inch equals 25.4 miles
One centimeter equals 16.1 kilometers

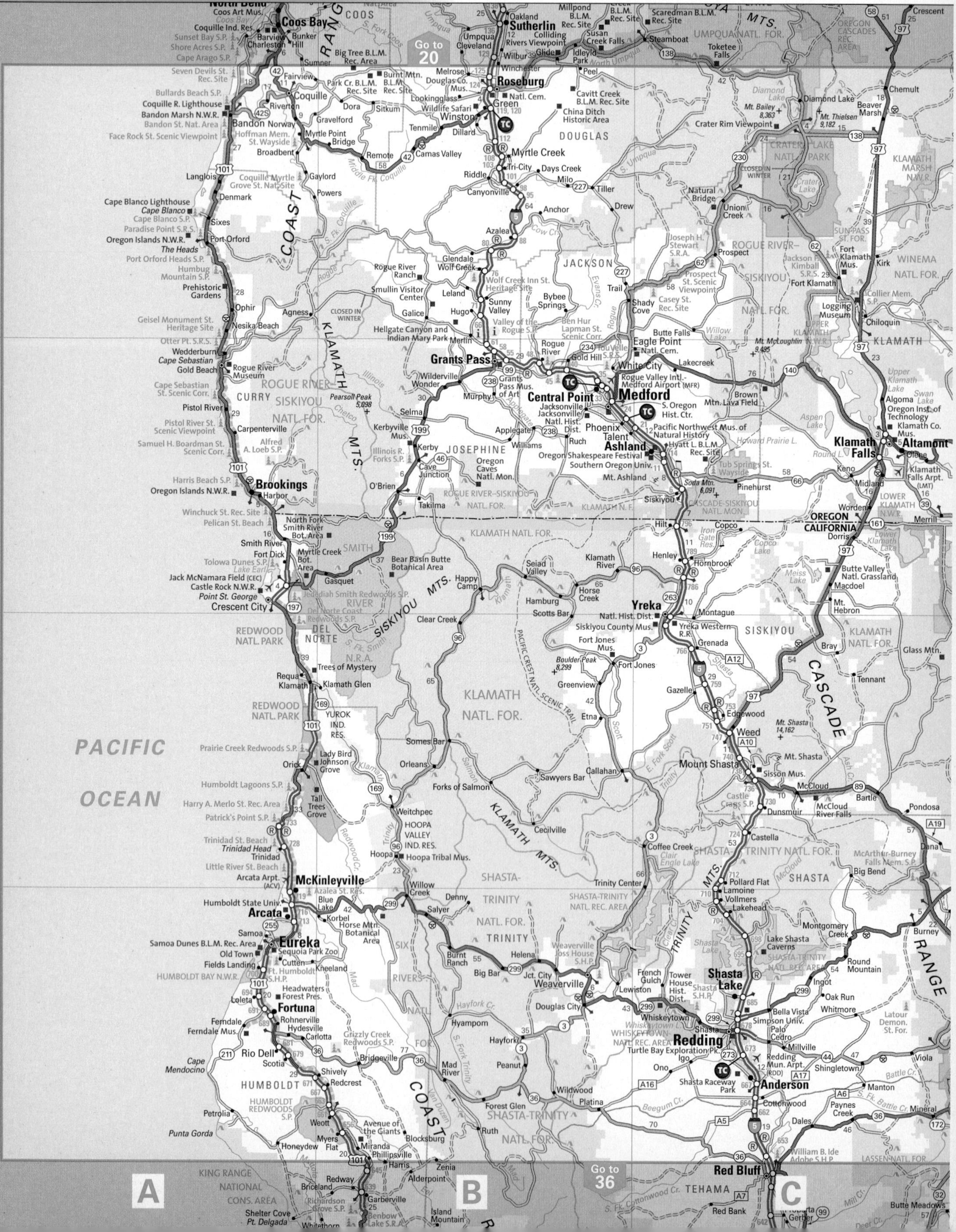

Oregon
California Nevada

DRIVING DISTANCES IN MILES

	ALTURAS, CA	CRATER LAKE NP, OR	CRESCENT CITY, CA	EUREKA, CA	KLAMATH FALLS, OR	LAKEVIEW, OR	LASSEN VOLCANIC NP, CA	MEDFORD, OR	REDDING, CA	ROSEBURG, OR	SUSANVILLE, CA	WINNEMUCCA, NV
LAKEVIEW, OR	56	153	282	332	98		192	171	199	265	161	212
MEDFORD, OR	176	80	111	192	76	171	208		148	94	221	383
REDDING, CA	143	198	189	133	141	199	63	148		242	114	364
SUSANVILLE, CA	105	226	303	247	170	161	74	221	114	315		250

SEE ALSO DISTANCE AND DRIVING TIME MAP ON PAGES 286–287

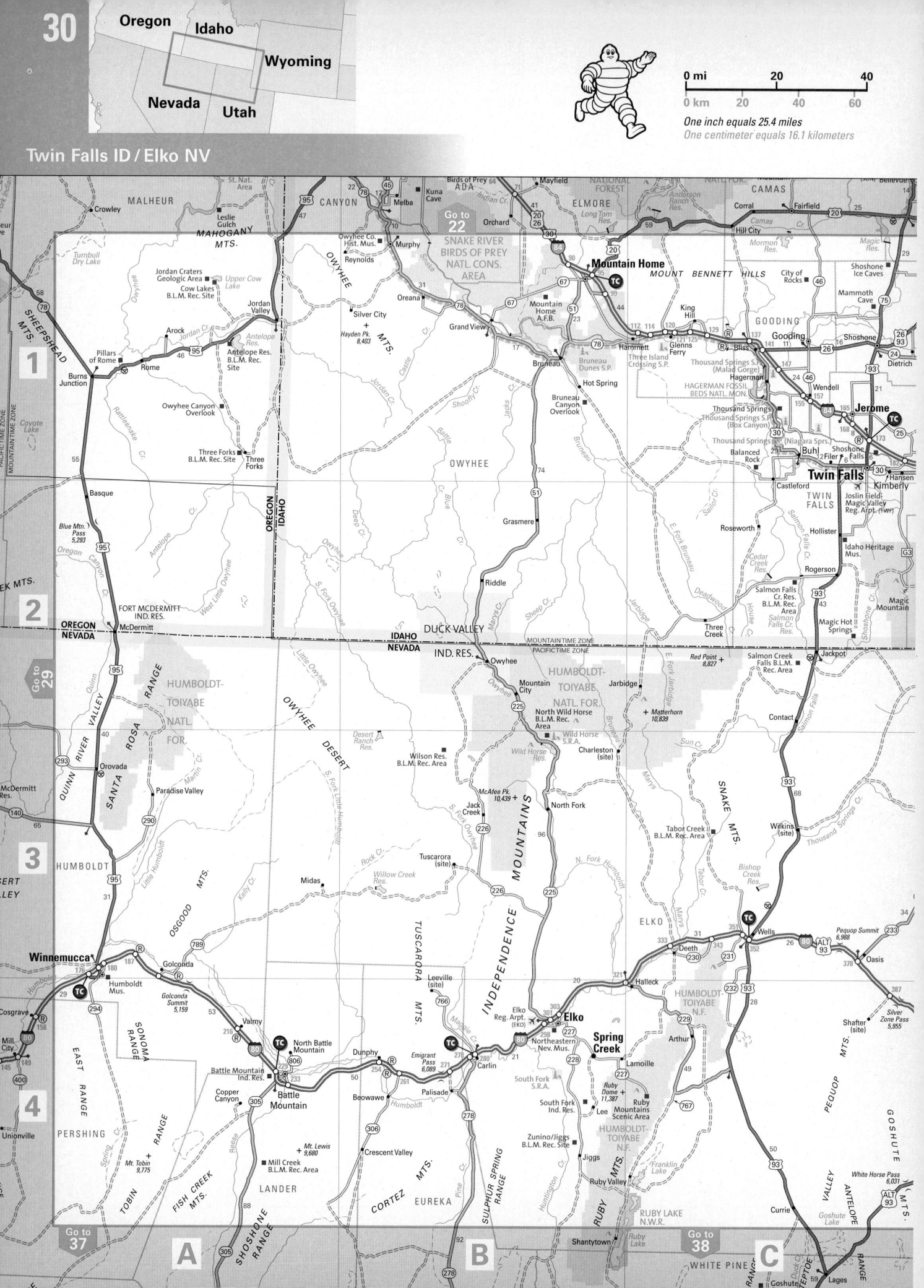

Oregon Idaho
Wyoming
Nevada Utah

0 mi 20 40
0 km 20 40 60
One inch equals 25.4 miles
One centimeter equals 16.1 kilometers

Wyoming — South Dakota — Nebraska — Utah — Colorado

One inch equals 25.4 miles
One centimeter equals 16.1 kilometers

0 mi   20   40
0 km   20   40   60

Rock Springs WY / Craig CO

WIND RIVER IND. RES.   COPPER MTN.

Go to 24

Hoback Junction   Doubletop Pk. 11,682   SHOSHONE   NATIONAL FOREST   Burris   Crowheart   ROCKY   Pavillion   Midvale   Bonneville   Lost Cabin

Grand Canyon of the Snake R.   Bondurant   Hoback Pk. 10,862   Highest Point in Wyoming 13,804   Gannett Pk.   Bull Lake   Morton   Kinnear   Riverton Reg. Arpt. (RIW)   Shoshoni   Moneta   Hiland   Arminto

Alpine   Grand Canyon   Upper Green River B.L.M. Rec. Area   New Fork Lakes   WIND RIVER IND. RES.   Ethete   St. Stephens   Riverton Mus.   Riverton

Thayne   Bedford   Merna   Cora   White Pine   Willow Lake   Fremont Lake   Wolverine Pk. 12,360   N. Fork Little Wind   Shoshone Cultural Ctr.   Fort Washakie   Hell's Half Acre   Powder River   Waltman

Gros   Afton   Intermittent Spring   Old Fort Bonneville   Daniel   Father de Smet Mon.   Pinedale   Boulder Lake B.L.M. Rec. Site   Roberts Mtn. 12,767   Northern Arapaho Cultural Mus.   Ampahoe   Milford   Hudson   Pioneer Museum   Lander   Castle Gardens   Ervay

Smoot   Halfway   Mus. of the Mountain Man   Boulder   Cirque of the Towers   Wind River Pk. 13,192   Popo Agie Falls   Sinks Canyon   Red Canyon   Sand Draw   FREMONT   GRANITE MTS.   Garfield Peak 8,234   RATTLESNAKE HILLS

Wyoming Pk. 11,378   Marbleton   Big Sandy   SHOSHONE   NATL.   FOR.   Granite Pk. 10,404   Miner's Delight   Atlantic City   South Pass City   Sweetwater Station   Three Crossings   Devils Gate & Mormon Handcart Interpretive Ctr.   Split Rock   Independence Rock S.H.S.   PATHFINDER N.W.R.

Cokeville   Pine Creek   Big Piney   SUBLETTE   South Pass City S.H.S.   Whitman Monument   South Pass 7,550   Jeffrey City   GREEN MTS.   Whiskey Pk. 9,225   Muddy Gap   FERRIS MTS.   Ferris Mtn. 10,037   Pathfinder Res.

Calpet   Monument Butte 7,204   CONTINENTAL DIVIDE   Eden Res.   Bairoil   Lamont

La Barge   Names Hill S.H.S.   Mormon Ferry   Farson   GREAT DIVIDE BASIN   Stratton Draw   Dugway B.L.M. Rec. Site   Ft. Fred Steele S.H.S.

Frontier   Fontenelle   Eden   SWEETWATER   Killpecker Sand Dunes   Steamboat Mtn. 8,683   MOUNTAINS   Frontier Prison Mus.   Rawlins   Sinclair

Kemmerer   Opal   Fontenelle Creek B.L.M. Rec. Area   Spring Butte 7,591   Red Desert   Wamsutter   Creston   Riner   Fort Steele

Diamondville   Elkol   J.C. Penney House   SEEDSKADEE N.W.R.   Superior   Point of Rocks Stage Sta.   Point of Rocks   Table Rock   Hadsell   Teton Reservoir B.L.M. Rec. Site

Go to 31   Fossil   Granger   Little America   Bryan   Reliance   Rock Springs - Sweetwater Co. Arpt. (RKS)   Bitter Creek   CLOSED IN WINTER   Bridger Pk. 11,004   Battle Pass   SIERRA

Granger Stage Station S.H.S.   James Town   Sweetwater Co. Hist. Mus.   Rock Springs   Qualey   ASPEN MTS.   Closed in winter   Baggs

UINTA   Carter   Green River   Three Patches B.L.M. Rec. Area   Dixon   Savery

Fort Bridger S.H.S.   Lyman   Fort Bridger   Mountain View   FLAMING GORGE NATL. REC. AREA   WYOMING / COLORADO   Slater

Piedmont Charcoal Kilns S.H.S.   Millburne   Piedmont   Robertson   Lonetree   Burntfork   McKinnon   Pine Mtn. 9,467   Great Divide   ELKHEAD MTS.   Columbine   Steamboat Lake S.P.

WYOMING / UTAH   Sheep Creek Canyon   Manila   The Flaming Gorge   Dutch John   Sparks   Powder Wash   Hiawatha   MOFFAT   Steamboat Lake S.P.

WASATCH-CACHE NATL. FOR.   Gilbert Pk. 13,442   Flaming Gorge Dam   John Jarvie Hist. Site   BROWNS PARK N.W.R.   Sunbeam   LITTLE YAMPA CANYON B.L.M. REC. AREA   Museum of Northwest Colorado

Mt. Lovenia 13,227   Kings Pk. Highest Pt. in Utah 13,528   Red Canyon Overlook & Visitor Ctr.   Oaks Park Res.   Gates of Lodore   Maybell   Lay   Craig   Hayden   Milner

Hayden Pk. 12,479   UINTA MTS.   Mt. Emmons 13,440   Marsh Pk. 12,240   Greystone   DINOSAUR NATL. MON.   ROUTT

Moon Lake   ASHLEY NATL. FOR.   Steinaker S.P.   Utah Field House of Natural History S.P. Mus.   Red Fleet Res.   Dinosaur Quarry Visitor Center   Yampa Valley Reg. Arpt. (HDN)

Whiterocks   Neola   Tridell   Lapoint   Maeser   Vernal   Vernal Reg. Arpt. (VEL)   Naples   Jensen   Elk Springs   Hamilton   Pagoda

Altonah   Altamont   Bluebell   Gusher   Blue Mountain   Massadona   Axial   Oak Creek

Mountain Home   Talmage   Roosevelt   Ballard   Fort Duchesne   UINTAH   Dinosaur   DANFORTH HILLS

Upalco   Bridgeland   Myton   Randlett   UINTAH AND OURAY IND. RES.   UTAH / COLORADO   Yampa Valley Reg. Arpt. (HDN)

Duchesne   Starvation S.P.   Leota   Ouray   Bonanza   White River Mus.   Maple Creek Pass 10,343

Go to 39   DUCHESNE   Go to 40   White   CATHEDRAL BLUFFS   ROUTT NATL. FOR.

A   B   C

1   2   3   4

DRIVING DISTANCES IN MILES

	CASPER, WY	CHEYENNE, WY	CRAIG, CO	FORT COLLINS, CO	KEMMERER, WY	LANDER, WY	LARAMIE, WY	PINEDALE, WY	RAWLINS, WY	ROCK SPRINGS, WY	SCOTTSBLUFF, NE	VERNAL, UT
CASPER, WY		175	234	217	297	144	148	271	117	214	173	322
CHEYENNE, WY	175		221	44	342	276	52	355	151	260	111	367
CRAIG, CO	234	221		194	257	221	171	269	117	149	331	123
ROCK SPRINGS, WY	214	260	149	273	86	118	210	98	110		370	111

SEE ALSO DISTANCE AND DRIVING TIME MAP ON PAGES 286–287

South Dakota

Nebraska   Iowa

Colorado

0 mi   20   40
0 km   20   40   60

One inch equals 25.4 miles
One centimeter equals 16.1 kilometers

Go to 26

Go to 33

Go to 42

PINE RIDGE IND. RES.   SHANNON   BENNETT   TODD   TRIPP   MELLETTE

FALL RIVER   DAWES   SIOUX   PINE RIDGE   SHERIDAN   CHERRY   ROSEBUD IND. RES.   BROWN

SOUTH DAKOTA
NEBRASKA

BUFFALO GAP NATL. GRASSLAND

OGLALA NATL. GRASSLAND

Chadron   Crawford   Ft. Robinson   Valentine

SURVEY VALLEY   SAND HILLS   NIOBRARA N.W.R.   VALENTINE N.W.R.

SAMUEL R. McKELVIE NATL. FOR.

BOX BUTTE   Alliance   Hemingford   GRANT   HOOKER   THOMAS   BLAINE

Scottsbluff   MORRILL   GARDEN   ARTHUR   McPHERSON   LOGAN   CUSTER

NEBRASKA NATL. FOR.

CRESCENT LAKE N.W.R.

MOUNTAIN TIME ZONE
CENTRAL TIME ZONE

Bridgeport   Oshkosh   Lake McConaughy   KEITH   LINCOLN

CHEYENNE   Sidney   DEUEL   Ogallala   North Platte

Buffalo Bill Ranch S.R.A. & S.H.P.
North Platte Reg. Arpt. (LBF)

NEBRASKA
COLORADO

KIMBALL   Lodgepole   Chappell   Big Springs   Brule   Paxton   Sutherland   Hershey   Maxwell   Brady   Gothenburg   Cozad   Lexington

PEETZ TABLE   SEDGWICK   Julesburg   PERKINS   Grant   Madrid   Wallace   Dickens   PERKINS

Sterling   LOGAN   Sedgwick   Crook   Holyoke   PHILLIPS   CHASE   Imperial   HAYES   FRONTIER   GOSPER

Atwood   St. Petersburg   Haxtun   Paoli   Lamar   Enders   Wauneta   Hamlet   Palisade   McCook   RED WILLOW   HITCHCOCK   FURNAS

WASHINGTON   YUMA   COLORADO
NEBRASKA   DUNDY   Stratton   Trenton   McCook   Cambridge   Edison

Akron   Wray   Haigler   Benkelman   RED WILLOW

California Nevada

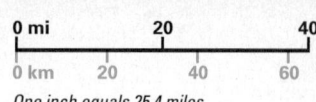

0 mi 20 40
0 km 20 40 60
One inch equals 25.4 miles
One centimeter equals 16.1 kilometers

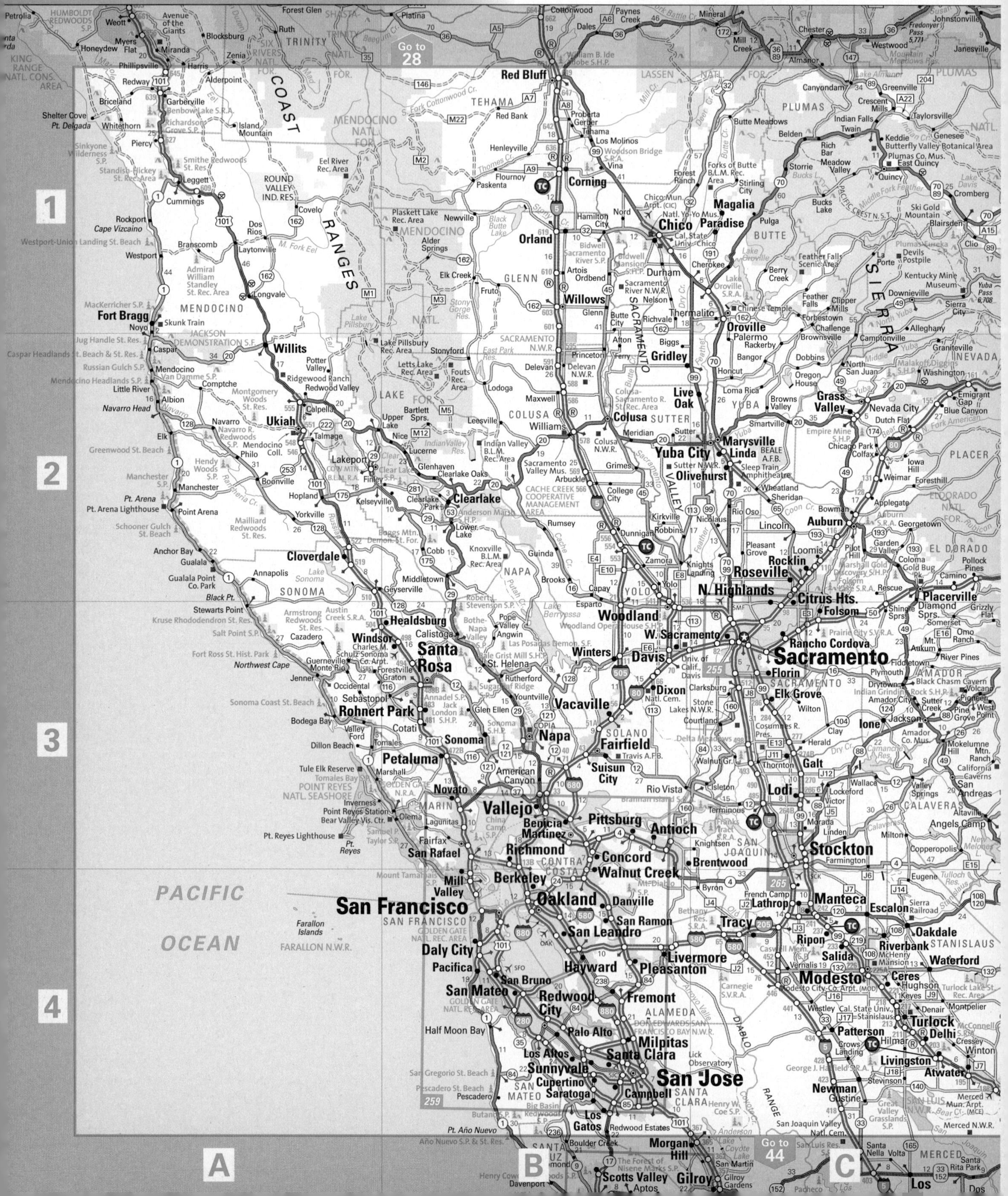

DRIVING DISTANCES IN MILES	AUSTIN, NV	CHICO, CA	MERCED, CA	RENO, NV	SACRAMENTO, CA	SAN FRANCISCO, CA	SAN JOSE, CA	S. LAKE TAHOE, CA	STOCKTON, CA	TONOPAH, NV	UKIAH, CA	YOSEMITE VIL., CA
RENO, NV	171	164	243		132	217	245	59	177	237	261	199
SACRAMENTO, CA	302	88	118	132		87	115	100	48	329	153	170
SAN FRANCISCO, CA	387	182	131	217	87		43	185	82	352	116	183
YOSEMITE VIL., CA	280	257	79	199	170	183	168	180	123	199	289	

SEE ALSO DISTANCE AND DRIVING TIME MAP ON PAGES 286–287

0 mi   20   40
0 km   20   40   60
One inch equals 25.4 miles
One centimeter equals 16.1 kilometers

1

B.L.M. Rec. Area
305
FISH CREEK MTS.
SHOSHONE RANGE
CORTEZ MTS.
Pine Cr.
278
RANGE
SULPHUR SPRING RANGE
Ruby Valley
Ruby Lake N.W.R.
HUMBOLDT-TOIYABE NATL. FOR.
Shantytown
ELKO
Go to 30
93
Currie
ALT 93
STEPTOE VALLEY
ANTELOPE MTS.
White Horse Pass 6,031
Deep Cr.
Dutch Mtn. 7,794
Gold Hill Ghost Town
GR

88
LANDER
92
Henderson Cr.
DIAMOND MTS.
Newark Lake
BUTTE MOUNTAINS
Goshute Lake
50
59
Lages
RANGE
Ibapah
GOSHUTE IND. RES.
Callao
DEEP CREEK RANGE

62
50
Austin
Austin Summit 7,484
Hickison Petroglyph B.L.M. Rec. Area
58
Eureka
Eureka Sentinel Mus.
Diamond Pk. 10,614
892
WHITE PINE
Goshute Canyon and Cave
Duck Cr.
Cherry Creek
CHERRY CREEK RANGE
59
Tippett
Ibapah Pk. 12,087
Trout Creek
Blue Mass Scenic Area
NEVADA UTAH
Salt Marsh Lake

305
12
RANGE
EUREKA
Bob Scotts Summit 7,195
Eureka Opera House
50
Robinson Summit 7,539
Steptoe (site)
93
Spring Valley Cr.
HUMBOLDT-
Gandy

722
Stokes Castle
TOIYABE RANGE
Summit Mtn. 10,461
50
77
Little Antelope Summit 7,438
McGill
North Schell Pk. 11,883
893
TOIYABE NATL.
Mt. Moriah 12,050
Eskdale
CONFUSION RANGE

Toiyabe Pk. 10,793
376
Mt. Hamilton 10,745
Illipah Res. B.L.M. Rec. Area
Garnet Hill
Ely Arpt. (ELY)
Nev. Northern Railway Mus.
FOR.
Sacramento Pass 7,136

Kingston
Kingston Canyon
Ruth
Ward Mtn. B.L.M. Rec. Area
Lane
E. Ely
Ely
93
Cleve Lake B.L.M. Rec. Site
Cave Lake S.R.A.
Connors Pass 7,733
30
Baker
488
487
50

2
376
Womba Ind. Res.
100
HUMBOLDT-TOIYABE NATL. FOR.
23
6
HUMBOLDT-TOIYABE NATL. FOR.
26
50
Majors Place
894
Wheeler Pk. 13,063
Lehman Caves
GREAT BASIN NATL. PARK
Garrison
Pruess Lake
159
DESERT RANGE EXPERIMENTAL STATION

376
J. Res.
EGAN RANGE
White
Ward Charcoal Ovens S.H.P.
6
50
Minerva (site)
93
Shoshone
HUMBOLDT-TOIYABE NATL. FOR.
21

HUMBOLDT-Arc Dome 11,773
Carvers
Hadley
Mt. Jefferson 11,949
Round Mountain
Belmont (site)
TOOUIMA RANGE
Duckwater
Duckwater Ind. Res.
Currant Mtn. 11,513
Preston
Lund
SNAKE RANGE

3
377
Manhattan
Go to 37
MONITOR RANGE
HUMBOLDT-TOIYABE NATL. FOR.
Belmont Courthouse S.H.P.
Potts (site)
Currant Summit 6,999
HOT CREEK RANGE
93
Currant
6
318
White
81
Mt. Wilson 9,296
WILSON CREEK RANGE
77

BIG SMOKY VALLEY
HUMBOLDT-TOIYABE NATL. FOR.
Lunar Crater Volcanic Field Natl. Natural Landmark
6
PANCAKE RANGE
RAILROAD VALLEY
93
Adams-McGill Res.
Sunnyside
Troy Pk. 11,298
GRANT RANGE
Meadow Valley Wash
LAKE VALLEY

4
Warm Springs Summit 6,293
Warm Springs (site)
44
Nyala (site)
REVEILLE RANGE
Spring Valley S.P.
Meadow Valley B.L.M. Rec. Site
Ursine
Hamlin Valley
INDIAN PEAK RANGE

6
5
ah
Central Nev. Mus.
Tonopah Hist. Mining Park
NYE
KAWICH RANGE
375
EXTRATERRESTRIAL HIGHWAY
Queen City Summit 5,935
98
318
320
Pioche
322
Caselton
Zane
Beryl
NEVADA UTAH
Modena
56

26
95
Mud Lake
CACTUS RANGE
TONOPAH TEST RANGE
BELTED RANGE
GROOM RANGE
Tempiute (site)
Rachel
Hiko
SEAMAN RANGE
White
375
Cathedral Gorge S.P.
Panaca
93
11
Echo Canyon S.P.
20
319
Uvada
25
DIXIE NATL. FOR.
Newcastle
18

Goldfield
15
PAHUTE MESA
NELLIS AIR FORCE RANGE COMPLEX
Groom Lake
Ash Springs
Ash Springs B.L.M. Rec. Site
Alamo
LINCOLN
93
42
Caliente
Caliente Railroad Depot
Rainbow Canyon
Kershaw-Ryan S.P.
14
317
Elgin
CLOVER MTS.
Beaver Dam S.P.
Lost Pk. 7,514
WASHINGTON
Mountain Meadows Monument
Baker Dam B.L.M. Rec. Site
Enterprise
Pinto
Veyo
Pine Valley

Scotty's Junction
16
Amargosa
YUC
Go to 45
NEVADA TEST SITE
A
DESERT NATL. WILDLIFE RANGE
B
Go to 46
62
Carp
DELAMAR MTS.
Delamar Lake
PAHRANAGAT N.W.R.
PAHRANAGAT RANGE
MEADOW VALLEY MTS.
MORMON MTS.
C
St. George
St. George Mun. Arpt.
PAIUTE IND. RES.
Shivwits
Santa Clara
Ivins
Jacob Hamblin Home
Snow Canyon S.P.
Gunlock
Gunlock S.P.
Brigham Young Winter Home
Joshua Tree Natl. Area
18
Grapevine Pk. 8,738
67
95
Beatty

PACIFIC TIME ZONE
MOUNTAIN TIME ZONE

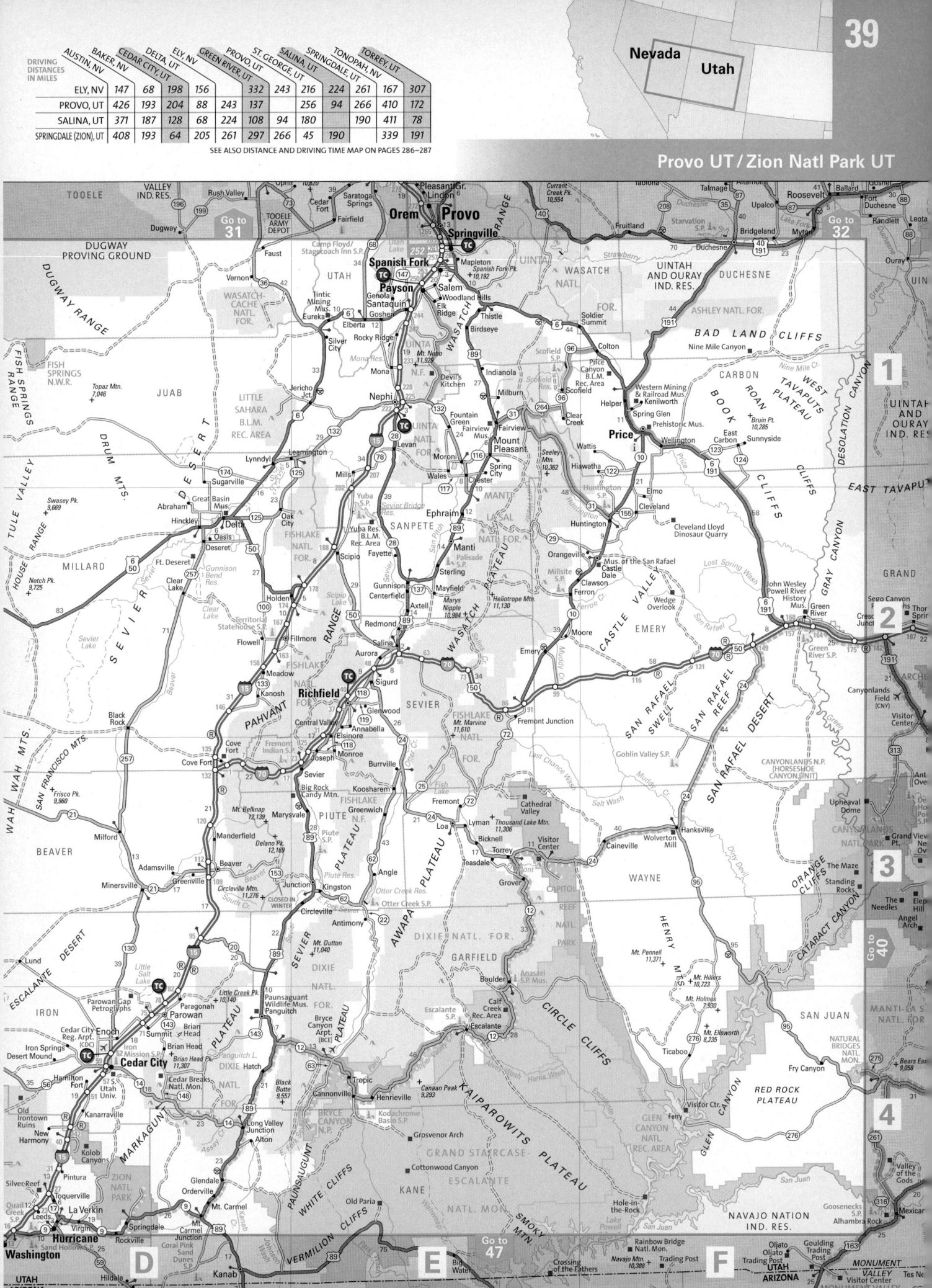

DRIVING DISTANCES IN MILES	AUSTIN, NV	BAKER, NV	CEDAR CITY, UT	DELTA, UT	ELY, NV	GREEN RIVER, UT	PROVO, UT	ST. GEORGE, UT	SALINA, UT	SPRINGDALE, UT	TONOPAH, NV	TORREY, UT
ELY, NV	147	68	198	156		332	243	216	224	261	167	307
PROVO, UT	426	193	204	88	243	137		256	94	266	410	172
SALINA, UT	371	187	128	68	224	108	94	180		190	411	78
SPRINGDALE (ZION), UT	408	193	64	205	261	297	266	45	190		339	191

SEE ALSO DISTANCE AND DRIVING TIME MAP ON PAGES 286–287

Utah | Colorado

0 mi   20   40
0 km   20   40   60

One inch equals 25.4 miles
One centimeter equals 16.1 kilometers

Go to 32
Go to 39
Go to 48

Major places and features:

Roosevelt, Ballard, Gusher, Fort Duchesne, Myton, Randlett, Leota, Bridgeland, Upalco, Bluebell, Duchesne, Ouray, Bonanza, Rangely, Dinosaur, Blue Mountain, Massadona, Elk Springs, Hamilton, Pagoda, Axial, Meeker, Buford, Yampa, Toponas, Radium, McCoy, Bond, State Bridge, Gypsum, Eagle, Edwards, Avon, Wolcott

UINTAH AND OURAY INDIAN RESERVATION

DESOLATION CANYON, EAST TAVAPUTS PLATEAU, ROAN CLIFFS, BOOK CLIFFS, GRAY CANYON

RIO BLANCO, ROAN PLATEAU, GARFIELD, NAVAL OIL SHALE RES., ROAN CLIFFS

Rifle, Silt, Glenwood Springs, Carbondale, El Jebel, Basalt, Snowmass, Snowmass Village, Aspen, Redstone, Marble, Crested Butte

WHITE RIVER NATL. FOR., THE FLAT TOPS, SAWATCH, PITKIN, ELK MTS.

De Beque, Collbran, Molina, Mesa, Cameo, Palisade, Clifton, Grand Junction, Fruita, Loma, Mack, Westwater, Cisco, Thompson Springs, Crescent Junction

COLORADO NATL. MON., GRAND MESA NATL. FOR., GRAND MESA, BUCK MESA, BATTLEMENT MESA

Orchard City, Cedaredge, Paonia, Bowie, Somerset, Hotchkiss, Crawford, Maher, Delta, Austin, Olathe, Montrose, Gunnison, Almont, Parlin, Ohio, Sapinero, Cimarron

UNCOMPAHGRE NATL. FOR., UNCOMPAHGRE PLATEAU, GATEWAY B.L.M. REC. AREA, DOMINGUEZ CANYON, GUNNISON, WEST ELK MTS., CURECANTI NATL. REC. AREA

Moab, Gateway, Paradox, Bedrock, Uravan, Nucla, Naturita, Redvale, Norwood, Placerville, Sawpit, Ridgway, Colona, Montrose, Lake City

ARCHES NATL. PARK, MANTI-LA SAL NATL. FOR., Delicate Arch, Fisher Towers, Castle Valley, Castleton Tower, The Windows, Mt. Waas 12,311, Mt. Peale 12,721, Mt. Tukuhnikivatz

Canyonlands Field (CNY), Visitor Center, Dead Horse Point S.P., Grand View Pt., Needles Overlook, Looking Glass Rock, Wilson Arch, La Sal, La Sal Junction, Church Rock, Summit Point, Newspaper Rock

CANYONLANDS NATL. PARK, The Maze, The Needles, Standing Rocks, Elephant Hill, Angel Arch, Cataract Canyon, GLEN CANYON NATL. REC. AREA

Monticello, Eastland, Ucolo, Dove Creek, Cahone, Pleasant View, Yellow Jacket, Lewis, Arriola, Dolores, Cortez, Mancos, Hesperus, Durango, Bayfield, Ignacio, Arboles

San Juan, Blanding, Bluff, Mexican Hat, Montezuma Creek, Aneth, Navajo Twin Rocks, Valley of the Gods, Goosenecks S.P.

MANTI-LA SAL NATL. FOR., Abajo Pk. 11,360, Mt. Linnaeus 10,961, Shay Mtn. 9,988, Bears Ears 9,058, Edge of the Cedars S.P.

Dinosaur Mus. of Blanding, Hovenweep Natl. Mon., Anasazi Heritage Center, Lowry Pueblo Ruins, McPhee Res., Yucca House Natl. Mon., MESA VERDE NATL. PARK, Towaoc

UTE MOUNTAIN IND. RES., NAVAJO NATION IND. RES., SOUTHERN UTE IND. RES., Four Corners Mon. & Navajo Tribal Park, Ute Mountain Tribal Park Visitor Center, Red Mesa

SAN MIGUEL, Telluride, Mountain Village, Ophir, Silverton, Ouray, Ouray Hot Springs, Camp Bird, Pandora, Bridal Veil Falls, Red Mtn. Pass, Molas Pass 10,910, Coal Bank Pass 10,640, Rico, Stoner, Rockwood, Hermosa, Trimble

SAN JUAN NATL. FOR., SAN JUAN MOUNTAINS, WEMINUCHE WILDERNESS, LA PLATA MTS., Mt. Eolus 14,083, Mt. Wilson 14,246, Lizard Head Pass, Lone Mesa S.P.

DOLORES, Disappointment Cr., TAYLOR MESA, SAN JUAN NATL. FOR.

RIO GRANDE NATL. FOR., LA GARITA, HINSDALE, MINERAL NATL. FOR., Creede, South Fork, Wolf Creek Pass, Pagosa Springs, Chimney Rock, Chimney Rock Archaeological Area, Nutria, Lonetree, Platoro, Summitville

COCHETOPA, GUNNISON NATL. FOR., North Pass 10,149, Cochetopa Pass 10,032, Spring Creek Pass 10,901, Slumgullion Pass 11,361, San Luis Pk. 14,014, Wheeler Geologic Area, Wagon Wheel Gap, Spar City

Durango & Silverton Narrow Gauge RR, Fort Lewis Coll., Grandview, Durango-La Plata Co. Arpt. (DRO), Oxford, Gem Village, Tiffany, Allison, Chromo

MONUMENT VALLEY, Mexican Hat, Poncho House, Alhambra Rock, NAVAJO NATION IND. RES.

UTAH / COLORADO, UTAH / ARIZONA, COLORADO / NEW MEXICO

A   B   C

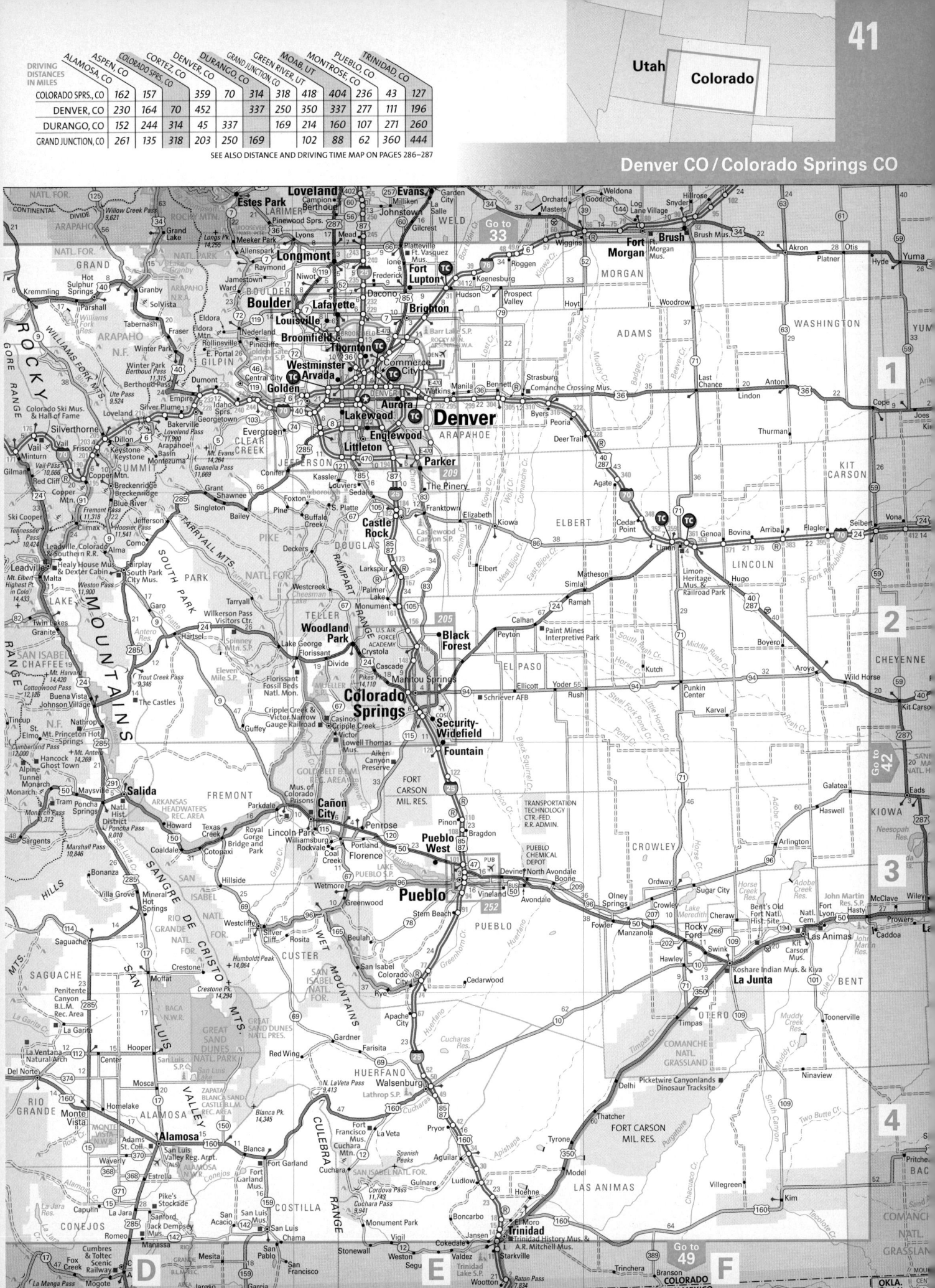

Utah   Colorado

DRIVING DISTANCES IN MILES	ALAMOSA, CO	ASPEN, CO	COLORADO SPRS., CO	CORTEZ, CO	DENVER, CO	DURANGO, CO	GRAND JUNCTION, CO	GREEN RIVER, UT	MOAB, UT	MONTROSE, CO	PUEBLO, CO	TRINIDAD, CO
COLORADO SPRS., CO	162	157		359	70	314	318	418	404	236	43	127
DENVER, CO	230	164	70	452		337	250	350	337	277	111	196
DURANGO, CO	152	244	314	45	337		169	214	160	107	271	260
GRAND JUNCTION, CO	261	135	318	203	250	169		102	88	62	360	444

SEE ALSO DISTANCE AND DRIVING TIME MAP ON PAGES 286–287

Nebraska

Colorado

Kansas

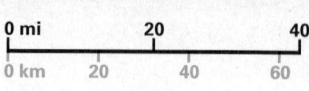

0 mi | 20 | 40
0 km | 20 | 40 | 60

One inch equals 25.4 miles
One centimeter equals 16.1 kilometers

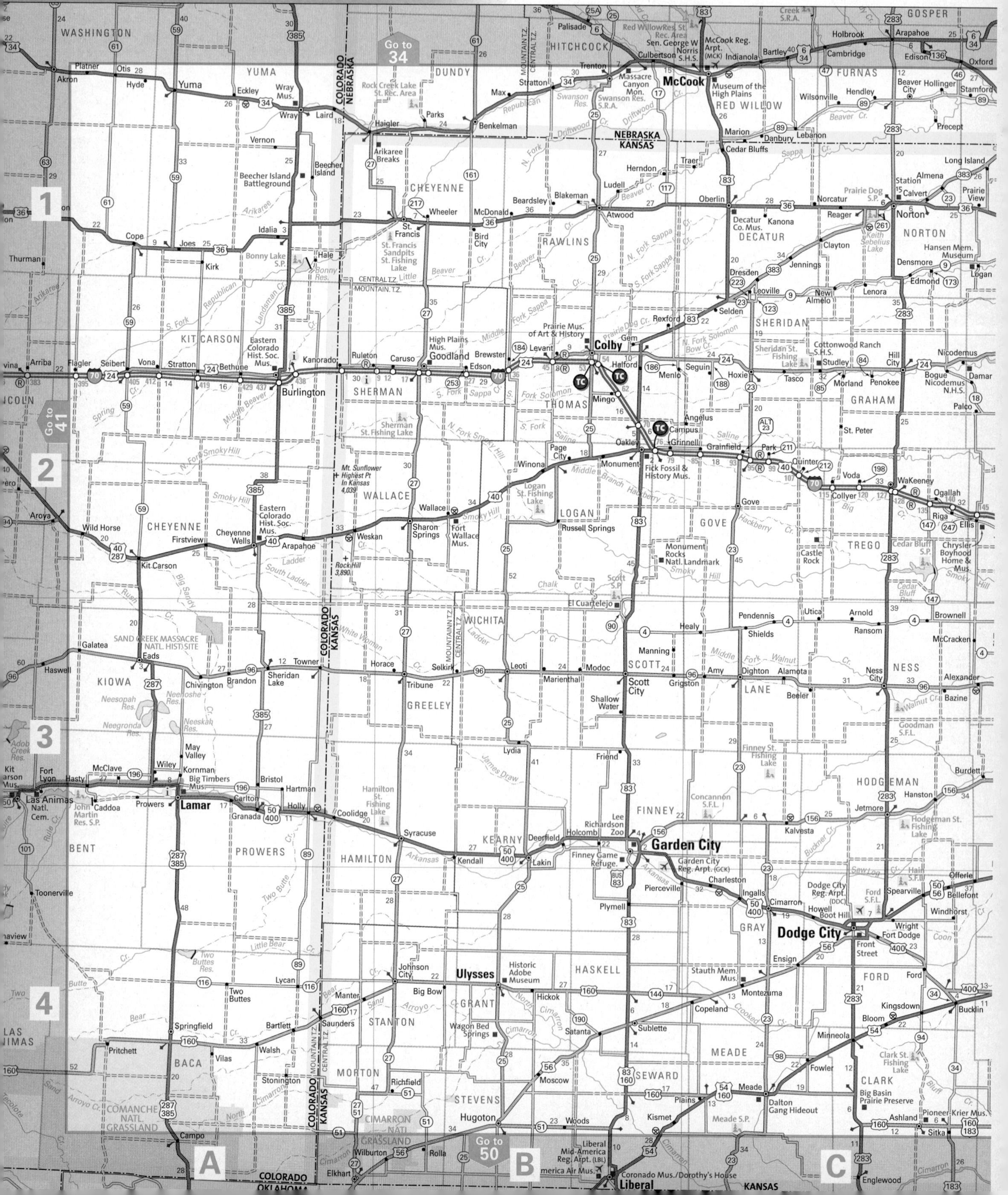

DRIVING DISTANCES IN MILES	BURLINGTON, CO	DODGE CITY, KS	EMPORIA, KS	GARDEN CITY, KS	HAYS, KS	LAMAR, CO	MANHATTAN, KS	McCOOK, NE	OAKLEY, KS	SALINA, KS	TOPEKA, KS	WICHITA, KS
GARDEN CITY, KS	167	52	290		139	98	272	167	79	204	311	205
OAKLEY, KS	88	136	293	79	87	156	247	88		179	286	268
SALINA, KS	266	164	118	204	93	335	72	240	179		111	92
WICHITA, KS	354	153	85	205	181	303	131	329	268	92	137	

SEE ALSO DISTANCE AND DRIVING TIME MAP ON PAGES 286–287

Nevada

California

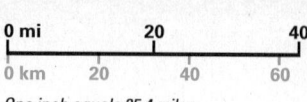

0 mi   20   40

0 km   20   40   60

One inch equals 25.4 miles
One centimeter equals 16.1 kilometers

San Jose CA / Fresno CA

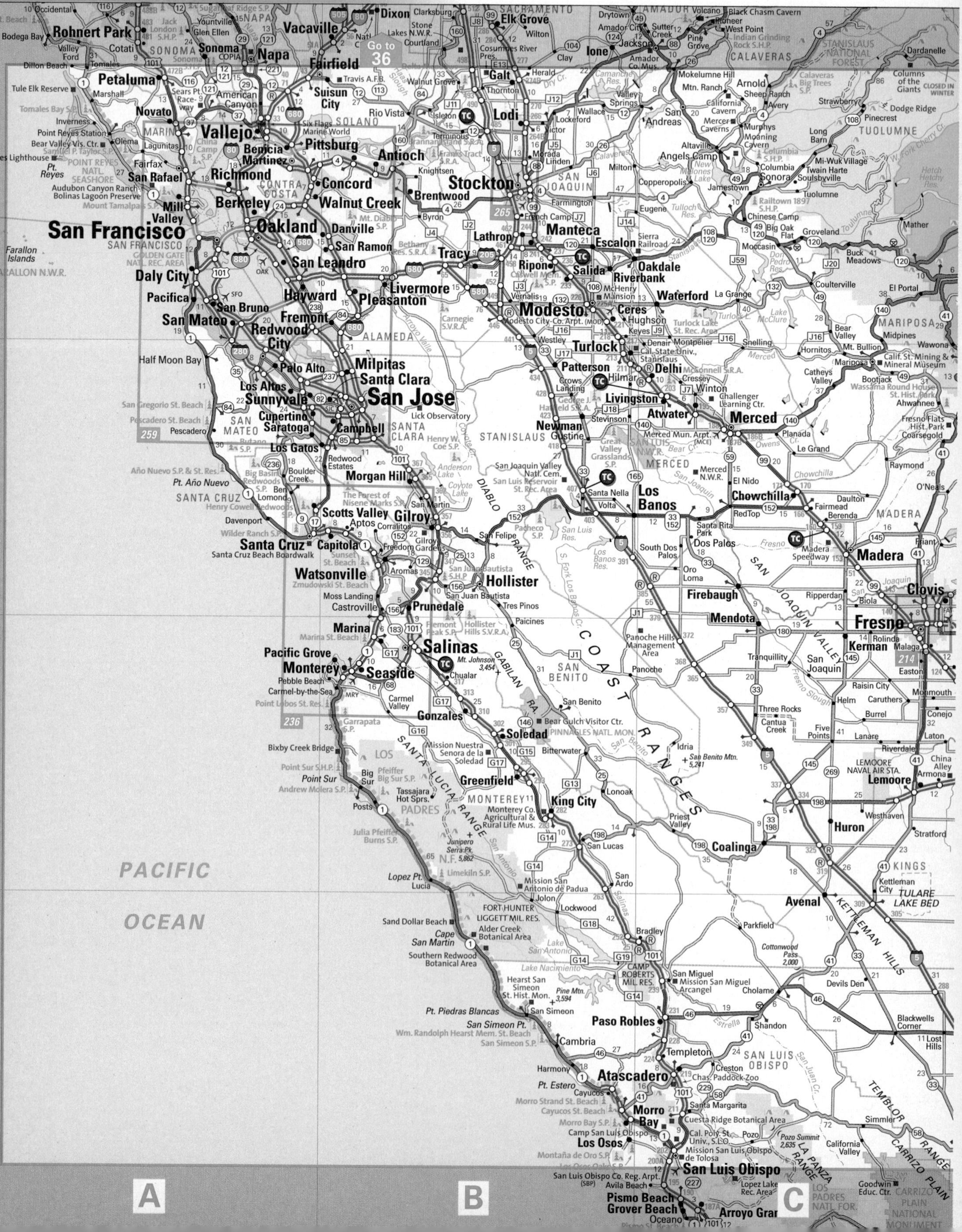

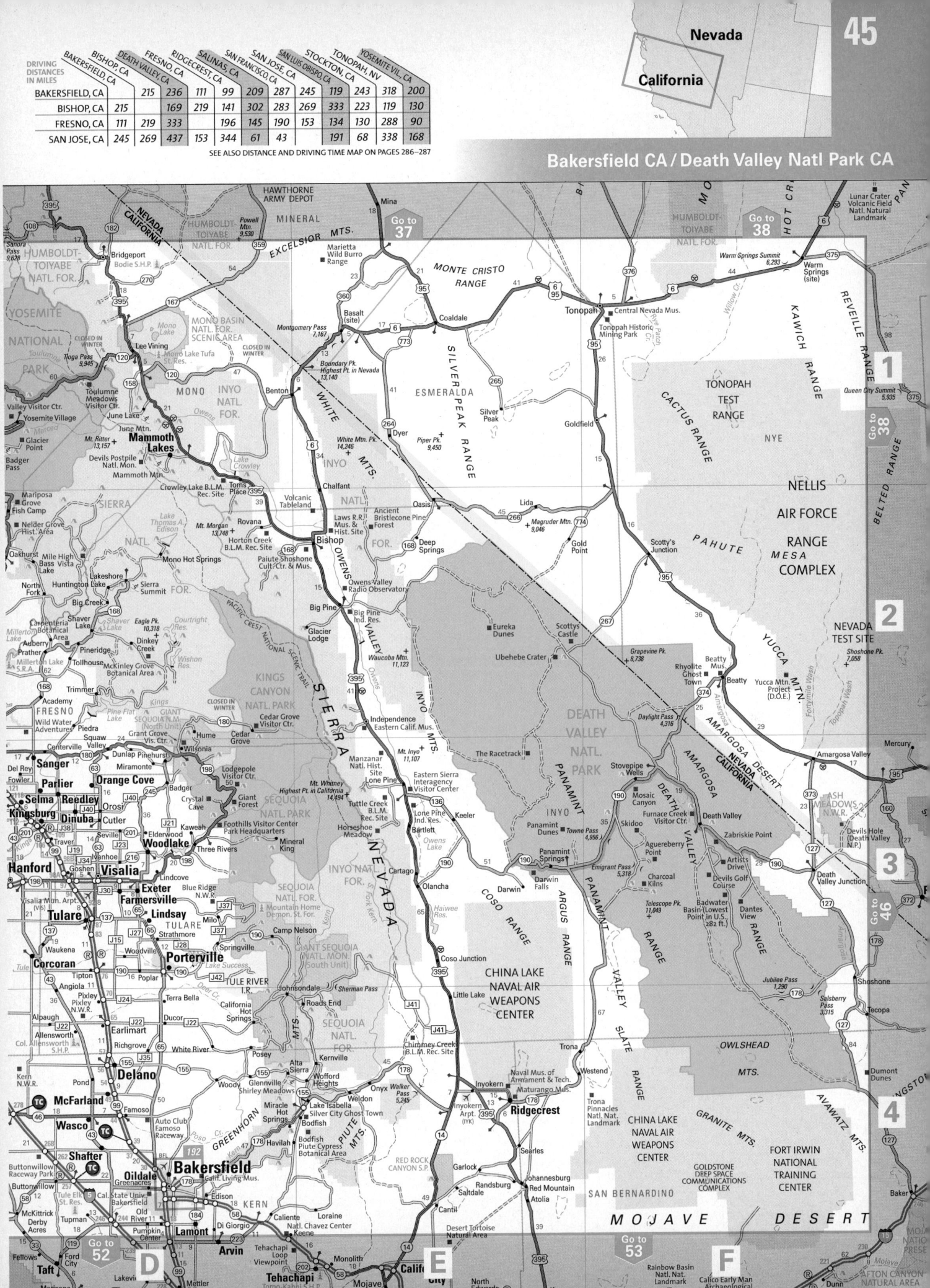

Nevada

California

DRIVING DISTANCES IN MILES	BAKERSFIELD, CA	BISHOP, CA	DEATH VALLEY, CA	FRESNO, CA	RIDGECREST, CA	SALINAS, CA	SAN FRANCISCO, CA	SAN JOSE, CA	SAN LUIS OBISPO, CA	STOCKTON, CA	TONOPAH, NV	YOSEMITE VIL., CA
BAKERSFIELD, CA		215	236	111	99	209	287	245	119	243	318	200
BISHOP, CA	215		169	219	141	302	283	269	333	223	119	130
FRESNO, CA	111	219	333		196	145	190	153	134	130	288	90
SAN JOSE, CA	245	269	437	153	344	61	43		191	68	338	168

Nevada Utah
California
Arizona

0 mi | 20 | 40
0 km | 20 | 40 | 60
One inch equals 25.4 miles
One centimeter equals 16.1 kilometers

Las Vegas NV / St George UT

MESA

NELLIS
AIR FORCE
RANGE
COMPLEX

NYE

NEVADA
TEST SITE

Shoshone Pk. + 7,058

Yucca Lake

Groom Lake

PAHRANAGAT N.W.R.

LINCOLN

DELAMAR MTS.

MORMON MTS.

Go to 38

PAIUTE IND. RES.

Gunlock
Veyo
Silver Reef
Brigham Young Winter Home
Snow Canyon S.P.
Santa Clara
Shivwits
Ivins
Jacob Hamblin Home
Joshua Tree Natural Area
St. George Mun. Arpt.
WASHINGTON
Washington
St. George
Leeds
Toquerville
La Verkin
Hurricane
Virgin
Rockville
Springdale
ZION NATL. PARK

UTAH
ARIZONA
Colorado City
Cane Beds
Hildale

Amargosa Valley
Mercury
Indian Springs

SPOTTED RANGE
DESERT
Desert Lake
Dog Bone Lake

SHEEP RANGE
NATL. WILDLIFE RANGE
Hayford Pk. + 9,912

CLARK

Mormon Pk. + 7,411

Carp
Moapa Valley N.W.R.
Glendale
Moapa
Logandale
Overton
Lost City Mus.
VALLEY OF FIRE S.P.

Mesquite
Bunkerville
Littlefield
Beaver Dam
Virgin River Canyon B.L.M. Rec. Area
Mt. Bangs + 8,012

VIRGIN MTS.

Virgin River Rec. Area

SHIVWITS

Poverty Mtn. + 6,791
Mt. Trumbull + 8,028
Ranger Station

GRAND CANYON-PARASHANT NATL. MONUMENT

UINKARET PLATEAU

Toroweap Overlook

LAKE MEAD NATL. REC. AREA

ASH MEADOWS N.W.R.
Devils Hole (Death Valley N.P.)
Death Valley Junction

SPRING MOUNTAINS N.R.A.
Las Vegas Ski and Snowboard
Charleston Pk. + 11,918

Floyd Lamb S.P.
Pahrump

Las Vegas
North Las Vegas
RED ROCK CANYON N.C.A.
Spring Mtn. Ranch S.P.
Blue Diamond

Nellis Air Force Range Complex

MUDDY MTS.

Fortification Hill 3,718
Temple Bar
Meadview

Lake Mead

Henderson
Hoover Dam
Boulder City
Sloan
SLOAN CANYON N.C.A.

Grand Canyon West & Skywalk
Grand Canyon West Arpt. (1G4)

GRAND CANYON NATL. PARK

Shoshone
Tecopa
Pass 3,315

INYO
KINGSTON RANGE

Goodsprings
Sandy Valley
Jean

Willow Beach

Nelson

ELDORADO MTS.

BLACK MTS.

Mt. Perkins + 5,456

WHITE HILLS

Joshua Tree Forest

Garnet Mtn. + 8,440

Red Lake
Natural Bridge

Dumont Dunes

Mesquite Lake
Roach Lake
Primm
Buffalo Bill's
Desert

Mt. Tipton + 7,148
Windy Point B.L.M. Rec. Site
Chloride
Dolan Springs

MOHAVE

HUALAPAI IND. RES.

Grand Canyon Caverns

Clark Mtn. + 7,929
Mountain Pass
Ivanpah Lake

Nipton
Searchlight

Cottonwood Cove
Lake Mohave

Dolan Springs

Peach Springs
Truxton
Nelson
Yampai

Halloran Springs
Mountain Pass 4,730
Ivanpah

Cal Nev Ari

Hackberry
Valentine

AQUARIUS MTS.

Cross Mtn. + 6,463

Silver Lake
Baker
Cima Dome
Cima
Cinder Cones

NEW YORK MTS.
LANFAIR VALLEY

NEVADA
CALIFORNIA

Davis Dam
Colorado River Museum
LAKE MEAD N.R.A.
ROAD CLOSED INDEFINITELY

Kingman Arpt. (IGM)
Kingman
McConnico
Mohave Mus. of History & Arts and Historic Rt. 66 Mus.
Hualapai Mtn. Park

SACRAMENTO MTS.

Snow Mtn. + 5,879
Mohon Pk. + 7,499
Mt. Hope + 7,263

MOJAVE NATIONAL PRESERVE
DEVILS PLAYGROUND

Providence Mountains St. Rec. Area
Kelso

Laughlin/Bullhead Intl. Arpt. (IFP)
Laughlin
Bullhead City
Oatman

Hualapai Pk. + 8,417
Wild Cow Springs B.L.M. Rec. Site

HUALAPAI MTS.

Hyde Creek Mtn. + 7,272

PRESCOTT NATL. FOR.

MOJAVE DESERT

AFTON CANYON NATURAL AREA

SAN BERNARDINO
Kelso Dunes
Mitchell Caverns

Goffs

Big Bend of the Colorado S.R.A.

Mohave Valley
FORT MOJAVE IND. RES.

Yucca

BLACK MESA

Wikieup

Granite Pk. + 7,069
Burro Creek B.L.M. Rec. Site
Bagdad

Mohon Pk.
Cypress Mtn. + 6,251

CADY MTS.
Pisgah Crater
Ludlow
Bagdad

BRISTOL MTS.

Fenner
Essex

Needles
South Pass 2,750

Topock
HAVASU N.W.R.
Golden Shores

AUBREY PK. + 5,078

MC CRACKEN MTS.

Burro Creek

POACHIE RANGE

Hillside

WEAVER MTS.

Go to 53

BULLION MTS.

Amboy Crater Natl. Nat. Landmark
Amboy
Cadiz
Danby

OLD NATIONAL TRAIL HWY

PIUTE MTS.

OLD WOMAN MTS.

CHEMEHUEVI VALLEY

Moabi Reg. Park
Lake Havasu City Arpt. (HII)

MOHAVE MTS.

Havasu Lake
London Bridge
Lake Havasu City
Lake Havasu S.P.

Twentynine Palms
TWENTYNINE PALMS MARINE CORPS AIR GROUND COMBAT CENTER
Bristol Lake

CHEMEHUEVI IND. RES.

CHEMEHUEVI VALLEY

TURTLE MTS.

WHIPPLE MTS.

ARIZ.
CALIF.

Parker Dam
Bill Williams River N.W.R.
Buckskin Mountain S.P.

BUCKSKIN MTS.

Alamo Lake
Tres Alamos + 4,293

LA PAZ

Joshua Tree
Yucca Valley
Hidden Valley
Lost Horse Mine
Oasis Visitor Ctr.
Twentynine Palms Ind. Res.

JOSHUA TREE NATL. PARK

Cholla Cactus Garden

RIVERSIDE

Rice

Vidal Jct.
Earp
Vidal
Big River
Parker
Parker Strip B.L.M. Rec. Area
Parker Dam

Colorado River Indian Tribes Arpt.
Poston

CACTUS PLAIN

Swansea Ghost Town

Go to 54

Robson's Mining World

Congress
Date
Forepaugh
Aquila
Bouse
Wenden

Nevada   Utah
California
Arizona

DRIVING DISTANCES IN MILES

	CHINLE, AZ	FLAGSTAFF, AZ	GRAND CANYON, AZ	HOLBROOK, AZ	KAYENTA, AZ	KINGMAN, AZ	LAKE HAVASU CITY, AZ	LAS VEGAS, NV	LAUGHLIN, NV	PAGE, AZ	PRESCOTT, AZ	ST. GEORGE, UT
FLAGSTAFF, AZ	216		89	93	152	148	209	249	182	135	89	271
GRAND CANYON, AZ	232	89		182	153	175	236	276	209	136	131	272
LAS VEGAS, NV	465	249	276	341	374	103	154		94	277	251	118
ST. GEORGE, UT	358	271	272	353	255	221	272	118	212	159	369	

SEE ALSO DISTANCE AND DRIVING TIME MAP ON PAGES 286–287

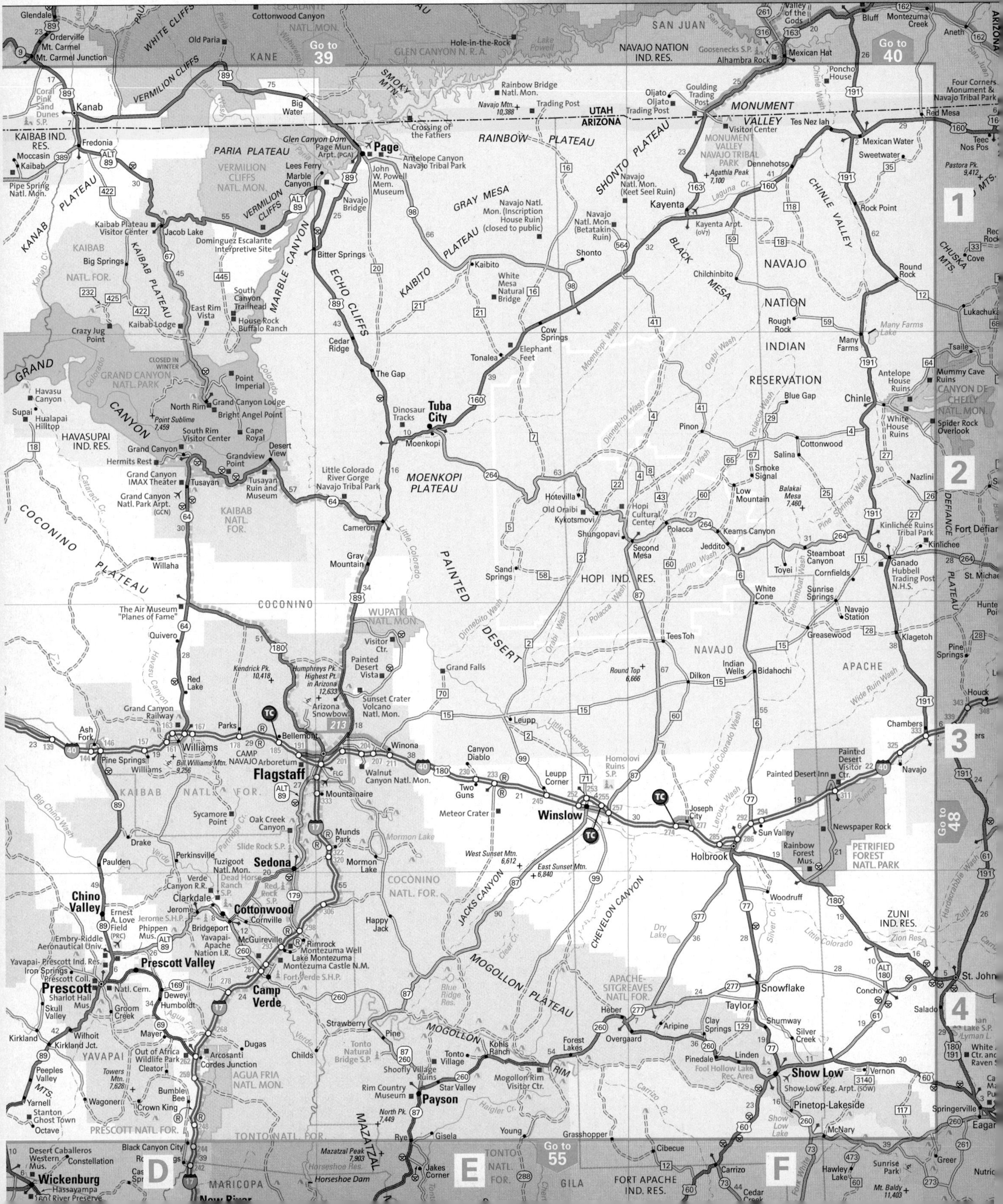

Utah Colorado

Arizona **New Mexico** Okla.

Texas

0 mi 20 40
0 km 20 40 60
One inch equals 25.4 miles
One centimeter equals 16.1 kilometers

Go to 40

Go to 47

Go to 40

Go to 56

Durango

Shiprock

Aztec

Farmington **Bloomfield**

Chinle

Gallup

Grants

Espanola

Los Alamos

White Rock

Rio Rancho

Albuquerque

Los Lunas

Belen

Socorro

A B C

1 2 3 4

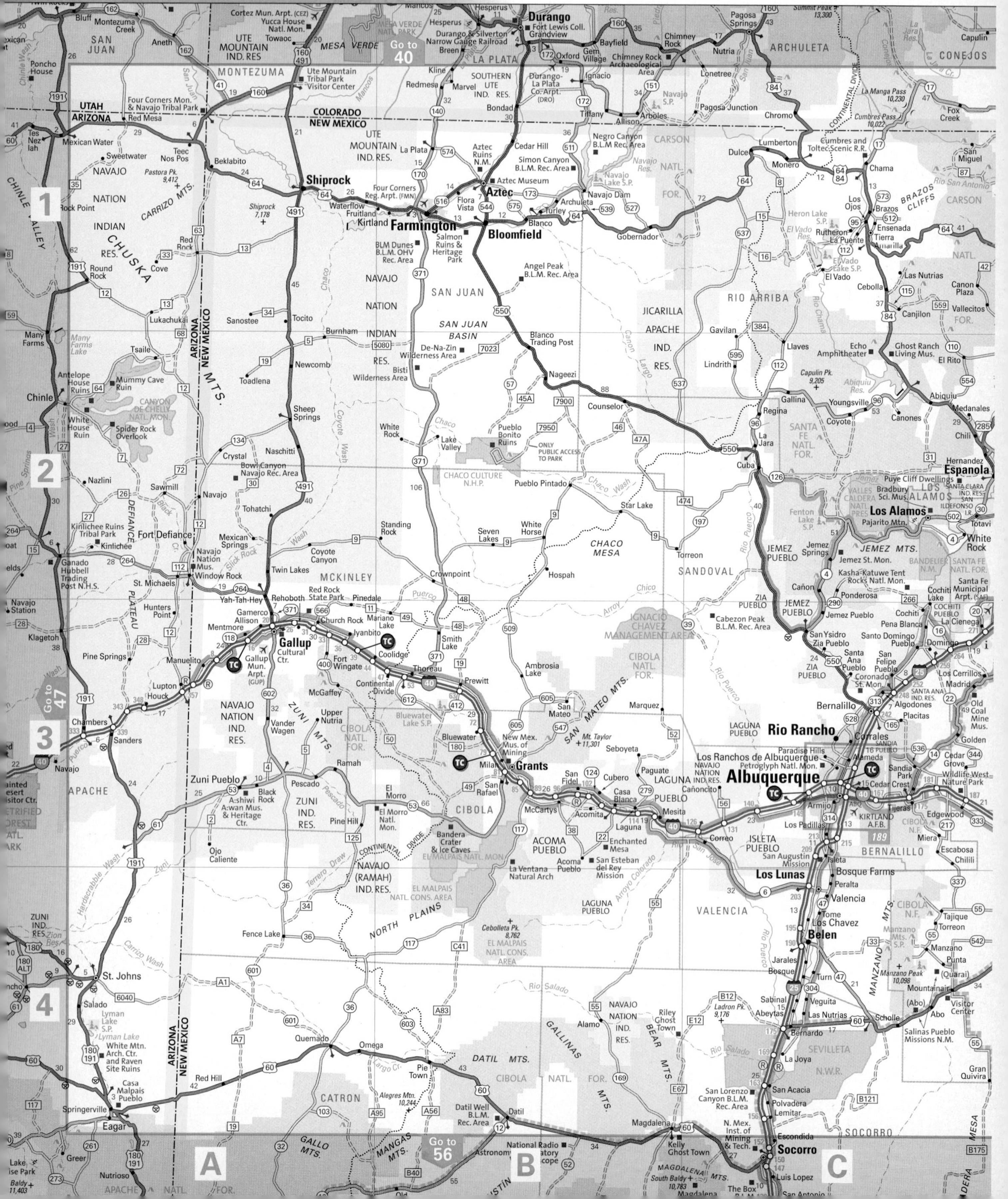

Go to 41
Go to 50
Go to 57

DRIVING DISTANCES IN MILES	ALBUQUERQUE, NM	CLAYTON, NM	CLOVIS, NM	DURANGO, CO	FARMINGTON, NM	GALLUP, NM	SANTA FE, NM	SOCORRO, NM	TAOS, NM	TRINIDAD, CO	TUCUMCARI, NM	VAUGHN, NM
ALBUQUERQUE, NM		266	220	212	181	141	55	77	123	242	174	104
FARMINGTON, NM	181	368	401	50		120	205	263	211	300	355	284
SANTA FE, NM	55	216	213	207	205	197		132	68	192	167	96
TUCUMCARI, NM	174	111	82	386	355	316	167	251	195	198		98

SEE ALSO DISTANCE AND DRIVING TIME MAP ON PAGES 286–287

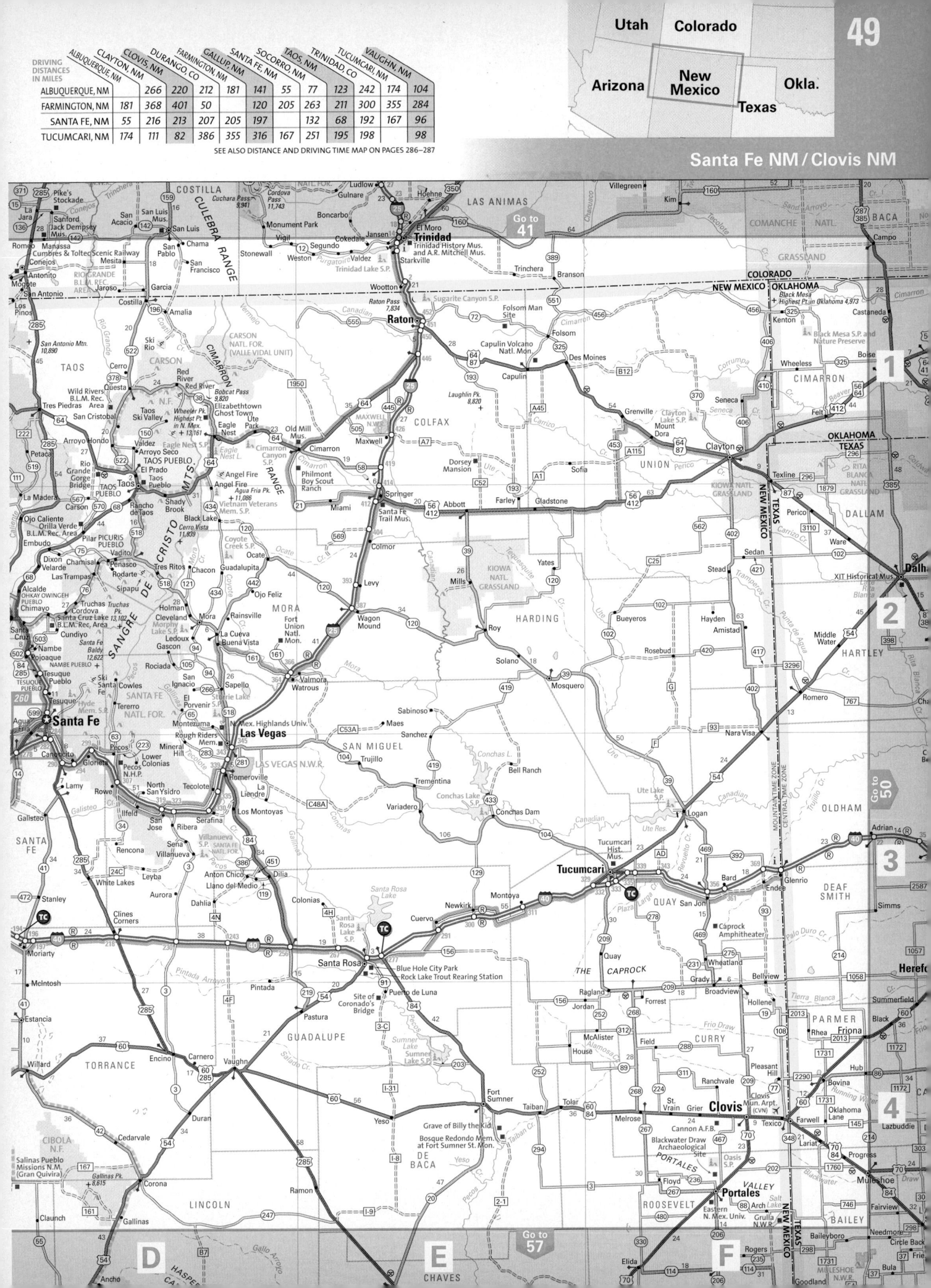

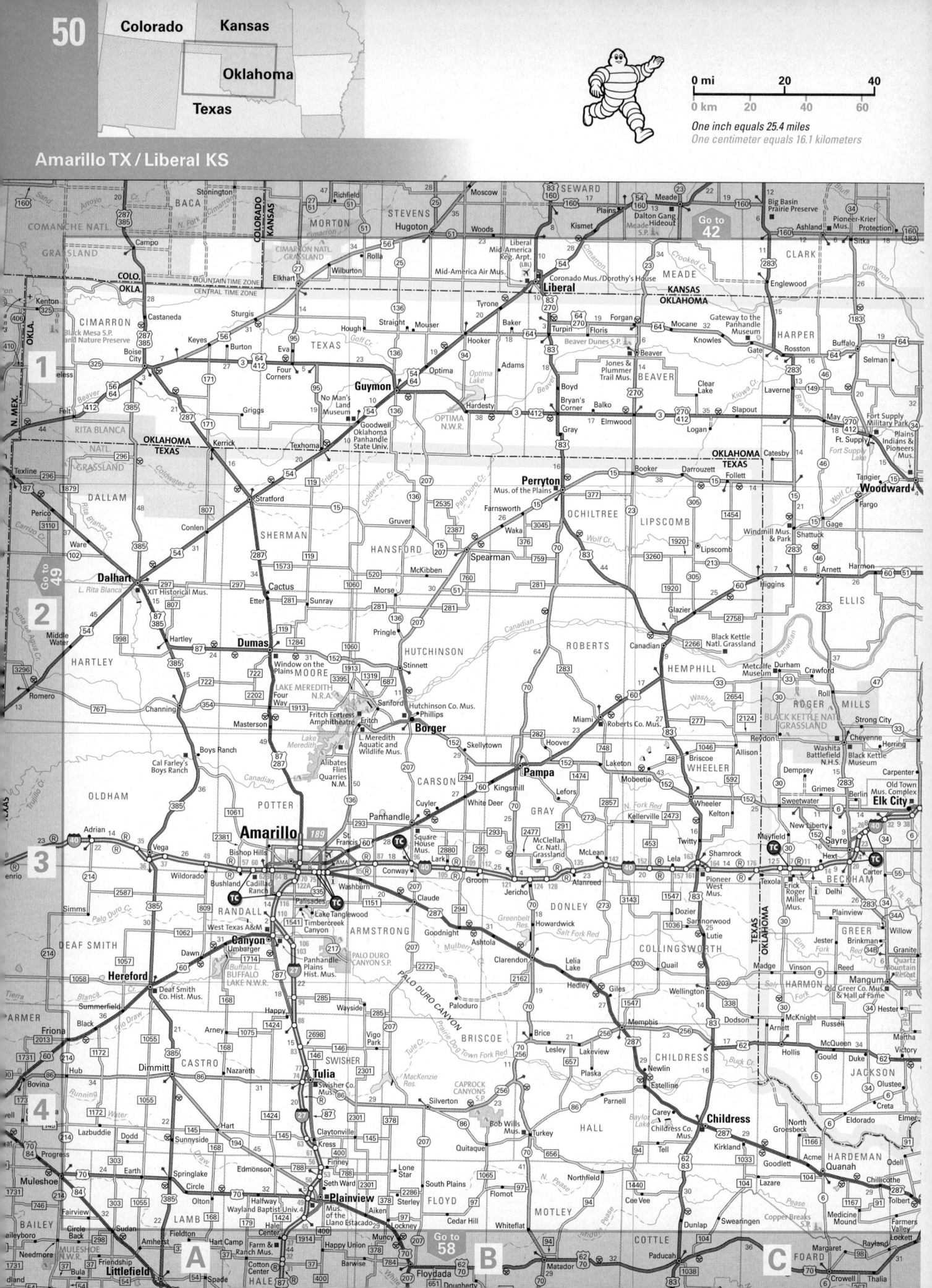

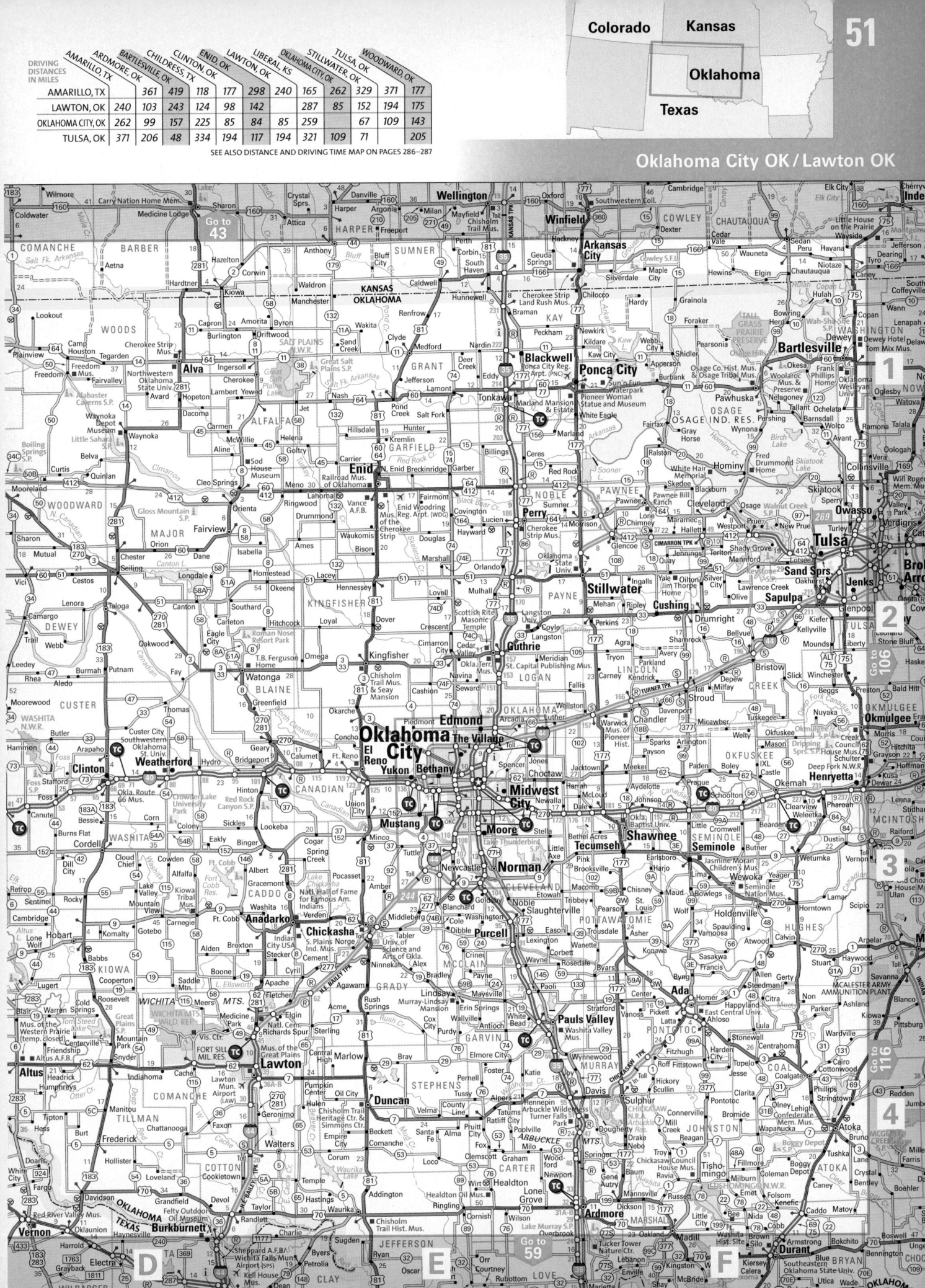

DRIVING DISTANCES IN MILES	AMARILLO, TX	ARDMORE, OK	BARTLESVILLE, OK	CHILDRESS, TX	CLINTON, OK	ENID, OK	LAWTON, OK	LIBERAL, KS	OKLAHOMA CITY, OK	STILLWATER, OK	TULSA, OK	WOODWARD, OK
AMARILLO, TX		361	419	118	177	298	240	165	262	329	371	177
LAWTON, OK	240	103	243	124	98	142		287	85	152	194	175
OKLAHOMA CITY, OK	262	99	157	225	85	84	85	259		67	109	143
TULSA, OK	371	206	48	334	194	117	194	321	109	71		205

SEE ALSO DISTANCE AND DRIVING TIME MAP ON PAGES 286–287

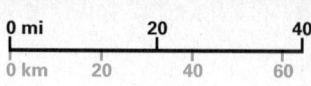

One inch equals 25.4 miles
One centimeter equals 16.1 kilometers

Los Angeles CA / Santa Barbara CA

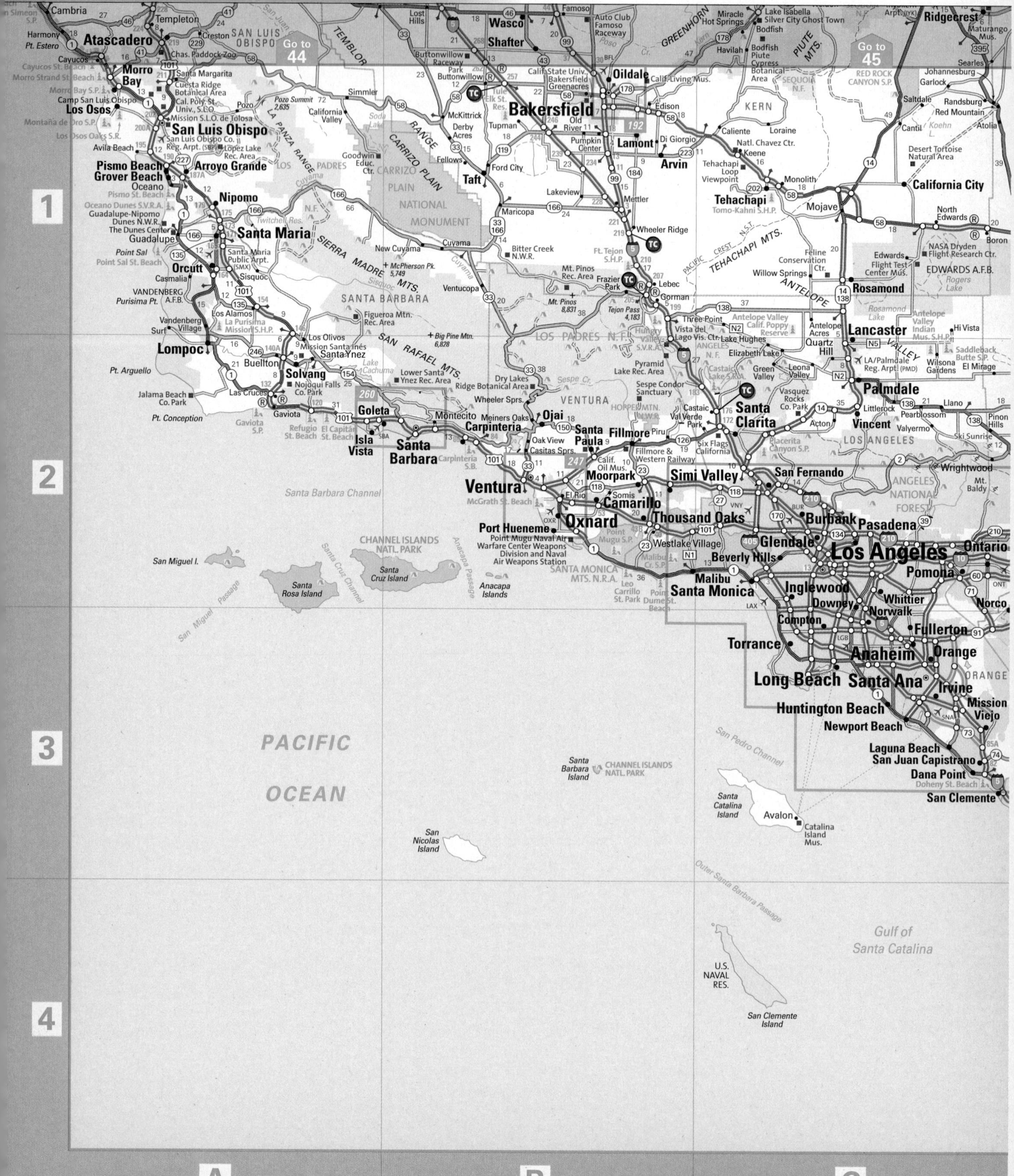

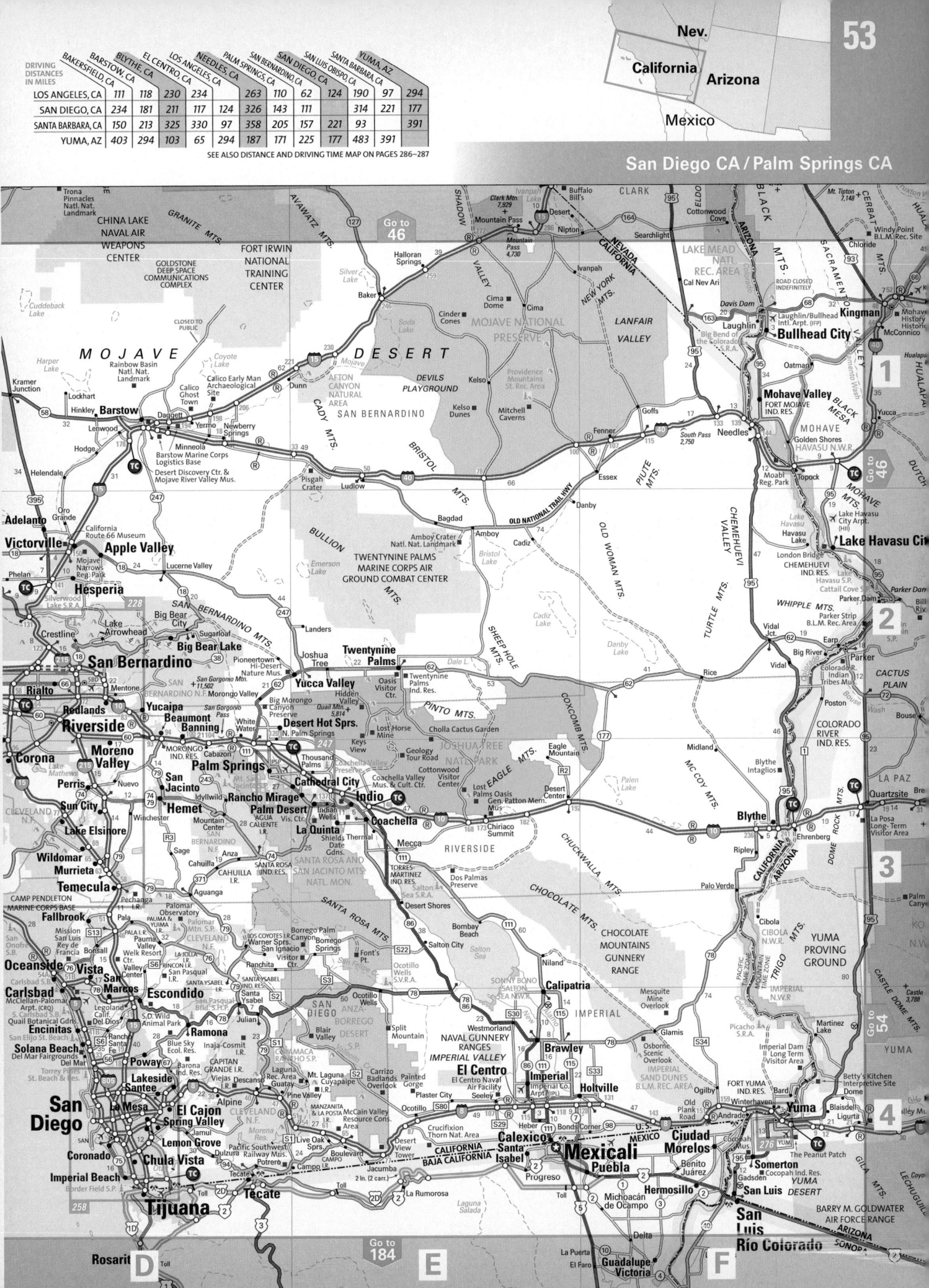

DRIVING DISTANCES IN MILES	BAKERSFIELD, CA	BARSTOW, CA	BLYTHE, CA	EL CENTRO, CA	LOS ANGELES, CA	NEEDLES, CA	PALM SPRINGS, CA	SAN BERNARDINO, CA	SAN DIEGO, CA	SAN LUIS OBISPO, CA	SANTA BARBARA, CA	YUMA, AZ
LOS ANGELES, CA	111	118	230	234		263	110	62	124	190	97	294
SAN DIEGO, CA	234	181	211	117	124	326	143	111		314	221	177
SANTA BARBARA, CA	150	213	325	330	97	358	205	157	221	93		391
YUMA, AZ	403	294	103	65	294	187	171	225	177	483	391	

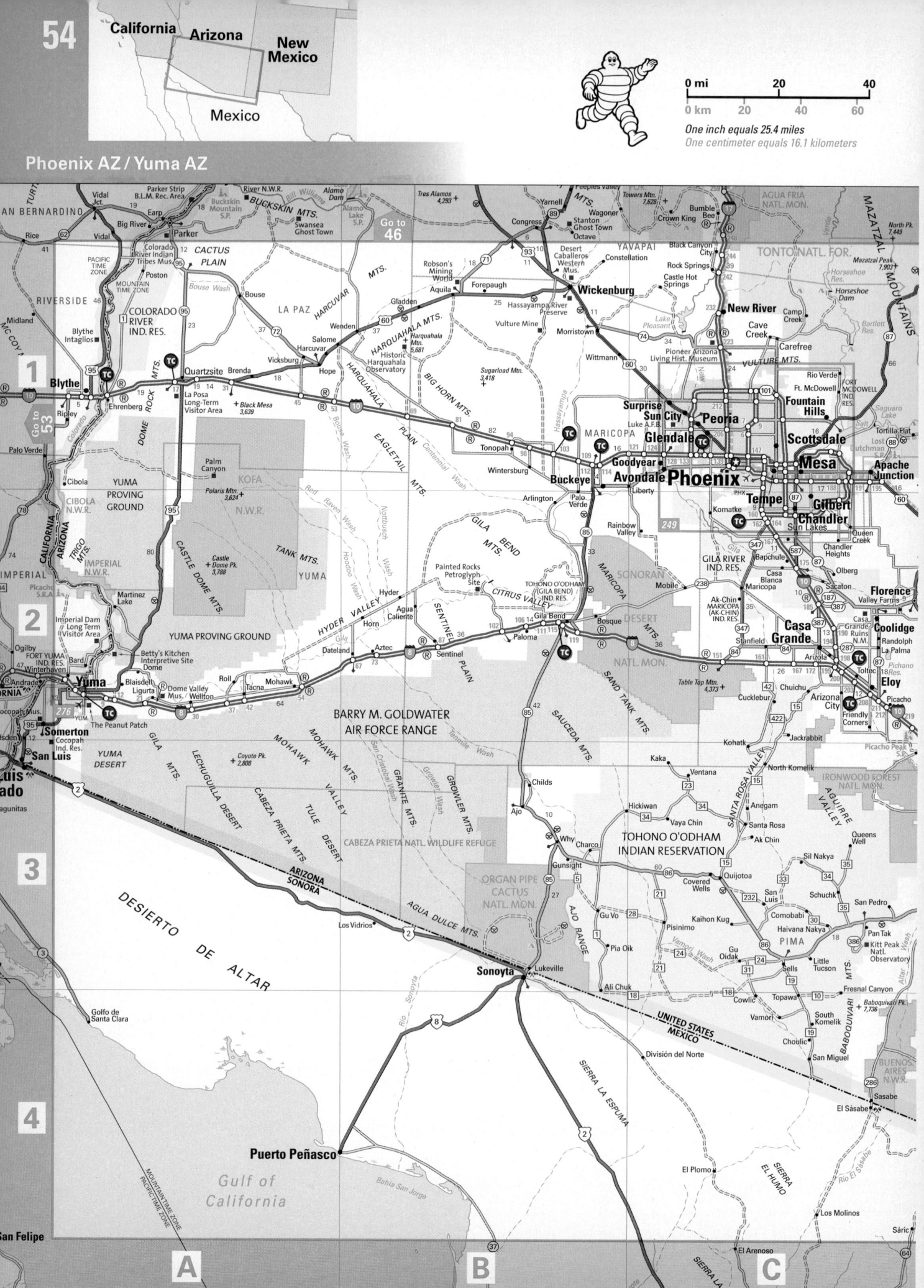

California   Arizona   New Mexico

Mexico

0 mi   20   40
0 km   20   40   60
One inch equals 25.4 miles
One centimeter equals 16.1 kilometers

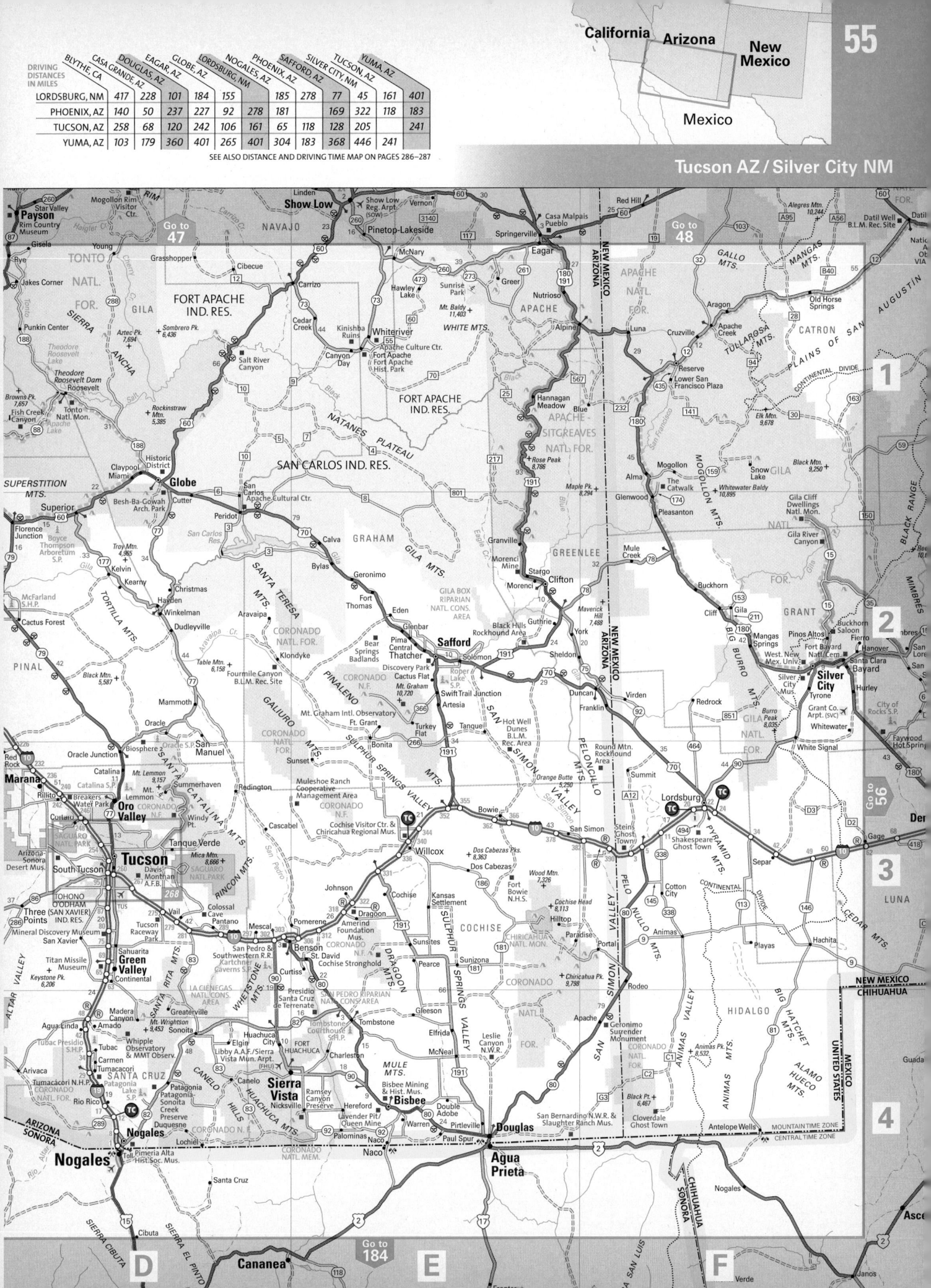

New
Mexico

Texas

Mexico

El Paso TX / Las Cruces NM

One inch equals 25.4 miles
One centimeter equals 16.1 kilometers

0 mi   20   40
0 km 20   40   60

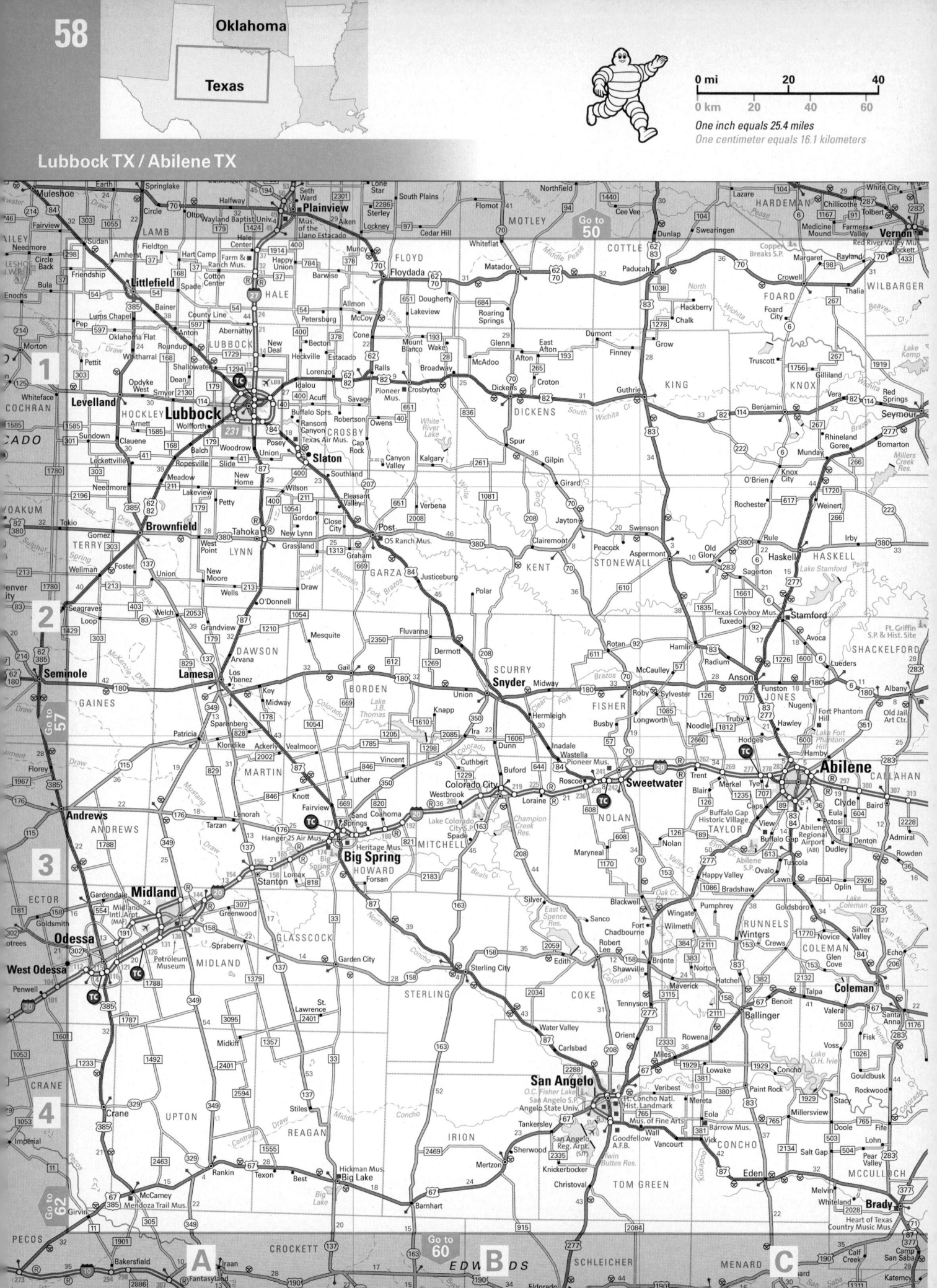

One inch equals 25.4 miles
One centimeter equals 16.1 kilometers

0 mi   20   40
0 km 20   40   60

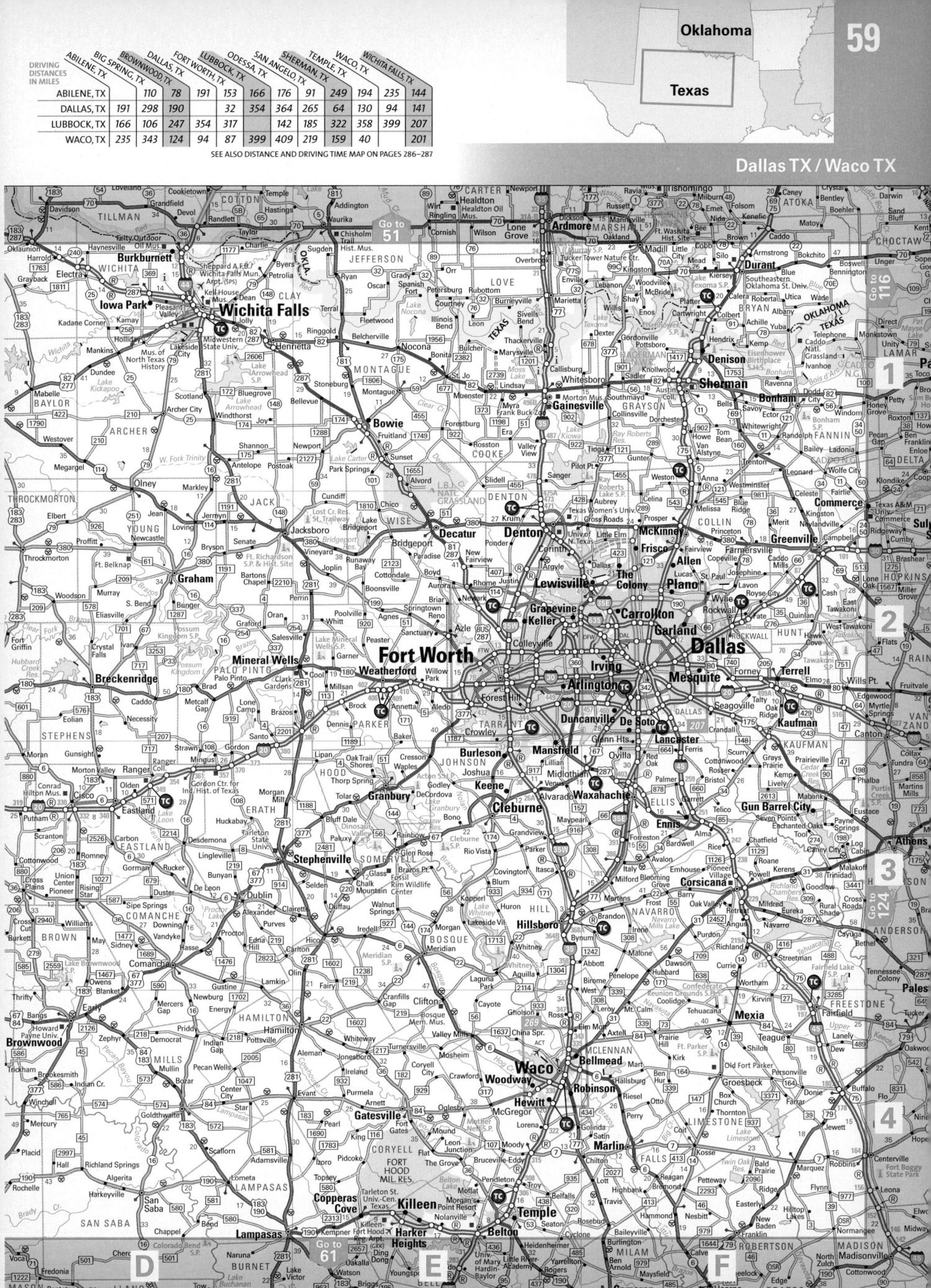

DRIVING DISTANCES IN MILES	ABILENE, TX	BIG SPRING, TX	BROWNWOOD, TX	DALLAS, TX	FORT WORTH, TX	LUBBOCK, TX	ODESSA, TX	SAN ANGELO, TX	SHERMAN, TX	TEMPLE, TX	WACO, TX	WICHITA FALLS, TX
ABILENE, TX		110	78	191	153	166	176	91	249	194	235	144
DALLAS, TX	191	298	190		32	354	364	265	64	130	94	141
LUBBOCK, TX	166	106	247	354	317		142	185	322	358	399	207
WACO, TX	235	343	124	94	87	399	409	219	159	40		201

SEE ALSO DISTANCE AND DRIVING TIME MAP ON PAGES 286–287

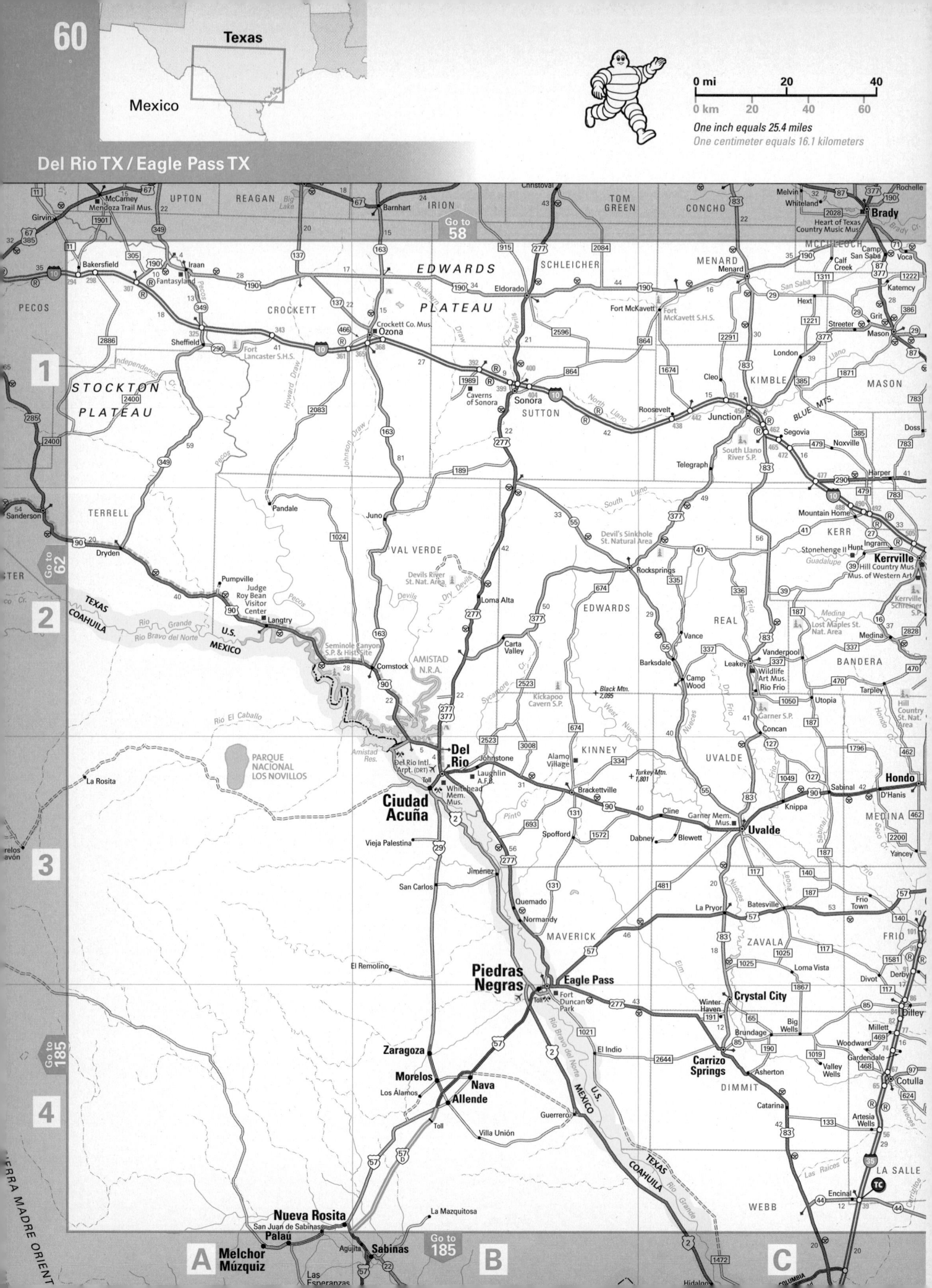

One inch equals 25.4 miles
One centimeter equals 16.1 kilometers

0 mi 20 40
0 km 20 40 60

Go to 58

Go to 62

Go to 185

Go to 185

UPTON REAGAN IRION TOM GREEN CONCHO McCULLOCH

EDWARDS PLATEAU SCHLEICHER MENARD MASON

Brady

Heart of Texas Country Music Mus.

McCamey
Mendoza Trail Mus.
Girvin
Bakersfield
Iraan
Fantasyland
Sheffield
Fort Lancaster S.H.S.
Ozona
Crockett Co. Mus.

STOCKTON PLATEAU
CROCKETT

PECOS

Sanderson
TERRELL
Dryden
Pandale
Juno

STOCKTON PLATEAU

Eldorado
Fort McKavett
Fort McKavett S.H.S.
Menard
Hext
Cleo
London
Roosevelt
Junction
Segovia
Noxville
Doss
Harper

Caverns of Sonora
Sonora
SUTTON

KIMBLE
BLUE MTS.
Telegraph
South Llano River S.P.
Mountain Home
KERR
Stonehenge II Hunt
Ingram
Kerrville
Hill Country Mus.
Mus. of Western Art
Kerrville-Schreiner S.P.

Guadalupe

VAL VERDE
Devils River St. Nat. Area
Loma Alta
Carta Valley
Rocksprings
EDWARDS
Vance
Barksdale
Camp Wood
Leakey
Vanderpool
Wildlife Art Mus.
Rio Frio
Lost Maples St. Nat. Area
Medina
BANDERA
Utopia
Tarpley
Hill Country St. Nat. Area

REAL
Concan
Garner S.P.

Pumpville
Judge Roy Bean Visitor Center
Langtry
TEXAS
COAHUILA
Rio Grande
Rio Bravo del Norte
U.S.
MEXICO
Seminole Canyon S.P. & Hist. Site
Comstock

AMISTAD N.R.A.

Kickapoo Cavern S.P.
Black Mtn. 2,095

Del Rio Intl. Arpt. (DRT)
Del Rio
Johnstone
Alamo Village
Laughlin A.F.B.
Whitehead Mem. Mus.
Ciudad Acuña
KINNEY
Brackettville
Turkey Mtn. 1,801
UVALDE
Concan
Garner Mem. Mus.
Uvalde
Knippa
Sabinal
D'Hanis
Hondo
MEDINA
Yancey

PARQUE NACIONAL LOS NOVILLOS
La Rosita
Amistad Res.
Rio El Caballo

Vieja Palestina
Jiménez
San Carlos
Quemado
Normandy
MAVERICK

Spofford
Dabney
Blewett
Cline
La Pryor
Batesville
Frio Town

Cotulla

El Remolino
Piedras Negras
Eagle Pass
Fort Duncan Park
Winter Haven
Brundage
Big Wells
Crystal City
ZAVALA
Loma Vista
Woodward
Gardendale
Divot
Derby
Dilley
FRIO
Millett

Zaragoza
Morelos
Los Álamos
Nava
Allende
Guerrero
El Indio
Carrizo Springs
Asherton
Catarina
Valley Wells
Artesia Wells
DIMMIT

Villa Unión

TEXAS
COAHUILA
Rio Bravo del Norte
U.S.
MEXICO
Rio Grande
Las Raices
WEBB
Encinal
LA SALLE

Nueva Rosita
La Mazquitosa
San Juan de Sabinas
Palau
Aguita
Sabinas
Melchor Múzquiz
Las Esperanzas
Hidalgo

SIERRA MADRE ORIENTAL

Go to 185

A B C
1 2 3 4

Texas

Mexico

DRIVING DISTANCES IN MILES	AUSTIN, TX	BEEVILLE, TX	COLLEGE STATION, TX	COLUMBUS, TX	DEL RIO, TX	EAGLE PASS, TX	FREDERICKSBURG, TX	SAN ANTONIO, TX	SONORA, TX	TEMPLE, TX	UVALDE, TX	VICTORIA, TX
AUSTIN, TX		136	108	92	229	226	78	78	244	67	159	123
DEL RIO, TX	229	235	322	277		55	178	152	89	295	70	268
SAN ANTONIO, TX	78	110	171	128	152	145	67		172	144	82	118
VICTORIA, TX	123	56	160	87	268	254	186	118	292	187	198	

SEE ALSO DISTANCE AND DRIVING TIME MAP ON PAGES 286–287

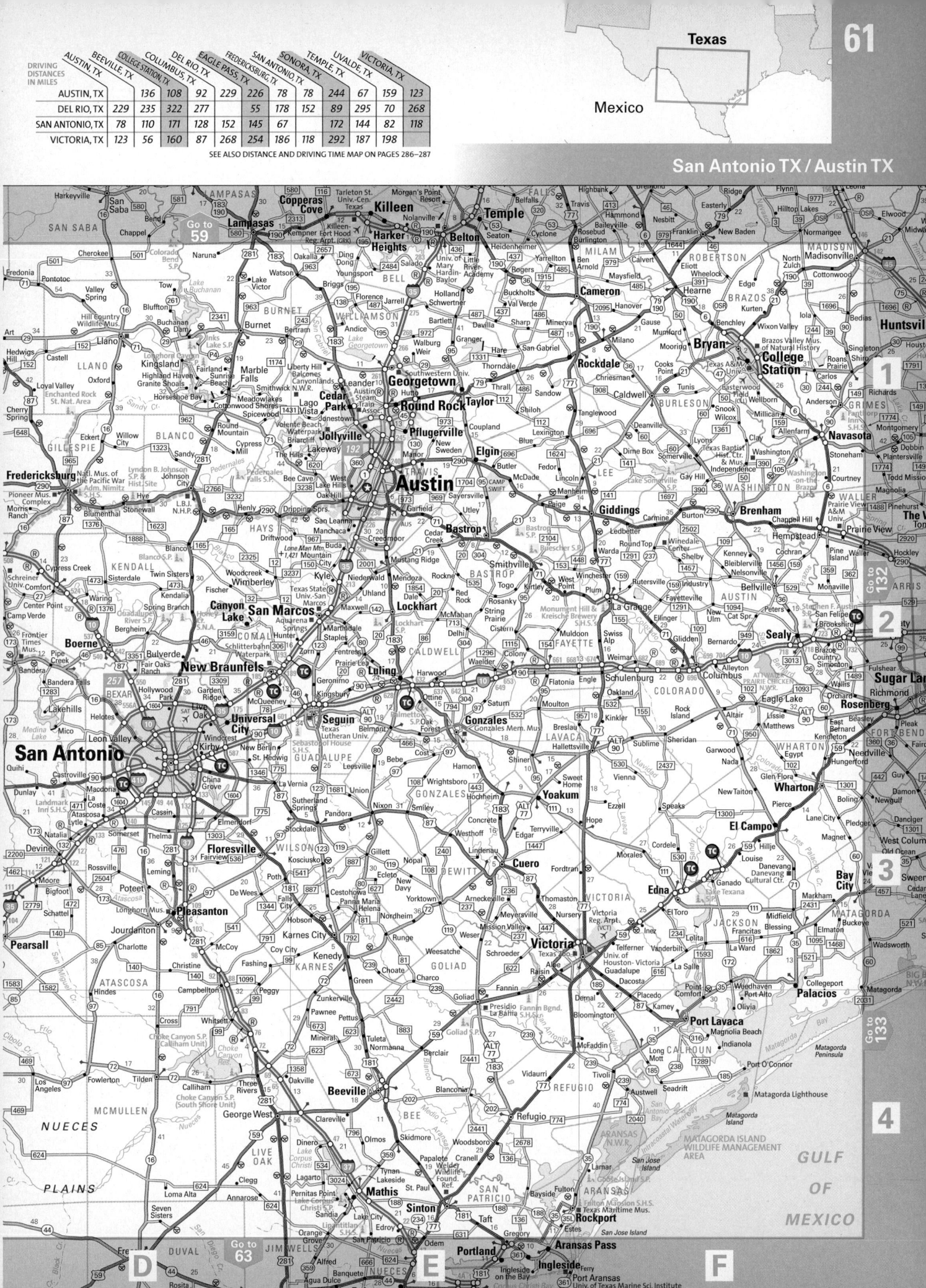

Texas

Mexico

DRIVING DISTANCES IN MILES	ALPINE, TX	BIG BEND NP, TX	FORT STOCKTON, TX	ODESSA, TX	PECOS, TX	VAN HORN, TX
ALPINE, TX		97	65	151	96	110
FORT STOCKTON, TX	65	123		86	58	119
ODESSA, TX	151	209	86		76	163
VAN HORN, TX	110	207	119	163	87	

SEE ALSO DISTANCE AND DRIVING TIME MAP ON PAGES 286–287

0 mi 10 20 30
0 km 20 40
One inch equals 25.4 miles
One centimeter equals 16.1 kilometers

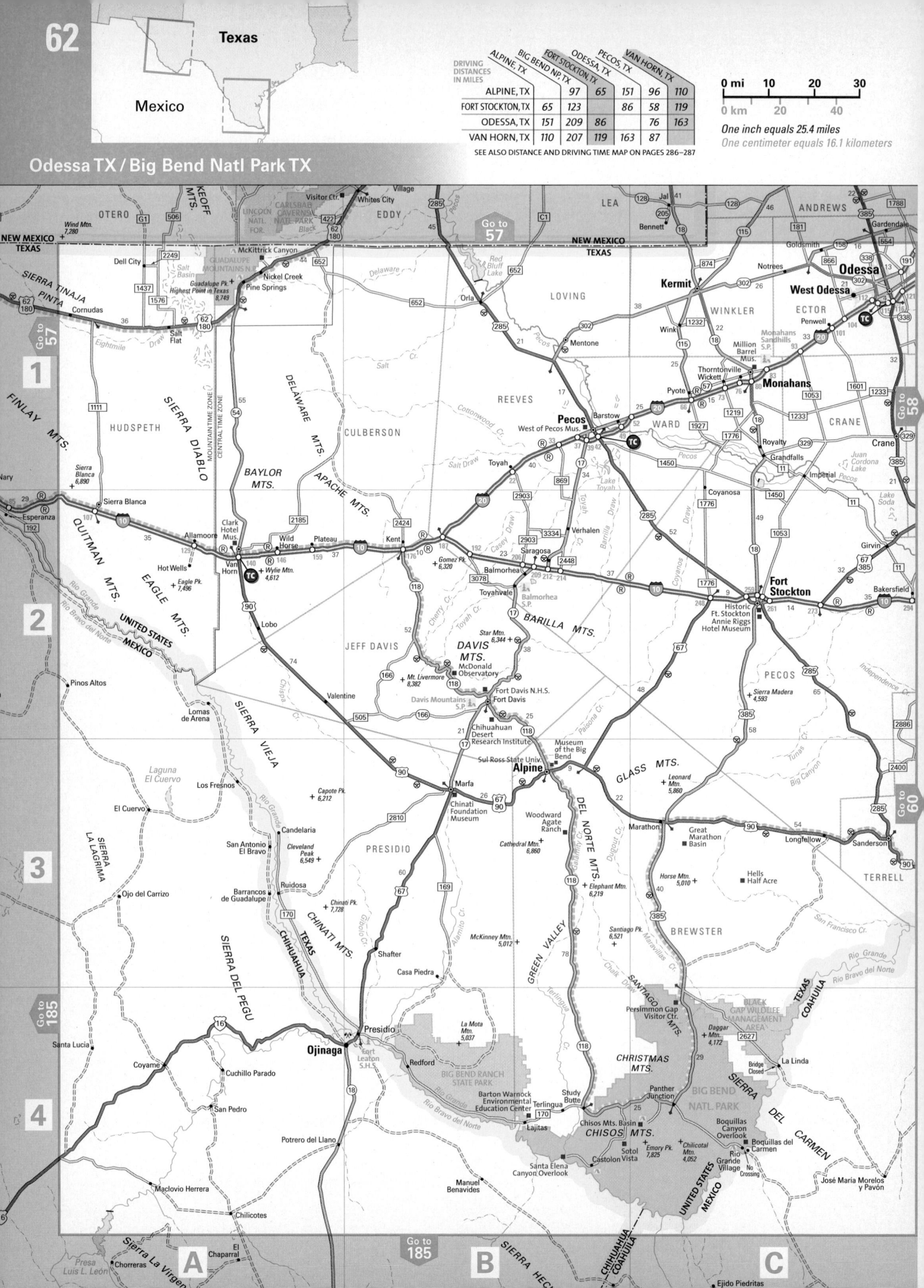

SEE ALSO DISTANCE AND DRIVING TIME MAP ON PAGES 286–287

DRIVING DISTANCES IN MILES	BEEVILLE, TX	BROWNSVILLE, TX	CARRIZO SPRS., TX	CORPUS CHRISTI, TX	HARLINGEN, TX	KINGSVILLE, TX	LAREDO, TX	MCALLEN, TX	VICTORIA, TX
BROWNSVILLE, TX	192		282	157	27	119	202	61	226
CORPUS CHRISTI, TX	59	157	199		131	38	141	152	94
LAREDO, TX	130	202	79	141	176	124		144	186
MCALLEN, TX	168	61	223	152	35	114	144		221

64

Manitoba

Ontario

Minnesota

Michigan

Wisconsin

Duluth MN / International Falls MN

0 mi   20   40

0 km   20   40   60

One inch equals 25.4 miles

One centimeter equals 16.1 kilometers

Go to 168

Go to 19

Go to 66

Go to 67

DRIVING DISTANCES IN MILES	ASHLAND, WI	BEMIDJI, MN	BRAINERD, MN	DETROIT LAKES, MN	DULUTH, MN	GRAND PORTAGE, MN	HOUGHTON, MI	INTERNAT'L FALLS, MN	IRONWOOD, MI	ISHPEMING, MI	THUNDER BAY, ON	VIRGINIA, MN
BEMIDJI, MN	239		96	91	153	295	362	109	254	384	314	124
DULUTH, MN	92	153	116	202		143	215	157	107	238	183	61
HOUGHTON, MI	132	362	325	412	215	358		370	108	87	654	274
INTERNAT'L FALLS, MN	247	109	190	200	157	245	370		262	393	205	97

SEE ALSO DISTANCE AND DRIVING TIME MAP ON PAGES 286–287

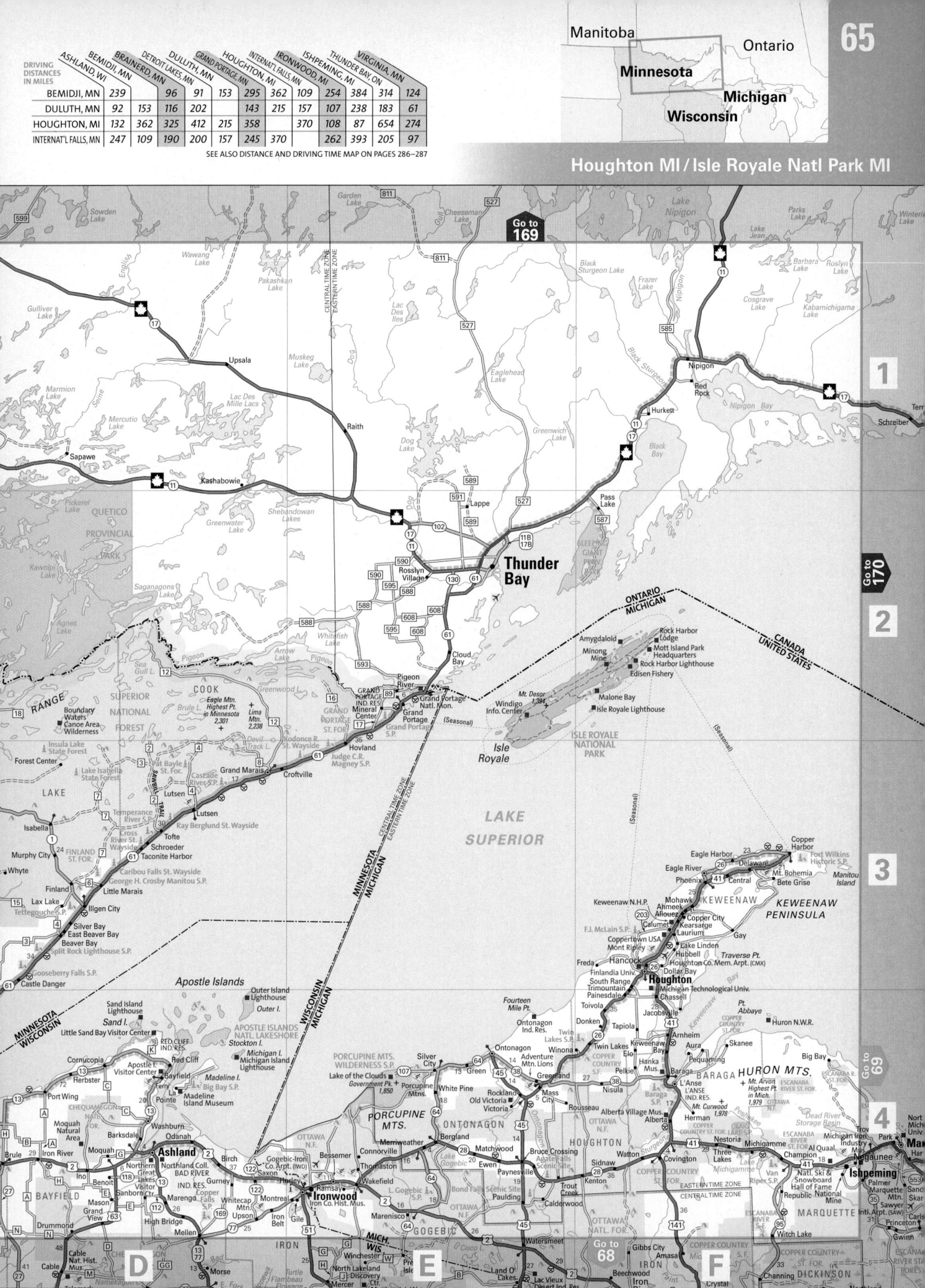

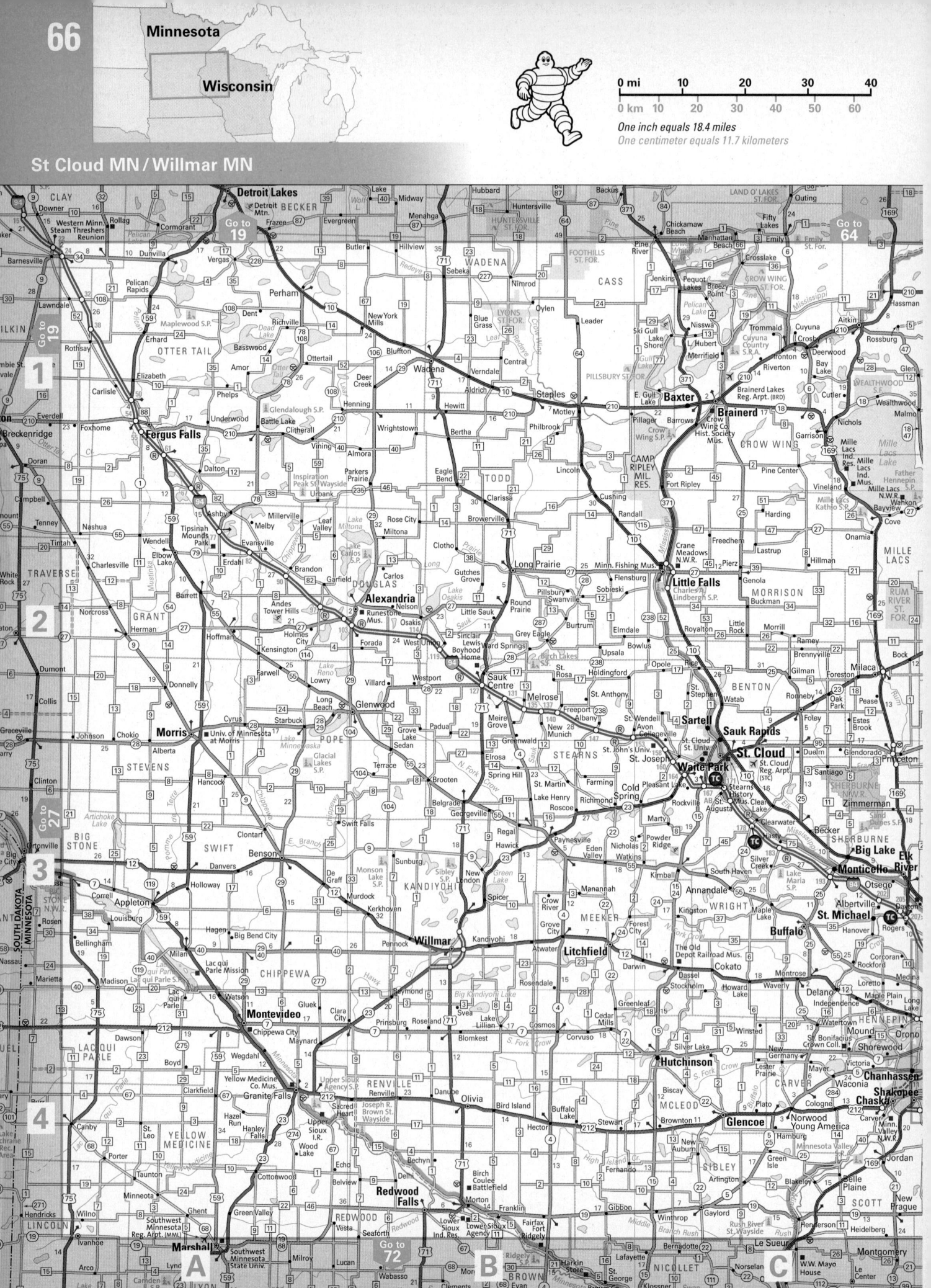

One inch equals 18.4 miles
One centimeter equals 11.7 kilometers

DRIVING DISTANCES IN MILES	ASHLAND, WI	BRAINERD, MN	DULUTH, MN	EAU CLAIRE, WI	FERGUS FALLS, MN	MARSHALL, MN	MINNEAPOLIS, MN	MORRIS, MN	RICE LAKE, WI	ST. CLOUD, MN	ST. PAUL, MN	WILLMAR, MN
EAU CLAIRE, WI	167	220	155		267	236	93	247	57	156	83	193
MINNEAPOLIS, MN	196	129	158	93	176	148		156	103	64	10	92
ST. CLOUD, MN	205	62	149	156	117	131	64	98	155		73	63
WILLMAR, MN	263	112	206	193	113	68	92	57	196	63	102	

SEE ALSO DISTANCE AND DRIVING TIME MAP ON PAGES 286–287

Wisconsin

Michigan

0 mi 10 20 30 40
0 km 10 20 30 40 50 60
One inch equals 18.4 miles
One centimeter equals 11.7 kilometers

Go to 65
Go to 67
Go to 74

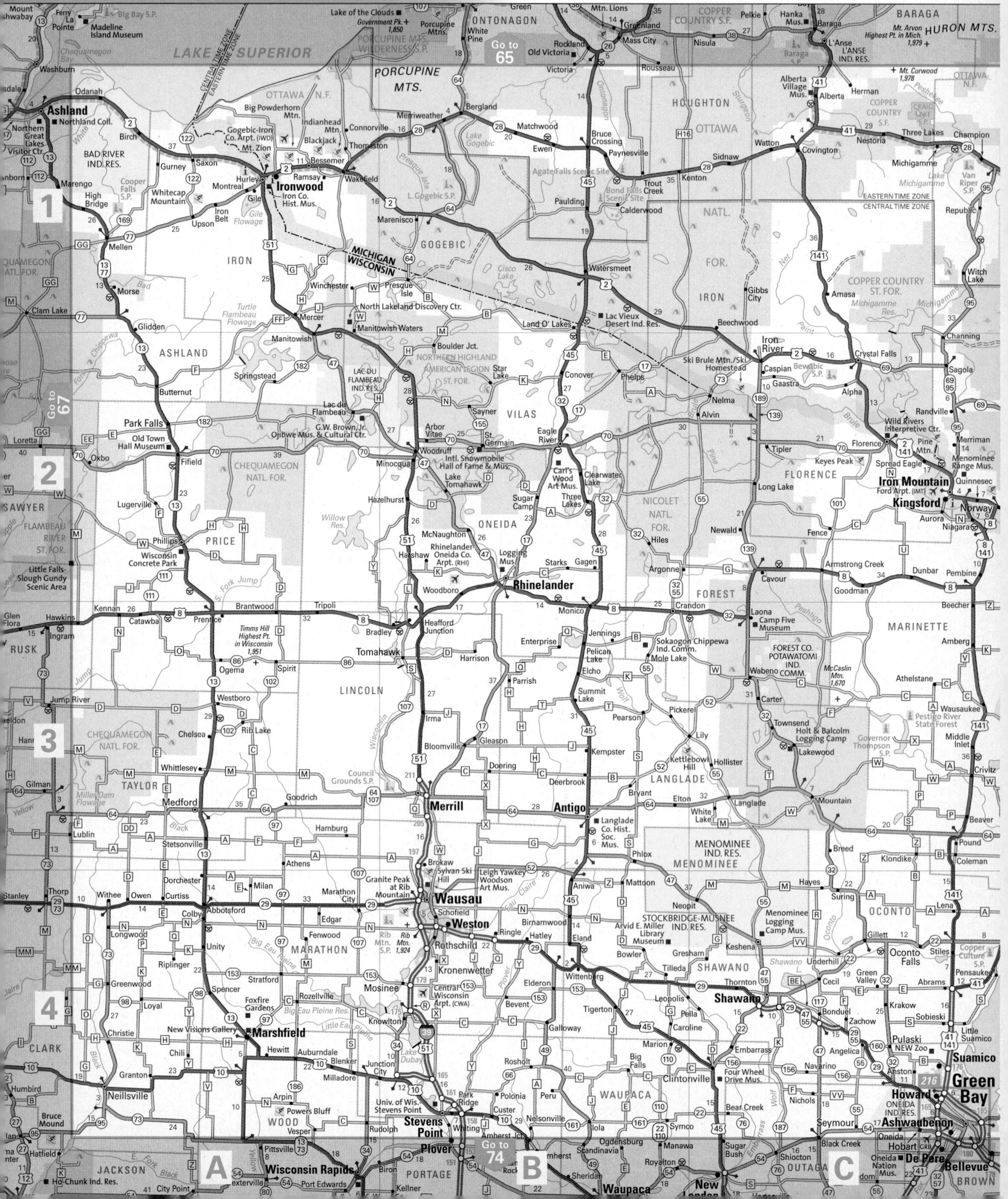

DRIVING DISTANCES IN MILES	ESCANABA, MI	GREEN BAY, WI	IRON MOUNTAIN, MI	IRONWOOD, MI	L'ANSE, MI	MANISTIQUE, MI	MARINETTE, WI	MARQUETTE, MI	RHINELANDER, WI	STEVENS POINT, WI	TRAVERSE CITY, MI	WAUSAU, WI
ESCANABA, MI		111	52	178	134	54	57	65	132	185	252	171
GREEN BAY, WI	111		96	202	178	165	54	175	124	87	363	93
MARQUETTE, MI	65	175	79	145	70	86	122		147	238	269	204
WAUSAU, WI	171	93	133	121	176	225	112	204	58	35	423	

SEE ALSO DISTANCE AND DRIVING TIME MAP ON PAGES 286–287

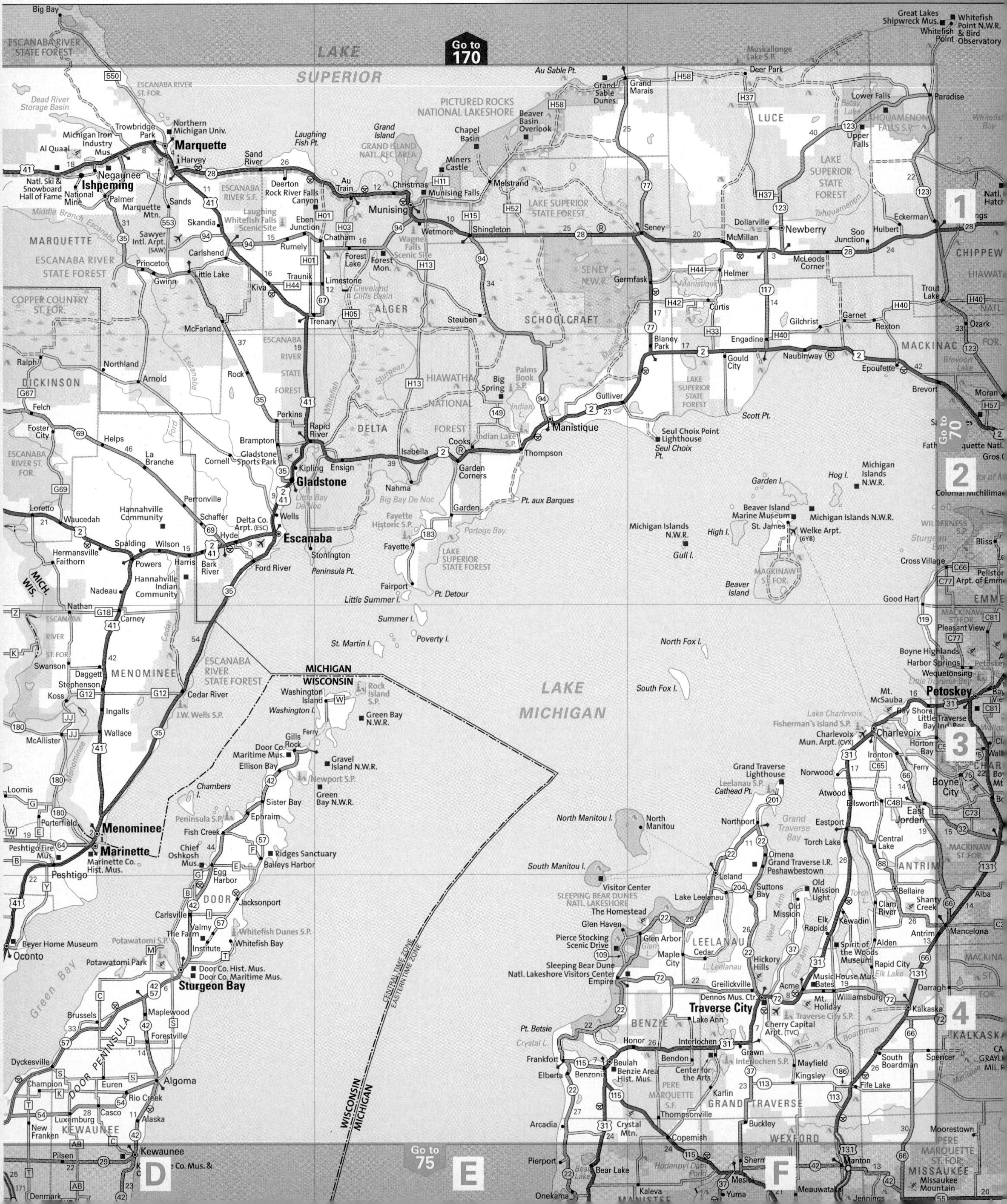

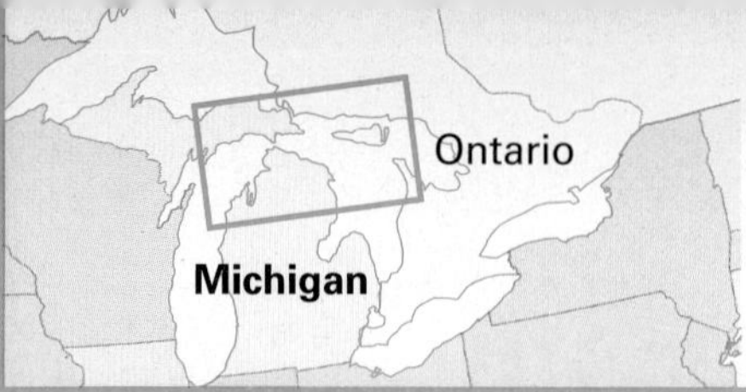

Ontario

Michigan

0 mi 10 20 30 40

0 km 10 20 30 40 50 60

One inch equals 18.4 miles
One centimeter equals 11.7 kilometers

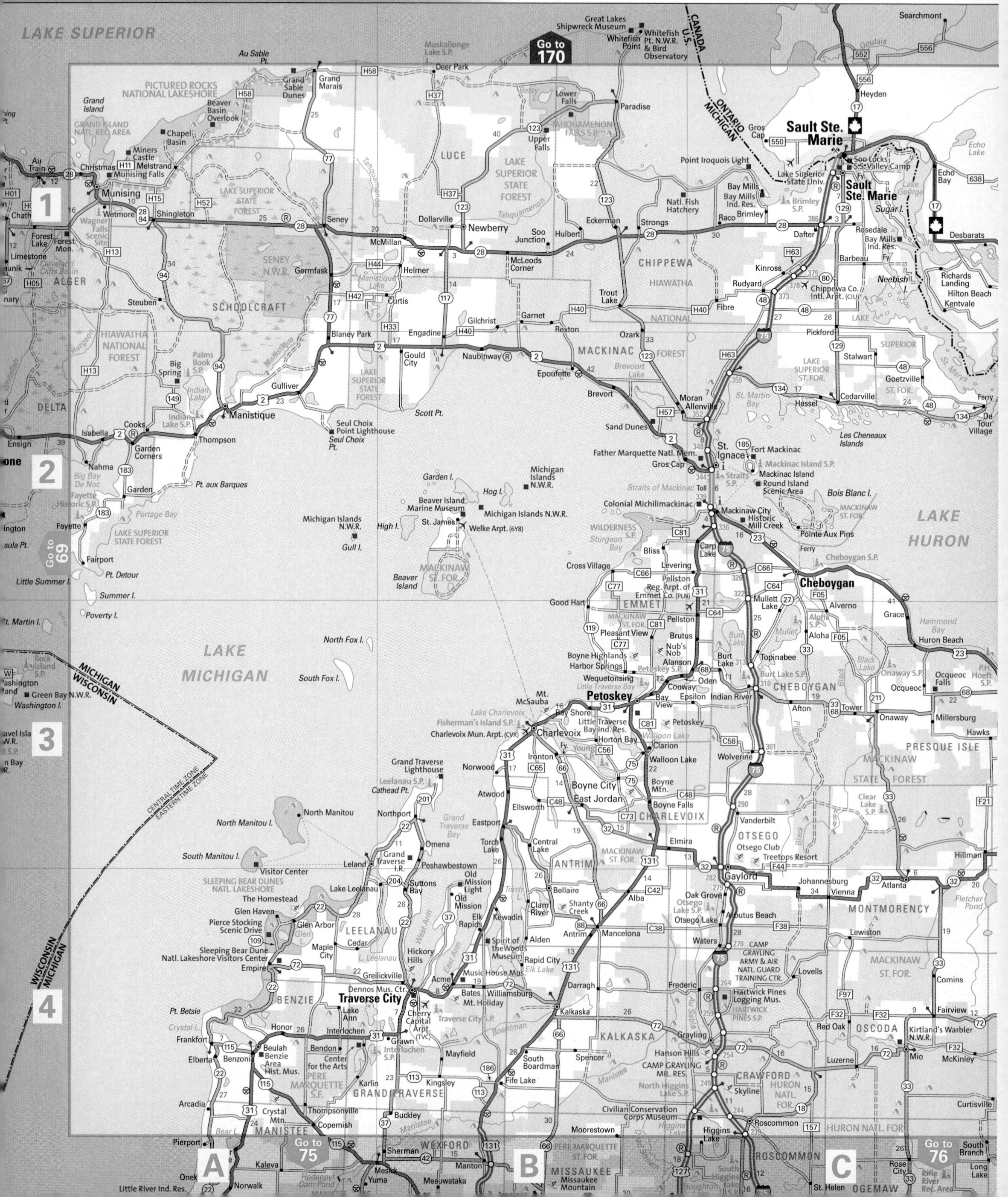

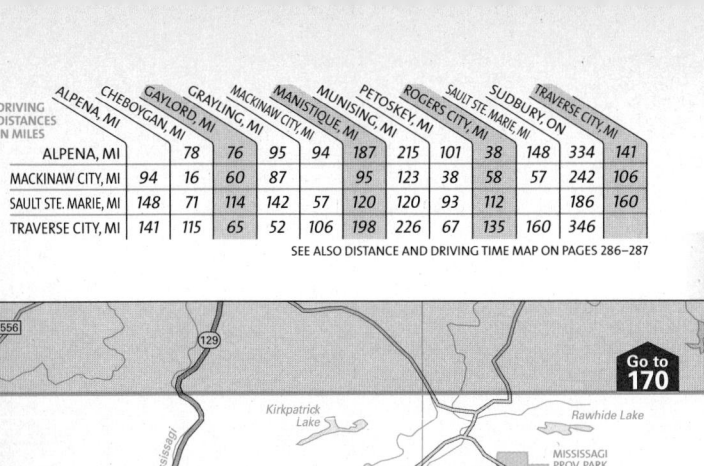

DRIVING DISTANCES IN MILES	ALPENA, MI	CHEBOYGAN, MI	GAYLORD, MI	GRAYLING, MI	MACKINAW CITY, MI	MANISTIQUE, MI	MUNISING, MI	PETOSKEY, MI	ROGERS CITY, MI	SAULT STE. MARIE, MI	SUDBURY, ON	TRAVERSE CITY, MI
ALPENA, MI		78	76	95	94	187	215	101	38	148	334	141
MACKINAW CITY, MI	94	16	60	87		95	123	38	58	57	242	106
SAULT STE. MARIE, MI	148	71	114	142	57	120	120	93	112		186	160
TRAVERSE CITY, MI	141	115	65	52	106	198	226	67	135	160	346	

SEE ALSO DISTANCE AND DRIVING TIME MAP ON PAGES 286–287

Minn. Wisconsin

Iowa Illinois

0 mi 10 20 30 40
0 km 10 20 30 40 50 60
One inch equals 18.4 miles
One centimeter equals 11.7 kilometers

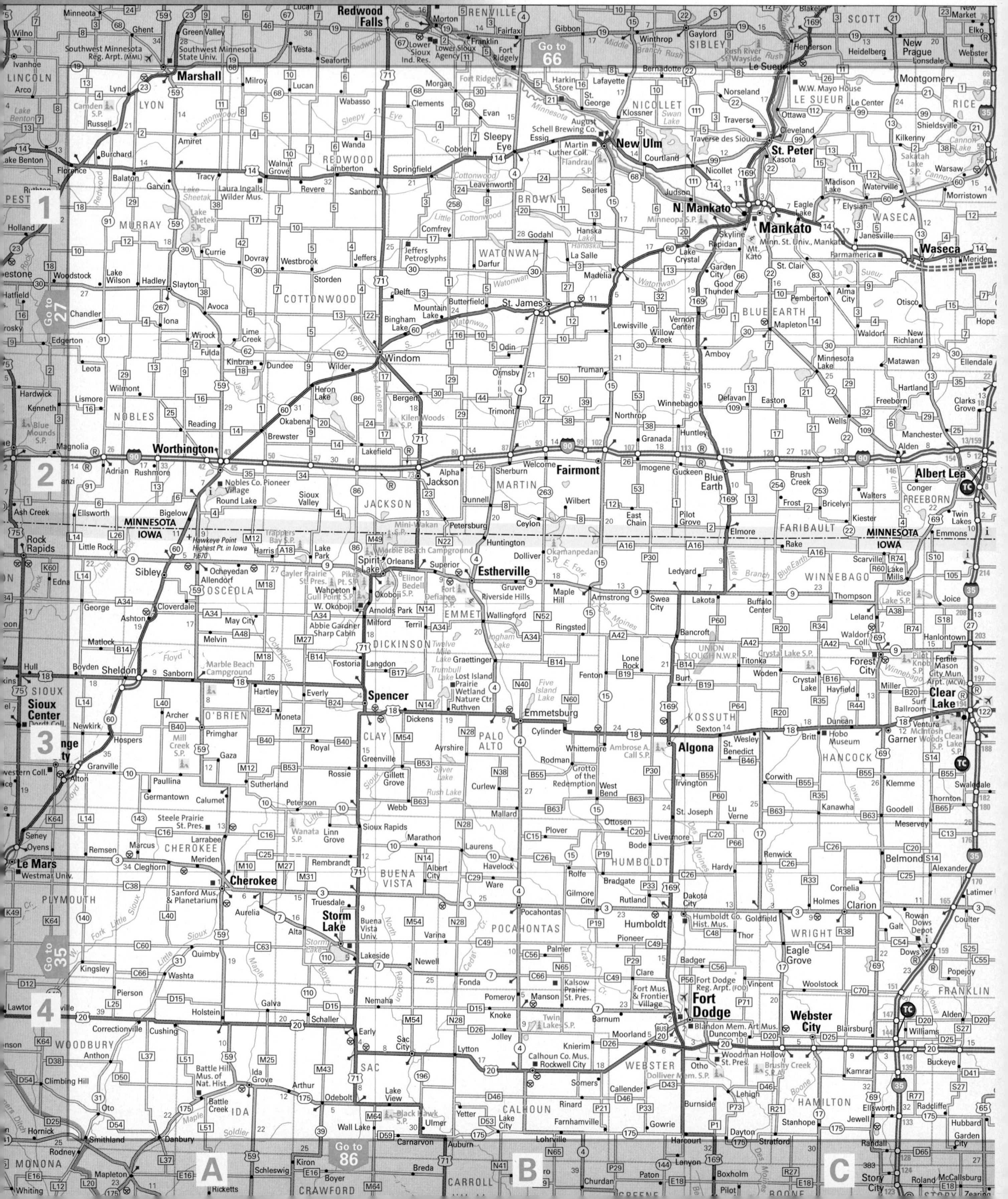

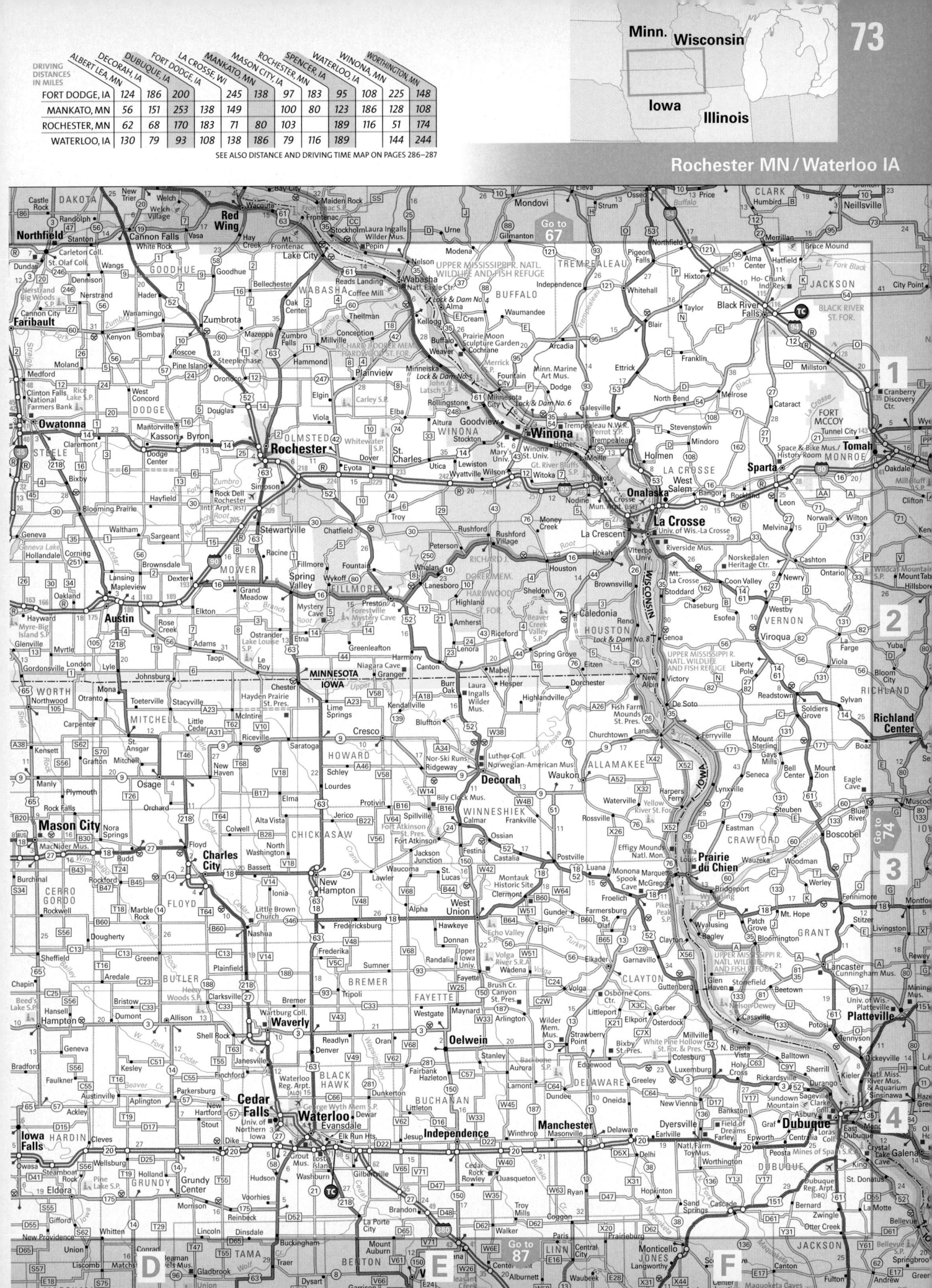

DRIVING DISTANCES IN MILES	ALBERT LEA, MN	DECORAH, IA	DUBUQUE, IA	FORT DODGE, IA	LA CROSSE, WI	MANKATO, MN	MASON CITY, IA	ROCHESTER, MN	SPENCER, IA	WATERLOO, IA	WINONA, MN	WORTHINGTON, MN
FORT DODGE, IA	124	186	200		245	138	97	183	95	108	225	148
MANKATO, MN	56	151	253	138	149		100	80	123	186	128	108
ROCHESTER, MN	62	68	170	183	71	80	103		189	116	51	174
WATERLOO, IA	130	79	93	108	138	186	79	116	189		144	244

SEE ALSO DISTANCE AND DRIVING TIME MAP ON PAGES 286–287

Wisconsin
Michigan
Iowa
Illinois

0 mi 10 20 30 40
0 km 10 20 30 40 50 60
One inch equals 18.4 miles
One centimeter equals 11.7 kilometers

Milwaukee WI / Madison WI

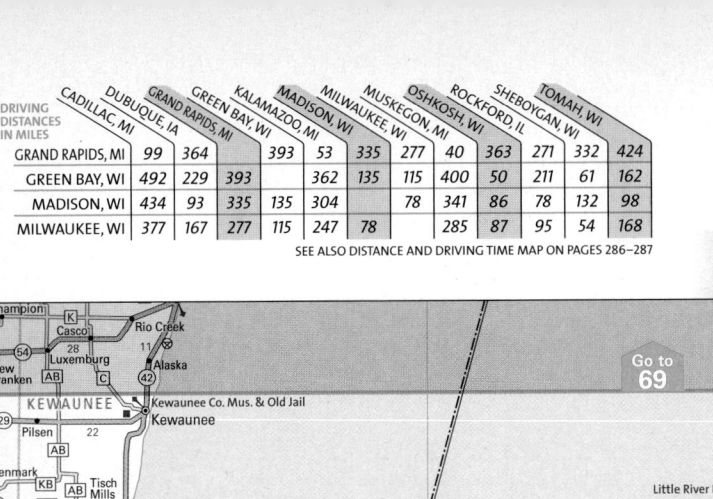

DRIVING DISTANCES IN MILES	CADILLAC, MI	DUBUQUE, IA	GRAND RAPIDS, MI	GREEN BAY, WI	KALAMAZOO, MI	MADISON, WI	MILWAUKEE, WI	MUSKEGON, MI	OSHKOSH, WI	ROCKFORD, IL	SHEBOYGAN, WI	TOMAH, WI
GRAND RAPIDS, MI	99	364		393	53	335	277	40	363	271	332	424
GREEN BAY, WI	492	229	393		362	135	115	400	50	211	61	162
MADISON, WI	434	93	335	135		304	78	341	86	78	132	98
MILWAUKEE, WI	377	167	277	115	247	78		285	87	95	54	168

SEE ALSO DISTANCE AND DRIVING TIME MAP ON PAGES 286–287

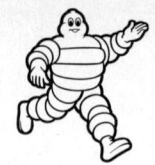

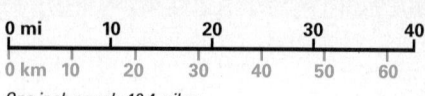

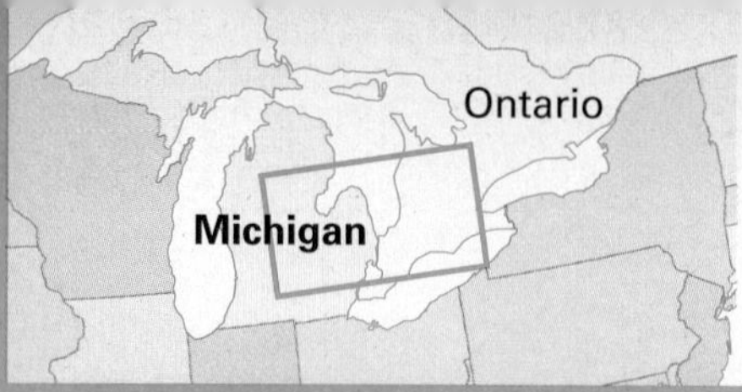
Ontario
Michigan

0 mi 10 20 30 40
0 km 10 20 30 40 50 60
One inch equals 18.4 miles
One centimeter equals 11.7 kilometers

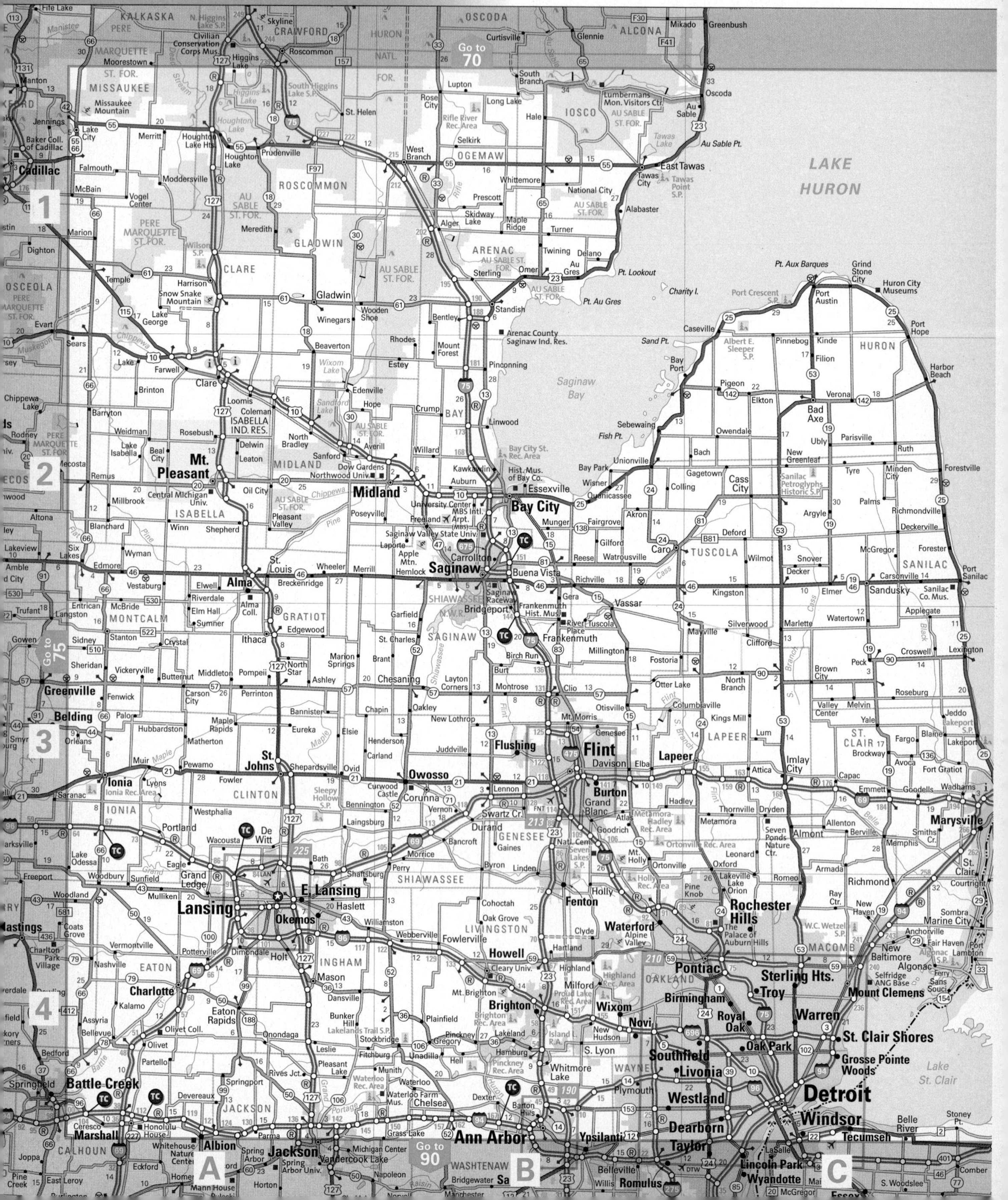
Go to 70
Go to 75
Go to 90
LAKE HURON
Saginaw Bay
Lake St. Clair
KALKASKA
CRAWFORD
OSCODA
ALCONA
MISSAUKEE
ROSCOMMON
OGEMAW
IOSCO
CLARE
GLADWIN
ARENAC
OSCEOLA
ISABELLA
MIDLAND
BAY
HURON
MONTCALM
GRATIOT
SAGINAW
TUSCOLA
SANILAC
IONIA
CLINTON
SHIAWASSEE
GENESEE
LAPEER
ST. CLAIR
EATON
INGHAM
LIVINGSTON
OAKLAND
MACOMB
CALHOUN
JACKSON
WASHTENAW
WAYNE
Cadillac
Mt. Pleasant
Midland
Bay City
Saginaw
Alma
Flint
Owosso
Lapeer
Lansing
E. Lansing
Okemos
Howell
Brighton
Pontiac
Sterling Hts.
Troy
Warren
Rochester Hills
Southfield
Livonia
Westland
Dearborn
Taylor
Detroit
Windsor
Ann Arbor
Ypsilanti
Jackson
Battle Creek
Marshall
Albion
Charlotte
Greenville
Belding
Ionia
St. Johns
Port Huron
Marysville
St. Clair Shores
Mount Clemens
Grosse Pointe Woods
Tawas City
East Tawas
Oscoda
Standish
Frankenmuth
Caro
Sandusky
Bad Axe
Port Austin
Harbor Beach
A
B
C
1
2
3
4

DRIVING DISTANCES IN MILES

	ANN ARBOR, MI	BAD AXE, MI	BATTLE CREEK, MI	CADILLAC, MI	DETROIT, MI	FLINT, MI	HAMILTON, ON	LANSING, MI	LONDON, ON	MT. PLEASANT, MI	PORT HURON, MI	SAGINAW, MI
DETROIT, MI	42	107	116	209		62	203	86	128	149	58	97
LANSING, MI	63	140	56	131	86	53	270		191	67	117	86
PORT HURON, MI	101	81	175	211	58	64	154	117	75	155		100
SAGINAW, MI	87	64	142	116	97	36	253	86	174	60	100	

SEE ALSO DISTANCE AND DRIVING TIME MAP ON PAGES 286–287

Go to 71

Go to 172

Go to 91

Go to 78

Go to 92

Ontario

New York

0 mi 10 20 30 40
0 km 10 20 30 40 50 60
One inch equals 18.4 miles
One centimeter equals 11.7 kilometers

Buffalo NY / Rochester NY

Go to 173
Go to 173
Go to 77
Go to 92

LAKE ONTARIO

LAKE ERIE

ONTARIO / NEW YORK
CANADA / UNITED STATES
PENNSYLVANIA / NEW YORK

Wasaga Beach, Barrie, Angus, Keswick, Sutton, Newmarket, Aurora, Bradford, Uxbridge, Port Perry, Lindsay, Peterborough, Belleville, Trenton, Markham, Oshawa, Port Hope, Cobourg, Brighton, Picton, Brampton, Toronto, Mississauga, Milton, Oakville, Burlington, Hamilton, St. Catharines, Grimsby, Beamsville, Thorold, Niagara Falls, Welland, Dunnville, Port Colborne, Crystal Beach, Buffalo, Lackawanna, Cheektowaga, West Seneca, Hamburg, Kenmore, Tonawanda, N. Tonawanda, Lockport, Medina, Albion, Brockport, Rochester, Irondequoit, Gates, Brighton, Fairport, Batavia, Le Roy, Avon, Geneseo, Mount Morris, Dansville, Canandaigua, Newark, Penn Yan, Bath, Hornell, Dunkirk, Fredonia, Salamanca

LAKE ONTARIO STATE PKWY

MONROE, ORLEANS, GENESEE, WYOMING, LIVINGSTON, ALLEGANY, STEUBEN, CATTARAUGUS, CHAUTAUQUA, ONTARIO, YATES, NIAGARA

N.Y. STATE THRUWAY

DRIVING DISTANCES IN MILES

	BATH, NY	BUFFALO, NY	ITHACA, NY	NIAGARA FALLS, NY	ONEONTA, NY	OSWEGO, NY	ROCHESTER, NY	SYRACUSE, NY	TORONTO, ON	TUPPER LAKE, NY	UTICA, NY	WATERTOWN, NY
BUFFALO, NY	113		153	20	263	158	74	152	106	321	199	210
ROCHESTER, NY	78	74	89	88	200	73		88	181	257	135	146
SYRACUSE, NY	105	152	59	166	118	38	88		260	176	53	65
UTICA, NY	152	199	108	213	65	81	135	53	307	131		86

SEE ALSO DISTANCE AND DRIVING TIME MAP ON PAGES 286–287

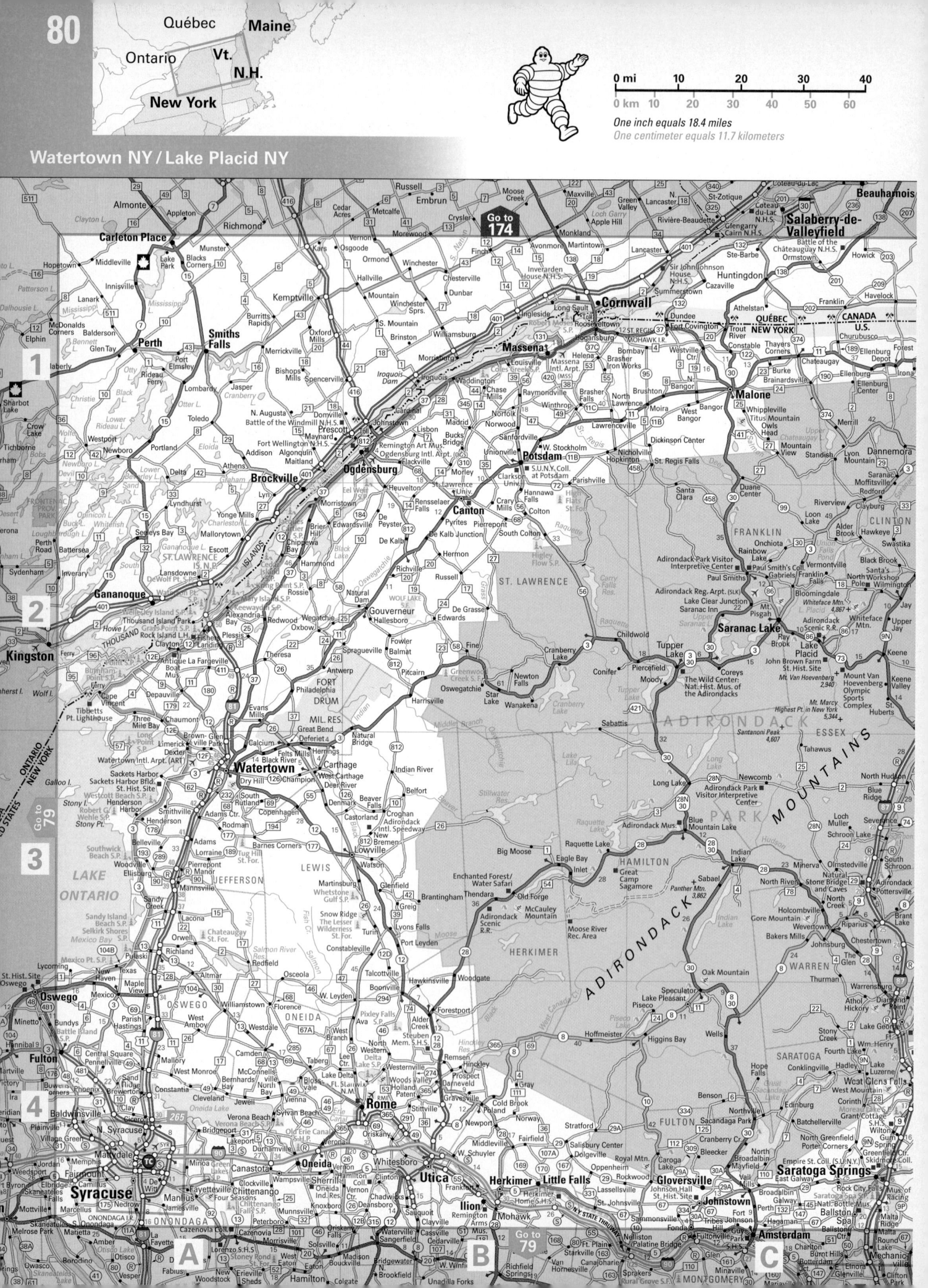

Québec Maine
Ontario Vt.
N.H.
New York

0 mi   10   20   30   40
0 km 10 20 30 40 50 60
One inch equals 18.4 miles
One centimeter equals 11.7 kilometers

Québec Maine
Ontario Vt.
New York N.H.

DRIVING DISTANCES IN MILES	BURLINGTON, VT	CONCORD, NH	LAKE PLACID, NY	OGDENSBURG, NY	PLATTSBURGH, NY	RUTLAND, VT	ST. JOHNSBURY, VT	SARATOGA SPRS., NY	SYRACUSE, NY	UTICA, NY	WATERTOWN, NY	WHITE RIVER JCT., VT
BURLINGTON, VT		150	68	208	51	69	76	115	230	183	195	91
CONCORD, NH	150		215	357	198	104	104	173	280	228	312	59
LAKE PLACID, NY	68	215		96	49	133	141	106	192	148	126	156
WATERTOWN, NY	195	312	126	68	167	244	319	179	65	86		289

SEE ALSO DISTANCE AND DRIVING TIME MAP ON PAGES 286–287

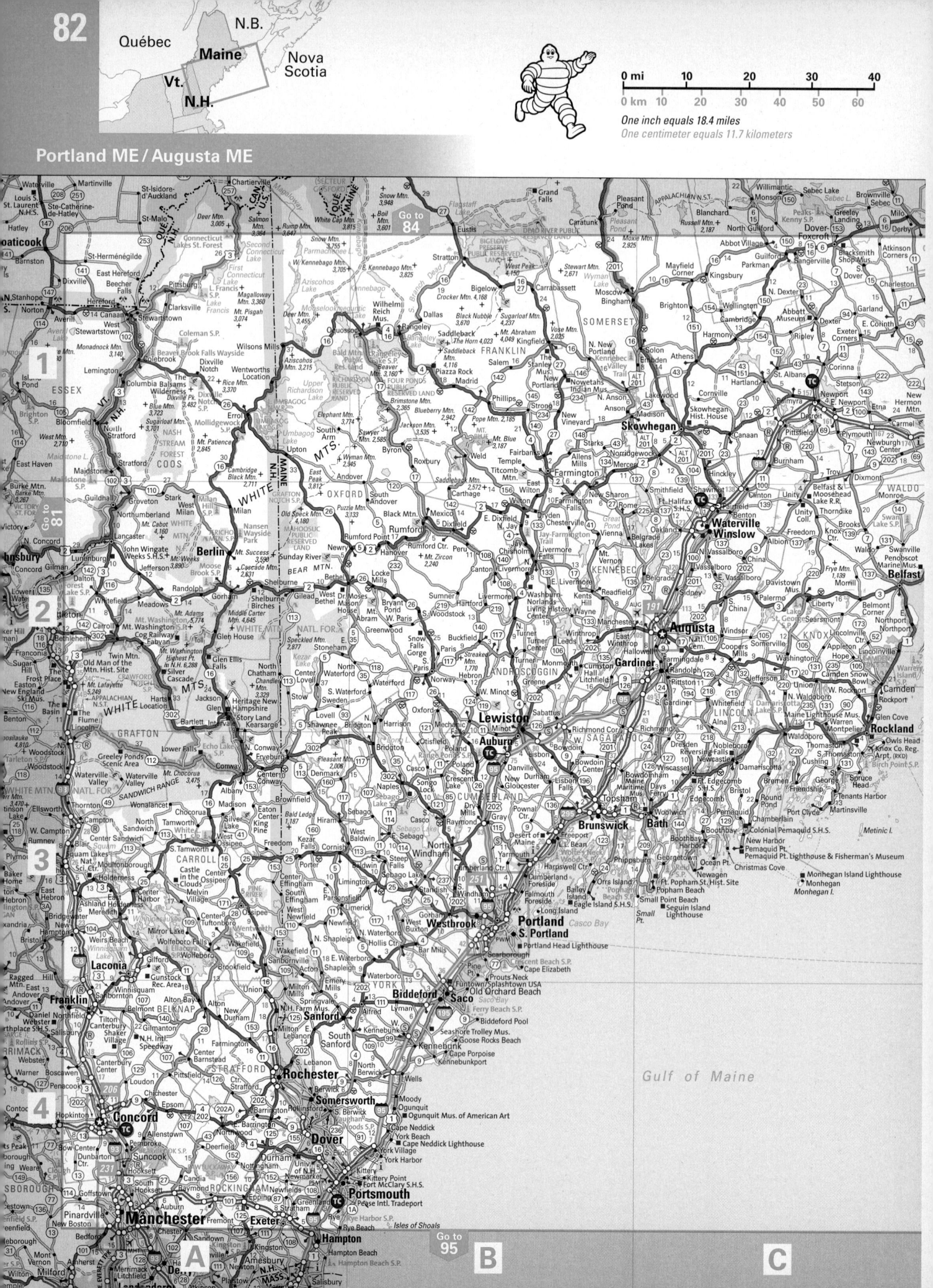

Québec   N.B.
          Maine
Vt.   Nova
      N.H.   Scotia

One inch equals 18.4 miles
One centimeter equals 11.7 kilometers

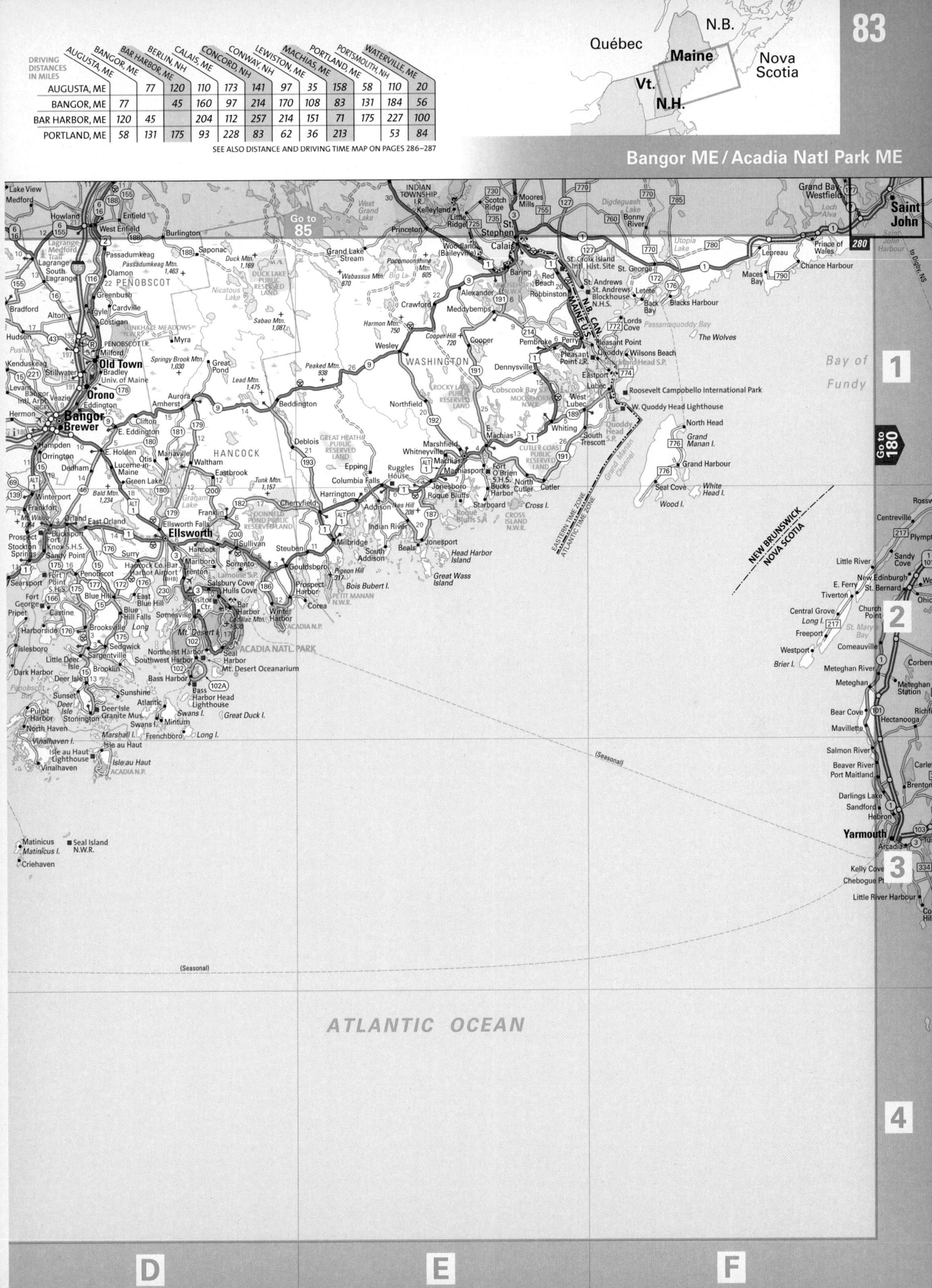

DRIVING DISTANCES IN MILES

	AUGUSTA, ME	BANGOR, ME	BAR HARBOR, ME	BERLIN, NH	CALAIS, ME	CONCORD, NH	CONWAY, NH	LEWISTON, ME	MACHIAS, ME	PORTLAND, ME	PORTSMOUTH, NH	WATERVILLE, ME
AUGUSTA, ME		77	120	110	173	141	97	35	158	58	110	20
BANGOR, ME	77		45	160	97	214	170	108	83	131	184	56
BAR HARBOR, ME	120	45		204	112	257	214	151	71	175	227	100
PORTLAND, ME	58	131	175	93	228	83	62	36	213		53	84

SEE ALSO DISTANCE AND DRIVING TIME MAP ON PAGES 286–287

Québec

N.B.

Maine

Nova Scotia

Vt.

N.H.

N.B.
Québec
Maine
N.H.

0 mi 10 20 30 40
0 km 10 20 30 40 50 60
One inch equals 18.4 miles
One centimeter equals 11.7 kilometers

Greenville ME / Allagash ME

1

Lac des Passes
Lac à Morse
Lac des Rognons
RÉS. FAUNIQUE DES LAURENTIDES
Petit Lac Jacques-Cartier
Lac Saulauriski
Lac aux Écorces
Lac des Neiges
Go to 176
St-Urbain
St-Joseph-de-la-Rive
St-Placide-de-Charlevoix
Baie-St-Paul
Les Éboulements
St-Bernard-sur-Mer
La Baleine
Rivière-Ouelle
Mont-Carmel
St-Pacôme
St-Denis
St-Pascal
St-Philippe-de-Néri
St-Bruno-de-Kamouraska
St-Athanase
St-Éleuthère
Pohénégamook
Pied-du-Lac

PARC DE LA JACQUES-CARTIER
Lac Tourilli
Lac Ste-Anne
St-Cassien-des-Caps
Petite-Rivière-St-François
Village-des-Aulnaies
St-Roch-des-Aulnaies
La Pocatière
Ste-Louise
Lac-de-l'Est
Lac de l'Est
Glazier Lake

ZEC BATISCAN-NEILSON
FAUNIQUE PORTNEUF
Lac Picard
Lac Batiscan
Lac Croche
ZEC CHAPAIS
Kelly Brook Mtn. 1,483
Allagash Hist. Soc.
Dickey
Gate
Allagash

St-Raymond
STATION FORESTIÈRE DE DUCHESNAY
371
St-Ferréol-les-Neiges
St-Tite-des-Caps
La Miche
Grosse Île Natl. Hist. Site
Cap-Tourmente
Île aux Oies
L'Islet-sur-Mer
Lac Trois Saumons
Ste-Anne
Tourville
St-Omer
St-Johns
Gate

2

St-Léonard-d'Aston
Chute-Panet
Shannon
371
280
Charlesbourg
Loretteville
40
369
Québec
Ste-Foy
Charny
Château-Richer
L'Ange-Gardien
Ste-Famille
Île d'Orléans
St-Jean
Beaupré
St-François
Cap-St-Ignace
L'Islet
St-Eugène
St-Cyrille-de-l'Islet
St-Perpétue
Montmagny
Bras-d'Apic
Ste-Félicité
St-Pamphile
Gate
Black
Big
RESTRICTED ROADS
ROUND POND PUBLIC RESERVED LAND
Round Pond

St-Catherine-de-la-Jacques-Cartier
Pont-Rouge
Ste-Croix
St-Apollinaire
St-Michel-de-Bellechasse
St-Charles-de-Bellechasse
St-Raphaël
Notre-Dame-du-Rosaire
St-Marcel
St-Adalbert
Depot Lake
ALLAGASH WILDERNESS WATERWAY
First Musquacook Lake

Donnacona
Deschambault-Grondines
Bernières-St-Nicolas
St-Henri
St-Gervais
Armagh
St-Euphémie
St-Paul-de-Montminy
St-Apolline
Ste-Lucie-de-Beauregard
Clayton Lake
Long Lake
Second Musquacook Lake

Lotbinière
St-Croix
Honfleur
St-Damien-de-Buckland
Buckland
St-Philémon
St-Fabien-de-Panet
Lac-Frontière
Gate
Daaquam
PARC RÉGIONAL DU MASSIF DU SUD
Priestly Mtn. 1,900
Priestly Lake
Fourth Musquacook Lake

Go to 175
Joly
St-Agapit
St-Anselme
Ste-Claire
St-Isidore
Ste-Hénédine
St-Nazaire-de-Buckland
St-Léon-de-Standon
St-Luc
St-Camille-de-Lellis
Hudson Mtn. 1,935
Harrow Lake
Clear Lake
Pleasant Lake

3

Val-Alain
Lyster
Laurier-Station
St-Flavien
Dosquet
St-Gilles
Ste-Marie
St-Elzéar
St-Sylvestre
Vallée-Jonction
St-Édouard-de-Frampton
Ste-Sabine
St-Sabine-Station
St-Justine
Lac-Etchemin
Spider Lake
CHAMBERLAIN LAKE PUBLIC RESERVED LAND
Crescent Pond
Churchill Lake
Munsungan Lake
Haymock Lake

Laurierville
St-Jacques-de-Leeds
St-Frédéric
St-Séverin
St-Odilon
Ste-Germaine-Station
Ste-Rose-de-Watford
St-Cyprien
Hardwood Mtn. 1,518
Allagash L.
Baker Lake
Poland Mtn. 1,870
Chamberlain Lake
TELOS PUBLIC RESERVED LAND

Plessisville
Princeville
Inverness
Kinnear's Mills
St-Pierre-de-Broughton
Tring-Jonction
St-Joseph-de-Beauce
St-Benjamin
St-Louis-de-Gonzague
St-Prosper
Caucomgomoc Lake
Chemquasabamticook Lake
BAXTER STATE PARK
Webster Lake

Norbertville
Victoriaville
St-Jean-de-Brébeuf
East Broughton
Broughton Station
Robertsonville
Ste-Clotilde-de-Beauce
St-Victor
Morisset-Station
Beauceville
Notre-Dame-des-Pins
St-Georges
Ste-Aurélie
St-Zacharie
Gate
Dole Pond
Seboomook Mtn. 2,390
Little Russell Mtn. 2,376
Loon Lake
GERO ISLAND PUBLIC RESERVED LAND
ALLAGASH WILDERNESS WATERWAY
Telos Mtn. 1,329
Strickland Mtn. 2,390

4

Warwick
St-Christophe
St-Rémi-de-Tingwick
St-Adrien-d'Irlande
Thetford Mines
Black Lake
Vimy-Ridge
St-Daniel
Adstock
St-Joseph-de-Coleraine
La Guadeloupe
St-Honoré
St-Martin
St-Théophile
St-Côme—Linière
St-René
Jersey Mills
Green Mtn. 2,395
Chesuncook Village
Center Mtn. 2,902
Chesuncook Lake (no park access)
North Brother 4,143
Doubletop Mtn. 3,488

Asbestos
Wottonville
Disraëli
St-Fortunat
Ham-Nord
St-Praxède
St-Évariste-de-Forsyth
Courcelles
St-Hilaire-de-Dorset
St-Gédéon
Armstrong
Boundary Bald Mtn. 3,640
Seboomook Lake
Pittston Farm
Penobscot Lake
Gate
W. Branch Penobscot
Big Spencer Mtn. 3,230
NAHMAKANTA PUBLIC RESERVED LAND

Sts-Martyrs-Canadiens
St-Adrien
Beaulac
PARC DE FRONTENAC
Lambton
St-Sébastien
St-Romain
Stratford
St-Gérard
Ham-Sud
Lac Aylmer
St-Ludger
Lac-Drolet
St-Robert-Bellarmin
QUÉBEC MAINE
Sandy Bay Mtn. 2,869
Sandy Stream Mtn. 3,117
Dennistown
Rockwood
Mt. Kineo 1,789
Kokadjo
Little Spencer Mtn. 3,040

Weedon Centre
Marbleton
Fontainebleau
Lac Louise
Stornoway
St-Samuel Station
Ste-Cécile-de-Whitton
Audet
Jackman
Long Pond
Moosehead
Lily Bay
Lily Bay S.P.
Brassua Lake
Moose River
MOOSEHEAD LAKE PUBLIC RESERVED LAND
Baker Mtn. 3,520
Jo-Mary Mtn. 2,904
Upper Jo-Mary Lake

East Angus
Ascot Corner
Cookshire-Eaton
West Ditton
Milan
Nantes
Lac-Mégantic
Frontenac
Marsboro
Val-Racine
Piopolis
Skinner
ZEC LOUISE GOSFORD (SECTEUR GOSFORD)
HOLEB PUBLIC RESERVED LAND
Lake Parlin
Attean Pond
Indian Pond
Gerard
Coburn Mtn. 3,718
Spencer Lake
SOMERSET
Big Moose Mtn. 3,196
Big Squaw
Gulf Hagas
Greenville Junction
Greenville
Moosehead Marine Mus.
White Cap Mtn. 3,644
Saddleback Mtn. 2,998
41

Sherbrooke
Lennoxville
Bury
Gould
Dudswell (Bishopton)
Scotstown
La Patrie
Notre-Dame-des-Bois
Woburn
Coburn Gore
Chain of Ponds Public Reserved Land
Snow Mtn. 3,948
Kibby Mtn. 3,638
Tumbledown Mtn. 3,542
Three Slide Mtn. 3,112
Attean Mtn. 2,442
West Forks
Lake Moxie
Moxie Pond
The Forks
Caratunk
Shirley Mills
Barren Mtn. 2,660
Little Wilson Falls
Katahdin Iron Works S.H.S.
Bodfish
Onawa
Brownville Junction

Coaticook
East Hereford
QUE. N.H.
Deer Mtn. 3,005
Salmon Mtn. 3,364
White Cap Mtn. 3,815
Snow Mtn. 3,755
Boil Mtn. 3,601
ZEC LOUISE GOSFORD (SECTEUR GOSFORD)
Stratton
Go to 82
Eustis
Flagstaff L.
Dead River
Grand Falls
Pleasant Pond
Russell Mtn. 2,187
North Guilford
Abbot Village
Moxie Mtn. 2,925
Monson
North Guilford
Willimantic
Sebec Lake
Greeley Landing
Dover-Foxcroft
Sangerville
Guilford
Milo
Derby
Sebec
Bowerbank
Brownville

Barnston
Dixville
East Angus
Waterville
St-Malo
St-Hermenegilde
Martinville
St-Isidore-d'Auckland
Chartierville
Magalloway
NEW HAMPSHIRE
MAINE
Kennebago
W. Kennebago Mtn. 3,705
E. Kennebago Mtn. 3,825
West Peak 4,150
Stewart Mtn. 2,671
Bigelow
Carrabassett
Kingsbury
Abbot
Mayfield Corner
Blanchard
North Guilford
Dover
S. Dover
Atkinson Corners
Blacksmith Shop Mus.
Charleston

A
B
C

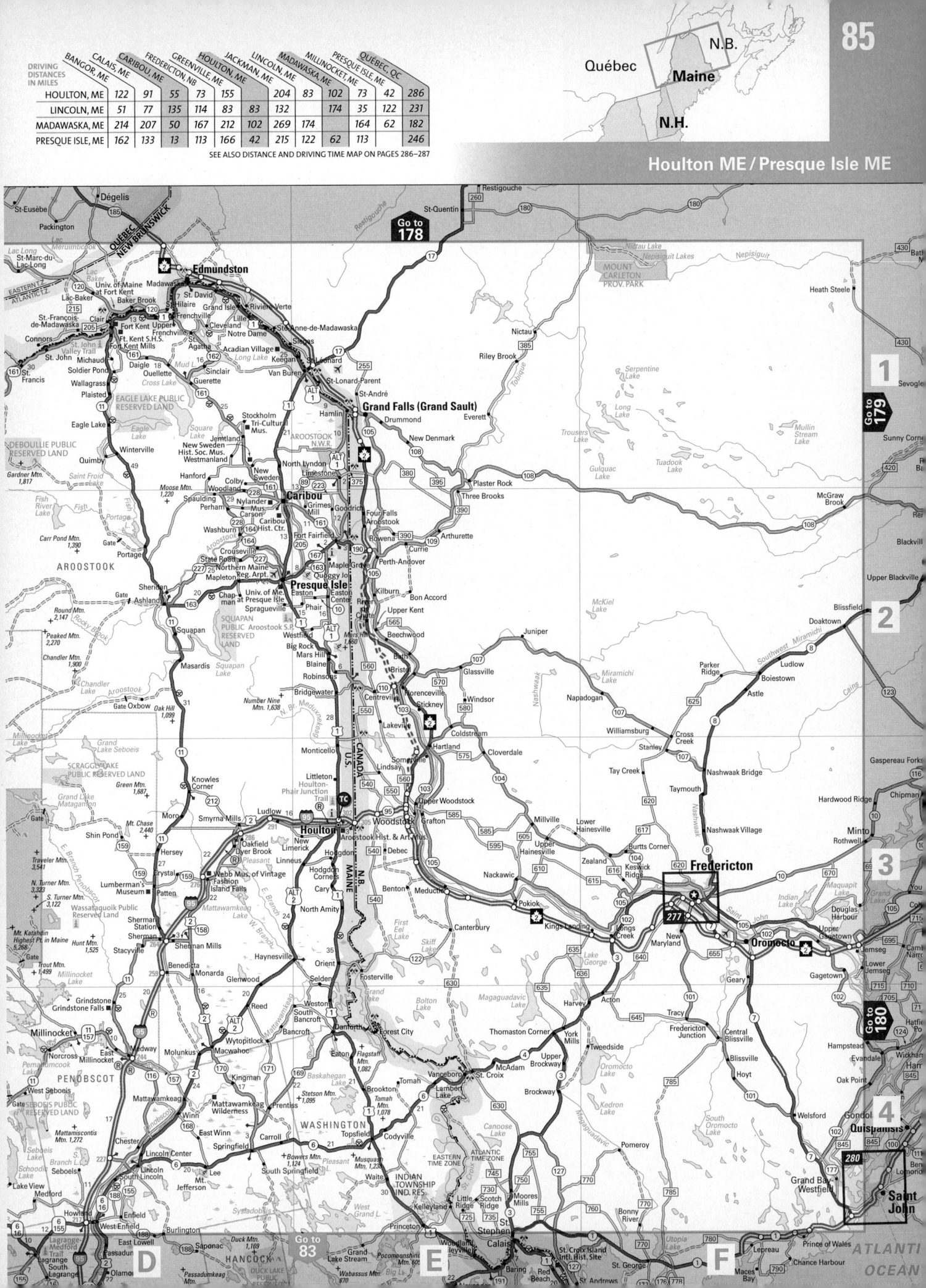

DRIVING DISTANCES IN MILES	BANGOR, ME	CALAIS, ME	CARIBOU, ME	FREDERICTON, NB	GREENVILLE, ME	HOULTON, ME	JACKMAN, ME	LINCOLN, ME	MADAWASKA, ME	MILLINOCKET, ME	PRESQUE ISLE, ME	QUEBEC, QC
HOULTON, ME	122	91	55	73	155		204	83	102	73	42	286
LINCOLN, ME	51	77	135	114	83	83	132		174	35	122	231
MADAWASKA, ME	214	207	50	167	212	102	269	174		164	62	182
PRESQUE ISLE, ME	162	133	13	113	166	42	215	122	62	113		246

SEE ALSO DISTANCE AND DRIVING TIME MAP ON PAGES 286–287

Nebraska Iowa Illinois Missouri

0 mi 10 20 30 40
0 km 10 20 30 40 50 60

One inch equals 18.4 miles
One centimeter equals 11.7 kilometers

Des Moines IA / Omaha NE

DRIVING DISTANCES IN MILES

	AMES, IA	BURLINGTON, IA	CARROLL, IA	CEDAR RAPIDS, IA	CRESTON, IA	DAVENPORT, IA	DES MOINES, IA	IOWA CITY, IA	KIRKSVILLE, MO	MARYVILLE, MO	OMAHA, NE	OTTUMWA, IA
CEDAR RAPIDS, IA	108	106	173		211	87	129	28	170	276	266	111
DES MOINES, IA	34	157	90	129	81	171		113	145	146	136	86
IOWA CITY, IA	136	82	195	28	195	59	113		143	260	250	83
OMAHA, NE	171	328	97	266	98	308	136	250	275	112		221

SEE ALSO DISTANCE AND DRIVING TIME MAP ON PAGES 286–287

Nebraska Iowa Illinois Missouri

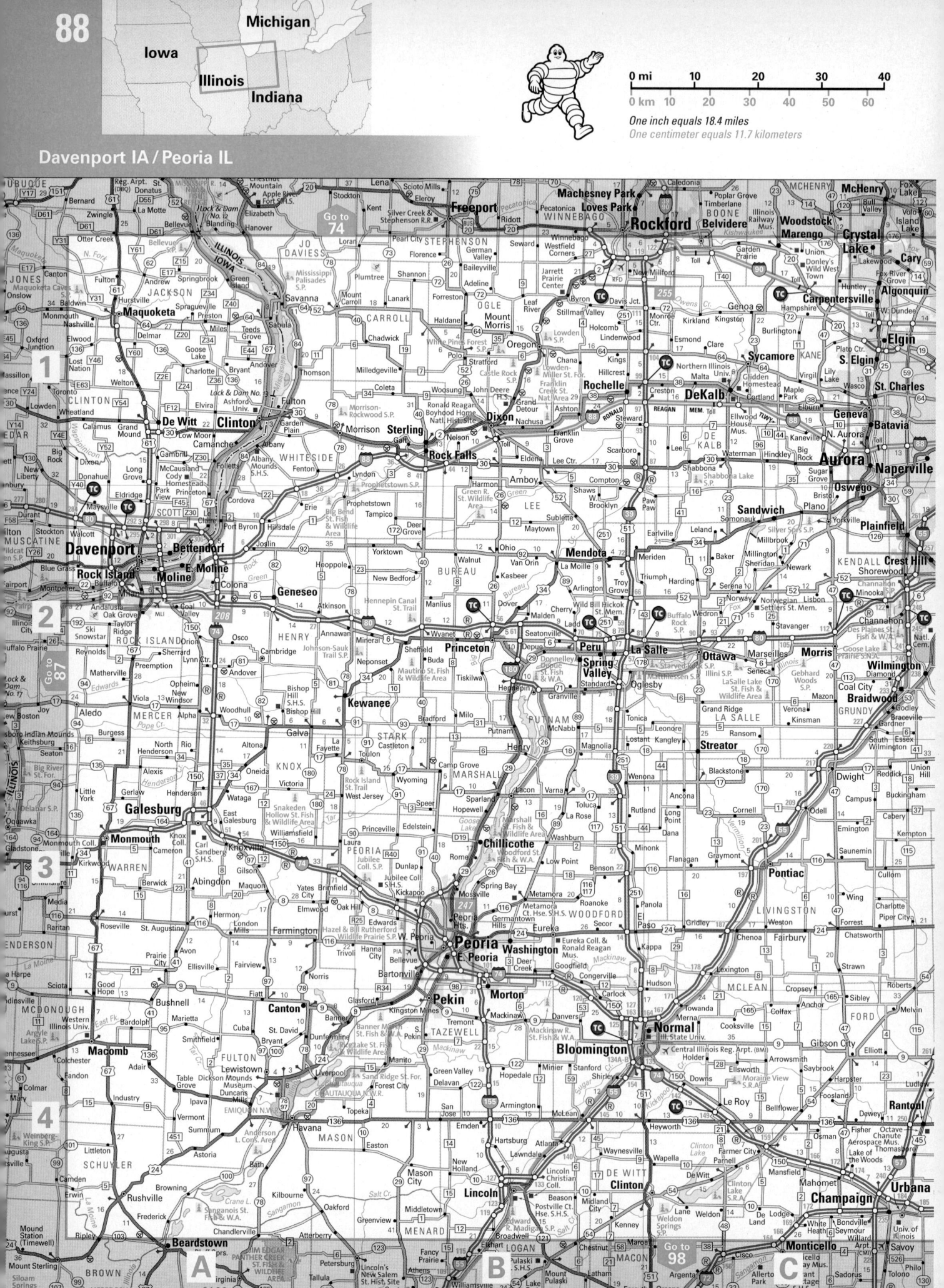

One inch equals 18.4 miles
One centimeter equals 11.7 kilometers

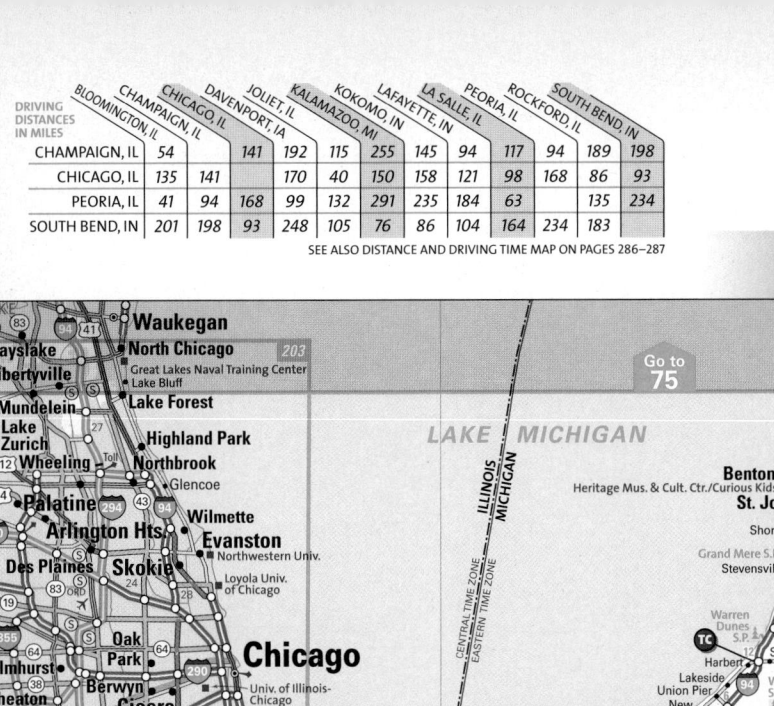

DRIVING DISTANCES IN MILES	BLOOMINGTON, IL	CHAMPAIGN, IL	CHICAGO, IL	DAVENPORT, IA	JOLIET, IL	KALAMAZOO, MI	KOKOMO IN	LAFAYETTE, IN	LA SALLE, IL	PEORIA, IL	ROCKFORD, IL	SOUTH BEND, IN
CHAMPAIGN, IL	54		141	192	115	255	145	94	117	94	189	198
CHICAGO, IL	135	141		170	40	150	158	121	98	168	86	93
PEORIA, IL	41	94	168	99	132	291	235	184	63		135	234
SOUTH BEND, IN	201	198	93	248	105	76	86	104	164	234	183	

SEE ALSO DISTANCE AND DRIVING TIME MAP ON PAGES 286–287

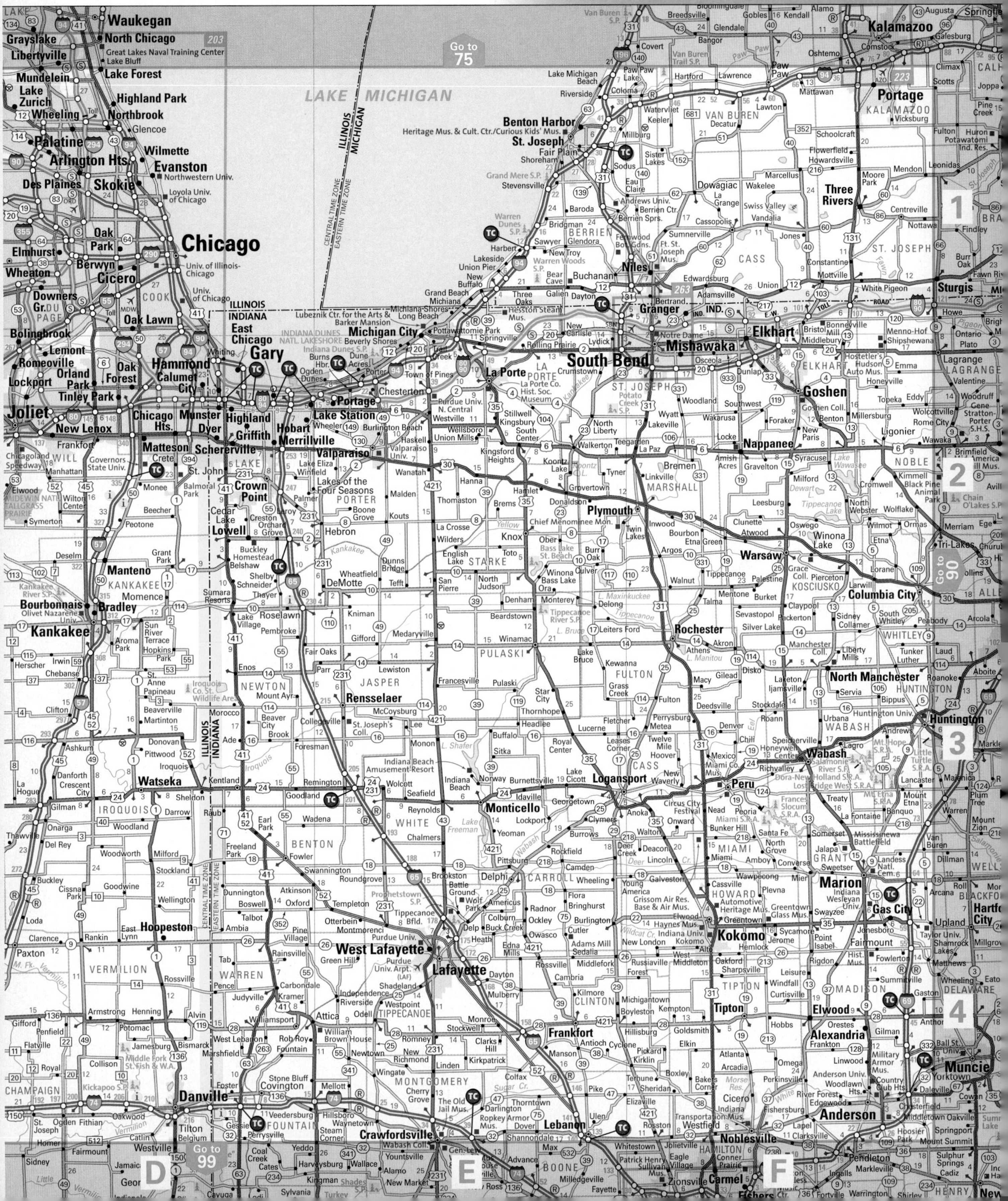

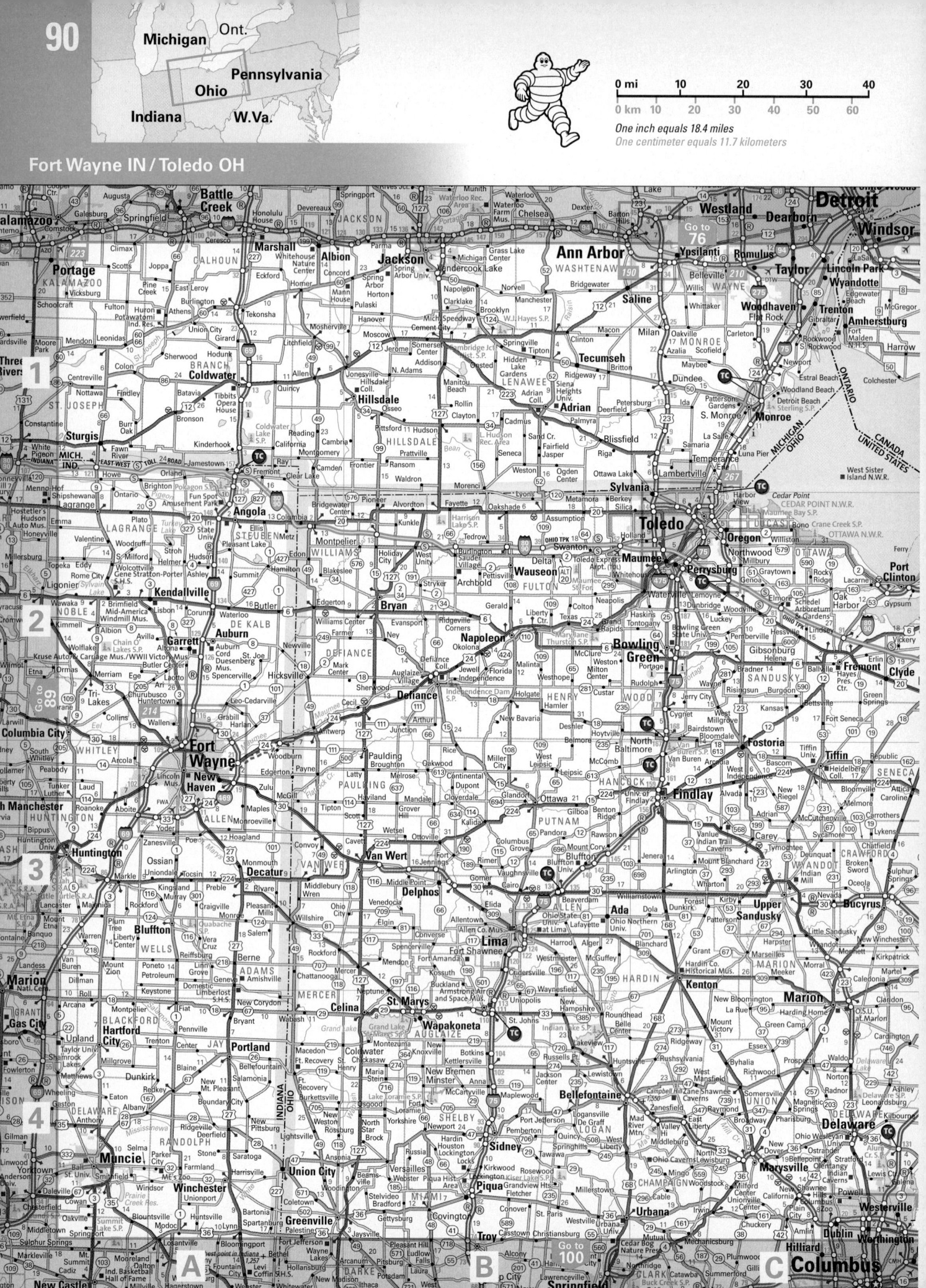

One inch equals 18.4 miles
One centimeter equals 11.7 kilometers

DRIVING DISTANCES IN MILES	AKRON, OH	CLEVELAND, OH	COLUMBUS, OH	DETROIT, MI	ERIE, PA	FORT WAYNE, IN	LIMA, OH	MANSFIELD, OH	MUNCIE, IN	TOLEDO, OH	WHEELING, WV	YOUNGSTOWN, OH
CLEVELAND, OH	38		144	171	106	214	163	81	287	119	16	275
FORT WAYNE, IN	237	214	186	170	322		66	151	75	109	290	274
MANSFIELD, OH	66	81	67	156	179	151	93		209	105	141	112
TOLEDO, OH	142	119	148	60	227	109	83	105	180		261	179

SEE ALSO DISTANCE AND DRIVING TIME MAP ON PAGES 286–287

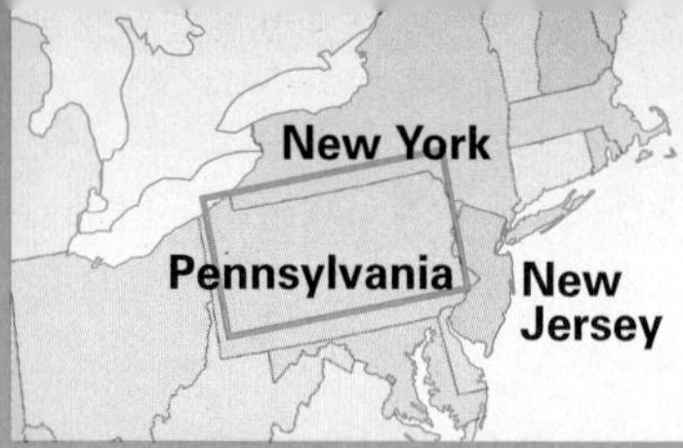

New York

Pennsylvania   New Jersey

0 mi   10   20   30   40
0 km   10   20   30   40   50   60
One inch equals 18.4 miles
One centimeter equals 11.7 kilometers

LAKE ERIE

Go to 77   Go to 78

Go to 91   Go to 102

Erie   Edinboro   Meadville   Titusville   Oil City   Franklin   Sugarcreek   Grove City   New Castle   Butler   Kittanning   Indiana   Pittsburgh   McKeesport   Mt. Lebanon   Bethel Park   Monroeville   Murrysville   Greensburg   Latrobe   Johnstown   Altoona   Hollidaysburg   State College   Bellefonte   Clearfield   DuBois   Punxsutawney   Brookville   Clarion   St. Marys   Ridgway   Kane   Warren   Bradford   Olean   Salamanca   Jamestown   Corry   Washington   Connellsville   Somerset

ONT.
S.   PA.

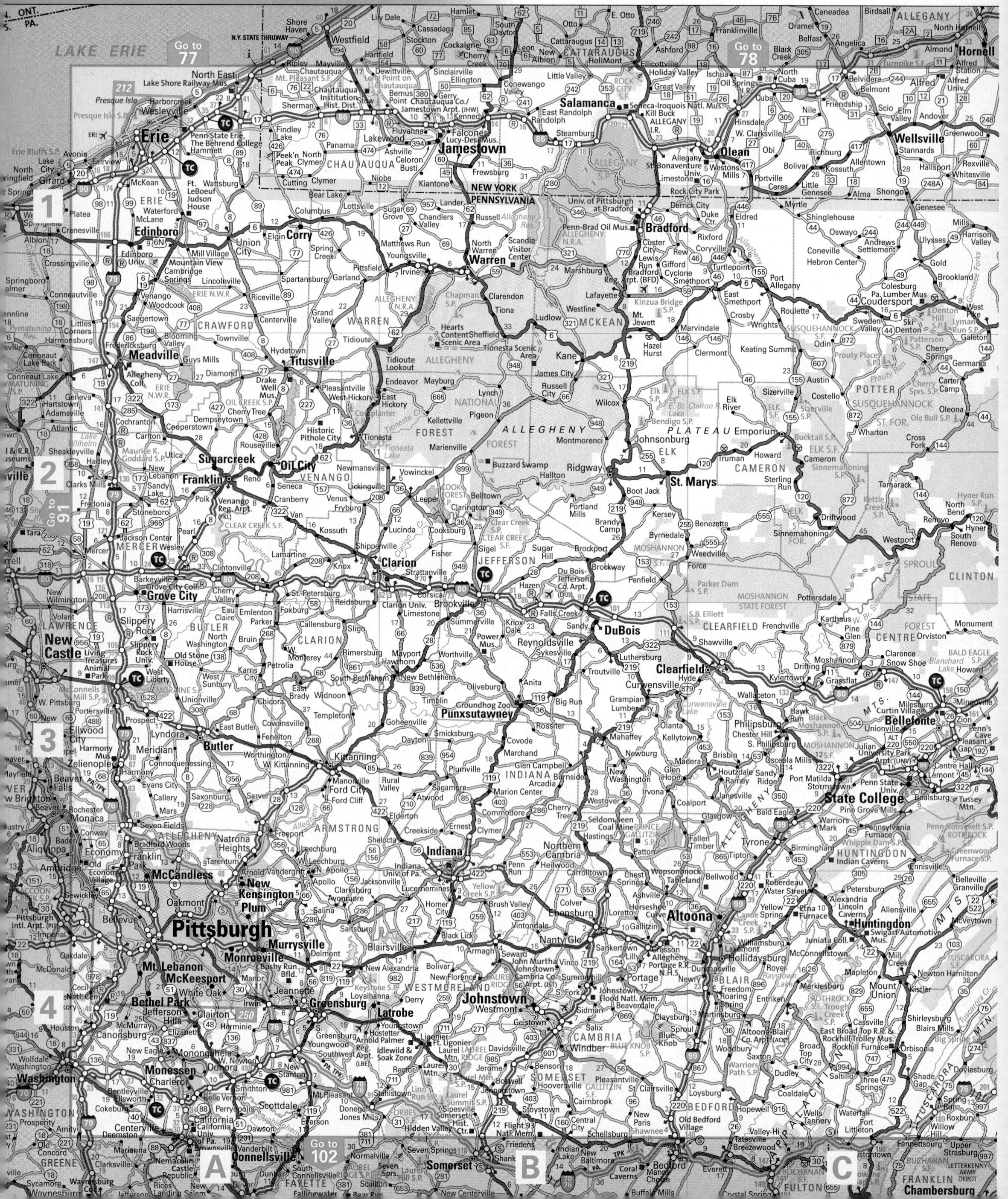

DRIVING DISTANCES IN MILES	ALLENTOWN, PA	ALTOONA, PA	BINGHAMTON, NY	ELMIRA, PA	ERIE, PA	HARRISBURG, PA	JOHNSTOWN, PA	PITTSBURGH, PA	READING, PA	SCRANTON, PA	STATE COLLEGE, PA	WILLIAMSPORT, PA
ALLENTOWN, PA		218	132	188	361	82	217	284	37	76	165	116
HARRISBURG, PA	82	140	181	157	298		138	205	65	119	88	83
PITTSBURGH, PA	284	99	363	284	126	205	73		262	301	139	215
SCRANTON, PA	76	185	61	117	317	119	233	301	103		149	83

SEE ALSO DISTANCE AND DRIVING TIME MAP ON PAGES 286–287

New York
Pennsylvania   New Jersey

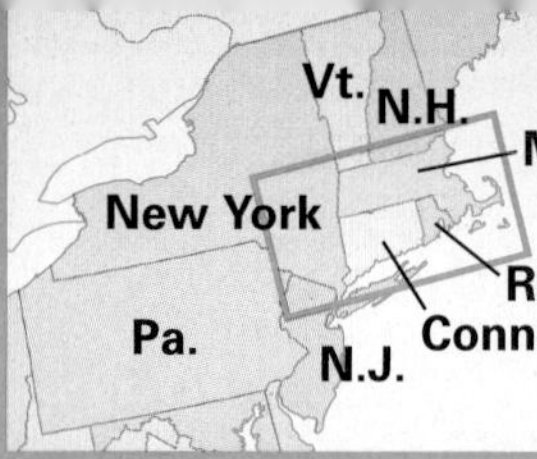

Vt.
N.H.
Massachusetts
New York
Rhode Island
Connecticut
Pa.
N.J.

0 mi 10 20 30 40
0 km 10 20 30 40 50 60
One inch equals 18.4 miles
One centimeter equals 11.7 kilometers

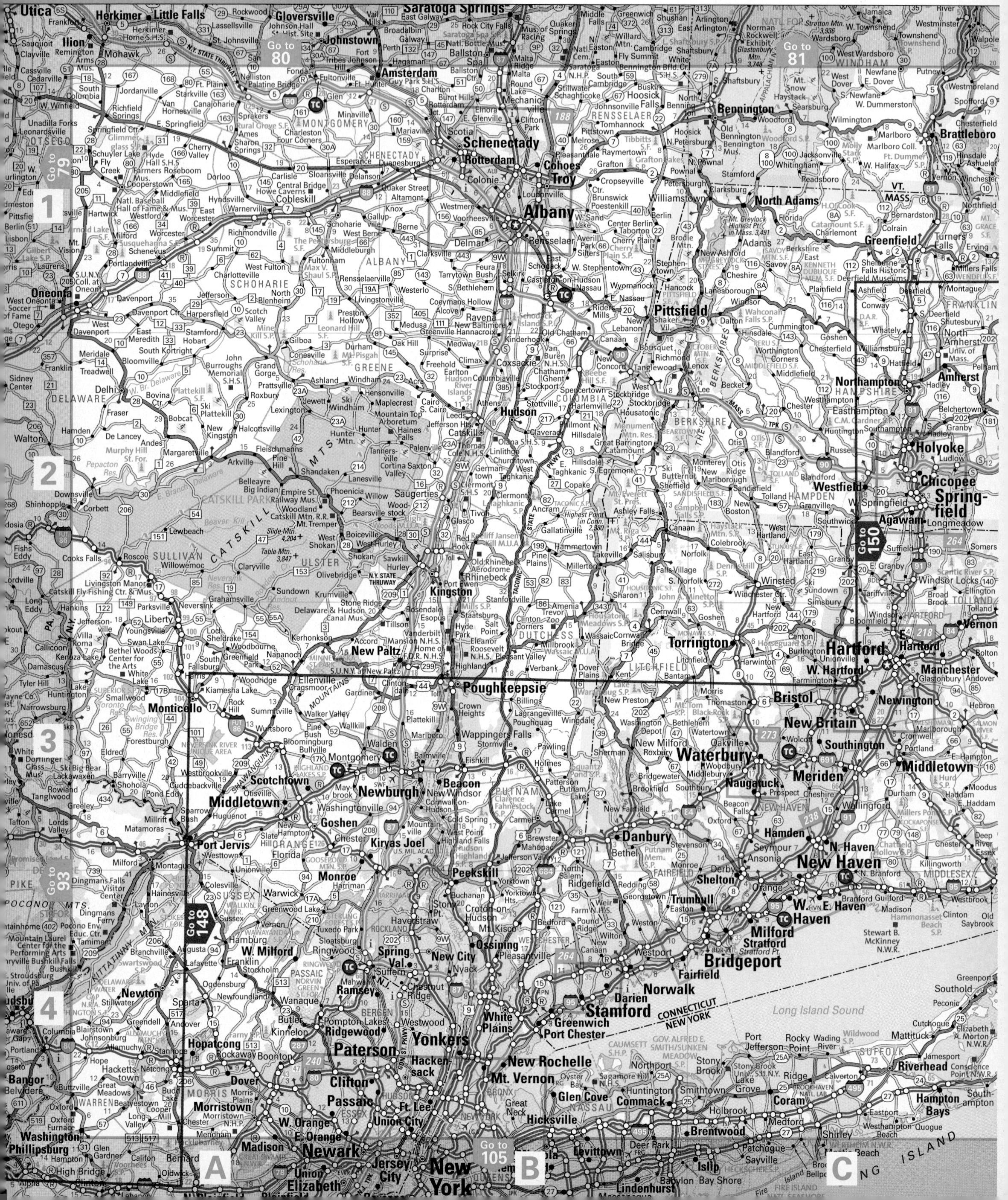

Go to 82

Go to 151

Go to 149

DRIVING DISTANCES IN MILES	BOSTON, MA	HARTFORD CT	MANCHESTER, NH	NEWBURGH, NY	NEW HAVEN, CT	NEW YORK, NY	ONEONTA, NY	PROVIDENCE, RI	PROVINCETOWN, MA	SPRINGFIELD MA	WORCESTER MA
ALBANY, NY	172	111	145	89	150	151	81	170	271	86	133
BOSTON, MA		102	54	201	139	215	251	52	117	95	46
HARTFORD, CT	111	102	131	99	39	115	190	73	200	25	62
NEW YORK, NY	151	215	115	245	56	78	193	177	292	141	176

SEE ALSO DISTANCE AND DRIVING TIME MAP ON PAGES 286–287

FOR DETAIL OF AREA
INSIDE PURPLE FRAME,
SEE PAGES 148–151

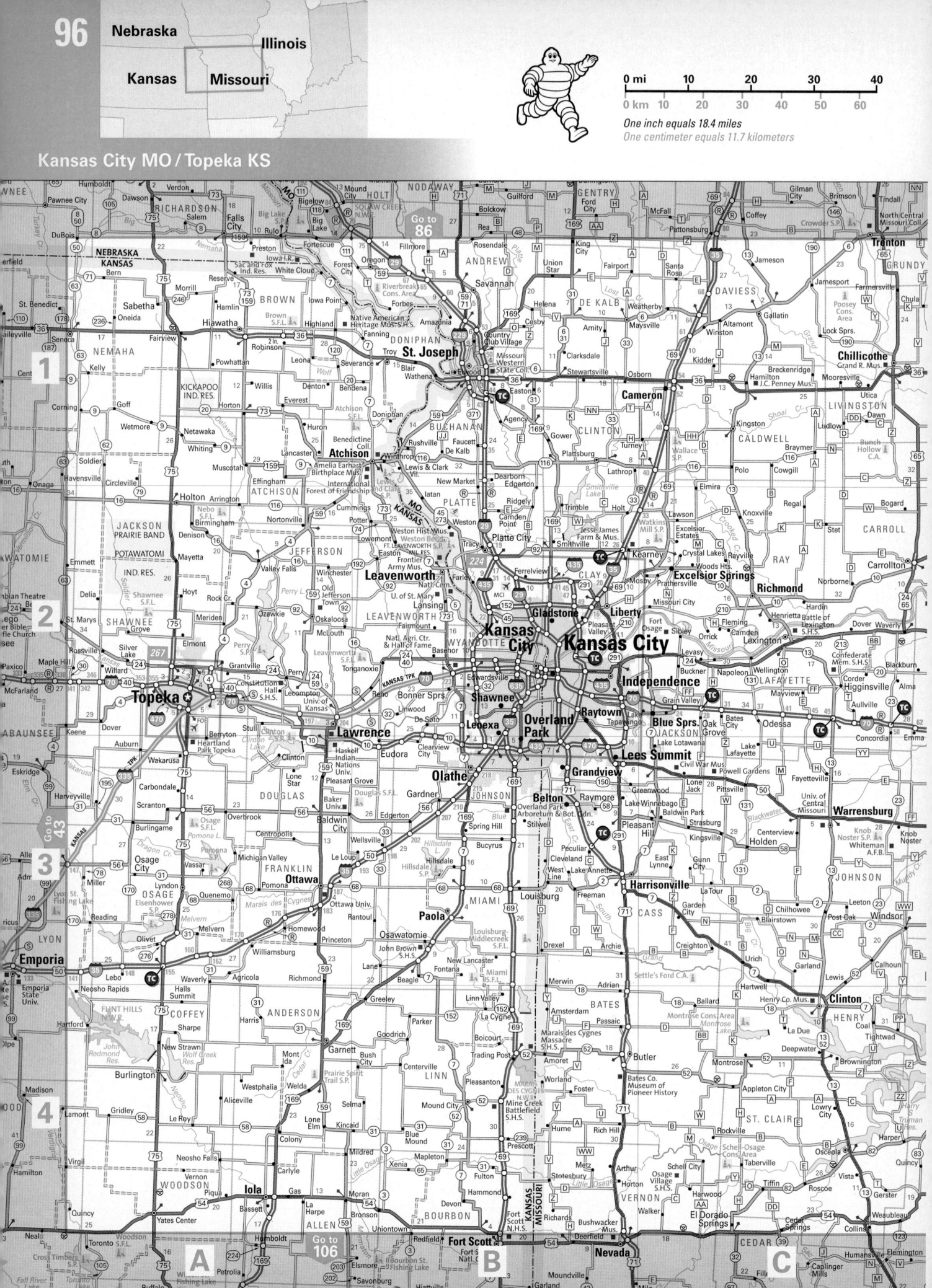

One inch equals 18.4 miles
One centimeter equals 11.7 kilometers

0 mi   10   20   30   40
0 km 10 20   30   40   50   60

Kansas City MO / Topeka KS

Nebraska
Illinois
Kansas
Missouri

DRIVING DISTANCES IN MILES	IOLA, KS	JEFFERSON CITY, MO	KANSAS CITY, MO	LAWRENCE, KS	MACON, MO	OSAGE BEACH, MO	QUINCY, IL	ROLLA, MO	ST. JOSEPH, MO	SEDALIA, MO	TOPEKA, KS
COLUMBIA, MO											
JEFFERSON CITY, MO	32	263		161	198	88	44	131	65	217	64	225
KANSAS CITY, MO	129	106	161		37	148	173	251	226	56	97	63
ST. JOSEPH, MO	185	154	217	56	76	131	229	210	282		153	71
TOPEKA, KS	193	100	225	63	26	209	236	314	289	71	161	

SEE ALSO DISTANCE AND DRIVING TIME MAP ON PAGES 286–287

Go to 87
Go to 98
Go to 107

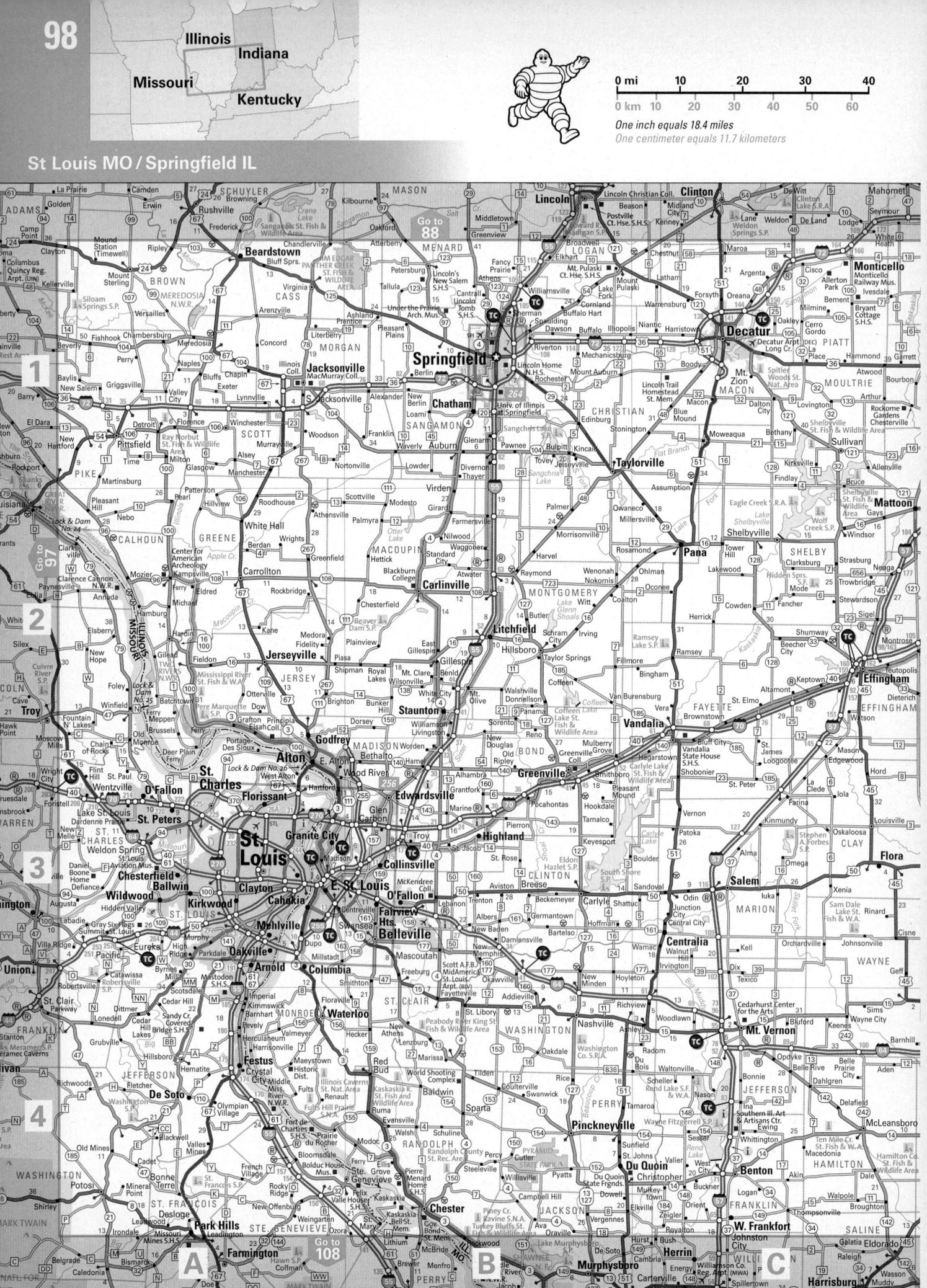

Illinois
Indiana
Missouri
Kentucky

0 mi 10 20 30 40
0 km 10 20 30 40 50 60
One inch equals 18.4 miles
One centimeter equals 11.7 kilometers

DRIVING DISTANCES IN MILES	BLOOMINGTON, IN	CHAMPAIGN, IL	DECATUR, IL	EFFINGHAM, IL	EVANSVILLE, IN	INDIANAPOLIS, IN	LOUISVILLE, KY	MT. VERNON, IL	ST. LOUIS, MO	SPRINGFIELD, IL	TERRE HAUTE, IN	VINCENNES, IN
EVANSVILLE, IN	117	192	184	117		166	114	90	170	247	107	51
INDIANAPOLIS, IN	47	123	177	137	166		112	205	239	212	77	123
ST. LOUIS, MO	223	179	116	103	170	239	264	81		97	169	185
SPRINGFIELD, IL	209	87	40	89	247	212	326	158	97		155	169

SEE ALSO DISTANCE AND DRIVING TIME MAP ON PAGES 286–287

Ohio

Indiana   W.Va.

Kentucky

0 mi   10   20   30   40
0 km 10   20   30   40   50   60
One inch equals 18.4 miles
One centimeter equals 11.7 kilometers

Cincinnati OH / Louisville KY

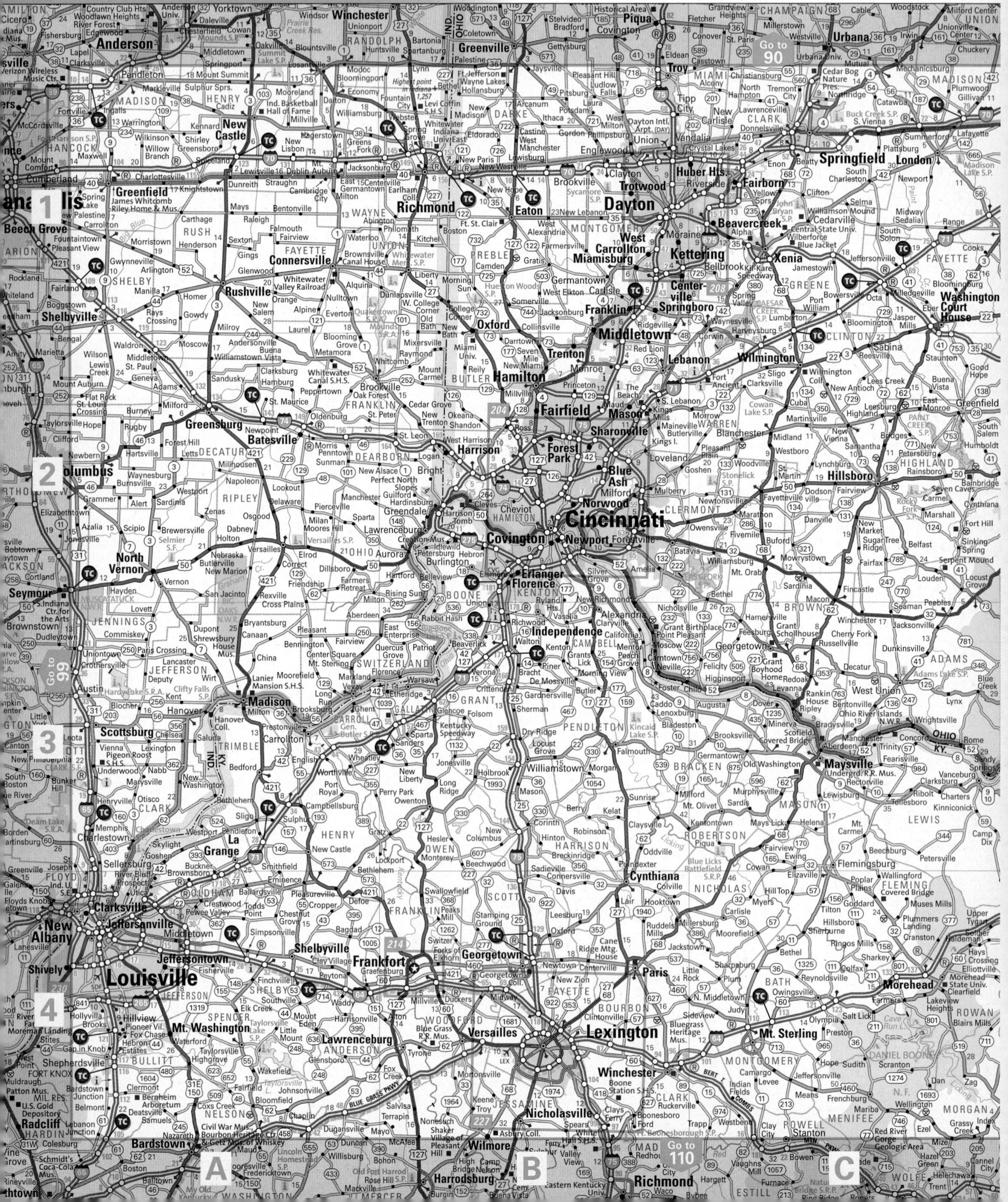

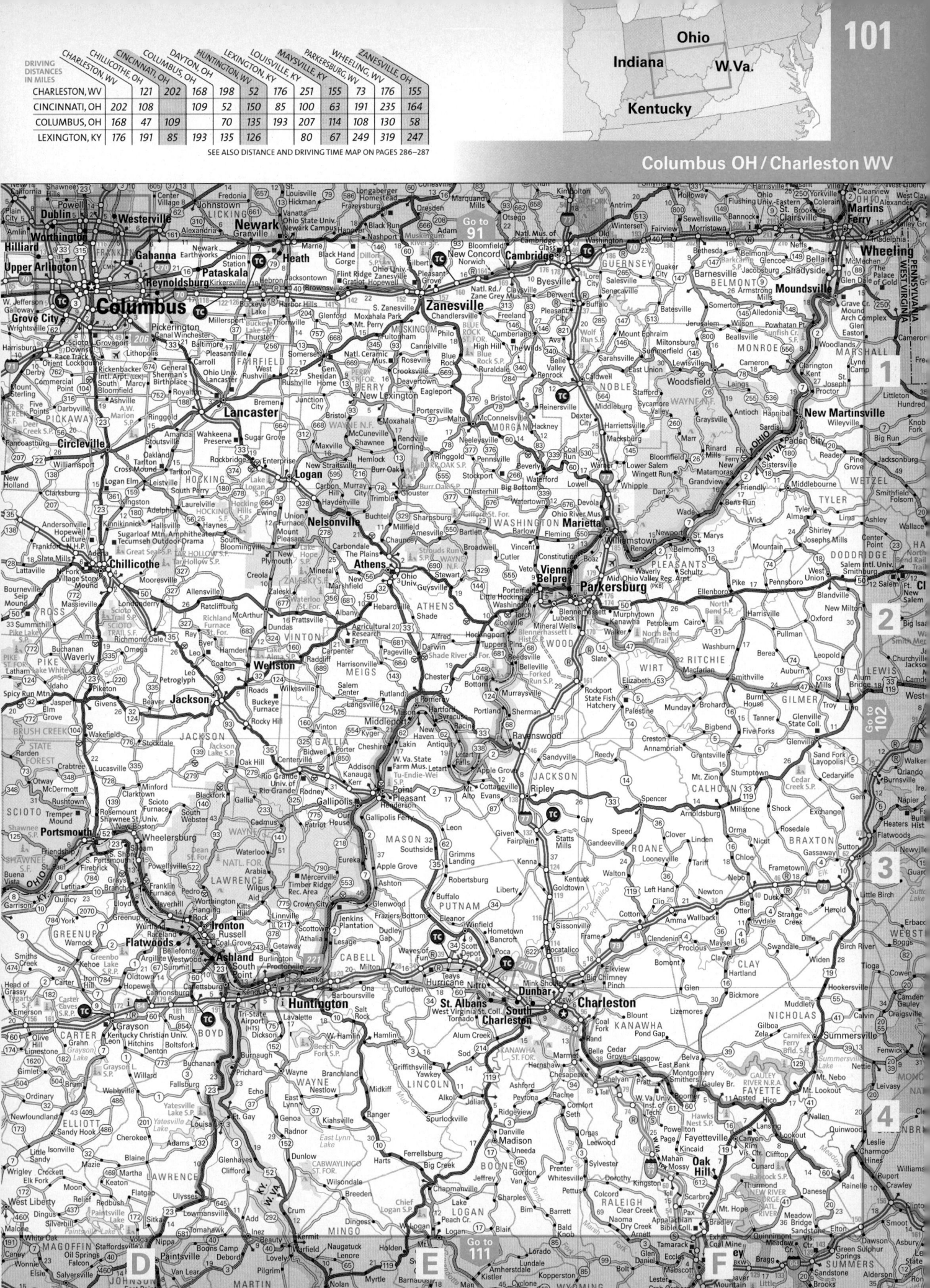

DRIVING DISTANCES IN MILES	CHARLESTON, WV	CHILLICOTHE, OH	CINCINNATI, OH	COLUMBUS, OH	DAYTON, OH	HUNTINGTON, WV	LEXINGTON, KY	LOUISVILLE, KY	MAYSVILLE, KY	PARKERSBURG, WV	WHEELING, OH	ZANESVILLE, OH
CHARLESTON, WV		121	202	168	198	52	176	251	155	73	176	155
CINCINNATI, OH	202	108		109	52	150	85	100	63	191	235	164
COLUMBUS, OH	168	47	109		70	135	193	207	114	108	130	58
LEXINGTON, KY	176	191	85	193	135	126		80	67	249	319	247

SEE ALSO DISTANCE AND DRIVING TIME MAP ON PAGES 286–287

Pennsylvania
Ohio
Md. — Delaware
W.Va.
Virginia

0 mi 10 20 30 40
0 km 10 20 30 40 50 60
One inch equals 18.4 miles
One centimeter equals 11.7 kilometers

Charlottesville VA / Morgantown WV

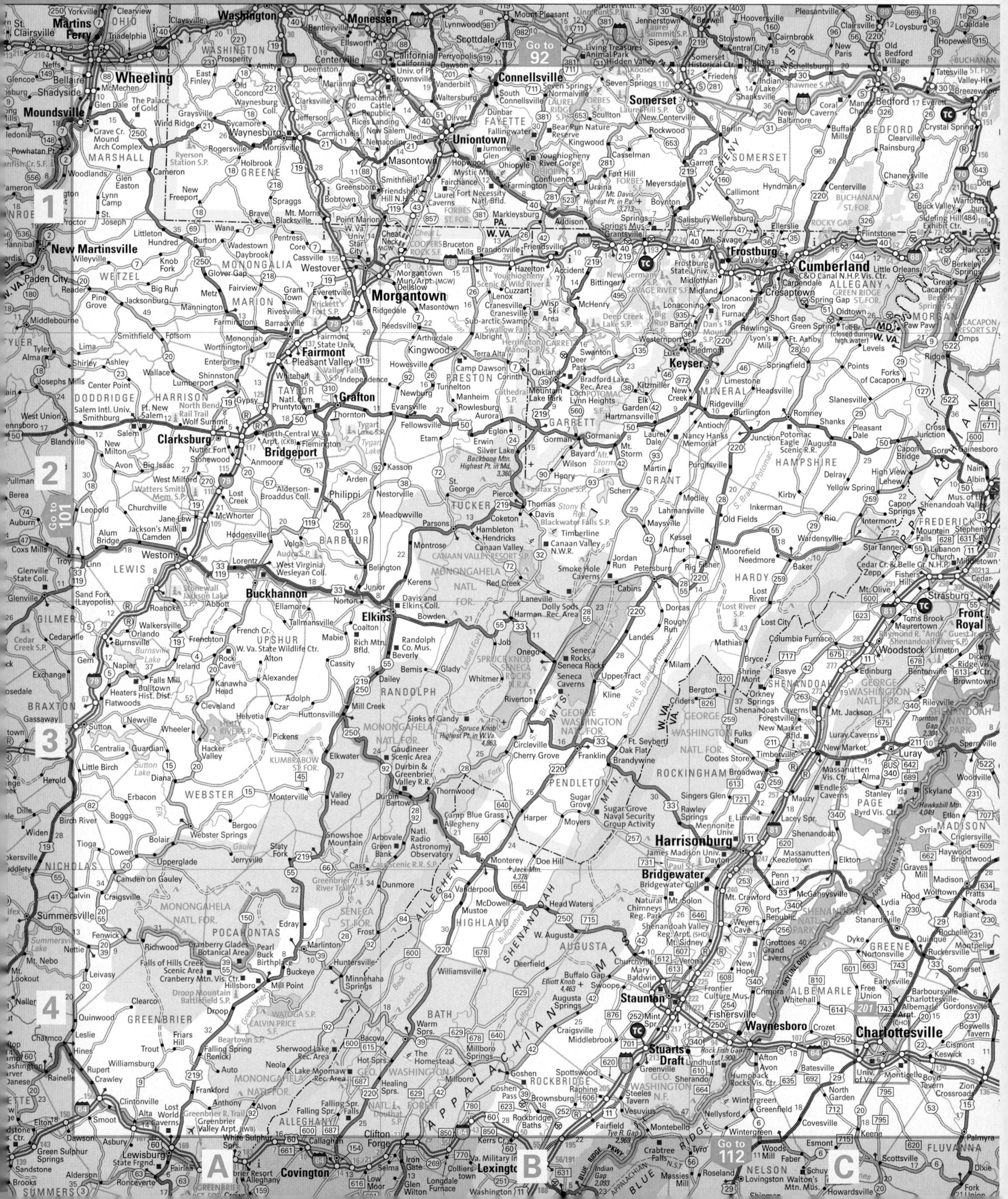

Go to 92
Go to 101
Go to 112

Martins Ferry, Wheeling, Moundsville, New Martinsville, Paden City, Middlebourne, Washington, Monessen, Connellsville, Uniontown, Somerset, Cumberland, Frostburg, Keyser, Morgantown, Fairmont, Clarksburg, Bridgeport, Grafton, Buckhannon, Weston, Elkins, Harrisonburg, Bridgewater, Staunton, Waynesboro, Charlottesville, Stuarts Draft, Lexington, Covington, Front Royal, Strasburg, Woodstock, Luray

103

Pennsylvania
Ohio   Md. — Delaware
W.Va.
Virginia

Washington DC / Baltimore MD

DRIVING DISTANCES IN MILES	CHARLOTTESVILLE, VA	CUMBERLAND, MD	ELKINS, WV	FREDERICKSBURG, VA	FRONT ROYAL, VA	GETTYSBURG, PA	HAGERSTOWN, MD	MORGANTOWN, WV	SALISBURY, MD	WASHINGTON, DC	WHEELING, WV
BALTIMORE, MD	161	140	229	98	110	62	76	211	106	38	290
CHARLOTTESVILLE, VA	161	163	142	70	74	190	141	204	235	118	279
MORGANTOWN, WV	211	204	71	62	252	161	181	138	317	205	76
WASHINGTON, DC	38	118	134	192	54	73	80	70	205	115	284

SEE ALSO DISTANCE AND DRIVING TIME MAP ON PAGES 286–287

FOR DETAIL OF AREA INSIDE PURPLE FRAME, SEE PAGES 144–147

Go to 93
Go to 146
Go to 144
Go to 145
Go to 104
Go to 114
Go to 113

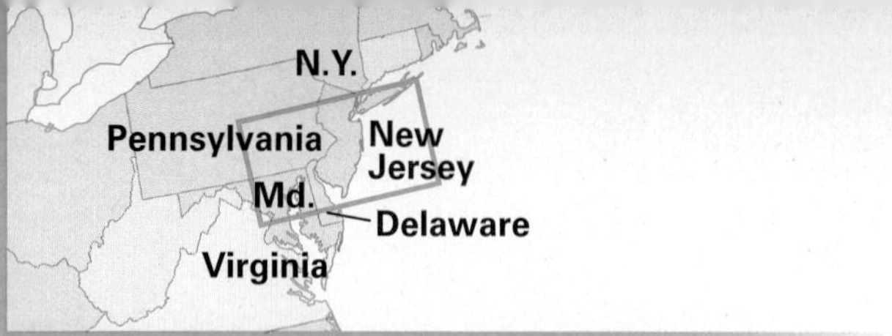

N.Y.

Pennsylvania — New Jersey

Md. — Delaware

Virginia

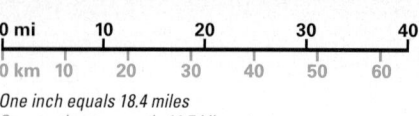

0 mi · 10 · 20 · 30 · 40
0 km · 10 · 20 · 30 · 40 · 50 · 60

One inch equals 18.4 miles
One centimeter equals 11.7 kilometers

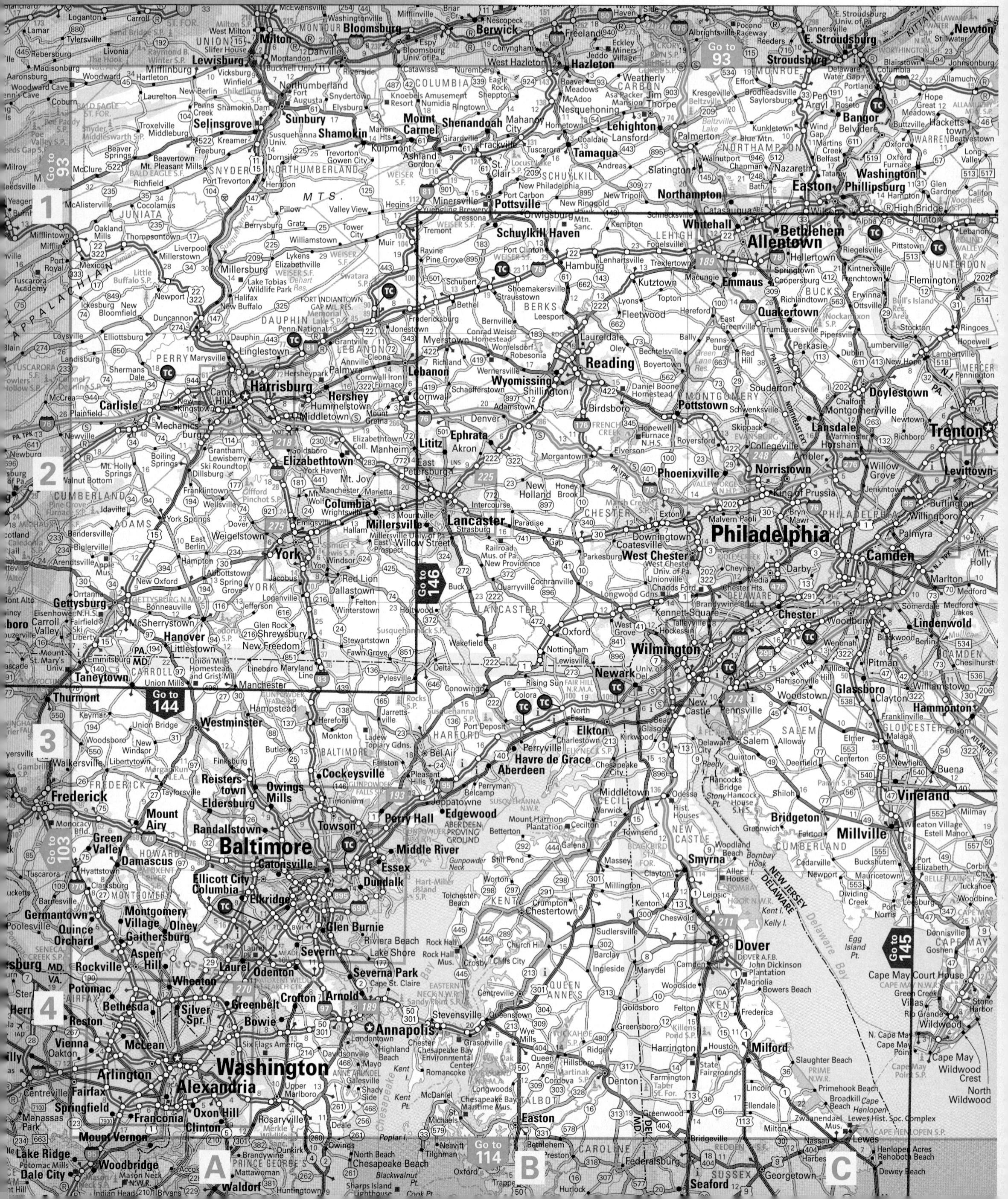

Philadelphia PA / Harrisburg PA

Go to 93 · Go to 146 · Go to 144 · Go to 103 · Go to 114 · Go to 145

A · B · C · 1 · 2 · 3 · 4

N.Y.
Pennsylvania — New Jersey
Md. — Delaware
Virginia

DRIVING DISTANCES IN MILES	ALLENTOWN, PA	ATLANTIC CITY, NJ	BALTIMORE, MD	DOVER, DE	HARRISBURG, PA	LANCASTER, PA	NEWARK, NJ	NEW YORK, NY	PHILADELPHIA, PA	TRENTON, NJ	WASHINGTON, DC	WILMINGTON, DE
HARRISBURG, PA	82	171	83	126		44	154	165	109	135	123	102
NEW YORK, NY	84	125	192	160	165	165	11		91	55	228	120
PHILADELPHIA, PA	63	62	104	74	109	79	80	91		34	140	30
WASHINGTON, DC	188	186	38	94	123	123	218	228	140	179		110

SEE ALSO DISTANCE AND DRIVING TIME MAP ON PAGES 286–287

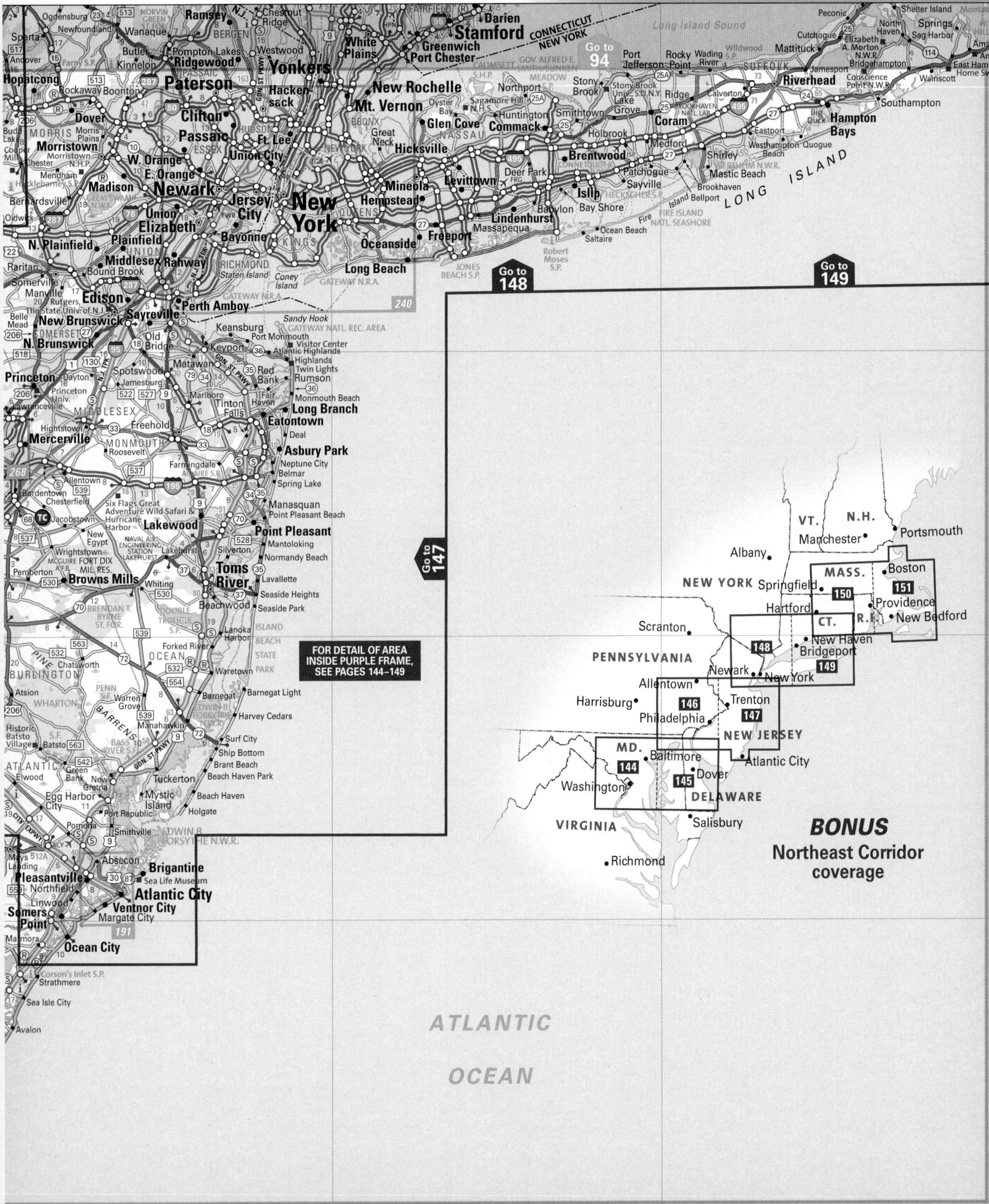

Go to 94
Go to 148
Go to 149
Go to 147

FOR DETAIL OF AREA INSIDE PURPLE FRAME, SEE PAGES 144–149

BONUS
Northeast Corridor coverage

ATLANTIC OCEAN

| 1 |
| 2 |
| 3 |
| 4 |

D   E   F

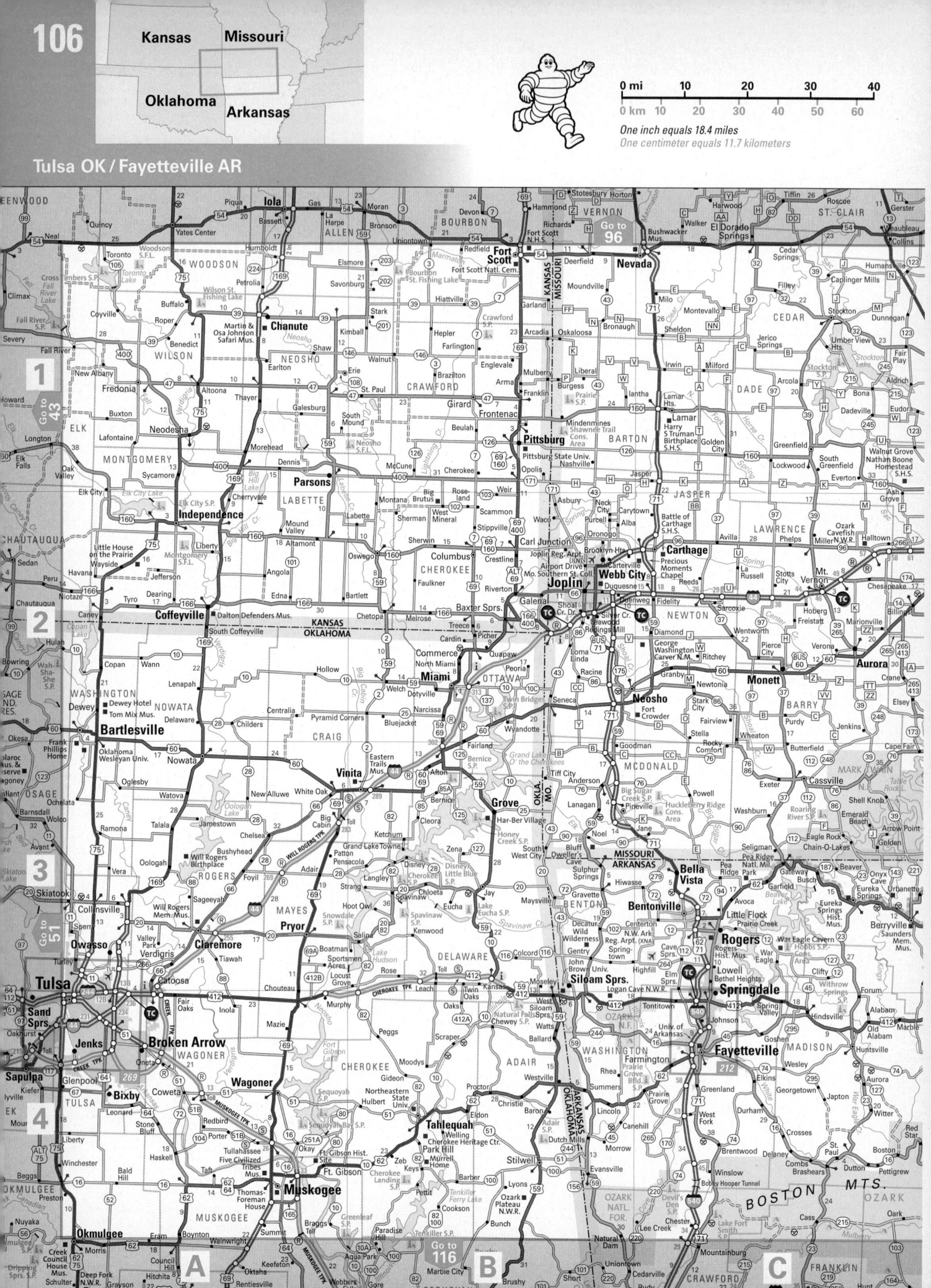

0 mi   10   20   30   40

0 km   10   20   30   40   50   60

One inch equals 18.4 miles
One centimeter equals 11.7 kilometers

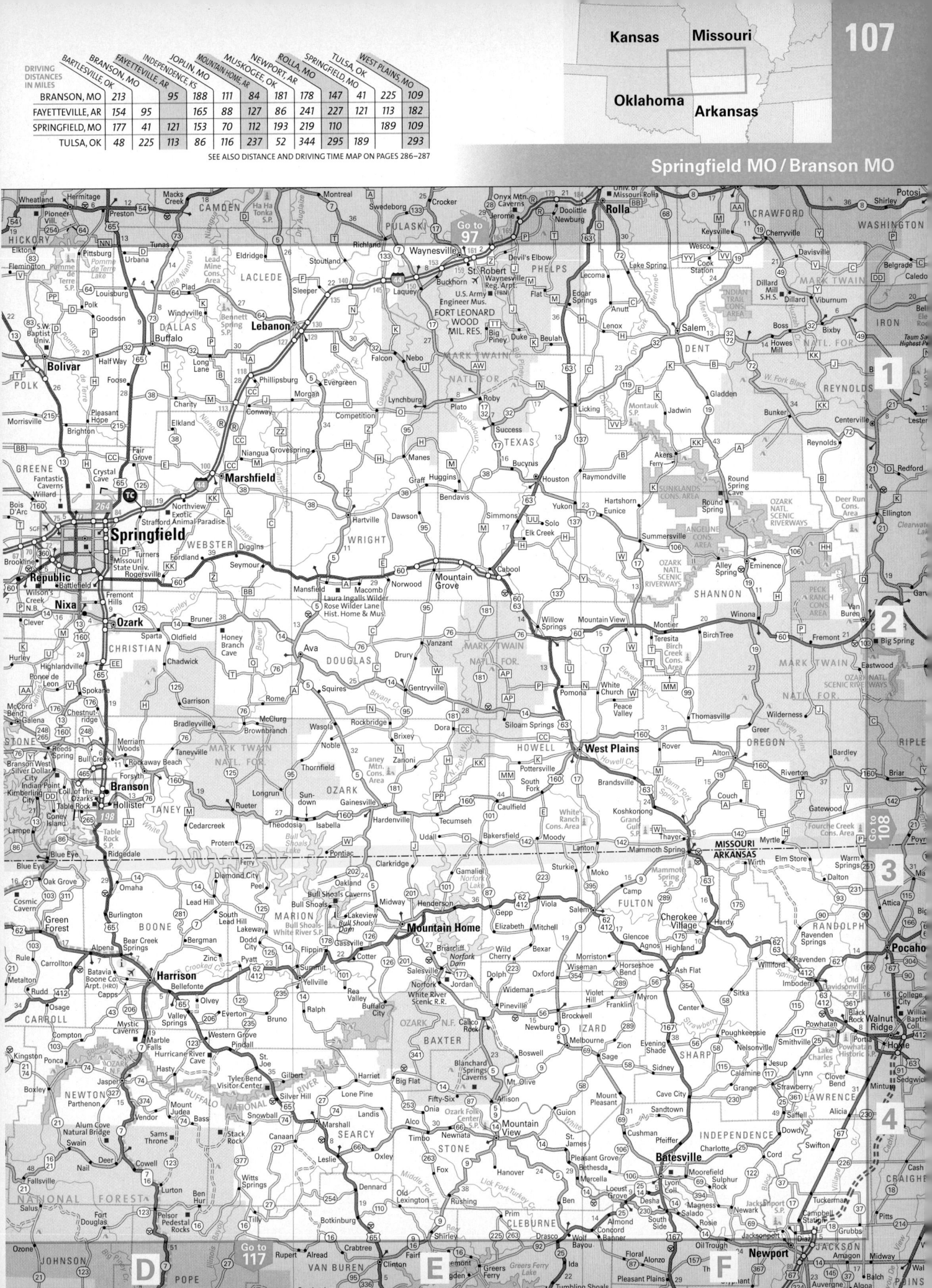

DRIVING DISTANCES IN MILES	BARTLESVILLE, OK	BRANSON, MO	FAYETTEVILLE, AR	INDEPENDENCE, KS	JOPLIN, MO	MOUNTAIN HOME, AR	MUSKOGEE, OK	NEWPORT, AR	ROLLA, MO	SPRINGFIELD, MO	TULSA, OK	WEST PLAINS, MO
BRANSON, MO	213		95	188	111	84	181	178	147	41	225	109
FAYETTEVILLE, AR	154	95		165	88	127	86	241	227	121	113	182
SPRINGFIELD, MO	177	41	121	153	70	112	193	219	110		189	109
TULSA, OK	48	225	113	86	116	237	52	344	295	189		293

SEE ALSO DISTANCE AND DRIVING TIME MAP ON PAGES 286–287

Kansas   Missouri

Oklahoma   Arkansas

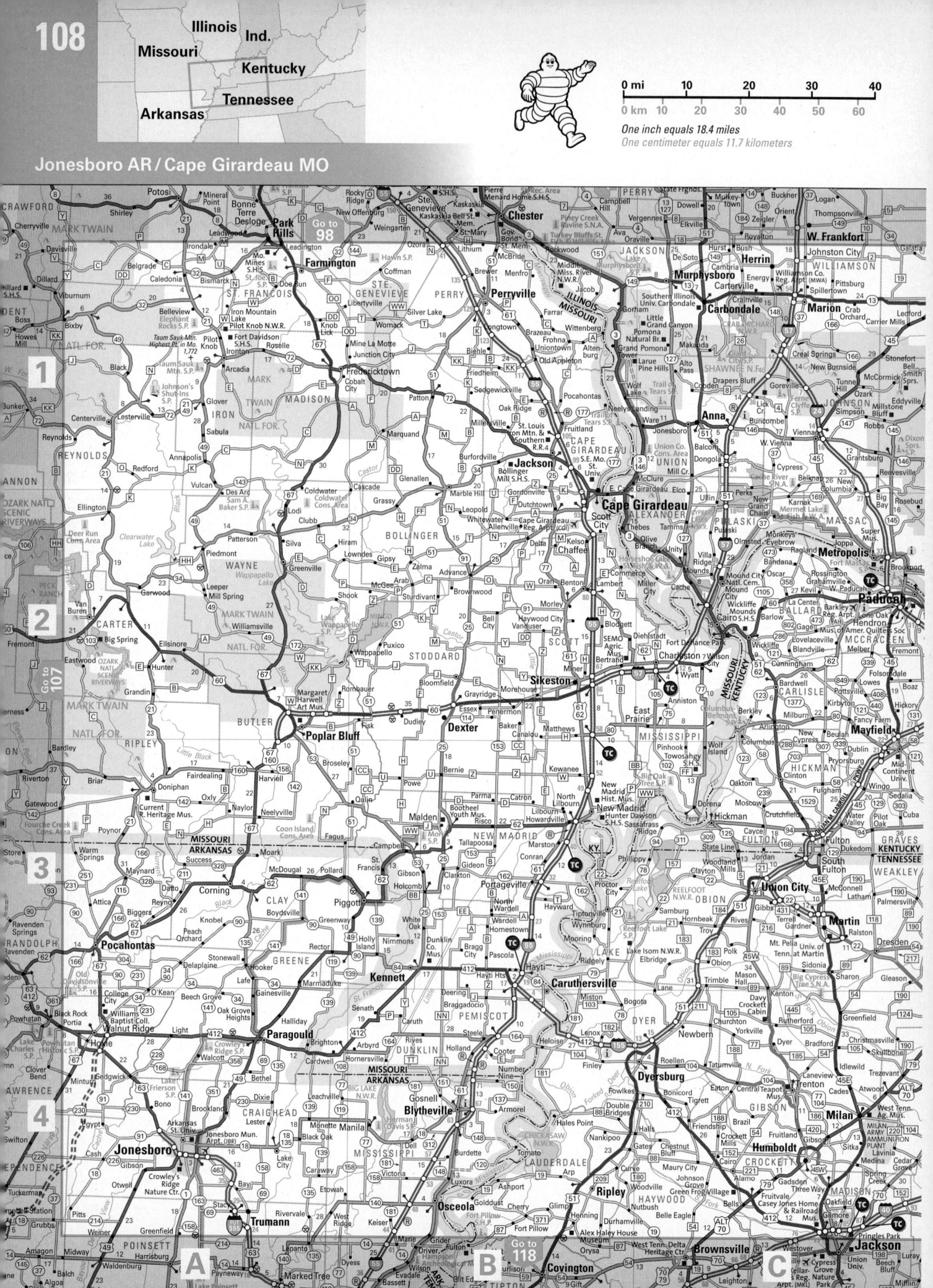

Illinois | Ind.
Missouri | Kentucky
Arkansas | Tennessee

Go to 99
Go to 110
Go to 119

DRIVING DISTANCES IN MILES

	BOWLING GREEN, KY	CAPE GIRARDEAU, MO	CARBONDALE, IL	CLARKSVILLE, TN	DYERSBURG, TN	HOPKINSVILLE, KY	JACKSON, TN	JONESBORO, AR	NASHVILLE, TN	OWENSBORO, KY	PADUCAH, KY	POPLAR BLUFF, MO
BOWLING GREEN, KY		199	206	63	217	63	196	349	68	76	135	239
CAPE GIRARDEAU, MO	199		46	155	112	136	161	155	197	168	67	75
JONESBORO, AR	349	155	199	268	101	249	160		285	304	178	81
NASHVILLE, TN	68	197	204	46	178	68	132	285		141	133	237

SEE ALSO DISTANCE AND DRIVING TIME MAP ON PAGES 286–287

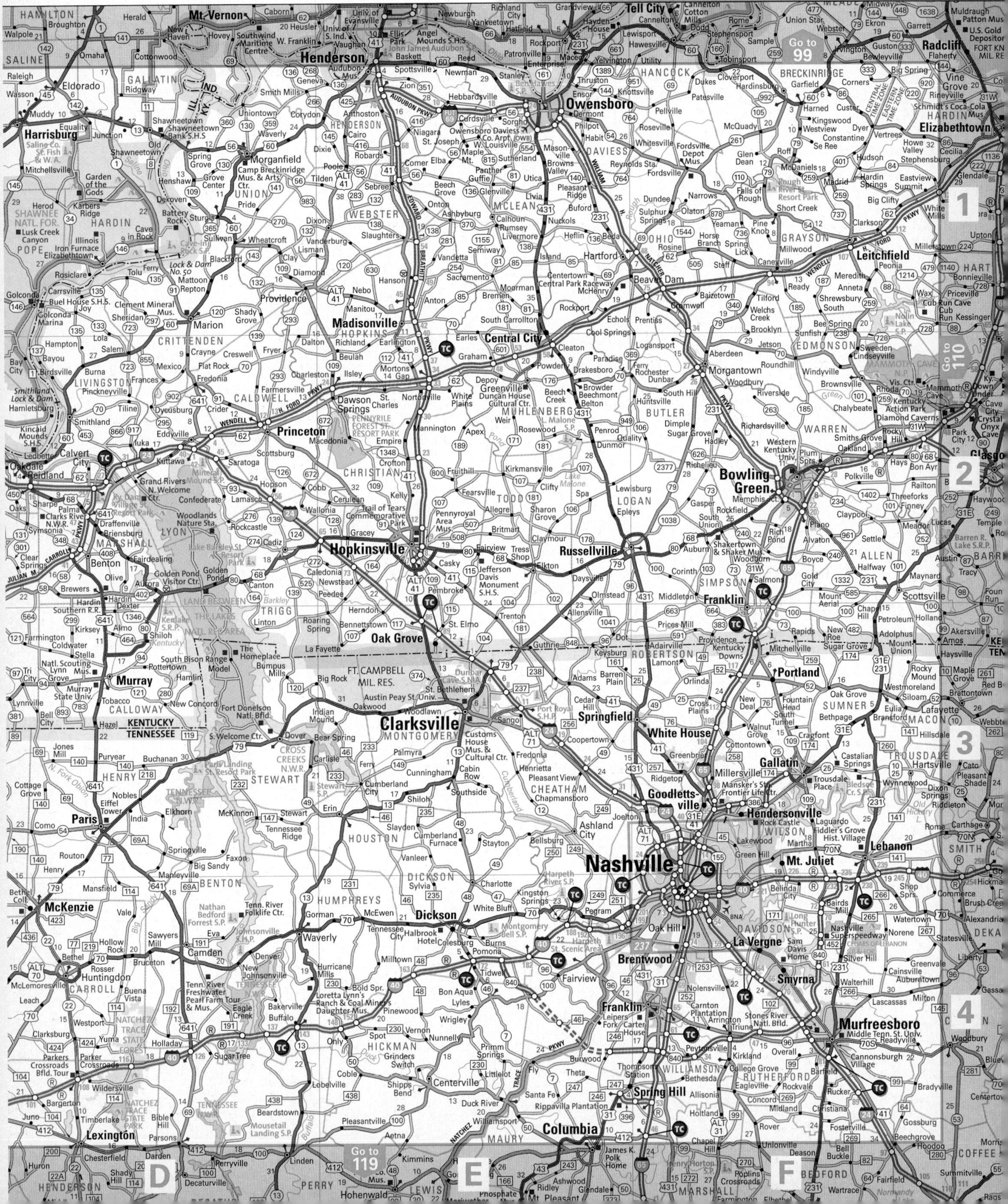

110

W.Va.
Virginia
Kentucky
North
Tennessee   Carolina

Knoxville TN / Richmond KY

0 mi   10   20   30   40
0 km 10   20   30   40   50   60
One inch equals 18.4 miles
One centimeter equals 11.7 kilometers

A   B   C

1

2

3

4

Go to
100

Go to
109

Go to
120

Radcliff
Bardstown
Elizabethtown
Hodgenville
Leitchfield
Glasgow
Campbellsville
Columbia
Lebanon
Danville
Harrodsburg
Richmond
Berea
Stanford
Somerset
Monticello
London
Corbin
Barbourville
Williamsburg
Middlesboro
Harrogate
La Follette
Clinton
Oak Ridge
Farragut
Knoxville
Maryville
Cookeville
Crossville
Harriman
Rockwood
Kingston
McMinnville
Lebanon
Nicholasville
Wilmore
Springfield
Bardstown

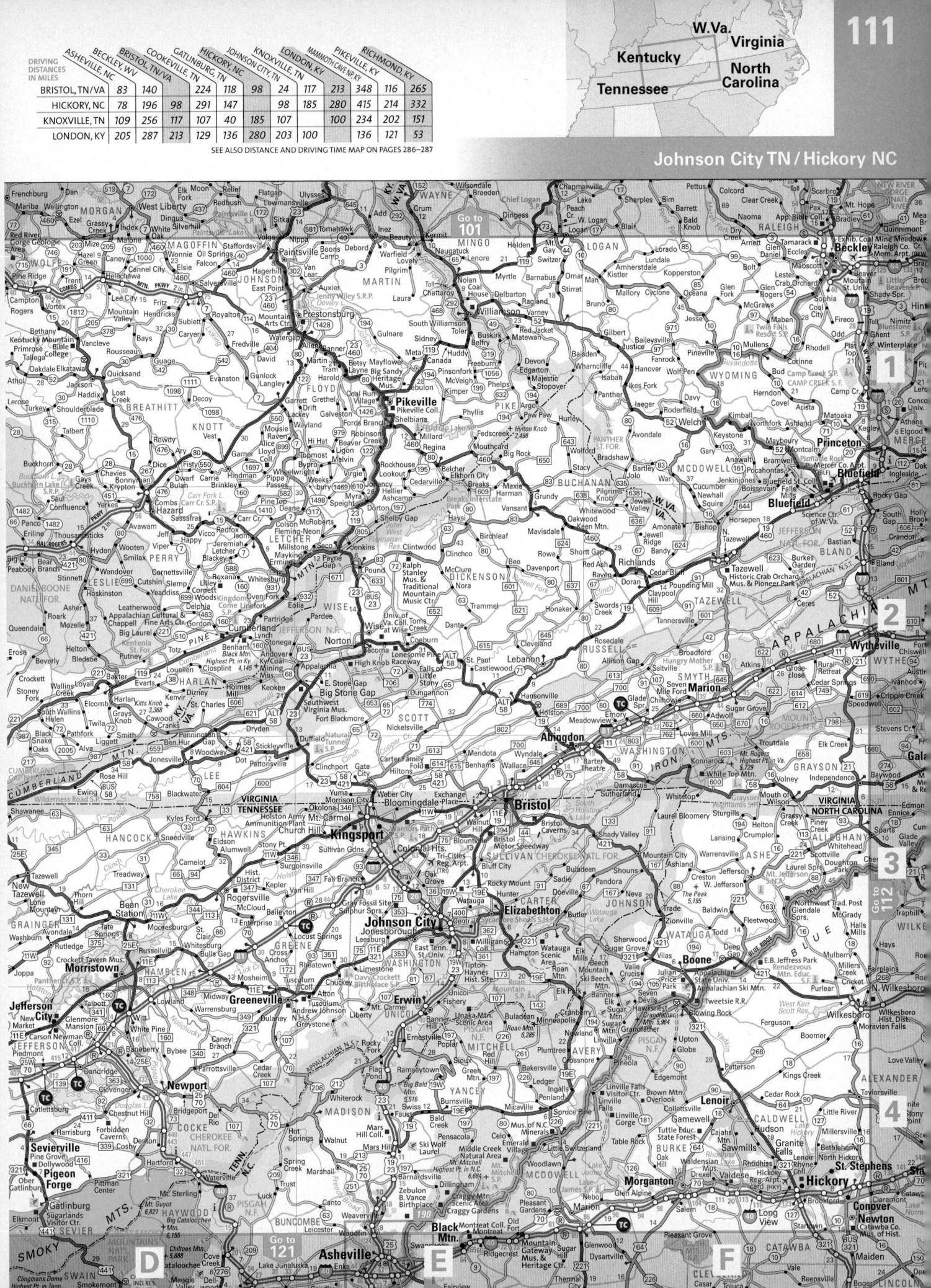

W. Va.
Virginia
North Carolina

0 mi 10 20 30 40
0 km 10 20 30 40 50 60
One inch equals 18.4 miles
One centimeter equals 11.7 kilometers

Greensboro NC / Roanoke VA

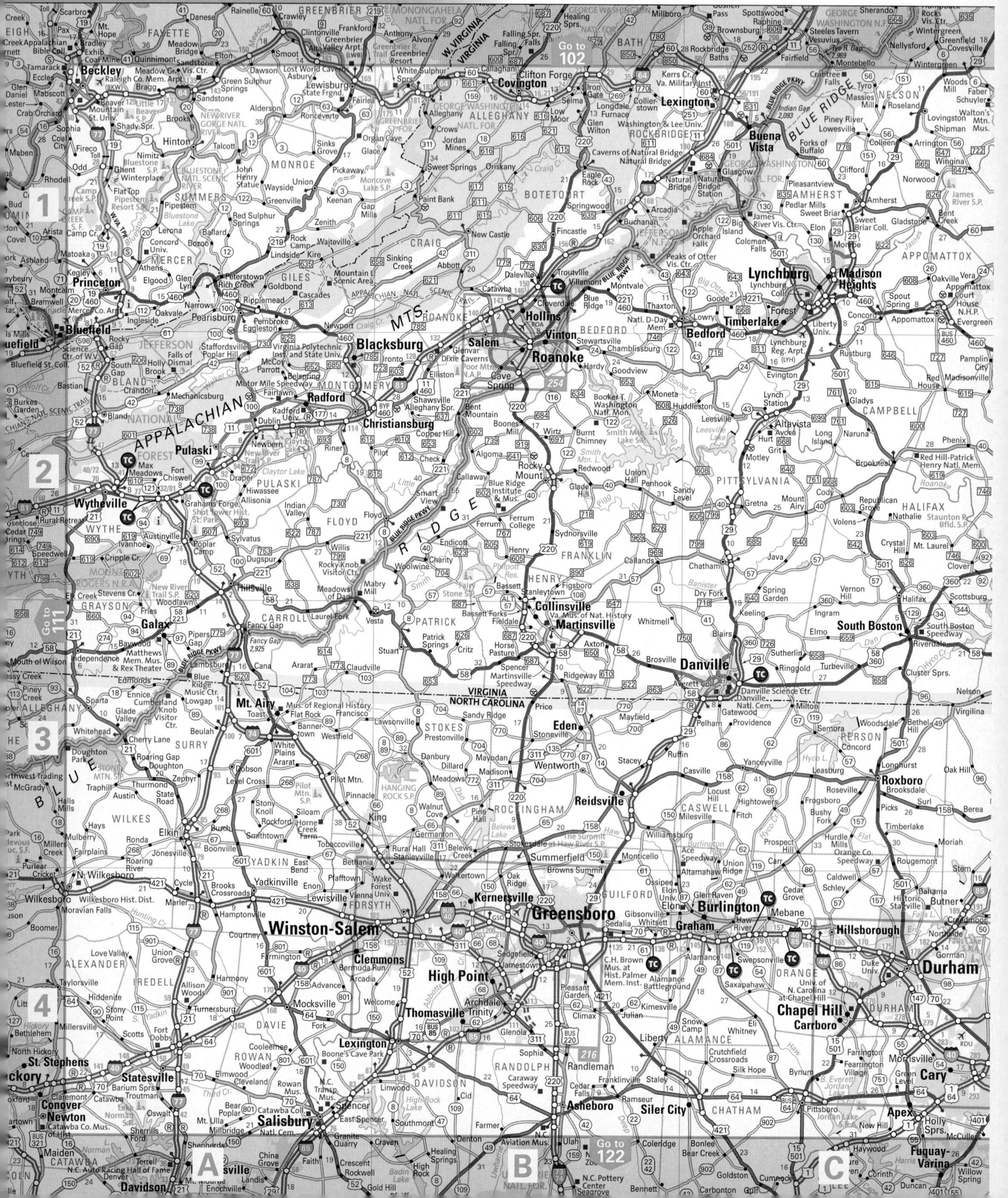

Go to 102
Go to 111
Go to 122

DRIVING DISTANCES IN MILES

	DANVILLE, VA	GREENSBORO, NC	LYNCHBURG, VA	NORFOLK, VA	RALEIGH, NC	RICHMOND, VA	ROANOKE, VA	ROANOKE RAPIDS, NC	ROCKY MOUNT, NC	WILLIAMSBURG, VA	WINSTON-SALEM, NC	WYTHEVILLE, VA
GREENSBORO, NC	46		106	230	69	200	101	132	124	237	30	120
RALEIGH, NC	89	69	140	179		157	156	84	54	204	96	186
RICHMOND, VA	160	200	114	91	157		192	91	127	49	228	256
ROANOKE, VA	83	101	55	285	156	192		190	211	243	107	78

SEE ALSO DISTANCE AND DRIVING TIME MAP ON PAGES 286–287

Md. — Delaware
Virginia
North Carolina

0 mi   10   20   30   40
0 km   10   20   30   40   50   60
One inch equals 18.4 miles
One centimeter equals 11.7 kilometers

FOR DETAIL OF AREA INSIDE PURPLE FRAME, SEE PAGES 144–145

ATLANTIC OCEAN

A   B   C

1
2
3
4

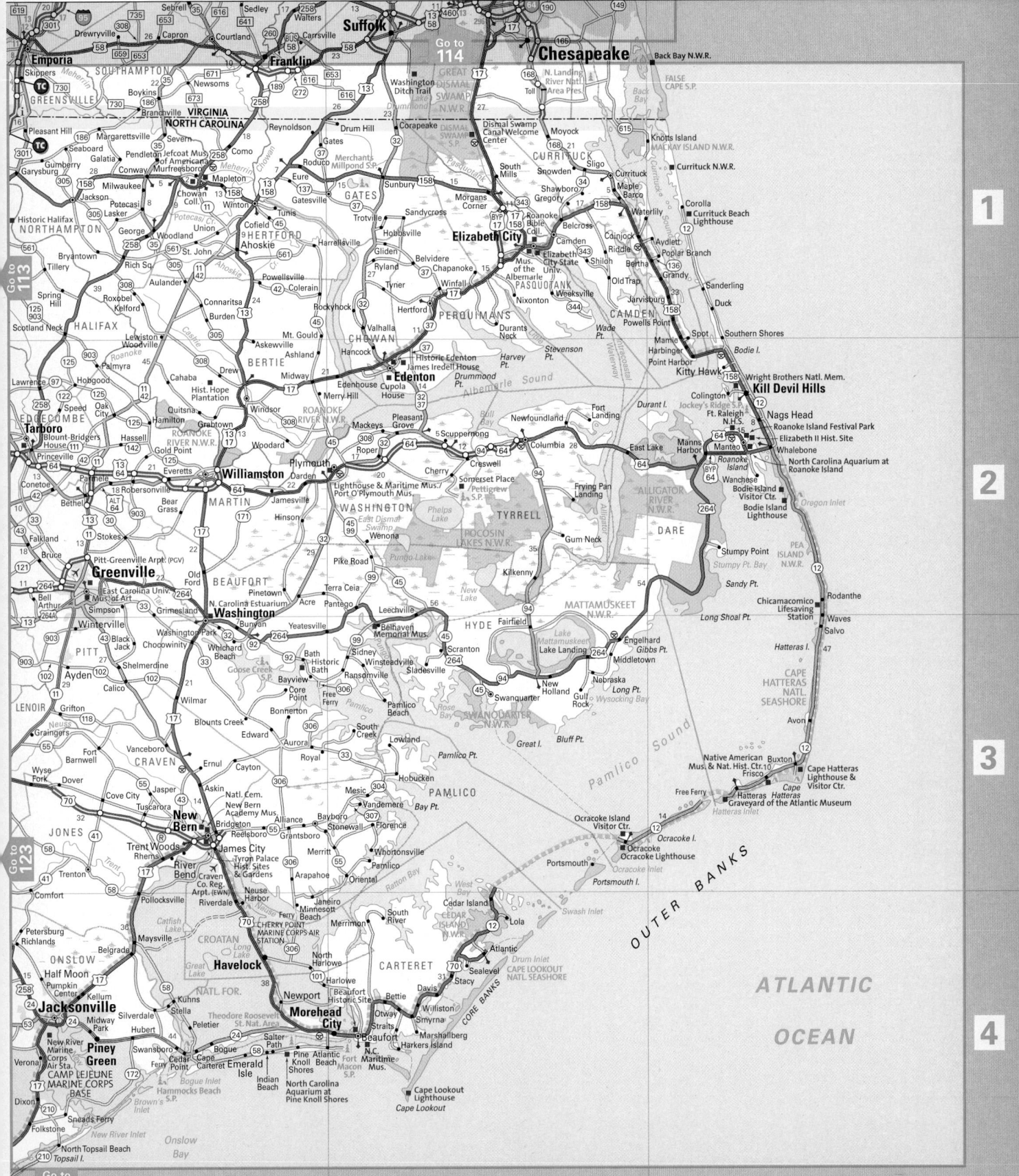

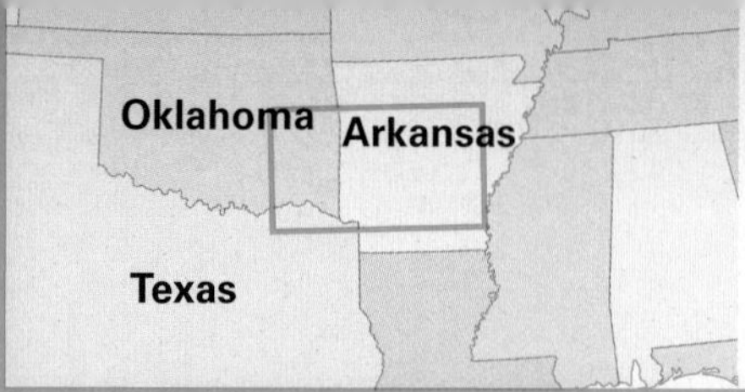

0 mi 10 20 30 40
0 km 10 20 30 40 50 60

One inch equals 18.4 miles
One centimeter equals 11.7 kilometers

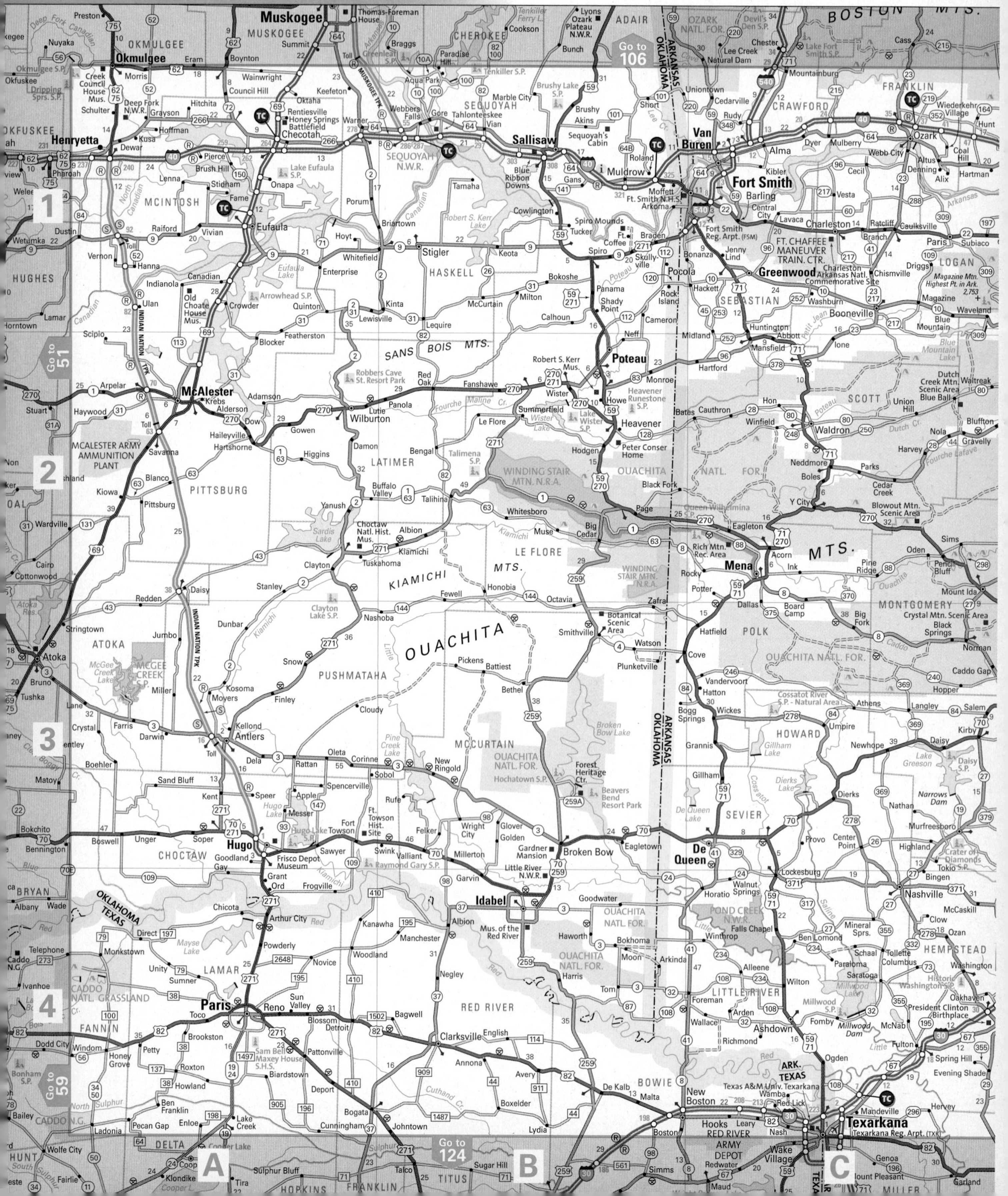

Go to 106

Go to 51

Go to 59

Go to 124

1 2 3 4

A B C

DRIVING DISTANCES IN MILES

	Arkadelphia, AR	Fort Smith, AR	Henryetta, OK	Hot Springs, AR	Little Rock, AR	McAlester, OK	Mena, AR	Newport, AR	Paris, TX	Pine Bluff, AR	Russellville, AR	Texarkana, AR/TX
FORT SMITH, AR	152		100	126	165	114	81	220	214	210	87	180
HOT SPRINGS, AR	37	126	224		65	193	75	154	207	76	67	117
LITTLE ROCK, AR	72	165	263	65		278	141	89	242	45	81	153
TEXARKANA, AR/TX	83	180	227	117	153	188	99	241	92	163	180	

SEE ALSO DISTANCE AND DRIVING TIME MAP ON PAGES 286–287

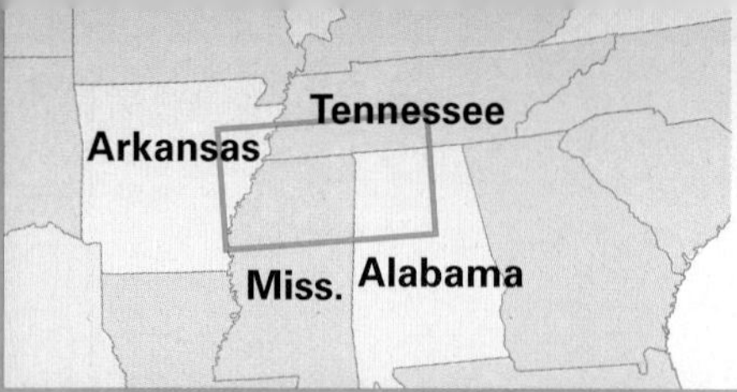

Tennessee
Arkansas
Miss. Alabama

0 mi 10 20 30 40
0 km 10 20 30 40 50 60
One inch equals 18.4 miles
One centimeter equals 11.7 kilometers

Go to 108
Go to 117
Go to 126

Memphis · West Memphis · Germantown · Collierville · Olive Branch · Bartlett · Millington · Southaven · Horn Lake · Hernando · Senatobia · Batesville · Oxford · Pontotoc · Holly Springs · New Albany · Ripley · Bolivar · Brownsville · Jackson · Covington · Wynne · Forrest City · Marianna · Helena–W. Helena · Clarksdale · Marks · Grenada · Winona · Greenwood · Indianola · Cleveland · Greenville · Leland · Newport · Osceola · Trumann · Starkville · Oktibbeha

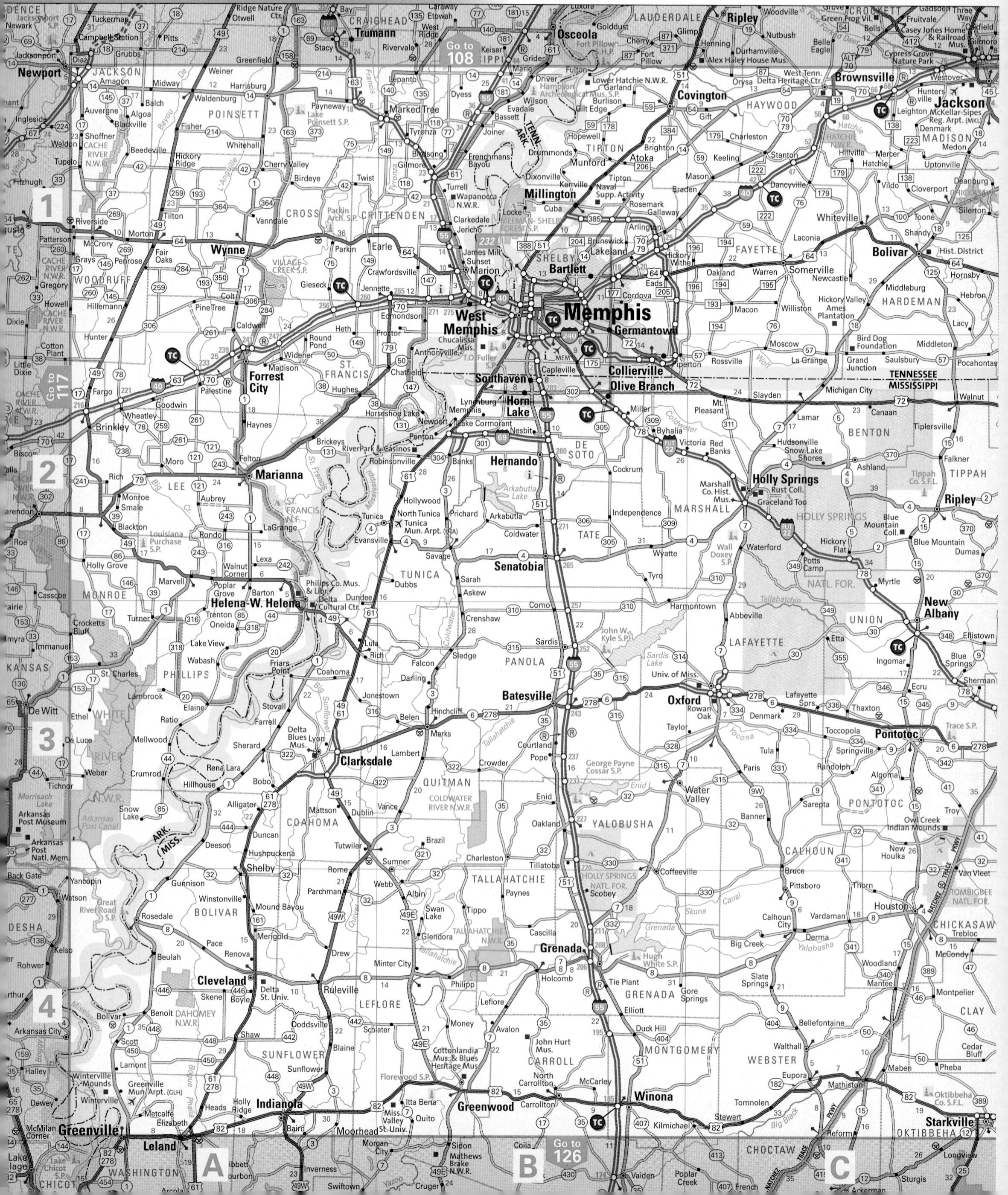

DRIVING DISTANCES IN MILES	Birmingham, AL	Clarksdale, MS	Columbia, TN	Columbus, MS	Decatur, AL	Florence, AL	Greenville, MS	Huntsville, AL	Jackson, TN	Memphis, TN	Oxford, MS	Tupelo, MS
BIRMINGHAM, AL		248	161	122	83	121	286	101	223	241	185	136
HUNTSVILLE, AL	101	260	79	163	25	65	318		205	216	196	148
MEMPHIS, TN	241	76	210	175	191	156	148	216	91			85	109
TUPELO, MS	136	113	159	66	123	92	172	148	107	109	50	

SEE ALSO DISTANCE AND DRIVING TIME MAP ON PAGES 286–287

Tennessee
North Carolina
South Carolina
Alabama
Georgia

0 mi 10 20 30 40
0 km 10 20 30 40 50 60
One inch equals 18.4 miles
One centimeter equals 11.7 kilometers

Atlanta GA / Chattanooga TN

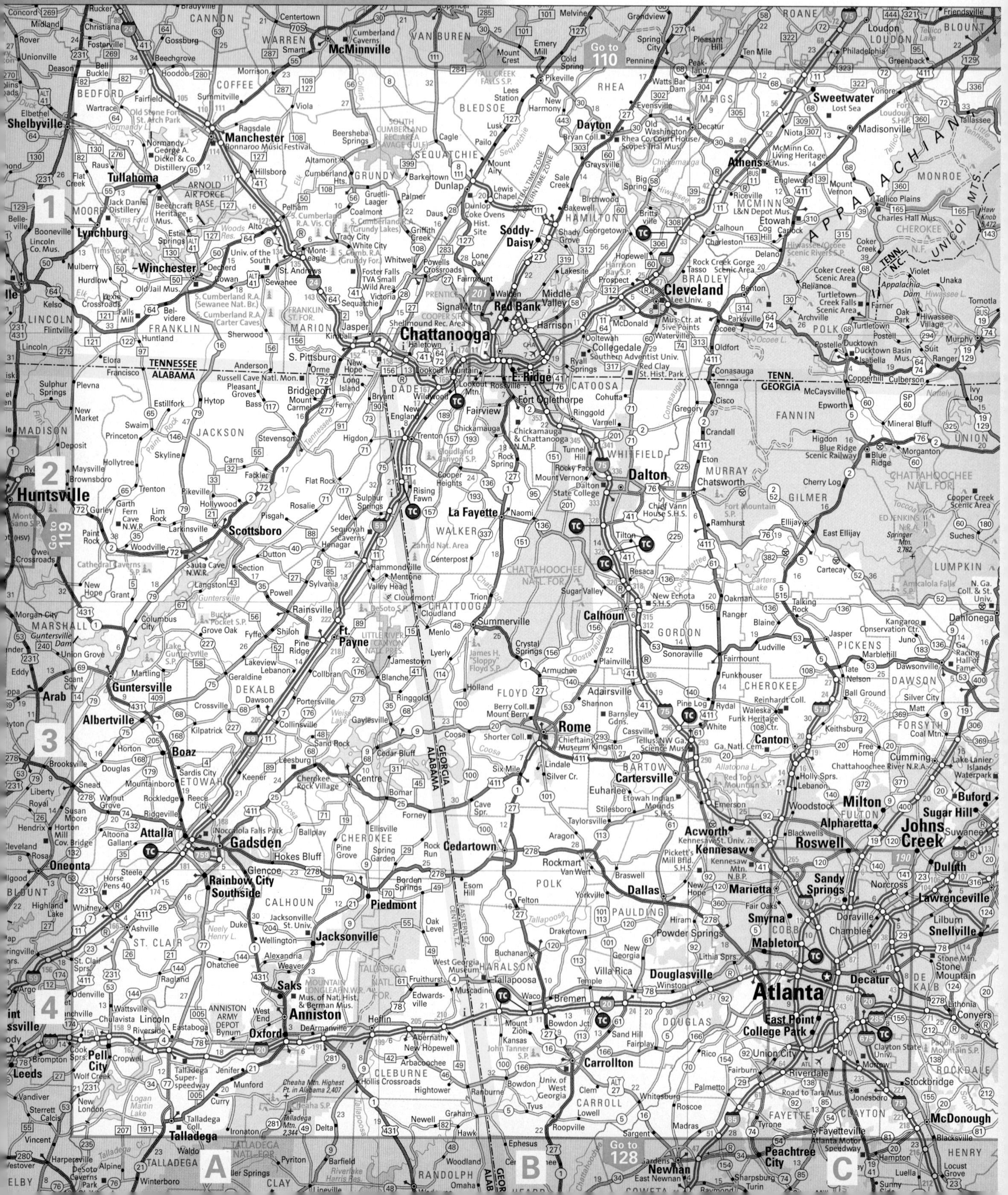

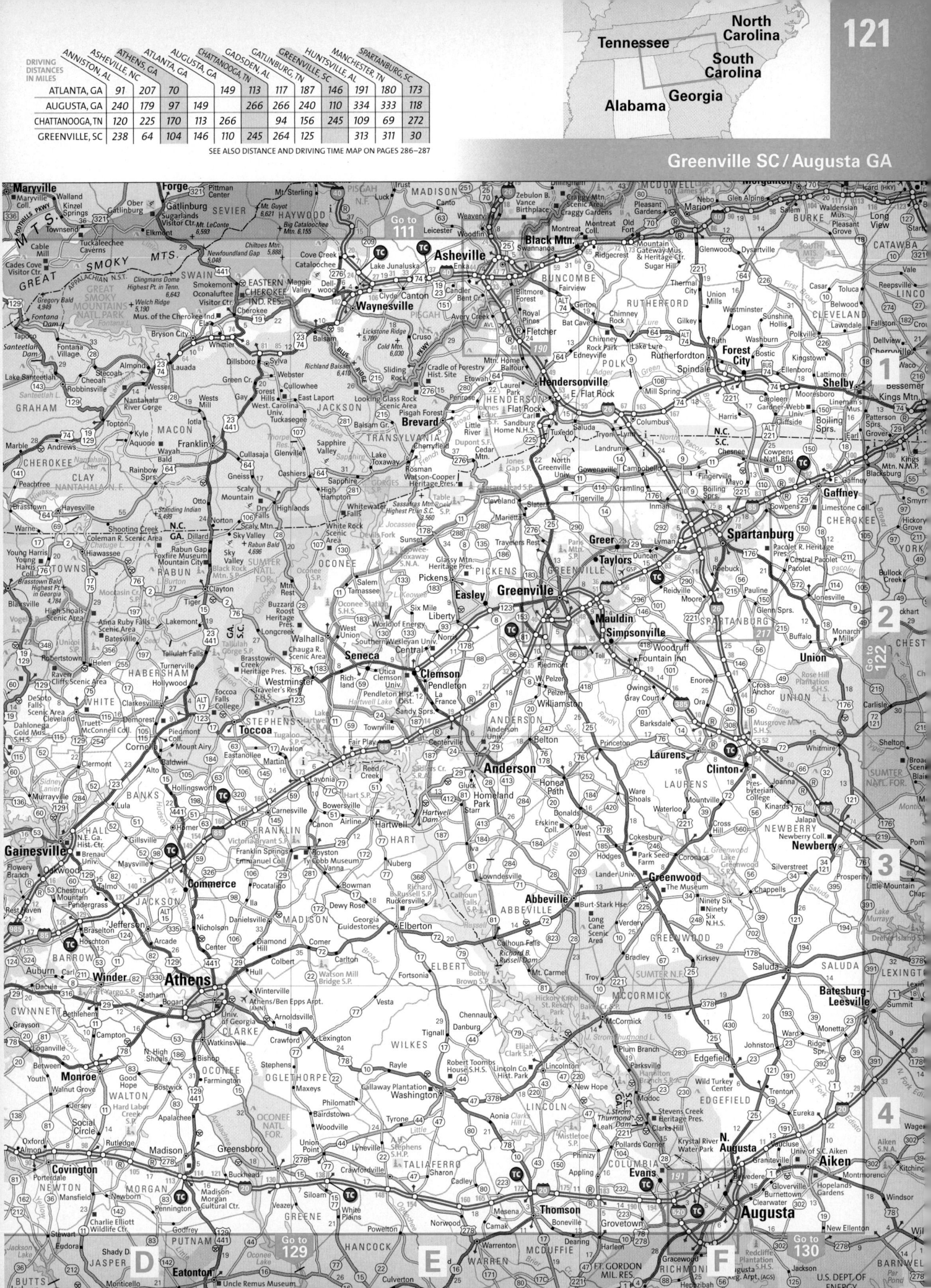

DRIVING DISTANCES IN MILES	ANNISTON, AL	ASHEVILLE, NC	ATHENS, GA	ATLANTA, GA	AUGUSTA, GA	CHATTANOOGA, TN	GADSDEN, AL	GATLINBURG, TN	GREENVILLE, SC	HUNTSVILLE, AL	MANCHESTER, TN	SPARTANBURG, SC
ATLANTA, GA	91	207	70		149	113	117	187	146	191	180	173
AUGUSTA, GA	240	179	97	149		266	266	240	110	334	333	118
CHATTANOOGA, TN	120	225	170	113	266		94	156	245	109	69	272
GREENVILLE, SC	238	64	104	146	110	245	264	125		313	311	30

SEE ALSO DISTANCE AND DRIVING TIME MAP ON PAGES 286–287

Tennessee North Carolina South Carolina Alabama Georgia

0 mi   10   20   30   40
0 km   10   20   30   40   50   60
One inch equals 18.4 miles
One centimeter equals 11.7 kilometers

Charlotte NC / Columbia SC

Go to 111
Go to 112
Go to 121
Go to 130
Go to 131

Hickory, Conover, Newton, Salisbury, Spencer, Asheboro, Siler City, Mooresville, Davidson, Cornelius, Kannapolis, Concord, Huntersville, Albemarle, Lincolnton, Shelby, Kings Mountain, Gastonia, Belmont, Charlotte, Mint Hill, Matthews, Pineville, Indian Trail, Stallings, Weddington, Monroe, Wingate, Wadesboro, Rockingham, Hamlet, Pinehurst, Southern Pines, Aberdeen, Gaffney, York, Rock Hill, Lancaster, Cheraw, Bennettsville, Laurinburg, Maxton, Pembroke, Dillon, Chester, Pageland, Chesterfield, Society Hill, Darlington, Marlboro, Little Rock, Mullins, Marion, Union, Newberry, Winnsboro, Camden, Hartsville, Florence, Aiken, Batesburg-Leesville, Lexington, Columbia, Cayce, Irmo, Dentsville, Sumter, Lake City, Manning, Kingstree, Orangeburg, Georgetown

N. CAROLINA / S. CAROLINA

U.S. DEPT. OF ENERGY SAVANNAH

North Carolina

South Carolina

SEE ALSO DISTANCE AND DRIVING TIME MAP ON PAGES 286–287

DRIVING DISTANCES IN MILES	CHARLOTTE, NC	COLUMBIA, SC	FAYETTEVILLE, NC	FLORENCE, SC	GOLDSBORO, NC	HICKORY, NC	LUMBERTON, NC	MOREHEAD CITY, NC	MYRTLE BEACH, SC	ROCK HILL, SC	SUMTER, SC	WILMINGTON, NC
CHARLOTTE, NC		91	139	107	208	47	128	298	173	26	115	205
COLUMBIA, SC	91		170	80	240	139	139	289	146	70	45	199
MYRTLE BEACH, SC	173	146	116	66	170	220	83	165		181	93	71
WILMINGTON, NC	205	199	92	120	100	292	77	95	71	220	158	

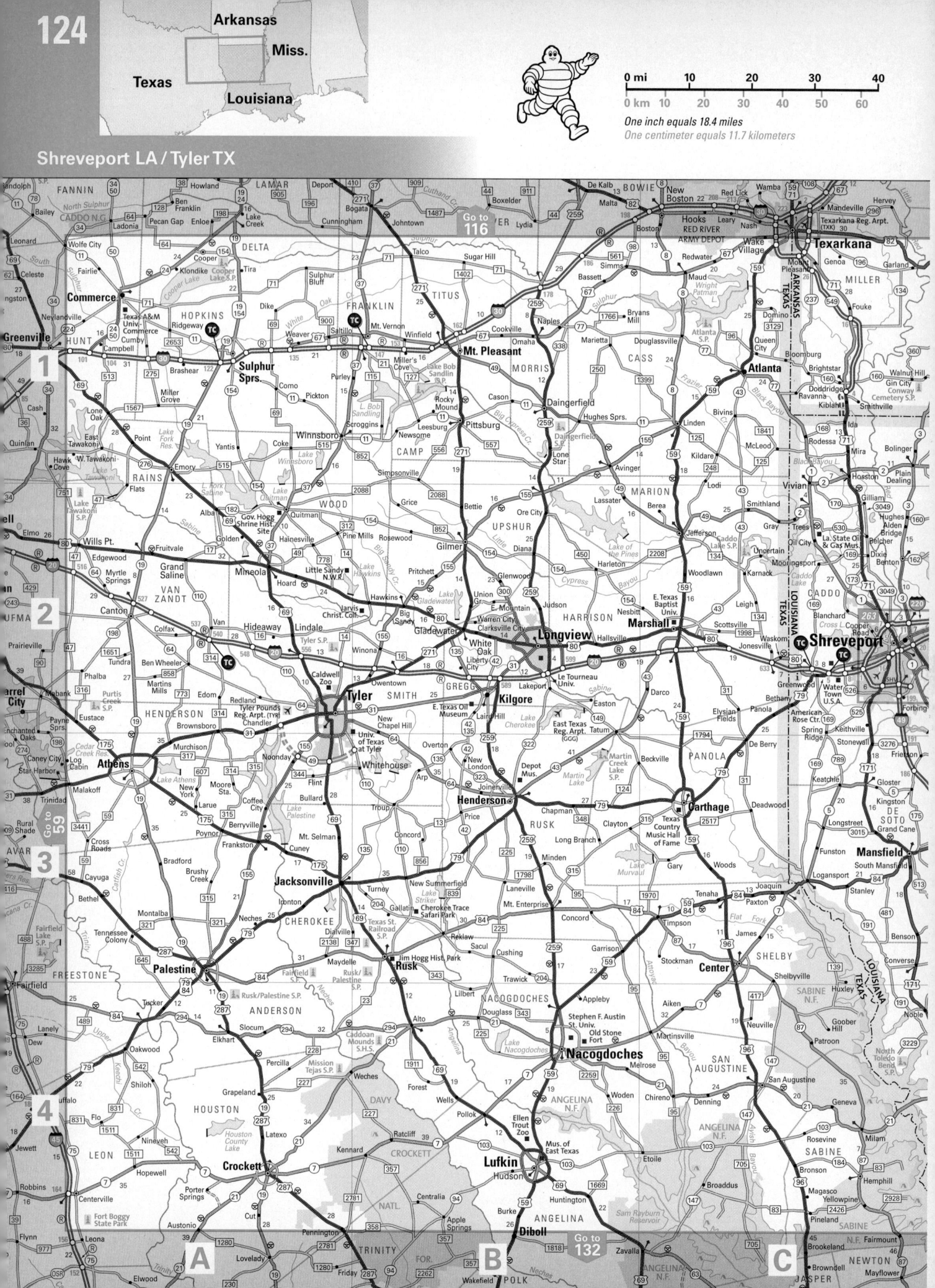

Arkansas

Miss.

Texas

Louisiana

0 mi   10   20   30   40
0 km 10 20 30 40 50 60
One inch equals 18.4 miles
One centimeter equals 11.7 kilometers

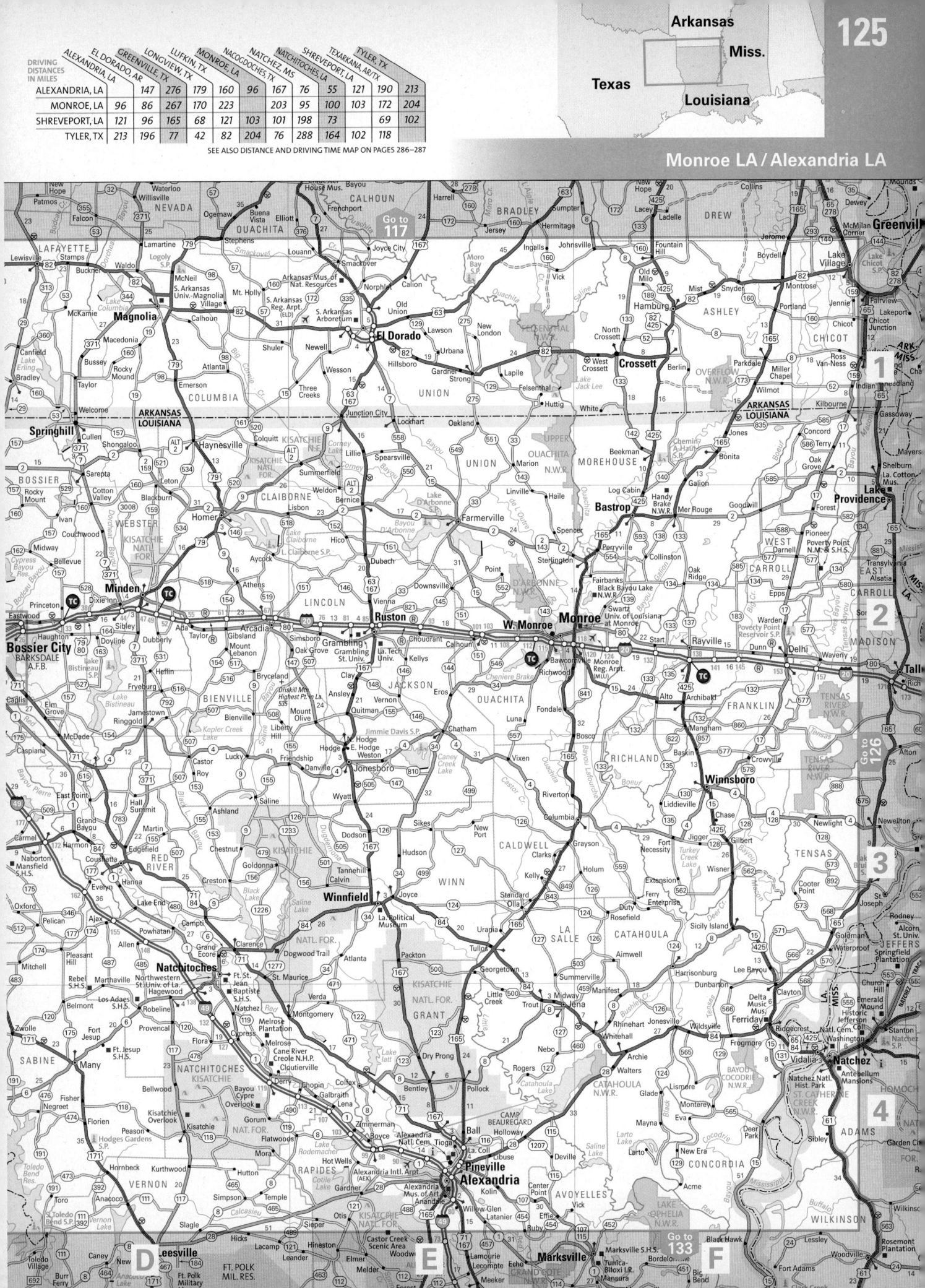

DRIVING DISTANCES IN MILES	ALEXANDRIA, LA	EL DORADO, AR	GREENVILLE, TX	LONGVIEW, TX	LUFKIN, TX	MONROE, LA	NACOGDOCHES, TX	NATCHEZ, MS	NATCHITOCHES, LA	SHREVEPORT, LA	TEXARKANA, AR/TX	TYLER, TX
ALEXANDRIA, LA		147	276	179	160	96	167	76	55	121	190	213
MONROE, LA	96		86	267	170	223		203	95	100	103	172	204
SHREVEPORT, LA	121	96	165	68	121	103	101	198	73		69	102
TYLER, TX	213	196	77	42	82	204	76	288	164	102	118	

SEE ALSO DISTANCE AND DRIVING TIME MAP ON PAGES 286–287

Arkansas
Miss. Alabama
Louisiana

0 mi 10 20 30 40
0 km 10 20 30 40 50 60
One inch equals 18.4 miles
One centimeter equals 11.7 kilometers

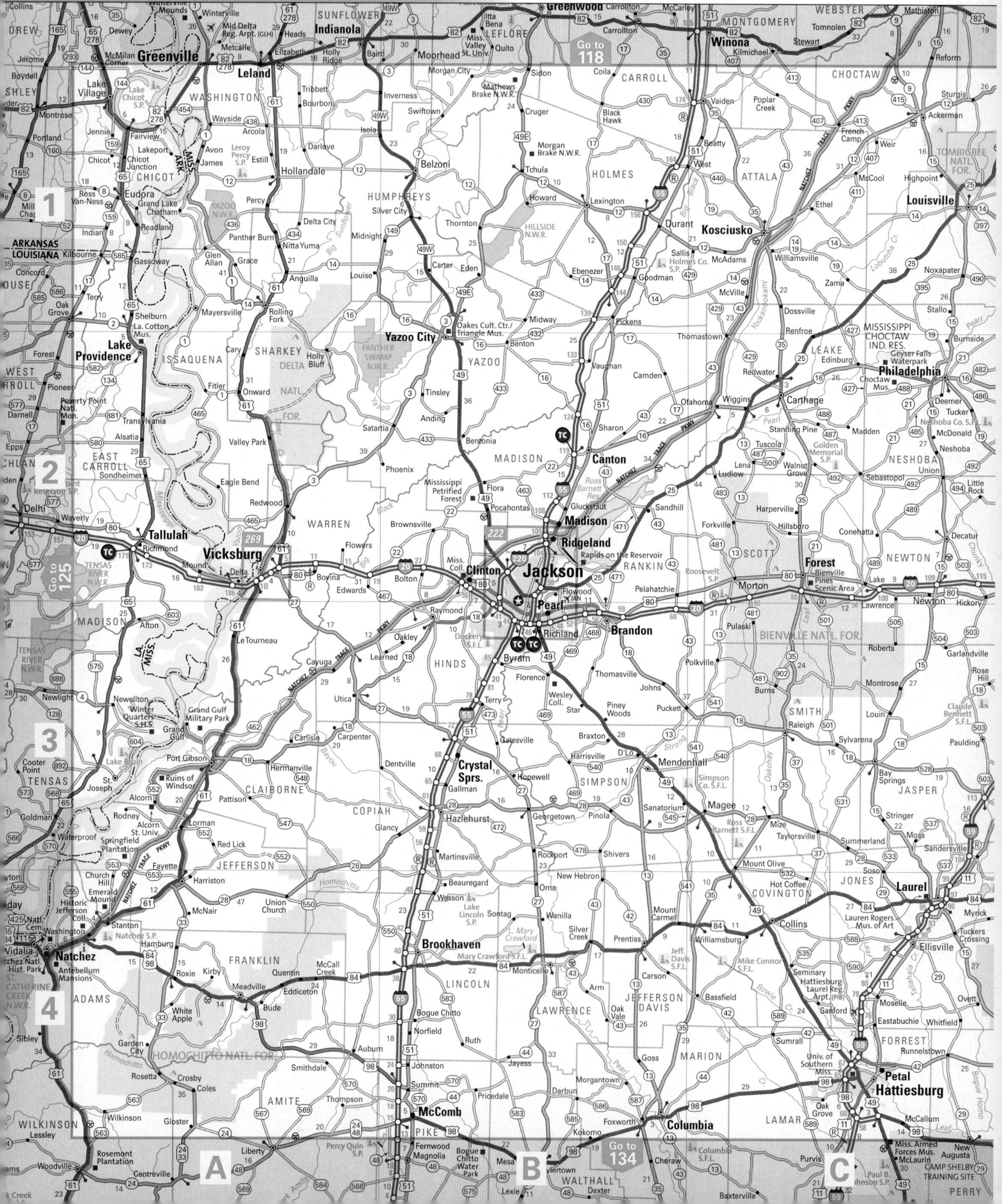

Arkansas

Miss. Alabama

Louisiana

Go to 119

Go to 128

Go to 135

DRIVING DISTANCES IN MILES	BIRMINGHAM, AL	EVERGREEN, AL	GREENVILLE, AL	HATTIESBURG, MS	JACKSON, MS	McCOMB, MS	MERIDIAN, MS	NATCHEZ, MS	SELMA, AL	TUSCALOOSA, AL	VICKSBURG, MS	WINONA, MS
HATTIESBURG, MS	239	184	215		90	75	89	142	193	183	132	180
JACKSON, MS	241	243	125	90		76	91	102	195	185	42	94
MERIDIAN, MS	149	152	216	89	91	167		194	104	94	133	113
TUSCALOOSA, AL	61	211	225	183	185	261	94	287	82		227	144

SEE ALSO DISTANCE AND DRIVING TIME MAP ON PAGES 286–287

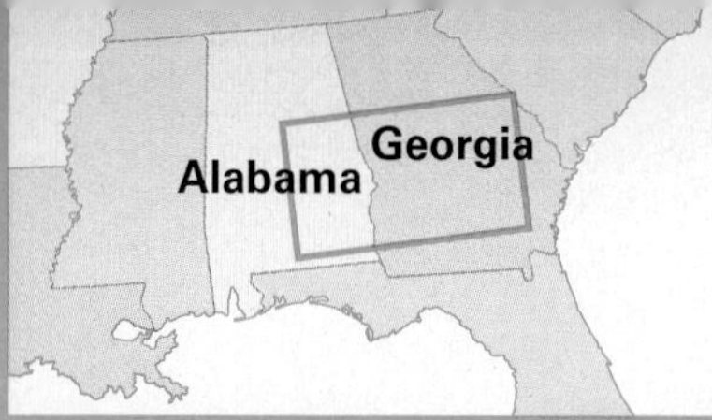

Alabama Georgia

0 mi 10 20 30 40
0 km 10 20 30 40 50 60
One inch equals 18.4 miles
One centimeter equals 11.7 kilometers

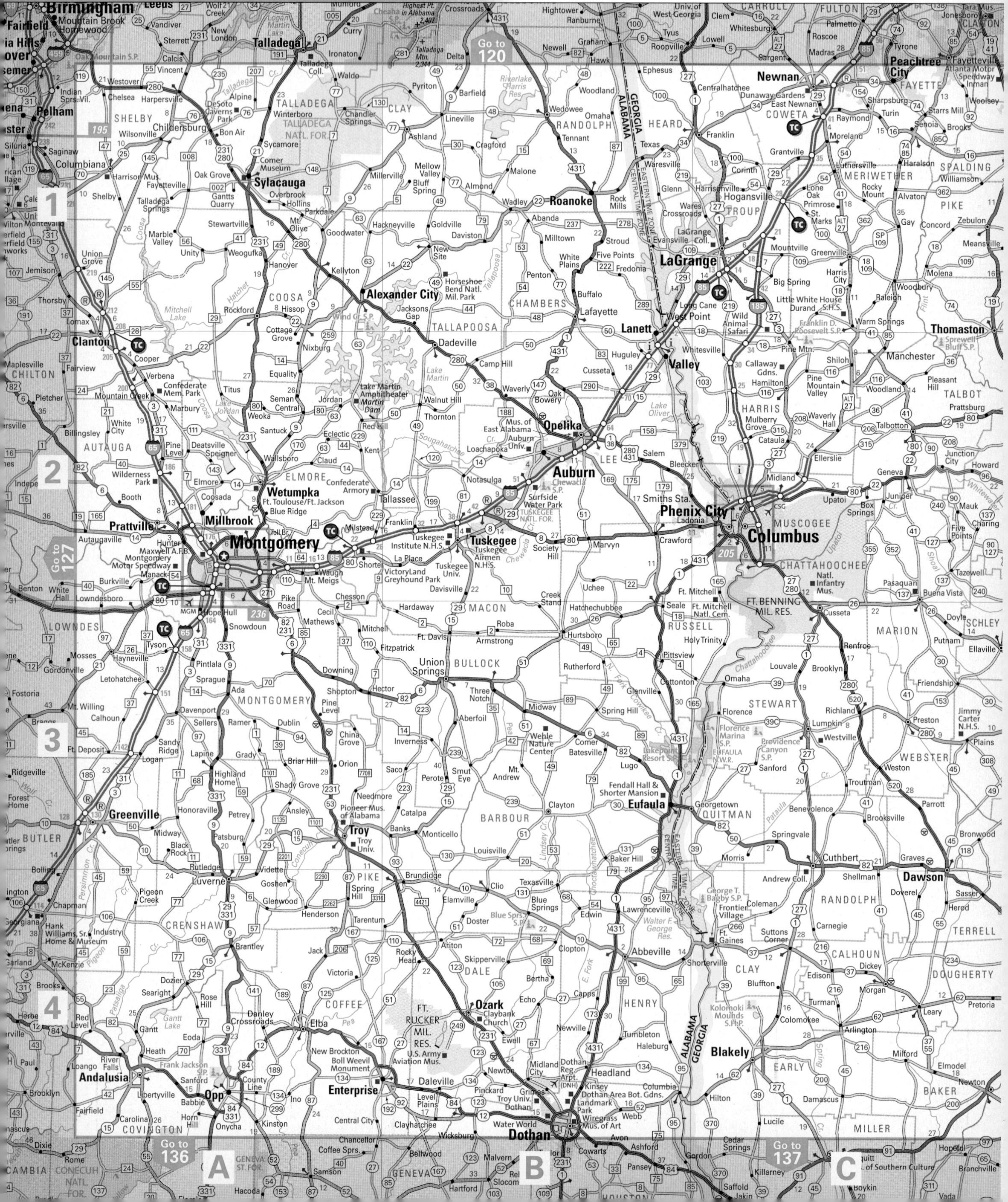

Georgia
Alabama

DRIVING DISTANCES IN MILES	ALBANY, GA	ATLANTA, GA	AUBURN, AL	AUGUSTA, GA	BIRMINGHAM, AL	COLUMBUS, GA	DOTHAN, AL	LA GRANGE, GA	MACON, GA	MONTGOMERY, AL	TIFTON, GA	WAYCROSS, GA
ALBANY, GA		180	121	226	253	86	83	97	102	165	43	116
COLUMBUS, GA	86	106	34	249	167		97	46	95	79	135	208
MACON, GA	102	84	151	123	234	95	186	114		203	102	159
MONTGOMERY, AL	165	158	54	301	88	79	103	95	203		214	287

SEE ALSO DISTANCE AND DRIVING TIME MAP ON PAGES 286–287

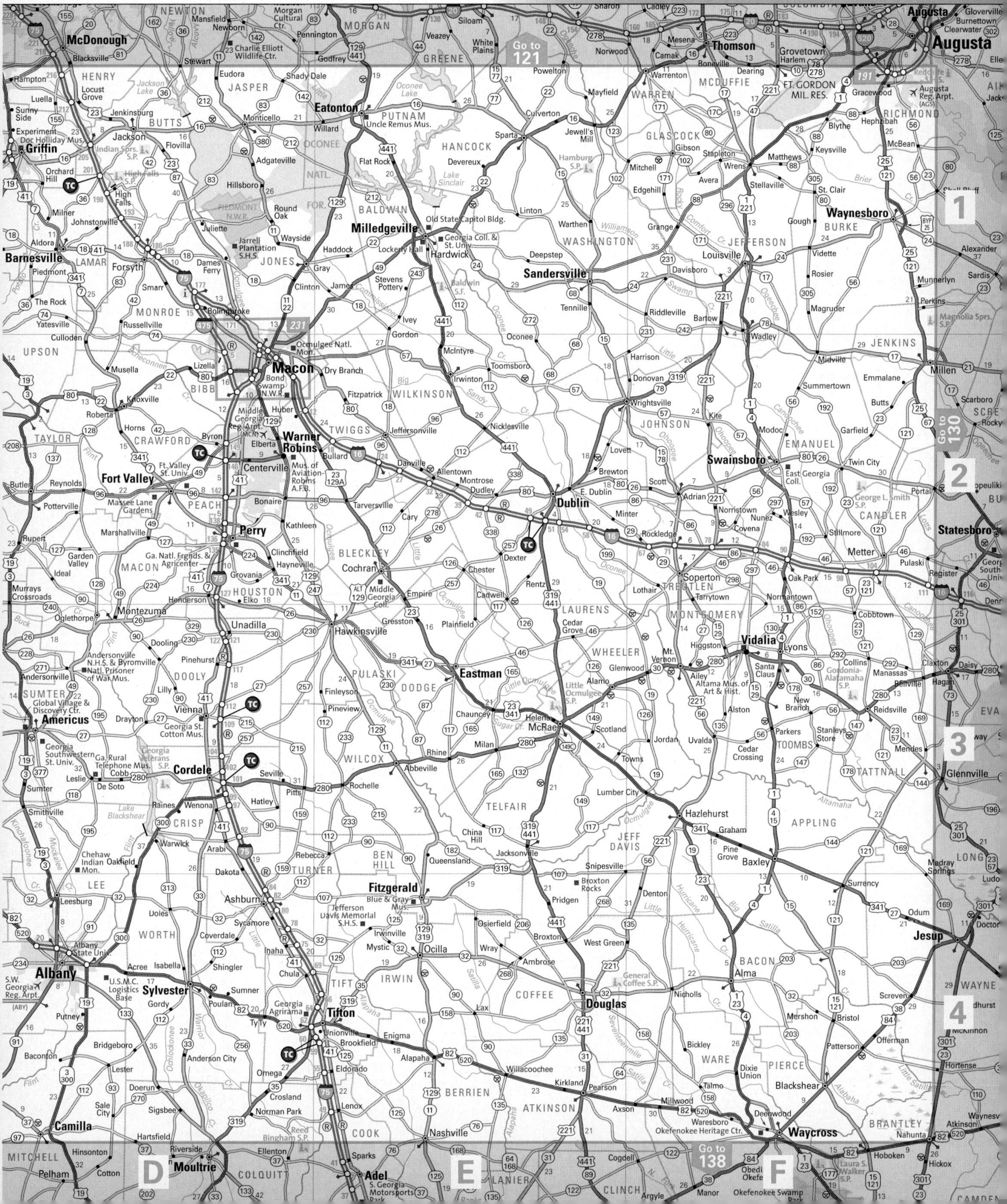

Go to 121

Go to 130

Go to 138

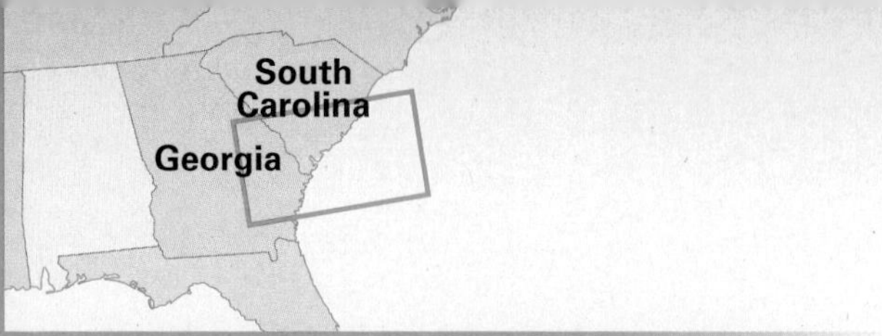

South
Carolina

Georgia

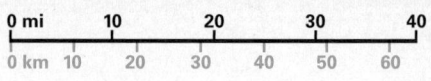

One inch equals 18.4 miles
One centimeter equals 11.7 kilometers

Savannah GA / Hilton Head Island SC

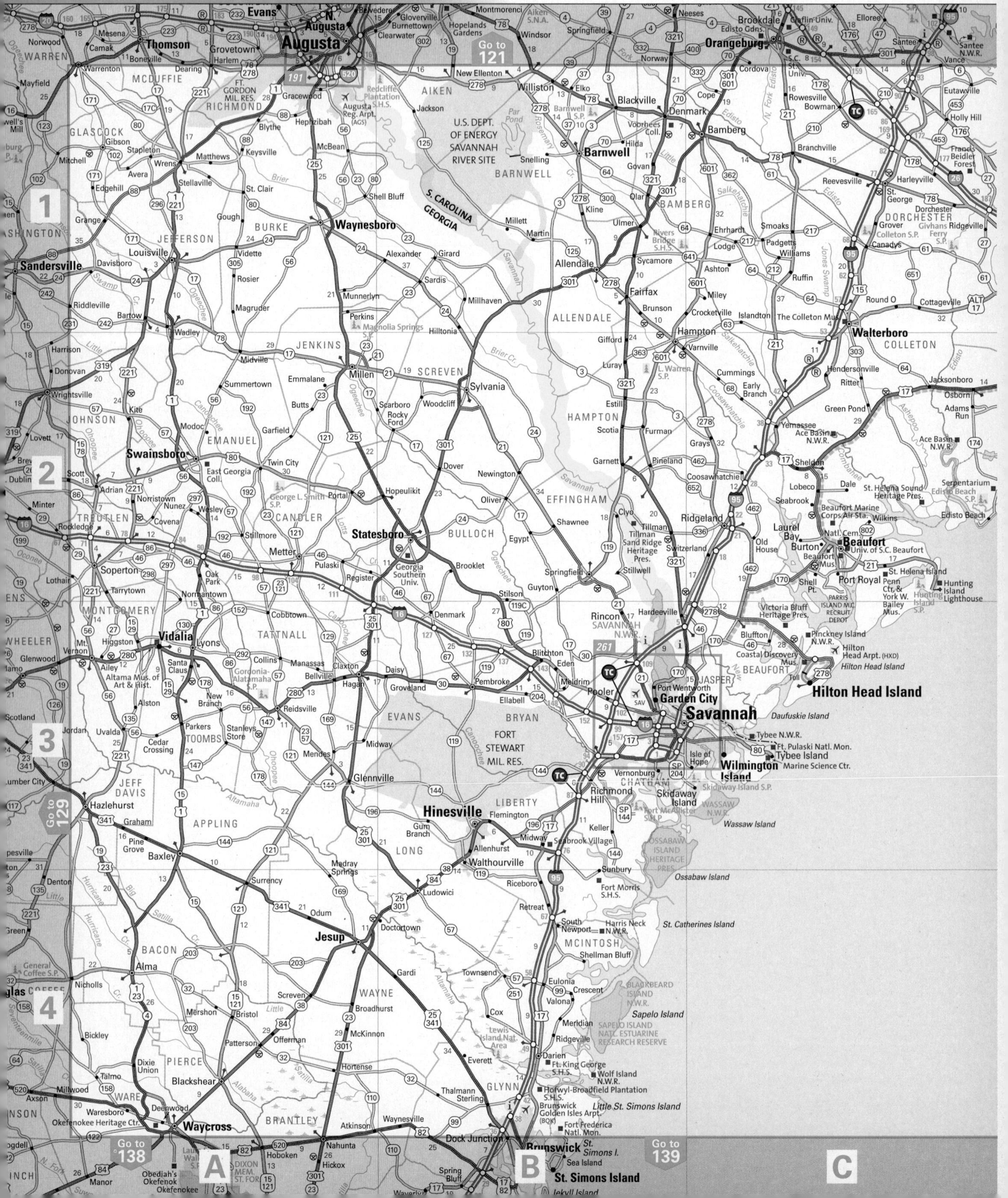

SEE ALSO DISTANCE AND DRIVING TIME MAP ON PAGES 286–287

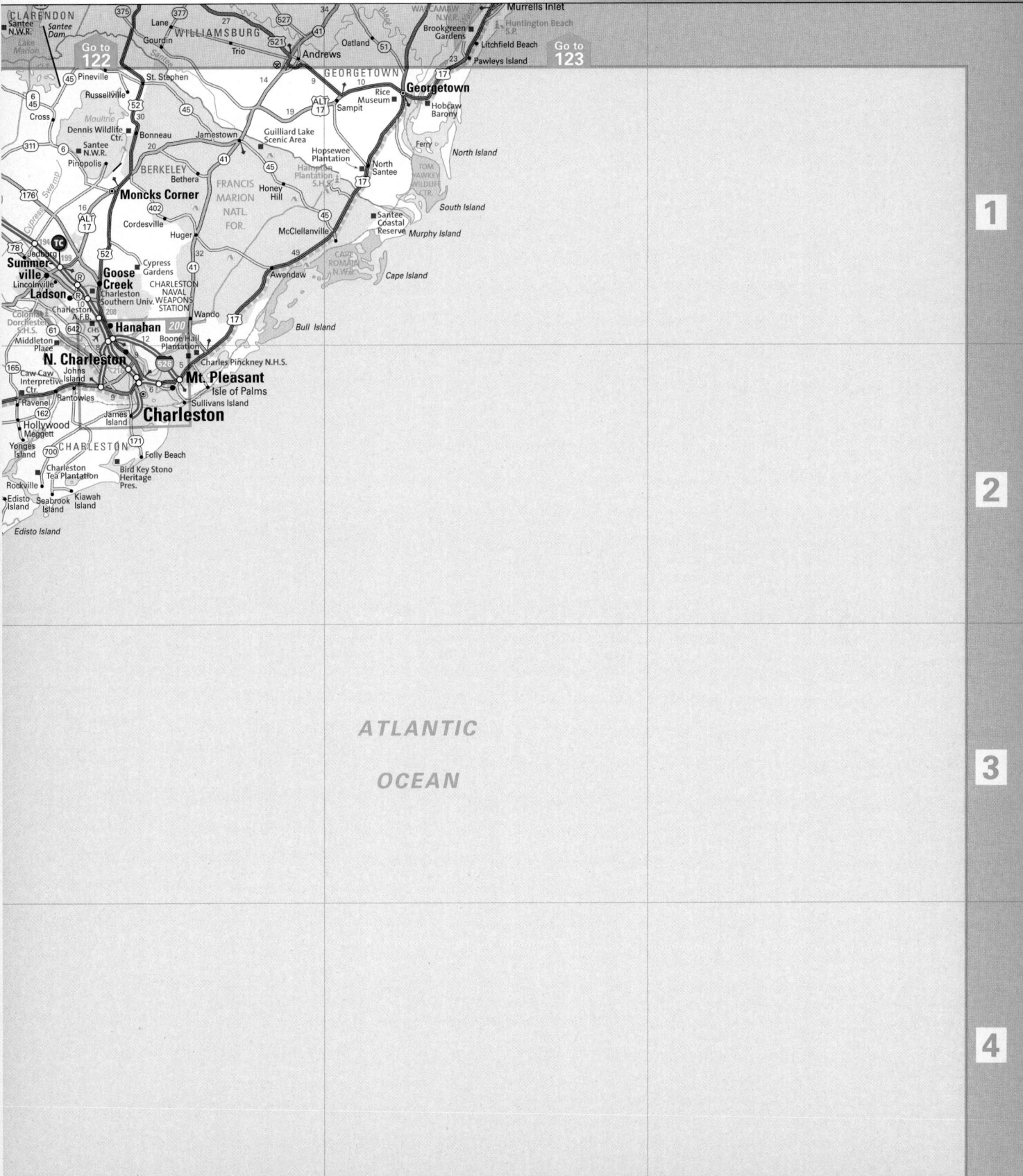

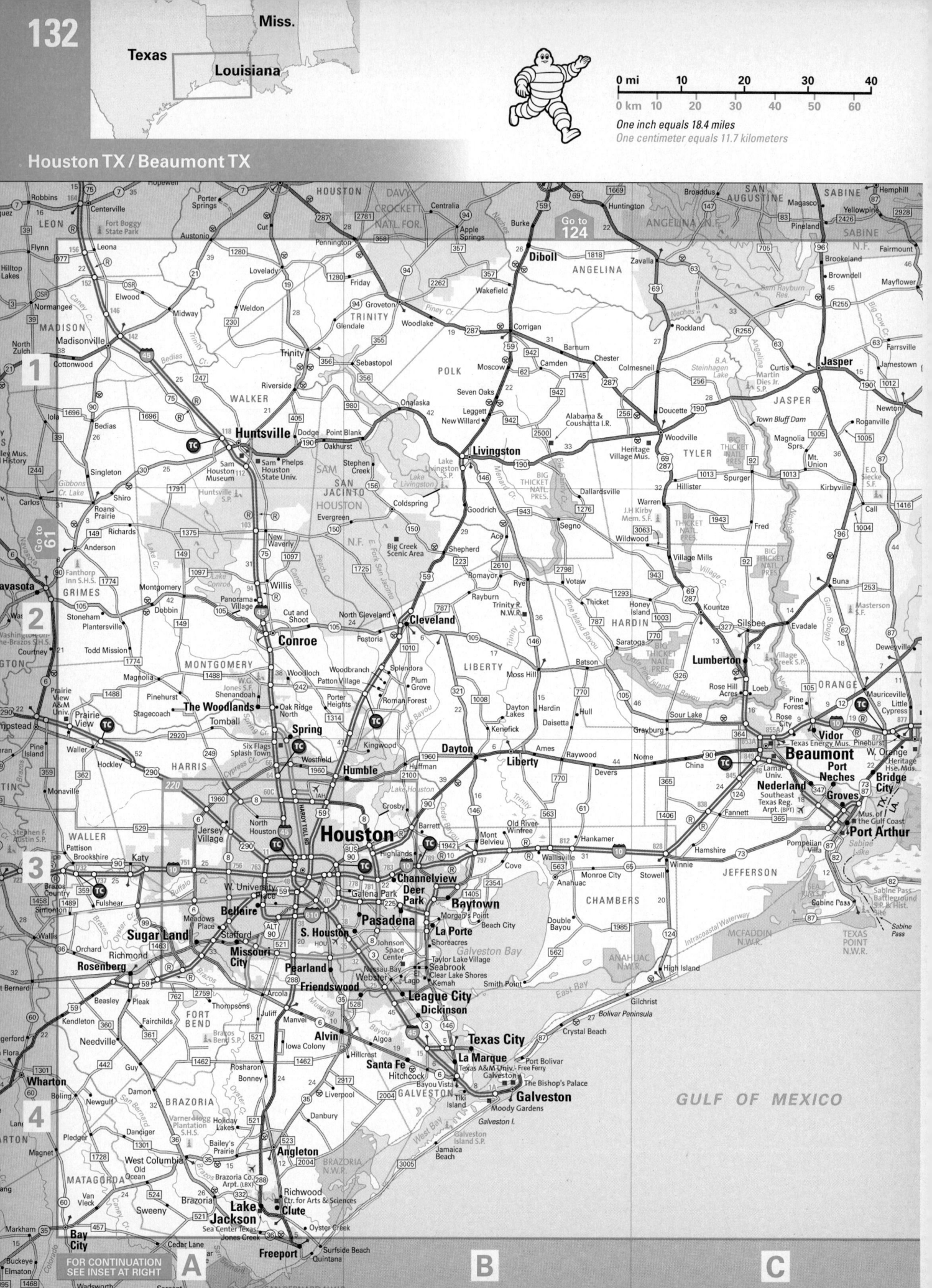

Miss.

Texas

Louisiana

DRIVING DISTANCES IN MILES	Alexandria, LA	Beaumont, TX	De Ridder, LA	Freeport, TX	Galveston, TX	Houston, TX	Huntsville, TX	Lafayette, LA	Lake Charles, LA	Lufkin, TX	Opelousas, LA	Port Arthur, TX
BEAUMONT, TX	157		82	143	75	84	157	133	57	112	144	18
HOUSTON, TX	241	84	166	61	53		75	217	141	121	228	93
LAFAYETTE, LA	87	133	119	276	208	217	290		76	216	27	130
LAKE CHARLES, LA	100	57	49	200	132	141	214	76		140	87	54

SEE ALSO DISTANCE AND DRIVING TIME MAP ON PAGES 286–287

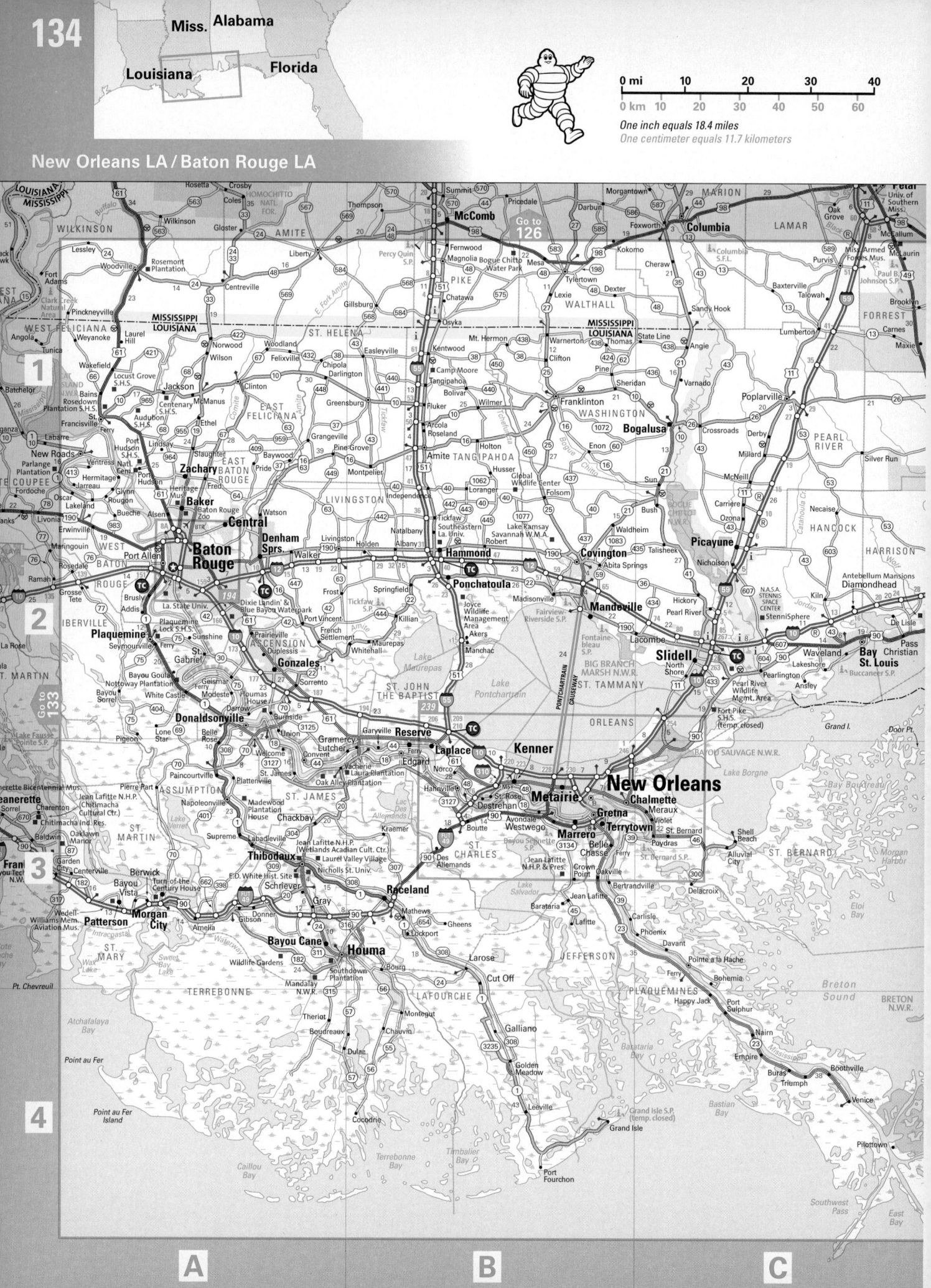

DRIVING DISTANCES IN MILES	BATON ROUGE, LA	BILOXI, MS	GULFPORT, MS	GULF SHORES, AL	HAMMOND, LA	HATTIESBURG, MS	HOUMA, LA	McCOMB, MS	MOBILE, AL	NEW ORLEANS, LA	PASCAGOULA, MS	PENSACOLA, FL
BATON ROUGE, LA		151	140	254	51	174	101	102	205	91	170	264
BILOXI, MS	151		12	110	106	82	148	161	61	93	20	120
MOBILE, AL	205	61	75	48	159	97	201	215		146	41	58
NEW ORLEANS, LA	91	93	81	195	57	115	57	111	146		112	205

SEE ALSO DISTANCE AND DRIVING TIME MAP ON PAGES 286–287

Alabama Georgia

Florida

0 mi   10   20   30   40
0 km   10   20   30   40   50   60
One inch equals 18.4 miles
One centimeter equals 11.7 kilometers

GULF OF MEXICO

A   B   C

1

2

3

4

Alabama Georgia

Florida

DRIVING DISTANCES IN MILES

	BREWTON, AL	DE FUNIAK SPRS., FL	DOTHAN, AL	FT. WALTON BEACH, FL	MARIANNA, FL	MOBILE, AL	PANAMA CITY, FL	PENSACOLA, FL	PERRY, FL	TALLAHASSEE, FL	THOMASVILLE, GA	VALDOSTA, GA
PANAMA CITY, FL	143	65	82	64	61	160		102	160	104	134	186
PENSACOLA, FL	57	82	152	39	138	58	102		256	200	230	282
TALLAHASSEE, FL	201	123	110	166	68	247	104	200	52		35	85
VALDOSTA, GA	283	204	133	247	149	329	186	282	66	85	42	

SEE ALSO DISTANCE AND DRIVING TIME MAP ON PAGES 286–287

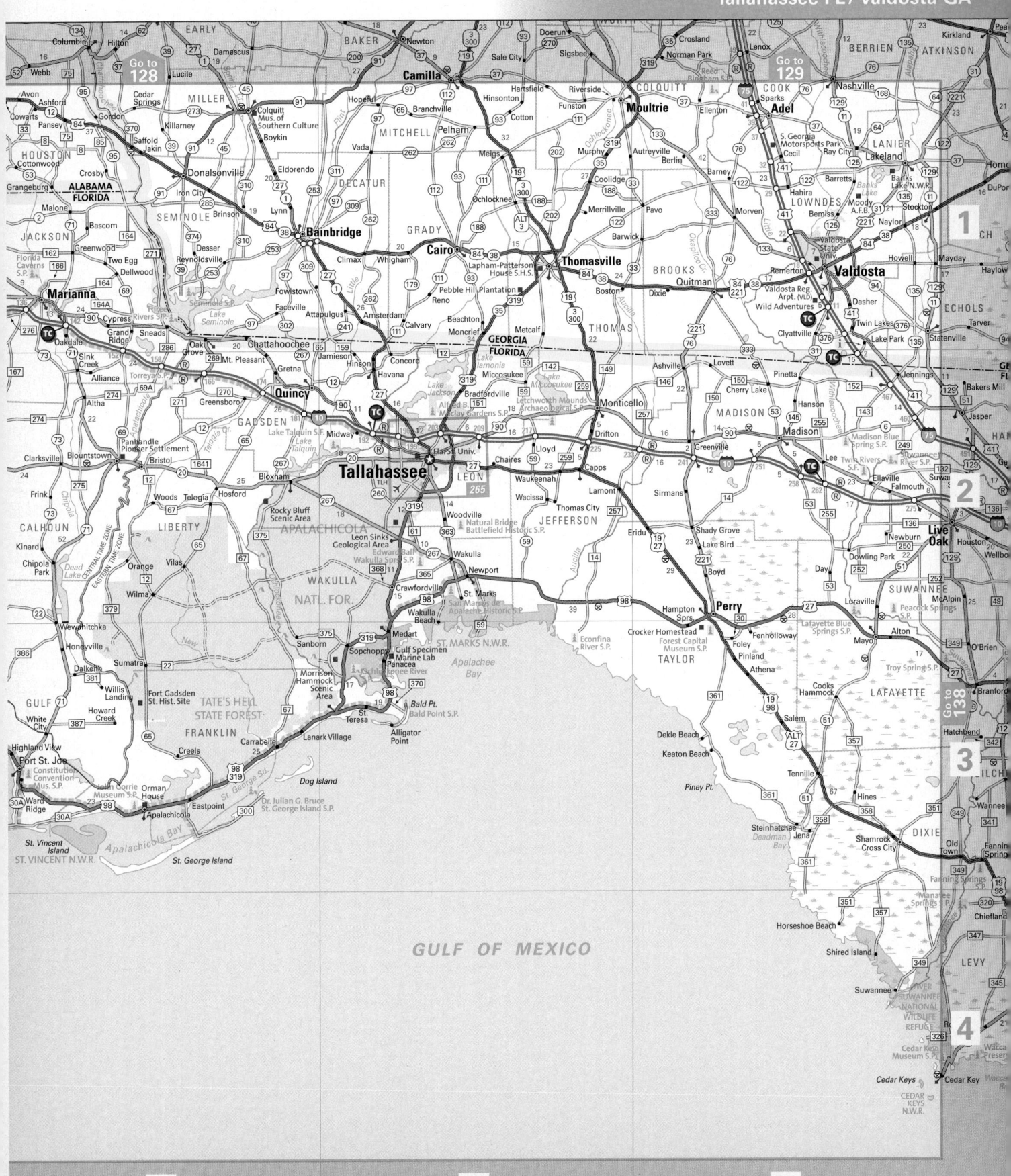

Georgia

Florida

0 mi   10   20   30   40
0 km   10   20   30   40   50   60

One inch equals 18.4 miles
One centimeter equals 11.7 kilometers

GULF

OF

MEXICO

Go to 129

Go to 137

Go to 140

A   B   C

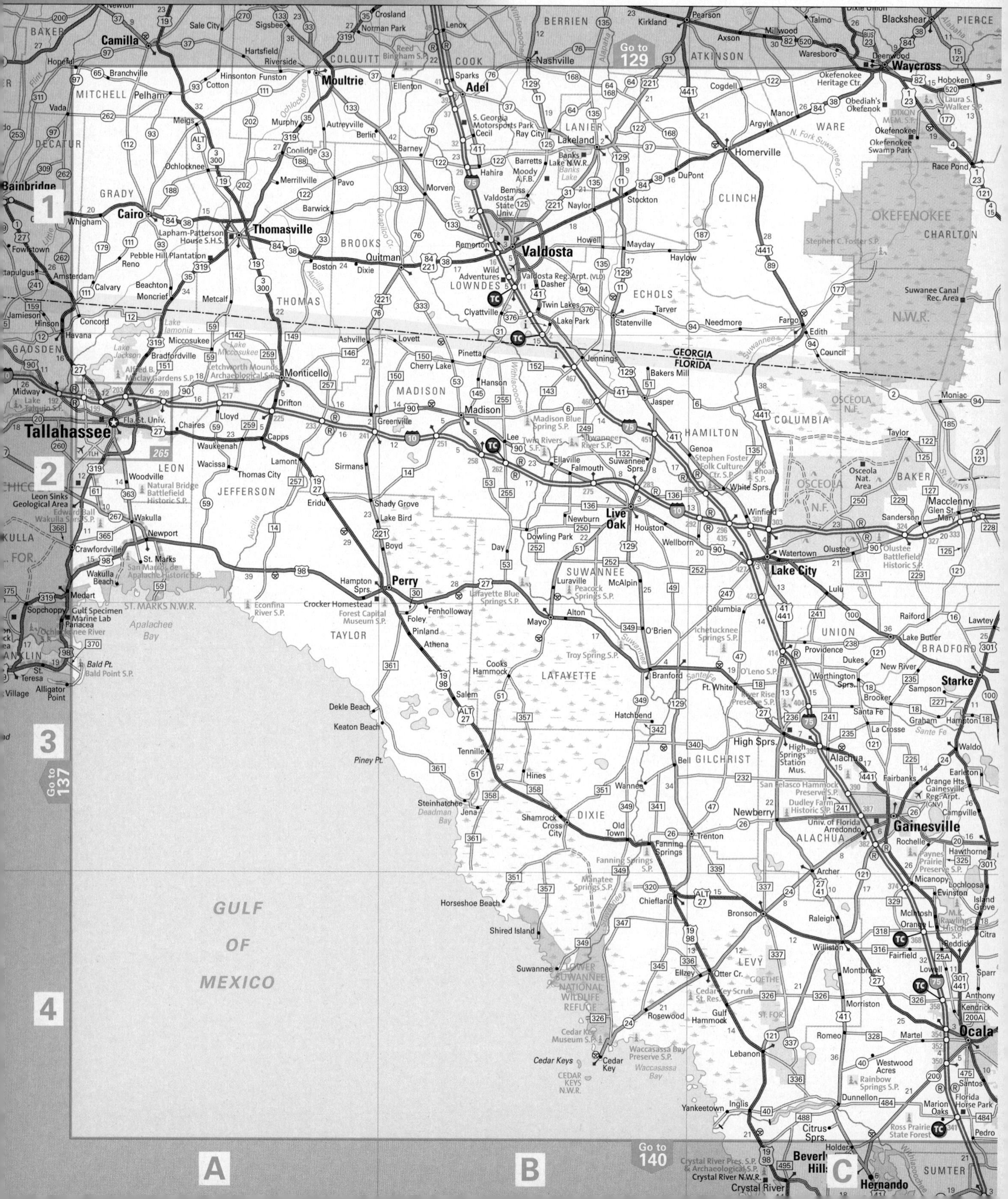

Georgia

Florida

DRIVING DISTANCES IN MILES

	BRUNSWICK, GA	DAYTONA BEACH, FL	GAINESVILLE, FL	JACKSONVILLE, FL	LAKE CITY, FL	OCALA, FL	PERRY, FL	ST. AUGUSTINE, FL	STARKE, FL	TALLAHASSEE, FL	VALDOSTA, GA	WAYCROSS, GA
DAYTONA BEACH, FL	160		99	91	154	77	225	53	92	258	209	173
JACKSONVILLE, FL	69	91	70		62	101	133	41	45	166	117	78
OCALA, FL	171	77	40	101	80		120	81	57	186	137	170
TALLAHASSEE, FL	235	258	152	166	109	186	52	207	145		85	146

SEE ALSO DISTANCE AND DRIVING TIME MAP ON PAGES 286–287

Go to 130

Go to 141

ATLANTIC OCEAN

GEORGIA

GLYNN
Brunswick
St. Simons Island
Jekyll Island
Jekyll Island Natl. Hist. Landmark District

BRANTLEY

CAMDEN
Kingsland
St. Marys
Cumberland Island Natl. Seashore

NASSAU
Fernandina Beach
Amelia Island
Callahan

DUVAL
Jacksonville
Atlantic Beach
Neptune Beach
Jacksonville Beach
Ponte Vedra Beach
Baldwin
Orange Park
Palm Valley
Fruit Cove
Middleburg

CLAY
Green Cove Sprs.
Orangedale
World Golf Vill.

ST. JOHNS
St. Augustine
St. Augustine Beach
St. Augustine Shores
Butler Beach
Crescent Beach
Fort Matanzas Natl. Mon.
Marineland of Florida
Washington Oaks Gardens S.P.

PUTNAM
Palatka
E. Palatka
San Mateo
Crescent City
Georgetown

FLAGLER
Palm Coast
Beverly Beach
Flagler Beach
Bunnell
Korona
Ormond-by-the-Sea

OCALA NATIONAL FOREST

Lake George

VOLUSIA
Ormond Beach
Holly Hill
Daytona Beach
Daytona Beach Shores
S. Daytona
Port Orange
Daytona Intl. Speedway
De Land
De Bary
Deltona
Orange City
New Smyrna Beach
Edgewater
Ponce Inlet
Ponce de Leon Inlet Lighthouse

MARION
Belleview
Silver Sprs. Shores
Lady Lake

Turtle Mound & Seashore Visitor Center
CANAVERAL NATL. SEASHORE

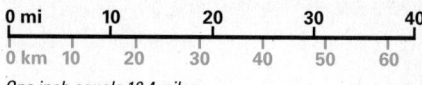

One inch equals 18.4 miles
One centimeter equals 11.7 kilometers

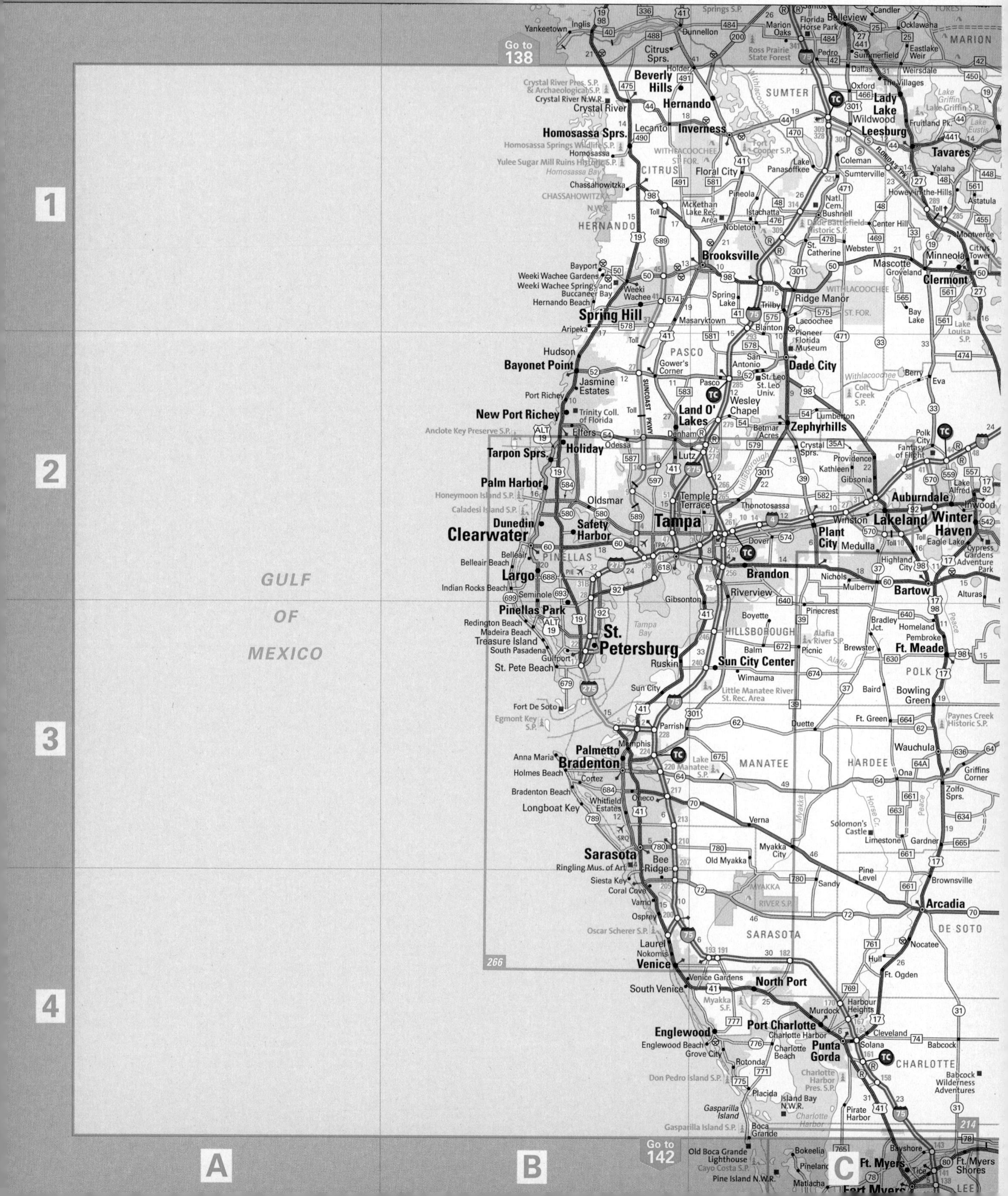

Florida

1

2

3

4

A

B

C

GULF

OF

MEXICO

Go to
138

Go to
142

266

214

Yankeetown
Inglis
Dunnellon
Springs S.P.
Marion
Oaks
Candler
Ocklawana
MARION

Crystal River Pres. S.P.
& Archaeological S.P.
Crystal River N.W.R.
Crystal River
**Beverly
Hills**
Hernando

Homosassa
Yulee Sugar Mill Ruins Historic S.P.
Homosassa Sprs.
Homosassa Bay
Chassahowitzka
CHASSAHOWITZKA
N.W.R.

HERNANDO

Inverness
CITRUS
Floral City
Pineola
Istachatta
Nobleton

Bayport
Weeki Wachee Gardens
Weeki Wachee Springs and
Buccaneer Bay
Hernando Beach
Spring Hill
Aripeka

Hudson
Bayonet Point
Port Richey
Jasmine
Estates
New Port Richey
Elfers
Tarpon Sprs.
Holiday

Palm Harbor
Honeymoon Island S.P.
Caladesi Island S.P.
Oldsmar
Dunedin
Clearwater
Safety
Harbor

Belleair
Belleair Beach
Indian Rocks Beach
Largo

Redington Beach
Madeira Beach
Treasure Island
South Pasadena
Gulfport
Pinellas Park
**St.
Petersburg**
St. Pete Beach

Fort De Soto
Egmont Key
S.P.

Anna Maria
Holmes Beach
Palmetto
Bradenton
Cortez
Bradenton Beach
Longboat Key

Sarasota
Ringling Mus. of Art
Siesta Key
Coral Cove
Osprey

Oscar Scherer S.P.

Laurel
Nokomis
Venice
South Venice
Myakka
S.P.

Englewood
Englewood Beach
Grove City
Rotonda

Don Pedro Island S.P.
Gasparilla
Island
Gasparilla Island S.P.
Old Boca Grande
Lighthouse
Cayo Costa S.P.
Pine Island N.W.R.
Bokeelia
Pinelland
Matlacha

Crystal
Sprs.
Holder

Lecanto
Homosassa Springs Wildlife S.P.

Chassahowitzka

McKethan
Lake Rec.
Area

Brooksville

Weeki
Wachee

Masaryktown

Spring
Lake
Trilby
Ridge Manor
ST. FOR.

PASCO
Gower's
Corner
San
Antonio
Pasco
St. Leo
Univ.
Wesley
Chapel
Betmar
Acres

Trinity Coll.
of Florida
Odessa
Lutz

Winston

Lakeland

Land O'
Lakes
Denham

Temple
Terrace
Thonotosassa
Tampa

Dover

**Plant
City**
Medulla

Brandon
Nichols
Mulberry

Gibsonton
Riverview
Boyette

Ruskin
Sun City Center
Wimauma
Balm
Alafia
River S.P.
Brewster
Ft. Meade

Sun City
Little Manatee River
St. Rec. Area
Baird
Bowling
Green

Parrish
Memphis
Duette
Ft. Green
Paynes Creek
Historic S.P.

MANATEE
Lake
Manatee
S.P.
HARDEE
Wauchula
Griffins
Corner

Oneco
Whitfield
Estates
Verna
Solomon's
Castle
Limestone
Gardner
Zolfo
Sprs.

Bee
Ridge
Old Myakka
Myakka
City
Pine
Level
Brownsville

Vamo
MYAKKA
RIVER S.P.
Sandy
Arcadia
DE SOTO

North Port
Murdock
Harbour
Heights
Cleveland
Nocatee
Hull
Ft. Ogden

Port Charlotte
Charlotte Harbor
Solana
**Punta
Gorda**
Babcock
CHARLOTTE
Babcock
Wilderness
Adventures

Placida
Island
Bay
N.W.R.
Charlotte
Harbor
Pirate
Harbor
Boca
Grande

Bayshore
Ft. Myers
Shores
Ft. Myers

POLK
Bartow
Alturas
Homeland
Pembroke
Bradley
Jct.
Pinecrest
Highland
City
Eagle Lake
Cypress
Gardens
Adventure
Park
**Winter
Haven**
Auburndale
Lake
Alfred
Inwood

SUMTER
Bushnell
Webster
Center Hill
St.
Catherine
Mascotte
Groveland
Clermont
Minneola
Citrus
Tower
Montverde
Clermont
Bay
Lake
Lake
Louisa
S.P.

Leesburg
**Lady
Lake**
Wildwood
Tavares
Yalaha
Howey-in-the-Hills
Astatula
Lake
Eustis
Minneola

Oxford
Dallas
The Villages
Weirsdale
Lake
Griffin S.P.
Lake
Griffin
Fruitland Pk.

Belleview
Summerfield
Eastlake
Weir

DRIVING DISTANCES IN MILES	FORT MYERS, FL	FORT PIERCE, FL	LAKELAND, FL	MELBOURNE, FL	OKEECHOBEE, FL	ORLANDO, FL	PUNTA GORDA, FL	ST. PETERSBURG, FL	SARASOTA, FL	TAMPA, FL	TITUSVILLE, FL	W. PALM BEACH, FL
FORT PIERCE, FL	126		122	57	36	120	127	197	150	172	95	57
ORLANDO, FL	155	120	56	72	108		131	107	130	82	40	169
SARASOTA, FL	74	150	85	190	114	130	50	35		60	170	184
TAMPA, FL	123	172	37	142	162	82	99	25	60		121	223

SEE ALSO DISTANCE AND DRIVING TIME MAP ON PAGES 286–287

Go to 139

Go to 143

Florida

0 mi 10 20 30 40
0 km 10 20 30 40 50 60
One inch equals 18.4 miles
One centimeter equals 11.7 kilometers

1

Go to **140**

Don Pedro Island S.P.
Charlotte Harbor
Babcock Wilderness Adventures
775
771 Placida Toll
Gasparilla Island
Island Bay N.W.R.
765
158
23
31
Boca Grande
Old Boca Grande Lighthouse
Gasparilla Island S.P.
Pine Island N.W.R.
Bokeelia
Pineland
765
Pirate Harbor
31
R
41
Bayshore
143
N. Ft. Myers
78
Tice
80
Ft. Myers Shores
Cayo Costa S.P.
Matlacha
78
Fort Myers
41
884
136
82
TC
Captiva I.
Cape Coral
767
Ft. Myers Villas
131
RSW
Captiva
767
Punta Rassa
Iona
869
128
LEE
St. James City
Sanibel
Toll
San Carlos Park
39
Sanibel I.
Ft. Myers Beach
865
Estero
123
41
Everglades Wonder Gardens
36
Lovers Key S.P.
214
Bonita Springs
116
Delnor-Wiggins Pass S.P.
865
846
111
Naples Park
951
Golden Gate
North Naples
31
107
Philharmonic Ctr. for the Arts
102
Naples Zoo at Caribbean Gardens
84
Naples Municipal Arpt. (APF)
7
Naples
7
Naples Botanical Garden
8
E. Naples
Naples Manor
8
951
Marco Island
Marco Island
Marco I. Trolley Tours
Cape Romano

2

GULF

OF

MEXICO

3

4

DRY TORTUGAS NATL. PARK
Fort Jefferson

KEY WEST N.W.R.
224
Stock Island
1
Marquesas Keys
Key West
EYW
Naval Air Station Key West

A   **B**   **C**

DRIVING DISTANCES IN MILES	BELLE GLADE, FL	BOCA RATON, FL	FLAMINGO, FL	FORT LAUDERDALE, FL	FORT MYERS, FL	HOMESTEAD, FL	KEY LARGO, FL	KEY WEST, FL	MARATHON, FL	MIAMI, FL	NAPLES, FL	W. PALM BEACH, FL
FORT MYERS, FL	84	155	227	139		174	195	308	260	155	36	125
KEY WEST, FL	235	211	181	190	308	133	113		48	168	273	234
MIAMI, FL	83	44	87	23	155	34	55	168	120		121	67
W. PALM BEACH, FL	41	28	153	48	125	100	121	234	186	67	144	

SEE ALSO DISTANCE AND DRIVING TIME MAP ON PAGES 286–287

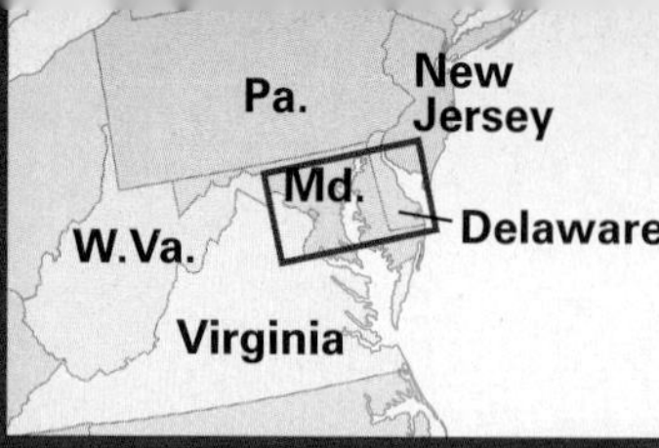

Pa. | New Jersey
W.Va. | Md. | Delaware
Virginia

BONUS MAPS!

0 mi — 5 — 10 — 15 — 20
0 km 5 — 10 — 15 — 20 — 25 — 30
One inch equals 9.85 miles
One centimeter equals 6.25 kilometers

Northeast Corridor / Washington DC

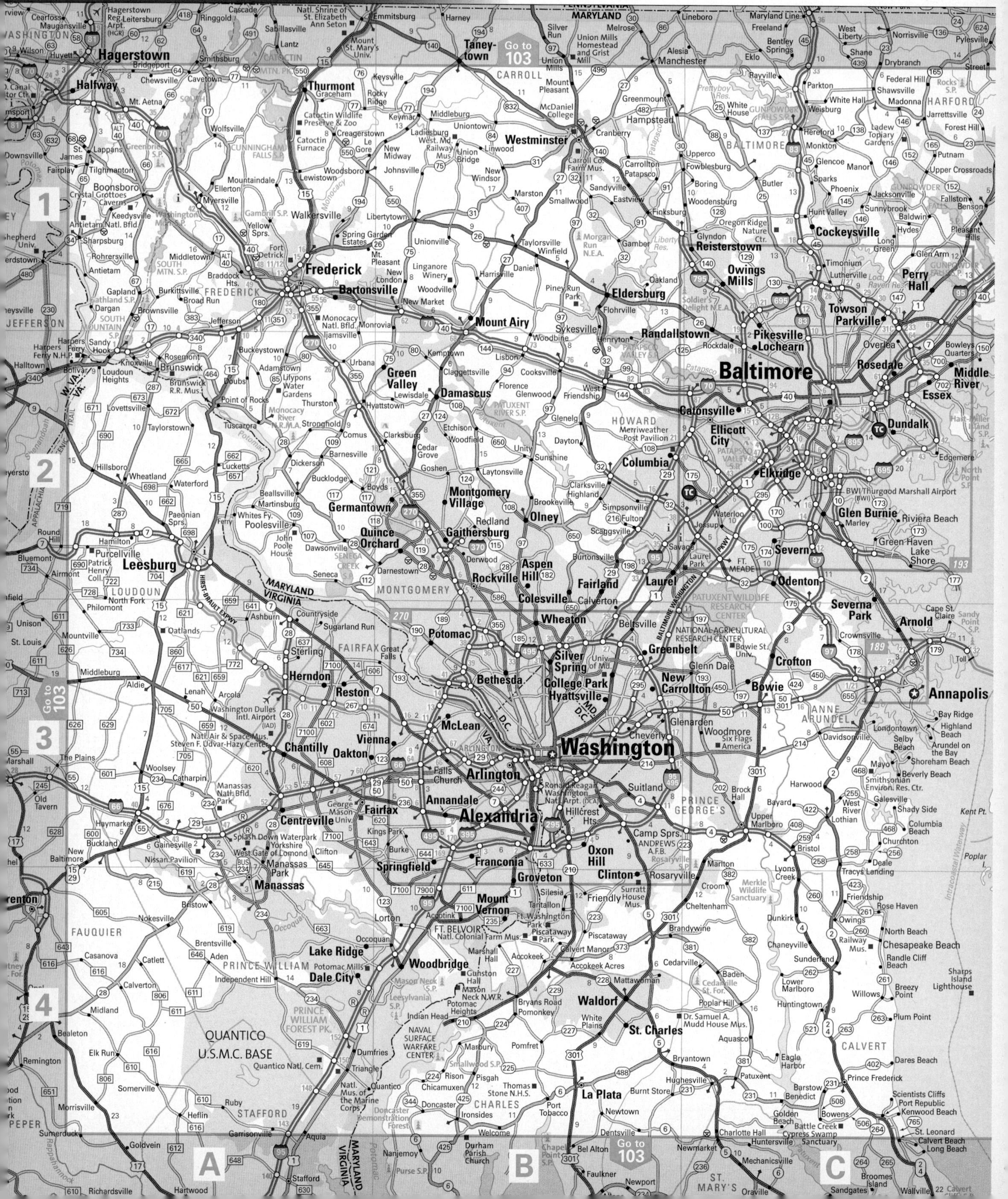

BONUS MAPS!

Pa. | New Jersey
Md. — Delaware
W.Va. | Virginia

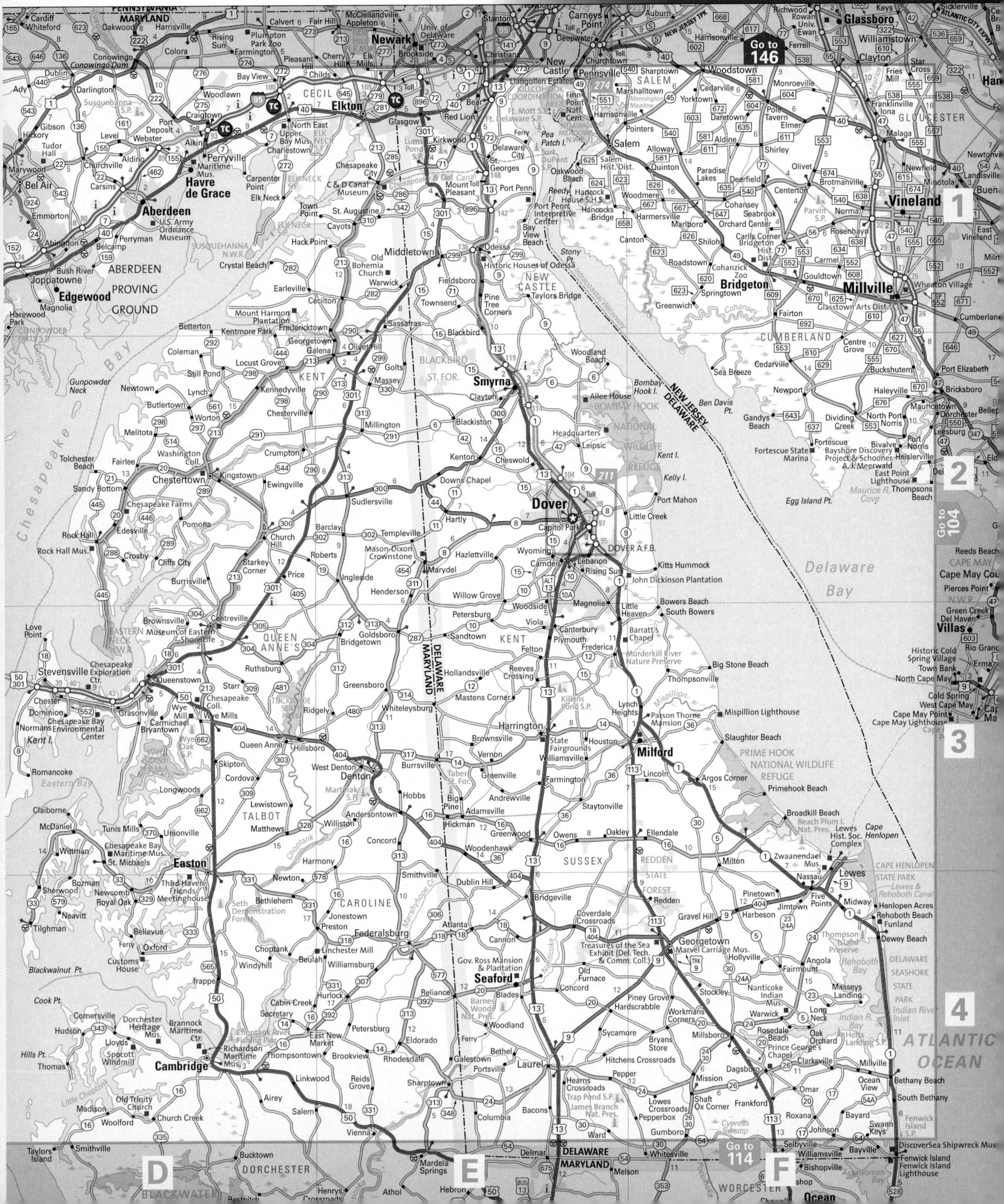

DRIVING DISTANCES IN MILES	ANNAPOLIS, MD	BALTIMORE, MD	CAMBRIDGE, MD	DOVER, DE	ELKTON, MD	FREDERICK, MD	HAGERSTOWN, MD	LEESBURG, VA	MANASSAS, VA	REHOBOTH BEACH, DE	VINELAND, NJ	WASHINGTON, DC
BALTIMORE, MD	25		78	98	58	51	76	71	67	111	109	38
DOVER, DE	62	98	64		40	135	160	135	131	43	77	94
FREDERICK, MD	73	51	128	135	106		28	25	61	161	158	44
WASHINGTON, DC	31	38	87	94	94	44	70	38	31	120	145	

SEE ALSO DISTANCE AND DRIVING TIME MAP ON PAGES 286–287

Go to 146

Go to 104

Go to 114

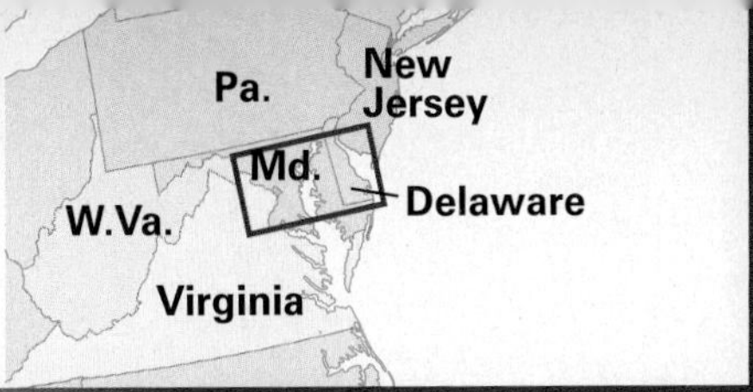

New York
Penn.
Md.
New Jersey
Delaware

BONUS MAPS!

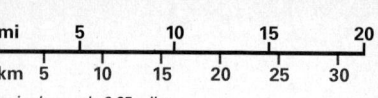

0 mi 5 10 15 20
0 km 5 10 15 20 25 30
One inch equals 9.85 miles
One centimeter equals 6.25 kilometers

Northeast Corridor / Philadelphia PA

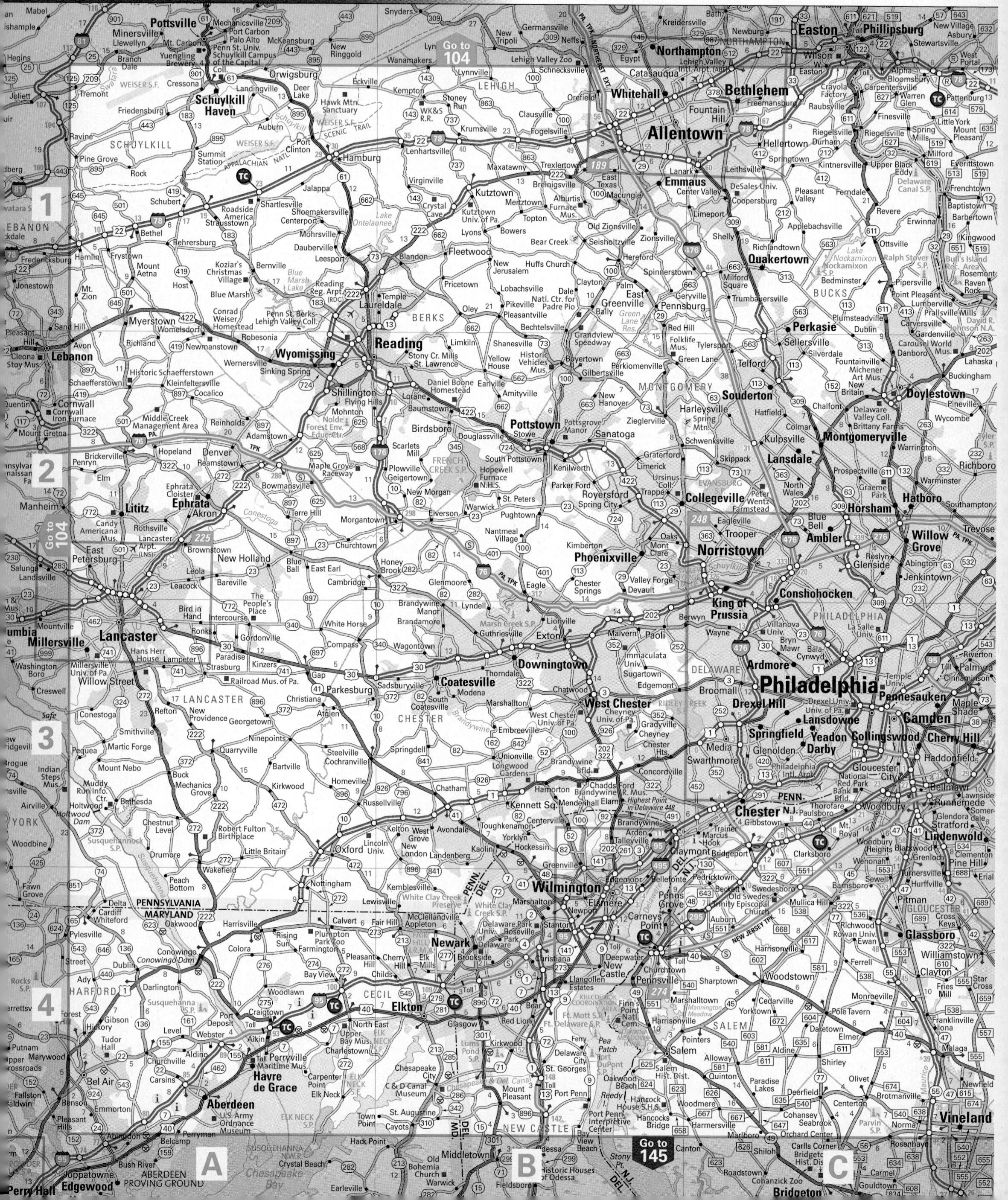

BONUS MAPS!

New York

Penn.

New Jersey

Md.

Delaware

DRIVING DISTANCES IN MILES	ALLENTOWN, PA	ATLANTIC CITY, NJ	ELKTON, MD	LANCASTER, PA	LONG BRANCH, NJ	NEW BRUNSWICK, NJ	NEW YORK, NY	PHILADELPHIA, PA	READING, PA	TOMS RIVER, NJ	TRENTON, NJ	WILMINGTON, DE
NEW YORK, NY	84	125	137	165	55	34		91	118	75	55	120
PHILADELPHIA, PA	63	62	50	79	77	55	91		63	58	34	30
TRENTON, NJ	66	77	88	105	53	22	55	34	89	48		68
WILMINGTON, DE	77	86	20	53	106	90	120	30	56	85	68	

SEE ALSO DISTANCE AND DRIVING TIME MAP ON PAGES 286–287

Go to 148

Go to 105

FOR CONTINUATION SEE INSET AT RIGHT

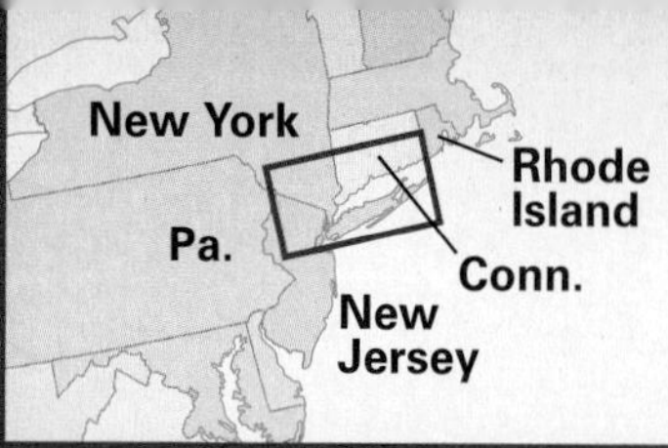

New York
Pa.
Rhode Island
Conn.
New Jersey

BONUS MAPS!

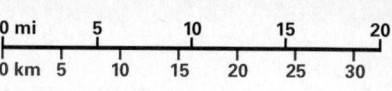

0 mi   5   10   15   20
0 km 5   10   15   20   25   30

One inch equals 9.85 miles
One centimeter equals 6.25 kilometers

Northeast Corridor / New York NY

BONUS MAPS!

DRIVING DISTANCES IN MILES	DANBURY, CT	HARTFORD, CT	NEWARK, NJ	NEWBURGH, NY	NEW HAVEN, CT	NEW LONDON, CT	NEW YORK, NY	PATERSON, NJ	RIVERHEAD, NY	STAMFORD, CT	WATERBURY, CT
BRIDGEPORT, CT	31	56	69	73	19	64	60	71	115	21	33
NEWARK, NJ	69	79	125	66	88	134	11	18	88	48	108
NEW HAVEN, CT	19	35	39	88	78		46	78	89	133	40	30
NEW YORK, NY	60	69	115	11	56	78	124		16	78	38	69

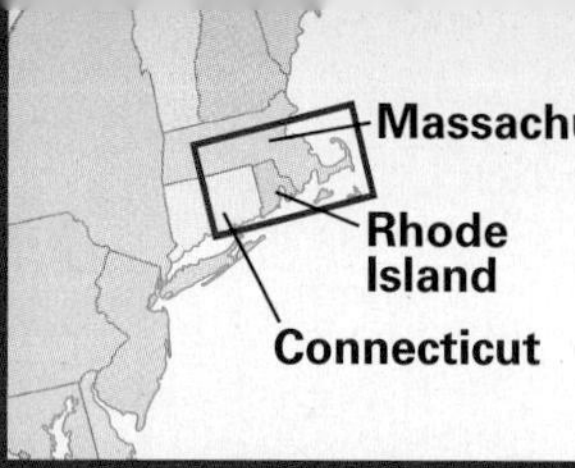

Massachusetts
Rhode Island
Connecticut

BONUS MAPS!

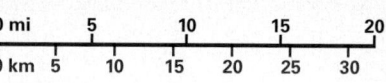

0 mi   5   10   15   20
0 km 5   10   15   20   25   30

One inch equals 9.85 miles
One centimeter equals 6.25 kilometers

Northeast Corridor / Hartford CT

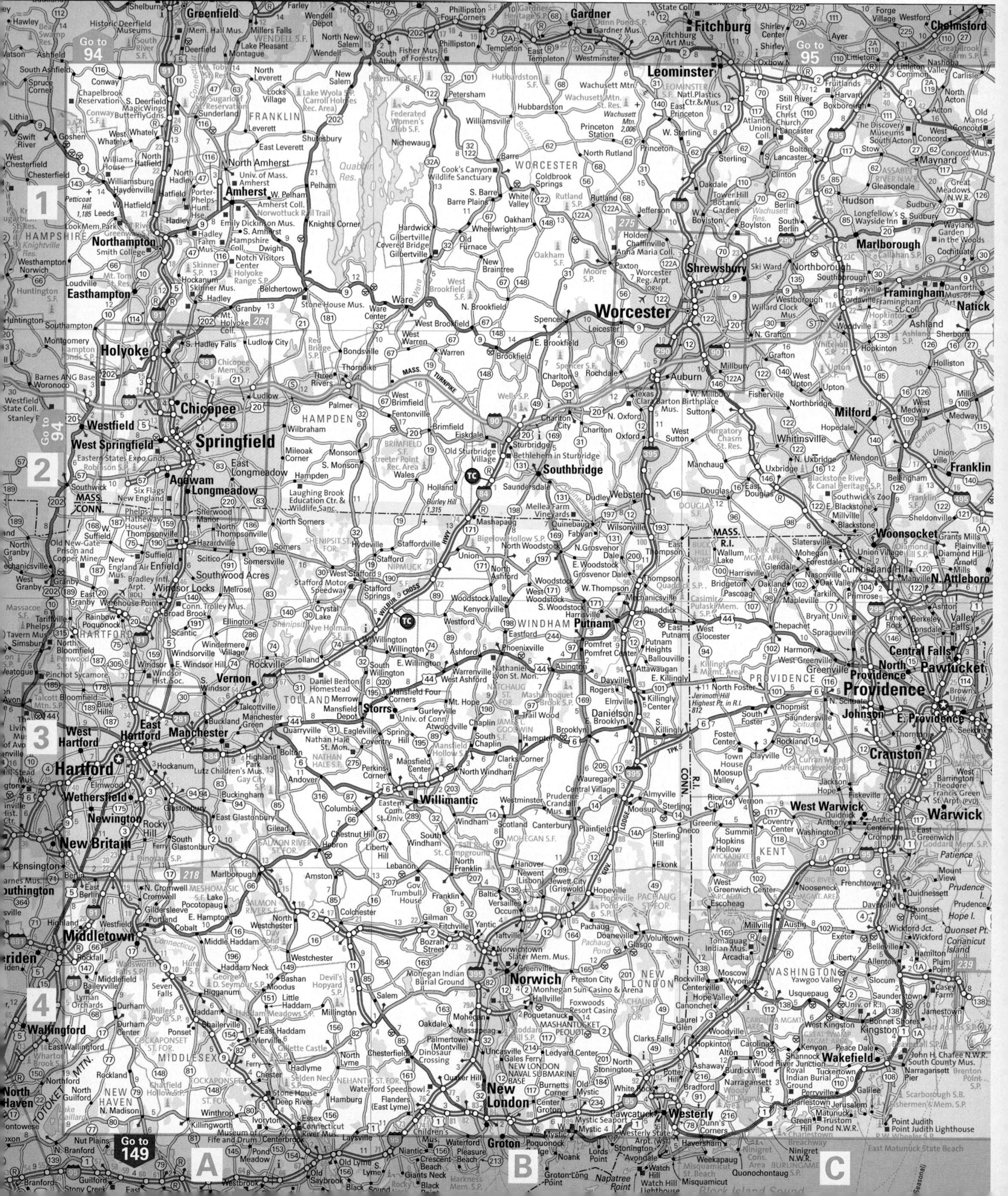

BONUS MAPS!

Massachusetts
Rhode Island
Connecticut

DRIVING DISTANCES IN MILES	BOSTON, MA	GLOUCESTER, MA	HARTFORD, CT	HYANNIS, MA	NEW BEDFORD, MA	NEW LONDON, CT	NEWPORT, RI	PLYMOUTH, MA	PROVIDENCE, RI	PROVINCETOWN, MA	SPRINGFIELD, MA	WORCESTER, MA	
BOSTON, MA		35	102	72	60	109	73	41	52	117	95	46
HARTFORD, CT	102	136		155	104	46	85	127	73	200	25	62
PROVIDENCE, RI	52	92	73	71	33	58	33	41		111	75	43
SPRINGFIELD, MA	95	129	25	148	127	71	111	120	75	193		55

SEE ALSO DISTANCE AND DRIVING TIME MAP ON PAGES 286–287

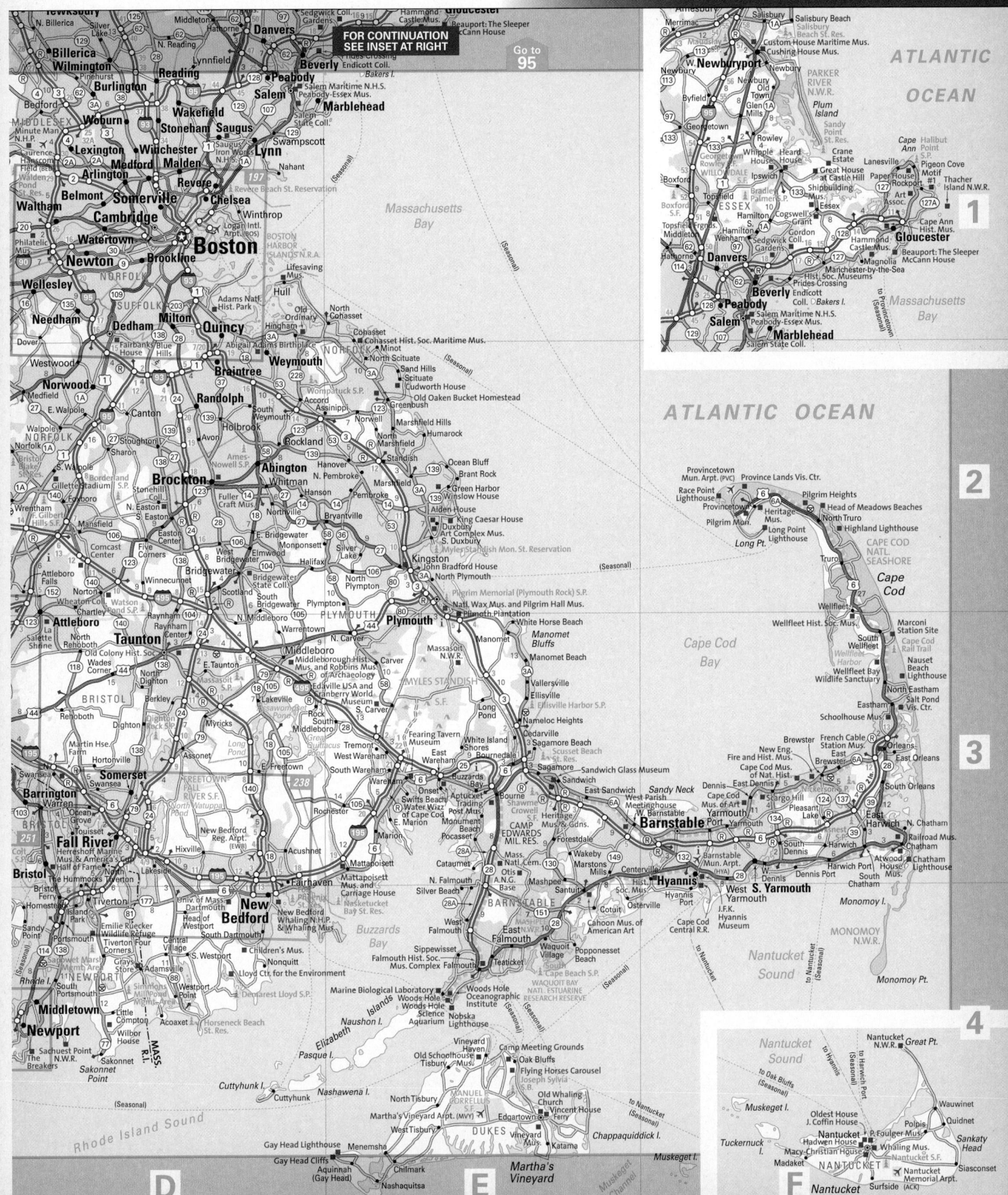

FOR CONTINUATION
SEE INSET AT RIGHT

Go to
95

CANADA
UNITED STATES
MEXICO
HAWAII

One inch equals 18.4 miles
One centimeter equals 11.7 kilometers

0 mi · 10 · 20 · 30 · 40
0 km 10 · 20 · 30 · 40 · 50 · 60

Honolulu HI / Lihue HI

1

Hā'ena S.P.
Princeville
Hanalei N.W.R.
Kilauea Pt. N.W.R.
NĀPALI COAST STATE WILDERNESS PARK
Hā'ena
Hanalei
Kalihiwai
Kilauea
Kaua'i
HONO O NĀPALI NAT. AREA RES.
NĀPALI COAST
560
56
MOLOA'A FOR. RES.
Anahola
KU'IA NAT. AREA RES.
PU'UKAPELE FOR. RES.
Pu'uokila Lookout
Wai'ale'ale (World's Rainiest Spot) 5,148
MAKALEHA MTS.
15
KŌKE'E
KEĀLIA FOR. RES.
Keālia
NĀPALI-KONA FOR. RES.
Waimea Canyon Lookout
Kawaikini 5,243
NONOU FOR. RES.
580
583
Kapa'a
Pollhale S.P.
Nohili Pt.
WAIMEA CANYON S.P.
Wailua River S.P.
56
Wailua
Hanamā'ulu
BARKING SANDS PACIFIC MISSILE RANGE FACILITY
Mānā
550
Kekaha
Waimea
Pākalā Village
Kaumakani
Hanapēpē 'Ele'ele
3
Waimea Falls
Olu Pua Bot. Gdns. & Plantation
Kalāheo
Numila
Lāwa'i
'Ōma'o
Kōloa
Kukui'ula
Po'ipū
Spouting Horn
Līhu'e
Ahukini St. Rec. Pier
Lihu'e Arpt. (LIH)
50
Puhi
58
Hulē'ia N.W.R.
51
KAUA'I COUNTY
Lehua
Kīkepa Pt.
Keawanui Bay
Pāni'au 1,281
Pu'uwai
Pueo Pt.
Ni'ihau (RESTRICTED PUBLIC ACCESS)
Kawaihoa
Kaulakahaki Channel
Kaua'i Channel

PACIFIC OCEAN

FOR CONTINUATION SEE MAP BELOW

2

FOR CONTINUATION SEE MAP ABOVE

Kauai Channel
Kahuku Pt.
James C. Campbell N.W.R.
Kawela Bay
Waiale'e
Sunset Beach
Kahuku
12
Mālaekahana S.R.A.
Waimea
Pūpūkea
Lā'ie
Kawailoa Beach
Waimea Falls
Polynesian Cultural Center
Hau'ula
Kawailoa
Pu'u Ka'inapua'a 2,360
SACRED FALLS S.P.
83
Mokulē'ia
Hale'iwa
Kamo'oloa
Punalu'u
Ka'ena Pt. S.P.
930
Waialua
Ka'ena Pt.
99
Kahana
Ka'a'awa
MĀKUA MIL. RES.
Whitmore Village
AHUPUA'A O KAHANA
Ka'a'awa Beach Park
O'ahu
8
KUALOA REG. PARK
93
Waikāne
CLOSED TO PUBLIC
Wahiawā
O'AHU FOR. N.W.R.
Kahalu'u
750
Mililani Town
Waipi'o Acres
He'eia
HAWAII MARINE CORPS BASE
Mākaha
LUALUALEI NAVAL RES.
99
Pearl City
'Āhuimanu
Wai'anae
Mā'ili
Waipahu
Kāne'ohe
Kailua
Nānākuli
Makakilo City
76
NAVAL RES.
U.S. 15
83
Maunawili
Honokai Hale
61
Waimānalo
Ewa Villages
63
Waimānalo Bay Park
Kapolei
'Ewa Beach
Waimānalo Beach
Sea Life Park
Makapu'u Pt.
Waimalu
HNL
219
17
72
Blow Hole
HONOLULU COUNTY
Honolulu
Hanauma Bay St. Underwater Park

PACIFIC OCEAN

Kalaupapa Airport (LUP)
KALAWAO COUNTY
'Īlio Pt.
Kahi'u Pt.
Pālā'au S.P.
KALAUPAPA NATL. HIST. PARK
Pāpōhaku Beach
Moloka'i Airport (MKK)
Ho'olehua
480
Kalaupapa
Hipuapua Falls
Hālawa Bay
Maunaloa
460
Kualapu'u
Hālawa
Cape Hālawa
Moloka'i Ranch Headquarters
Pu'u Nānā
'Ili'ili'ōpae
Mo'a'ula Falls
MOLOKA'I FOR. RES.
470
'Oloku'i Nat. Area Res.
Lā'au Pt.
Pu'u Ali'i Nat. Area Res.
Kamakou 4,970 Heiau
Waialua
Moloka'i
460
Kaunakakai
24
Pūko'o
Kalaohai'i N.W.R.
450
'Ualapu'e
Honolua Pt.
Nākālele Pt.
Kamalō
MAUI COUNTY
Honokōhau
Kalohi Channel
Honokahua
Honokōwai
Haleki'i-Pīhana Heiau St. Mon.
Kalaeloa Channel
Kahakuloa
Kalohi Channel
Pailolo Channel

3

Kalohi Channel
Kawi Channel

PACIFIC OCEAN

Shipwreck Beach
Garden of the Gods
Keanapapa Pt.
WEST MAUI NAT. AREA
Honokōwai
Kā'anapali
Kā'anapali & Pacific R.R.
Pu'u Kukui 5,788
Waihe'e
Kahului
36
340
Kahului Bay
Lāna'i
Keōmuku Village
Lahaina
Lahaina
Kahana
Waiehu
Waikapū
37
'Īao
Kaumalapau
Lāna'i City
Lāna'i hale 3,370
Lahaina Hist. Dist.
WEST MAUI FOR. RES.
Wailuku
Pu'u'unēne Sugar Mus.
380
Lāna'i Airport (LNY)
440
Olowalu
Mā'alaea
311
Keālia Pond N.W.R.
310
Kaunolū Village
Palaoa Pt.
Pu'u Pehe
Hulopo'e Beach Park
30
Papawai Pt.
Maui Ocean Ctr.
Mā'alaea Bay
Kīhei
Maui
Kama'ole
'Ulupalakua
Keōkea
37
Lao o Kukui
Pu'u Moa'ilanui 1,483
Mākena
Mākena Beach N.W.R.
Mākena S.P.
8
Lao o Kealaikahiki
Lao o Kākā
Molokini
'ĀHIHI-KĪNA'U NAT. AREA RES.
Kaho'olawe
26
Kealaikahiki Channel
Alalākeiki Channel

4

FOR CONTINUATION SEE MAP AT RIGHT

A · **B** · **C**

DRIVING DISTANCES IN MILES

	HĀNA	HILO	HONOLULU	HOʻOLEHUA	KAHULUI	KAILUA	KAILUA-KONA	LAHAINA	LANAI CITY	LIHUE	WAHIAWĀ	WAIMEA	
HILO	149*		217*		169*	121*	235*	88	142*	155*	319*	234*	54
HONOLULU	129*	217*		101*	54*	101*	14	185*	92*	74*	102*	23	172*
KAHULUI	42	121*	101*		76*		119*	109*	23	57*	202*	118*	79*
LIHUE	230*	319*	102*	156*		202*	120*	285*	225*	176*		119*	174*

*DISTANCE INCLUDES AIR TRAVEL   SEE ALSO DISTANCE AND DRIVING TIME MAP ON PAGES 286–287

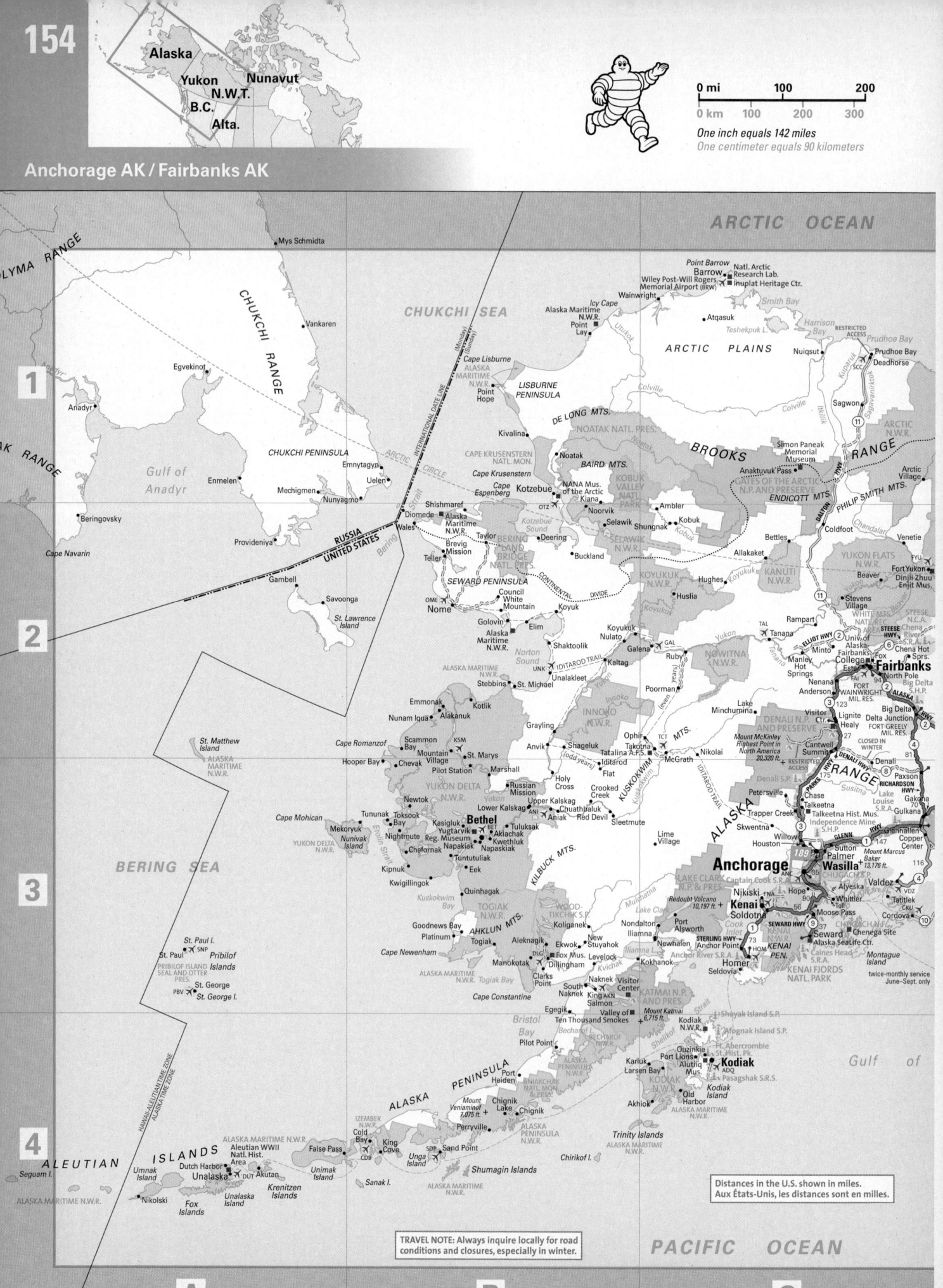

Alaska
Yukon Nunavut
N.W.T.
B.C.
Alta.

0 mi 100 200
0 km 100 200 300
One inch equals 142 miles
One centimeter equals 90 kilometers

ARCTIC OCEAN

CHUKCHI SEA

BERING SEA

PACIFIC OCEAN

Gulf of

Distances in the U.S. shown in miles.
Aux États-Unis, les distances sont en milles.

TRAVEL NOTE: Always inquire locally for road
conditions and closures, especially in winter.

A | B | C

DRIVING DISTANCES IN MILES	ANCHORAGE, AK	DAWSON CREEK, BC	DENALI NP, AK	FAIRBANKS, AK	HOMER, AK	JUNEAU, AK	PRINCE GEORGE, BC	PRINCE RUPERT, BC	SKAGWAY, AK	TOK, AK	WHITEHORSE, YT	YELLOWKNIFE, NT
ANCHORAGE, AK		1516	275	378	225	841*	1679	1514	807	323	697	1844
DAWSON CREEK, BC	1516		1503	1400	1740	963*	224	625	862	1193	819	741
FAIRBANKS, AK	378	1400	103		603	726*	1564	1398	691	207	581	1729
WHITEHORSE, YT	697	819	684	581	921	211*	982	817	110	374		1147

*DISTANCE INCLUDES FERRY TRAVEL

SEE ALSO DISTANCE AND DRIVING TIME MAP ON PAGES 286–287

Distances in Canada shown in kilometers.
Au Canada, les distances sont en kilomètres.

The Alaska Marine Highway—with ferry service to 30 communities in Alaska, plus Bellingham WA and Prince Rupert BC—is an All-American Road

Go to 158
Go to 156
Go to 157
Go to 164

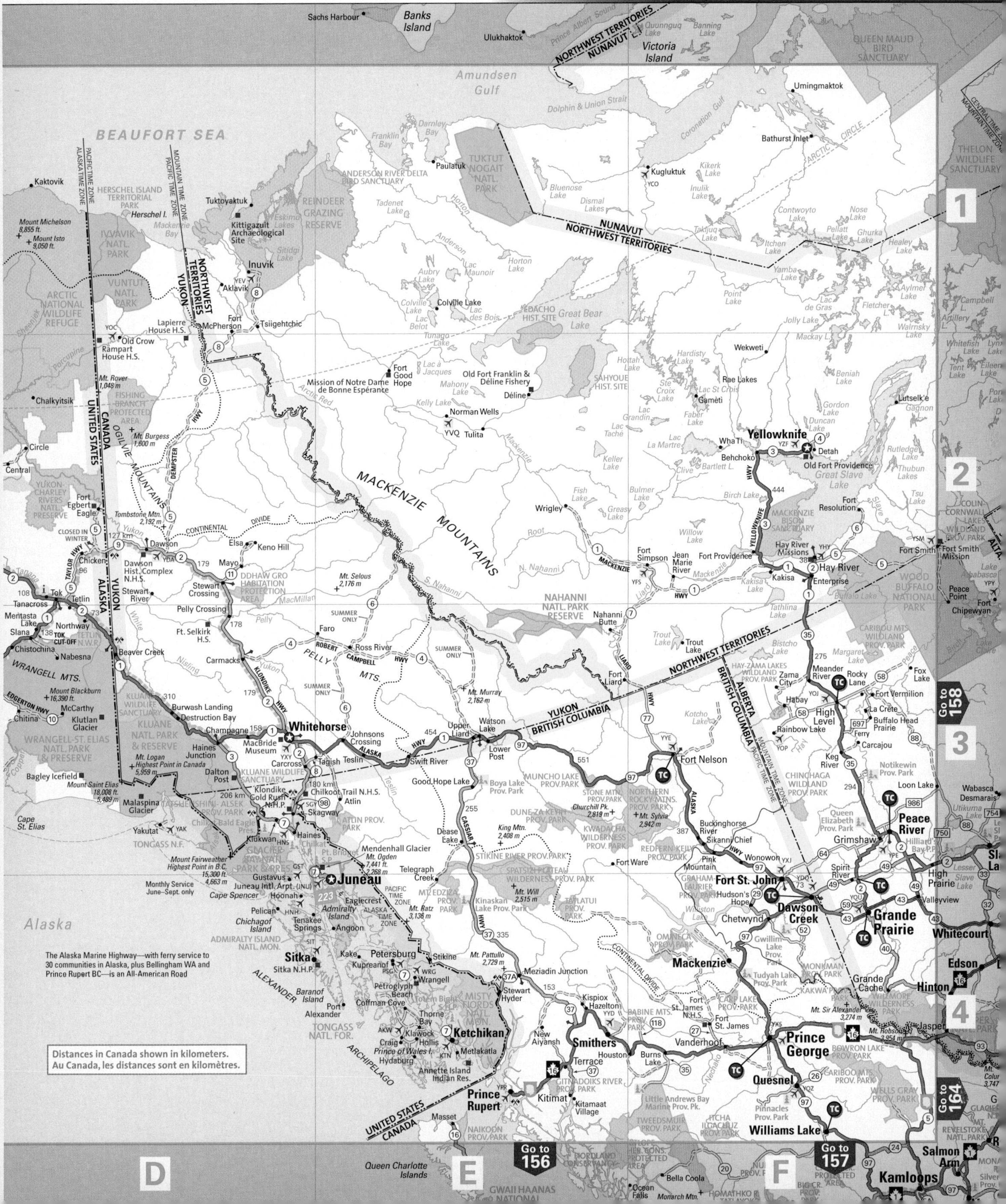

0 mi   20   40   60
0 km 20   40   60   80
One inch equals 40.3 miles/Un pouce équivaut à 40.3 milles
One centimeter equals 25.4 km/Un cm équivaut à 25.4 km

Go to 155

Go to 155

Mt. Pattullo 2,729 m Meziadin Lake
Meziadin Lake Provincial Park
Meziadin Junction
Stewart
Hyder
ALASKA B.C.
CASSIAR HWY.
CONTINENTAL DIVIDE
Motase Pk. 2,411 m
Bear Lake
USTUT PROVINCIAL PARK

MISTY FIORDS NATIONAL MONUMENT

TONGASS NATIONAL FOREST
Coffman Cove
Heceta I.
Meyers Chuck
Cleveland Peninsula
Revillagigedo Island
Thorne Bay
Klawock AKW
Noyes I.
Craig Hollis Kasaan
Baker I.
Waterfall
Prince of Wales Island
Hydaburg
Suemez I.
Sukkwan I.
Dall I.
Long I.
Forrester I.
ALASKA MARITIME N.W.R.
Ketchikan
KTN Saxman
Gravina Island
Metlakatla
ANNETTE ISLAND IND. RES.
Cordova Bay
Clarence Strait
Boom Canal
Behm Canal
Portland Inlet
Portland Canal

SWAN LAKE-KISPIOX RIVER PROVINCIAL PARK
Kinskuch Lake
Lavender Pk. 2,323 m
Cranberry Junction
Alice Arm
Mt. Weber 2,007 m
Shelagyote Pk. 2,466 m
Kisgegas Pk. 2,347 m
Cutoff Mtn. 1,649 m
BABINE RIVER CORRIDOR PROVINCIAL PARK
Centre Pk. 1,990 m
Mt. Lovell 1,995 m
Mt. Thomlinson 2,591 m
New Aiyansh
Gitwinksihlkw
Nass Camp
Kitwancool Lake
Gitanyow Totem Poles
Kispiox
New Hazelton
Hazelton Ksan Hist. Village & Mus.
Nilkitkwa L.
Fort Babine
Babine Lake-Smithers Landing Marine Prov. Park
Laxgalts'ap
Gingolx
NISGA'A MEMORIAL LAVA BED PROVINCIAL PARK
Seeley Lake Prov. Pk.
Kitwanga Fort N.H.S.
Kitwanga
South Hazelton
Ross Lake Prov. Park
Blunt Mtn. 2,286 m
Moricetown
Smithers Landing
Red Bluff Prov. Pk.
Nass Bay
Nasoga Gulf
Alder Pk. 2,220 m
Oscar Pk. 2,304 m
Lava Lake
Kitsumkalum Lake
Cedarvale
SEVEN SISTERS PROV. PARK
BABINE MOUNTAINS PROV. PARK
Granisle
Rosswood
Smithers Arpt. (YYD)
Kitseguecla
Smithers
Telkwa
Tyhee Lake Provincial Park
Fulton Lake
U.S. CANADA
ALASKA TIME ZONE PACIFIC TIME ZONE
Dixon Entrance
Lax Kw'alaams
Dundas I.
Chatham Sound
KHUTZEYMATEEN GRIZZLY BEAR SANCTUARY
Mt. Kenney 2,073 m
Heritage Park Mus.
Usk
Kleanza Creek Prov. Park
Ski Smithers
Eagle Pk. 2,093 m
257
118
Topley
16
Exchamsiks River Prov. Pk.
Shames Mountain
Terrace
Terrace Arpt. (YXT)
Lakelse Lake Prov. Park
Lakelse Lake
Houston
Masset Arpt. (ZMT)
Masset
NAIKOON PROV. PARK
Graham Island
Ian Lake
Port Clements
Juskatla Tlell
101
16
Mus. of Northern B.C.
Prudhomme Lake
Prince Rupert Arpt. (YPR)
Prince Rupert
North Pacific Hist. Fishing Village
Port Edward
Diana Lake Prov. Park
Stephens I.
Port Essington
Porcher Island
Oona River
Kitkatla
147
16
Skeena
Khtada Lake
GITNADOIKS RIVER PROVINCIAL PARK
58 37
Kitimat
Kitamaat Village
McBride
Tagetochlain Lake
Noralee
Morice Lake
Kidprice Lake
Nadina Lake
Tahtsa L.
Little Andrews Bay Marine Prov. Park
Wistaria Prov. Park
Dokdaon L.
Tweedsmuir Prov. Pk. 2,182 m
McCauley
Pitt Island
Klewnuggit Inlet Marine Prov. Park
Hawkesbury Island
Powell Pk. 2,012 m
Nanika Lake
Troitsa L.
Whtesail Lake
Michel Pk. 2,252 m
Fenton L.
Hecate Strait
Banks Island
Lowe Inlet Marine Prov. Park
Hartley Bay
Gribbell Island
Kemano
Glatheli L.
Knope Lake
COAST
Surel L.
TWEEDSMUIR PROVINCIAL PARK
Eutsuk Lake
Oppy L.
Queen Charlotte Islands
Qay'llnagaay Heritage Center
Skidegate Sandspit Arpt. (YZP)
Queen Charlotte
Sandspit
Alliford Bay
Moresby Camp
Yakoun L.
Anchor Lake
Campania I.
Princess Royal Island
FIORDLAND CONSERVANCY
KITLOPE HERITAGE CONSERVANCY PROTECTED AREA
PROVINCIAL PARK
Tesla L.
Kimsquit
Dean
Sewell Inlet
Moresby Island
GWAII HAANAS NATIONAL PARK RESERVE
Aristazabal Island
Gil I.
Laredo Inlet
Pooley I.
YKT Roderick
Klemtu
Jackson Narrows Marine Prov. Park
Swindle I.
Kynoch Inlet
Link Inlet
Sir Alexander Mackenzie Provincial Park
Kalone Pk. 2,557 m
Thunder Mtn. 2,681 m
Firvale
Bella Coola
Hagensborg
Mt. Saugstad 2,972 m
COAST MOUNTAINS
Price I.
Ocean Falls
Mussel Inlet
Bella QBC Coola
20
Oliver Cove Marine Prov. Pk.
Codville Lagoon Marine Prov. Pk.
King I.
ZEL Shearwater
Bella Bella
Goose I.
Hunter I.
Burke Channel
Namu
HAKAI CONSERVANCY AREA
Mt. Buxton 1,045 m
Calvert I.
Dawsons Landing
Good Hope
Rivers Inlet
Oweikeno Lake
Rivers Inlet
Draney Inlet
Penrose Island Marine Prov. Pk.
Smith Sound
Long L.
Belize Inlet

PACIFIC OCEAN

Distances in Canada shown in kilometers.
Au Canada, les distances sont en kilomètres.

Go to 162

To Port Hardy Hope I.
LANZ & COX ISLANDS PROV. PARK
CAPE SCOTT PROV. PARK
Niget
God's Pocket
Sullivan Bay
Lanz I. Cox I.
Seymour Inlet

A   **B**   **C**

1 2 3 4

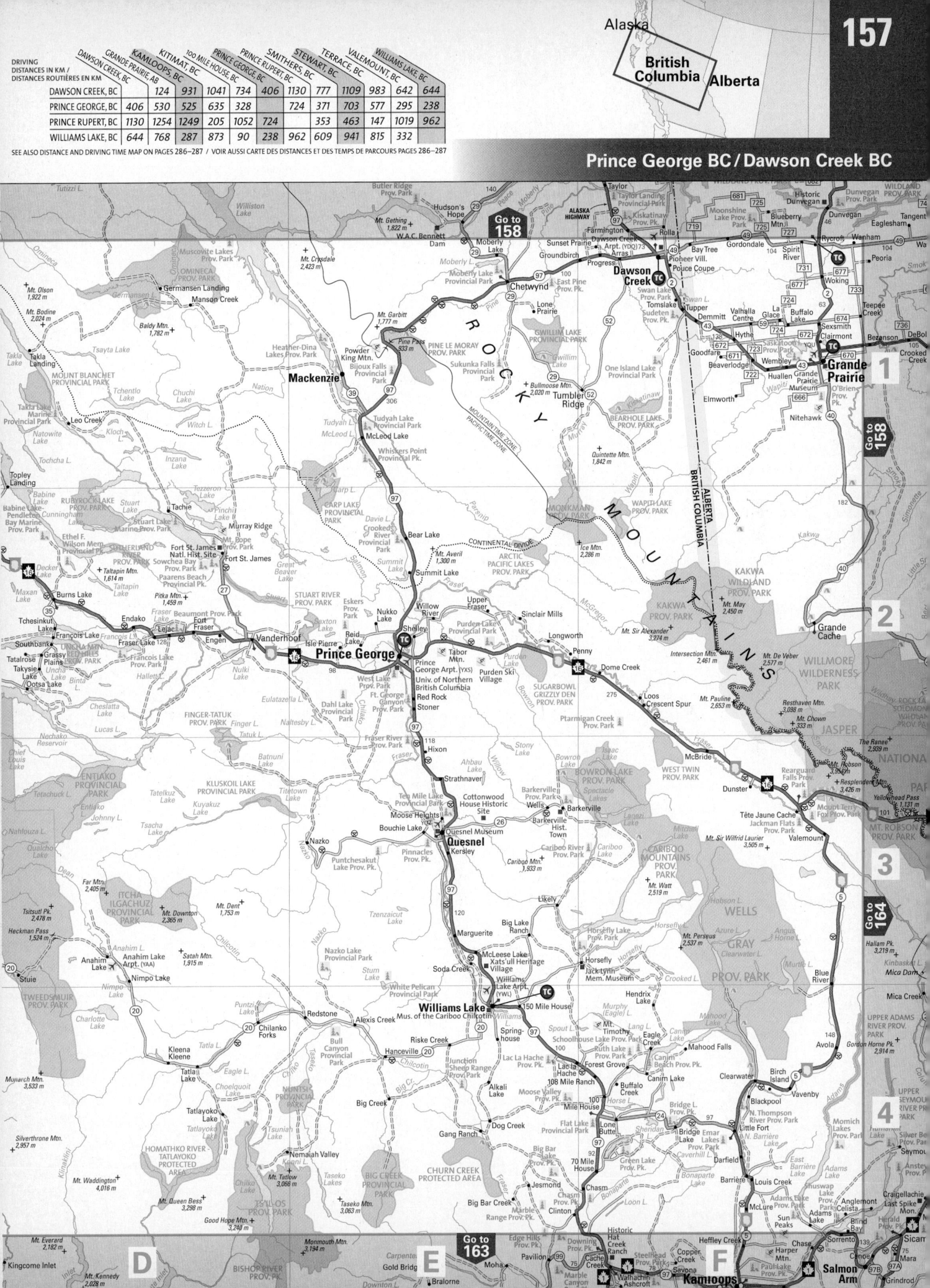

DRIVING
DISTANCES IN KM /
DISTANCES ROUTIÈRES EN KM

	DAWSON CREEK, BC	GRANDE PRAIRIE, AB	KAMLOOPS, BC	KITIMAT, BC	100 MILE HOUSE, BC	PRINCE GEORGE, BC	PRINCE RUPERT, BC	SMITHERS, BC	TERRACE, BC	VALEMOUNT, BC	WILLIAMS LAKE, BC	
DAWSON CREEK, BC		124	931	1041	734	406	1130	777	1109	983	642	644
PRINCE GEORGE, BC	406	530	525	635	328		724	371	703	577	295	238
PRINCE RUPERT, BC	1130	1254	1249	205	1052	724		353	463	147	1019	962
WILLIAMS LAKE, BC	644	768	287	873	90	238	962	609	941	815		332

SEE ALSO DISTANCE AND DRIVING TIME MAP ON PAGES 286–287 / VOIR AUSSI CARTE DES DISTANCES ET DES TEMPS DE PARCOURS PAGES 286–287

British Columbia
Alberta Sask.

0 mi 20 40 60
0 km 20 40 60 80
One inch equals 40.3 miles/Un pouce équivaut à 40.3 milles
One centimeter equals 25.4 km/Un cm équivaut à 25.4 km

Go to 155

Go to 155

Go to 157

Go to 164

Paddle Prairie · Buffalo Head Prairie · Carcajou · Keg River · Wadlin Lake · Mikkwa · Talbot Lake · Hotchkiss · Notikewin · Manning · North Star · Deadwood · Dixonville · Cadotte Lake · Little Buffalo · Red Earth Creek · Loon Lake · Peerless Lake · Trout Lake · Gods Lake · Peace River · St. Isidore · Grimshaw · Berwyn · Brownvale · Whitelaw · Marie-Reine · Nampa · Reno · Atikameg · Gift Lake · Marten Beach · Worsley · Eureka River · Hines Creek · Fairview · Historic Dunvegan · Bluesky · Jean Côté · Donnelly · McLennan · Grouard · High Prairie · Kinuso · Widewater · Slave Lake

Beatton River · Prespatou · Altona · Buick · Wonowon · Pink Mountain · Montney · North Pine · Goodlow · Cleardale · Bear Canyon · Cherry Point · Spirit River · Rycroft · Wanham · Eaglesham · Girouxville · Falher · Kathleen · Guy · Enilda · Joussard · Driftpile · Faust

Fort St. John · Taylor · Baldonnel · Charlie Lake · Hudson's Hope · Moberly Lake · Groundbirch · Chetwynd · Dawson Creek · Pouce Coupe · Rolla · Farmington · Blueberry Mountain · Dunvegan · Woking · Sexsmith · Clairmont · Bezanson · DeBolt · Crooked Creek · Valleyview · Sunset House · Little Smoky · Fox Creek · Whitecourt · Blue Ridge · Barrhead

Lone Prairie · Tumbler Ridge · Hythe · Buffalo Lake · Goodfare · Beaverlodge · Huallen · Elmworth · Wembley · Grande Prairie · O'Brien Prov. Park · Nitehawk · Sturgeon Heights · Williamson Prov. Park · Swan Hills · Fort Assiniboine · Mayerthorpe · Sangudo · Barrhead

Upper Fraser · Sinclair Mills · Longworth · Penny · Dome Creek · Grande Cache · Silver Summit · Carson-Pegasus Prov. Park · Carrot Creek · MacKay · Evansburg · Edson · Marlboro · Peers · Niton Junction · Nojack · Entwistle · Seba Beach

Wells · Barkerville · McBride · Crescent Spur · Dunster · Tête Jaune Cache · Valemount · Jasper · Hinton · Brûlé · Pocahontas · Robb · Cadomin · Drayton Valley · Lodgepole · Cynthia · Rocky Rapids · Breton · Warburg

ROCKY MOUNTAINS · JASPER NATIONAL PARK · WILLMORE WILDERNESS PARK · KAKWA WILDLAND PROV. PARK

Go to 164

British
Columbia Alberta Sask.

DRIVING DISTANCES IN KM / DISTANCES ROUTIÈRES EN KM

	DAWSON CREEK, BC	EDMONTON, AB	FORT McMURRAY, AB	GRANDE PRAIRIE, AB	JASPER, AB	LLOYDMINSTER, AB/SK	MEADOW LAKE, SK	N. BATTLEFORD, SK	PEACE RIVER, AB	SLAVE LAKE, AB	VALEMOUNT, BC	WHITECOURT, AB
EDMONTON, AB	597		439	462	367	238	415	375	484	251	488	177
GRANDE PRAIRIE, AB	124	462	756		397	700	824	837	197	318	521	279
JASPER, AB	521	367	796	397		605	782	742	578	464	121	271
N. BATTLEFORD, SK	972	375	814	837	742	137	158		866	633	863	559

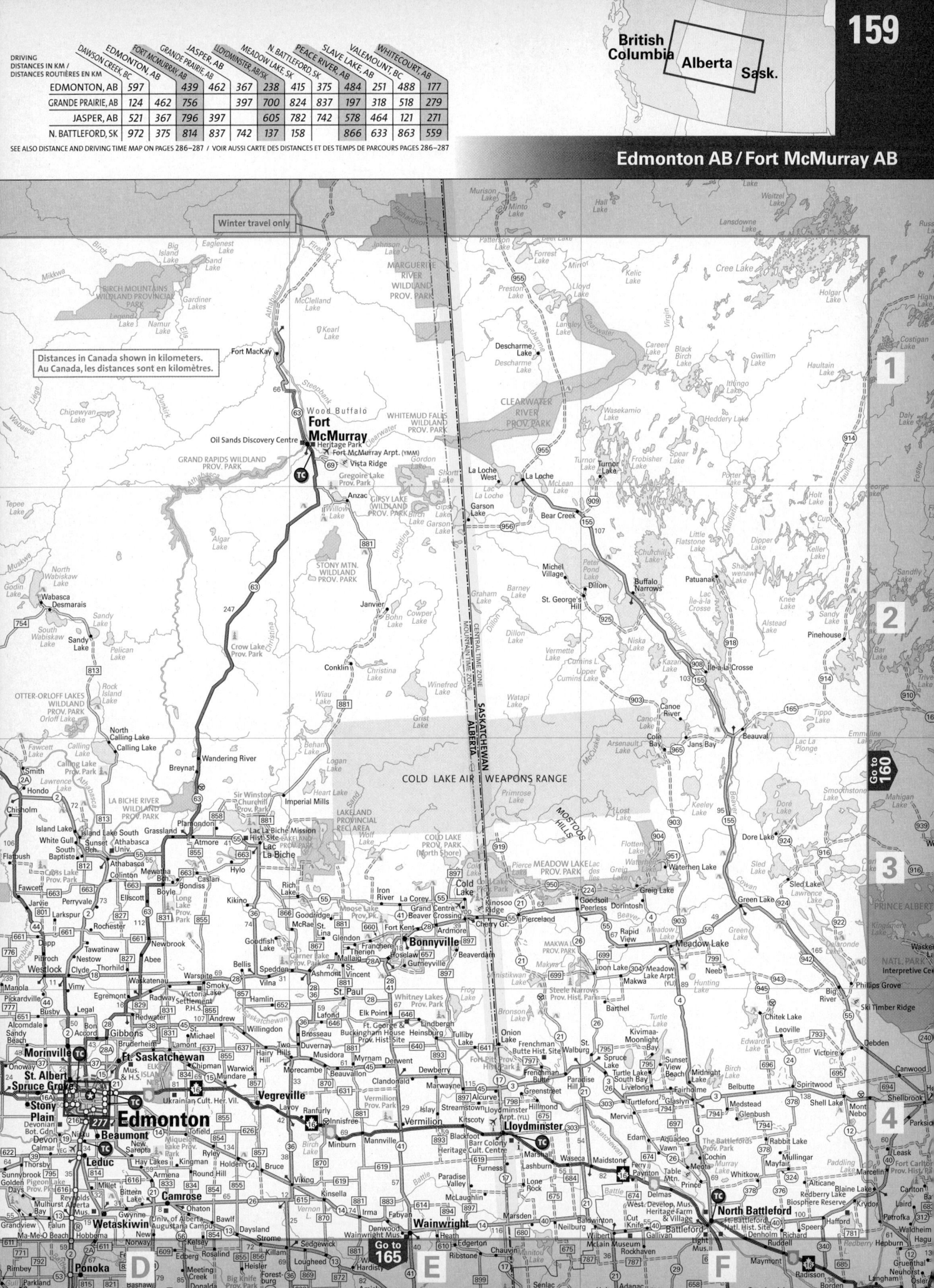

Distances in Canada shown in kilometers.
Au Canada, les distances sont en kilomètres.

Winter travel only

Alberta Sask. Manitoba

Ontario

0 mi 20 40 60

0 km 20 40 60 80

One inch equals 40.3 miles/Un pouce équivaut à 40.3 milles
One centimeter equals 25.4 km/Un cm équivaut à 25.4 km

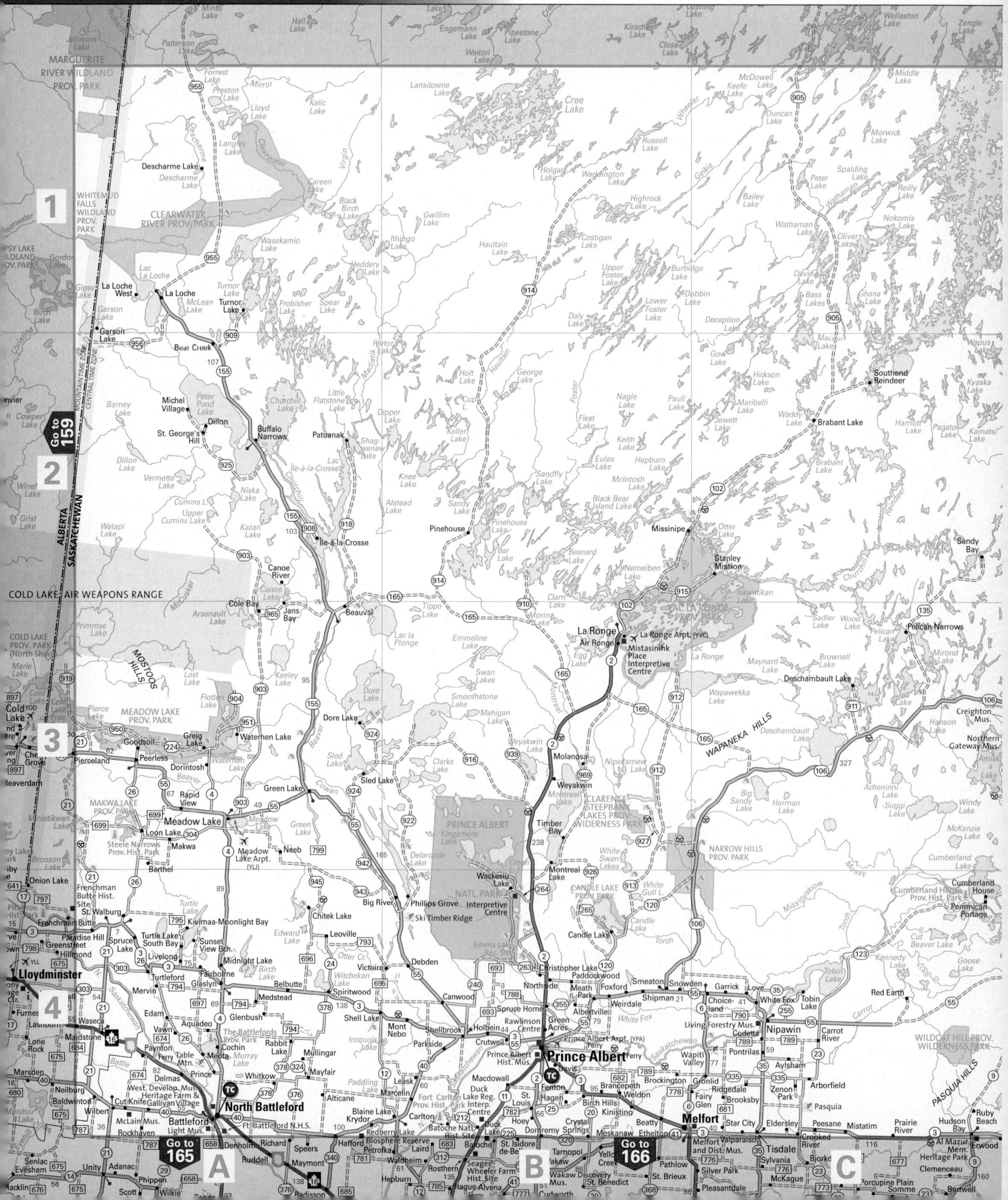

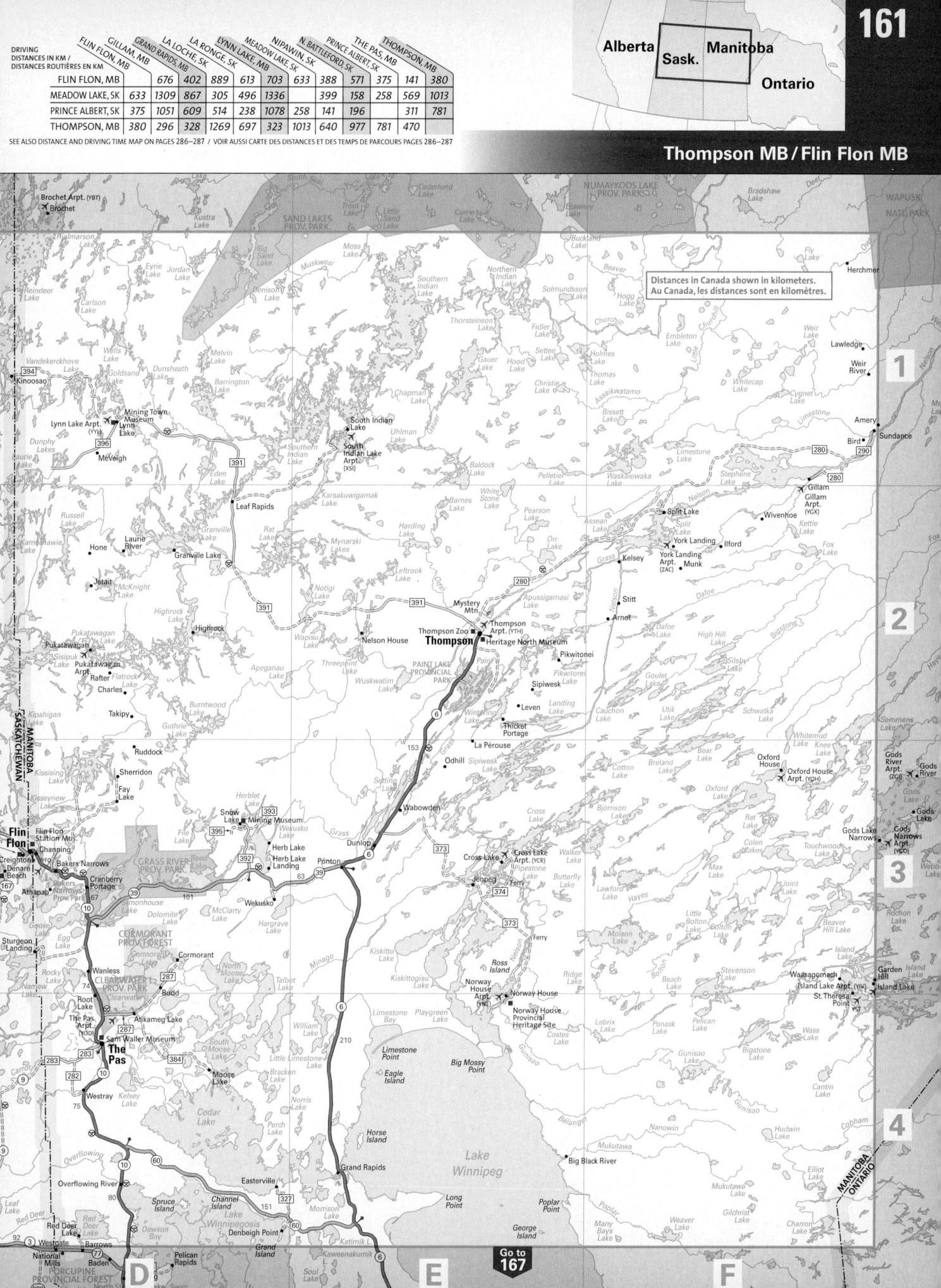

Alberta | Sask. | Manitoba
Ontario

DRIVING DISTANCES IN KM / DISTANCES ROUTIÈRES EN KM	FLIN FLON, MB	GILLAM, MB	GRAND RAPIDS, MB	LA LOCHE, SK	LA RONGE, SK	LYNN LAKE, MB	MEADOW LAKE, SK	NIPAWIN, SK	N. BATTLEFORD, SK	PRINCE ALBERT, SK	THE PAS, MB	THOMPSON, MB
FLIN FLON, MB		676	402	889	613	703	633	388	571	375	141	380
MEADOW LAKE, SK	633	1309	867	305	496	1336		399	158	258	569	1013
PRINCE ALBERT, SK	375	1051	609	514	238	1078	258	141	196		311	781
THOMPSON, MB	380	296	328	1269	697	323	1013	640	977	781	470	

Distances in Canada shown in kilometers.
Au Canada, les distances sont en kilomètres.

D   E   F

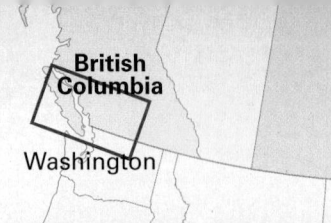

British Columbia
Washington

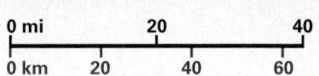

0 mi | 20 | 40
0 km | 20 | 40 | 60

One inch equals 25.4 miles/Un pouce équivaut à 25.4 milles
One cm equals 16.1 km/Un cm équivaut à 16.1 km

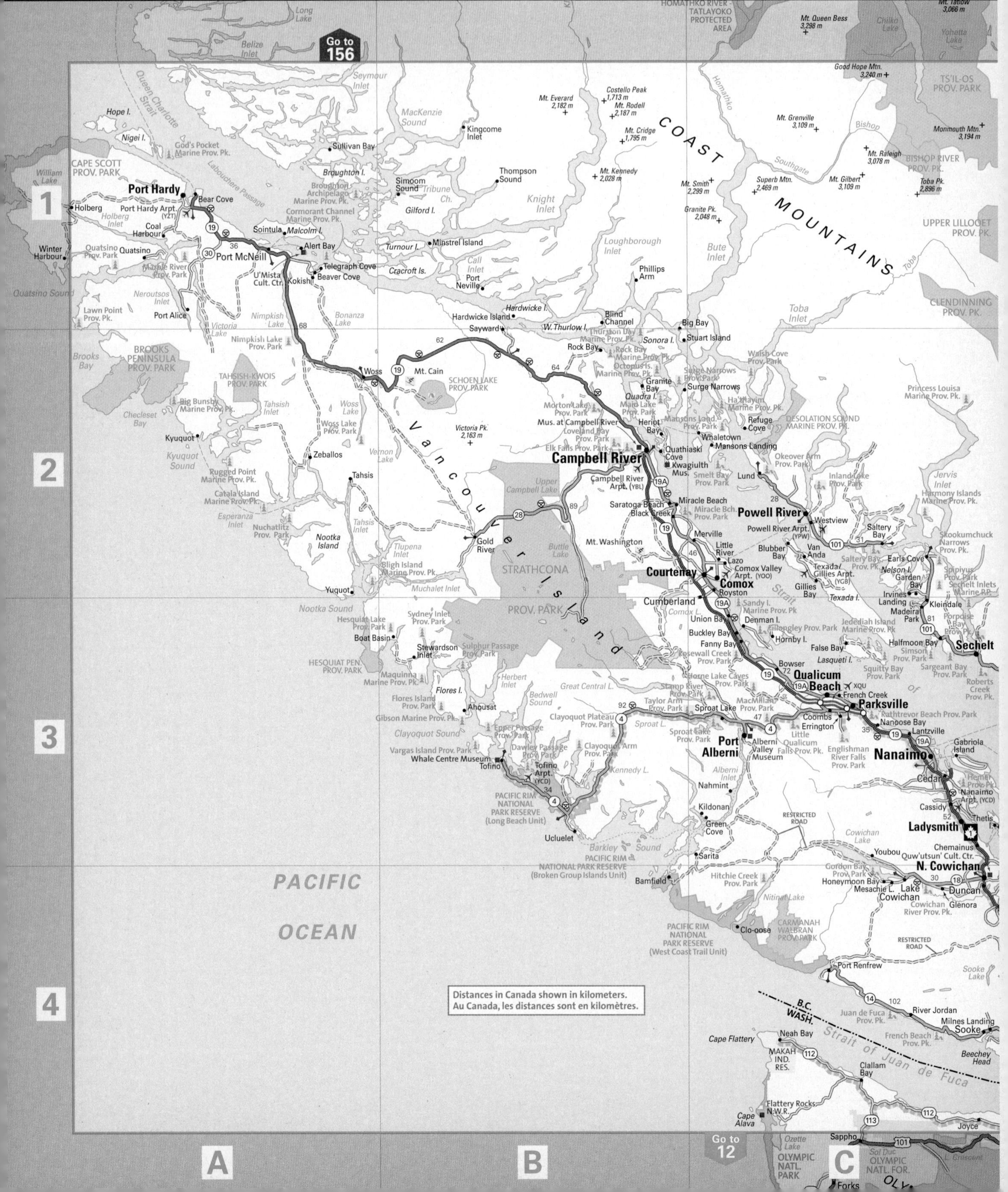

Nanaimo BC / Campbell River BC

Go to 156

Distances in Canada shown in kilometers.
Au Canada, les distances sont en kilomètres.

PACIFIC

OCEAN

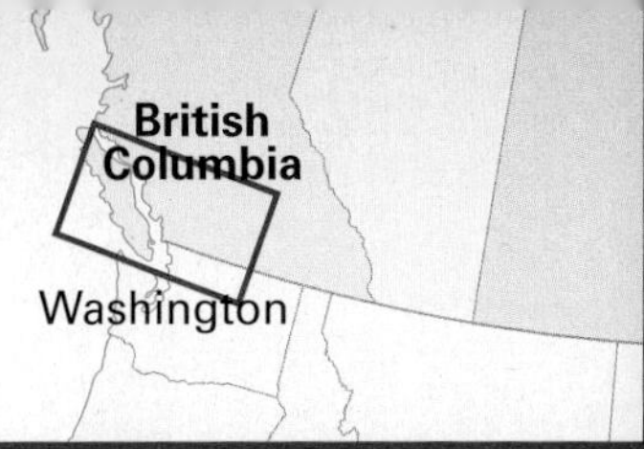

British Columbia

Washington

DRIVING DISTANCES IN KM / DISTANCES ROUTIÈRES EN KM	CAMPBELL RIVER, BC	KAMLOOPS, BC	KELOWNA, BC	MERRITT, BC	NANAIMO, BC	OSOYOOS, BC	PORT ALBERNI, BC	PORT HARDY, BC	SALMON ARM, BC	VANCOUVER, BC	VICTORIA, BC	WHISTLER, BC
KAMLOOPS, BC	512		163	87	363	231	441	750	108	355	393	475
NANAIMO, BC	153	363	403	279		404	82	391	471	23	113	104
VANCOUVER, BC	172	355	395	271	23	396	101	410	463		69	123
VICTORIA, BC	266	393	433	309	113	434	195	504	501	69		192

SEE ALSO DISTANCE AND DRIVING TIME MAP ON PAGES 286–287 / VOIR AUSSI CARTE DES DISTANCES ET DES TEMPS DE PARCOURS PAGES 286–287

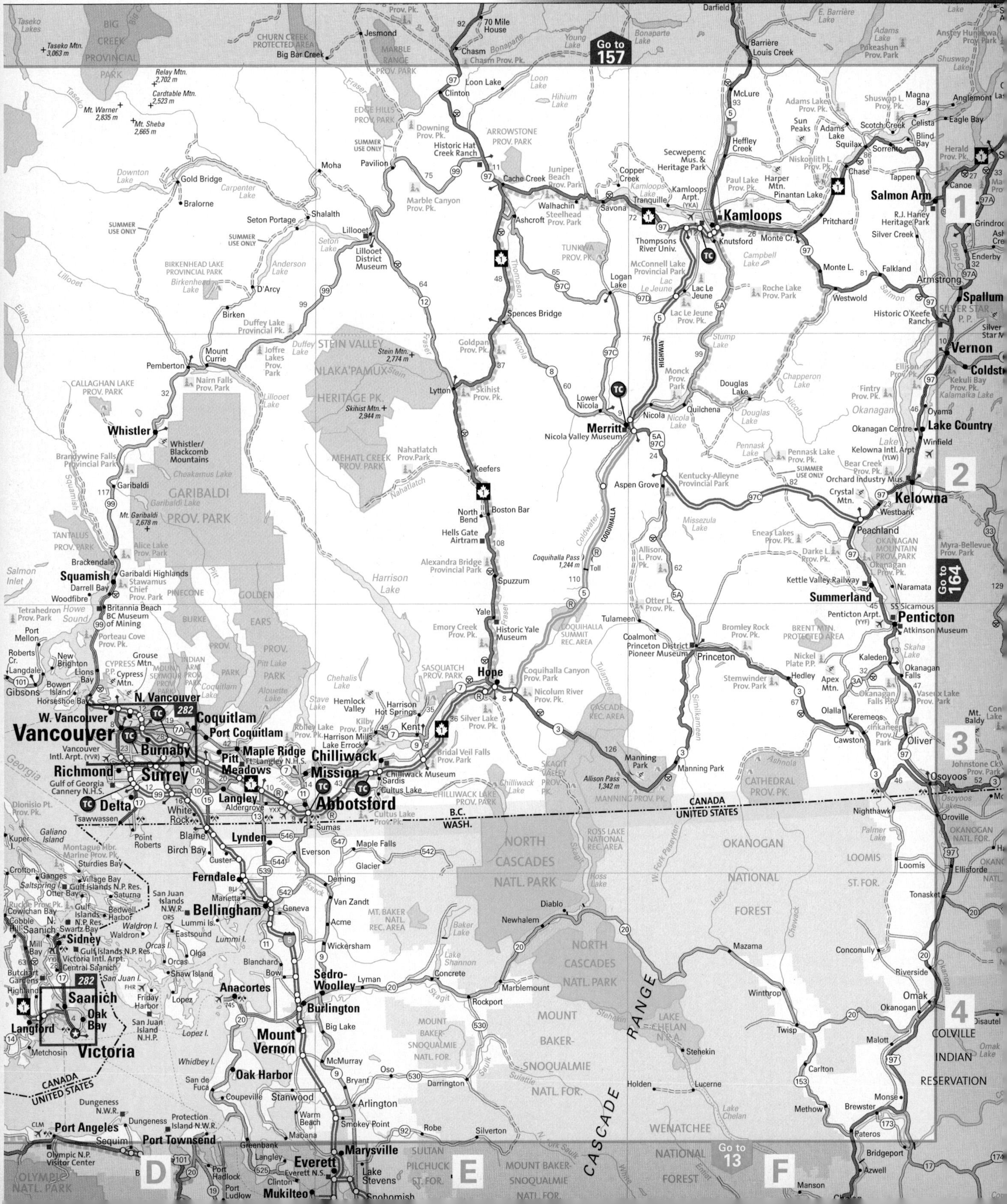

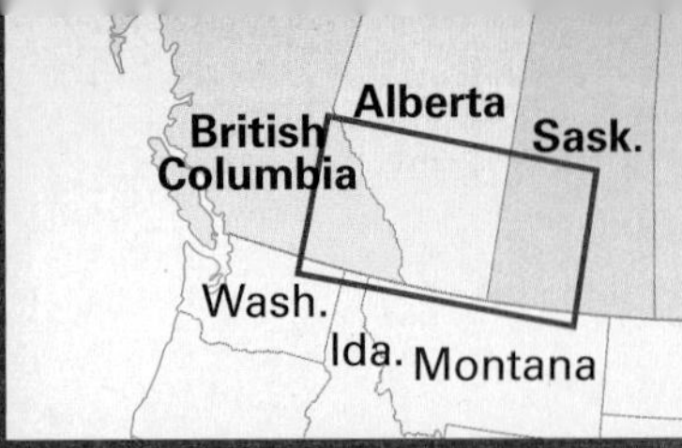

British Columbia · Alberta · Sask.

Wash.

Ida. Montana

0 mi 20 40 60

0 km 20 40 60 80

One inch equals 40.3 miles/Un pouce équivaut à 40.3 milles
One centimeter equals 25.4 km/Un cm équivaut à 25.4 km

Calgary AB / Banff AB

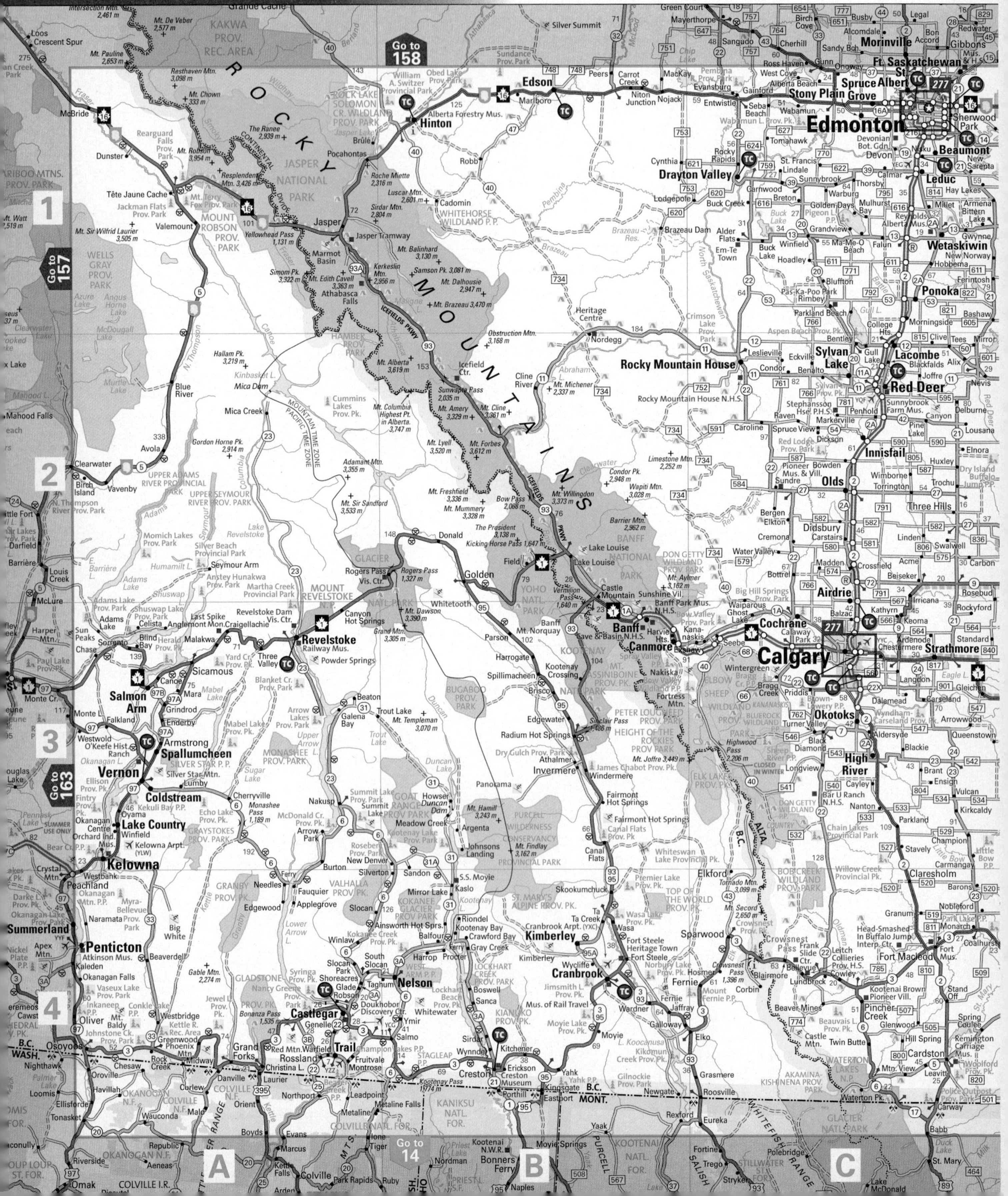

Go to 158
Go to 157
Go to 163
Go to 14

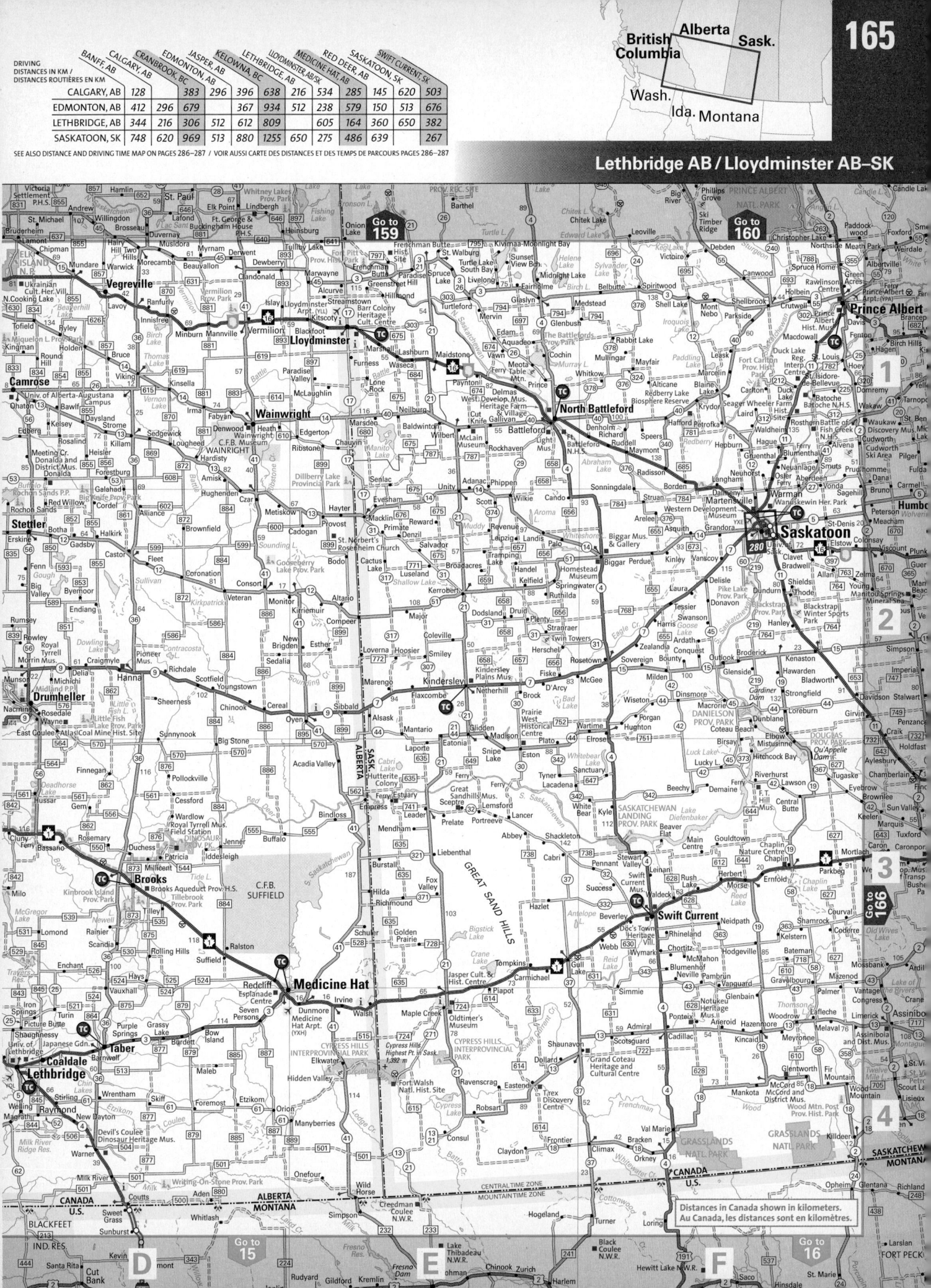

DRIVING DISTANCES IN KM / DISTANCES ROUTIÈRES EN KM	BANFF, AB	CALGARY, AB	CRANBROOK, BC	EDMONTON, AB	JASPER, AB	KELOWNA, BC	LETHBRIDGE, AB	LLOYDMINSTER, AB/SK	MEDICINE HAT, AB	RED DEER, AB	SASKATOON, SK	SWIFT CURRENT, SK
CALGARY, AB	128		383	296	396	638	216	534	285	145	620	503
EDMONTON, AB	412	296	679		367	934	512	238	579	150	513	676
LETHBRIDGE, AB	344	216	306	512	612	809		605	164	360	650	382
SASKATOON, SK	748	620	969	513	880	1255	650	275	486	639		267

Sask. Manitoba

Ontario

Montana   N.D.   Minn.

Saskatoon SK / Regina SK

0 mi · 20 · 40 · 60
0 km 20 · 40 · 60 · 80
One inch equals 40.3 miles/Un pouce équivaut à 40.3 milles
One centimeter equals 25.4 km/Un cm équivaut à 25.4 km

Go to 160
Go to 165
Go to 17
Go to 18

A   B   C

1   2   3   4

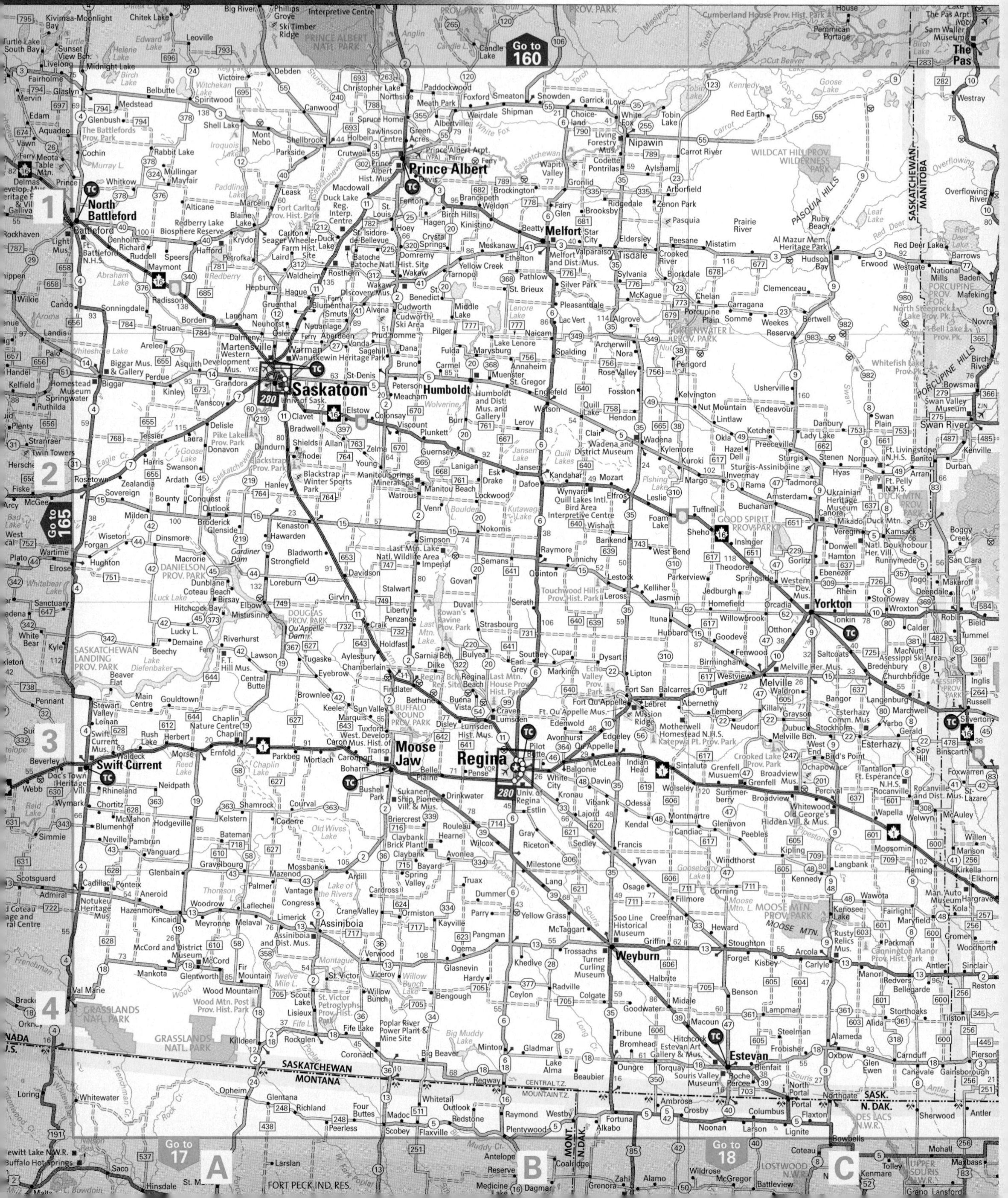

DRIVING DISTANCES IN KM / DISTANCES ROUTIÈRES EN KM	BRANDON, MB	DAUPHIN, MB	GRAND RAPIDS, MB	MOOSE JAW, SK	PORTAGE LA PRAIRIE, MB	PRINCE ALBERT, SK	REGINA, SK	SASKATOON, SK	SWIFT CURRENT, SK	THE PAS, MB	WINNIPEG, MB	YORKTON, SK
BRANDON, MB		166	525	448	134	745	377	639	618	570	216	270
REGINA, SK	377	366	787	68	511	368		261	241	557	593	195
SASKATOON, SK	639	502	689	224	691	141	261		267	578	773	331
WINNIPEG, MB	216	322	430	664	82	819	593	773	834	611		442

SEE ALSO DISTANCE AND DRIVING TIME MAP ON PAGES 286–287 / VOIR AUSSI CARTE DES DISTANCES ET DES TEMPS DE PARCOURS PAGES 286–287

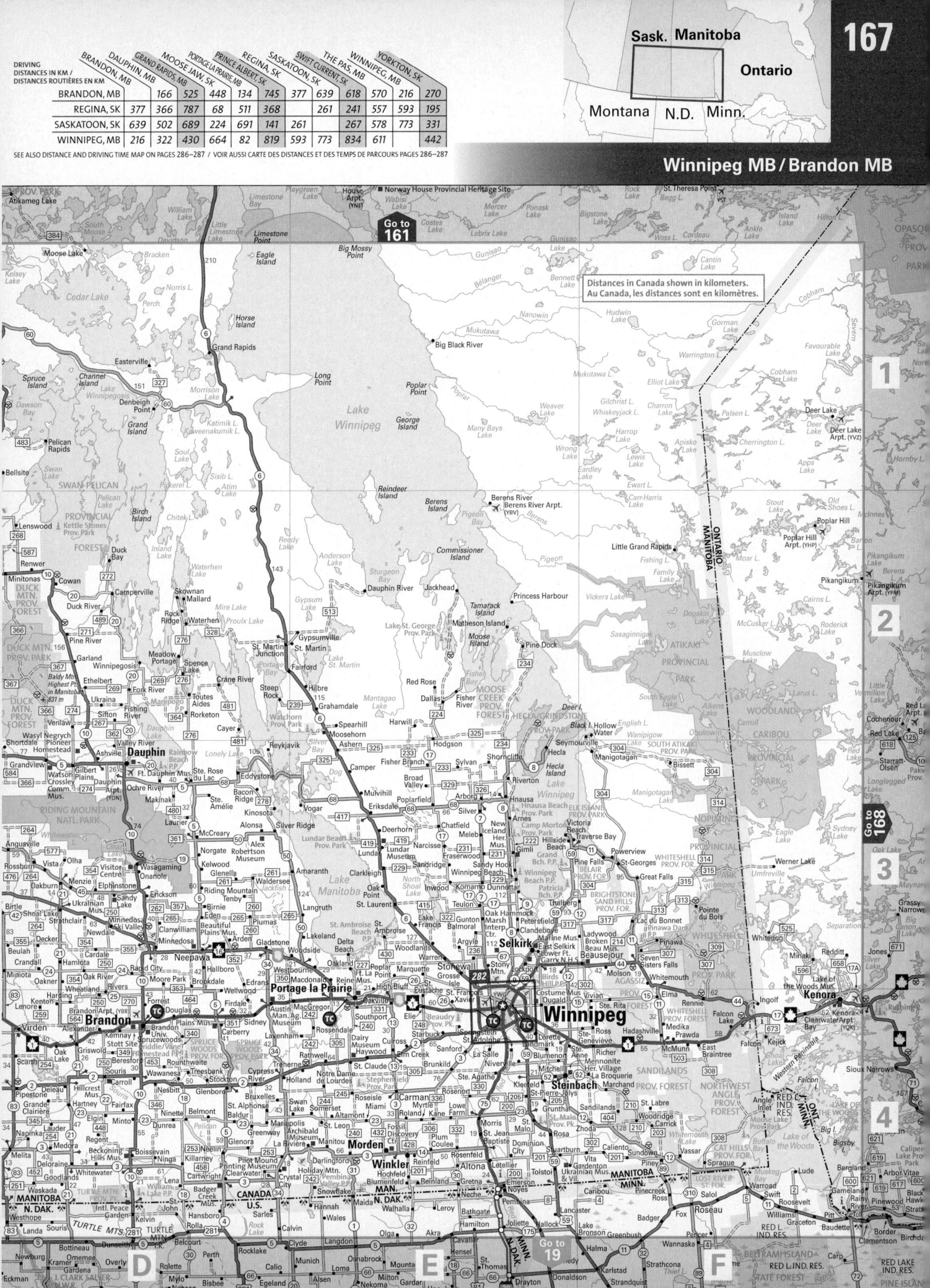

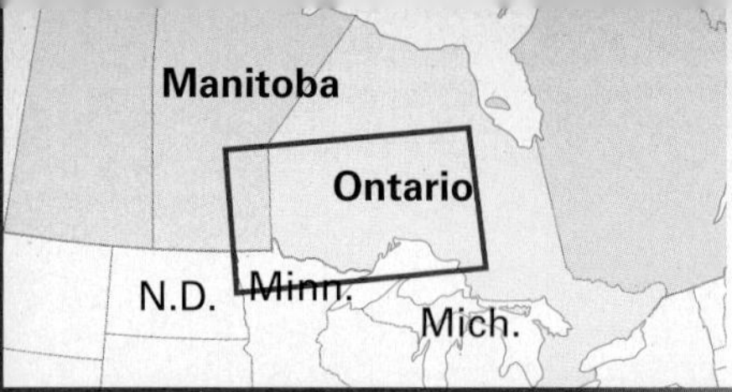

0 mi 20 40 60

0 km 20 40 60 80

One inch equals 40.3 miles/Un pouce équivaut à 40.3 milles
One centimeter equals 25.4 km/Un cm équivaut à 25.4 km

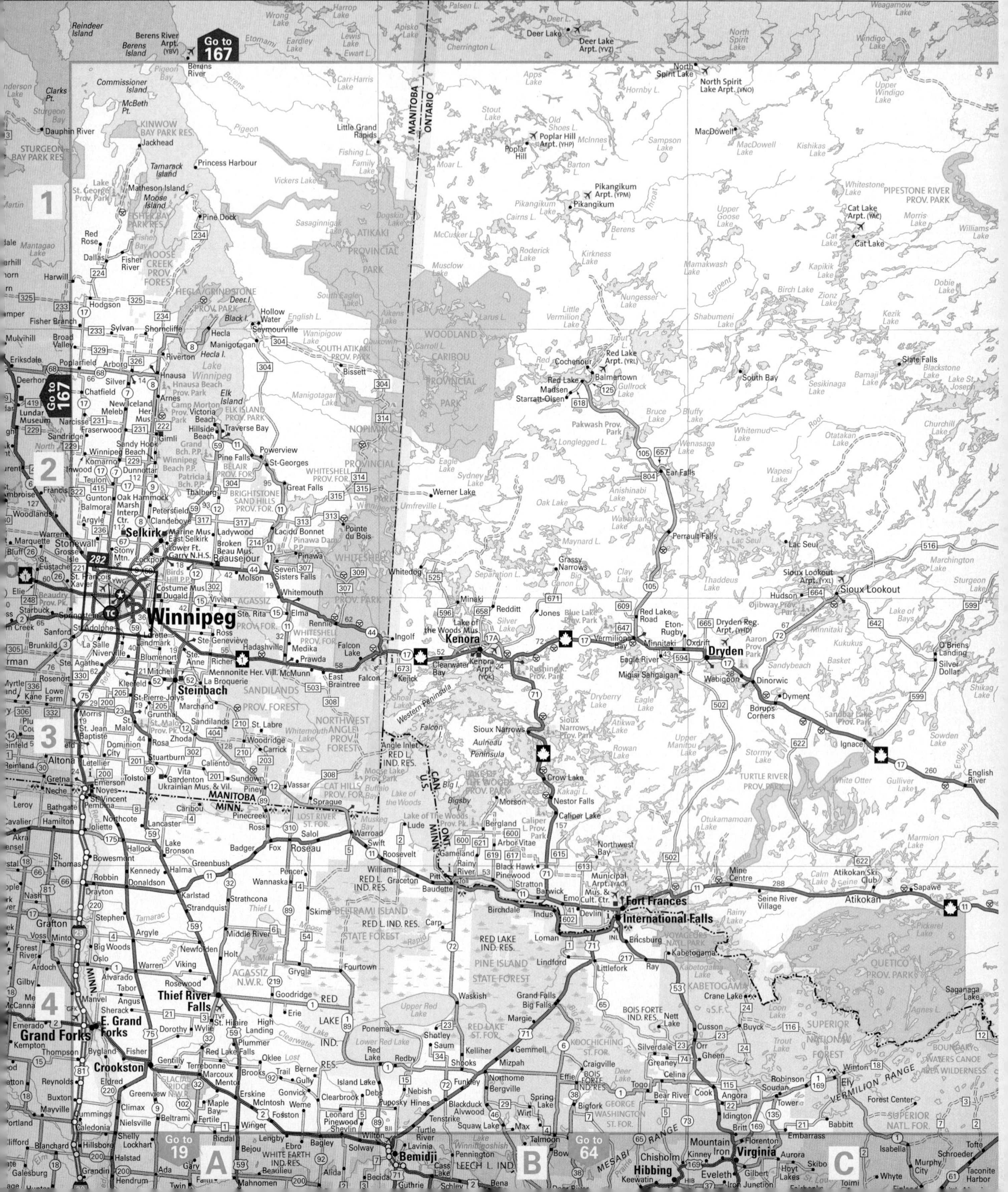

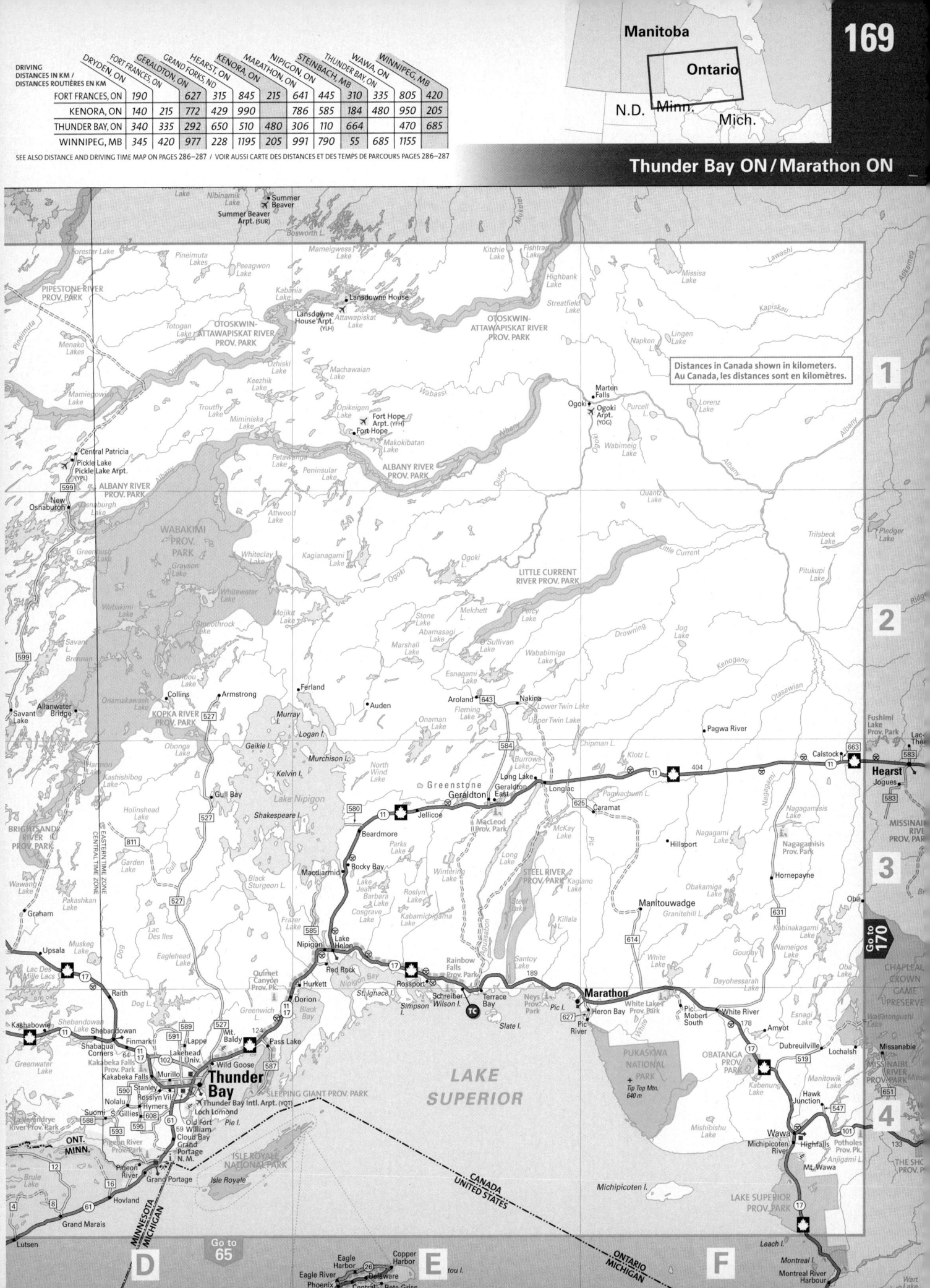

Manitoba

Ontario

N.D. Minn. Mich.

DRIVING
DISTANCES IN KM /
DISTANCES ROUTIÈRES EN KM

	DRYDEN, ON	FORT FRANCES, ON	GERALDTON, ON	GRAND FORKS, ND	HEARST, ON	KENORA, ON	MARATHON, ON	NIPIGON, ON	STEINBACH, MB	THUNDER BAY, ON	WAWA, ON	WINNIPEG, MB
FORT FRANCES, ON	190		627	315	845	215	641	445	310	335	805	420
KENORA, ON	140	215	772	429	990		786	585	184	480	950	205
THUNDER BAY, ON	340	335	292	650	510	480	306	110	664		470	685
WINNIPEG, MB	345	420	977	228	1195	205	991	790	55	685	1155	

SEE ALSO DISTANCE AND DRIVING TIME MAP ON PAGES 286–287 / VOIR AUSSI CARTE DES DISTANCES ET DES TEMPS DE PARCOURS PAGES 286–287

Distances in Canada shown in kilometers.
Au Canada, les distances sont en kilomètres.

Ontario   Québec

Mich.   N.Y.

0 mi   20   40   60
0 km 20   40   60   80

One inch equals 40.3 miles/Un pouce équivaut à 40.3 milles
One centimeter equals 25.4 km/Un cm équivaut à 25.4 km

Go to 169

Distances in Canada shown in kilometers.
Au Canada, les distances sont en kilomètres.

ONTARIO / MICHIGAN

CANADA / UNITED STATES

LAKE SUPERIOR

LAKE MICHIGAN

LAKE HURON

Georgian Bay

Sault Ste. Marie

Sudbury

Timmins

Kapuskasing

Hearst

Iroquois Falls

Cochrane

Marathon

Wawa

Chapleau

Elliot Lake

Espanola

Blind River

Manitoulin Island

Escanaba

Gladstone

Manistique

Munising

Newberry

St. Ignace

Cheboygan

Petoskey

Traverse City

Gaylord

Alpena

Go to 169

Go to 65

Go to 70

Go to 172

PUKASKWA NATIONAL PARK

LAKE SUPERIOR PROV. PARK

CHAPLEAU CROWN GAME PRESERVE

Manitoulin Island

BRUCE PENINSULA NATL. PARK

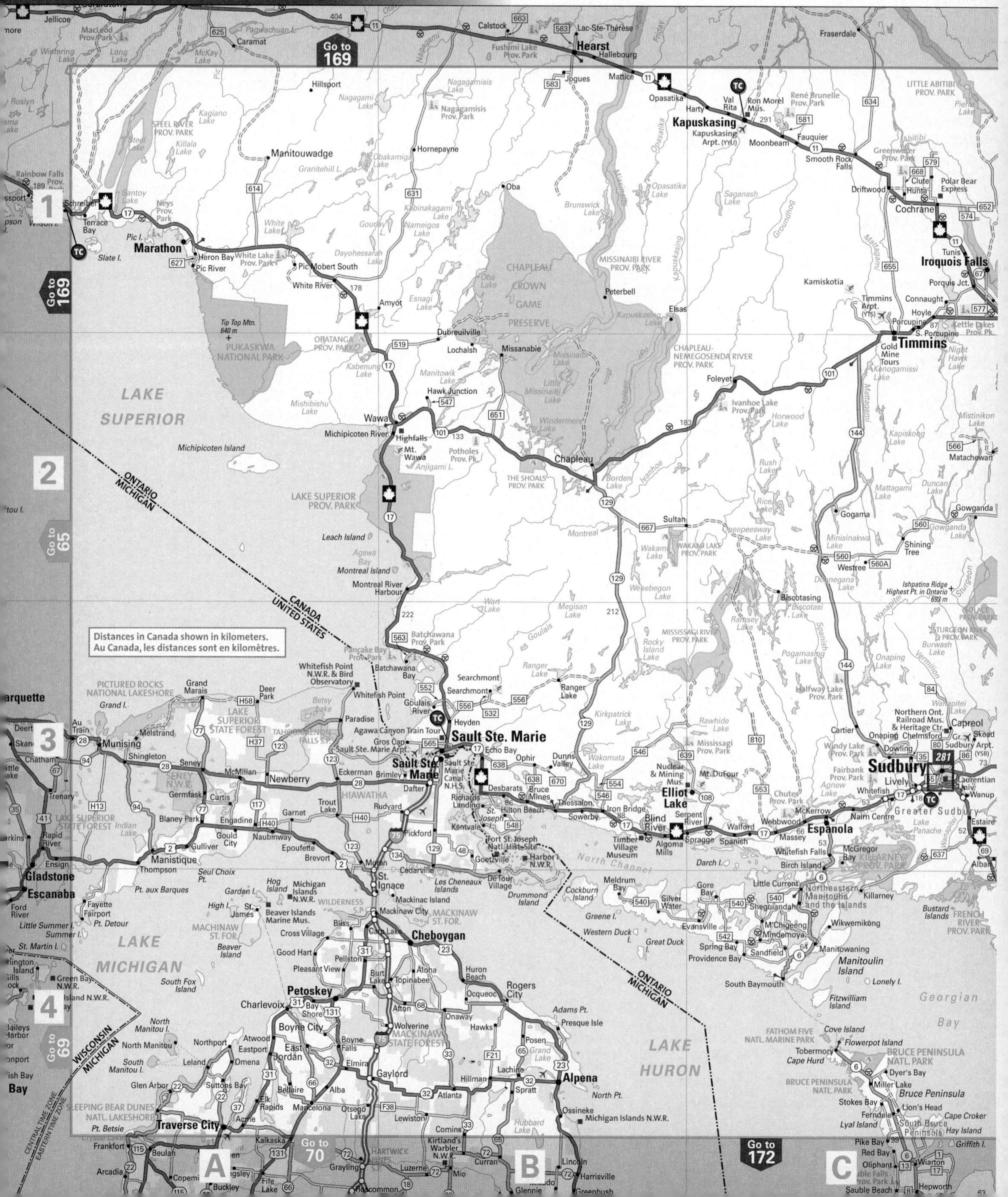

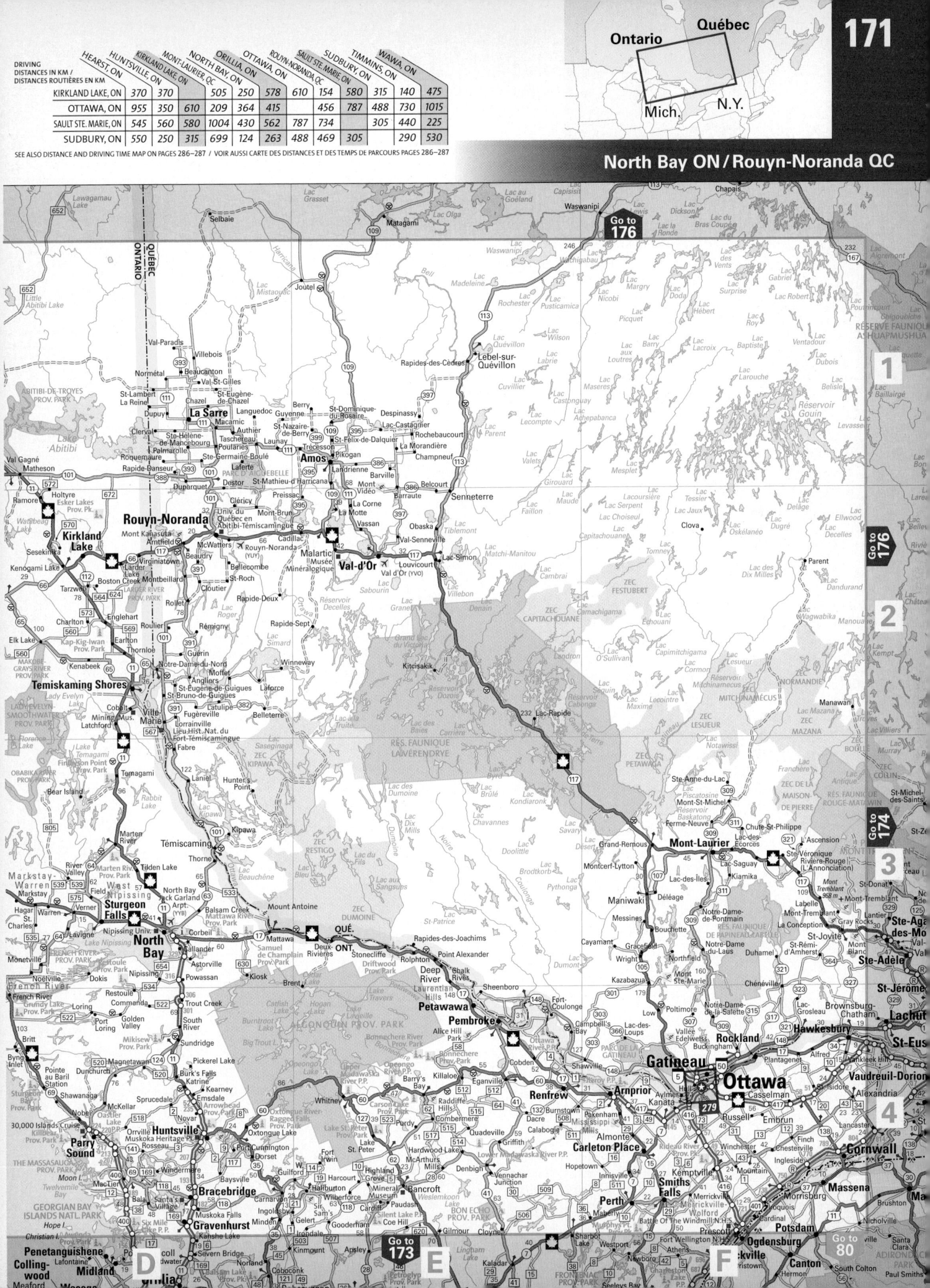

Ontario   Québec

Mich.   N.Y.

DRIVING
DISTANCES IN KM /
DISTANCES ROUTIÈRES EN KM

	HEARST, ON	HUNTSVILLE, ON	KIRKLAND LAKE, ON	MONT-LAURIER, QC	NORTH BAY, ON	ORILLIA, ON	OTTAWA, ON	ROUYN-NORANDA, QC	SAULT STE. MARIE, ON	SUDBURY, ON	TIMMINS, ON	WAWA, ON	
KIRKLAND LAKE, ON	370	370		505	250	578	610	154	580	315	140	475	
OTTAWA, ON	955	350	610	209	364	415		456	787	488	730	1015	
SAULT STE. MARIE, ON	545	560	580	1004	562	209	787	734		305	440	225	
SUDBURY, ON	550	250	315	699	124	263	488	469	305		290	530	

SEE ALSO DISTANCE AND DRIVING TIME MAP ON PAGES 286–287 / VOIR AUSSI CARTE DES DISTANCES ET DES TEMPS DE PARCOURS PAGES 286–287

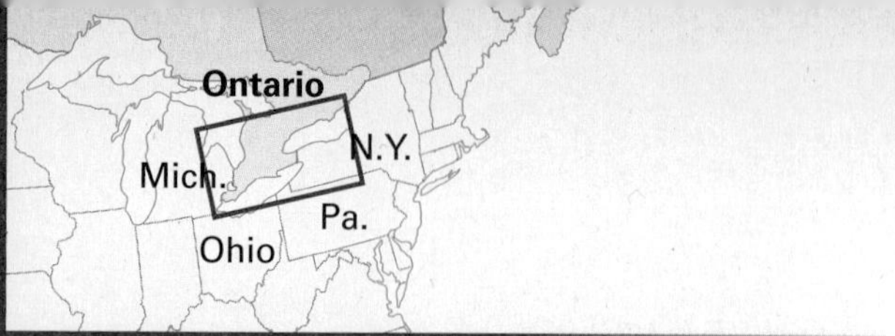

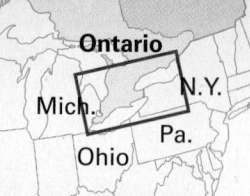

Ontario
Mich.
N.Y.
Ohio
Pa.

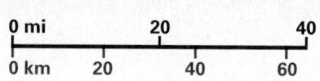

0 mi   20   40
0 km 20   40   60
One inch equals 25.4 miles/Un pouce équivaut à 25.4 milles
One cm equals 16.1 km/Un cm équivaut à 16.1 km

London ON / Windsor ON

Go to 170

Distances in Canada shown in kilometers.
Au Canada, les distances sont en kilomètres.

LAKE HURON

LAKE ST. CLAIR

LAKE ERIE

Georgian Bay

Go to 90

Go to 91

A   B   C

Ontario
Mich.   N.Y.
Ohio   Pa.

SEE ALSO DISTANCE AND DRIVING TIME MAP ON PAGES 286–287 / VOIR AUSSI CARTE DES DISTANCES ET DES TEMPS DE PARCOURS PAGES 286–287

Ontario Québec Me.
N.Y. N.H. Vermont

Ottawa ON / Montréal QC

0 mi — 20 — 40
0 km — 20 — 40 — 60
One inch equals 25.4 miles/Un pouce équivaut à 25.4 milles
One cm equals 16.1 km/Un cm équivaut à 16.1 km

Go to **171**
Go to **176**

1
2
3
4

Go to **171**

QUÉBEC
ONTARIO

Distances in Canada shown in kilometers.
Au Canada, les distances sont en kilomètres.

RÉSERVE FAUNIQUE LA VÉRENDRYE

ZEC MITCHINAMÉCUS
ZEC NORMANDIE
ZEC LESUEUR
ZEC PETAWAGA
ZEC MAZANA
ZEC BOULLÉ
ZEC DE LA MAISON-DE-PIERRE
RÉSERVE FAUNIQUE ROUGE-MATAWIN
PARC DU MONT-TREMBLANT
RÉS. FAUNIQUE DE PAPINEAU-LABELLE
ZEC DES NYMPHES

Mont-Laurier
Maniwaki
Gatineau
Ottawa
Nepean
Kanata
Renfrew
Arnprior
Pembroke
Carleton Place
Perth
Smiths Falls
Brockville
Gananoque
Napanee
Kingston

Rockland
Hawkesbury
Lachute
St-Jérôme
Ste-Agathe-des-Monts
Ste-Adèle
Mont-Tremblant
St-Jovite
Joliette
Terrebonne
Laval
Montréal
Longueuil
Blainville
St-Eustache
Vaudreuil-Dorion
Châteauguay
Salaberry-de-Valleyfield
Cornwall
Massena
Malone
Plattsburgh
Potsdam
Canton
Ogdensburg
Saranac Lake

ADIRONDACK PARK

Go to **80**

A   **B**   **C**

Go to **173**

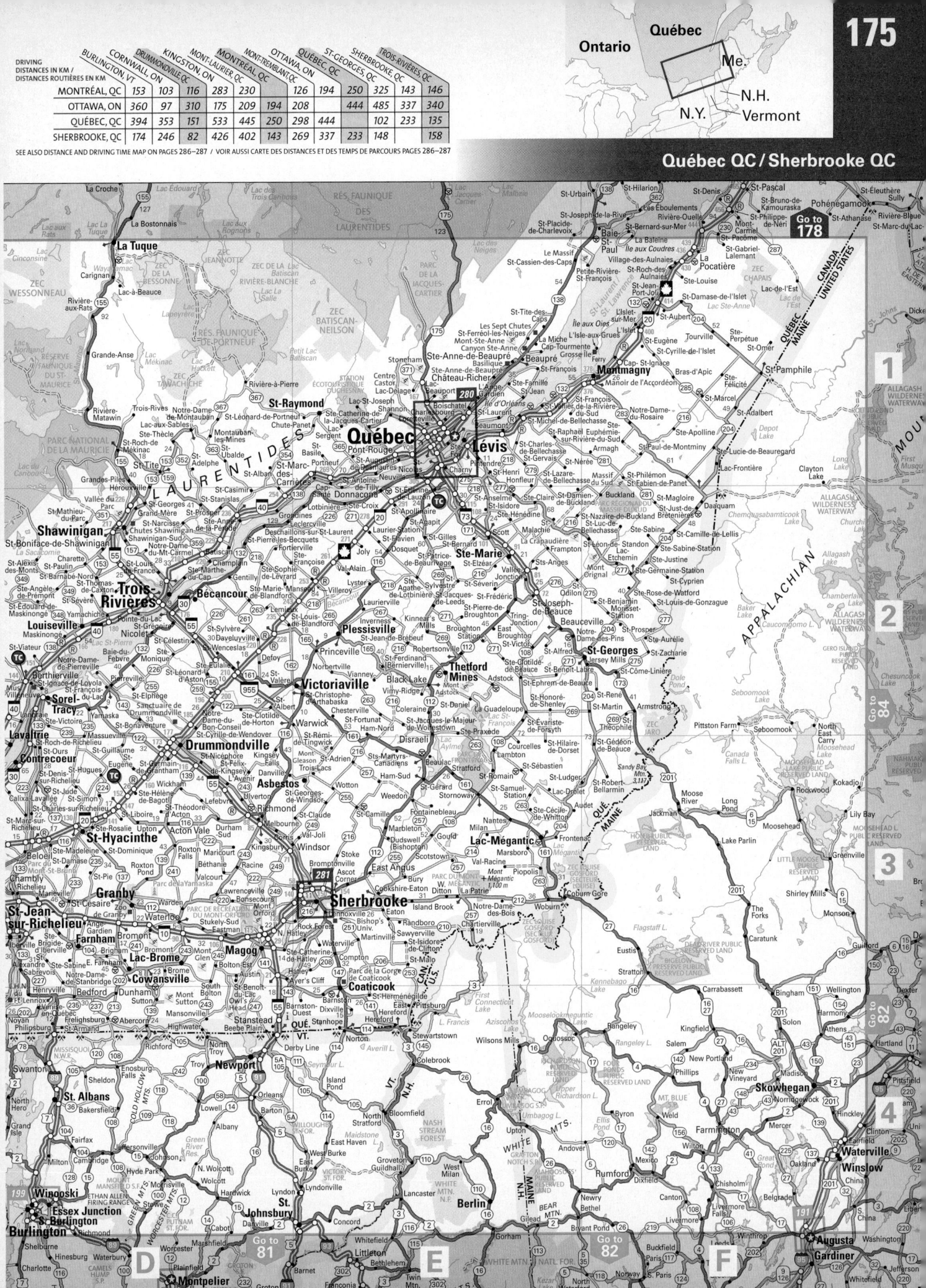

DRIVING DISTANCES IN KM /
DISTANCES ROUTIÈRES EN KM

	BURLINGTON, VT	CORNWALL, ON	DRUMMONDVILLE, QC	KINGSTON, ON	MONT-LAURIER, QC	MONT-TREMBLANT, QC	OTTAWA, ON	QUÉBEC, QC	ST-GEORGES, QC	SHERBROOKE, QC	TROIS-RIVIÈRES, QC
MONTRÉAL, QC	153	103	116	283	230	126	194	250	325	143	146
OTTAWA, ON	360	97	310	175	209	194		208	444	485	337	340
QUÉBEC, QC	394	353	151	533	445	250	298	444		102	233	135
SHERBROOKE, QC	174	246	82	426	402	143	269	337	233		148	158

SEE ALSO DISTANCE AND DRIVING TIME MAP ON PAGES 286–287 / VOIR AUSSI CARTE DES DISTANCES ET DES TEMPS DE PARCOURS PAGES 286–287

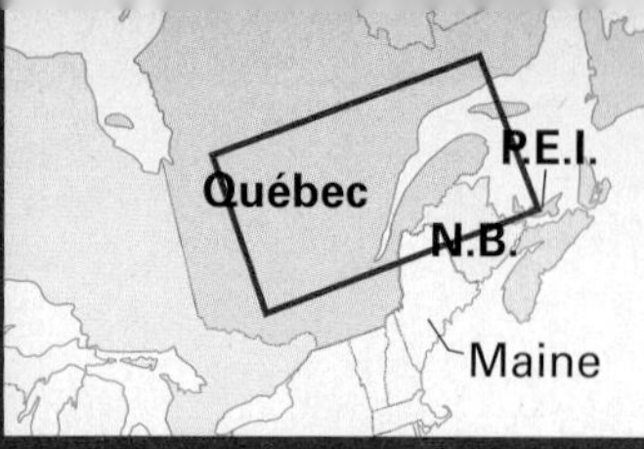

Québec
P.E.I.
N.B.
Maine

0 mi 20 40 60
0 km 20 40 60 80
One inch equals 40.3 miles/Un pouce équivaut à 40.3 milles
One centimeter equals 25.4 km/Un cm équivaut à 25.4 km

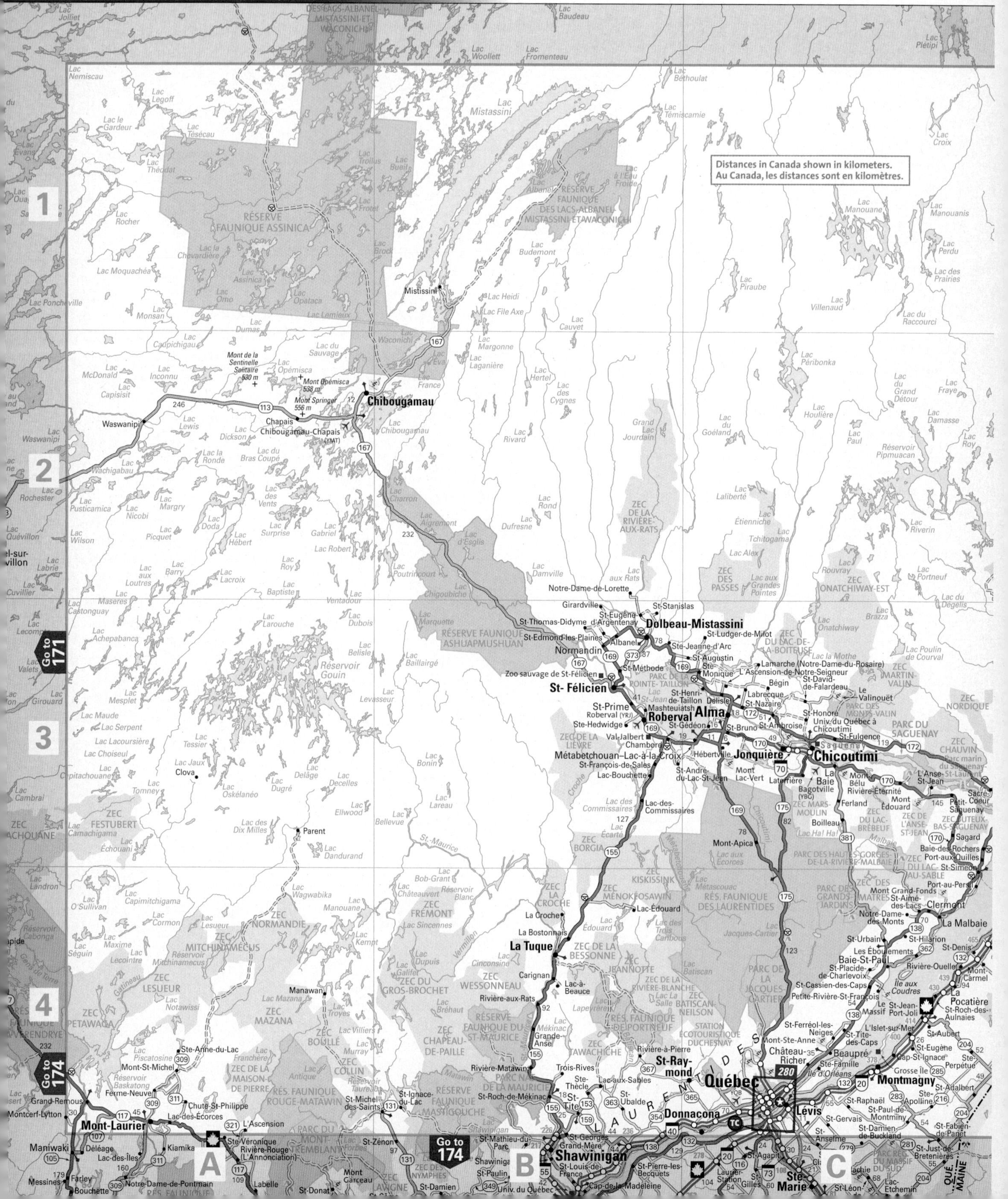

Distances in Canada shown in kilometers.
Au Canada, les distances sont en kilomètres.

Go to 171

Go to 174

Go to 174

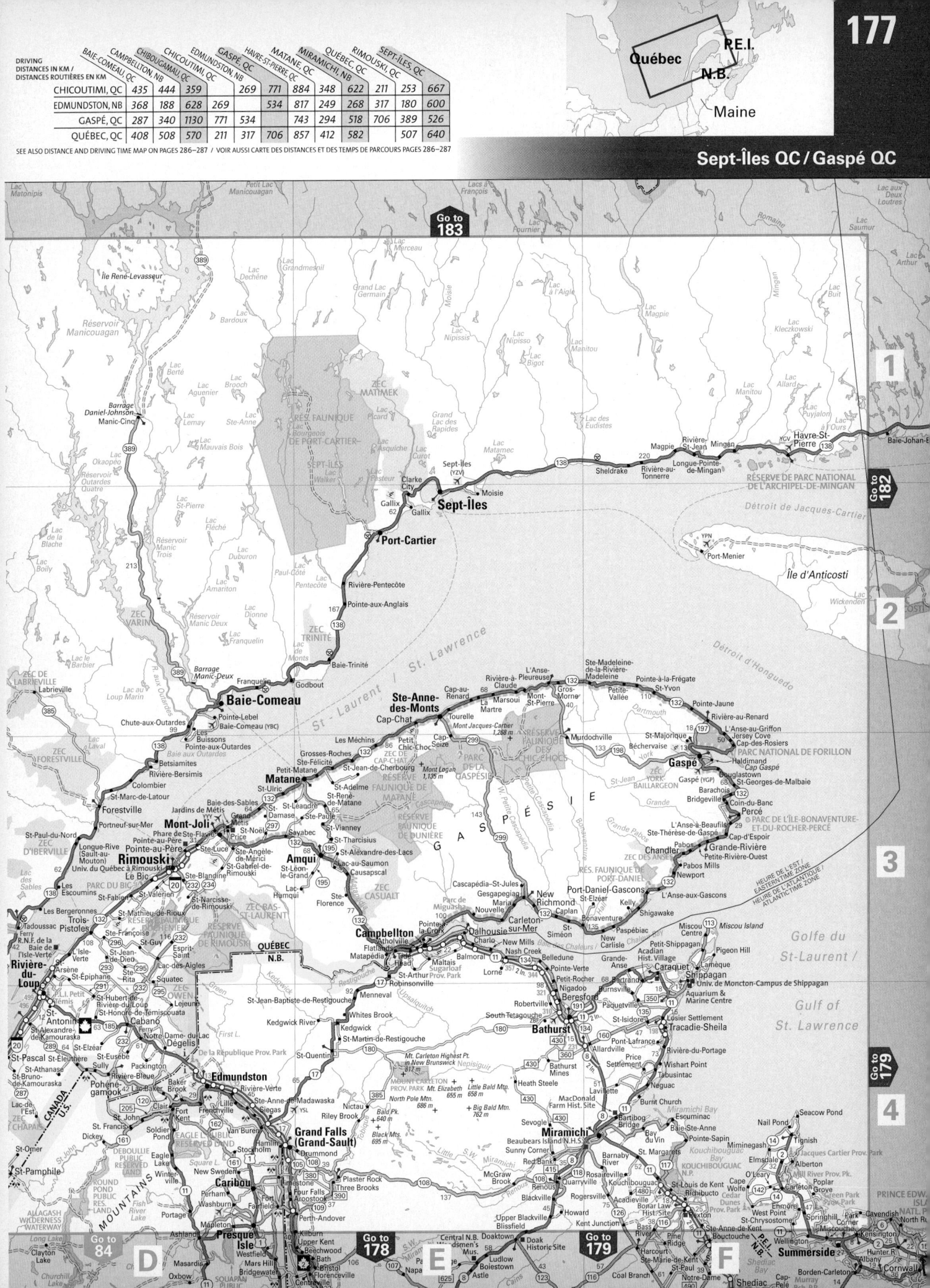

Go to 183
Go to 182
Go to 179
Go to 84
Go to 178
Go to 179

DRIVING DISTANCES IN KM / DISTANCES ROUTIÈRES EN KM	BAIE-COMEAU, QC	CAMPBELLTON, NB	CHIBOUGAMAU, QC	CHICOUTIMI, QC	EDMUNDSTON, NB	GASPÉ, QC	HAVRE-ST-PIERRE, QC	MATANE, QC	MIRAMICHI, NB	QUÉBEC, QC	RIMOUSKI, QC	SEPT-ÎLES, QC
CHICOUTIMI, QC	435	444	359		269	771	884	348	622	211	253	667
EDMUNDSTON, NB	368	188	628	269		534	817	249	268	317	180	600
GASPÉ, QC	287	340	1130	771	534		743	294	518	706	389	526
QUÉBEC, QC	408	508	570	211	317	706	857	412	582		507	640

SEE ALSO DISTANCE AND DRIVING TIME MAP ON PAGES 286–287 / VOIR AUSSI CARTE DES DISTANCES ET DES TEMPS DE PARCOURS PAGES 286–287

Québec
P.E.I.
N.B.
Maine

0 mi — 20 — 40
0 km — 20 — 40 — 60
One inch equals 25.4 miles/Un pouce équivaut à 25.4 milles
One cm equals 16.1 km/Un cm équivaut à 16.1 km

Go to 177
Go to 176
Go to 175
Go to 84
Go to 85
Go to 180

Baie-Comeau

Pointe-Lebel
Chute-aux-Outardes
Baie-Comeau (YBC)
Les Buissons
Pointe-aux-Outardes
vers/to Sept-Îles
Betsiamites
Rivière-Bersimis
Colombier
St-Marc-de-Latour
Forestville
Pointe-à-Boisvert
Portneuf-sur-Mer
St-Paul-du-Nord
Longue-Rive (Sault-au-Mouton)
Baie-des-Bacon
Les Escoumins
Les Bergeronnes
Petites-Bergeronnes
Sacré-Cœur
Vieille Chapelle
Tadoussac Ferry
Baie-Ste-Catherine
Trois-Pistoles
Notre-Dame-des-Sept-Douleurs
L'Isle-Verte
St-Éloi
St-Médard
Ste-Françoise
St-Paul-de-la-Croix
St-Arsène
St-Épiphane
St-François-Xavier-de-Viger
St-Hubert-de-Rivière-du-Loup
St-Modeste
St-Antonin
St-Cyprien
Biencourt
Squatec
Lejeune
Auclair
Rivière-du-Loup
Notre-Dame-du-Portage
Chemin-du-Lac
St-Honoré-de-Témiscouata
Fort Ingall
Cabano
St-Juste-du-Lac
Notre-Dame-du-Lac
St-Elzéar
St-Eusèbe
Dégelis
Pohénégamook
Packington
St-Jean-de-la-Lande
St-Marc-du-Lac-Long
Rivière-Bleue
Connors
St-François de Madawaska
Clair
Baker Brook
St-Hilaire
Edmundston
Rivière-Verte
Ste-Anne-de-Madawaska
St-Léonard (St-Léonard)
Siegas
Van Buren
St-Léonard-Parent
Grand Falls (Grand-Sault)
Grand Falls Gorge
Drummond
New Denmark
Everett
Limestone
New Sweden
Caribou
Four Falls
Aroostook
Plaster Rock
Three Brooks
Perth-Andover
Arthurette
Presque Isle
Fort Fairfield
Washburn
Perham
Mapleton
Portage
Ashland
Currie
Rowena
Bon Accord
Upper Kent
Mars Hill
Beechwood
Bath
Bristol
Glassville
Windsor
Florenceville
Stickney
Hartland Covered Bridge (World's Longest)
Bridgewater
Centreville
Lakeville
Coldstream
Hartland
Cloverdale
Masardis
Oxbow
Monticello
Littleton
Somerville
Williamsburg
Stanley
Houlton
Smyrna Mills
Linneus
Hodgdon
Woodstock
Debec
Grafton
Millville
Lower Hainesville
Upper Hainesville
Zealand
Burtts Corner
Keswick Ridge
Fredericton
Nackawic
Meductic
Pokiok
Kings Landing
Canterbury

Matane
Ste-Félicité
St-Jean-de-Cherbourg
St-Ulric
Petit-Matane
St-Adelme
St-Luc-de-Matane
Baie-des-Sables
Métis-sur-Mer
Grand-Métis
St-Léandre
Mont-Castor
St-Damase
St-René-de-Matane
Ste-Flavie
Ste-Luce
Les Jardins Boules de Métis
St-Noël
Sayabec
Mont-Joli
Price
Padoue
St-Donat
Ste-Angèle-de-Mérici
La Rédemption
Val-Brillant
St-Cléophas
St-Vianney
Ste-Paule
St-Gabriel-de-Rimouski
Les Hauteurs
Amqui
Pointe-au-Père
Phare de Pointe-au-Père
Rimouski-Est
Univ. du Québec à Rimouski
Rimouski
Le Bic
St-Valérien
Ste-Blandine
Mont-Lebel
St-Narcisse-de-Rimouski
St-Charles-Garnier
St-Fabien
St-Simon
St-Eugène-de-Ladrière
St-Mathieu-de-Rioux
St-Mathieu
St-Guy
Esprit-Saint
Ste-Rita
Lac-des-Aigles
St-Léon-le-Grand
Lac-au-Saumon
St-Tharcisius
St-Alexandre-des-Lacs
Causapscal
Lac-Humqui
Albertville
Ste-Marguerite
Ste-Florence
St-André-de-Restigouche
Pointe-à-la-Croix
Flatlands
Campbellton
Atholville
L'Ascension-de-Patapédia
L'Ascension
St-François-d'Assise
Matapédia
Mann Mtn.
Glencoe
Tide Head
Dalhousie
Balmoral
Dawsonville
Sugarloaf Prov. Park
Maltais
St-Arthur
Charlo
Black Point
Nash Creek
Belledune
Menneval
Robinsonville
St-Jean-Baptiste-de-Restigouche
Lorne
Pointe-Verte
Whites Brook
Kedgwick River
Kedgwick
St-Martin-de-Restigouche
Nicholas Denys
Robertville
North Tetagouche
South Tetagouche
St-Quentin
Nouvelle
Escuminac
Point La Nim
Miguasha
Carleton-sur-Mer
Maria
Gesgapegiag
Cascapédia-St-Jules
New Richmond
Eel River Crossing
New Mills
Heron I.
Herron Mills

Mont Jacques-Cartier 1,268 m
Mont Logan 1,135 m
Mt. Carleton Highest Pt. in New Brunswick 817 m
Mt. Carleton 817 m
Mt. Elizabeth 655 m
Little Bald Mtn. 658 m
North Pole Mtn. 686 m
Bald Pk. 640 m
Big Bald Mtn. 762 m
Black Mts. 695 m

Nictau
Riley Brook
Nepisiguit
Bathurst Mines
Heath Steele
Sevogle
Sunny Corner
Red Bank
Quarryville
McGraw Brook
Renous
Blackville
Upper Blackville
Blissfield
Doaktown
Doak Historic Site
Central N.B. Woodsmen's Mus.
Parker Ridge
Ludlow
Boiestown
Napadogan
Astle
Cross Creek
Tay Creek
Nashwaak Bridge
Taymouth
Nashwaak Village
Hardwood Ridge
Chipman
Minto
Gaspereau Forks
Cumberland Bay

ZEC FORESTVILLE
ZEC D'IBERVILLE
ZEC NORDIQUE
ZEC HAUVIN
ZEC SAGUENAY
ZEC BAS-SAGUENAY
ZEC CHAPAIS
ZEC BAS-ST-LAURENT
ZEC DE CAP-CHAT
RÉSERVE FAUNIQUE DE MATANE
RÉSERVE FAUNIQUE DE DUNIÈRE
PARC DE LA GASPÉSIE
GASPÉSIE
RÉSERVE FAUNIQUE DUCHÉNIER
RÉSERVE FAUNIQUE DE RIMOUSKI
PARC DU BIC
ZEC BAS-ST-LAURENT
CASUALT
QUÉBEC
NEW BRUNSWICK
MAINE
CANADA / UNITED STATES
QUÉBEC / MAINE
APPALACHIAN MOUNTAINS
ALLAGASH WILDERNESS WATERWAY
DEBOULLIE PUBLIC RESERVED LAND
EAGLE LAKE PUBLIC RESERVED LAND
SQUAPAN PUBLIC RESERVED LAND
ROUND POND PUBLIC RESERVED LAND
SCRAGGLY LAKE PUBLIC RESERVED LAND
GERO ISLAND PUBLIC RESERVED LAND
BAXTER STATE PARK
DE LA RÉPUBLIQUE PROV. PARK
MOUNT CARLETON PROV. PARK
HEURE DE L'EST / EASTERN TIME ZONE
HEURE DE L'ATLANTIQUE / ATLANTIC TIME ZONE
OWEN

St. Lawrence / St. Laurent
Réservoir Outardes Quatre
Baie aux Outardes
Lac Laval
Lac des Sables
Lac Témiscouata
Lac Pohénégamook
Lac de l'Est
Lac Touladi
Lac Baker
Eagle Lake
Square Lake
Portage L.
Fish River Lake
Rocky Brook
Musquacook Lake
Munsungan Lake
Millinocket Lake
Grand Lake Seboeis
Chesuncook Lake
Lac Matapédia
Lac Inférieur
Lac Mistigougèche
Green
Patapédia
Restigouche
Upsalquitch
Tobique
Little Southwest Miramichi
Trousers Lake
Long Lake
Nashwaak
Cains
St. John
Nepisiguit

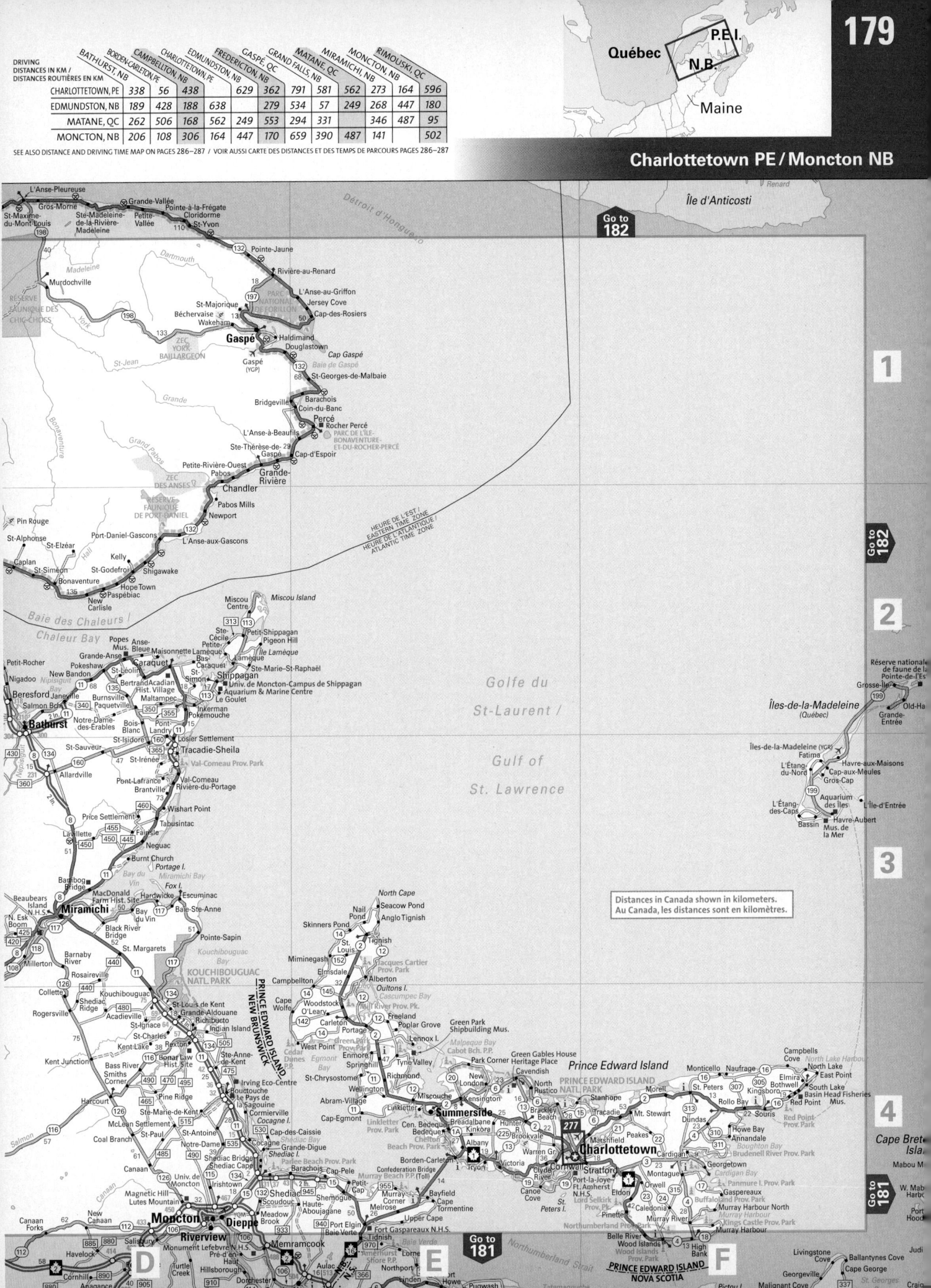

DRIVING DISTANCES IN KM / DISTANCES ROUTIÈRES EN KM

	BATHURST, NB	BORDEN-CARLETON, PE	CAMPBELLTON, NB	CHARLOTTETOWN, PE	EDMUNDSTON, NB	FREDERICTON, NB	GASPÉ, QC	GRAND FALLS, NB	MATANE, QC	MIRAMICHI, NB	MONCTON, NB	RIMOUSKI, QC
CHARLOTTETOWN, PE	338	56	438		629	362	791	581	562	273	164	596
EDMUNDSTON, NB	189	428	188	638		279	534	57	249	268	447	180
MATANE, QC	262	506	168	562	249	553	294	331		346	487	95
MONCTON, NB	206	108	306	164	447	170	659	390	487	141		502

SEE ALSO DISTANCE AND DRIVING TIME MAP ON PAGES 286–287 / VOIR AUSSI CARTE DES DISTANCES ET DES TEMPS DE PARCOURS PAGES 286–287

Distances in Canada shown in kilometers.
Au Canada, les distances sont en kilomètres.

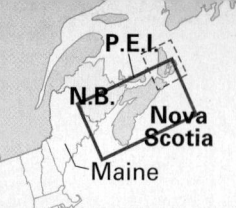

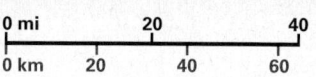

0 mi   20   40
0 km   20   40   60
One inch equals 25.4 miles/Un pouce équivaut à 25.4 milles
One cm equals 16.1 km/Un cm équivaut à 16.1 km

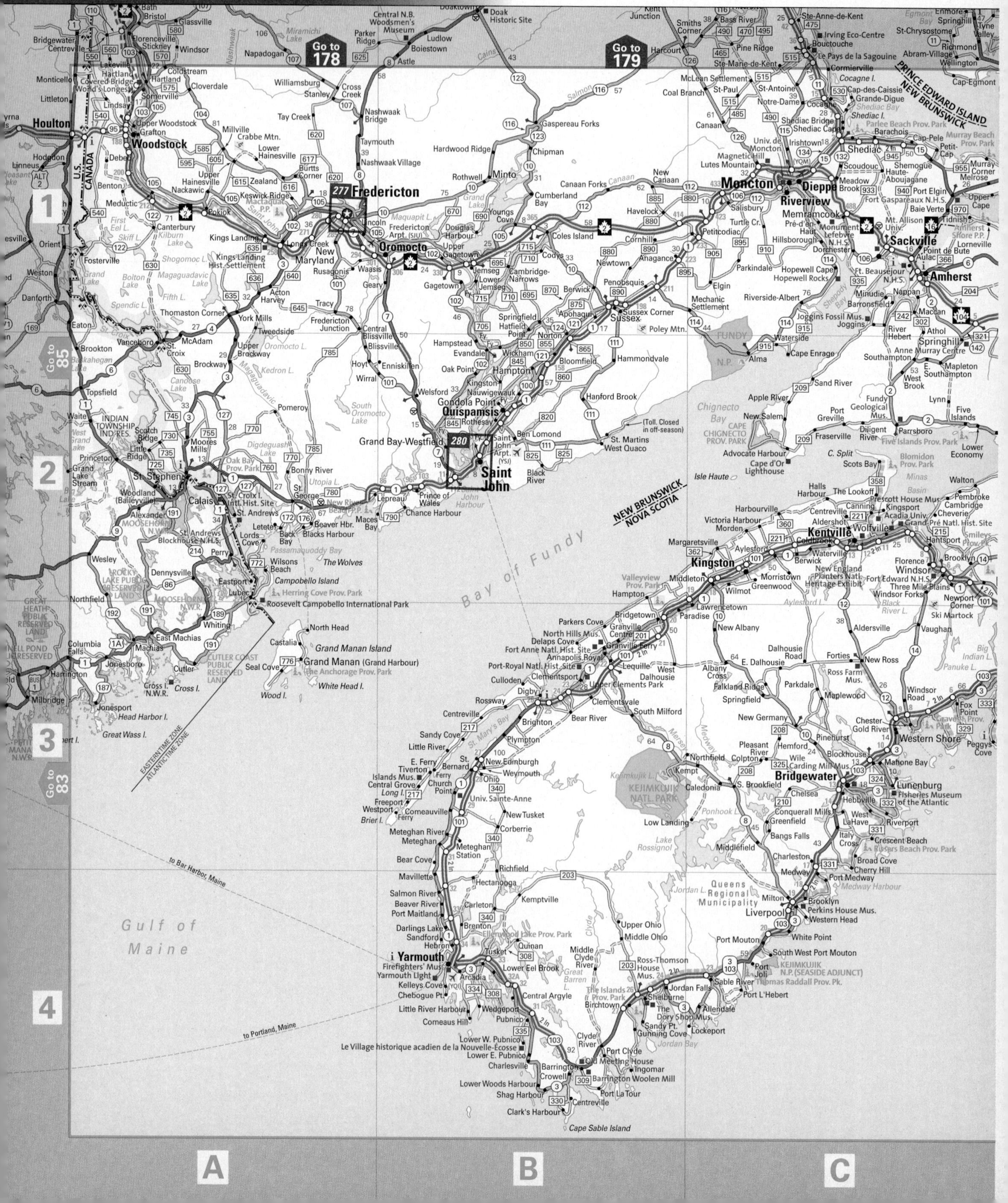

SEE ALSO DISTANCE AND DRIVING TIME MAP ON PAGES 286–287 / VOIR AUSSI CARTE DES DISTANCES ET DES TEMPS DE PARCOURS PAGES 286–287

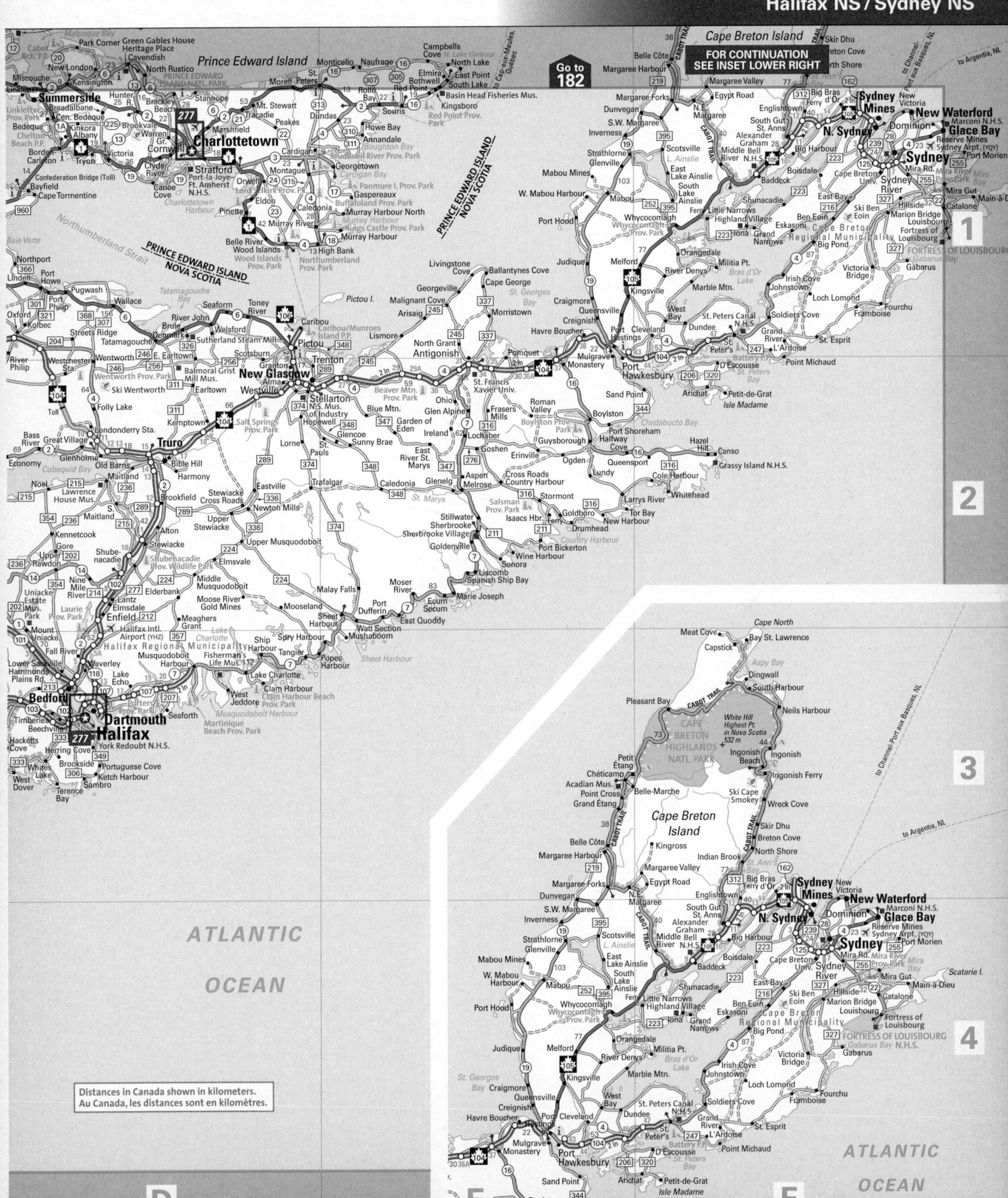

Go to 182

FOR CONTINUATION SEE INSET LOWER RIGHT

Distances in Canada shown in kilometers.
Au Canada, les distances sont en kilomètres.

ATLANTIC OCEAN

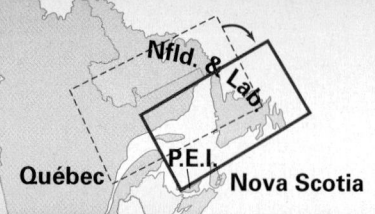

Nfld. & Lab
P.E.I.
Québec   Nova Scotia

0 mi   20   40   60
0 km   20   40   60   80

One inch equals 40.3 miles/Un pouce équivaut à 40.3 milles
One centimeter equals 25.4 km/Un cm équivaut à 25.4 km

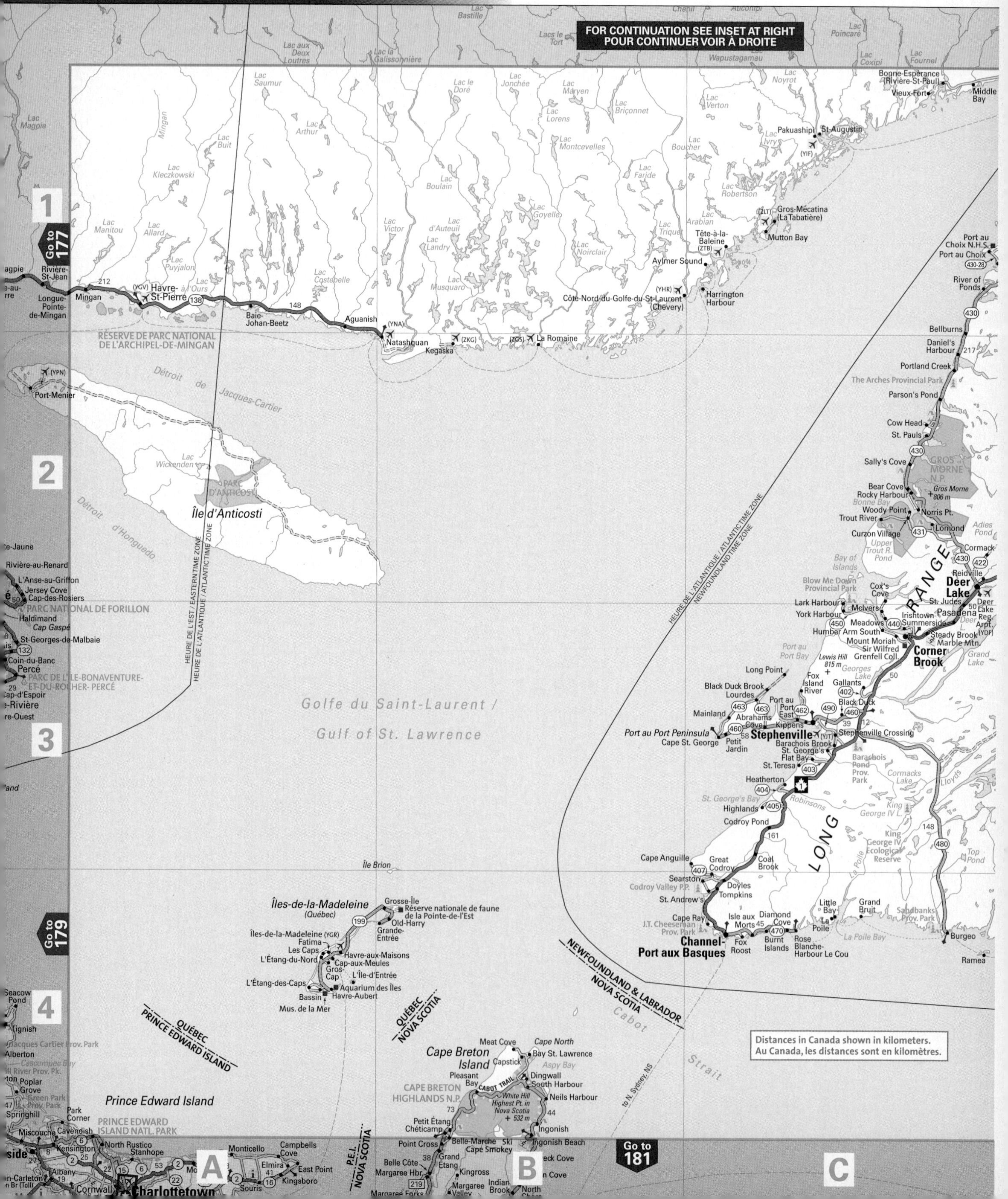

FOR CONTINUATION SEE INSET AT RIGHT
POUR CONTINUER VOIR À DROITE

1
Go to 177

2

3

4
Go to 179

Lac Bastille
Lac aux Deux Loutres
Lacs la Galissonnière
Lac le Doré
Lac Maryen
Lac Briçonnet
Lac Verton
Lac Noyrot
Lac Coxipi
Lac Fournel
Bonne-Espérance (Rivière-St-Paul)
Vieux-Fort
Middle Bay
Lac Poincaré

Mingan
Lac Saumur
Lac Arthur
Lac Buit
Lac Doré
Lac Boulain
Lac Goyelle
Lac Montcevelles
Lac Faride
Lac Robertson
Lac Ivry
Pakuaship
St-Augustin
(YIF)

Lac Magpie
Lac Manitou
Lac Allard
Lac Kleczkowski
Lac Puyjalon
Lac Victor
Lac d'Auteuil
Lac Landry
Lac Arabian
Lac Triquet
Tête-à-la-Baleine
(ZTB)
Gros-Mécatina (La Tabatière)
(ZLT)
Mutton Bay
Port au Choix N.H.S.
Port au Choix
(430-28)

Go to 177
Rivière-St-Jean
Longue-Pointe-de-Mingan
Mingan
212
(YGV) Havre-St-Pierre
138
Lac à l'Ours
Lac Costebelle
148
Aguanish
Baie-Johan-Beetz
(YNA)
Natashquan
Kegaska
(ZKG)
(ZGS)
La Romaine
Côte-Nord-du-Golfe-du-St-Laurent (Chevery)
(YHR)
Harrington Harbour
Aylmer Sound
River of Ponds
(430)
Bellburns
Daniel's Harbour
217
Portland Creek
The Arches Provincial Park
Parson's Pond

RÉSERVE DE PARC NATIONAL DE L'ARCHIPEL-DE-MINGAN

(YPN)
Port-Menier
Détroit de Jacques-Cartier

Cow Head
St. Pauls
Sally's Cove
(430)
Bear Cove
Rocky Harbour
Gros Morne + 806 m
Woody Point
Trout River
Curzon Village
Lomond
(431)
Norris Pt.
GROS MORNE N.P.
Bonne Bay
Upper Trout R. Pond
Adies Pond
Cormack
(430)

Lac Wickenden
Détroit d'Honguedo
PARC D'ANTICOSTI
Île d'Anticosti

RANGE
Bay of Islands
Blow Me Down Provincial Park
Cox's Cove
Lark Harbour
York Harbour
Melvers
Meadows
(450)
Humber Arm South
Mount Moriah
Sir Wilfred Grenfell Coll
(440)
Irishtown
Summerside
Steady Brook
Marble Mtn.
(YDP)
Reidville
St. Judes
Deer Reg Arpt.
Deer Lake
(422)
Corner Brook
Grand Lake
50
Georges Lake

-Jaune
L'Anse-au-Griffon
Jersey Cove
Cap-des-Rosiers
PARC NATIONAL DE FORILLON
Haldimand
Cap Gaspé
St-Georges-de-Malbaie
132
Coin-du-Banc
Percé
PARC DE L'ÎLE-BONAVENTURE-ET-DU-ROCHER-PERCÉ
Cap d'Espoir
29
re-Rivière
re-Ouest

Golfe du Saint-Laurent / Gulf of St. Lawrence

HEURE DE L'EST / EASTERN TIME ZONE
HEURE DE L'ATLANTIQUE / ATLANTIC TIME ZONE
HEURE DE L'ATLANTIQUE / ATLANTIC TIME ZONE
NEWFOUNDLAND TIME ZONE

Lewis Hill 815 m +
Port au Port Bay
Long Point
Fox Island River
Gallants
(402)
Black Duck
(460)
12
(490)
(462)
Black Duck Brook
Lourdes
(463)
Mainland
Abrahams Cove
Port au Port East
West
(YJT)
Stephenville Crossing
Port au Port Peninsula
Cape St. George
(460)
Petit Jardin
58
Kippens
Stephenville
39
Barachois Brook
St. George's
Flat Bay
St. Teresa
(403)
Barachois Pond Prov. Park
Cormacks Lake

Île Brion

St. George's Bay
Heatherton
(404)
Highlands
(405)
Codroy Pond
161
Robinsons
King George IV L.
King George IV Ecological Reserve
148
(480)
Top Pond
Lloyds

LONG

Îles-de-la-Madeleine (Québec)
Grosse-Île
Réserve nationale de faune de la Pointe-de-l'Est
Old-Harry
199
Grande-Entrée
Fatima
Les Caps
(YGR)
Havre-aux-Maisons
Îles-de-la-Madeleine
L'Étang-du-Nord
Cap-aux-Meules
Gros-Cap
L'Île-d'Entrée
L'Étang-des-Caps
Aquarium des Îles
Bassin
Havre-Aubert
Mus. de la Mer

Cape Anguille
Great Codroy
Coal Brook
(407)
Searston
Codroy Valley P.P.
J.T. Cheeseman Prov. Park
Doyles
Tompkins
St. Andrew's
Cape Ray
Isle aux Morts
45
Diamond Cove
Little Bay
Grand Bruit
La Poile
Sandbanks Prov. Park
Burgeo
Channel-Port aux Basques
(470)
Fox Roost
Burnt Islands
Rose Blanche
Harbour Le Cou
La Poile Bay
Ramea

Seacow Pond
Tignish

Jacques Cartier Prov. Park
Casoumpec Bay
Poplar Grove
Green Park
Park Corner
Springhill
Miscouche
Cavendish
-side
North Carleton
Albany
19
Barr (Toll)
Kensington
North Rustico
Stanhope
25
15
22
53
2
Cornwall
Charlottetown
22
Green Park
PRINCE EDWARD ISLAND NATL. PARK
Prince Edward Island
PRINCE EDWARD ISLAND

QUÉBEC
PRINCE EDWARD ISLAND
Monticello
Campbells Cove
41
Elmira
East Point
Souris
2
18
Kingsboro

QUÉBEC
NOVA SCOTIA

NEWFOUNDLAND & LABRADOR
NOVA SCOTIA

Cabot Strait
To N. Sydney, NS

Meat Cove
Cape North
Bay St. Lawrence
Capstick
Aspy Bay
Dingwall
South Harbour
Neils Harbour
Pleasant Bay
CAPE BRETON HIGHLANDS N.P.
Cape Breton Island
White Hill Highest Pt. in Nova Scotia + 532 m
CABOT TRAIL
73
Ingonish
44
Ingonish Beach
Petit Étang
Chéticamp
Point Cross
Belle-Marche
Cape Smokey
Belle Côte
Grand Étang
38
Margaree Hbr.
219
Margaree Valley
Margaree Forks
Kingross
Indian Brook
North
Ski
Neck Cove

A   **B**   Go to 181   **C**

Distances in Canada shown in kilometers.
Au Canada, les distances sont en kilomètres.

DRIVING DISTANCES IN KM / DISTANCES ROUTIÈRES EN KM

	ARGENTIA, NL	BISHOP'S FALLS, NL	BONAVISTA, NL	CHAN.-PT. AUX BASQUES, NL	CORNER BROOK, NL	DEER LAKE, NL	GANDER, NL	GRAND FALLS-WINDSOR, NL	MARYSTOWN, NL	ST. ANTHONY, NL	ST. JOHN'S, NL	STEPHENVILLE, NL
BISHOP'S FALLS, NL	363		307	482	280	225	72	18	384	628	393	339
CHAN.-PT. AUX BASQUES, NL	845	482	789		202	257	554	464	866	660	875	151
CORNER BROOK, NL	643	280	587	202		55	352	262	664	458	673	59
ST. JOHN'S, NL	134	393	296	875	673	618	321	411	293	1021		732

SEE ALSO DISTANCE AND DRIVING TIME MAP ON PAGES 286–287 / VOIR AUSSI CARTE DES DISTANCES ET DES TEMPS DE PARCOURS PAGES 286–287

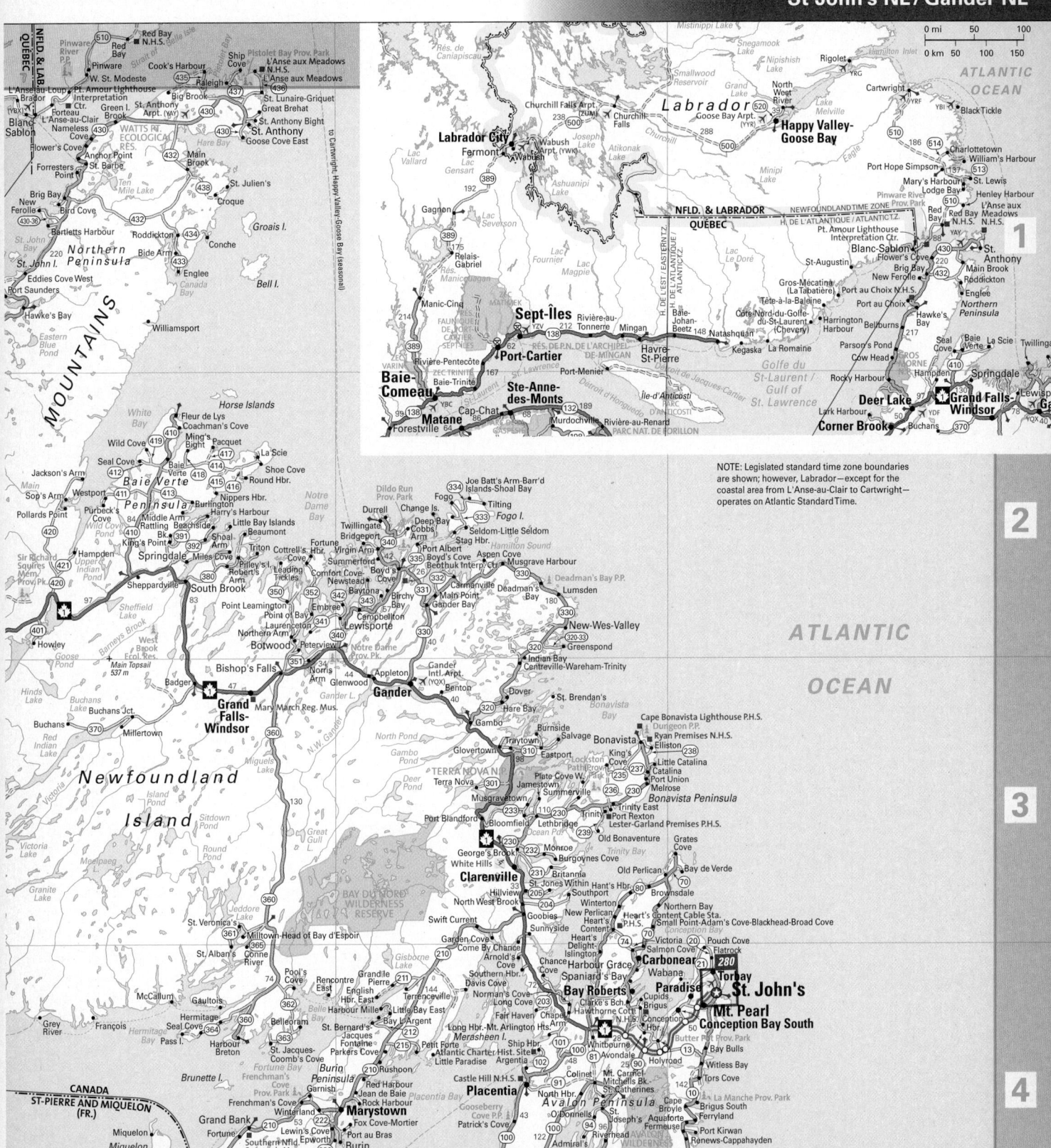

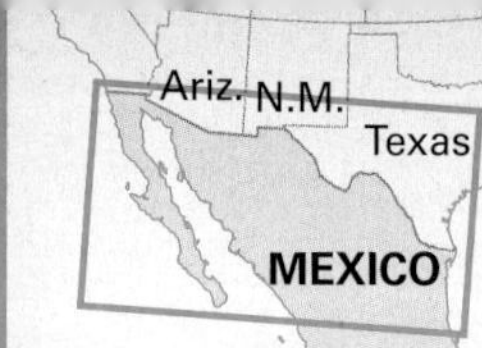

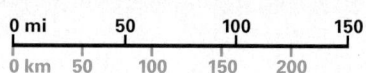

One inch equals 83.75 miles/Una pulgada igual a 83.75 millas
One centimeter equals 53 km/Un centímetro igual a 53 km

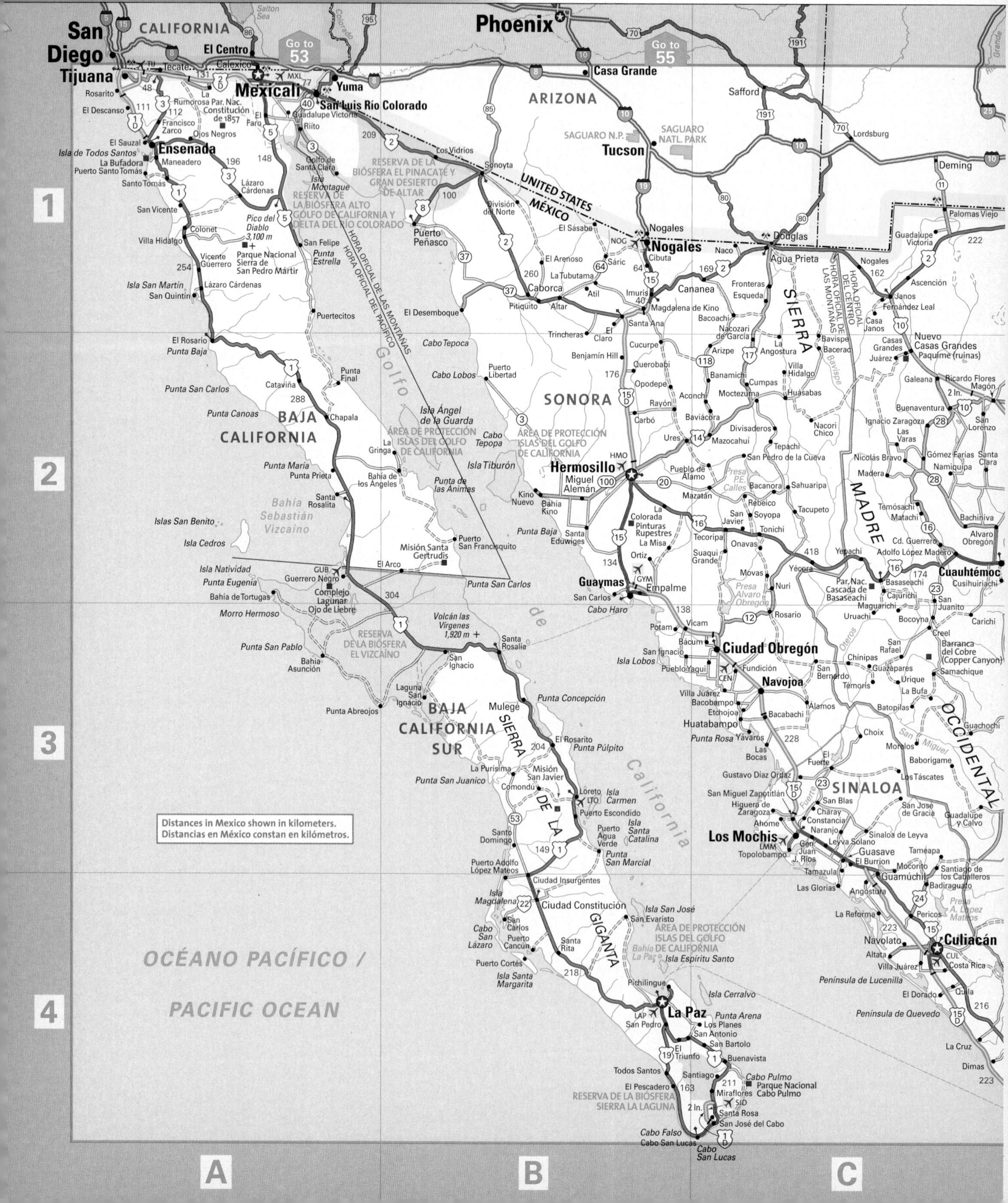

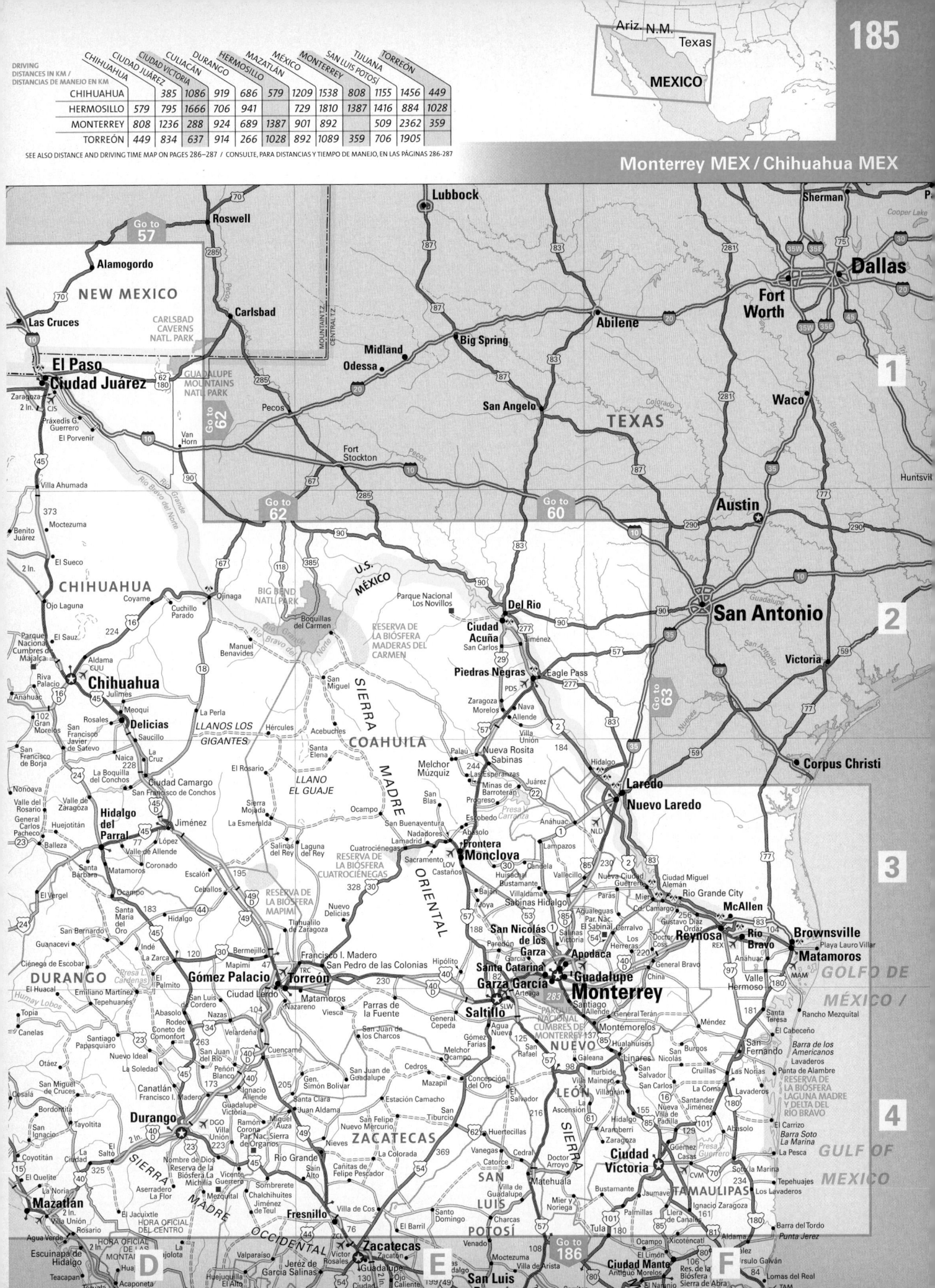

Ariz. N.M.
Texas
MEXICO

DRIVING DISTANCES IN KM / DISTANCIAS DE MANEJO EN KM	CHIHUAHUA	CIUDAD JUÁREZ	CIUDAD VICTORIA	CULIACÁN	DURANGO	HERMOSILLO	MAZATLÁN	MÉXICO	MONTERREY	SAN LUIS POTOSÍ	TIJUANA	TORREÓN
CHIHUAHUA		385	1086	919	686	579	1209	1538	808	1155	1456	449
HERMOSILLO	579	795	1666	706	941		729	1810	1387	1416	884	1028
MONTERREY	808	1236	288	924	689	1387	901	892		509	2362	359
TORREÓN	449	834	637	914	266	1028	892	1089	359	706	1905	

SEE ALSO DISTANCE AND DRIVING TIME MAP ON PAGES 286–287 / CONSULTE, PARA DISTANCIAS Y TIEMPO DE MANEJO, EN LAS PÁGINAS 286–287

MEXICO

Puerto Rico

0 mi 50 100 150
0 km 50 100 150 200

One inch equals 83.75 miles/Una pulgada igual a 83.75 millas
One centimeter equals 53 km/Un centímetro igual a 53 km

México MEX / Guadalajara MEX

Go to 185

Go to 184

OCÉANO PACÍFICO / PACIFIC OCEAN

Distances in Mexico shown in kilometers.
Distancias en México constan en kilómetros.

DURANGO · ZACATECAS · NAYARIT · JALISCO · AGU · GUANAJUATO · SAN LUIS POTOSÍ · NUEVO LEÓN · TAMAULIPAS · QUERÉTARO · HIDALGO · MICHOACÁN · MÉXICO · MORELOS · PUEBLA · GUERRERO · SIERRA MADRE DEL SUR · SIERRA MADRE OCCIDENTAL · SIERRA MADRE ORIENTAL

Gómez Palacio · Torreón · Saltillo · Garza García · Monterrey · Guadalupe · Santiago · Ciudad Victoria · Durango · Mazatlán · Fresnillo · Zacatecas · San Luis Potosí · Soledad de Graciano Sánchez · Ciudad Mante · Tampico · Ciudad Madero · Tepic · Aguascalientes · Lagos de Moreno · León · Guanajuato · Silao · Puerto Vallarta · Zapopan · Guadalajara · Tonala · Ocotlán · La Piedad de Cabadas · Irapuato · Salamanca · Celaya · San Juan del Río · Querétaro · Pachuca · Poza Rica · Tuxpam · Xalapa · Córdoba · Orizaba · Tehuacán · Puebla · Cholula · Tlaxcala · México · Netzahualcóyotl · Toluca · Cuernavaca · Cuautla · Morelia · Zamora de Hidalgo · Ciudad Guzmán · Uruapan · Colima · Manzanillo · Tecomán · Apatzingán · Lázaro Cárdenas · Zihuatanejo · Chilpancingo · Iguala · Acapulco · Oaxaca

A · B · C

1 · 2 · 3 · 4

MEXICO · Puerto Rico

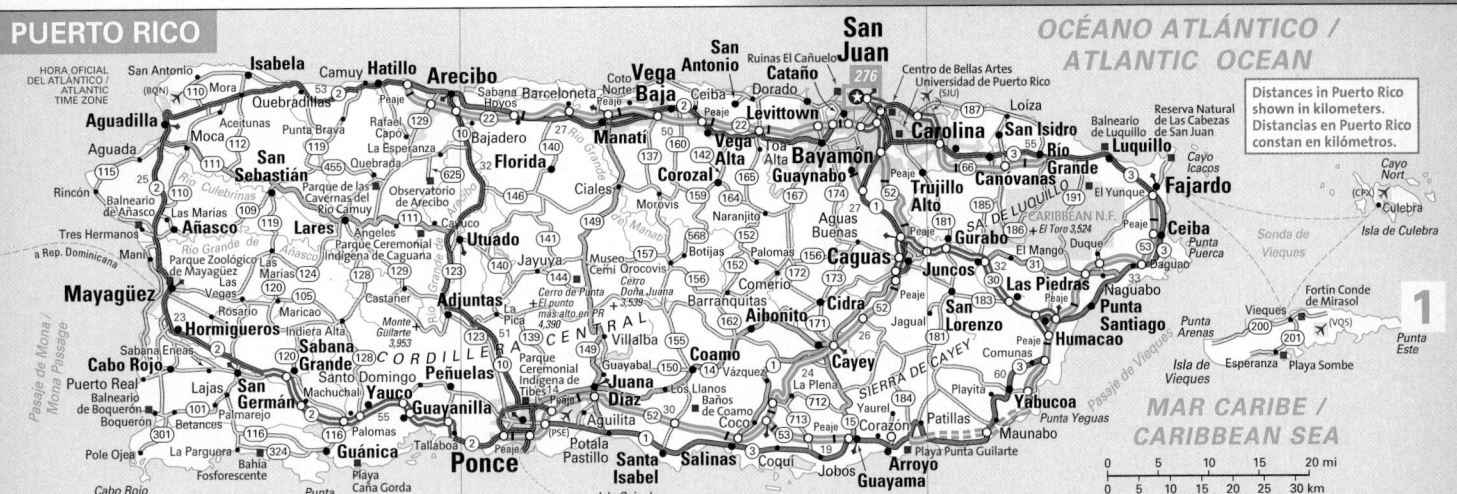

DRIVING DISTANCES IN KM / DISTANCIAS DE MANEJO EN KM

	ACAPULCO	CANCÚN	CIUDAD VICTORIA	DURANGO	GUADALAJARA	MAZATLÁN	MÉRIDA	MÉXICO	PUEBLA	SAN LUIS POTOSÍ	TUXTLA GUTIÉRREZ	VERACRUZ
GUADALAJARA	897	2275	774	599		523	1904	578	691	336	1510	943
MÉRIDA	1777	321	1725	2182	1904	2408		1326	1282	1707	786	365
MÉXICO	422	1736	682	856	578	1081	1326		133	381	932	365
SAN LUIS POTOSÍ	834	2161	438	475	336	687	1707	381	496		1313	747

SEE ALSO DISTANCE AND DRIVING TIME MAP ON PAGES 286–287 / CONSULTE, PARA DISTANCIAS Y TIEMPO DE MANEJO, EN LAS PÁGINAS 286–287

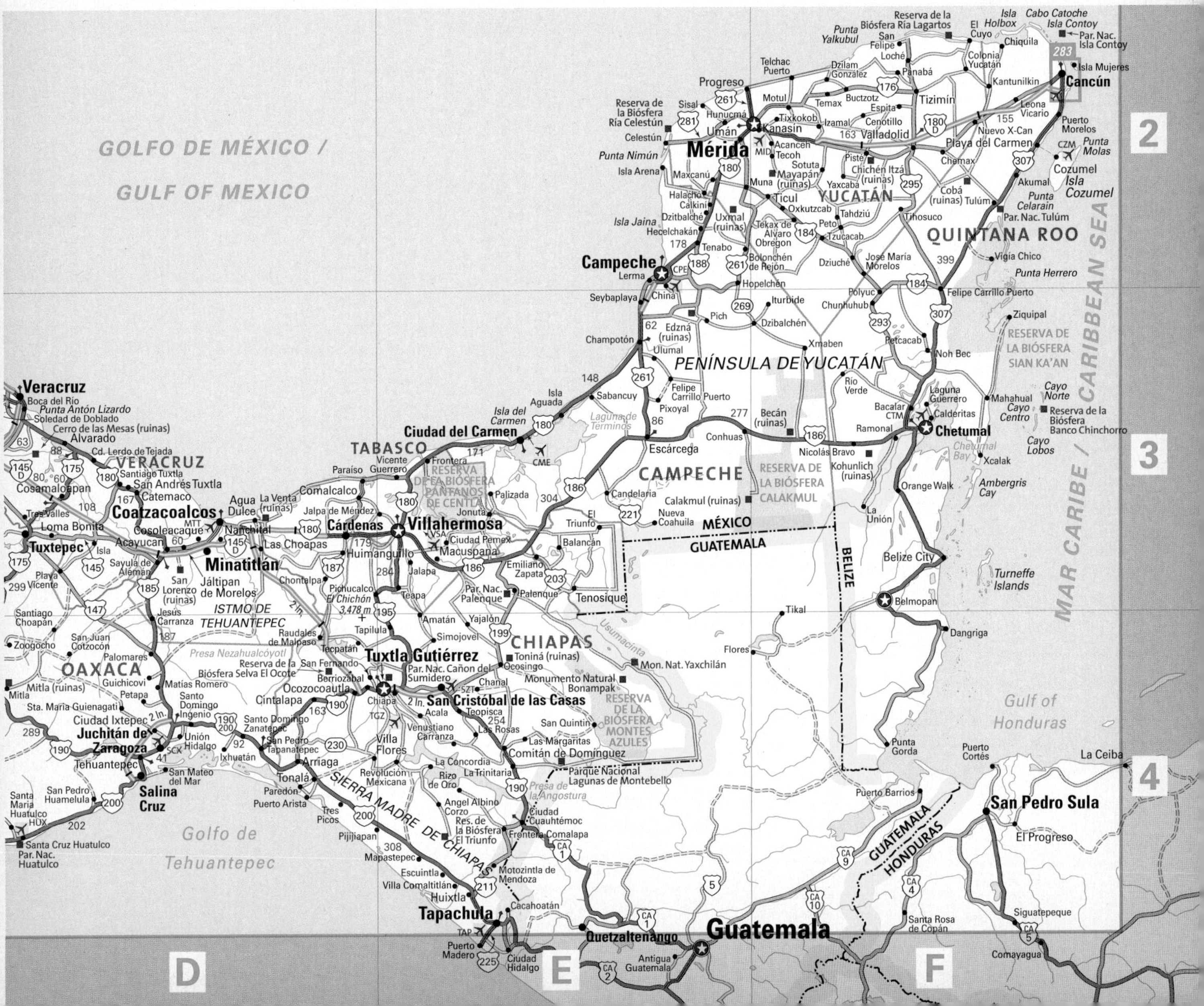

PUERTO RICO

HORA OFICIAL DEL ATLÁNTICO / ATLANTIC TIME ZONE

OCÉANO ATLÁNTICO / ATLANTIC OCEAN

Distances in Puerto Rico shown in kilometers. Distancias en Puerto Rico constan en kilómetros.

MAR CARIBE / CARIBBEAN SEA

Pasaje de Mona / Mona Passage

GOLFO DE MÉXICO / GULF OF MEXICO

PENÍNSULA DE YUCATÁN

RESERVA DE LA BIÓSFERA SIAN KA'AN

MAR CARIBE / CARIBBEAN SEA

Gulf of Honduras

Figures after entries indicate population, page number, and grid reference.

UNITED STATES

A

Abbeville AL, *2987*	128 B4
Abbeville GA, *2298*	129 E3
Abbeville LA, *11887*	133 F3
Abbeville MS, *423*	118 C3
Abbeville SC, *5840*	121 E3
Abbeville Co. SC, *26167*	121 E3
Abbotsford WI, *1956*	68 A4
Abbottstown PA, *905*	103 E1
Abercrombie ND, *296*	19 F4
Aberdeen ID, *1840*	31 E1
Aberdeen MD, *13842*	145 D1
Aberdeen MS, *6415*	119 D4
Aberdeen NC, *3400*	122 C1
Aberdeen OH, *1603*	100 C3
Aberdeen SD, *24658*	27 E2
Aberdeen WA, *16461*	12 B4
Abernathy TX, *2839*	58 A1
Abilene KS, *6543*	43 E2
Abilene TX, *115390*	58 C3
Abingdon IL, *3612*	88 A3
Abingdon MD, *950*	145 D1
Abingdon VA, *7780*	111 E3
Abington MA, *14605*	151 D2
Abita Sprs. LA, *1957*	134 B2
Absarokee MT, *1234*	24 B2
Absecon NJ, *7638*	147 F4
Acadia Par. LA, *58861*	133 E2
Accokeek MD, *7349*	144 B4
Accokeek Acres MD, *1500*	144 B4
Accomac VA, *547*	114 C3
Accomack Co. VA, *38305*	114 C3
Accord MA, *2300*	151 D2
Accord NY, *622*	94 A3
Achille NE, *506*	59 F1
Achilles VA, *650*	113 F2
Ackerman MS, *1626*	118 C4
Ackley IA, *1809*	73 D4
Acme MI, *650*	69 F4
Acomita NM, *288*	48 B3
Acton CA, *2390*	52 C2
Acton MA, *2100*	150 C1
Acushnet MA, *3171*	151 D3
Acworth GA, *13422*	120 C3
Ada MN, *1657*	19 F3
Ada OK, *5582*	90 B3
Ada OK, *15691*	51 F4
Ada Co. ID, *300904*	22 B4
Adair IA, *839*	86 B2
Adair OK, *704*	106 A3
Adair Co. IA, *8243*	86 B2
Adair Co. KY, *17244*	110 B2
Adair Co. MO, *24977*	87 D4
Adair Co. OK, *21038*	106 B4
Adair Vil. OR, *536*	20 B3
Adairsville GA, *2542*	120 B3
Adairville KY, *920*	109 F3
Adams MA, *5784*	94 C1
Adams MN, *800*	73 D2
Adams NE, *489*	35 F4
Adams NY, *1624*	79 E2
Adams OR, *297*	21 F1
Adams TN, *566*	109 E3
Adams Ctr. NY, *1502*	79 E2
Adams WI, *1914*	74 A1
Adams Co. CO, *348618*	41 F1
Adams Co. ID, *3476*	22 B2

Adams Co. IL, *68277*	87 F4
Adams Co. IN, *33625*	90 A3
Adams Co. IA, *4482*	86 B3
Adams Co. MS, *34340*	126 A4
Adams Co. NE, *31151*	35 D4
Adams Co. ND, *2593*	26 A1
Adams Co. OH, *27330*	100 C3
Adams Co. PA, *91292*	103 E1
Adams Co. WA, *16428*	13 F4
Adams Co. WI, *18643*	74 A2
Adamston NJ, *4900*	147 E3
Adamstown MD, *650*	144 A2
Adamstown PA, *1203*	146 A2
Adamsville AL, *4965*	119 F4
Adamsville RI, *550*	151 D4
Adamsville TN, *1983*	119 D1
Addis LA, *2238*	134 A3
Addison AL, *723*	119 E3
Addison IL, *35914*	203 C4
Addison ME, *300*	83 E2
Addison MI, *627*	90 B1
Addison NY, *1797*	93 D1
Addison TX, *14166*	207 D1
Addison Co. VT, *35974*	81 D3
Adel GA, *5307*	137 F1
Adel IA, *3435*	86 C2
Adelanto CA, *18130*	53 D2
Adelphi MD, *14998*	270 E1
Adelphia NJ, *700*	147 E2
Adena OH, *815*	91 F4
Adrian GA, *579*	129 E4
Adrian MI, *21574*	90 B1
Adrian MN, *1234*	72 A2
Adrian MO, *1780*	96 B4
Advance IN, *562*	99 E1
Advance MO, *1244*	108 B2
Adwolf VA, *1457*	111 F2
Afton IA, *917*	86 C3
Afton NY, *836*	93 F1
Afton OK, *1118*	106 B3
Afton WY, *1818*	31 F1
Agawam MA, *28144*	150 A2
Agency IA, *622*	87 E3
Agency MO, *624*	96 B1
Agoura Hills CA, *20537*	228 A2
Agua Dulce TX, *737*	63 D3
Agua Fria NM, *2051*	49 D2
Aguilar CO, *593*	41 E4
Ahoskie NC, *5039*	113 F3
Ahuimanu HI, *8506*	152 A3
Aiken SC, *25337*	121 F4
Aiken Co. SC, *142552*	122 A4
Ainsworth IA, *524*	87 F2
Ainsworth NE, *1862*	34 C1
Airmont NY, *7799*	148 B3
Airport Drive MO, *622*	106 B2
Airway Hts. WA, *4500*	13 F3
Aitkin MN, *1984*	64 B4
Aitkin Co. MN, *15301*	64 B4
Ajo AZ, *3705*	54 B3
Ak-Chin AZ, *600*	54 C2
Akiachak AK, *585*	154 B3
Akins OK, *449*	116 B1

Akron NY, *3085*	78 B3
Akron CO, *1711*	41 F1
Akron PA, *4046*	146 A2
Akron IA, *1489*	35 F1
Akron MI, *461*	76 B2

Alachua FL, *6098*	138 C3
Alachua Co. FL, *217955*	138 C3
Alakanuk AK, *652*	154 B2
Alamance Co. NC, *130880*	112 C4
Alameda CA, *72259*	259 C3
Alameda NM, *4200*	48 C3
Alameda Co. CA, *1443741*	36 A4
Alamo CA, *15626*	259 D2
Alamo GA, *1943*	129 E4
Alamo NM, *1183*	48 B4
Alamo TN, *2392*	108 C4
Alamo TX, *14760*	63 E4
Alamogordo NM, *35582*	56 C2
Alamo Hts. TX, *7319*	257 E2
Alamosa CO, *7960*	41 D4
Alamosa Co. CO, *14966*	41 D4
Alanson MI, *785*	70 C3
Alapaha GA, *682*	129 E4
Alba MO, *588*	106 B2
Albany CA, *16444*	259 C2
Albany GA, *76939*	129 D4
Albany IL, *895*	88 B1
Albany IN, *2368*	90 A4
Albany KY, *2220*	110 B3
Albany LA, *865*	134 B2
Albany MN, *1796*	66 B2
Albany MO, *1937*	86 B4
Albany NY, *95658*	94 B1
Albany OH, *808*	101 E2
Albany OR, *40852*	20 B3
Albany TX, *1921*	58 C2
Albany WI, *1191*	74 B4
Albany Co. NY, *294565*	94 B1
Albany Co. WY, *32014*	33 E2
Albemarle NC, *15680*	122 B1
Albemarle Co. VA, *79236*	102 C4
Albers IL, *878*	98 B3
Albert City IA, *709*	72 B4
Albert Lea MN, *18356*	72 C2
Alberton MT, *374*	15 D4
Albertville AL, *17247*	120 A3
Albertville MN, *3621*	66 C3
Albia IA, *3706*	87 D3
Albion CA, *700*	102 C2
Albion ID, *262*	31 D2
Albion IL, *1933*	99 D4
Albion IN, *2284*	90 A2
Albion IA, *592*	87 D1

Albion MI, *9144*	76 A4
Albion NE, *1797*	35 E3
Albion NY, *7438*	78 B3
Albion PA, *1607*	91 F1
Albion WA, *616*	14 A4
Albuquerque NM, *448607*	48 C3
Alburg VT, *488*	81 D1
Alburnett IA, *559*	87 E1
Alburtis PA, *2117*	146 B1
Alcalde NM, *377*	49 D2
Alcester SD, *880*	35 F1
Alcoa TN, *8378*	110 C4
Alcona Co. MI, *11719*	71 D4
Alcorn MS, *1200*	126 A3
Alcorn Co. MS, *34558*	119 D2
Alda NE, *652*	35 D4
Aldan PA, *4313*	248 B4
Alden IA, *904*	72 C4
Alden MN, *652*	69 D4
Alden NY, *2666*	78 B3
Alderson WV, *1091*	112 A1
Alderwood Manor WA, *15329*	262 B2
Aldine TX, *13979*	220 C1
Aledo IL, *3613*	87 F2
Aledo TX, *1726*	59 E2
Alex OK, *635*	51 E3
Alexander AR, *614*	117 E2
Alexander ND, *217*	17 F2
Alexander City AL, *15008*	128 A1
Alexander Co. IL, *9590*	108 C2
Alexander Co. NC, *33603*	111 F4
Alexandria AL, *3692*	120 A4

Albany	D3
Alplaus	C1
Best	E3
Bethlehem Ctr.	D3
Boght Corners	E1
Calico Colony	D1
Clifton Gardens	D1
Clifton Park	D1
Clifton Park Ctr.	D1
Clinton Park	E3
Cohoes	E2
Colonie	D2
Crescent	E1
Defreestville	E3
Delmar	D3
Dunnsville	C2
Dunsbach Ferry	E1

E. Greenbush	E3
Elsmere	D3
Ft. Hunter	C2
Glenmont	D3
Glenridge	C1
Grant Hollow	E1
Green Island	E2
Grooms Corners	D1
Guilderland	C2
Guilderland Ctr.	C2
Halfmoon	E1
Hartmans Corners	C2
Hawthorne Hill	D1
Latham	D2
Loudonville	E2
Maple Wood	E2

Maywood	D2
McCormack Corners	C2
McKownville	C3
Meadowdale	C2
Menands	E2
Mohawk View	C2
New Salem	C3
New Scotland	C3
Newtonville	E2
Niskayuna	C1
Normanville	D3
N. Bethlehem	D3
Rensselaer	E3
Rexford	D1
Roessleville	D2
Rotterdam	C1

Scotia	C1
Sherwood Park	E3
Slingerlands	D3
Snyders Corners	E3
Speigletown	E1
Sycaway	E2
Troy	E2
Unionville	D3
Verdoy	D2
Vischer Ferry	D1
Voorheesville	C3
Waterford	E1
Watervliet	E2
W. Hill	C1
Westmere	C2
Wynantskill	E2

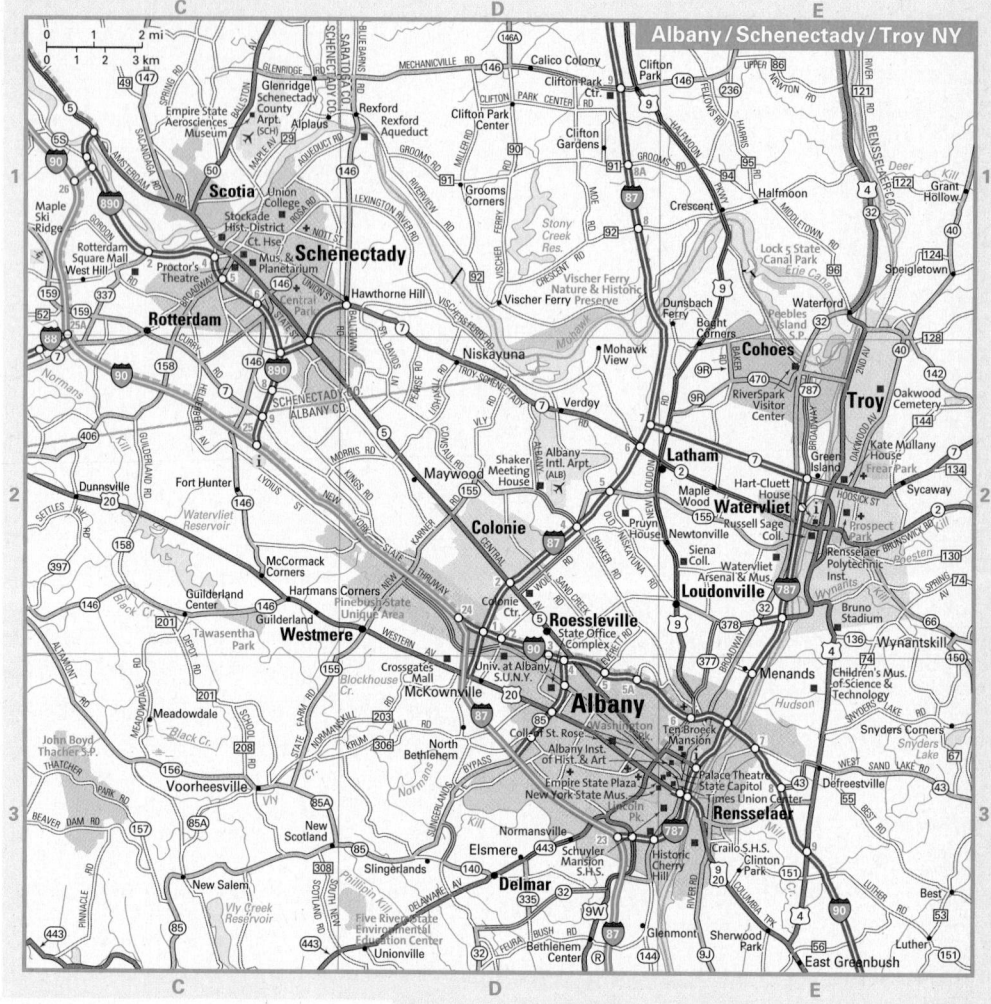

Albany / Schenectady / Troy NY

Alexandria IN, *6260*	89 F4
Alexandria KY, *8286*	100 B3
Alexandria LA, *46342*	125 E4
Alexandria MN, *8820*	66 B2
Alexandria SD, *563*	27 E4
Alexandria TN, *814*	110 A4
Alexandria Bay NY, *1088*	79 E1
Alexandria VA, *128283*	144 B3
Alexis IL, *863*	88 A3
Alfalfa Co. OK, *6105*	51 D1
Alford FL, *466*	136 C1
Alfred ME, *700*	82 B4
Alfred NY, *3954*	92 C1
Alger OH, *888*	90 B3
Alger Co. MI, *9862*	69 D3
Algodones NM, *688*	48 C3
Algoma MS, *508*	118 C3
Algoma WI, *3357*	69 D4
Algona IA, *5741*	72 B3
Algona WA, *2460*	262 B5
Algonac MI, *4613*	76 C4
Algonquin IL, *23276*	88 C1
Algood TN, *2942*	110 B3
Alhambra CA, *85004*	228 D3
Alhambra IL, *630*	98 B3
Alice TX, *19010*	63 E2
Aliceville AL, *2567*	127 E1
Ali Chuk AZ, *450*	54 B3
Aliquippa PA, *11734*	91 F3
Aliso Viejo CA, *40596*	229 G6
Allamakee Co. IA, *14675*	73 F3

Allamuchy NJ, *3125*	94 A4
Allardt TN, *642*	110 B3
Allegan MI, *4838*	75 F4
Allegan Co. MI, *105665*	75 F4
Allegany NY, *1883*	92 C1
Allegany Co. MD, *74930*	102 C1
Allegany Co. NY, *49927*	78 C4
Alleghany Co. NC, *10677*	111 F3
Alleghany Co. VA, *17215*	102 A4
Allegheny Co. PA, *1281666*	92 A4
Allen NE, *411*	35 F2
Allen OK, *951*	51 F3
Allen SD, *419*	26 B4
Allen TX, *43554*	59 F2
Allen Co. IN, *331849*	90 A3
Allen Co. KS, *14385*	96 A4
Allen Co. KY, *17800*	109 F2
Allen Co. OH, *108473*	90 B3
Allendale NJ, *6699*	148 B3
Allendale SC, *4052*	130 B1
Allendale Co. SC, *11211*	130 B1
Allenhurst GA, *788*	130 B3
Allenhurst NJ, *718*	147 F2
Allen Par. LA, *25440*	133 E1
Allen Park MI, *29376*	210 B4
Allensboro PA, *496*	41 D1
Allenton RI, *1400*	150 C4
Allenton WI, *850*	74 C2
Allentown NJ, *1882*	147 E2
Allentown PA, *106632*	146 B1
Allenwood NJ, *935*	147 E2

Akron OH

Akron	A1
Barberton	A2
Copley	A1
Cuyahoga Falls	B1
Fairlawn	A1
Ghent	A1
Lakemore	B2
Mogadore	B2
Montrose	A1
Munroe Falls	B1
Norton	A2
Portage Lakes	A2
Silver Lake	B1
Stow	B1
Tallmadge	B1

Entries in **bold black** indicate counties or parishes.
Entries in **bold color** indicate cities with detailed inset maps.

Allerton IA, *559* **87** D3	Alpharetta GA, *34854* **120** C3	Alton KY, *750* **100** B4	Amawalk NY, *1500* **148** B2	Amherstdale WV, *1785* **111** F1	Anahola HI, *1932* **152** B1	**Anderson Co. SC**, *165740* **121** E2
Allgood AL, *629* **119** F4	Alpine CA, *13143* **53** D4	Alton MO, *668* **107** F3	Amber OK, *490* **51** E3	Amidon ND, *26* **18** A4	Anahuac TX, *2210* **132** B3	**Anderson Co. TN**, *71330* **110** C4
Alliance NE, *8959* **34** A2	Alpine NJ, *2183* **148** B3	Alton NH, *650* **81** F4	Amberley OH, *3425* **204** B2	Amissville VA, *550* **103** D3	Anamoose ND, *282* **18** C2	**Anderson Co. TX**, *55109* **124** A4
Alliance NC, *781* **115** D3	Alpine TX, *5786* **62** B3	Alton IL, *570* **88** A3	Ambler PA, *6426* **146** C2	Amite LA, *4110* **134** B1	Andersonville OH, *800* **101** D2	**Anderson Co. TX**, *13004* **57** F3
Alliance OH, *23253* **91** E3	Alpine UT, *7146* **31** F4	Altona NY, *1056* **81** D1	Amboy IL, *2561* **88** B1	**Amite Co. MS**, *13599* **126** A4	Anchorage AK, *260283* **154** C3	**Andrew Co. MO**, *16492* **96** B1
Allison IA, *1006* **73** D4	Alpine WY, *550* **37** F1	Alton Bay NH, *400* **81** F4	Amboy MN, *570* **72** C2	Amity AR, *762* **117** D3	Anchorage KY, *2264* **230** F1	Andrews IN, *1290* **89** F3
Allison Gap VA, *900* **111** F2	**Alpine Co. CA**, *1208* **37** D3	Altona AL, *984* **120** A3	Amboy WA, *2085* **20** C1	Amity OR, *1478* **20** B2	Anchor Pt. AK, *1845* **154** C3	Andrews NC, *1602* **121** D1

Albuquerque NM

Amarillo TX

Anderson SC, *3068* **122** C4				
Andrews NC, *9652* **57** F3				
Andrews TX, *13004* **57** F3				
Androscoggin Co. ME, *103793* **82** B2				
Aneta ND, *284* **19** E3				
Aneth UT, *598* **40** A4				
Angel Fire NM, *1048* **49** D2				
Angelica NY, *903* **78** B4				
Angelina Co. TX, *80130* **124** B4				
Angels Camp CA, *3004* **36** C3				
Angier NC, *3419* **123** D1				
Angleton TX, *18130* **132** A4				
Angola IN, *7344* **90** A2				
Angola NY, *2266* **78** A4				
Angola on the Lake NY, *1771* **78** A4				
Angoon AK, *572* **155** E4				
Anguilla MS, *907* **126** A1				
Angwin CA, *3148* **36** B3				
Aniak AK, *572* **154** B3				
Anita IA, *1049* **86** B2				
Ankeny IA, *27117* **86** C1				
Anmoore WV, *685* **102** A3				
Anna IL, *5136* **108** C1				
Anna OH, *1319* **90** B4				
Anna TX, *1225* **59** F1				
Annabella UT, *603* **39** E2				
Anna Maria FL, *1814* **140** B3				
Annandale MN, *2684* **66** C3				
Annandale NJ, *1276* **147** D1				
Annandale VA, *54943* **144** B3				
Annapolis MD, *35838* **144** C3				
Ann Arbor MI, *114024* **76** B4				

Alloway NJ, *1128* **145** F1	Alsen LA, *950* **134** A2	Altoona IA, *10345* **86** C2	Amityville NY, *9441* **148** C4	Anchorville MI, *3200* **76** C4
Allyn WA, *2004* **12** C3	Alsip IL, *19725* **203** D6	Altoona KS, *485* **106** A1	Ammon ID, *6187* **23** E4	Andale KS, *766* **43** E4
Alma AR, *4160* **116** C1	Alta IA, *1865* **72** A4	Altoona PA, *49523* **92** C4	Amory MS, *6956* **119** D4	Andalusia AL, *8794* **128** A4
Alma GA, *3236* **129** F4	Alta UT, *370* **31** F4	Altoona WI, *6698* **67** F4	Amsterdam MT, *727* **23** F1	Andalusia IL, *1300* **87** F2
Alma KS, *797* **43** F2	Alta WY, *400* **23** F4	Alturas CA, *2892* **29** D3	Amsterdam NY, *18355* **94** A1	Anderson CA, *9022* **28** C4
Alma MI, *9275* **76** A2	Altadena CA, *42610* **228** D1	Altus OK, *21447* **51** D4	Amsterdam OH, *568* **91** E4	Anderson IA, *54* **89** F4
Alma NE, *1214* **43** D1	Altamahaw NC, *996* **112** B4	Altus AR, *817* **116** C1	Amenia NY, *1115* **94** B3	Anacoco LA, *866* **125** D4
Alma WI, *942* **73** E1	Altamont IL, *2283* **98** C2	Alum Creek WV, *1839* **101** E4	American Beach FL, *800* **139** D2	Anderson MO, *1856* **106** B3
Almena KS, *469* **42** C1	Altamont KS, *1092* **106** A2	Alva FL, *2182* **143** D1	American Canyon CA, *9774* **36** B3	Anderson SC, *25514* **121** E3
Almena WI, *607* **67** E3	Altamont NY, *1737* **94** B1	Alva OK, *5288* **51** D1	American Falls ID, *4111* **31** E1	Anderson TX, *257* **61** F1
Almon GA, *1000* **121** D4	Altamont OR, *19603* **28** C2	Alvarado TX, *3288* **59** E3	American Fork UT, *21941* **31** F4	**Anderson Co. KS**, *8110* **96** A1
Almont ND, *2803* **76** C3	Altamont TN, *1136* **120** A1	Alvin TX, *21413* **132** B4	Americus GA, *17013* **129** D3	**Anderson Co. KY**, *19111* **100** A4
Aloe TX, *850* **61** E3	Altamonte Sprs. FL, *41200* **141** D1	Alvord TX, *1007* **59** E1	Americus KS, *938* **43** F3	
Aloha OR, *41741* **20** B2	Alta Vista KS, *442* **43** F2	Ama LA, *1285* **239** B2	Amery WI, *2845* **67** E3	
Alorton IL, *2749* **256** C4	Altavista VA, *3425* **112** C2	Amado AZ, *275* **55** D4	Ames IA, *50731* **86** C1	
Alpaugh CA, *761* **45** D4	Altha FL, *506* **137** D2	**Amador Co. CA**, *35100* **36** C3	Ames TX, *1079* **132** B3	
Alpena MI, *11304* **71** D3	Altheimer AR, *1192* **117** F3	Amagansett NY, *1067* **149** F3	Amesbury MA, *12327* **95** E1	
Alpena SD, *265* **27** E3	Alto GA, *876* **121** D3	Amalga UT, *427* **31** E2	Amherst MA, *17050* **150** A1	
Alpena Co. MI, *31314* **71** D4	Alton TX, *1190* **124** B4	Amanda OH, *700* **101** D1	Amherst NH, *1600* **95** D1	
Alpha IL, *726* **88** A2	Alton IL, *30496* **98** A3	Amherst NY, *13200* **78** B3		
Alpha NJ, *2482* **146** C1	Alton IA, *1095* **35** F1	Amherst OH, *11797* **91** D2		
			Amherst TX, *791* **57** F1		
		Amarillo TX, *173627* **50** A3	Amherst WI, *964* **74** B1		
			Amherst Co. VA, *31894* **112** C1		

Anchorage AK

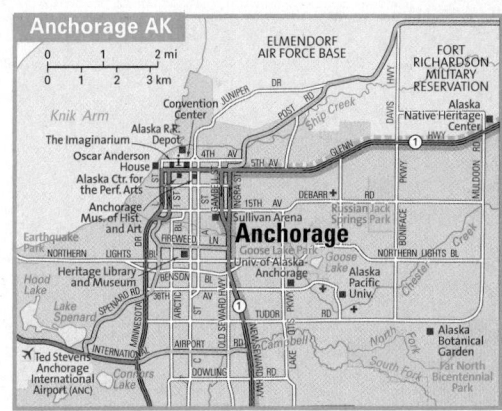

Allentown / Bethlehem PA

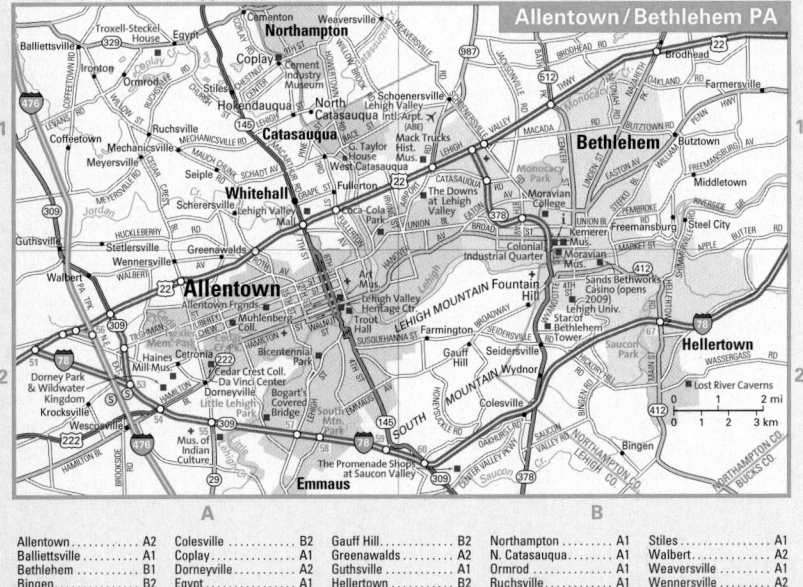

Annapolis MD

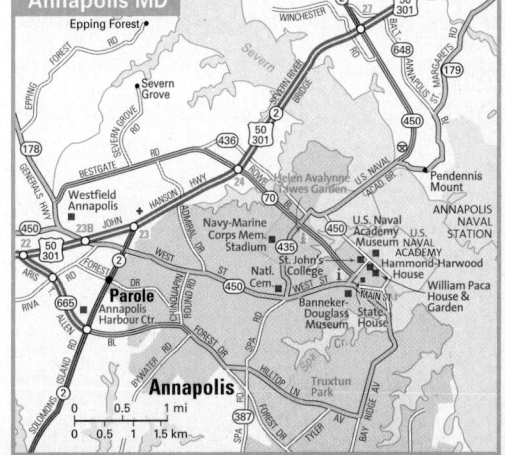

Allentown A2	Colesville B2	Gauff Hill B2	Northampton A1	Stiles A1
Balliettsville A1	Coplay A1	Greenawalds A2	N. Catasauqua A1	Walbert A2
Bethlehem B1	Dorneyville A2	Guthsville A1	Ormrod A1	Weaversville A1
Bingen B2	Egypt A1	Hellertown B2	Ruchsville A1	Wennersville A2
Brodhead B1	Emmaus A2	Hokendauqua A1	Schererville A1	Wescosville A2
Butztown B1	Farmersville B1	Ironton A1	Schoenersville B1	W. Catasauqua A1
Catasauqua A1	Farmington A2	Krocksville A2	Seidersville B2	Whitehall A1
Cementon A1	Fountain Hill B2	Mechanicsville A1	Seiple A1	Wydnor B2
Cetronia A2	Freemansburg B1	Meyersville A1	Steel City B1	
Coffeetown A1	Fullerton A1	Middletown B1	Stetlersville A1	

Figures after entries indicate population, page number, and grid reference.

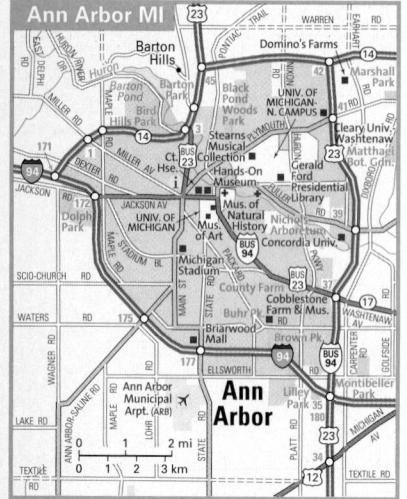

Ann Arbor MI

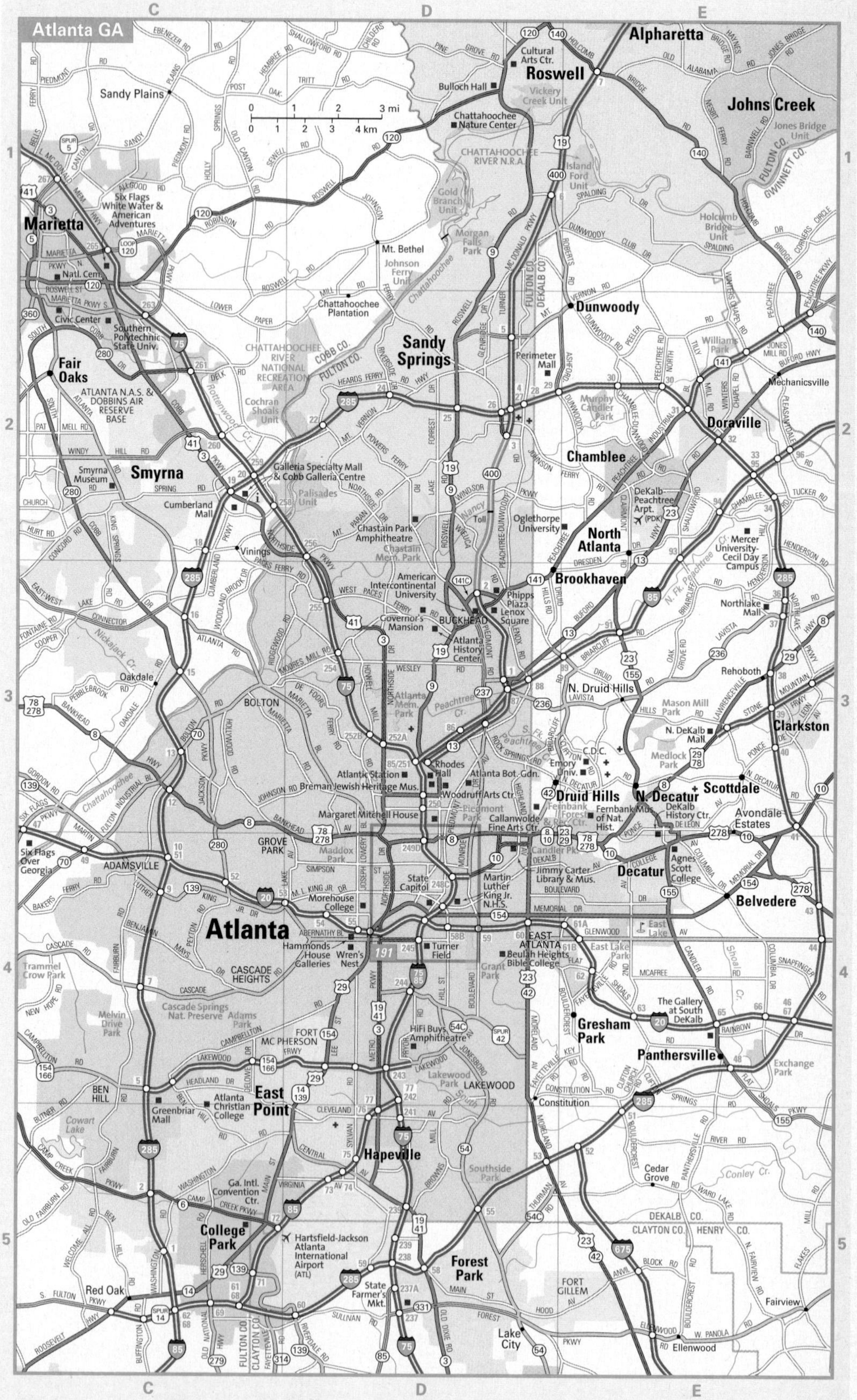

Atlanta GA

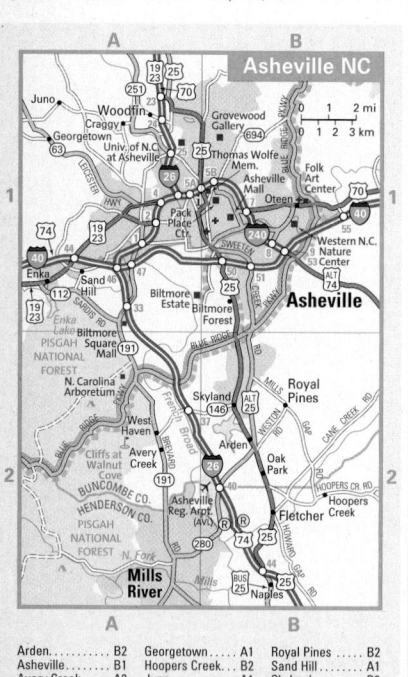

Asheville NC

Entries in **bold black** indicate counties or parishes.
Entries in **bold color** indicate cities with detailed inset maps.

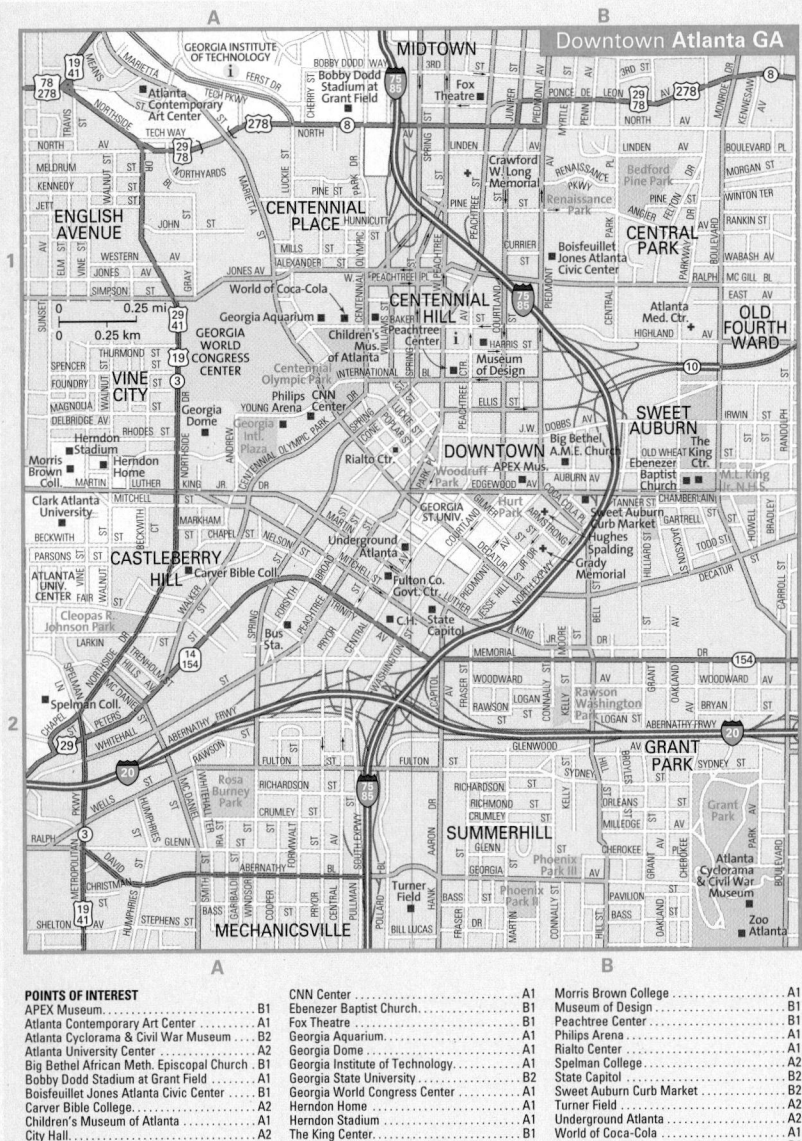

Downtown Atlanta GA

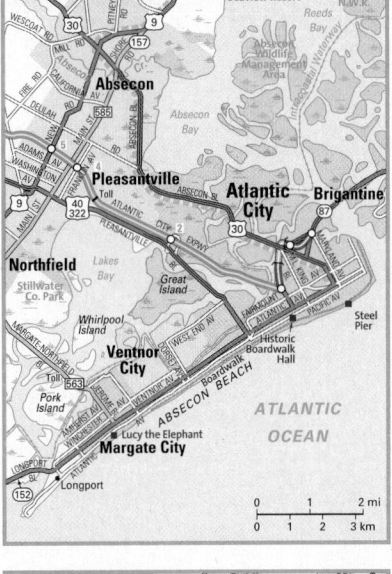

Atlantic City NJ

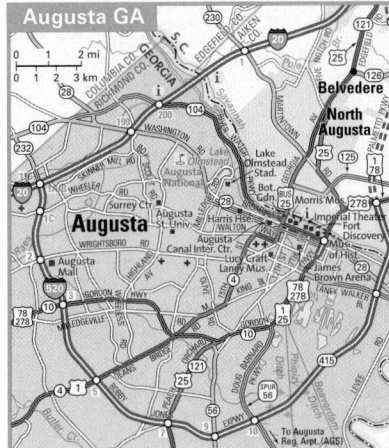

Augusta GA

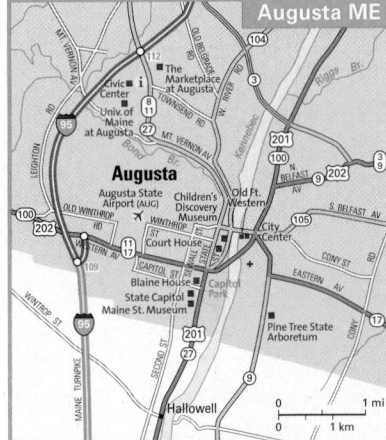

Augusta ME

POINTS OF INTEREST

APEX Museum B1	Morris Brown College A1
Atlanta Contemporary Art Center A1	Museum of Design A1
Atlanta Cyclorama & Civil War Museum ... B2	Peachtree Center B1
Atlanta University Center A2	Philips Arena A1
Big Bethel African Meth. Episcopal Church . B1	Rialto Center A1
Bobby Dodd Stadium at Grant Field A1	Spelman College A2
Boisfeuillet Jones Atlanta Civic Center B1	State Capitol B2
Carver Bible College A2	Sweet Auburn Curb Market B2
Children's Museum of Atlanta A1	Turner Field A2
City Hall A2	Underground Atlanta A1
Clark Atlanta University A2	World of Coca-Cola A1
CNN Center A1	Zoo Atlanta B2
Ebenezer Baptist Church B1	
Fox Theatre B1	
Georgia Aquarium A1	
Georgia Dome A1	
Georgia Institute of Technology A1	
Georgia State University B2	
Georgia World Congress Center A1	
Herndon Home A1	
Herndon Stadium A1	
The King Center B1	
Martin Luther King, Jr. Natl. Hist. Site ... B1	

Figures after entries indicate population, page number, and grid reference.

Entries in **bold black** indicate counties or parishes.
Entries in **bold color** indicate cities with detailed inset maps.

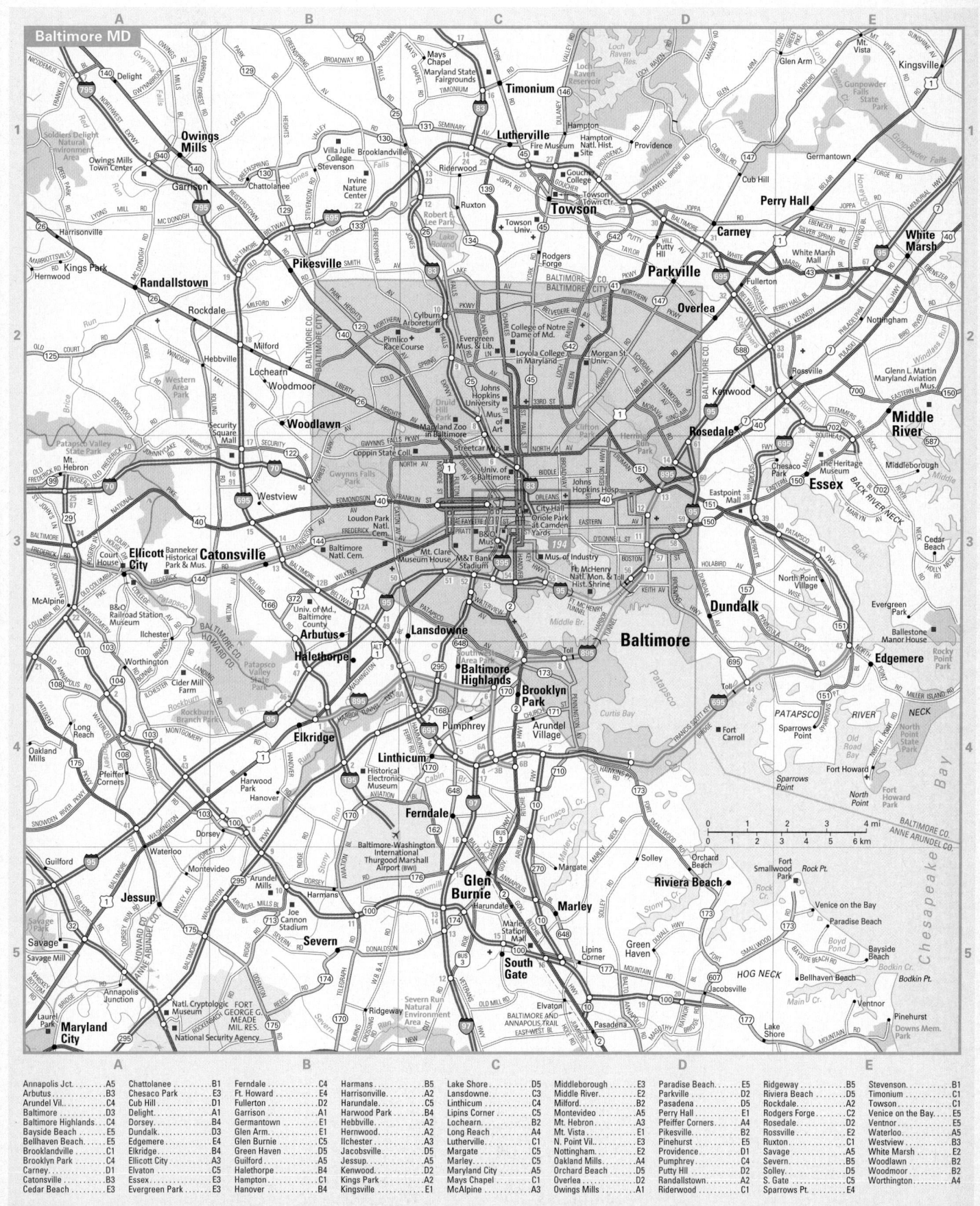

Baltimore MD

Figures after entries indicate population, page number, and grid reference.

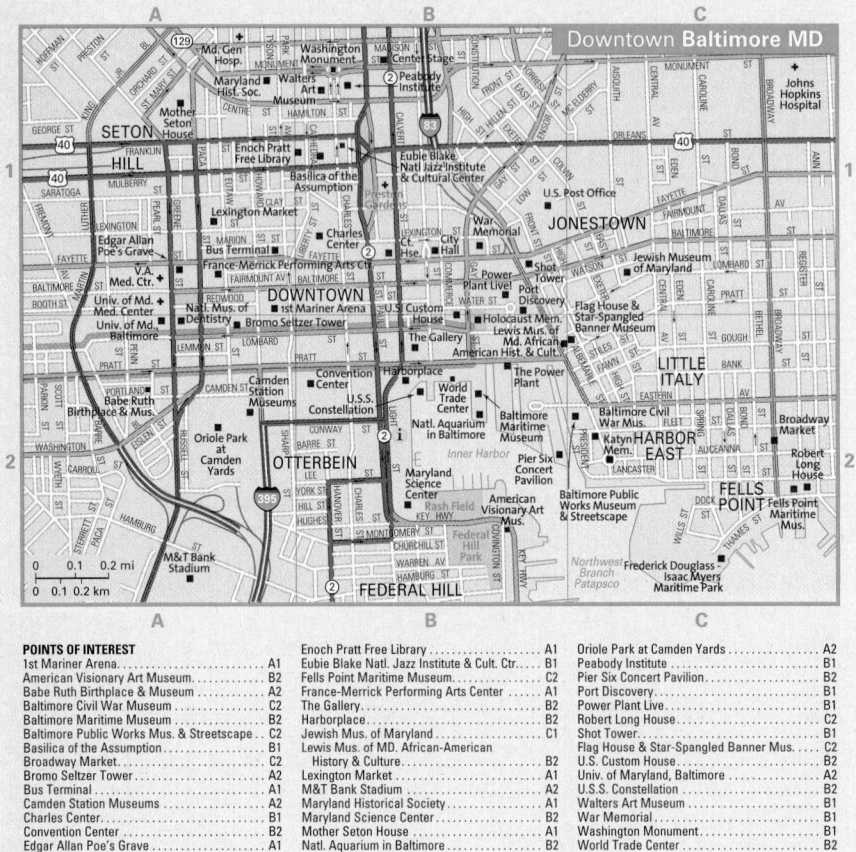

Downtown Baltimore MD

POINTS OF INTEREST

1st Mariner Arena	A1	Enoch Pratt Free Library	A1	Oriole Park at Camden Yards	A2
American Visionary Art Museum	B2	Eubie Blake Natl. Jazz Institute & Cult. Ctr.	B1	Peabody Institute	B1
Babe Ruth Birthplace & Museum	A2	Fells Point Maritime Museum	C2	Pier Six Concert Pavilion	B2
Baltimore Civil War Museum	C2	France-Merrick Performing Arts Center	A1	Port Discovery	B1
Baltimore Maritime Museum	B2	The Gallery	B2	Power Plant Live	B1
Baltimore Public Works Mus. & Streetscape	C2	Harborplace	B2	Robert Long House	C2
Basilica of the Assumption	B1	Jewish Mus. of Maryland	C1	Shot Tower	B1
Broadway Market	C2	Lewis Mus. of MD. African-American		Flag House & Star-Spangled Banner Mus.	B2
Bromo Seltzer Tower	A2	History & Culture	B2	U.S. Custom House	B2
Bus Terminal	A1	Lexington Market	A1	Univ. of Maryland, Baltimore	A2
Camden Station Museums	A2	M&T Bank Stadium	A2	U.S.S. Constellation	B2
Charles Center	B1	Maryland Historical Society	A1	Walters Art Museum	B1
Convention Center	B2	Maryland Science Center	B2	War Memorial	B1
Edgar Allan Poe's Grave	A1	Mother Seton House	A1	Washington Monument	B1
		Natl. Aquarium in Baltimore	B2	World Trade Center	B2

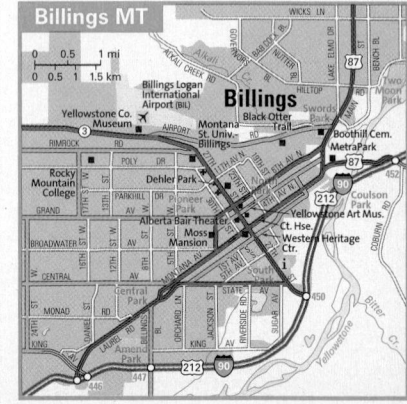

Billings MT

Entries in **bold black** indicate counties or parishes.
Entries in **bold color** indicate cities with detailed inset maps.

Biloxi/Gulfport MS

Birmingham AL

Figures after entries indicate population, page number, and grid reference.

Bowdoinham ME, 600 82 B3
Bowdon GA, 1959 120 B4
Bowen IL, 535 87 F4
Bowers Beach DE, 305 145 F3
Bowie AZ, 550 55 E3
Bowie MD, 50269 144 C3
Bowie TX, 5219 59 E1
Bowie Co. TX, 89306 116 B4
Bowleys Quarters MD, 6314 144 C2
Bowling Green FL, 2892 140 C3
Bowling Green KY, 49296 109 F2
Bowling Green MO, 3260 97 F2
Bowling Green OH, 29636 90 C2
Bowling Green VA, 936 103 D4
Bowman GA, 898 121 E3
Bowman ND, 1600 25 F1
Bowman SC, 1198 130 C1
Bowman Co. ND, 3242 25 F1
Bow Mar CO, 847 209 B4
Boxborough MA, 1400 150 C1
Box Butte Co. NE, 12158 34 A2
Box Elder MT, 794 16 B2
Box Elder SD, 2841 26 A3
Box Elder Co. UT, 42745 31 D3
Boxford MA, 2340 151 F1
Boyce LA, 1190 125 E4
Boyce VA, 426 103 D2
Boyceville WI, 1043 67 E3
Boyd TX, 1099 59 E2
Boyd WI, 680 67 F4
Boyd Co. KY, 49752 101 D4
Boyd Co. NE, 2438 35 D1
Boyden IA, 672 35 F1
Boydton VA, 454 113 D3
Boyertown PA, 3940 146 B2
Boyette FL, 5895 140 C3
Boykins VA, 620 113 E3
Boyle MS, 720 118 A4
Boyle Co. KY, 27697 110 B1
Boyne City MI, 3503 70 B3
Boynton Beach FL, 60389 143 F1
Boys Town NE, 818 245 A2
Bozeman MT, 27509 23 F1
Braceville IL, 792 88 C2
Bracken Co. KY, 8279 100 C3
Brackettville TX, 1876 60 B3
Bradbury CA, 855 228 E2
Braddock PA, 2912 250 C2
Braddock Hts. MD, 4627 144 A1
Braddock Hills PA, 1998 250 C2
Bradenton FL, 49504 140 B3
Bradenton Beach FL, 1482 140 B3
Bradford AR, 800 117 F1
Bradford IL, 787 88 B2
Bradford NH, 600 81 E4
Bradford OH, 1859 90 B4
Bradford PA, 9175 92 B1
Bradford RI, 1497 150 C4
Bradford TN, 1113 108 C4
Bradford VT, 815 81 E3
Bradford Co. FL, 26088 138 C3
Bradford Co. PA, 62761 93 E2
Bradfordville FL, 1100 137 E2
Bradford Woods PA, 1149 92 A3
Bradley AR, 563 125 D1

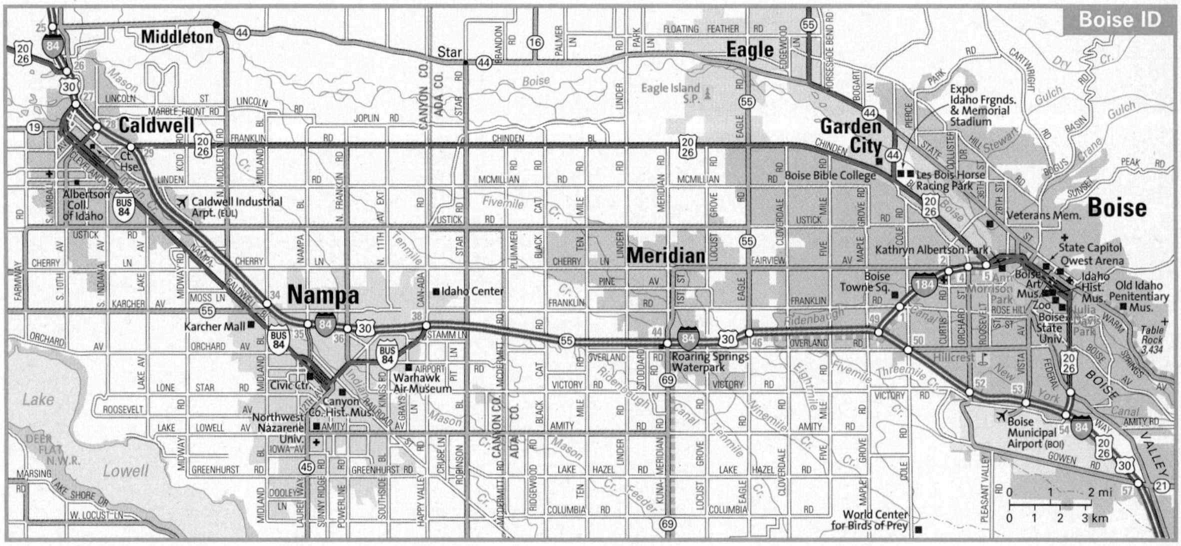
Boise ID
Middleton
Star
Eagle
Caldwell
Garden City
Boise
Meridian
Nampa
Kuna
Eagle Island S.P.
Expo Idaho Frgnds. & Memorial Stadium
Boise Bible College
Les Bois Horse Racing Park
Veterans Mem.
State Capitol
Qwest Arena
Idaho Hist. Mus.
Old Idaho Penitentiary Mus.
Boise Art Mus.
Zoo Boise
Boise State Univ.
Kathryn Albertson Park
Boise Towne Sq.
Albertson Coll. of Idaho
Caldwell Industrial Arpt. (EUL)
Idaho Center
Karcher Mall
Civic Ctr.
Canyon Co. Hist. Mus.
Northwest Nazarene Univ.
Warhawk Air Museum
Roaring Springs Waterpark
Boise Municipal Airport (BOI)
World Center for Birds of Prey
Deer Flat N.W.R.
Lake Lowell
Table Rock 3,434
0 1 2 mi
0 1 2 3 km

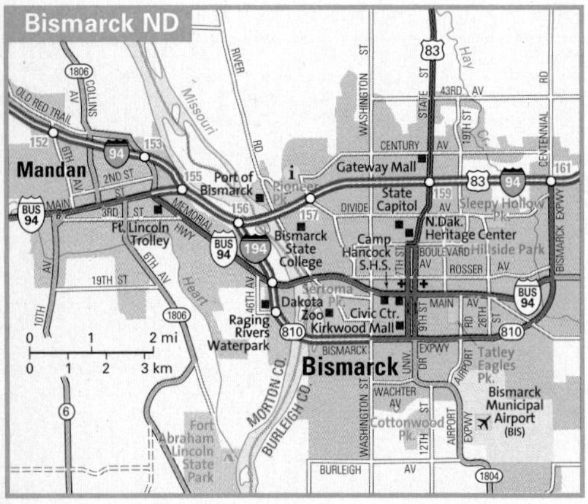
Bismarck ND
Mandan
Bismarck
Port of Bismarck
Gateway Mall
State Capitol
N.Dak. Heritage Center
Sleepy Hollow Pk.
Hillside Park
Camp Hancock S.H.S.
Bismarck State College
Ft. Lincoln Trolley
Dakota Zoo
Raging Rivers Waterpark
Civic Ctr.
Kirkwood Mall
Sertoma Pk.
Pioneer Pk.
Tatley Eagles Pk.
Bismarck Municipal Airport (BIS)
Cottonwood Pk.
Fort Abraham Lincoln State Park
Missouri
Heart
0 1 2 mi
0 1 2 3 km

Bradley IL, 12784 89 D3
Bradley ME, 650 83 D1
Bradley WV, 2371 101 F4
Bradley Beach NJ, 4793 147 F2
Bradley Co. AR, 12600 117 E4
Bradley Co. TN, 87965 120 C1
Bradley Jct. FL, 850 140 C3
Bradner OH, 1171 90 C2
Brady TX, 5523 58 C4
Braham MN, 1276 67 D2
Braidwood IL, 5203 88 C2
Brainerd MN, 13178 64 B4
Braintree MA, 33698 151 D2
Bramwell WV, 426 111 F1
Branch Co. MI, 45787 90 A1
Branchville AL, 825 119 F4
Branchville NJ, 845 94 A4
Branchville SC, 1083 130 C1
Brandenburg KY, 2049 99 F4
Brandon FL, 77895 140 C2
Brandon MS, 16436 126 B3
Brandon SD, 5693 27 F4
Brandon VT, 1684 81 D3
Brandon WI, 912 74 C2
Brandywine MD, 1410 144 B4
Brandywine Manor PA, 1200 146 B3
Branford CT, 5735 149 D2
Branford FL, 695 138 B3
Branson MO, 6050 107 D3
Brant Beach NJ, 800 147 E4
Brantley AL, 920 128 A4
Brantley Co. GA, 14629 129 F4
Brant Rock MA, 5100 151 E2
Braselton GA, 1206 121 D3
Brasher Falls NY, 1140 80 B1
Bratenahl OH, 1337 204 F1
Brattleboro VT, 8289 94 C1
Brawley CA, 22052 53 E4
Braxton Co. WV, 14702 101 F3
Bray OK, 1035 51 E4
Braymer MO, 910 96 C1
Brazil IN, 8188 99 E1
Brazoria TX, 2787 132 A4
Brazoria Co. TX, 241767 132 A4
Brazos Co. TX, 152415 61 F1
Brea CA, 35410 229 F3
Breathitt Co. KY, 16100 111 D1
Breaux Bridge LA, 7281 133 F2
Breckenridge CO, 2408 41 D1
Breckenridge MI, 1339 76 A2
Breckenridge MN, 3559 27 F1
Breckenridge TX, 5868 59 D2
Breckenridge Hills MO, 4817 256 B2
Breckinridge Co. KY, 18648 99 F4
Brecksville OH, 13382 204 F3
Breese IL, 4048 98 B3
Breezy Pt. MD, 800 144 C4
Breezy Pt. MN, 979 64 B4
Breinigsville PA, 1700 146 B1
Bremen GA, 4579 120 B4
Bremen IN, 4486 89 F2
Bremen KY, 365 109 E1
Bremen OH, 1265 101 D1
Bremer Co. IA, 23325 73 E3
Bremerton WA, 37259 12 C3
Bremond TX, 876 59 F4
Brenham TX, 13507 61 F2
Brent AL, 4024 127 F1
Brent FL, 22257 135 F2
Brentsville VA, 650 144 A4
Brentwood CA, 23302 36 B3
Brentwood MD, 2844 270 E2
Brentwood MO, 7693 256 B2
Brentwood NY, 53917 149 D4
Brentwood PA, 10466 250 B3
Brentwood TN, 23445 109 F4
Bressler PA, 2809 218 C2
Brevard NC, 6789 121 E1
Brevard Co. FL, 476230 141 E2
Brewer ME, 8987 83 D1
Brewerton NY, 3453 79 D3
Brewster MA, 2212 151 F3
Brewster MN, 502 72 A2
Brewster NE, 29 34 C2
Brewster NY, 2162 148 C2
Brewster OH, 2324 91 E3
Brewster WA, 2189 13 E2
Brewster Co. TX, 8866 62 C3
Brewster Hill NY, 2226 148 C1
Brewton AL, 5498 135 F1
Briar TX, 5350 59 E2
Briarcliff TX, 895 61 D1
Briarcliffe Acres SC, 470 123 D4
Briarcliff Manor NY, 7696 148 B2
Briar Creek PA, 651 93 E3
Briarwood KY, 554 230 F1
Briceville TN, 650 110 C4
Brickerville PA, 1287 146 A2
Bridge City LA, 8323 239 B2
Bridge City TX, 8651 132 C3
Bridgehampton NY, 1381 149 F3
Bridgeport AL, 2728 120 A2
Bridgeport CA, 200 37 E3
Bridgeport CT, 139529 149 D2
Bridgeport IL, 2168 99 D3
Bridgeport MD, 2700 144 A1
Bridgeport MI, 7849 76 B3
Bridgeport NE, 1594 34 A3
Bridgeport NY, 1665 79 E3
Bridgeport PA, 4371 248 A1
Bridgeport TX, 4309 59 E2
Bridgeport WA, 2059 13 E2
Bridgeport WV, 7306 102 A2
Bridger MT, 745 24 B2
Bridgeton MO, 15550 256 B1
Bridgeton NJ, 22771 145 F1
Bridgetown OH, 12569 204 A2
Bridgeview IL, 15335 203 D5
Bridgeville DE, 1436 145 E4
Bridgeville PA, 5341 250 A3
Bridgewater MA, 6664 151 D2
Bridgewater NJ, 3200 147 D1
Bridgewater NY, 579 79 E3
Bridgewater SD, 607 27 E4
Bridgewater VA, 5203 102 C4
Bridgman MI, 2428 89 E1
Bridgton ME, 2359 82 B3
Brielle NJ, 4893 147 E2
Brier WA, 6383 262 B2
Brigantine NJ, 12594 147 F4
Brigham City UT, 17411 31 E3
Bright IN, 5405 100 B2
Brighton AL, 3640 195 D2
Brighton CO, 20905 41 E1
Brighton IL, 2196 98 A2
Brighton IA, 687 87 E2
Brighton MI, 6701 76 B4
Brighton NY, 35584 78 C3
Brighton TN, 1719 118 B1
Brightwaters NY, 3248 149 D4
Brightwood VA, 500 102 C3
Brilliant AL, 762 119 E3
Brilliant OH, 1600 91 F4
Brillion WI, 2937 74 C1
Brimfield IL, 933 88 B3
Brinckerhoff NY, 2734 148 B1
Brinkley AR, 3940 117 F2
Brinnon WA, 803 12 C3
Brisbane CA, 3597 259 B3
Briscoe Co. TX, 1790 50 B4
Bristol CT, 60062 149 D1
Bristol FL, 845 137 D2
Bristol IN, 1382 89 F1
Bristol NH, 1670 81 F3
Bristol PA, 9923 147 D2
Bristol RI, 22469 151 D3
Bristol SD, 377 27 E2
Bristol TN, 24821 111 E3
Bristol VT, 1800 81 D2
Bristol VA, 17367 111 E3
Bristol WI, 1100 74 C4
Bristol Co. MA, 534678 151 D3
Bristol Co. RI, 50648 151 D3
Bristow OK, 4325 51 F2
Britt IA, 2052 72 C3
Brittany Farms PA, 3268 146 C2
Britton MI, 699 90 B1
Britton SD, 1328 27 E1
Broadalbin NY, 1411 80 C4
Broad Brook CT, 3469 150 A3
Broadmoor CA, 4026 259 B3
Broadus MT, 451 25 E2
Broadview IL, 8264 203 C4
Broadview Hts. OH, 15967 204 F3
Broadwater Co. MT, 4385 15 F4
Broadway NC, 1015 123 D1
Broadway VA, 2192 102 C3
Brock Hall MD, 1200 144 C3
Brockport NY, 8103 78 C3
Brockton MA, 94304 151 D2
Brockton MT, 245 17 E2
Brockway PA, 2182 92 B2
Brocton NY, 1547 78 A4
Brodhead KY, 1193 110 C1
Brodhead WI, 3180 74 B4
Brodheadsville PA, 1637 93 F3
Brogden NC, 2907 123 E1
Broken Arrow OK, 75427 106 A4
Broken Bow NE, 3491 35 D3
Broken Bow OK, 4230 116 B3
Bromley KY, 838 204 A3
Bronson FL, 964 138 C4
Bronson MI, 2421 90 A1
Bronte TX, 1076 58 C3
Bronwood GA, 513 128 C3
Bronx Co. NY, 1332650 148 B4
Brook IN, 1062 89 D3
Brookdale SC, 4724 122 A4
Brooke VA, 650 103 D4
Brooke Co. WV, 25447 91 F4
Brookfield CT, 2700 148 C1
Brookfield IL, 19085 203 C5
Brookfield MA, 1200 150 B2
Brookfield MO, 4769 97 D1
Brookfield OH, 1288 276 C1
Brookfield WI, 38649 234 B2
Brookfield Ctr. CT, 1800 148 C1
Brookhaven MS, 9861 126 B4
Brookhaven NY, 3570 149 D4
Brookhaven PA, 7985 248 A4
Brookings OR, 5447 28 A2
Brookings SD, 18504 27 F3
Brookings Co. SD, 28220 27 F3
Brookland AR, 1332 108 A4
Brooklandville MD, 2200 193 C1
Brooklawn NJ, 2354 248 C4
Brooklet GA, 1113 130 B2
Brookline MA, 57107 151 D1
Brookline NH, 650 95 D1
Brooklyn CT, 1100 150 B3
Brooklyn IL, 676 256 C2
Brooklyn IN, 1545 99 F1
Brooklyn IA, 1367 87 E1
Brooklyn MI, 1176 90 B1
Brooklyn OH, 11586 204 E2
Brooklyn WI, 916 74 B3
Brooklyn Ctr. MN, 29172 235 B1
Brooklyn Hts. OH, 1558 204 F2
Brooklyn Park MD, 10938 193 C4
Brooklyn Park MN, 67388 235 B1
Brookneal VA, 1259 112 C2
Brook Park OH, 21218 204 E3
Brookport IL, 1054 108 C2
Brooks GA, 553 128 C1
Brooks KY, 2678 100 A4
Brooks ME, 550 82 C2
Brooks Co. GA, 16450 137 F1
Brooks Co. TX, 7976 63 E3
Brookshire TX, 3450 61 F2
Brookside AL, 1393 195 D1
Brookside DE, 14806 146 B4
Brookside OH, 644 91 F4
Brookside Vil. TX, 1960 220 C4
Brookston IN, 1717 89 E3
Brooksville FL, 7264 140 C1
Brooksville KY, 589 100 C3
Brooksville MS, 1182 127 D1
Brookville IN, 2652 100 A2
Brookville NY, 2126 148 C4
Brookville OH, 5289 100 B1
Brookville PA, 4230 92 B2
Brookwood AL, 1483 127 F1
Broomall PA, 11046 146 C3
Broome Co. NY, 200536 93 F1
Broomfield CO, 38272 41 E1
Broomfield Co. CO, 38272 41 E1
Brooten MN, 649 66 B3
Broussard LA, 5874 133 F2
Broward Co. FL, 1623018 143 E1
Browerville MN, 735 66 B2
Brown City MI, 1334 76 C3
Brown Co. IL, 6950 87 F4
Brown Co. IN, 14957 99 F2
Brown Co. KS, 10724 96 A1
Brown Co. MN, 26911 72 B1
Brown Co. NE, 3525 34 C1
Brown Co. OH, 42285 100 C3
Brown Co. SD, 35460 27 E1
Brown Co. TX, 37674 59 D3
Brown Co. WI, 226778 74 C1
Brown Deer WI, 12170 234 C1
Brownfield TX, 9488 58 A2
Browning MT, 1065 15 E2
Brownsboro TX, 796 124 A3
Brownsburg IN, 14520 99 F1
Brownsdale MN, 718 73 D2
Browns Mills NJ, 11257 147 D3
Brownstown IL, 705 98 C2
Brownstown IN, 2978 99 F3
Browns Valley MN, 690 27 F1
Brownsville CA, 1069 36 C1
Brownsville KY, 921 109 F2
Brownsville MN, 517 73 F2
Brownsville OR, 1449 20 B3
Brownsville PA, 2804 102 B1
Brownsville TN, 10748 118 C1
Brownsville TX, 139722 63 F4
Brownsville WI, 570 74 C2
Brownton MN, 807 66 C4
Brownville NY, 1022 79 E1
Brownville Jct. ME, 750 84 C4
Brownwood TX, 18813 59 D4
Broxton GA, 1428 129 E4
Broyhill Park VA, 17000 270 B4
Bruce MS, 2097 118 C3
Bruce SD, 272 27 F3
Bruce WI, 787 67 F3
Bruceton TN, 1554 109 D4
Bruceville-Eddy TX, 1490 59 E4
Brule Co. SD, 5364 27 D4
Brundidge AL, 2341 128 B4
Brunson SC, 589 130 B1
Brunswick GA, 15600 139 D1
Brunswick ME, 14816 82 B3
Brunswick MD, 4894 144 A2
Brunswick MO, 925 97 D2
Brunswick OH, 33388 91 E2
Brunswick Co. NC, 73143 123 E3
Brunswick Co. VA, 18419 113 D3
Brush CO, 5117 33 F4
Brush Prairie WA, 2384 20 C1
Brushy OK, 787 116 B1
Brusly LA, 2020 134 A2
Bryan OH, 8333 90 B2
Bryan TX, 65660 61 F1
Bryan Co. GA, 23417 130 B3
Bryan Co. OK, 36534 59 F1
Bryans Road MD, 4912 144 B4
Bryant AR, 9764 117 E2
Bryant SD, 396 27 E3
Bryantville MA, 2600 151 E2
Bryn Athyn PA, 1351 248 D1
Bryn Mawr PA, 4382 146 C3
Bryson TX, 528 59 D2
Bryson City NC, 1411 121 D1
Buchanan GA, 941 120 B4
Buchanan MI, 4681 89 E1
Buchanan NY, 2189 148 B2
Buchanan VA, 1233 112 B1
Buchanan Co. IA, 21093 73 E4
Buchanan Co. MO, 85998 96 B1
Buchanan Co. VA, 26978 111 F2
Buchanan Dam TX, 1688 61 D1
Buchtel OH, 574 101 E2
Buckeye AZ, 6537 54 B1
Buckeye Lake OH, 3049 101 D1
Buckfield ME, 325 82 B2
Buckhannon WV, 5725 102 A2
Buckhead Ridge FL, 1390 141 E4
Buckingham PA, 1400 146 C2
Buckingham VA, 175 113 D1
Buckingham Co. VA, 15623 113 D1
Buckland AK, 406 154 B2
Buckley IL, 593 89 D4
Buckley MI, 550 69 F4
Buckley WA, 4145 12 C3
Bucklin KS, 725 42 C4
Bucklin MO, 524 97 D1
Buckner KY, 4000 100 A4
Buckner MO, 2725 96 C2
Bucks Co. PA, 597635 146 C1
Bucksport ME, 2970 83 D2
Bucksport SC, 1117 123 D4
Bucoda WA, 628 12 C4
Bucyrus OH, 13224 90 C3
Buda IL, 592 88 B2
Buda TX, 2404 61 E2
Budd Lake NJ, 8100 94 A4
Bude MS, 1037 126 A4
Buellton CA, 3828 52 A2
Buena NJ, 3873 147 D4
Buena WA, 950 13 D4
Buena Park CA, 78282 228 E3
Buena Ventura Lakes FL, 14100 246 C5
Buena Vista CO, 2195 41 D2
Buena Vista GA, 1664 128 C2
Buena Vista MI, 7845 76 B2
Buena Vista VA, 6349 112 C1
Buena Vista Co. IA, 20411 72 B4
Buffalo IN, 672 89 E3
Buffalo IA, 1321 87 F2
Buffalo KY, 475 110 A1
Buffalo MN, 10097 66 C3
Buffalo MO, 2781 107 D1
Buffalo NY, 292648 78 B3
Buffalo ND, 209 19 E4
Buffalo OK, 1200 50 C1
Buffalo SC, 1426 121 F2
Buffalo SD, 380 25 F1
Buffalo TX, 1804 59 F4
Buffalo WV, 1171 101 E3
Buffalo WI, 1040 73 E1
Buffalo WY, 3900 25 D3
Buffalo Ctr. IA, 963 72 C2
Buffalo Co. NE, 42259 35 D4
Buffalo Co. SD, 2032 27 D3
Buffalo Co. WI, 13804 67 E4
Buffalo Grove IL, 42909 203 C2
Buffalo Lake MN, 768 66 B4
Buford GA, 10668 120 C3
Buhl ID, 3985 30 C1
Buhl MN, 983 64 C3
Buhler KS, 1358 43 E3
Buies Creek NC, 2215 123 D1
Bullard TX, 1150 124 A3
Bullhead SD, 308 26 C1
Bullhead City AZ, 33769 46 B3
Bullitt Co. KY, 61236 99 F4
Bulloch Co. GA, 55983 130 B2
Bullock Co. AL, 11714 128 B3
Bulls Gap TN, 714 111 D3
Bull Shoals AR, 2000 107 E3
Bull Valley IL, 726 74 C4
Bulverde TX, 3761 61 D2
Buna TX, 2269 132 C2
Buncombe Co. NC, 206330 111 E4
Bunker Hill IL, 1801 98 B2
Bunker Hill IN, 987 89 F3
Bunker Hill OR, 1462 20 A4
Bunker Hill WV, 700 103 D2
Bunker Hill Vil. TX, 3654 220 B2
Bunkerville NV, 1014 46 B1
Bunkie LA, 4662 133 E1
Bunnell FL, 2122 139 E4
Buras LA, 3358 134 C4
Burbank CA, 100316 52 C2
Burbank IL, 27902 203 D5
Burbank WA, 3303 21 E1
Burden KS, 564 43 F4

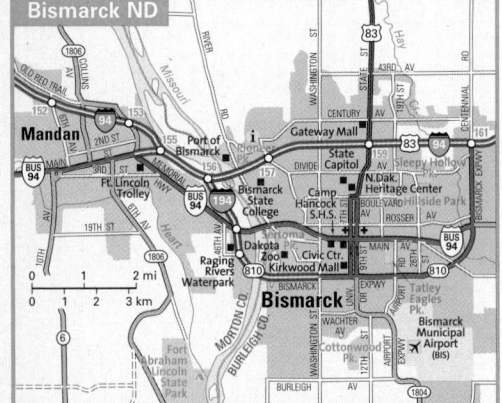

Entries in **bold black** indicate counties or parishes.
Entries in **bold color** indicate cities with detailed inset maps.

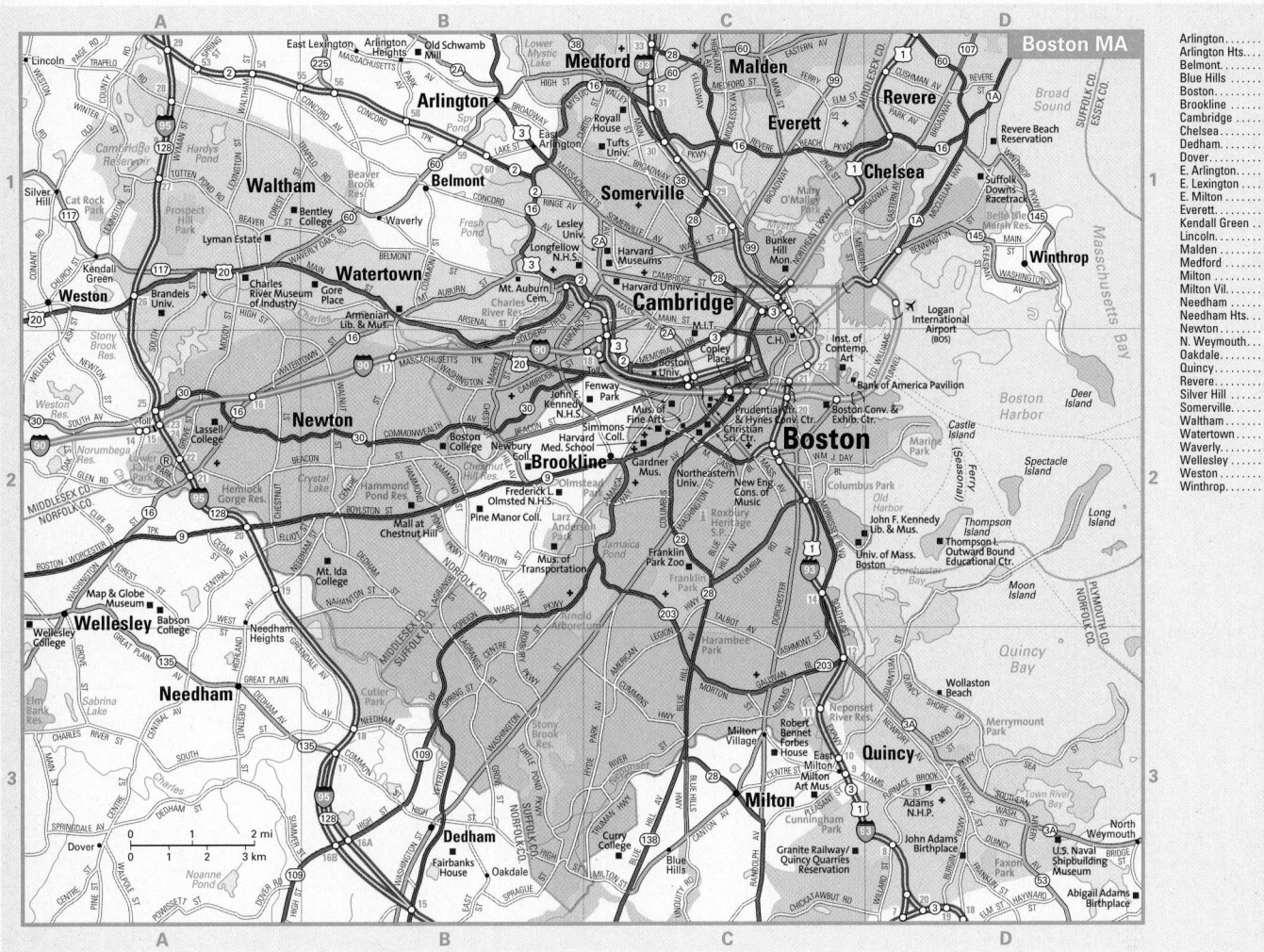

Boston MA

Downtown Boston MA

POINTS OF INTEREST

Arlington Street Church. E2
Boston Athenaeum. E2
Boston City Hall. F2
Boston Fire Museum F2
Boston Massacre Monument E2
Boston Massacre Site F2
Boston Tea Party Ship & Museum F2
Bunker Hill Pavilion F1
Central Burying Ground E2
Charles Street Meeting House E2
Children's Museum F2
Citi Performing Arts Center. E2
Copp's Hill Burying Ground F1
Custom House F2
Emerson College. E2
Faneuil Hall F2
Gibson House Museum E2
Granary Burying Ground E2
Hancock Tower. E2
Harrison Gray Otis Hse. E1
Hatch Memorial Shell E2
Hayden House E2
Hayden Planetarium E1
JFK Federal Building F2
King's Chapel F2
Moakley Federal Courthouse F2
Museum of Afro-American Hist. E2
Museum of Science E1
New England Aquarium F2
North Station F1
Old North Church F1
Old South Meeting House F2
Old State House F2
Old West Church E1
The Opera House E2
Park Street Church E2
Paul Revere House F1
Paul Revere Mall F1
Pierce Hichborn House F1
Quincy Market F2
St. Stephens Church. F1
Shaw Memorial E2
South Station (Amtrak) F2
State House E2
Suffolk County Court House E2
Suffolk Univ. E2
TD Banknorth Garden E1
Thomas P. O'Neill Federal Building E1
Trinity Church E2
U.S.S. Constitution F1

198

Butte County–Calion

Figures after entries indicate population, page number, and grid reference.

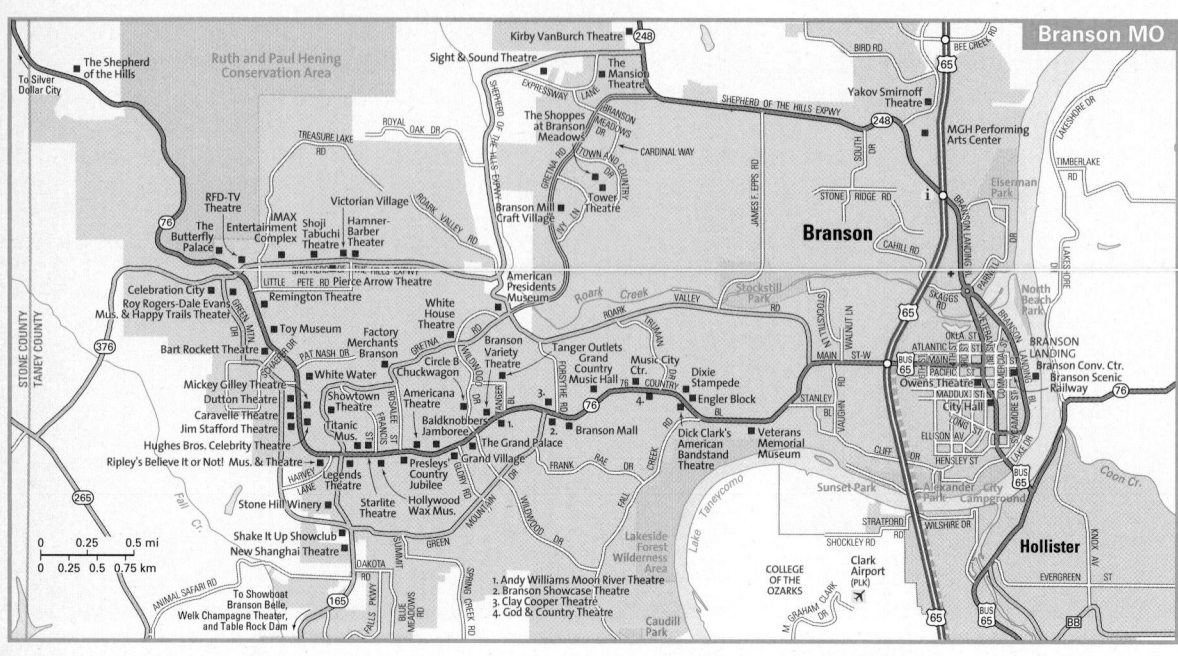

Branson MO

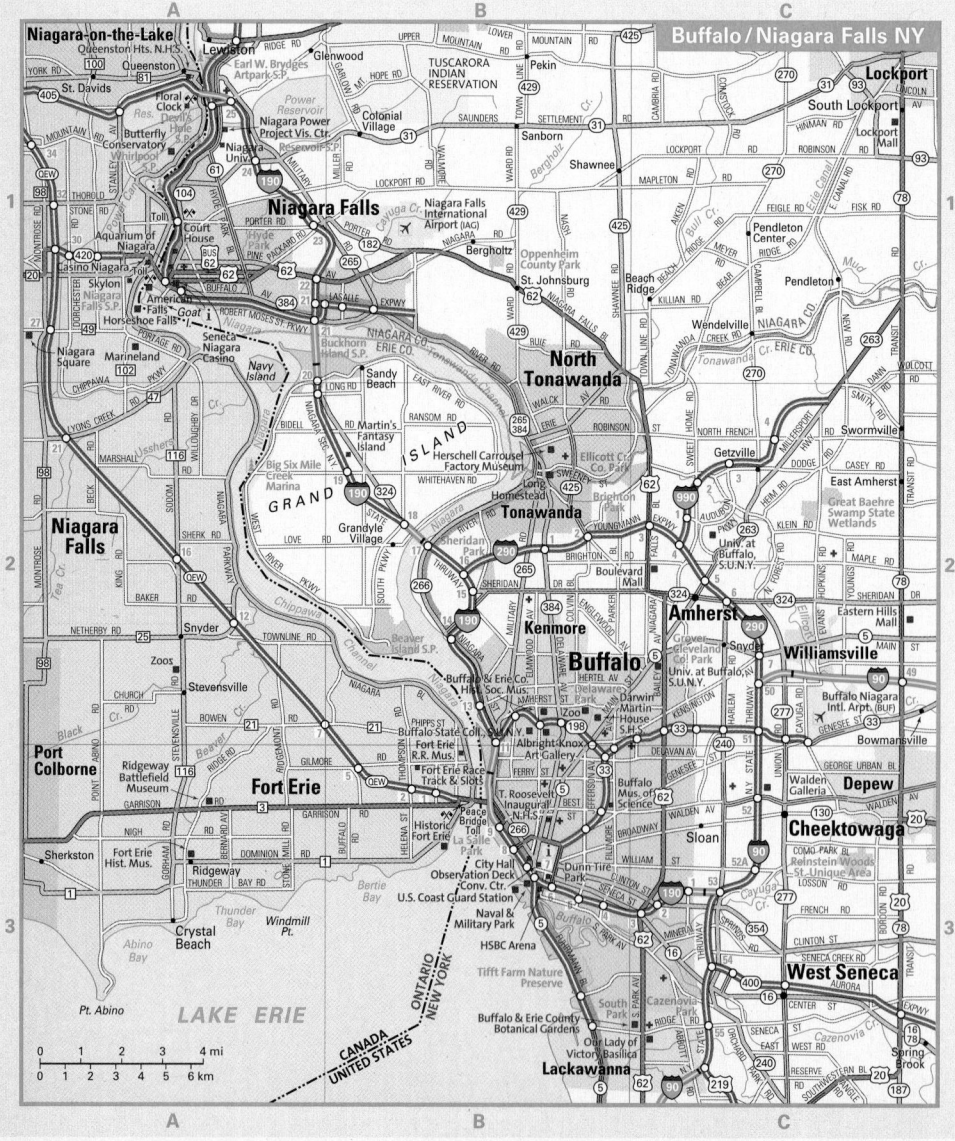

Buffalo / Niagara Falls NY

Entries in **bold black** indicate counties or parishes.
Entries in **bold color** indicate cities with detailed inset maps.

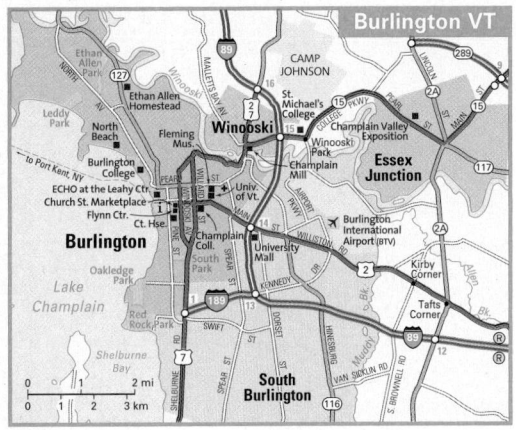

Burlington VT

Canton OH inset map

Green — A1
Canton — B1
Crystal Sprs. — A1
Fairhope — B1
Hills and Dales — A1
Louisville — B1
Massillon — A2
McDonaldsville — A1
Meyers Lake — A1
Middlebranch — B1
N. Canton — B1
Perry Hts. — A2
Reedurban — A2
Richville — A2
Waco — B2

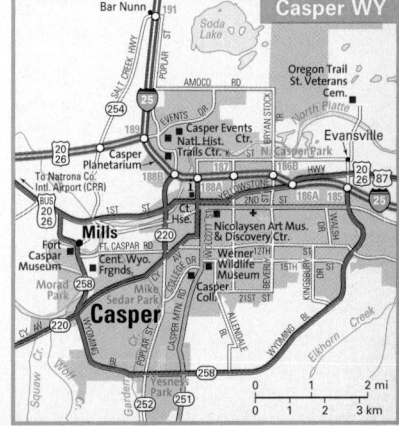

Carson City NV · Casper WY

200

Cattaraugus County–Chippewa Falls

Figures after entries indicate population, page number, and grid reference.

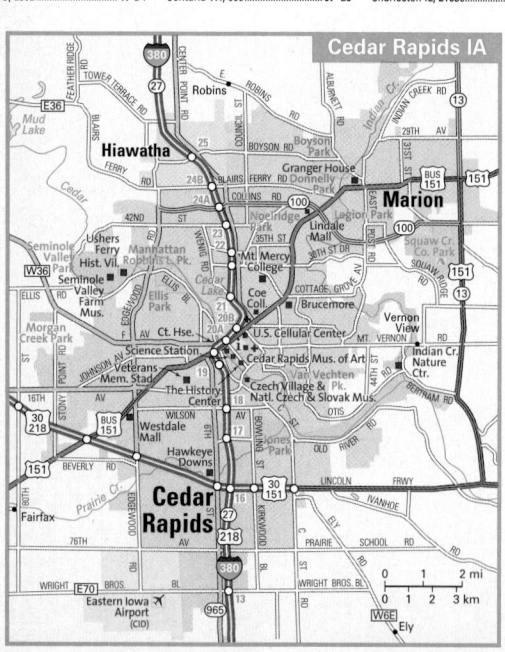

Cedar Rapids IA

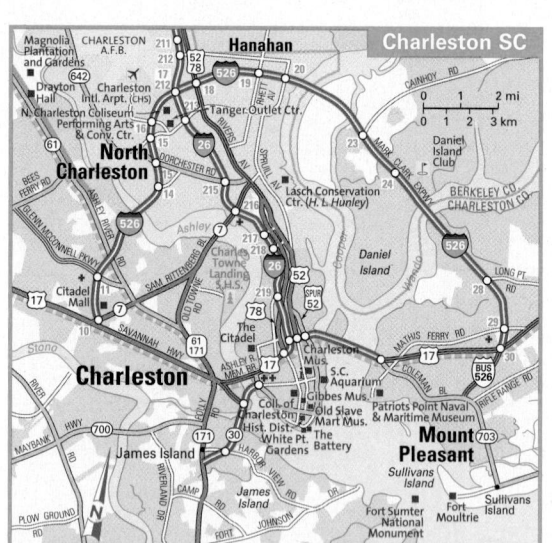

Charleston SC

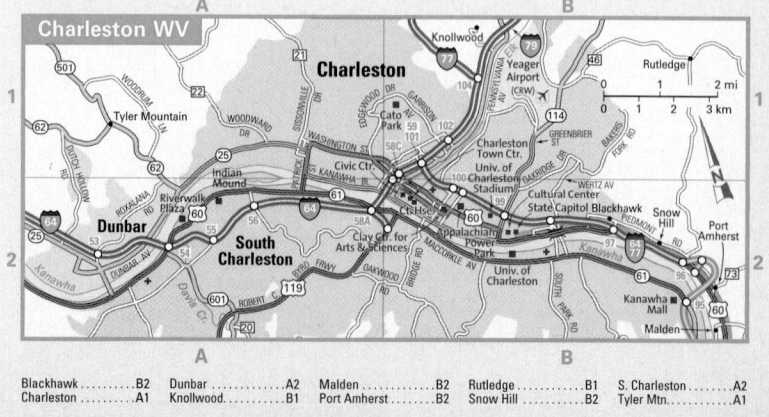

Charleston WV

Entries in **bold black** indicate counties or parishes.
Entries in **bold color** indicate cities with detailed inset maps.

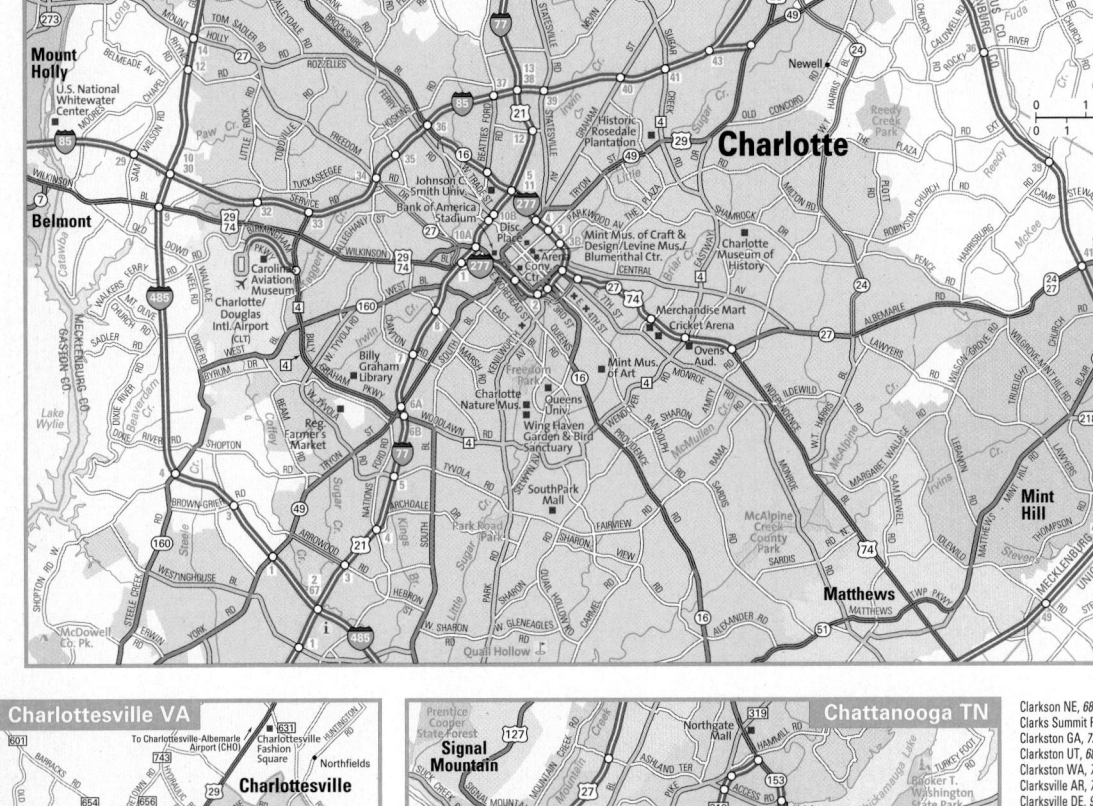

Charlotte NC

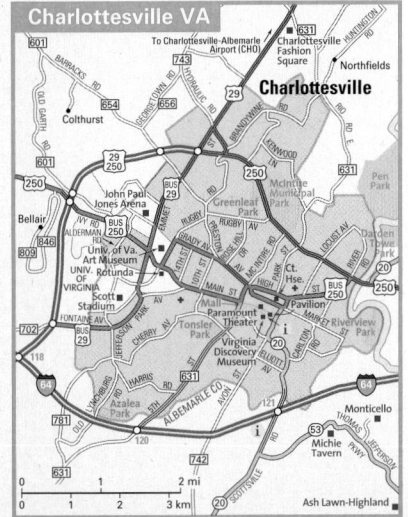

Charlottesville VA

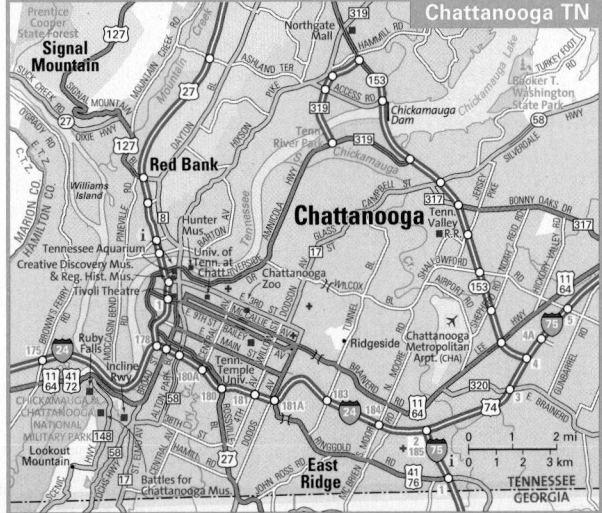

Chattanooga TN

202

Clinchco—Columbiana County

Figures after entries indicate population, page number, and grid reference.

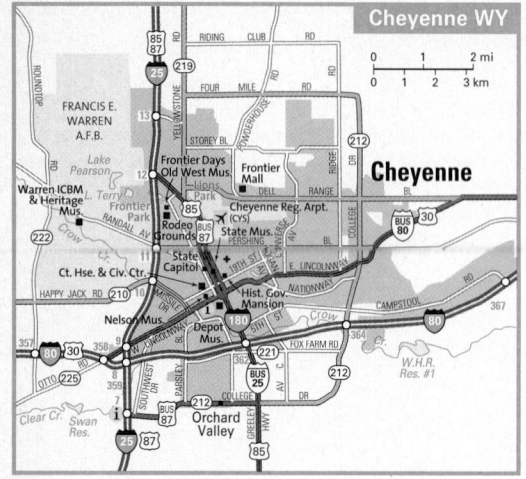

Cheyenne WY

POINTS OF INTEREST

900 North Michigan Avenue Shops ..B1
Adler Planetarium &
Astronomy Museum C3
Art Institute of Chicago B2
Auditorium Building B2
Buckingham Fountain B2
Cadillac Palace Theatre B2
Centennial Fountain & Arc B2
Chicago Architecture Foundation ..B2
Chicago Board of Trade B2
Chicago Ctr. for the Perform. Arts ..A1
Chicago Children's Museum C1
Chicago Cultural Center B2
Chicago Fire Marker A3
Chicago Mercantile Exchange A2
Chicago Place B1
Chicago Stock Exchange B2
Chicago Theatre B2
Chicago Yacht Club B2
City Hall B2
Civic Opera House A2
Cloud Gate B2
Crown Fountain B2
Daley Plaza B2
Dearborn Station B3
The Field Museum C3
Ford Center for the Performing Arts ..B2
Goodman Theatre B2
Harris Theater B2
Harold Washington Library Center ..B2
James R. Thompson Center B2
Jane Addams' Hull House Mus. A3
John G. Shedd Aquarium C3
John Hancock Center B1
LaSalle Bank Theatre A2
Merchandise Mart A2
Monadnock Building B2
Moody Bible Institute B1
Mus. of Broadcast Communications ..B1
Mus. of Contemporary Art B1
Mus. of Contemporary
Photography B3
Navy Pier C1
Newberry Library B1
New Maxwell Street Market A3
Northwestern University
(Chicago Campus) C1
Petrillo Band Shell B2
Pritzker Pavilion B2
River East Plaza C1
Sears Tower A2
Smith Museum of Stained Glass
Windows C1
Soldier Field C3
Spertus Museum B2
Symphony Center B2
Tribune Tower B1
Univ. of Illinois at Chicago A3
Water Tower B1
Water Tower Place B1
Wrigley Building B1

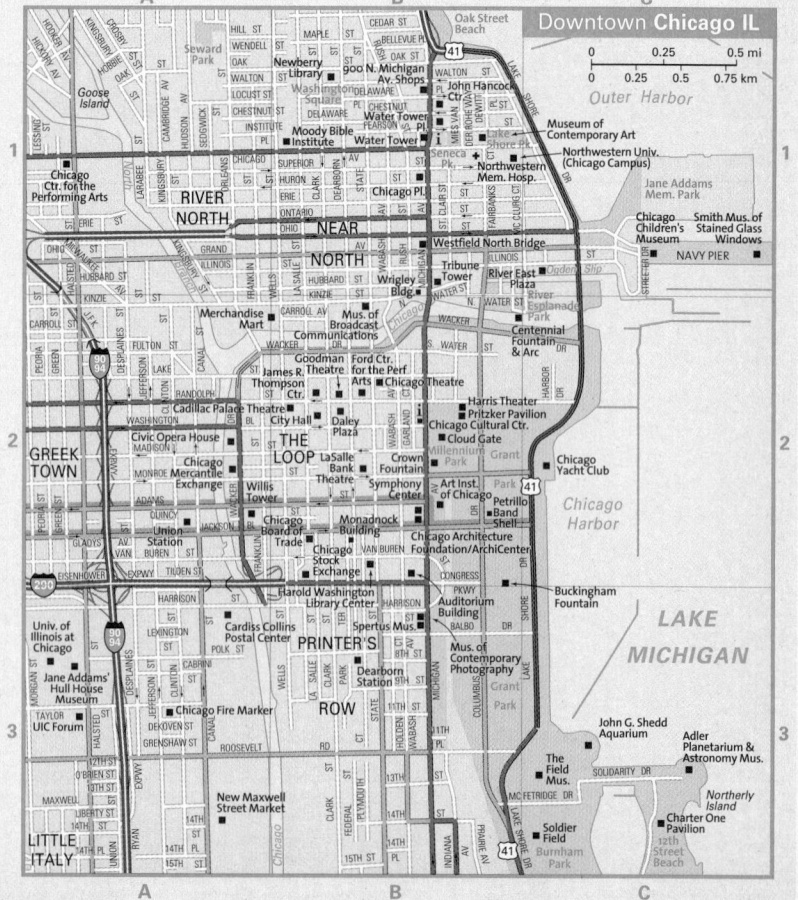

Downtown Chicago IL

Entries in **bold black** indicate counties or parishes.
Entries in **bold color** indicate cities with detailed inset maps.

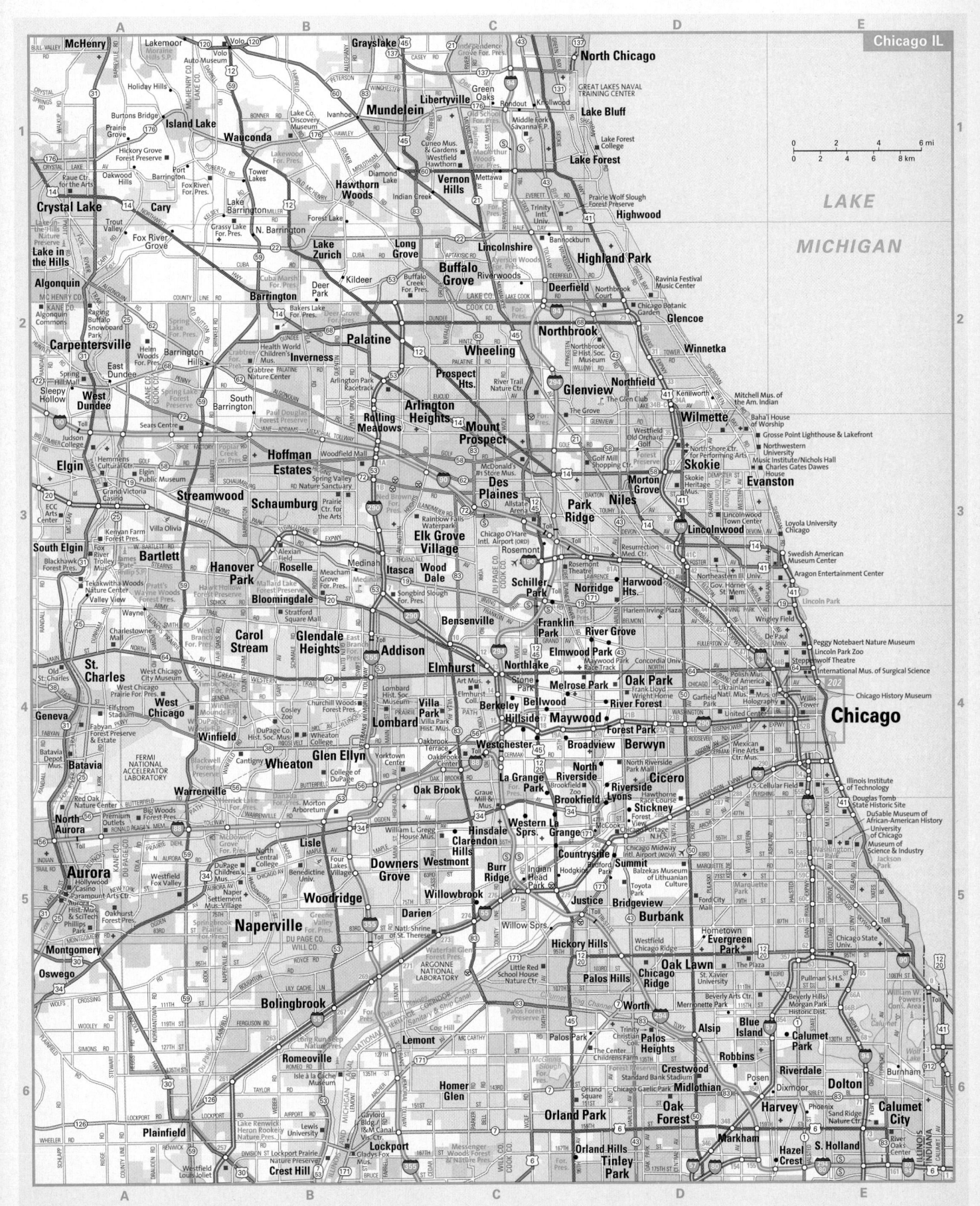

Chicago IL

LAKE

MICHIGAN

Figures after entries indicate population, page number, and grid reference.

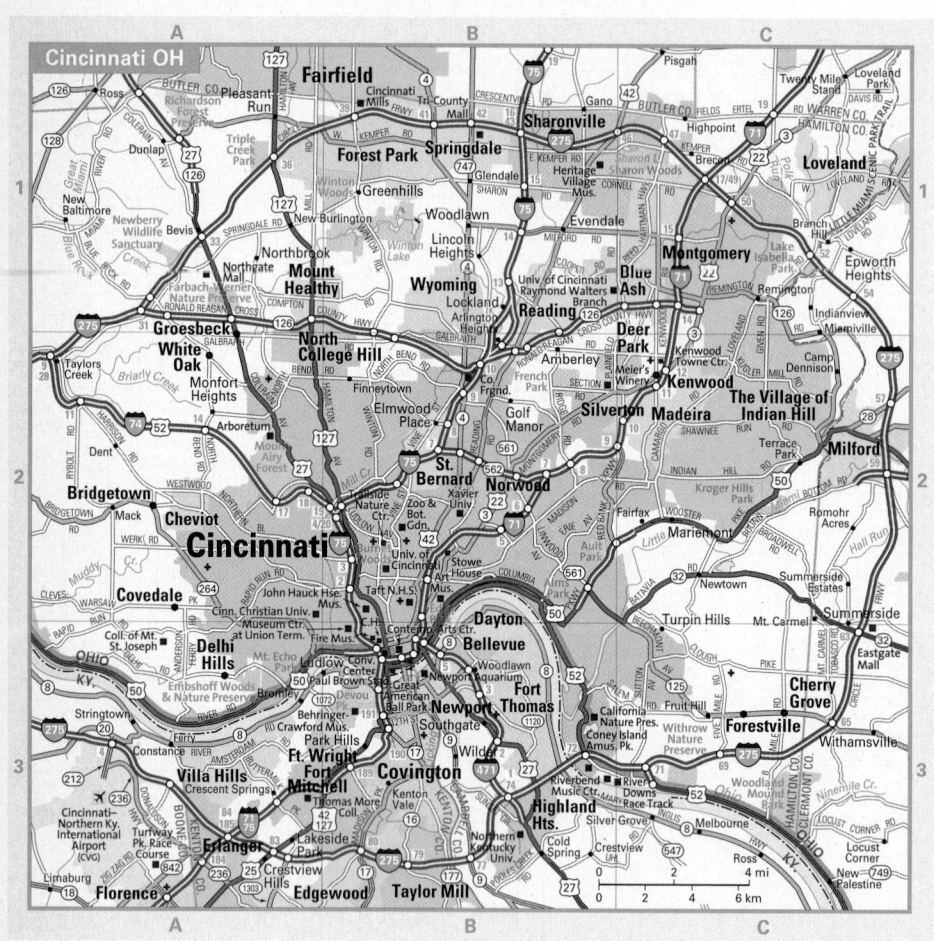

Cincinnati OH

Amberley	B2	Ft. Mitchell	A3	Newtown	C2
Arlington Hts.	B2	Ft. Thomas	B3	Northbrook	A1
Bellevue	B3	Ft. Wright	B3	N. College Hill	A2
Bevis	A1	Fruit Hill	C3	Norwood	B2
Blue Ash	C1	Gano	B1	Park Hills	B3
Branch Hill	C1	Glendale	B1	Pisgah	C1
Brecon	C1	Golf Manor	B2	Pleasant Run	A1
Bridgetown	A2	Greenhills	B1	Reading	B1
Bromley	A3	Groesbeck	A2	Remington	C2
Camp Dennison	C2	Highland Hts.	B3	Romohr Acres	C2
Cherry Grove	C3	Highpoint	C1	Ross, KY	C1
Cheviot	A2	Indianview	C1	Ross, OH	A1
Cincinnati	A2	Kenton Vale	B3	St. Bernard	B2
Cold Spr.	B3	Kenwood	C2	Sharonville	B1
Constance	A3	Lakeside Park	A3	Silver Grove	C3
Covedale	A2	Limaburg	A3	Silverton	B2
Covington	B3	Lincoln Hts.	B1	Southgate	B3
Crescent Sprs.	A3	Lockland	B1	Springdale	B1
Crestview	B3	Locust Corner	C3	Stringtown	A3
Crestview Hills	A3	Loveland	C1	Summerside	C2
Dayton	B2	Loveland Park	C1	Summerside
Deer Park	C2	Ludlow	A3	Estates	C2
Delhi Hills	A3	Mack	A2	Taylor Mill	B3
Dent	A1	Madeira	C2	Taylors Creek	A2
Dunlap	A1	Mariemont	C2	Terrace Park	C2
Edgewood	B3	Melbourne	C3	The Vil. of
Elmwood Place	B2	Miamiville	C1	Indian Hill	C2
Epworth Hts.	C1	Milford	C2	Turpin Hills	C3
Erlanger	A3	Monfort Hts.	A2	Twenty Mile Stand	C1
Evendale	B1	Montgomery	C1	Villa Hills	A3
Fairfax	C2	Mt. Carmel	C2	White Oak	A2
Fairfield	B1	Mt. Healthy	A1	Wilder	B3
Finneytown	B2	New Baltimore	A1	Withamsville	C3
Florence	A3	New Burlington	A1	Woodlawn, KY	B3
Forest Park	B1	New Palestine	C3	Woodlawn, OH	B1
Forestville	C3	Newport	B3	Wyoming	B1

Cleveland OH

205
Comstock Park–Crescent

Entries in **bold black** indicate counties or parishes.
Entries in **bold color** indicate cities with detailed inset maps.

Comstock Park MI, *10674* **75** F3
Concho Co. TX, *3966* **58** C4
Concord AL, *1809* **195** D2
Concord CA, *121780* **36** B3
Concord MA, *3500* **150** C1
Concord MI, *1101* **90** B1
Concord MO, *16689* **256** B3
Concord NH, *40687* **81** F4
Concord NC, *55977* **122** B1
Concord TN, *1700* **110** C4
Concord VA, *800* **112** C1
Concordia KS, *5714* **43** E1
Concordia MO, *2360* **96** C2
Concordia Par. LA, *20247* **125** F4
Concrete WA, *790* **12** C2
Condon OR, *759* **21** E2
Conecuh Co. AL, *14089* **127** F4
Conehatta MS, *997* **126** C2
Conejos CO, *125* **49** D1
Conejos Co. CO, *8400* **41** D4
Conestoga PA, *1400* **146** A3
Confluence PA, *834* **102** B1
Congers NY, *8303* **148** B2
Congress AZ, *1717* **46** C4
Conklin NY, *850* **93** F1
Conneaut OH, *12485* **91** F1
Conneaut Lake PA, *708* **91** F2
Conneaut Lake Park PA, *2502* **91** F2
Conneautville PA, *848* **91** F1
Connell WA, *2956* **13** F4
Connellsville PA, *9146* **102** B1
Connersville IN, *15411* **100** A1
Conover NC, *6604* **111** F4
Conovertown NJ, *1000* **147** F4
Conrad IA, *1055* **87** D1
Conrad MT, *2753* **15** E2
Conroe TX, *36811* **132** A2
Conshohocken PA, *7589* **146** C2
Constantia NY, *1107* **79** E3
Constantine MI, *2095* **89** F1
Continental OH, *1188* **90** B3
Contoocook NH, *1444* **81** F4
Contra Costa Co. CA, *948816* **36** B3
Convent LA, *250* **134** A3
Converse IN, *1137* **89** F3
Converse LA, *400* **124** C3
Converse TX, *11508* **257** F2
Converse Co. WY, *12052* **33** E1
Convoy OH, *1110* **90** A3
Conway AR, *43167* **117** E1
Conway FL, *14394* **246** C3
Conway MO, *743* **107** D1
Conway NH, *1692* **81** F3
Conway NC, *734* **113** E3
Conway PA, *2290* **91** F3
Conway SC, *11788* **123** D4
Conway Co. AR, *20336* **117** E1
Conway Sprs. KS, *1322* **43** E4
Conyers GA, *10689* **120** C4
Conyngham PA, *1958* **93** E3
Cook MN, *622* **64** C3
Cook Co. GA, *15771* **129** E4
Cook Co. IL, *5376741* **89** D1
Cook Co. MN, *5168* **65** D2
Cooke Co. TX, *36363* **59** E1
Cookeville TN, *23923* **110** A4
Cooleemee NC, *905* **112** A4
Coolidge AZ, *7786* **54** C2
Coolidge GA, *552* **137** E1
Coolidge TX, *848* **59** F4
Cool Valley MO, *1081* **256** B1
Coon Rapids IA, *1305* **86** B1
Coon Rapids MN, *61607* **67** D3
Coon Valley WI, *714* **73** F2
Cooper TX, *2150* **124** A1
Cooper City FL, *27939* **233** A3
Cooper Co. MO, *16670* **97** D3
Coopersburg PA, *2582* **146** C1
Coopers Mills ME, *350* **82** C2
Cooperstown NY, *2032* **79** F4
Cooperstown ND, *1053* **19** E3
Coopersville MI, *3910* **75** F3
Coopertown TN, *3027* **109** E3
Coosa Co. AL, *12202* **128** A1
Coosada AL, *1382* **128** A2
Coos Bay OR, *15374* **20** A4
Coos Co. NH, *33111* **81** F1
Coos Co. OR, *62779* **20** B4
Copalis Beach WA, *489* **12** B3
Copan OK, *796* **51** F1
Copenhagen NY, *865* **79** E2
Copiague NY, *21922* **148** C4
Copiah Co. MS, *28757* **126** A3
Coplay PA, *3387* **189** A1
Copley OH, *2000* **188** A1
Coppell TX, *35958* **207** C1
Copperas Cove TX, *29592* **59** E4
Copperhill TN, *511* **120** C2
Copperopolis CA, *2363* **36** C3
Coquille OR, *4184* **28** A1
Coral Gables FL, *42249* **143** E2
Coral Hills MD, *10720* **270** E4
Coral Sprs. FL, *117549* **143** E1
Coralville IA, *15123* **87** F2
Coram MT, *337* **15** D2
Coram NY, *34923* **149** D3
Coraopolis PA, *6131* **250** A1
Corbin KY, *7742* **110** C2
Corcoran CA, *14458* **45** D3
Corcoran MN, *5630* **66** C3
Cordaville MA, *2515* **150** C1
Cordele GA, *11608* **129** D3
Cordell OK, *2867* **51** D3
Cordova AL, *2423* **119** E4
Cordova AK, *2454* **154** C3
Cordova IL, *633* **88** A2
Cordova MD, *592* **145** D3
Cordova NC, *1100* **122** C2
Cordova TN, *2800* **118** B1
Corea ME, *450* **83** E2
Corfu NY, *795* **78** B3
Corinna ME, *600* **82** C1
Corinne UT, *621* **31** E3
Corinth MS, *14054* **119** D2
Corinth NY, *2474* **80** C4
Corinth TX, *11325* **59** E2
Corn OK, *591* **51** D3
Cornelia GA, *3674* **121** D3
Cornelius NC, *11969* **122** A1
Cornelius OR, *9652* **20** B2
Cornell WI, *1466* **67** F3
Cornersville TN, *962* **119** F1
Cornfields AZ, *300* **47** F2
Corning AR, *3679* **108** A3
Corning CA, *6741* **36** B1
Corning IA, *1783* **86** B3
Corning NY, *10842* **93** D1
Corning OH, *593* **101** E1
Cornish ME, *400* **82** A3
Cornville AZ, *3335* **47** D4
Cornwall PA, *3486* **93** E4
Cornwall-on-Hudson NY, *3058* **148** B1
Corona CA, *124966* **53** D3
Coronado CA, *24100* **53** D4
Corpus Christi TX, *277454* **63** F2

Black Forest........ D1
Cascade........... C1
Chipita Park........ C1
Colorado Sprs....... D1
Crystola........... C1
Fountain........... D2
Green Mtn. Falls.... C1
Manitou Sprs....... C2
Security-Widefield.. D2
Stratmoor Hills...... D2

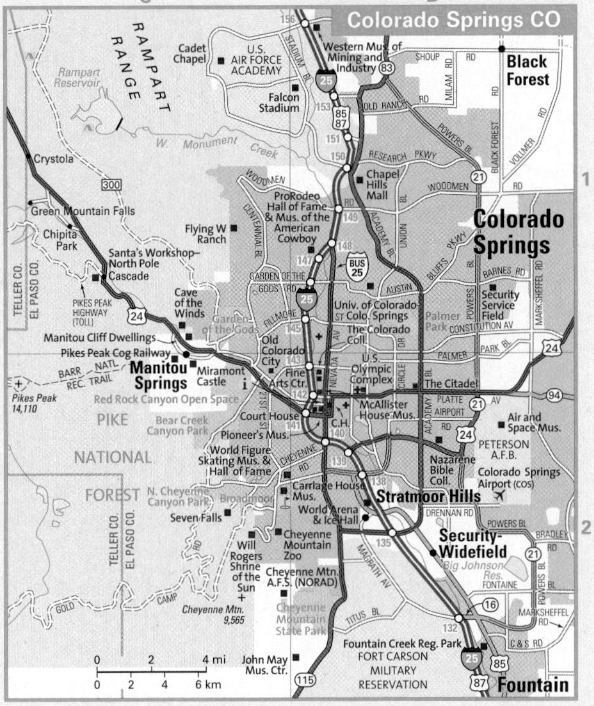
Colorado Springs CO
C
D
1
2
RAMPART RANGE
Rampart Reservoir
Cadet Chapel
U.S. AIR FORCE ACADEMY
Western Mus. of Mining and Industry
Black Forest
Falcon Stadium
W. Monument Creek
Crystola
Chapel Hills Mall
Green Mountain Falls
Chipita Park
ProRodeo Hall of Fame & Mus. of the American Cowboy
Flying W Ranch
Colorado Springs
Santa's Workshop-North Pole
Cascade
TELLER CO.
EL PASO CO.
PIKES PEAK HIGHWAY (TOLL)
Cave of the Winds
Garden of the Gods
Univ. of Colorado-Colo. Springs
The Colorado Coll.
Security Service Field
Palmer Park
Manitou Cliff Dwellings
Pikes Peak Cog Railway
Manitou Springs
Miramont Castle
Old Colorado City
Fine Arts Ctr.
U.S. Olympic Complex
The Citadel
Pikes Peak 14,110
Red Rock Canyon Open Space
Bear Creek Canyon Park
Court House
C.H.
McAllister House Mus.
Pioneer's Mus.
Air and Space Mus.
PIKE
NATIONAL
FOREST
World Figure Skating Mus. & Hall of Fame
Nazarene Bible Coll.
PETERSON A.F.B.
Colorado Springs Airport (COS)
N. Cheyenne Canyon Park
Carriage House Mus.
Stratmoor Hills
Seven Falls
World Arena & Ice Hall
Will Rogers Shrine of the Sun
Cheyenne Mountain Zoo
Cheyenne Mtn. A.F.S. (NORAD)
Security-Widefield
Big Johnson Res.
Cheyenne Mtn. 9,565
Cheyenne Mountain State Park
Fountain Creek Reg. Park
FORT CARSON MILITARY RESERVATION
John May Mus. Ctr.
Fountain
0 2 4 mi
0 2 4 6 km

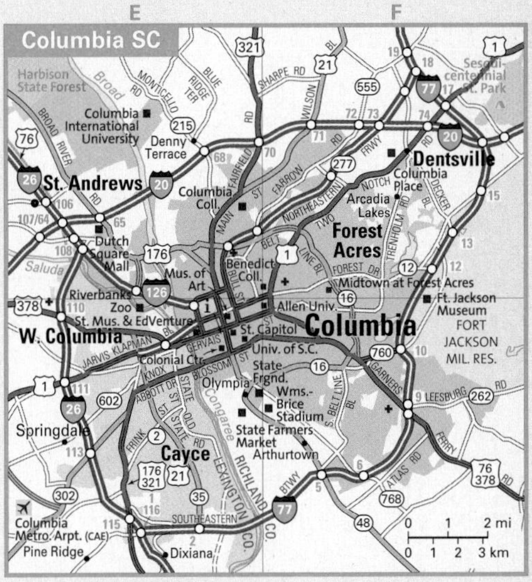
Columbia SC
E
F
1
2
Harbison State Forest
Columbia International University
Denny Terrace
St. Andrews
Dentsville
Columbia Place
Arcadia Lakes
Forest Acres
Sesquicentennial St. Park
Columbia Coll.
Dutch Square Mall
Mus. of Art
Benedict Coll.
Midtown at Forest Acres
Ft. Jackson Museum
FORT JACKSON MIL. RES.
Riverbanks Zoo
Allen Univ.
St. Mus. & EdVenture
St. Capitol
W. Columbia
Columbia
Colonial Ctr.
Univ. of S.C.
State Frgnd.
Olympia
Wms.-Brice Stadium
Springdale
State Farmers Market
Arthurtown
Cayce
Columbia Metro. Arpt. (CAE)
Pine Ridge
Dixiana
0 1 2 mi
0 1 2 3 km

Arcadia Lakes.............F1
Arthurtown..............F2
Cayce..................E2
Columbia................F2
Denny Terrace...........E1
Dentsville...............F1
Dixiana.................E2
Forest Acres............F1
Olympia.................E2
Pineridge...............E2
St. Andrews.............E1
Springdale..............E2
W. Columbia.............E2

Corrales NM, *7334* **48** C3
Corralitos CA, *2431* **44** B2
Correctionville IA, *851* **72** A4
Corrigan TX, *1721* **132** B1
Corry PA, *6834* **92** A1
Corryton TN, *650* **110** C4
Corsica SD, *644* **27** E4
Corsicana TX, *24485* **59** F3
Corson Co. SD, *4181* **26** C1
Cortaro AZ, *1700* **55** D3
Corte Madera CA, *9100* **259** A2
Cortez CO, *7977* **40** B4
Cortez FL, *4491* **140** B3
Cortland IL, *2066* **88** C1
Cortland NE, *488* **35** F4
Cortland NY, *18740* **79** D4
Cortland OH, *6830* **91** F2
Cortland Co. NY, *48599* **79** E4
Corunna MI, *3381* **76** B3
Corvallis MT, *443* **15** D4
Corvallis OR, *49322* **20** B3
Corydon IN, *2715* **99** F4
Corydon IA, *1591* **87** D3
Corydon KY, *744* **109** E1
Coryell Co. TX, *74978* **59** E4
Coshocton OH, *11682* **91** E4
Coshocton Co. OH, *36655* **91** E4
Cosmopolis WA, *1595* **12** B4
Cosmos MN, *582* **66** B4
Costa Mesa CA, *108724* **228** E5
Costilla Co. CO, *3663* **41** E4
Cotati CA, *6471* **36** B3
Coto de Caza CA, *13057* **229** G5
Cottage City MD, *1136* **270** E3
Cottage Grove MN, *30582* **67** D4
Cottage Grove OR, *8445* **20** B4
Cottage Grove WI, *4059* **74** B3
Cottage Hill FL, *1300* **135** F1
Cottageville SC, *707* **130** C1
Cottageville WV, *750* **101** E3
Cotter AR, *921* **107** E3
Cottle Co. TX, *1904* **58** B1
Cotton Co. OK, *6614* **51** D4
Cottondale AL, *2000* **127** E1
Cottondale FL, *869* **136** C1
Cotton Plant AR, *960* **117** F2
Cottonport LA, *2316* **133** F1
Cotton Valley LA, *1189* **125** D2
Cottonwood AL, *1170* **137** D1
Cottonwood AZ, *9179* **47** D4
Cottonwood CA, *2960* **28** C4
Cottonwood ID, *944* **22** B1
Cottonwood MN, *1148* **66** A4
Cottonwood Co. MN, *12167* **72** A1
Cottonwood Cove NV, *100* **46** B3
Cottonwood Falls KS, *966* **43** F3
Cottonwood Hts. UT, *27569* **257** B3
Cottonwood Shores TX, *877* **61** D1
Cotuit MA, *2400* **151** E4
Cotulla TX, *3614* **60** C4
Coudersport PA, *2650* **92** C1
Coulee City WA, *600* **13** E3
Coulee Dam WA, *1044* **13** E2
Coulterville IL, *1230* **98** B4
Council ID, *816* **22** B3
Council Bluffs IA, *58268* **86** A2
Council Grove KS, *2321* **43** F2
Country Club Hills MO, *1381* **256** B1
Country Club Vil. MO, *1846* **96** B1
Country Homes WA, *5203* **14** A3
Country Knolls NY, *2155* **94** B1
Countryside IL, *5991* **203** C5
Countryside VA, *8300* **144** A3
Coupeville WA, *1723* **12** C2
Courtdale PA, *791* **261** B1
Courtland AL, *769* **119** E2
Courtland MN, *538* **72** B1
Courtland MS, *460* **118** B3
Courtland VA, *1270* **113** E3
Courtney TX, *1500* **61** F1
Coushatta LA, *2299* **125** D3
Cove OR, *594* **21** F2
Covedale OH, *6360* **204** A2
Covelo CA, *1175* **36** A1
Coventry CT, *1381* **150** A3
Coventry Ctr. RI, *850* **150** C3
Covert MI, *650* **75** E4
Covina CA, *46837* **229** F2
Covington GA, *11547* **121** D4
Covington IN, *2565* **89** D4
Covington KY, *43370* **100** B2
Covington LA, *8483* **134** B2
Covington OH, *2559* **90** B4
Covington OK, *553* **51** E2
Covington TN, *8463* **118** B1
Covington VA, *6303* **112** B1
Covington WA, *13783* **262** B4
Covington Co. AL, *37631* **128** A4
Covington Co. MS, *19407* **126** C4
Cowan TN, *1770* **120** A1
Cowan Hts. CA, *4700* **229** F4
Coward SC, *650* **122** C4
Cowarts AL, *1546* **137** D1
Cowden IL, *612* **98** C2
Cowen WV, *513* **102** A3
Coweta OK, *7139* **106** A4
Coweta Co. GA, *89215* **128** C1
Cowley WY, *560* **24** C2
Cowley Co. KS, *36291* **43** F4
Cowlitz Co. WA, *92948* **20** C1
Cowpens SC, *2279* **121** F2
Coxsackie NY, *2895* **94** B2
Cozad NE, *4163* **34** C4
Crab Orchard KY, *842* **110** B1
Crab Orchard TN, *838* **110** B4
Crab Orchard WV, *2761* **111** F1
Crafton PA, *6706* **250** A2
Craig AK, *1397* **155** E4
Craig CO, *9189* **32** C4
Craig Beach OH, *1254* **91** F3
Craig Co. OK, *14950* **106** A2
Craig Co. VA, *5091* **112** B1
Craighead Co. AR, *82148* **108** A4
Craigmont ID, *556* **22** B1
Craigsville VA, *979* **102** B4
Craigsville WV, *2204* **102** A4
Crainville IL, *992* **108** C1
Cramerton NC, *2976* **122** A1
Cranbury NJ, *2008* **147** D2
Crandall TX, *2774* **59** F2
Crandon WI, *1961* **68** B3
Crane MO, *1390* **106** C2
Crane TX, *3191* **58** A4
Crane Co. TX, *3996* **57** F4
Cranesville PA, *600* **91** F1
Cranford NJ, *22578* **147** E1
Cranston RI, *79269* **150** C3
Craven Co. NC, *91436* **115** D3
Crawford CO, *366* **40** C2
Crawford GA, *807* **121** E4
Crawford MS, *655* **127** D1
Crawford NE, *1107* **33** F1
Crawford TX, *705* **59** E4
Crawford Co. AR, *53247* **116** C1
Crawford Co. GA, *12495* **129** D2
Crawford Co. IL, *20452* **99** D2
Crawford Co. IN, *10743* **99** F4
Crawford Co. IA, *16942* **86** A1
Crawford Co. KS, *38242* **106** B1
Crawford Co. MI, *14273* **70** C4
Crawford Co. MO, *22804* **97** F4
Crawford Co. OH, *46966* **90** C3
Crawford Co. PA, *90366* **91** F1
Crawford Co. WI, *17243* **73** F3
Crawfordsville AR, *514* **118** B1
Crawfordsville IN, *15243* **89** E4
Crawfordville FL, *750* **137** E2
Crawfordville GA, *572* **121** E4
Creal Sprs. IL, *702* **108** C1
Creede CO, *377* **40** C4
Creedmoor NC, *2232* **112** C4
Creek Co. OK, *67367* **51** F2
Creekside KY, *336* **230** F1
Creighton NE, *1270* **35** E2
Crenshaw MS, *916* **118** B3
Crenshaw Co. AL, *13665* **128** A4
Creola AL, *2002* **135** E1
Cresaptown MD, *5884* **102** C1
Crescent IA, *537* **86** A2

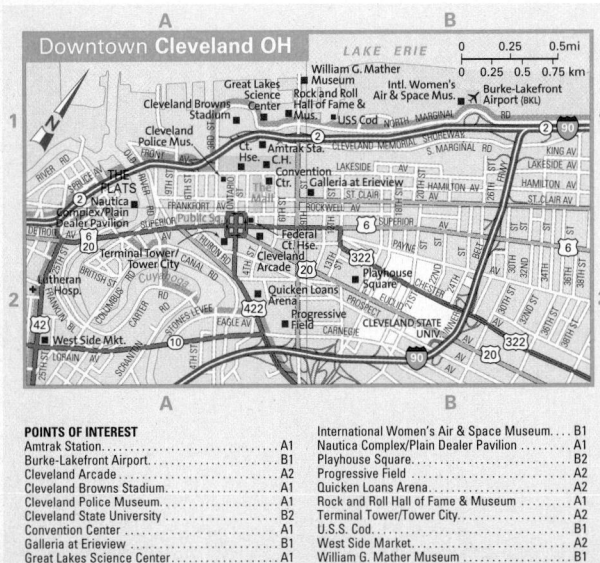

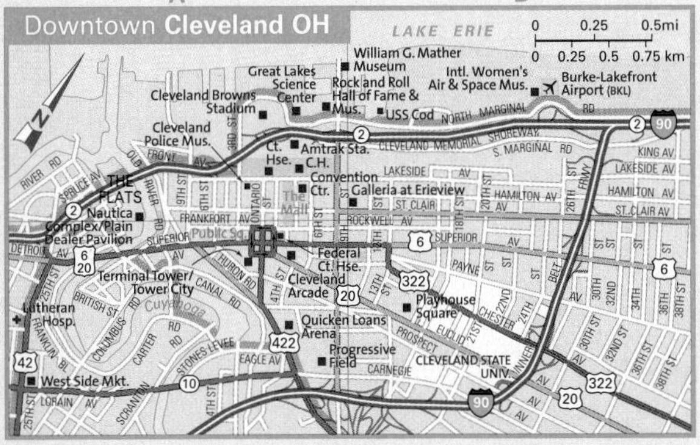
Downtown Cleveland OH
A
B
1
2
LAKE ERIE
0 0.25 0.5 mi
0 0.25 0.5 0.75 km
William G. Mather Museum
Great Lakes Science Center
Rock and Roll Hall of Fame & Mus.
Intl. Women's Air & Space Mus.
Burke-Lakefront Airport (BKL)
Cleveland Browns Stadium
USS Cod
Cleveland Police Mus.
Amtrak Sta.
Ct. Hse.
C.H.
Convention Ctr.
Galleria at Erieview
THE FLATS
Nautica Complex/Plain Dealer Pavilion
Public Sq.
Terminal Tower/Tower City
Federal Ct. Hse.
Cleveland Arcade
Playhouse Square
Lutheran Hosp.
Quicken Loans Arena
Progressive Field
CLEVELAND STATE UNIV.
West Side Mkt.

POINTS OF INTEREST

Amtrak Station.......................A1
Burke-Lakefront Airport...............B1
Cleveland Arcade....................A2
Cleveland Browns Stadium.............A1
Cleveland Police Museum..............A1
Cleveland State University.............B2
Convention Center...................A1
Galleria at Erieview..................B1
Great Lakes Science Center............A1
International Women's Air & Space Museum....B1
Nautica Complex/Plain Dealer Pavilion.........A1
Playhouse Square......................B2
Progressive Field......................A2
Quicken Loans Arena...................A2
Rock and Roll Hall of Fame & Museum.......A1
Terminal Tower/Tower City...............A2
U.S.S. Cod...........................B1
West Side Market.......................A2
William G. Mather Museum.................B1

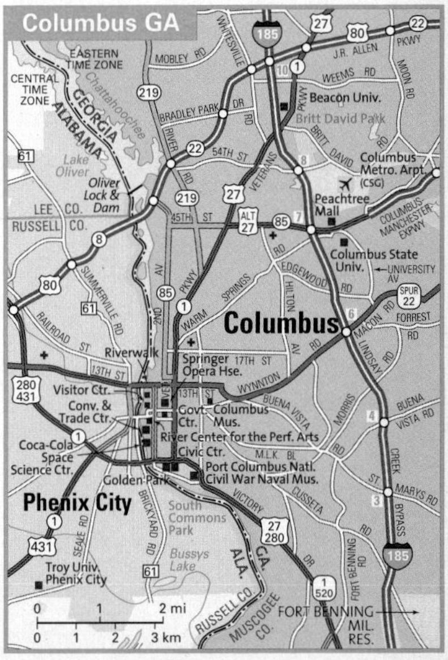
Columbus GA
EASTERN TIME ZONE
CENTRAL TIME ZONE
GEORGIA
ALABAMA
Chattahoochee
Beacon Univ.
Britt David Park
Columbus Metro. Arpt. (CSG)
Lake Oliver
Oliver Lock & Dam
LEE CO.
RUSSELL CO.
Peachtree Mall
Columbus State Univ.
UNIVERSITY AV
Columbus
Riverwalk
Springer Opera Hse.
Visitor Ctr.
Conv. & Trade Ctr.
Govt. Ctr.
Columbus Mus.
River Center for the Perf. Arts
Civic Ctr.
Coca-Cola Space Science Ctr.
Golden Park
Port Columbus Natl. Civil War Naval Mus.
Phenix City
South Commons Park
Bussys Lake
Troy Univ. Phenix City
MUSCOGEE CO.
FORT BENNING MIL. RES.
0 1 2 mi
0 1 2 3 km

206

Crescent–Decatur

Figures after entries indicate population, page number, and grid reference.

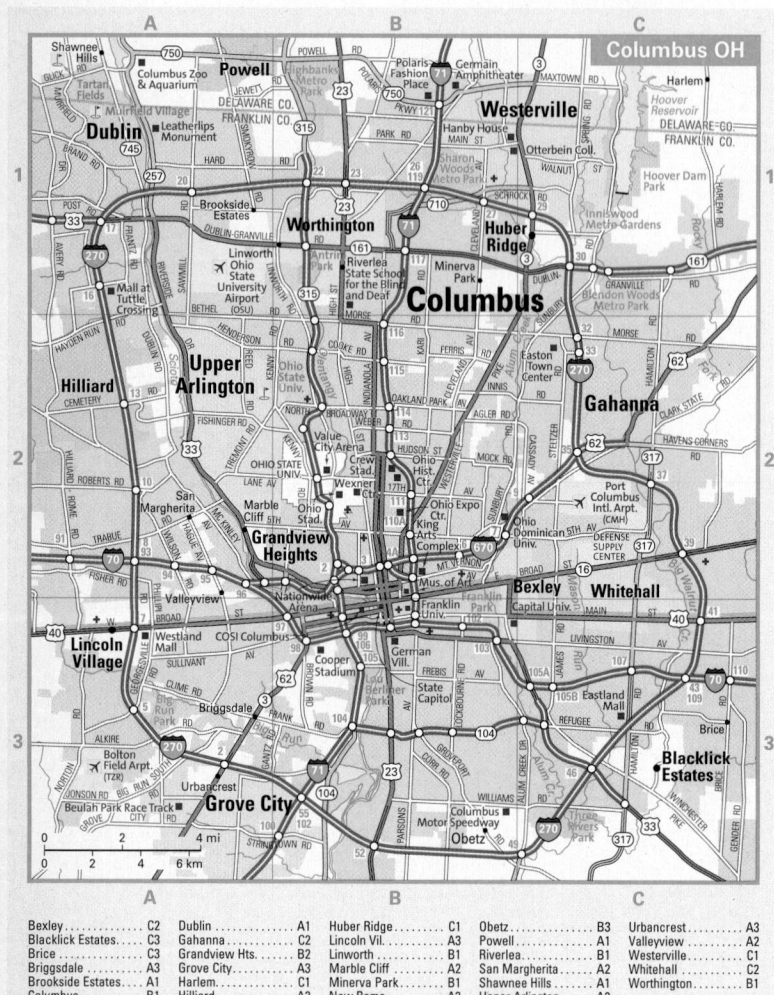

Columbus OH

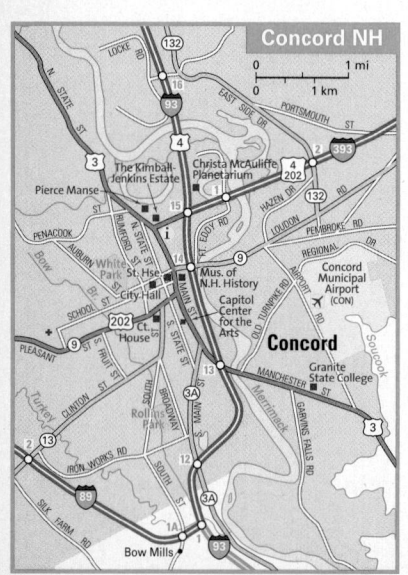

Concord NH

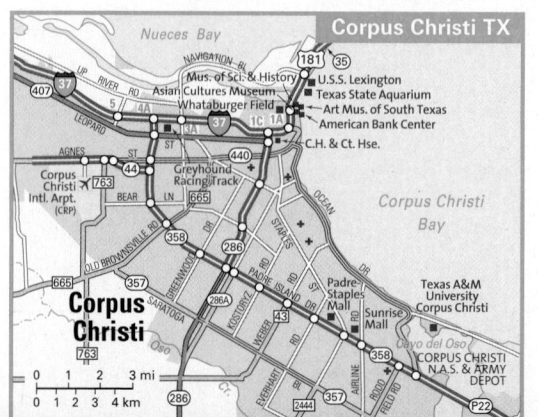

Corpus Christi TX

Entries in **bold black** indicate counties or parishes.
Entries in **bold color** indicate cities with detailed inset maps.

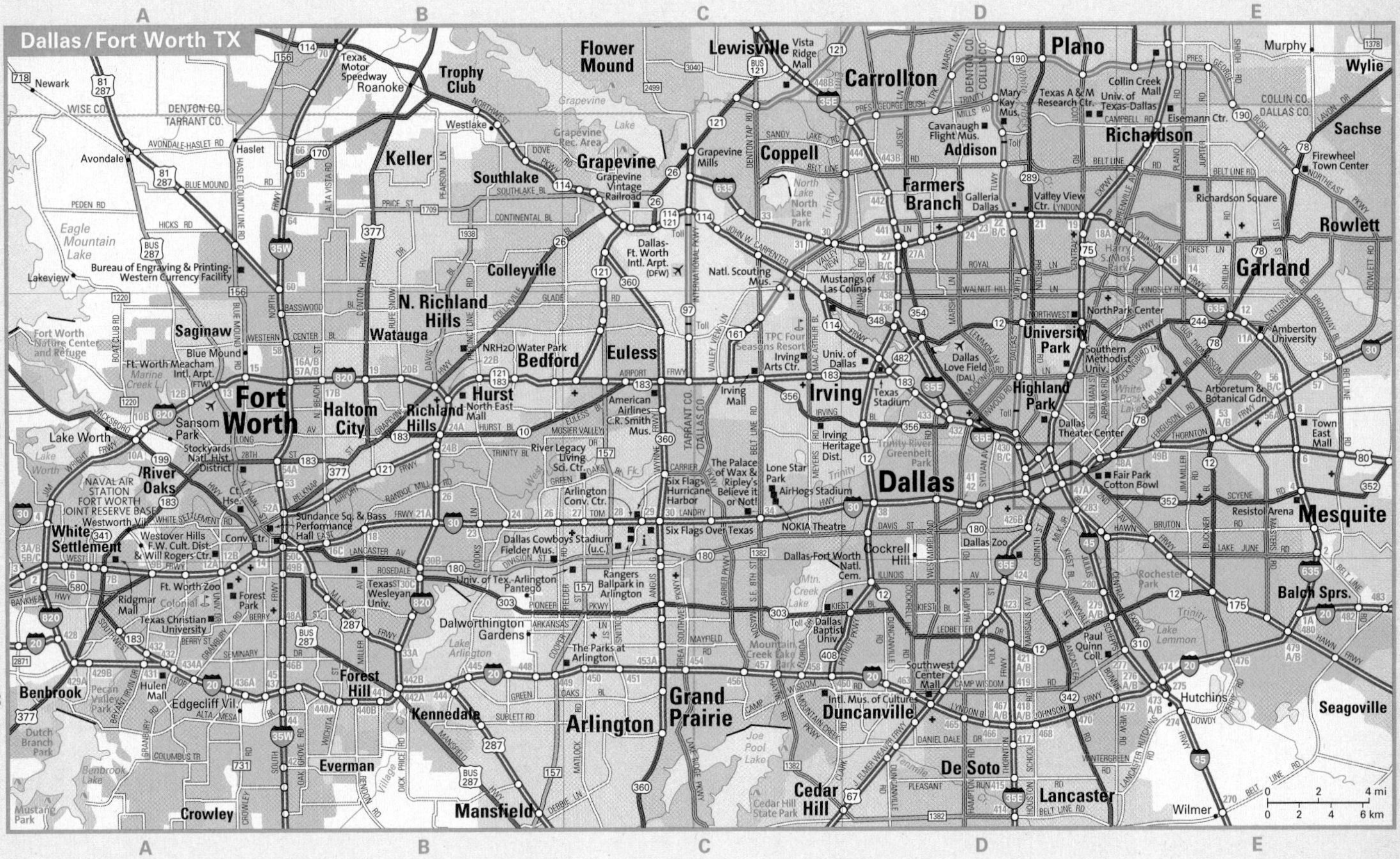

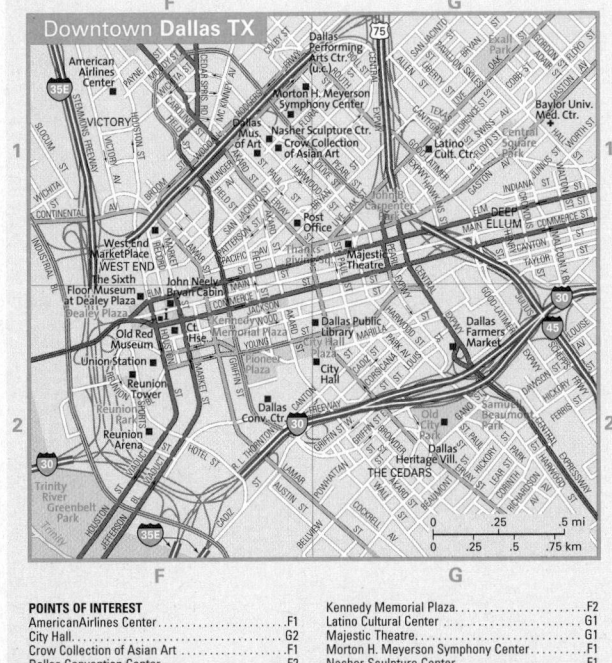

POINTS OF INTEREST

AmericanAirlines Center..............F1
City Hall...........................G2
Crow Collection of Asian Art........F1
Dallas Convention Center............F2
Dallas Heritage Village.............F2
Dallas Museum of Art................F1
Dallas Public Library...............G2
Farmers Market......................G2
John Neely Bryan Cabin..............F2

Kennedy Memorial Plaza..............F2
Latino Cultural Center..............G1
Majestic Theatre....................G1
Morton H. Meyerson Symphony Center..F1
Nasher Sculpture Ctr................F1
Old Red Museum......................F2
Reunion Arena.......................F2
Reunion Tower.......................F2
The Sixth Floor Museum at Dealey Plaza..F2
West End MarketPlace................F1

Figures after entries indicate population, page number, and grid reference.

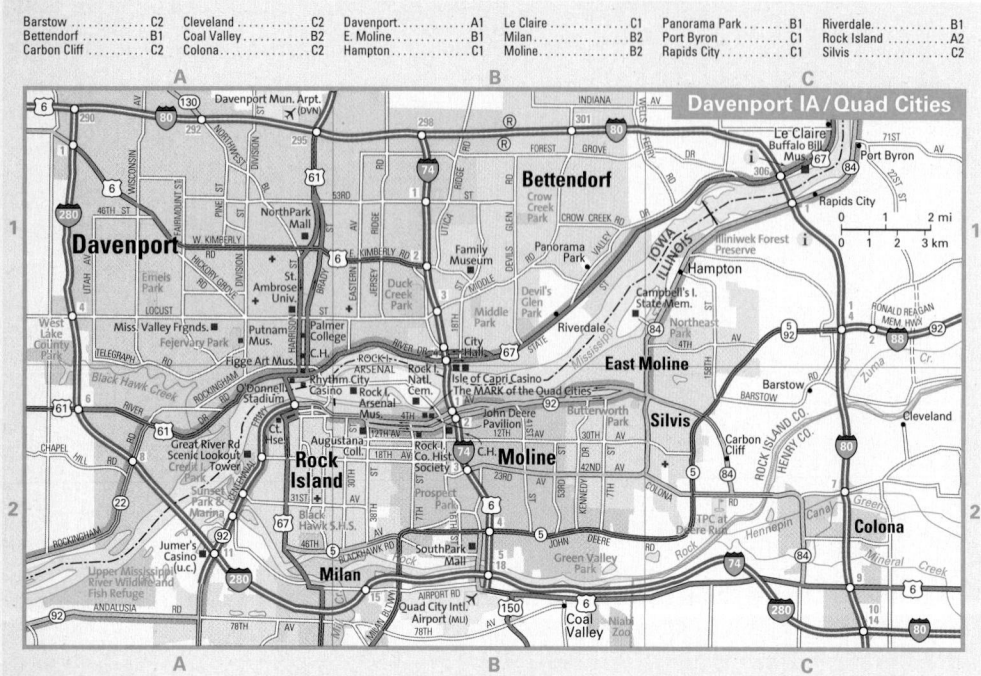

Davenport IA / Quad Cities

Barstow ... C2	Cleveland ... C2	Davenport ... A1	Le Claire ... C1	Panorama Park ... B1	Riverdale ... B1
Bettendorf ... B1	Coal Valley ... B2	E. Moline ... B1	Milan ... B2	Port Byron ... C1	Rock Island ... A2
Carbon Cliff ... C2	Colona ... C2	Hampton ... C1	Moline ... B2	Rapids City ... C1	Silvis ... C2

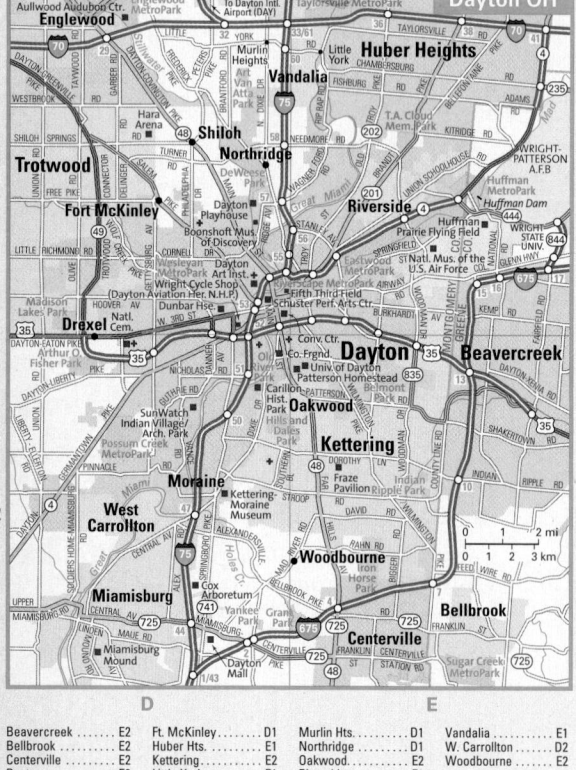

Dayton OH

Beavercreek ... E2	Ft. McKinley ... D1	Murlin Hts. ... D1	Vandalia ... E1
Bellbrook ... E2	Huber Hts. ... E1	Northridge ... D1	W. Carrollton ... D2
Centerville ... E2	Kettering ... E2	Oakwood ... E2	Woodbourne ... E2
Dayton ... D1	Little York ... E1	Riverside ... E1	
Drexel ... D1	Miamisburg ... D2	Shiloh ... D1	
Englewood ... D1	Moraine ... D2	Trotwood ... D1	

Des Plaines IL, *58720* ... 89 D1
Destin FL, *11119* ... 136 B2
Destrehan LA, *11260* ... 134 B3
Detroit MI, *951270* ... 76 C4
Detroit TX, *776* ... 116 A4
Detroit Beach MI, *2289* ... 90 C1
Detroit Lakes MN, *7348* ... 19 F4
Deuel Co. NE, *2098* ... 34 A3
Deuel Co. SD, *4498* ... 27 F2
De Valls Bluff AR, *783* ... 117 F2
Deville LA, *1007* ... 125 E4
Devils Lake ND, *7222* ... 19 D2
Devine TX, *4140* ... 61 D3

Devola OH, *2771* ... 101 F2
Devon PA, *5067* ... 248 A2
Dewar OK, *919* ... 116 A1
Dewey AZ, *6295* ... 47 D4
Dewey OK, *3179* ... 51 F1
Dewey Beach DE, *301* ... 145 F4
Dewey Co. OK, *4743* ... 51 D2
Dewey Co. SD, *5972* ... 26 C2
Deweyville TX, *1190* ... 132 C2
Deweyville UT, *278* ... 31 E3
De Witt AR, *3552* ... 117 F3
De Witt IA, *5049* ... 88 A1
De Witt MI, *4702* ... 76 A3

De Witt NE, *572* ... 35 F4
De Witt NY, *8200* ... 79 E3
De Witt Co. IL, *16798* ... 88 B4
DeWitt Co. TX, *20013* ... 61 E3
Dexter GA, *509* ... 129 E2
Dexter IA, *689* ... 86 C2
Dexter ME, *2201* ... 82 C1
Dexter MI, *2338* ... 76 B4
Dexter MO, *7356* ... 108 B2
Dexter NM, *1235* ... 57 E2
Dexter NY, *1120* ... 79 E1
Dexter OR, *2400* ... 20 C4
Diablo CA, *988* ... 259 D2

Daytona Beach FL

Allandale ... G2	Holly Hill ... F1	Port Orange ... G2
Daytona Beach ... F1	Ormond Beach ... F1	S. Daytona ... G2
Daytona Beach Shores ... G2	Ponce Inlet ... G2	Wilbur-by-the-Sea ... G2

Dilworth MN, *3001* ... 19 F4
Dimmit Co. TX, *10248* ... 60 C4
Dimmitt TX, *4375* ... 50 A4
Dimondale MI, *1342* ... 76 A4
Dinosaur CO, *319* ... 32 B4
Dinuba CA, *16844* ... 45 D3
Dinwiddie VA, *350* ... 113 E2
Dinwiddie Co. VA, *24533* ... 113 E2
Divernon IL, *1201* ... 98 B1
Divide Co. ND, *2283* ... 17 F1
Dixfield ME, *1137* ... 82 B2
Dixie Co. FL, *13827* ... 137 F3
Dixmoor IL, *3934* ... 203 E6
Dixon CA, *16103* ... 36 B3
Dixon IL, *15941* ... 88 B1
Dixon KY, *632* ... 109 E1
Dixon MO, *1570* ... 97 E4
Dixon MT, *216* ... 15 D3
Dixon Co. NE, *6339* ... 35 F1
D'Lo MS, *394* ... 126 B3
Dobbins Hts. NC, *936* ... 122 C2
Dobbs Ferry NY, *10622* ... 148 B3
Dobson NC, *1457* ... 112 B2
Dock Jct. GA, *6951* ... 139 D1
Doctor Phillips FL, *9548* ... 246 B3
Doctors Inlet FL, *1400* ... 139 D2
Doddridge Co. WV, *7403* ... 102 A2
Dodge NE, *700* ... 35 F2
Dodge Ctr. MN, *2226* ... 73 D1
Dodge City AL, *612* ... 119 F3
Dodge City KS, *25176* ... 42 C4
Dodge Co. GA, *19171* ... 129 E3
Dodge Co. MN, *17731* ... 73 D1
Dodge Co. NE, *36160* ... 35 F3
Dodge Co. WI, *85897* ... 74 C2
Dodgeville WI, *4220* ... 74 A3
Doerun GA, *828* ... 129 D4
Doland SD, *297* ... 27 E2
Dolan Sprs. AZ, *1867* ... 46 B3
Dolgeville NY, *2166* ... 79 F3
Dollar Bay MI, *950* ... 65 F3
Dolores CO, *857* ... 40 B4
Dolores Co. CO, *1844* ... 40 B4
Dolton IL, *25614* ... 203 E6
Doña Ana NM, *1379* ... 56 B3
Dona Ana Co. NM, *174682* ... 56 B3
Donald OR, *608* ... 20 B2
Donalsonville GA, *2796* ... 137 D1
Dongola IL, *806* ... 108 C1
Doniphan MO, *1932* ... 108 A3
Doniphan NE, *763* ... 35 E4
Doniphan Co. KS, *8249* ... 96 B1
Donna TX, *14768* ... 63 E4
Donnellson IA, *963* ... 87 F3
Donora PA, *5653* ... 92 A4
Dooly Co. GA, *11525* ... 129 D3
Doolittle MO, *644* ... 97 E4
Door Co. WI, *27961* ... 69 D4
Dora AL, *2413* ... 119 F4
Doraville GA, *9862* ... 120 C4
Dorchester NE, *615* ... 35 F4
Dorchester WI, *827* ... 68 A4

Dorchester Co. MD, *30674* ... 103 F4
Dorchester Co. SC, *96413* ... 130 C1
Dormont PA, *9305* ... 250 B3
Dorr MI, *2800* ... 75 F4
Dorris CA, *886* ... 28 C2
Dorset VT, *400* ... 81 D4
Dorsey MD, *1000* ... 193 B4
Dortches NC, *809* ... 113 D4
Dos Palos CA, *4581* ... 44 C2
Dothan AL, *57737* ... 128 B4
Double Sprs. AL, *1003* ... 119 E3
Doubs MD, *750* ... 144 A2
Dougherty Co. GA, *96065* ... 128 C4
Douglas AL, *530* ... 120 A3
Douglas AZ, *14312* ... 55 E4
Douglas GA, *10639* ... 129 E4
Douglas MA, *800* ... 150 C2
Douglas MI, *1214* ... 75 E4
Douglas WY, *5288* ... 33 E1
Douglas Co. CO, *175766* ... 41 E2
Douglas Co. GA, *92174* ... 120 C4
Douglas Co. IL, *19922* ... 99 D1
Douglas Co. KS, *99962* ... 96 A3
Douglas Co. MN, *32821* ... 66 B2
Douglas Co. MO, *13084* ... 107 E2
Douglas Co. NE, *463585* ... 35 F3
Douglas Co. NV, *41259* ... 37 D2
Douglas Co. OR, *100399* ... 20 B4
Douglas Co. SD, *3458* ... 27 E4
Douglas Co. WA, *32603* ... 13 E3
Douglas Co. WI, *43287* ... 64 C4
Douglass KS, *1813* ... 43 F4
Douglass Hills KY, *5718* ... 230 F2
Douglasville GA, *20065* ... 120 C4
Dousman WI, *1584* ... 74 C3
Dove Creek CO, *698* ... 40 A4
Dover AR, *1329* ... 117 D1
Dover DE, *32135* ... 145 E2
Dover FL, *2798* ... 140 C2
Dover ID, *342* ... 14 B2
Dover MA, *2216* ... 151 D1
Dover NH, *26884* ... 82 A4
Dover NJ, *18188* ... 148 A3
Dover OH, *12210* ... 91 E4
Dover PA, *1815* ... 103 E3
Dover TN, *1442* ... 109 D3
Dover-Foxcroft ME, *2592* ... 82 C1
Dover Plains NY, *1996* ... 94 B3
Dowagiac MI, *6147* ... 89 F1
Dow City IA, *503* ... 86 A1
Dowling Park FL, *650* ... 137 F2
Downers Grove IL, *48724* ... 89 D1
Downey CA, *107323* ... 52 C2
Downey ID, *613* ... 31 E2
Downieville CA, *80* ... 36 C1
Downingtown PA, *7589* ... 146 B3
Downs IL, *776* ... 88 C4
Downs KS, *1038* ... 43 D1
Dows IA, *675* ... 72 C4
Doyle TN, *525* ... 110 A4
Doylestown OH, *2799* ... 91 E3
Doylestown PA, *8227* ... 146 C2
Doyline LA, *841* ... 125 D2
Drain OR, *1021* ... 20 B4
Drake ND, *322* ... 18 C2
Drakesboro KY, *627* ... 109 E2
Drakes Branch VA, *504* ... 113 D2
Draper UT, *25220* ... 31 E4
Dravosburg PA, *2015* ... 250 C3
Drayton ND, *913* ... 19 E2
Dresden OH, *1423* ... 91 D4
Dresden TN, *2855* ... 108 C3
Dresser WI, *732* ... 67 D3
Drew MS, *2434* ... 118 A4
Drew Co. AR, *18723* ... 117 F4
Drexel MO, *1090* ... 96 B3
Drexel NC, *1938* ... 111 F4
Drexel OH, *2057* ... 208 D1
Drexel Hill PA, *29364* ... 146 C3
Driggs ID, *1100* ... 23 F4
Dripping Sprs. TX, *1548* ... 61 D2
Driscoll TX, *825* ... 63 F2
Druid Hills GA, *12741* ... 190 D3
Drummond MT, *318* ... 15 E4
Drumright OK, *2905* ... 51 F2
Dryden ME, *1100* ... 82 B2
Dryden MI, *815* ... 76 C3
Dryden NY, *1832* ... 79 D4
Dryden VA, *1253* ... 111 D2
Dry Mills ME, *700* ... 82 B3
Dry Prong LA, *421* ... 125 D4
Dry Ridge KY, *1995* ... 100 B3
Duarte CA, *21486* ... 228 E2
Dubach LA, *800* ... 125 E2
Dublin CA, *29973* ... 259 E3
Dublin GA, *15857* ... 129 E2
Dublin IN, *697* ... 100 A1
Dublin MD, *650* ... 145 D1
Dublin OH, *31392* ... 90 C4
Dublin PA, *2083* ... 146 C2
Dublin TX, *3754* ... 59 D3
Dublin VA, *2288* ... 112 A2
Dubois ID, *647* ... 23 E3
DuBois PA, *8123* ... 92 B4
Dubois WY, *962* ... 24 B4
Dubois Co. IN, *39674* ... 99 E3
Duboistown PA, *1280* ... 93 D2
Dubuque IA, *57686* ... 73 F4
Dubuque Co. IA, *89143* ... 73 F4
Duchesne UT, *1408* ... 31 F3
Duchesne Co. UT, *14371* ... 39 F1
Duck Hill MS, *746* ... 118 B4

Entries in **bold black** indicate counties or parishes.
Entries in **bold color** indicate cities with detailed inset maps.

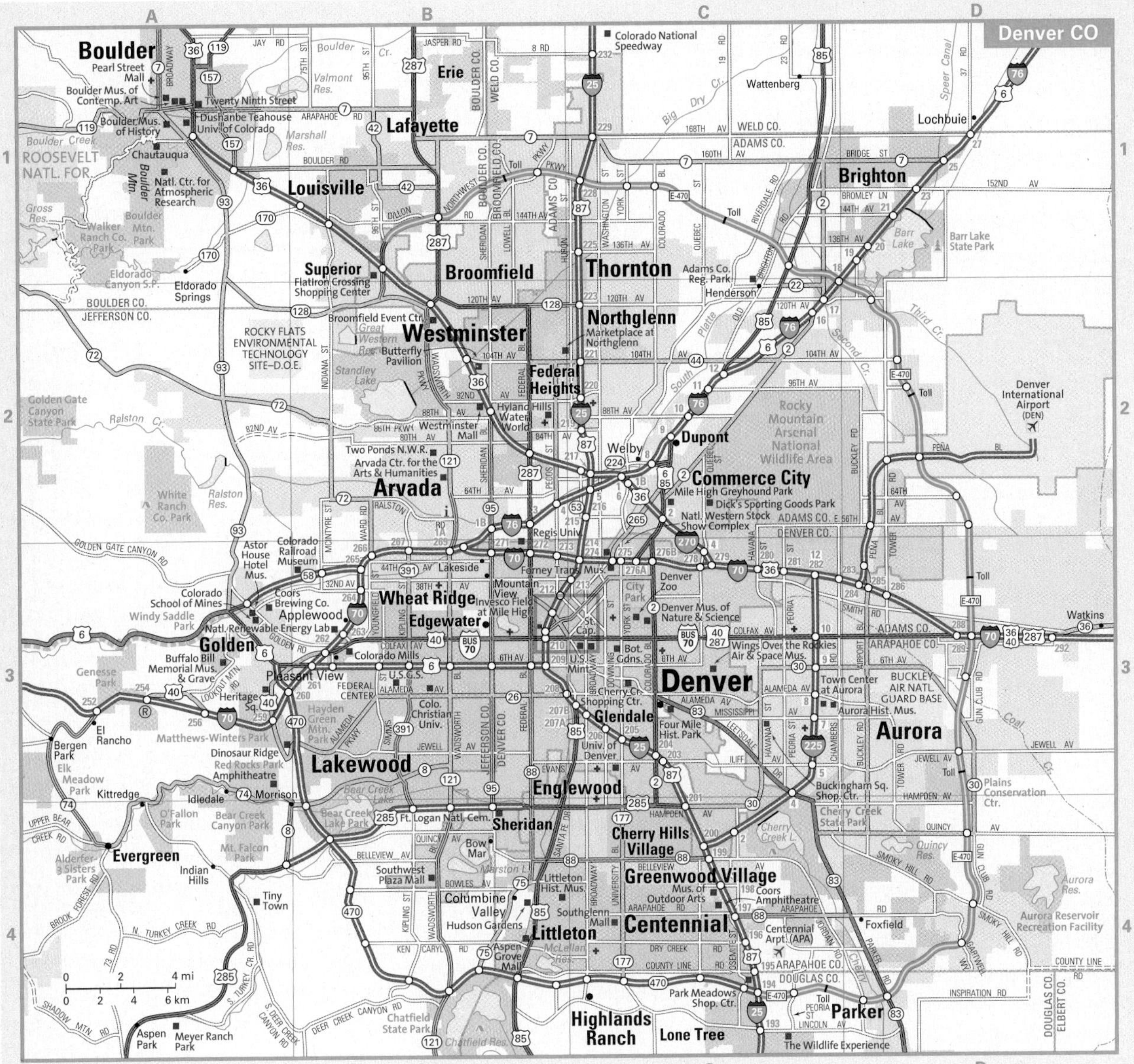

Denver CO

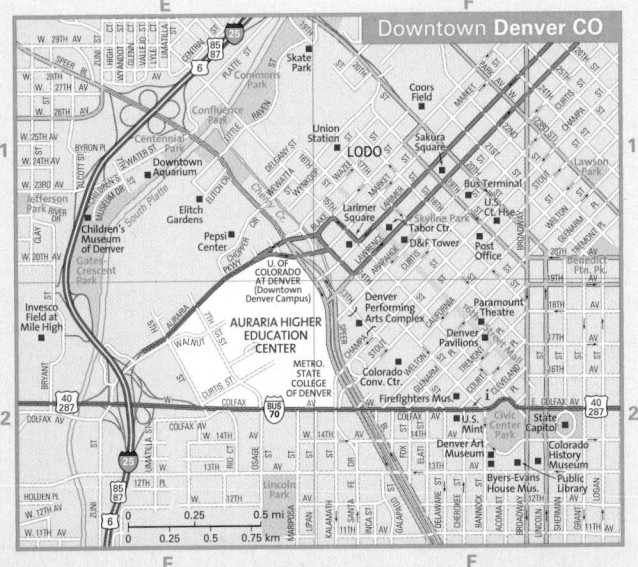

Downtown **Denver** CO

POINTS OF INTEREST

Figures after entries indicate population, page number, and grid reference.

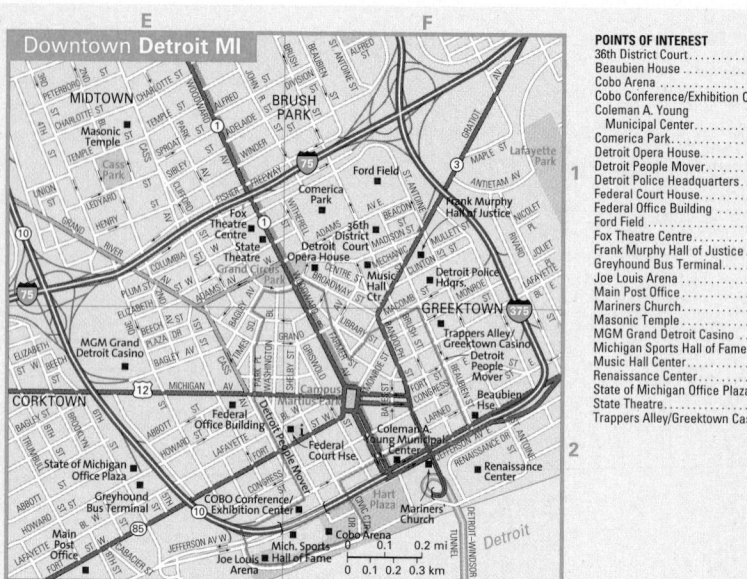

POINTS OF INTEREST

Des Moines IA

Downtown Detroit MI

Detroit MI

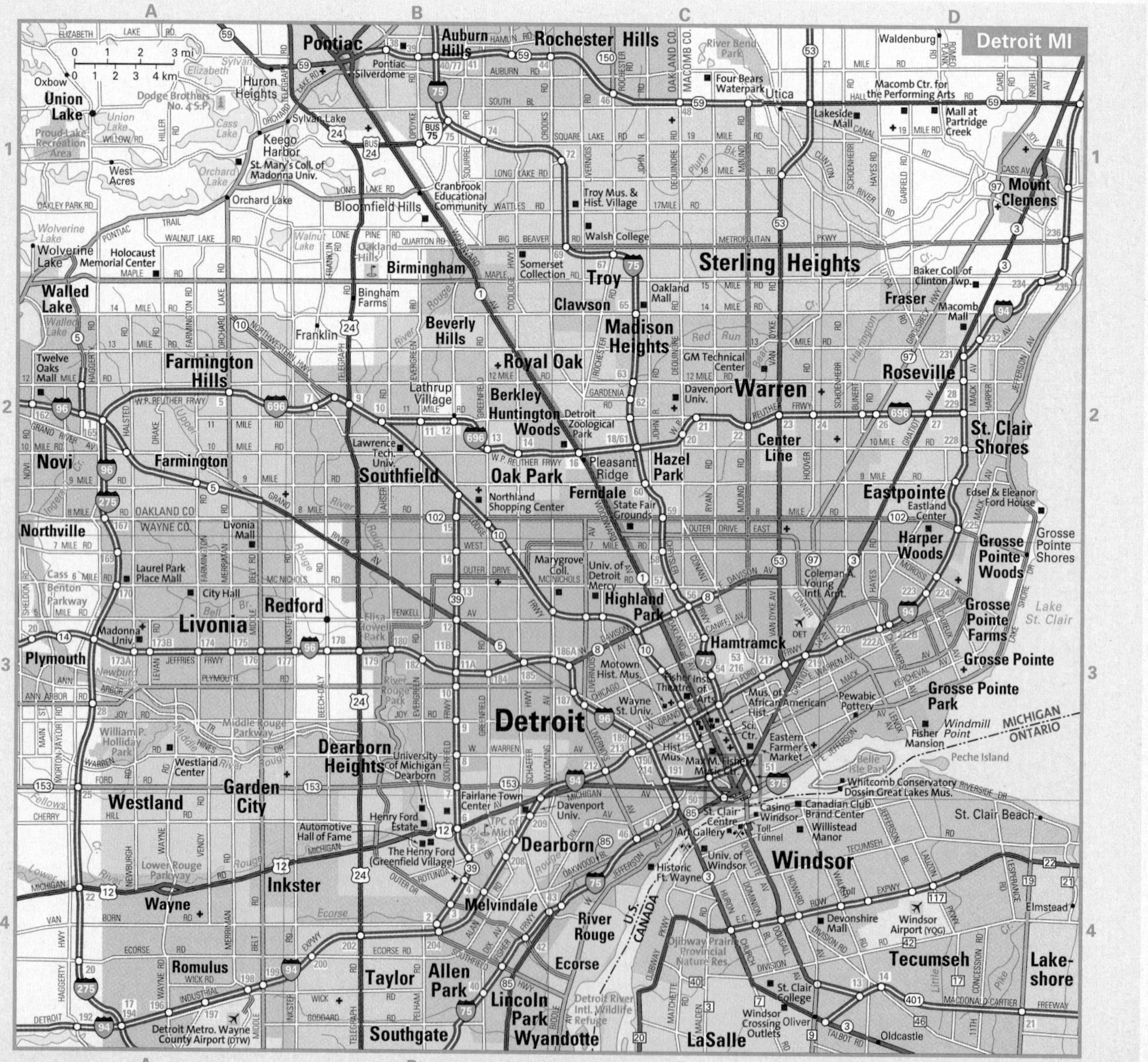

211
Durand–Elizabeth Lake

Entries in **bold black** indicate counties or parishes.
Entries in **bold color** indicate cities with detailed inset maps.

Durand WI, 1968 ... 67 E4
Durango CO, 13922 ... 40 B4
Durant IA, 1677 ... 87 F2
Durant MS, 2932 ... 126 B1
Durant OK, 13549 ... 59 F1
Durham CA, 5220 ... 36 B1
Durham CT, 2773 ... 149 E1
Durham NH, 9024 ... 82 A4
Durham NC, 187035 ... 112 C4
Durham OR, 1382 ... 251 C3
Durham Co. NC, 223314 ... 112 C4
Duryea PA, 4634 ... 93 F2
Dushore PA, 663 ... 93 E2
Duson LA, 1672 ... 133 E2
Dustin OK, 452 ... 51 F3
Dutchess Co. NY, 280150 ... 148 C1
Dutch Neck NJ, 4400 ... 147 D2
Dutton MT, 389 ... 15 F2
Duval Co. FL, 778879 ... 139 D2
Duval Co. TX, 13120 ... 63 E2
Duvall WA, 4616 ... 12 C3
Duxbury MA, 1426 ... 151 E2
Duxbury VT, 325 ... 81 E2
Dwaar Kill NY, 1400 ... 148 A1
Dwarf KY, 550 ... 111 D1
Dwight IL, 4363 ... 88 C3
Dyer AR, 585 ... 116 C1
Dyer IN, 13895 ... 89 D2
Dyer TN, 2406 ... 108 C4
Dyer Co. TN, 37279 ... 108 C4
Dyersburg TN, 17452 ... 108 C4
Dyersville IA, 4035 ... 73 F4
Dyess AR, 515 ... 118 B1
Dysart IA, 1303 ... 87 E1

E
Eads CO, 747 ... 42 A3
Eagan MN, 63557 ... 235 D4
Eagar AZ, 4033 ... 48 A4
Eagle CO, 3032 ... 40 C1
Eagle ID, 11085 ... 22 B4
Eagle NE, 1105 ... 35 F4
Eagle WI, 1707 ... 74 C3
Eagle Bend MN, 595 ... 66 B1
Eagle Butte SD, 619 ... 26 B2
Eagle Co. CO, 41659 ... 40 C1
Eagle Grove IA, 3712 ... 72 C4
Eagle Lake FL, 2496 ... 140 C2
Eagle Lake ME, 600 ... 85 D1
Eagle Lake MN, 1787 ... 72 C1
Eagle Lake TX, 3664 ... 61 F2
Eagle Mtn. UT, 2157 ... 31 E4
Eagle Nest NM, 306 ... 49 D1
Eagle Pass TX, 22413 ... 60 B4
Eagle Pt. OR, 4797 ... 28 C2
Eagle River MI, 20 ... 65 F3
Eagle River WI, 1443 ... 68 B2
Eagleton Vil. TN, 4883 ... 110 C4
Eagleville PA, 4458 ... 146 C2
Eagleville TN, 464 ... 109 F4
Earle AR, 3036 ... 118 A1
Earlham IA, 1298 ... 86 C2
Earlimart CA, 6583 ... 45 D4
Earlington KY, 1649 ... 109 E2
Earlsboro OK, 633 ... 51 F3
Earlville IL, 1778 ... 88 C2
Earlville IA, 900 ... 73 F4
Earlville NY, 791 ... 79 E4
Earlville PA, 800 ... 146 B2
Early IA, 605 ... 72 A4
Early TX, 2588 ... 59 D4
Early Co. GA, 12354 ... 128 C4
Earlysville VA, 750 ... 102 C4
Earth TX, 1109 ... 50 A4
Easley SC, 17754 ... 121 E2
E. Alton IL, 6830 ... 98 A3
E. Arcadia NC, 524 ... 123 E3
E. Arlington VT, 750 ... 81 D4
E. Atlantic Beach NY, 2257 ... 241 G5
E. Aurora NY, 6673 ... 78 B4
E. Bank WV, 933 ... 101 F4
E. Barre VT, 2136 ... 81 E2
E. Barrington NH, 400 ... 81 F4
E. Baton Rouge Par. LA, 412852 ... 134 A1
E. Bend NC, 659 ... 112 A3
E. Berlin PA, 1365 ... 103 E1
E. Bernard TX, 1729 ... 61 F2
E. Bernstadt KY, 774 ... 110 C2
E. Bethel MN, 10941 ... 67 D3
E. Blackstone MA, 1600 ... 150 C2
E. Brady PA, 1038 ... 92 A3
E. Brewster MA, 850 ... 151 F3
E. Brewton AL, 2496 ... 135 F1
E. Bridgewater MA, 4000 ... 151 D2
E. Brookfield MA, 1410 ... 150 B2
E. Brooklyn CT, 1473 ... 150 B3
E. Brunswick NJ, 46756 ... 147 E1
E. Butler PA, 679 ... 92 A3
E. Camden AR, 902 ... 117 E4
E. Canton OH, 1629 ... 91 E3
E. Carbon UT, 1393 ... 39 F1
E. Carroll Par. LA, 9421 ... 126 A2
Eastchester NY, 18564 ... 148 B3
E. Chicago IN, 32414 ... 89 D2
E. Cleveland OH, 27217 ... 91 E2
E. Dennis MA, 3299 ... 151 F3
E. Douglas MA, 2319 ... 150 C2
E. Dublin GA, 2484 ... 129 E2
E. Dubuque IL, 1995 ... 73 F4
E. Dundee IL, 2955 ... 203 A2
E. Ellijay GA, 707 ... 120 C2
E. End AR, 5623 ... 117 E2
E. Falmouth MA, 6615 ... 151 E4
E. Feliciana Par. LA, 21360 ... 134 A1
E. Flat Rock NC, 4151 ... 121 E1
E. Freehold NJ, 4936 ... 147 E2
E. Freetown MA, 1200 ... 151 D3
E. Gaffney SC, 3349 ... 121 F1
E. Galesburg IL, 839 ... 88 A3
Eastgate WA, 4558 ... 262 B3
E. Glacier Park MT, 396 ... 15 D2
E. Glastonbury CT, 1400 ... 149 E1
E. Glenville NY, 6064 ... 94 B1
E. Grand Forks MN, 7501 ... 19 E2
E. Grand Rapids MI, 10764 ... 215 B2
E. Greenbush NY, 4085 ... 188 E3
E. Greenville PA, 3103 ... 146 B1
E. Greenwich RI, 4300 ... 150 C3
E. Gull Lake MN, 978 ... 64 A4
E. Haddam CT, 550 ... 149 E1
Eastham MA, 1100 ... 151 F3
E. Hampton CT, 2254 ... 149 E1
Easthampton MA, 15994 ... 150 A1
E. Hampton NY, 1334 ... 149 F3
E. Hanover NJ, 9900 ... 148 A3
E. Hardwick VT, 300 ... 81 E2
E. Hartford CT, 49575 ... 150 A3
E. Harwich MA, 4744 ... 151 F3
E. Haven CT, 28189 ... 149 D2
E. Helena MT, 1642 ... 15 E4
E. Highland Park VA, 12488 ... 254 B1
E. Holden ME, 475 ... 83 D1
E. Hope ID, 200 ... 14 B2
E. Ithaca NY, 2192 ... 79 D4
E. Jordan MI, 2507 ... 69 F3
Eastlake OH, 20255 ... 91 E2
Eastland TX, 3769 ... 59 D3
Eastland Co. TX, 18297 ... 59 D3
E. Lansdowne PA, 2586 ... 248 B3
E. Lansing MI, 46525 ... 76 A4
E. Lebanon ME, 650 ... 82 A4
E. Liverpool OH, 13089 ... 91 F3
E. Longmeadow MA, 14100 ... 150 A2
E. Los Angeles CA, 124283 ... 228 D3
Eastman GA, 5440 ... 129 E3
E. Marion MA, 550 ... 151 E3
E. Marion NY, 756 ... 149 E2
E. McKeesport PA, 2343 ... 250 D3
E. Meadow NY, 37461 ... 148 C4
E. Middlebury VT, 650 ... 81 D3
E. Middletown NY, 5000 ... 148 A1
E. Millcreek UT, 21385 ... 257 B2
E. Millinocket ME, 1701 ... 85 D4
E. Moline IL, 20333 ... 88 A2
E. Montpelier VT, 450 ... 81 E2
E. Moriches NY, 4550 ... 149 E4
E. Mtn. TX, 580 ... 124 B2
E. Naples FL, 23000 ... 142 C2
E. Nassau NY, 571 ... 94 B1
E. Newark NJ, 2377 ... 240 B3
E. Newnan GA, 1305 ... 128 C1
E. Northport ME, 350 ... 82 C2
E. Northport NY, 20845 ... 148 C3
E. Olympia WA, 900 ... 12 C4
Easton CA, 1966 ... 44 C3
Easton CT, 750 ... 148 C2
Easton ME, 475 ... 85 E2
Easton MD, 11708 ... 145 D3
Easton PA, 26263 ... 93 F3
Easton TX, 524 ... 124 B2
E. Orange NJ, 69824 ... 148 A4
E. Orleans MA, 1800 ... 151 F3
Eastover NC, 1376 ... 123 D1
Eastover SC, 830 ... 122 B4
E. Palatka FL, 1707 ... 139 D3
E. Palestine OH, 4917 ... 91 F3
E. Palo Alto CA, 29506 ... 259 D5
E. Patchogue NY, 20824 ... 149 D4
E. Peoria IL, 22638 ... 88 B3
E. Petersburg PA, 4450 ... 146 A2
E. Pittsburgh PA, 2017 ... 250 D2
Eastpoint FL, 2158 ... 137 D3
E. Point GA, 39595 ... 120 C4
Eastpointe MI, 34077 ... 210 D2
Eastport ME, 1640 ... 83 F1
Eastport NY, 1454 ... 149 E3
E. Poultney VT, 400 ... 81 D3
E. Prairie MO, 3227 ... 108 C2
E. Prospect PA, 678 ... 103 E1
E. Providence RI, 48688 ... 150 C3
E. Quincy CA, 2398 ... 36 C1
E. Quogue NY, 4265 ... 149 E3
E. Randolph NY, 630 ... 92 B1
E. Ridge TN, 20640 ... 120 B2
E. Rochester NY, 6650 ... 254 G2
E. Rockaway NY, 10414 ... 147 F1
E. Rockingham NC, 3885 ... 122 C2
E. Rutherford NJ, 8716 ... 240 C2
E. St. Louis IL, 31542 ... 98 A3
E. Sandwich MA, 3720 ... 151 E3
E. Setauket NY, 15931 ... 149 D3
E. Shoreham NY, 5809 ... 149 D3
Eastsound WA, 750 ... 12 C1
E. Spencer NC, 1755 ... 112 A4
E. Stroudsburg PA, 9888 ... 93 F3
E. Swanzey NH, 475 ... 95 D1
E. Syracuse NY, 3178 ... 265 B2
E. Tawakoni TX, 775 ... 59 F2
E. Tawas MI, 2951 ... 76 B1
E. Texas PA, 6000 ... 146 B1
E. Thermopolis WY, 274 ... 24 C4
E. Troy WI, 3564 ... 74 C4
E. Vassalboro ME, 300 ... 82 C2
Eastview MD, 650 ... 144 B1
Eastview TN, 618 ... 119 D2
E. Village CT, 1500 ... 149 D2
Eastville VA, 203 ... 114 B3
E. Wareham MA, 1700 ... 151 E3
E. Washington PA, 1930 ... 92 A4
E. Wenatchee WA, 5757 ... 13 D3
E. Wilton ME, 550 ... 82 B2
E. Winthrop ME, 650 ... 82 B2
Eastwood LA, 3374 ... 125 D2
E. York PA, 8782 ... 275 F1
Eaton CO, 2690 ... 33 E4
Eaton IN, 1603 ... 90 A4
Eaton OH, 8133 ... 100 B1
Eaton Co. MI, 103655 ... 76 A4
Eaton Estates OH, 1409 ... 91 D2
Eaton Park FL, 3000 ... 266 E2
Eaton Rapids MI, 5330 ... 76 A4
Eatons Neck NY, 1388 ... 148 C3
Eatonton GA, 6764 ... 129 E1
Eatontown NJ, 14008 ... 147 E2
Eatonville FL, 2432 ... 246 C1
Eatonville WA, 2012 ... 12 C4
Eau Claire MI, 656 ... 89 F1
Eau Claire WI, 61704 ... 67 F4
Eau Claire Co. WI, 93142 ... 67 F4
Ebensburg PA, 3091 ... 92 B4
Eccles WV, 700 ... 111 F1
Echo OR, 650 ... 21 E1
Echols Co. GA, 3754 ... 138 B1
Eclectic AL, 1037 ... 128 A2
Economy PA, 9363 ... 92 A3
Ecorse MI, 11229 ... 210 C4
Ecru MS, 947 ... 118 C3
Ector TX, 600 ... 59 F1
Ector Co. TX, 121123 ... 57 F3
Edcouch TX, 3342 ... 63 E4
Eddington ME, 700 ... 83 D1
Eddy Co. NM, 51658 ... 57 E2
Eddy Co. ND, 2757 ... 19 D3
Eddystone PA, 2442 ... 248 A4
Eddyville IA, 1064 ... 87 D2
Eddyville KY, 2350 ... 109 D2
Eden ID, 411 ... 31 D1
Eden MD, 793 ... 103 F4
Eden NY, 3579 ... 78 A4
Eden NC, 15908 ... 112 B3
Eden TX, 2561 ... 58 C4
Eden WI, 687 ... 74 C2
Eden WY, 388 ... 32 A2
Eden Prairie MN, 54901 ... 235 A4
Edenton NC, 5394 ... 113 F4
Eden Valley MN, 866 ... 66 B3
Edenville NY, 650 ... 148 A2
Edgar NE, 539 ... 35 E4
Edgar WI, 1386 ... 68 A4
Edgar Co. IL, 19704 ... 99 D1
Edgard LA, 2637 ... 134 B3
Edgartown MA, 1100 ... 151 E4
Edgecliff Vil. TX, 2550 ... 207 A3
Edgecombe Co. NC, 55606 ... 113 E4
Edgefield SC, 4449 ... 121 F4
Edgefield Co. SC, 24595 ... 121 F4
Edgeley ND, 637 ... 19 D4
Edgemere MD, 9248 ... 144 C2
Edgemont SD, 867 ... 25 F4
Edgemoor DE, 5992 ... 146 B4
Edgerton KS, 1440 ... 96 B3
Edgerton MN, 1033 ... 27 F4
Edgerton MO, 533 ... 96 B2
Edgerton OH, 2117 ... 90 A2
Edgerton WI, 4933 ... 74 B3
Edgerton WY, 169 ... 25 D4
Edgewater AL, 730 ... 195 D2
Edgewater CO, 5445 ... 209 B3
Edgewater FL, 18668 ... 139 E4
Edgewater NJ, 7677 ... 240 D2
Edgewater Park NJ, 8400 ... 147 D3
Edgewood FL, 1901 ... 246 C3
Edgewood IN, 1988 ... 89 F4
Edgewood IA, 923 ... 73 F4
Edgewood KY, 9400 ... 204 B3
Edgewood MD, 25378 ... 145 D1
Edgewood NM, 1893 ... 48 C3
Edgewood OH, 4762 ... 91 F1
Edgewood PA, 3311 ... 250 C2
Edgewood TX, 1348 ... 124 A2
Edgewood WA, 9089 ... 262 B5
Edina MN, 47425 ... 67 D4
Edina MO, 1233 ... 87 E4
Edinboro PA, 6950 ... 92 A1
Edinburg IL, 1135 ... 98 B1
Edinburg NJ, 900 ... 147 D2
Edinburg ND, 252 ... 19 E2
Edinburg TX, 48465 ... 63 E4
Edinburg VA, 813 ... 102 C3
Edinburgh IN, 4505 ... 99 F2
Edison GA, 1340 ... 128 C4
Edison NJ, 97687 ... 147 E1
Edisto Beach SC, 641 ... 130 C2
Edmond OK, 68315 ... 51 E2
Edmonds WA, 39515 ... 12 C3
Edmondson AR, 513 ... 118 B1
Edmonson Co. KY, 11644 ... 109 F2
Edmonston MD, 959 ... 270 E2
Edmonton KY, 1586 ... 110 A2
Edmore MI, 1244 ... 76 A2
Edmore ND, 256 ... 19 D2
Edmunds Co. SD, 4367 ... 27 D2
Edmundson MO, 840 ... 256 B1
Edna KS, 423 ... 106 A2
Edna TX, 5899 ... 61 F3
Edon OH, 898 ... 90 A2
Edwards CO, 8257 ... 40 C1
Edwards MS, 1347 ... 126 A2
Edwardsburg MI, 1147 ... 89 F1
Edwards Co. IL, 6971 ... 99 D4
Edwards Co. KS, 3449 ... 43 D4
Edwards Co. TX, 2162 ... 60 B2
Edwardsville IL, 21491 ... 98 B3
Edwardsville KS, 4146 ... 96 B2
Edwardsville PA, 4984 ... 261 A1
Effingham IL, 12384 ... 98 C2
Effingham KS, 588 ... 96 A1
Effingham Co. GA, 37535 ... 130 B2
Effingham Co. IL, 34264 ... 98 C2
Effort PA, 900 ... 93 F3
Egan SD, 265 ... 27 F3
Egg Harbor City NJ, 4545 ... 147 D4
Egypt PA, 2700 ... 189 A1
Ehrenberg AZ, 1357 ... 53 F3
Ehrhardt SC, 614 ... 130 C1
Ekalaka MT, 410 ... 25 F1
Elaine AR, 865 ... 118 A3
Elam PA, 2000 ... 146 B3
Elba AL, 4185 ... 128 A4
Elba NY, 696 ... 78 B3
Elberfeld IN, 636 ... 99 E4
Elberta AL, 552 ... 135 F2
Elberta MI, 457 ... 69 E4
Elberta UT, 256 ... 39 E1
Elbert Co. CO, 19872 ... 41 E2
Elbert Co. GA, 20511 ... 121 E3
Elberton GA, 4743 ... 121 E3
Elbow Lake MN, 1275 ... 27 F1
Elbridge NY, 1103 ... 79 D3
Elburn IL, 2756 ... 88 C1
El Cajon CA, 94869 ... 53 D4
El Campo TX, 10945 ... 61 F3
El Cenizo TX, 3545 ... 63 D2
El Centro CA, 37835 ... 53 E4
El Cerrito CA, 4590 ... 229 H4
El Cerrito CA, 23171 ... 259 B2
Eldersburg MD, 27741 ... 144 B1
Eldon IA, 998 ... 87 E3
Eldon MO, 4895 ... 97 E4
Eldon OK, 991 ... 106 B4
Eldora IA, 3035 ... 73 D4
El Dorado AR, 21530 ... 125 E1
Eldorado IL, 4534 ... 109 D1
El Dorado KS, 12057 ... 43 F4
Eldorado OK, 527 ... 50 C4
Eldorado TX, 1951 ... 60 B1
El Dorado Co. CA, 156299 ... 36 C2
Eldorado Sprs. CO, 557 ... 209 A1
El Dorado Sprs. MO, 3775 ... 96 C4
Eldred PA, 858 ... 92 C1
Eldridge IA, 4159 ... 88 A2
Eleanor WV, 1345 ... 101 E3
Electra TX, 3168 ... 59 D1
Electric City WA, 922 ... 13 E2
Eleele HI, 2040 ... 152 B1
Elephant Butte NM, 1390 ... 56 B2
Eleva WI, 635 ... 67 F4
Elfers FL, 13161 ... 140 B2
Elfrida AZ, 475 ... 55 E4
Elgin AZ, 309 ... 55 D4
Elgin IL, 94487 ... 88 C1
Elgin IA, 676 ... 73 E3
Elgin MN, 826 ... 73 E1
Elgin NE, 735 ... 35 E2
Elgin ND, 659 ... 18 B4
Elgin OK, 1210 ... 51 D4
Elgin OR, 1654 ... 21 F1
Elgin SC, 806 ... 122 A3
Elgin SC, 2426 ... 122 B2
Elgin TX, 5700 ... 61 E1
El Granada CA, 5724 ... 259 B5
Elida OH, 1917 ... 90 B3
Elihu KY, 650 ... 110 B2
Elizabeth CO, 1434 ... 41 E2
Elizabeth IL, 682 ... 74 A4
Elizabeth LA, 574 ... 133 E1
Elizabeth NJ, 120568 ... 148 A4
Elizabeth PA, 1609 ... 92 A4
Elizabeth WV, 994 ... 101 F2
Elizabeth City NC, 17188 ... 113 F3
Elizabeth Lake CA, 750 ... 52 C2

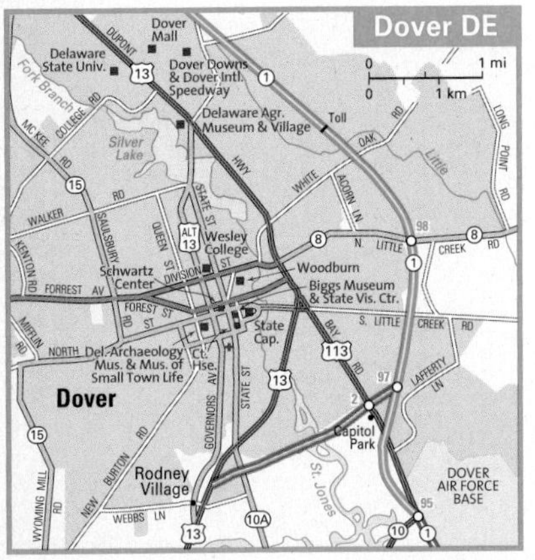

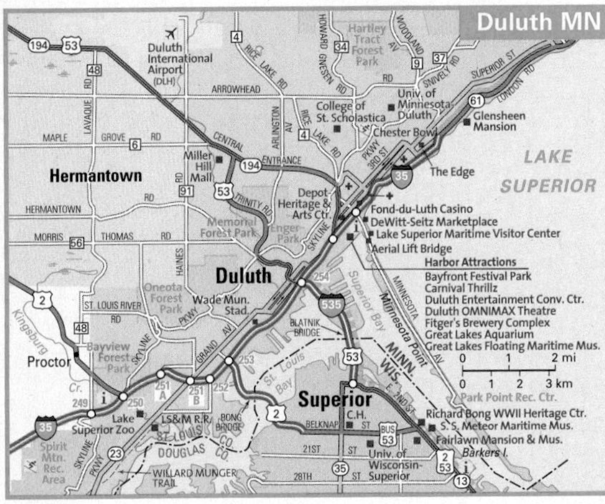

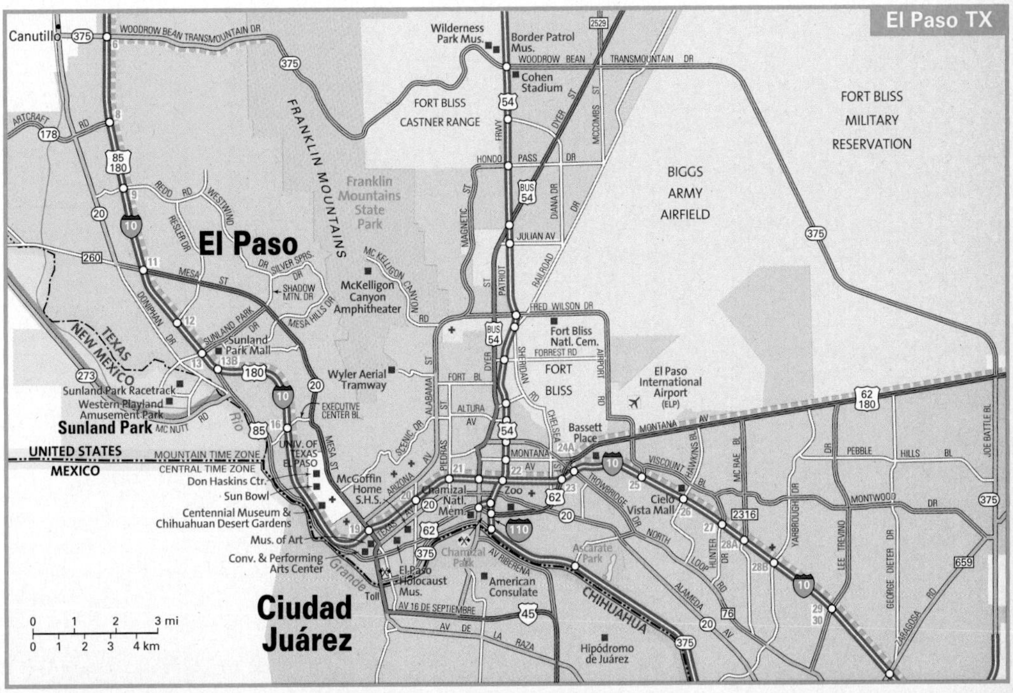

212
Elizabethton–Ewa Beach

Figures after entries indicate population, page number, and grid reference.

Elizabethton TN, 13372 **111** E3
Elizabethtown IL, 348 **109** D1
Elizabethtown KY, 22542 **110** A1
Elizabethtown NY, 750 **81** D2
Elizabethtown NC, 3698 **123** D2
Elizabethtown PA, 11887 **93** E4
Elizabethville PA, 1344 **93** D4
El Jebel CO, 4488 **40** C2
Elkader IA, 1465 **73** F3
Elk City OK, 10510 **50** C3
Elk Co. KS, 3261 **43** F4
Elk Co. PA, 35112 **92** B2
Elk Grove CA, 75175 **36** C3
Elk Grove Vil. IL, 34727 **203** C3
Elkhart IN, 51874 **89** F2
Elkhart KS, 2233 **50** A1
Elkhart TX, 1215 **124** A4
Elkhart Co. IN, 182791 **89** F2
Elkhart Lake WI, 1021 **74** C2
Elkhorn CA, 1591 **236** E2
Elk Horn IA, 649 **86** B2
Elkhorn NE, 6062 **35** F3
Elkhorn WI, 7305 **74** C4
Elkhorn City KY, 1060 **111** E1
Elkin NC, 4109 **112** A3
Elkins AR, 1251 **106** C4
Elkins WV, 7032 **102** A3
Elkland PA, 1786 **93** D1
Elkmont AL, 470 **119** F2
Elk Mound WI, 785 **67** E4
Elko NV, 16708 **30** B4
Elko Co. NV, 45291 **30** C3
Elk Pt. SD, 1714 **35** F1
Elk Rapids MI, 1700 **69** F4
Elkridge MD, 22042 **144** C2
Elk Ridge UT, 1838 **39** E1
Elk River MN, 16447 **66** C3
Elk Run Hts. IA, 1052 **73** E4
Elkton KY, 1984 **109** E2
Elkton MD, 11893 **145** E1
Elkton MI, 863 **76** C2
Elkton SD, 677 **27** F3
Elkton TN, 510 **119** F2
Elkton VA, 2042 **102** C3
Elkview WV, 1182 **101** F3
Elkville IL, 1001 **98** B4
El Lago TX, 3075 **132** B3
Ellaville GA, 1609 **129** D3
Ellenboro NC, 479 **121** F1
Ellenboro WV, 373 **101** F2
Ellendale DE, 327 **145** F3
Ellendale MN, 590 **72** C2
Ellendale ND, 1559 **27** D1
Ellensburg WA, 15414 **13** D4
Ellenton FL, 3142 **266** B4
Ellenville NY, 4130 **94** A3
Ellerbe NC, 1021 **122** C2
Ellerslie MD, 600 **102** C1
Ellettsville IN, 5078 **99** F2
Ellicott NY, 2200 **78** B4
Ellicott City MD, 56397 **144** C2
Ellijay GA, 1584 **120** C2
Ellington CT, 1300 **150** A3
Ellington MO, 1045 **108** A2
Ellinwood KS, 2164 **43** D3
Elliott Co. KY, 6748 **101** D4
Ellis KS, 1873 **42** C2
Ellis Co. KS, 27507 **43** D2
Ellis Co. OK, 4075 **50** C2
Ellis Co. TX, 111360 **59** F3
Ellisport WA, 1200 **262** A4
Elliston MT, 225 **15** E4
Elliston VA, 1241 **112** B2
Ellisville MS, 3465 **126** C4
Ellisville MO, 9104 **256** A2
Elloree SC, 742 **122** B4
Ellsworth IA, 531 **72** C4
Ellsworth KS, 2965 **43** E2
Ellsworth ME, 6456 **83** D2
Ellsworth MI, 483 **69** F3
Ellsworth MN, 540 **27** F4
Ellsworth PA, 1083 **92** A4
Ellsworth WI, 2909 **67** E4
Ellsworth Co. KS, 6525 **43** E3
Ellwood City PA, 8688 **91** F3
Elma IA, 598 **73** D3
Elma NY, 2491 **78** B3
Elma WA, 3049 **12** B4
Elm City NC, 1165 **113** D4
Elm Creek NE, 894 **35** D4
Elmendorf TX, 664 **61** D3
Elmer NJ, 1384 **145** F1
Elm Grove WI, 6249 **234** B2
Elmhurst IL, 42762 **89** D1
Elmira NY, 30940 **93** D1
El Mirage AZ, 7609 **249** A1
Elmira Hts. NY, 4170 **93** D1
Elm Mott TX, 1200 **59** E4
Elmo UT, 368 **39** F2
Elmont NY, 32657 **148** C4
Elmont VA, 500 **113** E1
El Monte CA, 115965 **228** E2
Elmore MN, 735 **72** C2
Elmore OH, 1426 **90** C2
Elmore City OK, 756 **51** E4
Elmore Co. AL, 65874 **128** A2
Elmore Co. ID, 29130 **22** B4
Elm Sprs. AR, 1044 **106** C3
Elmville CT, 1300 **150** B3
Elmwood IL, 1945 **88** A3
Elmwood NE, 668 **35** F4
Elmwood WI, 841 **67** E4
Elmwood Park IL, 25405 **203** D4
Elmwood Park NJ, 18925 **240** C1
Elmwood Place OH, 2681 **204** B2
Elnora IN, 721 **99** E3
Elnora NY, 2700 **94** B1
Elon NC, 6738 **112** C4
Eloy AZ, 10375 **54** C2
El Paso IL, 2695 **88** B3
El Paso TX, 563662 **56** C4
El Paso Co. CO, 516929 **41** E2
El Paso Co. TX, 679622 **56** C4
El Portal FL, 2505 **233** B4
El Prado NM, 400 **49** D1
El Reno OK, 16212 **51** E3
El Rio CA, 6193 **52** B2
El Rito NM, 425 **48** C2
Elroy WI, 1578 **74** A2
Elsa TX, 5549 **63** E4
Elsah IL, 635 **98** A2
Elsberry MO, 2047 **98** A2
El Segundo CA, 16033 **228** C3
Elsie MI, 1055 **76** A3
Elsinore UT, 733 **39** E3
Elsmere DE, 5800 **146** B4
Elsmere KY, 8139 **100** B2
Elsmere NY, 3200 **188** D3
El Sobrante CA, 12260 **259** C1
Elton LA, 1261 **133** E2
Elvaton MD, 3500 **193** C5
Elverson PA, 959 **146** B2
Elwood IL, 1620 **89** D2
Elwood IN, 9737 **89** F4
Elwood KS, 1145 **96** B1
Elwood NE, 761 **34** C4
Elwood NJ, 1392 **147** D4
Elwood UT, 678 **31** E3
Ely IA, 1149 **87** E1
Ely MN, 3724 **64** C2
Ely NV, 4041 **38** B2
Elyria OH, 55953 **91** D2
Elysburg PA, 2067 **93** E3
Elysian MN, 486 **72** C1
Emanuel Co. GA, 21837 **129** F2
Emerado ND, 510 **19** E2
Emerald Isle NC, 3488 **115** D4
Emerson GA, 1092 **120** C3
Emerson NE, 817 **35** F2
Emerson NJ, 7197 **148** B3
Emery SD, 439 **27** E4
Emery UT, 308 **39** E2
Emery Co. UT, 10860 **39** F2
Emery Mills ME, 350 **82** A4
Emeryville CA, 6882 **259** C2
Emigsville PA, 2467 **103** E1
Emily MN, 847 **64** B4
Eminence KY, 2231 **100** A4
Eminence MO, 548 **107** F2
Emlenton PA, 784 **92** A2
Emmaus PA, 11313 **146** B1
Emmet AR, 506 **117** D4
Emmet Co. IA, 11027 **72** B3
Emmet Co. MI, 31437 **70** B3
Emmetsburg IA, 3958 **72** B3
Emmett ID, 5490 **22** B4
Emmitsburg MD, 2290 **103** D1
Emmonak AK, 767 **154** B2
Emmons Co. ND, 4331 **18** C4
Emmorton MD, 4000 **145** D1
Emory TX, 1021 **124** A1
Emory VA, 2266 **111** F2
Empire CO, 355 **41** D1
Empire LA, 2211 **134** C4
Empire NV, 499 **29** E4
Empire City OK, 734 **51** E4
Emporia KS, 26760 **43** F3
Emporia VA, 5665 **113** E3
Emporium PA, 2526 **92** C2
Emsworth PA, 2598 **250** A1
Encampment WY, 443 **33** D3
Encinal TX, 629 **60** C4
Encinitas CA, 58014 **53** D4
Enderlin ND, 947 **19** E4
Endicott NY, 13038 **93** E1
Endicott WA, 621 **13** F4
Endwell NY, 11706 **93** E1
Energy IL, 1175 **108** C1
Enfield CT, 8125 **150** A2
Enfield IL, 625 **99** D4
Enfield NH, 1698 **81** E3
Enfield NC, 2347 **113** E4
Enfield Ctr. NH, 600 **81** E3
England AR, 2972 **117** E2
Englewood CO, 31727 **41** E1
Englewood FL, 16196 **140** C4
Englewood NJ, 26203 **148** B3
Englewood OH, 12235 **100** B1
Englewood TN, 1590 **120** C1
Englewood Beach FL, 1000 **140** C4
Englewood Cliffs NJ, 5322 **240** D1
English IN, 673 **99** F4
Englishtown NJ, 1764 **147** E2
Enhaut PA, 2809 **218** C2
Enid OK, 47045 **51** E1
Enigma GA, 869 **129** E4
Enka NC, 1500 **121** E1
Ennis MT, 840 **23** E2
Ennis TX, 16045 **59** F3
Enoch UT, 3467 **39** D4
Enochville NC, 2851 **122** B1
Enola PA, 5627 **218** A1
Enon OH, 2638 **100** C1
Enoree SC, 700 **121** F2
Enosburg Falls VT, 1473 **81** D1
Ensley FL, 18752 **135** F2
Ensor KY, 500 **109** E1
Enterprise AL, 21178 **128** B4
Enterprise KS, 836 **43** F2
Enterprise MS, 474 **127** D3
Enterprise OR, 1895 **22** A2
Enterprise UT, 1285 **38** C4
Enterprise WV, 939 **102** A2
Entiat WA, 957 **13** D3
Enumclaw WA, 11116 **12** C3
Ephraim UT, 4505 **39** E2
Ephrata PA, 13213 **146** A2
Ephrata WA, 6808 **13** E3
Epping NH, 1673 **81** F4
Epps LA, 1153 **125** F2
Epworth IA, 1428 **73** F4
Epworth Hts. OH, 3300 **204** C1
Equality IL, 721 **109** D1
Erath LA, 2187 **133** F3
Erath Co. TX, 33001 **59** D3
Erda UT, 2473 **31** E4
Erial NJ, 6200 **146** C4
Erick OK, 1023 **50** C3
Erie CO, 6291 **209** B1
Erie IL, 1589 **88** A2
Erie KS, 1211 **106** A1
Erie PA, 103717 **92** A1
Erie Co. NY, 950265 **78** B4
Erie Co. OH, 79551 **91** D2
Erie Co. PA, 280843 **92** A1
Erin TN, 1490 **109** E3
Erlanger KY, 16676 **100** B2
Erwin NC, 4537 **123** D1
Erwin TN, 5610 **111** E4
Erwinville LA, 700 **134** A2
Escalante UT, 818 **39** E4
Escalon CA, 5963 **36** C4
Escambia Co. AL, 38440 **136** A1
Escambia Co. FL, 294410 **135** F1
Escanaba MI, 13140 **69** D2
Escatawpa MS, 3566 **195** C1
Escobares TX, 1954 **63** D4
Escondido CA, 133559 **53** D4
Esko MN, 1300 **64** C4
Eskridge KS, 589 **43** F2
Esmeralda Co. NV, 971 **37** F4
Espanola NM, 9688 **49** D2
Espanong NJ, 2700 **148** A3
Esparto CA, 1858 **36** B2
Espy PA, 1428 **93** E3
Essex CT, 2573 **149** E2
Essex IA, 884 **86** A3
Essex MD, 39078 **144** C2
Essex MA, 1426 **151** F1
Essex MO, 524 **108** B2
Essex Co. MA, 723419 **151** F1
Essex Co. NJ, 793633 **148** A3
Essex Co. NY, 38851 **80** C3
Essex Co. VT, 6459 **81** F1
Essex Co. VA, 9989 **103** E4
Essex Fells NJ, 2162 **240** A2
Essex Jct. VT, 8591 **81** D2
Essexville MI, 3766 **76** B2
Estacada OR, 2371 **20** C2
Estancia NM, 1584 **49** D4
Estelle LA, 15880 **239** C2
Estelline SD, 675 **27** F3
Estell Manor NJ, 1585 **104** C3
Ester AK, 1680 **154** C2
Estero FL, 9503 **142** C1
Estes Park CO, 5413 **33** E4
Estherville IA, 6656 **72** B2
Estherwood LA, 807 **133** E2
Estill SC, 2425 **130** B2
Estill Co. KY, 15307 **110** C1
Estill Sprs. TN, 2152 **120** A1
Estral Beach MI, 486 **90** C1
Ethan SD, 330 **27** E4
Ethel MS, 452 **126** C1
Ethete WY, 1455 **32** B1
Ethridge TN, 536 **119** E1
Etna CA, 781 **28** B3
Etna PA, 3924 **250** C1
Etna Green IN, 663 **89** F2
Etowah NC, 2766 **121** E1
Etowah TN, 3663 **120** C1
Etowah Co. AL, 103459 **120** A3
Ettrick VA, 5627 **113** E2
Ettrick WI, 521 **73** F1
Eubank KY, 358 **110** B2
Euclid OH, 52717 **91** E2
Eudora AR, 2819 **126** A1
Eudora KS, 4307 **96** B3
Eufaula AL, 13908 **128** B3
Eufaula OK, 2639 **116** A1
Eugene OR, 137893 **20** B4
Euharlee GA, 3208 **120** B3
Euless TX, 46005 **207** C2
Eunice LA, 11499 **133** E2
Eunice NM, 2562 **57** F3
Eupora MS, 2326 **118** C4
Eureka CA, 26128 **28** A4
Eureka IL, 4871 **88** B3
Eureka KS, 2914 **43** F4
Eureka MO, 7676 **98** A3
Eureka MT, 1017 **14** C1
Eureka NV, 550 **38** A1
Eureka SD, 1101 **27** D1
Eureka UT, 766 **39** E1
Eureka Co. NV, 1651 **30** B4
Eureka Mill SC, 1737 **122** A2
Eureka Sprs. AR, 2278 **106** C3
Eustace TX, 798 **59** F3
Eustis FL, 15106 **140** C1
Eustis NE, 464 **34** C4
Eutaw AL, 1878 **127** E2
Eva AL, 491 **119** F3
Evadale TX, 1430 **132** C2
Evangeline Par. LA, 35434 **133** E1
Evans CO, 9514 **33** E4
Evans GA, 17727 **121** F4
Evans WV, 750 **101** E3
Evans City PA, 2009 **92** A3
Evans Co. GA, 10495 **130** B3
Evansdale IA, 4526 **73** E4
Evans Mills NY, 605 **79** E1
Evanston IL, 74239 **89** D1
Evanston WY, 11507 **31** F3
Evansville IL, 724 **98** B4
Evansville IN, 121582 **99** D4
Evansville MN, 566 **66** A2
Evansville WI, 4039 **74** B4
Evansville WY, 2255 **33** D1
Evaro MT, 329 **15** D4
Evart MI, 1738 **75** F1
Evarts KY, 1101 **111** D2
Eveleth MN, 3865 **64** C3
Evendale OH, 3090 **204** B1
Evening Shade AR, 465 **107** F4
Everett MA, 38037 **197** C1
Everett PA, 1905 **102** C1
Everett WA, 91488 **12** C2
Everglades City FL, 479 **143** D2
Evergreen AL, 3630 **127** F4
Evergreen CO, 9216 **41** D1
Evergreen MT, 6215 **15** D2
Evergreen Park IL, 20821 **203** D5
Everly IA, 647 **72** A3
Everman TX, 5836 **207** B3
Everson PA, 842 **92** A4
Everson WA, 2035 **12** C1
Evesboro NJ, 2400 **147** D3
Ewa Beach HI, 14650 **152** A3

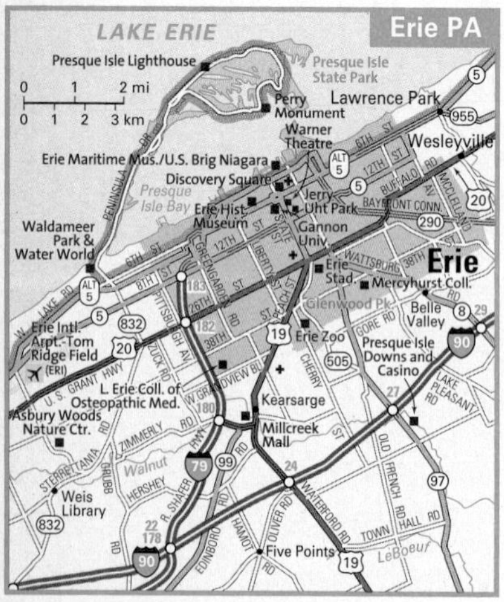
Erie PA
LAKE ERIE
Presque Isle Lighthouse
Presque Isle State Park
0 1 2 mi
0 1 2 3 km
Perry Monument
Lawrence Park
Warner Theatre
Wesleyville
Erie Maritime Mus./U.S. Brig Niagara
Discovery Square
Erie Hist. Museum
Gannon Univ.
Waldameer Park & Water World
Erie
Mercyhurst Coll.
Erie Intl. Arpt.-Tom Ridge Field (ERI)
Erie Zoo
Belle Valley
Presque Isle Downs and Casino
L. Erie Coll. of Osteopathic Med.
Asbury Woods Nature Ctr.
Kearsarge
Millcreek Mall
Weis Library
Five Points

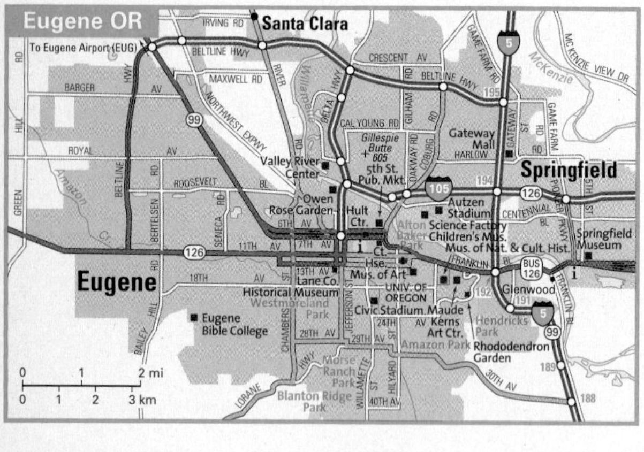
Eugene OR
Santa Clara
To Eugene Airport (EUG)
Gateway Mall
Springfield
Valley River Center
Owen Rose Garden
Hult Ctr.
5th St. Pub. Mkt.
Autzen Stadium
Science Factory Children's Mus.
Mus. of Nat. & Cult. Hist.
Springfield Museum
Eugene
Historical Museum
Lane Co.
Mus. of Art
UNIV. OF OREGON
Civic Stadium
Maude Kerns Art Ctr.
Hendricks Park
Rhododendron Garden
Amazon Park
Glenwood
Eugene Bible College
Morse Ranch Park
Blanton Ridge Park
0 1 2 mi
0 1 2 3 km

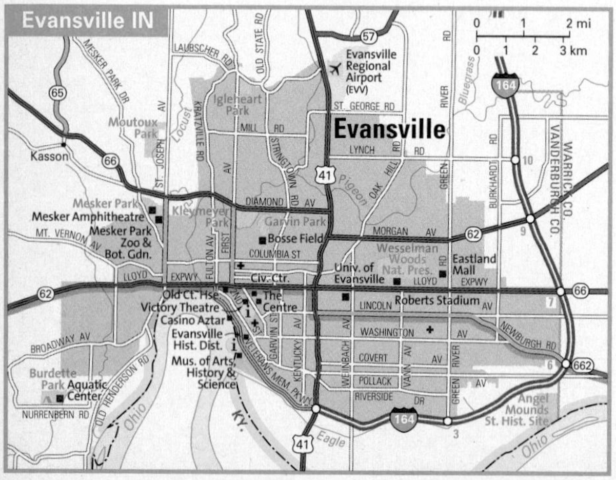
Evansville IN
0 1 2 mi
0 1 2 3 km
Evansville Regional Airport (EVV)
Igleheart Park
Evansville
Moutoux Park
Kasson
Mesker Park
Mesker Amphitheatre
Mesker Park Zoo & Bot. Gdn.
Kleymeyer Park
Garvin Park
Bosse Field
Wesselman Woods Nat. Pres.
Univ. of Evansville
Eastland Mall
Old Ct. Hse.
Victory Theatre
Casino Aztar
Evansville Hist. Dist.
Mus. of Arts History & Science
The Centre
Roberts Stadium
Burdette Park Aquatic Center
Angel Mounds St. Hist. Site

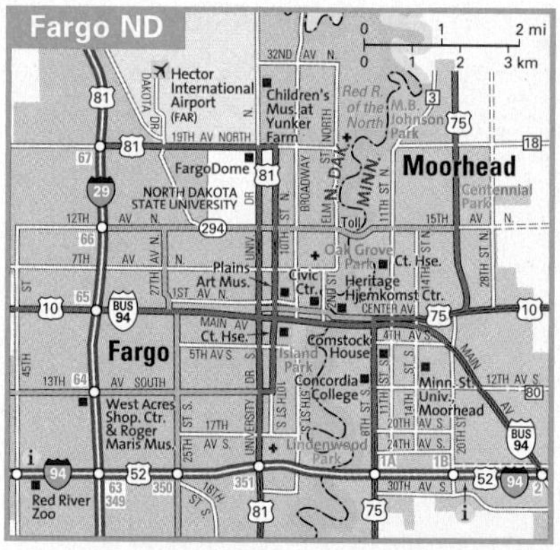
Fargo ND
0 1 2 mi
0 1 2 3 km
Hector International Airport (FAR)
Children's Mus. at Yunker Farm
FargoDome
NORTH DAKOTA STATE UNIVERSITY
Moorhead
Plains Art Mus.
Civic Ctr.
Heritage Hjemkomst Ctr.
Fargo
Comstock House
Concordia College
Minn. St. Univ. Moorhead
West Acres Shop. Ctr. & Roger Maris Mus.
Red River Zoo

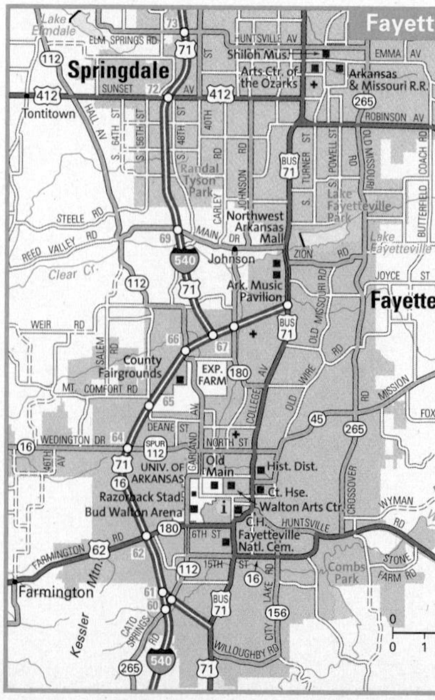
Fayetteville AR
Springdale
Tontitown
Shiloh Mus.
Arts Ctr. of the Ozarks
Arkansas & Missouri R.R.
Northwest Arkansas Mall
Johnson
Ark. Music Pavilion
Fayetteville
County Fairgrounds
EXP. FARM
UNIV. OF ARKANSAS
Old Main
Hist. Dist.
Razorback Stad.
Bud Walton Arena
Ct. Hse.
Walton Arts Ctr.
Fayetteville Natl. Cem.
Farmington
0 1 2 mi
0 1 2 3 km

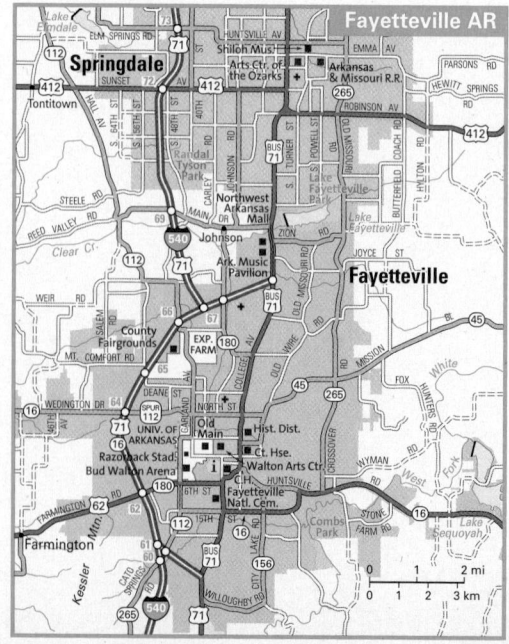

Entries in **bold black** indicate counties or parishes.
Entries in **bold color** indicate cities with detailed inset maps.

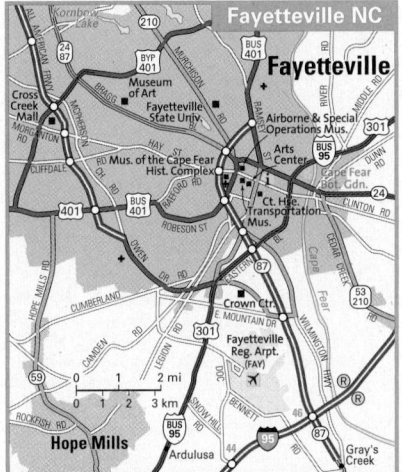

Fayetteville NC
Fayetteville · Hope Mills

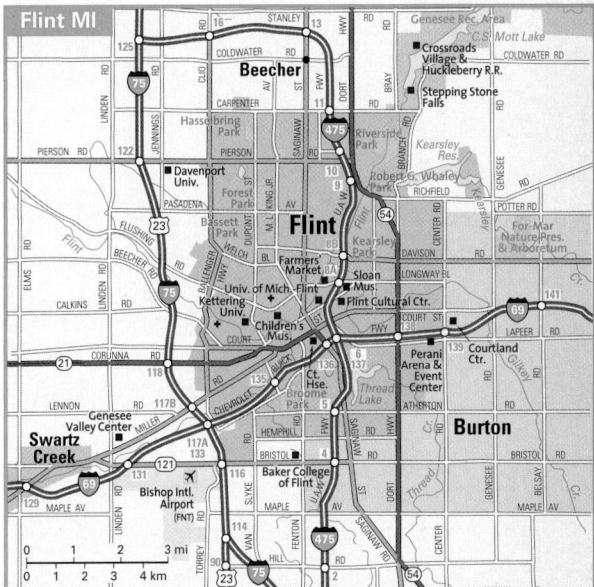

Flint MI
Beecher · Flint · Swartz Creek · Burton

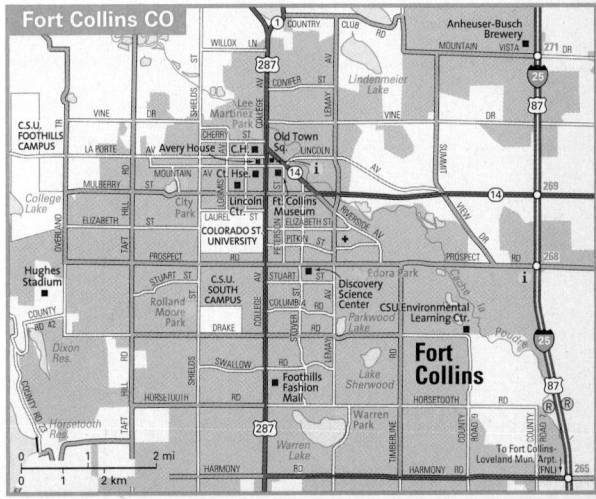

Flagstaff AZ
Flagstaff

Fort Collins CO
Fort Collins

Figures after entries indicate population, page number, and grid reference.

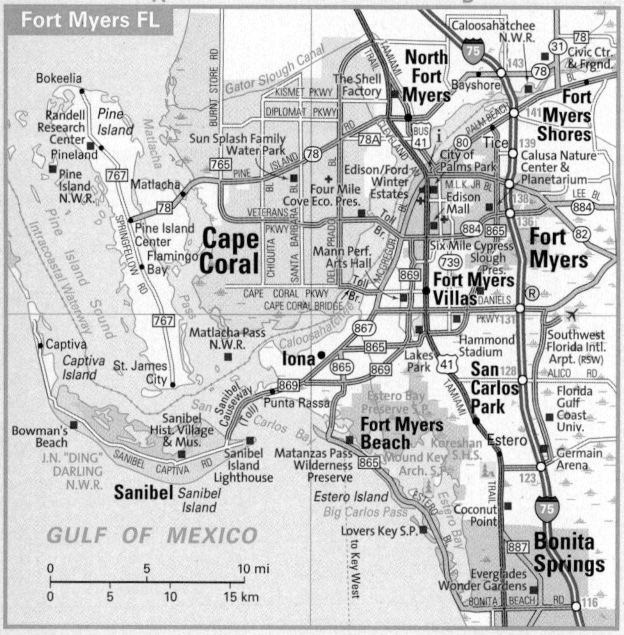

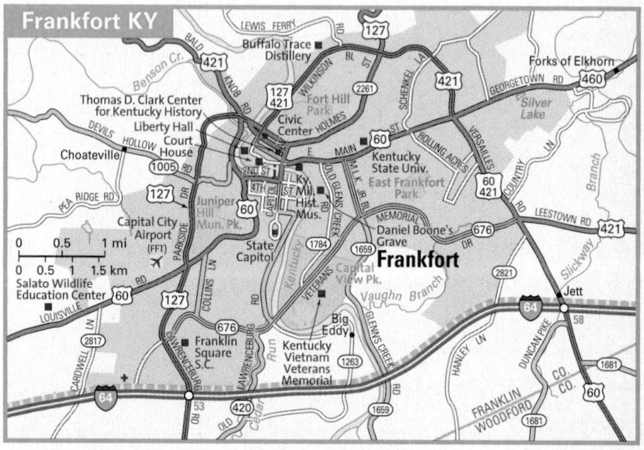

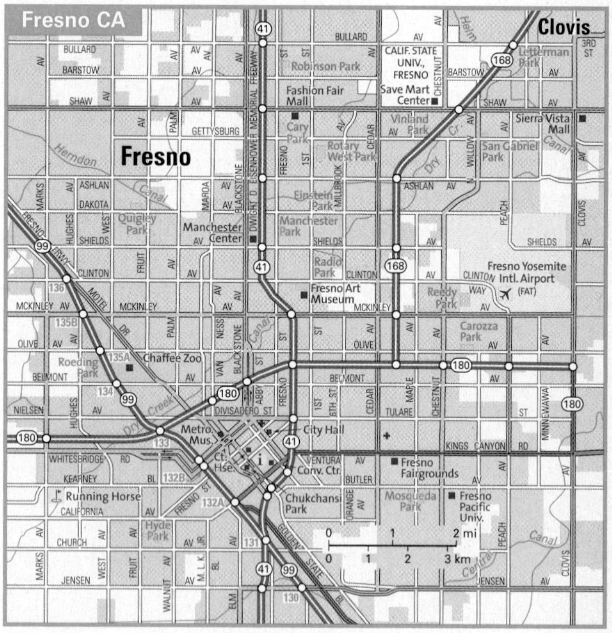

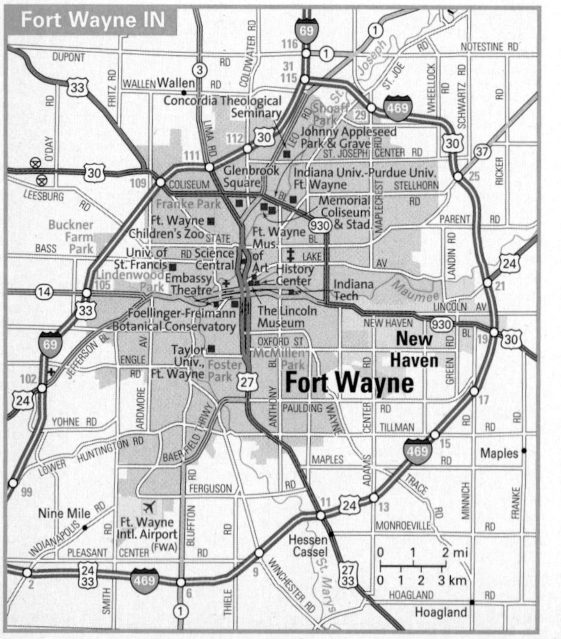

Fort Myers FL

Frankfort KY

Fresno CA

Fort Wayne IN

Entries in **bold black** indicate counties or parishes.
Entries in bold color indicate cities with detailed inset maps.

Franklin Co. IA, 10704.....72 C4
Franklin Co. KS, 24784.....96 A3
Franklin Co. KY, 47687.....100 B4
Franklin Co. ME, 29467.....82 B1
Franklin Co. MA, 71535.....150 A1
Franklin Co. MS, 8448.....126 A4
Franklin Co. MO, 93807.....97 F3
Franklin Co. NE, 3574.....43 D1
Franklin Co. NY, 51134.....80 C2
Franklin Co. NC, 47260.....113 D4
Franklin Co. OH, 1068978.....101 D1
Franklin Co. PA, 129313.....103 D1
Franklin Co. TN, 39270.....120 A1
Franklin Co. TX, 9458.....124 B1
Franklin Co. VT, 45417.....81 D1
Franklin Co. VA, 47286.....112 B2
Franklin Co. WA, 49347.....13 F4
Franklin Furnace OH, 1537.....101 D3
Franklin Grove IL, 1052.....88 B3
Franklin Par. LA, 21263.....125 F2
Franklin Park IL, 19434.....203 C4
Franklin Park PA, 11364.....92 A3
Franklin Sprs. GA, 762.....121 E3
Franklinton LA, 3657.....134 B1
Franklinton NC, 1745.....113 D4
Franklinville NJ, 1100.....145 F1
Franklinville NY, 1855.....78 B4
Franklinville NC, 1258.....112 B4
Frankston TX, 1209.....124 A3
Franksville WI, 1789.....74 C4
Frankton IN, 1905.....89 F4
Frannie WY, 209.....24 B2
Fraser CO, 910.....41 D1
Fraser MI, 15297.....210 D1
Frazee MN, 1377.....26 A4
Frazer MT, 452.....17 E2
Frazeysburg OH, 1201.....91 D4
Frazier Park CA, 2348.....52 B1
Frederic WI, 1262.....67 E2
Frederica DE, 648.....145 E3
Frederick CO, 2467.....41 E1
Frederick MD, 52767.....144 A1
Frederick OK, 4637.....51 D4
Frederick SD, 255.....27 D1
Frederick Co. MD, 195277.....144 A1
Frederick Co. VA, 59209.....102 C2
Fredericksburg IA, 933.....73 E3
Fredericksburg PA, 1140.....92 A3
Fredericksburg TX, 10432.....93 E4
Fredericksburg TX, 8911.....61 D2
Fredericksburg VA, 19279.....103 D3
Fredericktown MO, 3928.....108 A1
Fredericktown OH, 2428.....91 D4
Fredonia AZ, 1036.....47 D1
Fredonia KS, 2600.....106 A1
Fredonia KY, 420.....109 D2
Fredonia NY, 10706.....78 A4
Fredonia PA, 652.....91 F1
Fredonia WI, 1934.....74 C2
Freeborn Co. MN, 32584.....72 C4
Freeburg IL, 3872.....98 B3
Freeburg PA, 584.....93 D3
Freedom CA, 6000.....44 B2
Freedom WI, 1500.....74 C1
Freehold NJ, 10976.....147 E2
Freeland MI, 5147.....76 B2
Freeland PA, 3643.....93 E3
Freeland WA, 1313.....262 A1
Freeman MO, 521.....96 B3
Freeman SD, 1317.....27 E4
Freemansburg PA, 1897.....146 C1
Freeport FL, 1190.....136 B2
Freeport IL, 26443.....74 B4
Freeport ME, 1813.....82 B3
Freeport NY, 43783.....147 F1
Freeport PA, 1962.....92 A3
Freeport TX, 12708.....133 E4
Freer TX, 3241.....63 E2
Freestone Co. TX, 17867.....59 F4
Freetown IN, 600.....99 F2
Freetown NY, 2400.....149 F3
Freeville NY, 505.....79 D4
Freewood Acres NJ, 3100.....147 E2
Fremont CA, 203413.....36 B4
Fremont IN, 1696.....90 A1
Fremont IA, 704.....87 E2
Fremont MI, 4224.....75 F2
Fremont NE, 25174.....35 F3
Fremont NH, 500.....81 F4
Fremont NC, 1463.....123 E1
Fremont OH, 17375.....90 C2
Fremont WI, 666.....74 B1
Fremont Co. CO, 46145.....41 D3
Fremont Co. ID, 11819.....23 F3
Fremont Co. WY, 35804.....32 C1
Fremont Hills MO, 1007.....107 D2
Frenchburg KY, 551.....100 C4
French Camp CA, 4109.....36 C4
French Lick IN, 1941.....99 F3
French Settlement LA, 945.....134 A2
Frenchtown MT, 883.....15 D4
Frenchtown NJ, 1488.....146 C1
Frenchville ME, 350.....85 D1
Fresno CA, 427652.....44 C3
Fresno TX, 6603.....220 B4
Fresno Co. CA, 799407.....37 E4
Frewsburg NY, 1965.....92 B1
Friant CA, 519.....44 C3
Friars Pt. MS, 1480.....118 A3
Friday Harbor WA, 1989.....12 B2
Fridley MN, 27449.....67 D3

Friedens PA, 1673.....102 C1
Friedensburg PA, 828.....102 A1
Friend NE, 1174.....35 E4
Friendly MD, 10938.....144 B4
Friendship ME, 475.....82 C3
Friendship NY, 1176.....92 C1
Friendship TN, 608.....108 C4
Friendship WI, 698.....74 A1
Friendsville MD, 539.....102 C4
Friendsville TN, 890.....110 C4
Friendswood TX, 29037.....132 B4
Fries VA, 614.....112 A3
Frio Co. TX, 16252.....60 C3
Friona TX, 3854.....49 F4
Frisco CO, 2443.....41 D1
Frisco TX, 33714.....59 F2
Frisco City AL, 1460.....127 F4
Fritch TX, 2235.....50 B2
Froid MT, 195.....17 F2
Fromberg MT, 486.....24 B2
Frontenac FL, 1900.....232 A1
Frontenac KS, 2996.....106 B1
Frontenac MO, 3483.....256 B2
Frontier ND, 273.....19 F4
Frontier Co. NE, 3099.....34 C4
Fronton TX, 599.....63 D4
Front Royal VA, 13589.....102 C3
Frost TX, 648.....59 F3
Frostburg MD, 7873.....102 C1
Frostproof FL, 2975.....141 D3
Fruita CO, 6478.....40 B2
Fruit Cove FL, 16077.....139 D2
Fruit Hts. UT, 4701.....31 E3
Fruit Hill OH, 3945.....204 C3
Fruitland ID, 3805.....22 A4
Fruitland IA, 703.....87 F2
Fruitland MD, 3774.....103 F4
Fruitland NM, 650.....48 B1
Fruitland Park FL, 3186.....140 C1
Fruitport MI, 1124.....75 E3
Fruitvale TX, 399.....61 E4
Fryeburg ME, 1549.....81 F3
Fulda MN, 1283.....72 A2
Fullerton CA, 126003.....52 C3
Fullerton MD, 10100.....193 D2
Fullerton NE, 1378.....35 E3
Fulshear TX, 716.....132 A3
Fulton IL, 3881.....88 A1
Fulton KY, 2775.....108 C3
Fulton MD, 850.....144 B2
Fulton MS, 3882.....119 D3
Fulton MO, 12128.....97 E3
Fulton NY, 11855.....79 D3
Fulton TX, 1553.....61 E4
Fulton Co. AR, 11642.....107 F3
Fulton Co. GA, 816006.....120 C3
Fulton Co. IL, 38250.....88 A4
Fulton Co. IN, 20511.....89 F3
Fulton Co. KY, 7752.....108 C3
Fulton Co. NY, 55073.....79 F3
Fulton Co. OH, 42698.....90 B2
Fulton Co. PA, 14261.....103 D1
Fultondale AL, 6595.....119 F4
Fultonville NY, 710.....79 F3
Fuquay-Varina NC, 7898.....123 D1
Furnas Co. NE, 5324.....42 C1
Fyffe AL, 971.....120 A3

G
Gabbs NV, 318.....37 F2
Gackle ND, 319.....19 D4
Gadsden AL, 38978.....120 A3
Gadsden AZ, 9955.....53 F4
Gadsden TN, 553.....108 C4
Gadsden Co. FL, 45087.....137 D2
Gaffney SC, 12968.....121 F2
Gage Co. NE, 22993.....35 F4
Gahanna OH, 32636.....101 D1
Gail TX, 70.....58 B2
Gainesboro TN, 879.....110 A3
Gainesville FL, 95447.....138 C3
Gainesville GA, 25578.....121 D3
Gainesville MO, 632.....107 E3
Gainesville TX, 15538.....59 E1
Gainesville VA, 4382.....144 A3
Galatia IL, 1013.....108 C1
Galax VA, 6837.....112 A3
Galena AK, 675.....154 C2
Galena IL, 3460.....74 A4
Galena IN, 1831.....99 F4
Galena KS, 3287.....106 B2
Galena MO, 451.....107 D2
Galena Park TX, 10592.....220 C3
Galesburg IL, 33706.....88 A3
Galesburg MI, 1988.....75 F4
Gales Ferry CT, 2400.....149 F1
Galesville WI, 1427.....73 F1
Galeton PA, 1325.....92 C1
Galeville NY, 4476.....265 A1
Galien MI, 593.....89 E1
Galilee RI, 1400.....150 C4
Galion OH, 11341.....91 D3
Galisteo NM, 1304.....49 D3
Gallatin MO, 1789.....96 C1
Gallatin TN, 23230.....109 F3
Gallatin Co. IL, 6445.....109 D1
Gallatin Co. KY, 7870.....100 B3
Gallatin Gateway MT, 350.....23 F1
Gallaway TN, 666.....118 B1
Gallia Co. OH, 31069.....101 E3

Galliano LA, 7356.....134 B4
Gallipolis OH, 4180.....101 E3
Gallitzin PA, 1756.....92 B4
Gallup NM, 20209.....48 A3
Galt CA, 19472.....36 C3
Galva IL, 2758.....88 A2
Galva KS, 701.....43 E3
Galveston IN, 1532.....89 F4
Galveston KY, 450.....111 E1
Galveston TX, 57247.....132 B4
Galveston Co. TX, 250158.....132 B4
Gamaliel KY, 439.....110 A3
Gambell AK, 649.....154 A2
Gamber MD, 1000.....144 B1
Gambier OH, 1871.....91 D4
Gamewell NC, 3644.....111 F4
Ganado AZ, 1505.....47 F2
Ganado TX, 1915.....61 F3
Gang Mills NY, 3304.....93 D1
Gannvalley SD, 20.....27 D3
Gansevoort NY, 800.....81 D4
Gantt SC, 13962.....217 A2
Gap PA, 1611.....146 A3
Garber OK, 845.....51 E1
Gardena CA, 57746.....228 C4
Garden City AL, 564.....119 F3
Garden City CO, 357.....33 E4
Garden City GA, 11289.....130 B3
Garden City ID, 10624.....22 B4
Garden City KS, 28451.....42 B3
Garden City MI, 30047.....210 A3
Garden City MO, 1500.....96 C3
Garden City NY, 21672.....241 G3
Garden City SC, 9357.....123 D4
Garden City TX, 200.....58 A3
Garden City UT, 557.....31 E2
Garden City South NY, 3974.....241 G4
Garden City NE, 2292.....34 A3
Gardendale AL, 11626.....119 F4
Gardendale MI, 800.....76 C3
Gardendale TX, 1197.....58 A3
Garden Grove CA, 165196.....228 C4
Garden Home OR, 6931.....251 C2
Garden Plain KS, 797.....43 E4
Garden Ridge TX, 1882.....61 D2
Garden View PA, 2679.....93 D2
Gardenville PA, 1000.....146 C1
Gardiner ME, 6198.....82 C2
Gardiner MT, 851.....23 F2
Gardiner NY, 856.....148 B1
Gardner IL, 1406.....88 C2
Gardner KS, 9396.....96 B3
Gardner MA, 20770.....95 D1
Gardnertown NY, 4563.....148 B1
Gardnerville NV, 3357.....37 D2
Garfield AR, 490.....106 C3
Garfield NJ, 29786.....148 B3
Garfield TX, 1660.....61 E2
Garfield WA, 641.....14 B4
Garfield Co. CO, 43791.....40 B1
Garfield Co. MT, 1206.....17 D3
Garfield Co. NE, 1902.....35 D2
Garfield Co. OK, 57813.....51 E1
Garfield Co. UT, 4735.....39 E3
Garfield Co. WA, 2397.....14 A4
Garfield Hts. OH, 30734.....91 E2
Garibaldi OR, 899.....20 B2
Garland NC, 808.....123 D2
Garland TX, 215768.....59 F2
Garland UT, 1943.....31 E2
Garland Co. AR, 88068.....117 D2
Garnavillo IA, 754.....73 F3
Garner IA, 2922.....72 C3
Garner KY, 600.....111 D1
Garner NC, 17773.....113 D4
Garnett KS, 3368.....96 A4
Garrard Co. KY, 14792.....110 C1
Garretson SD, 1165.....27 F4
Garrett IN, 5803.....90 A3
Garrett Co. MD, 29846.....102 B2
Garrett Park MD, 917.....270 C1
Garrettsville OH, 2262.....91 F2
Garrison KY, 950.....101 D3
Garrison MN, 200.....67 D1
Garrison ND, 1318.....18 B3
Garrison TX, 844.....124 B3
Garrisonville VA, 2700.....144 A4
Garvin OK, 151.....51 E4
Garwin IA, 565.....87 D1
Gary IN, 102746.....89 D2
Gary SD, 231.....27 F2
Gary WV, 917.....111 F1
Garysburg NC, 1254.....113 E3
Garyville LA, 2775.....134 B3
Gas SC, 556.....96 A4
Gas City IN, 5940.....89 F4
Gasconade Co. MO, 15342.....97 F3
Gasport NY, 1248.....78 B3
Gassaway WV, 901.....101 F3
Gassville AR, 1706.....107 E3
Gaston IN, 1010.....89 F4
Gaston NC, 1097.....113 E3
Gaston OR, 600.....20 B1
Gaston SC, 1304.....122 A4
Gaston Co. NC, 190365.....122 A1
Gastonia NC, 66277.....122 A1
Gate City VA, 2159.....111 E1
Gates NY, 15138.....78 C3
Gates OR, 471.....20 C2
Gates TN, 695.....108 B4
Gates Co. NC, 10516.....113 F3
Gates Mills OH, 2493.....204 G1

Gatesville NC, 281.....113 F3
Gatesville TX, 15591.....59 E4
Gatlinburg TN, 3382.....111 D4
Gauley Bridge WV, 738.....101 F4
Gautier MS, 11681.....135 D2
Gayle Mill SC, 1094.....122 A2
Gaylord MI, 3681.....70 C3
Gaylord MN, 2282.....66 B2
Gaylordsville CT, 750.....148 C1
Gays Mills WI, 625.....73 F3
Geary OK, 1258.....51 D4
Geary Co. KS, 27947.....43 F2
Geauga Co. OH, 90895.....91 E2
Geddes SD, 252.....35 D1
Geistown PA, 2555.....92 B4
Gem Co. ID, 15181.....22 B3
Genesee ID, 946.....14 B4
Genesee Co. MI, 436141.....76 B3
Genesee Co. NY, 60370.....78 B3
Geneseo IL, 6480.....88 A2
Geneseo NY, 7579.....78 C4
Geneva AL, 4388.....136 C1
Geneva FL, 2601.....141 D1
Geneva IL, 19515.....88 C1
Geneva IN, 1368.....90 A3
Geneva NE, 2226.....35 E4
Geneva NY, 13617.....79 D3
Geneva OH, 6595.....91 F1
Geneva WA, 2257.....12 C1
Geneva Co. AL, 25764.....136 C1
Geneva-on-the-Lake OH, 1545.....91 F1
Genoa IL, 4169.....88 C1
Genoa OH, 2230.....90 C2
Genoa City WI, 1949.....74 C4
Genola UT, 965.....39 E1
Gentry AR, 2165.....106 B3
Gentry Co. MO, 6861.....86 B4
George IA, 1051.....72 A3
George WA, 528.....13 E4
George Co. MS, 19144.....135 D1
Georgetown CA, 962.....36 C2
Georgetown CO, 1088.....41 D1
Georgetown CT, 1650.....148 C2
Georgetown DE, 4643.....145 F4
Georgetown GA, 973.....128 C3
Georgetown ID, 538.....31 F1
Georgetown IN, 3628.....99 F1
Georgetown KY, 18080.....100 B4
Georgetown MA, 3000.....151 F1
Georgetown OH, 3691.....100 C2
Georgetown PA, 850.....146 A3
Georgetown SC, 8950.....131 E1
Georgetown TX, 28339.....61 E1
Georgetown Co. SC, 55797.....122 C4
George West TX, 2524.....61 D4
Georgia VT, 375.....81 D1
Georgiana AL, 1737.....127 F4
Gerald MO, 1171.....97 F3
Geraldine AL, 820.....120 A3

Geraldine MT, 284.....16 A3
Gerber CA, 1389.....36 B1
Gering NE, 7751.....33 F2
Gerlach NV, 499.....29 E4
Germania NJ, 750.....147 D4
Germantown IL, 1118.....98 B3
Germantown MD, 55419.....144 B2
Germantown NY, 862.....94 B2
Germantown OH, 4884.....100 B1
Germantown TN, 37348.....118 B1
Germantown WI, 18260.....74 C3
Germantown Hills IL, 2111.....88 B3
Geronimo OK, 959.....51 D4
Geronimo TX, 619.....61 E2
Gerrardstown WV, 550.....103 D2
Gettysburg OH, 558.....90 B4
Gettysburg PA, 7490.....103 E1
Gettysburg SD, 1352.....26 C2
Geyserville CA, 700.....36 A2
Ghent KY, 371.....100 A3
Ghent NY, 586.....94 B2
Ghent OH, 5261.....188 A1
Gholson TX, 922.....59 E4
Giants Neck CT, 1000.....149 F2
Gibbon MN, 808.....66 B4
Gibbon NE, 1759.....35 D4
Gibbsboro NJ, 2435.....147 D3
Gibbstown NJ, 3758.....146 C3
Gibraltar MI, 4264.....90 C1
Gibsland LA, 1119.....125 D2
Gibson GA, 694.....129 F1
Gibson MD, 650.....145 D1
Gibson Co. IN, 32500.....99 E4
Gibson Co. TN, 48152.....108 C4
Gibsonburg OH, 2506.....90 C2
Gibsonton FL, 8752.....140 C3
Gibsonville NC, 4722.....112 B4
Giddings TX, 5105.....61 F2

Gideon MO, 1113.....108 A3
Gifford FL, 7599.....141 E3
Gifford IL, 815.....89 D4
Gig Harbor WA, 6465.....12 C3
Gila Bend AZ, 1980.....54 B2
Gila Co. AZ, 51335.....55 D1
Gilbert AZ, 109697.....54 C2
Gilbert IA, 987.....86 C1
Gilbert LA, 561.....125 F3
Gilbert MN, 1847.....64 C3
Gilbert SC, 500.....122 A4
Gilbert WV, 417.....111 F1
Gilbertsville PA, 4242.....146 B2
Gilbertville IA, 767.....73 E4
Gilbertville MA, 1000.....150 B1
Gilby ND, 243.....19 E2
Gilchrist Co. FL, 14437.....138 C2
Gilcrest CO, 1162.....33 E4
Giles Co. TN, 29447.....119 F1
Giles Co. VA, 16657.....112 A2
Gilford NH, 600.....81 F3
Gilford Park NJ, 8700.....147 E3
Gillespie IL, 3412.....88 B3

Gillespie Co. TX, 20814.....61 D1
Gillett AR, 819.....117 F3
Gillett WI, 1256.....68 C4
Gilliam Co. OR, 1915.....21 D2
Gilman IL, 1793.....89 D3
Gilman IA, 600.....87 D1
Gilman VT, 375.....81 F2
Gilmer TX, 4799.....124 B2
Gilmer Co. GA, 23456.....120 C2
Gilmer Co. WV, 7160.....101 F2
Gilmore City IA, 556.....72 B4
Gilpin Co. CO, 4757.....41 D1
Gilroy CA, 41464.....44 B2
Gilt Edge TN, 489.....118 B1
Girard KS, 2773.....106 B1
Girard OH, 10902.....91 F2
Girard PA, 3164.....91 F1
Girardville PA, 1742.....93 E3
Gisela AZ, 532.....47 E4
Glacier Co. MT, 13247.....15 E1
Gladbrook IA, 1015.....87 D1
Glade Spr. VA, 1374.....111 F2
Glades Co. FL, 10576.....141 D4
Gladewater TX, 6078.....124 B2
Gladstone MI, 5032.....69 D2
Gladstone MO, 26365.....96 B2
Gladstone OR, 11438.....251 D3
Gladwin MI, 3001.....76 A1
Gladwin Co. MI, 26023.....76 A1
Glandorf OH, 919.....90 B3
Glasco KS, 536.....43 E2
Glasco NY, 1692.....94 B2
Glascock Co. GA, 2556.....129 F1
Glasford IL, 1076.....88 B3
Glasgow DE, 12840.....145 E2
Glasgow KY, 13019.....110 A3
Glasgow MO, 1263.....97 D2

Glasgow MT, 3253.....17 D2
Glasgow VA, 1046.....112 C1
Glasgow WV, 783.....101 F4
Glasgow Vil. MO, 5234.....256 C1
Glassboro NJ, 19068.....146 C4
Glasscock Co. TX, 1406.....58 B3
Glassmanor MD, 35355.....270 D5
Glassport PA, 4993.....250 D3
Glastonbury CT, 7157.....150 A3
Gleason TN, 1463.....108 C3
Glen Allen AL, 442.....119 E4
Glen Allen VA, 12562.....254 B1
Glen Alpine NC, 1090.....111 F4
Glenarden MD, 6318.....144 B3
Glen Avon CA, 14853.....229 H3
Glenburn ND, 374.....18 B2
Glenburn PA, 1212.....93 F2
Glen Burnie MD, 38922.....144 C2
Glen Carbon IL, 10425.....98 B3
Glencoe AL, 5152.....120 A4
Glencoe IL, 8762.....89 D1
Glencoe MN, 5453.....66 C3
Glencoe OK, 583.....51 F2
Glen Cove ME, 500.....82 C2
Glen Cove NY, 26622.....148 C3
Glendale AZ, 218812.....54 C1
Glendale CA, 194973.....52 C2
Glendale MO, 5767.....256 B2
Glendale OH, 2188.....204 B1
Glendale OR, 855.....28 B1
Glendale RI, 500.....150 C3
Glendale UT, 355.....39 D4
Glendale Hts. IL, 31765.....203 B4
Glendive MT, 4729.....17 F3
Glendo WY, 229.....33 E1
Glendora CA, 49415.....229 F2
Glendora NJ, 4907.....146 C3
Glen Elder KS, 439.....43 D1

Grand Rapids MI (inset map)

Ada B2
Cascade B2
Comstock Park A1
E. Grand Rapids B2
Grand Rapids B1
Grandville A2
Jenison A2
Kentwood B2
Marne A1
Tallmadge A1
Walker A2
Wyoming A2

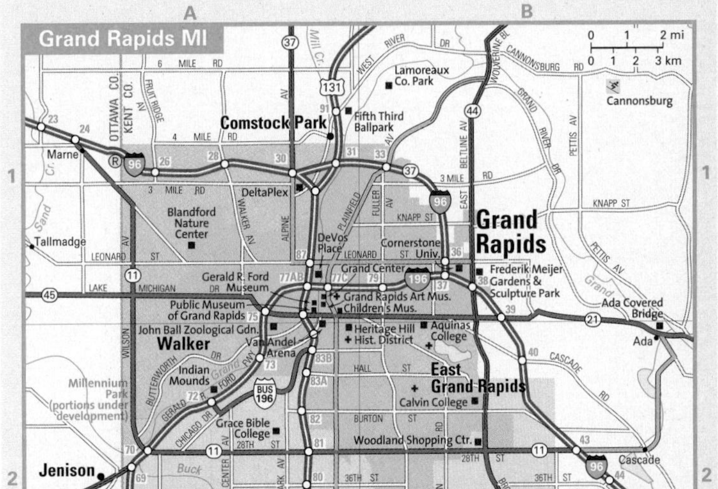

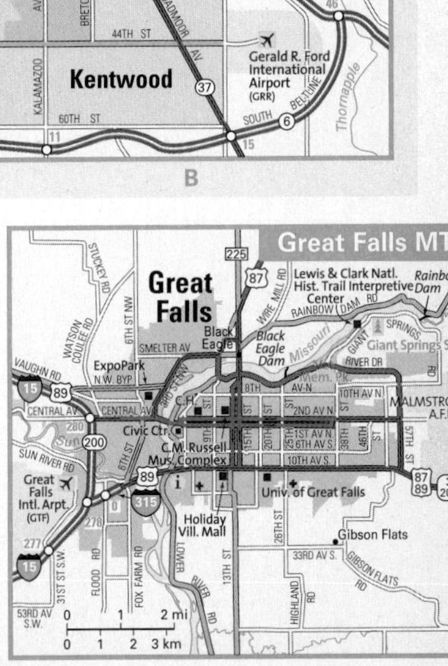

Great Falls MT (inset map)

Figures after entries indicate population, page number, and grid reference.

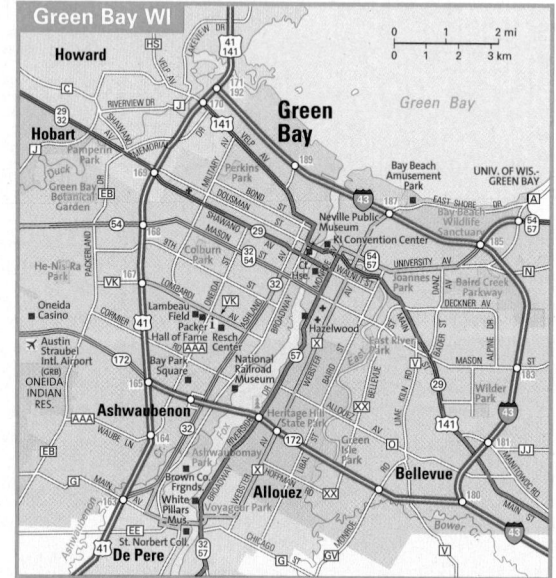

Green Bay WI

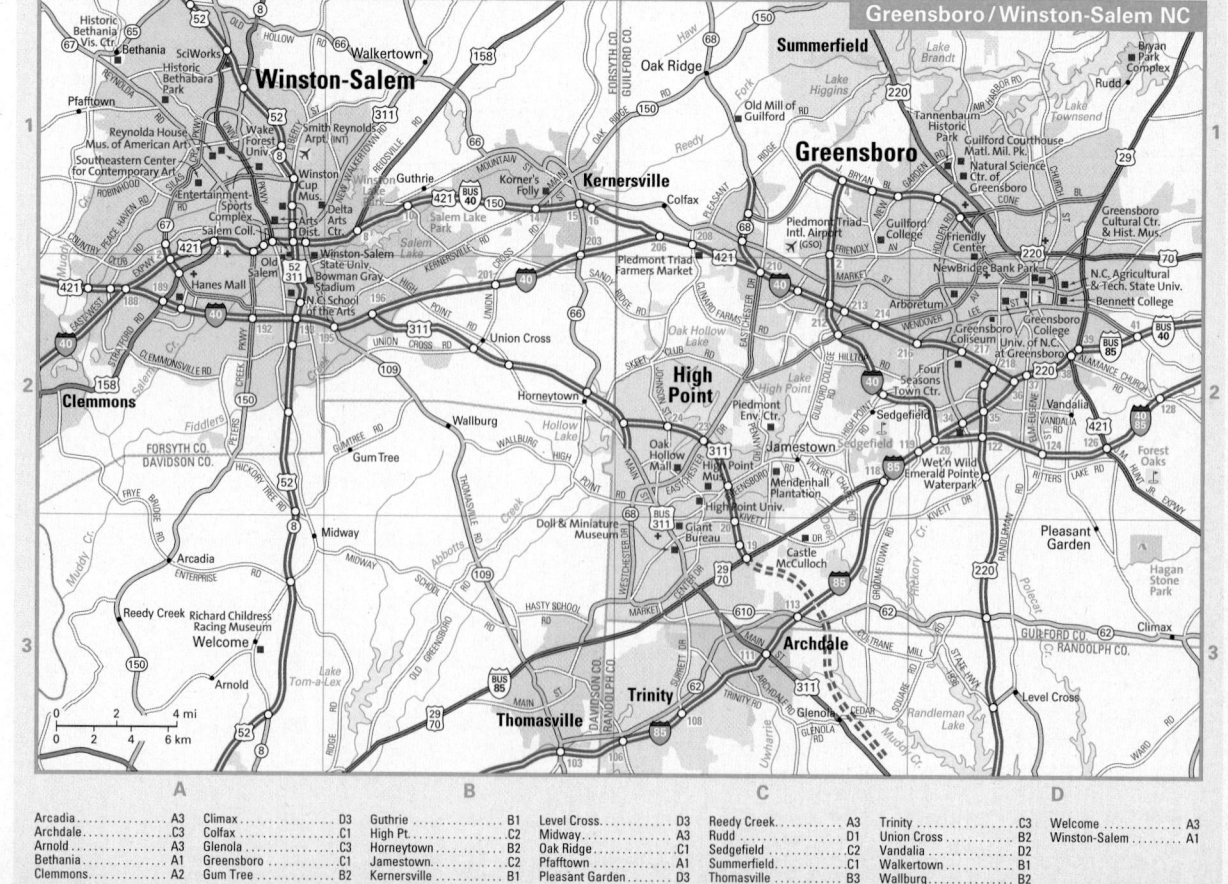

Greensboro / Winston-Salem NC

217
Grayson–Harrington

Entries in **bold black** indicate counties or parishes.
Entries in **bold color** indicate cities with detailed inset maps.

Grayson KY, 3877 101 D4
Grayson LA, 531 125 E3
Grayson Co. KY, 24053 109 F1
Grayson Co. TX, 110595 59 F1
Grayson Co. VA, 17917 111 F3
Gray Summit MO, 2640 98 A3
Graysville AL, 2344 119 F4
Graysville TN, 1411 120 B1
Grayville IL, 1725 99 D4
Greasewood AZ, 581 47 F3
Great Barrington MA, 2459 94 B2
Great Bend KS, 15345 43 D3
Great Bend NY, 801 79 E1
Great Bend PA, 700 93 F1
Great Falls MT, 56690 15 F3
Great Falls SC, 2194 122 A2
Great Falls VA, 8549 144 B3
Great Meadows NJ, 1264 94 A4
Great Mills MD, 2600 103 E4
Great Neck NY, 9538 148 B4
Great Neck Estates NY, 2756 241 G3
Great Neck Gardens NY, 1089 241 G2
Great Neck Plaza NY, 6433 241 G2
Great River NY, 1546 149 D4
Greece NY, 14614 78 C3
Greeley CO, 76930 33 E4
Greeley NE, 531 35 D3
Greeley Co. KS, 1534 42 B3
Greeley Co. NE, 2714 35 D3
Greeleyville SC, 452 122 B4
Green OH, 22817 91 E3
Green OR, 6174 28 B1
Greenacres CA, 7400 45 D4
Greenacres FL, 27569 143 F1
Greenback TN, 954 110 C4
Green Bay WI, 102313 68 C4
Greenbelt MD, 21456 144 B3
Greenbrier AR, 3042 117 E1
Greenbrier TN, 4940 109 F3
Greenbrier Co. WV, 34453 102 A4
Greenbush MA, 550 151 E2
Greenbush MN, 784 19 F1
Greencastle IN, 9880 99 E1
Greencastle PA, 3722 103 D1
Green City MO, 688 87 D4
Green Co. KY, 11518 110 A1
Green Co. WI, 33647 74 B4
Green Cove Sprs. FL, 5378 139 D3
Green Creek NJ, 1300 104 C4
Greendale IN, 4296 100 B2
Greendale MO, 722 256 B2
Greendale WI, 14405 234 C3
Greene IA, 1099 73 D3
Greene ME, 950 82 B2
Greene NY, 1701 79 E4
Greene Co. AL, 9974 127 E2
Greene Co. AR, 37331 108 A3
Greene Co. GA, 14406 121 E4
Greene Co. IL, 14761 98 A2
Greene Co. IN, 33157 99 E2
Greene Co. IA, 10366 86 B1
Greene Co. MS, 13299 127 D4
Greene Co. MO, 240391 107 D1
Greene Co. NY, 48195 94 A2
Greene Co. NC, 18974 115 C3
Greene Co. OH, 147886 100 C1
Greene Co. PA, 40672 102 A1
Greene Co. TN, 62909 111 D3
Greene Co. VA, 15244 102 C4
Greenevers NC, 560 123 E2
Greeneville TN, 15198 111 D4
Greenfield CA, 12583 44 B3
Greenfield IL, 1179 98 A2
Greenfield IN, 14600 99 F1
Greenfield IA, 2129 86 B2
Greenfield MA, 13716 94 C1
Greenfield MO, 1358 106 C1
Greenfield NH, 375 95 D1
Greenfield OH, 4906 100 C2
Greenfield TN, 2208 108 C4
Greenfield WI, 35476 234 C3
Green Forest AR, 2717 107 D3
Green Harbor MA, 2397 151 E2
Green Haven MD, 17415 144 C2
Green Haven NY, 3000 148 C1
Green Hill TN, 7068 109 F3
Greenhills OH, 4103 204 B1
Green Island NY, 2278 188 E2
Green Lake WI, 1100 74 B2
Green Lake Co. WI, 19105 74 B2
Greenland AR, 907 106 C4
Greenland NH, 1100 82 A4
Green Lane PA, 584 146 B2
Greenleaf ID, 862 22 A4
Greenlee Co. AZ, 8547 55 E2
Greenmount MD, 600 144 B1
Green Mtn. Falls CO, 773 205 C1
Green Oaks IL, 3572 203 C1
Green Park MO, 2666 256 B3
Green Pond NJ, 1400 148 A3
Greenport NY, 2048 149 E3
Green River UT, 973 39 F2
Green River WY, 11808 32 A3
Greensboro AL, 2731 127 E2
Greensboro FL, 619 137 D2
Greensboro GA, 3238 121 D4
Greensboro MD, 1632 145 E3
Greensboro NC, 223891 112 B4
Greensboro Bend VT, 350 81 E2
Greensburg IN, 10260 100 A2
Greensburg KS, 1574 43 D4
Greensburg KY, 2396 110 A2
Greensburg LA, 631 134 B1
Greensburg PA, 15889 92 A4
Green Sprs. OH, 1247 90 C2
Greensville Co. VA, 11560 113 E2
Greentown IN, 2546 89 F4
Greentown OH, 3154 91 E3
Green Tree PA, 4719 250 B2
Greenup IL, 1532 99 D2
Greenup KY, 1198 101 D3
Greenup Co. KY, 36891 101 D3
Green Valley AZ, 17283 55 D3
Green Valley CA, 600 52 C2
Green Valley IL, 728 88 B4
Green Valley MD, 12262 144 B2
Greenview IL, 862 88 B4
Green Vil. PA, 1100 103 D1
Greenville AL, 7228 128 A3
Greenville CA, 1160 36 C1
Greenville DE, 2332 146 B3
Greenville FL, 837 137 F2
Greenville GA, 946 128 C1
Greenville IL, 6955 98 B3
Greenville IN, 591 99 F4
Greenville KY, 4398 109 E2
Greenville ME, 1319 84 C4
Greenville MI, 7935 75 F3
Greenville MS, 41633 126 A1
Greenville MO, 451 108 A2
Greenville NH, 1131 95 D1
Greenville NY, 493 94 B2
Greenville NC, 60476 115 D2
Greenville OH, 13294 90 A4
Greenville PA, 6380 91 F2
Greenville RI, 8626 150 C3
Greenville SC, 56002 121 E2
Greenville TX, 23960 59 F2
Greenville VA, 886 102 B4
Greenville WI, 950 74 C1
Greenville Co. SC, 379616 121 E2
Greenville Jct. ME, 850 84 C4
Greenwich CT, 61101 148 C3
Greenwich NY, 1902 81 D4
Greenwich OH, 1525 91 D3
Greenwood AR, 7112 116 C1
Greenwood DE, 837 145 E3
Greenwood FL, 735 137 D1
Greenwood IN, 36037 99 F1
Greenwood LA, 2458 124 C2
Greenwood MS, 18425 118 B4
Greenwood MO, 3952 96 B3
Greenwood NE, 544 35 F3
Greenwood SC, 22071 121 F3
Greenwood WI, 1079 68 A4
Greenwood Co. KS, 7673 43 F3
Greenwood Co. SC, 66271 121 F3
Greenwood Lake NY, 3411 148 A2
Greenwood Vil. CO, 11035 209 C4
Greer SC, 16843 121 F2
Greer Co. OK, 6061 50 C3
Greers Ferry AR, 930 117 E1
Gregg Co. TX, 111379 124 B2
Gregory SD, 1342 35 D1
Gregory TX, 2318 63 F2
Gregory Co. SD, 4792 35 D1
Greilickville MI, 1415 69 F4
Grenada MS, 14879 118 B4
Grenada Co. MS, 23263 118 B4
Gresham OR, 90205 20 C2
Gresham WI, 575 68 C4
Gresham Park GA, 9215 190 E4
Gretna FL, 1709 137 D2
Gretna LA, 17423 134 B3
Gretna NE, 2355 35 F3
Gretna VA, 1257 112 C2
Greybull WY, 1815 24 C3
Gridley CA, 5382 36 B2
Gridley IL, 1411 88 C3
Gridley KS, 372 96 A4
Griffin GA, 23451 129 D1
Griffith IN, 17334 89 D2
Grifton NC, 2073 115 D3
Griggs Co. ND, 2754 19 D3
Griggsville IL, 1258 98 A1
Grimes AL, 459 128 B4
Grimes IA, 8246 86 C2
Grimes Co. TX, 23552 132 A2
Grinnell IA, 9105 87 D1
Griswold IA, 1039 86 B2
Groesbeck OH, 7202 204 A2
Groesbeck TX, 4291 59 F4
Groom TX, 587 50 B3
Grosse Pointe MI, 5670 210 D3
Grosse Pointe Farms MI, 9764 210 D3
Grosse Pointe Park MI, 12443 210 D3
Grosse Pointe Shores MI, 2823 210 D3
Grosse Pointe Woods MI, 17080 76 C4
Grosse Tete LA, 670 133 F2
Grosvenor Dale CT, 700 150 B2
Groton CT, 10010 149 F2
Groton MA, 1113 95 D1
Groton NY, 2470 79 D4
Groton SD, 1356 27 E2
Groton VT, 450 81 E2
Groton Long Pt. CT, 667 149 F2
Grottoes VA, 2114 102 C4
Grove OK, 5131 106 B3
Grove City FL, 2092 140 C4
Grove City MN, 608 66 B3
Grove City OH, 27075 101 D1
Grove City PA, 8024 92 A2
Grove Hill AL, 1438 127 E4
Groveland CA, 3388 37 D4
Groveland FL, 2360 140 C1
Groveland MA, 2800 95 E1
Groveport OH, 3865 101 D1
Grover NC, 698 122 A1
Grover Beach CA, 13067 52 A1
Groves TX, 15733 132 C3
Groveton NH, 1197 81 F2
Groveton TX, 1107 132 B1
Groveton VA, 21296 144 B4
Grovetown GA, 6089 121 F4
Grubbs AR, 438 107 F4
Gruetli-Laager TN, 1867 120 A1
Grundy VA, 1105 111 E2
Grundy Ctr. IA, 2596 73 D4
Grundy Co. IL, 37535 88 C2
Grundy Co. IA, 12369 73 D4
Grundy Co. MO, 10432 86 C4
Grundy Co. TN, 14332 120 A1
Gruver TX, 1162 50 B2
Guadalupe AZ, 5228 249 C3
Guadalupe CA, 5659 52 A1
Guadalupe Co. NM, 4680 49 E4
Guadalupe Co. TX, 89023 61 E3
Guerneville CA, 2441 36 A3
Guernsey WY, 1147 33 E2
Guernsey Co. OH, 40792 91 E4
Gueydan LA, 1598 133 E3
Guilderland NY, 1700 188 C2
Guildhall VT, 40 81 F2
Guilford CT, 2603 149 E2
Guilford ME, 945 82 C1
Guilford MD, 12918 193 A5
Guilford Co. NC, 421048 112 B4
Guin AL, 2389 119 E4
Gulf Breeze FL, 5665 135 F2
Gulf Co. FL, 13332 137 D3
Gulfport FL, 12527 140 B3
Gulfport MS, 71127 135 D2
Gulf Shores AL, 5044 135 E2
Gulf Stream FL, 716 143 F1
Gun Barrel City TX, 5145 59 F3
Gunnison CO, 5409 40 C3
Gunnison MS, 633 118 A4
Gunnison UT, 2394 39 E2
Gunnison Co. CO, 13956 40 C2
Gunter TX, 1230 59 F1
Guntersville AL, 7395 120 A3
Guntown MS, 1183 119 D3
Gurdon AR, 2276 117 D4
Gurley AL, 876 119 F2
Gurn Spr. NY, 600 80 C4
Gustavus AK, 429 155 D4
Gustine CA, 4698 36 C4
Guthrie KY, 1469 109 E3
Guthrie OK, 9925 51 E2
Guthrie TX, 10 58 C1
Guthrie Ctr. IA, 1668 86 B2
Guthrie Co. IA, 11353 86 B2
Guthriesville PA, 1800 146 B3
Guttenberg IA, 1987 73 F4
Guttenberg NJ, 10807 240 D2
Guymon OK, 10472 50 B1
Guys TN, 483 119 D2
Guyton GA, 917 130 B2
Gwinn MI, 1965 69 D1
Gwinner ND, 717 27 E1
Gwinnett Co. GA, 588448 121 D4
Gwynn VA, 600 113 F1
Gypsum CO, 3654 40 C1
Gypsum KS, 414 43 E2

H

Haakon Co. SD, 2196 26 B3
Habersham Co. GA, 35902 121 D2
Hacienda Hts. CA, 53122 228 E3
Hackberry LA, 1699 133 D3
Hackensack NJ, 42677 148 B3
Hackett AR, 694 116 C1
Hackettstown NJ, 10403 94 A4
Hackleburg AL, 1527 119 E3
Haddam CT, 650 149 E1
Haddonfield NJ, 11659 146 C3
Haddon Hts. NJ, 7547 248 D4
Hadley MA, 1200 150 A1
Hadley NY, 2240 80 C4
Hagaman NY, 1357 80 C4
Hagan GA, 898 129 F3
Hagerhill KY, 900 111 D1
Hagerman ID, 656 30 C1
Hagerman NM, 1168 57 E2
Hagerstown IN, 1768 100 A1
Hagerstown MD, 36687 144 A1
Hahira GA, 1626 137 F1
Hahnville LA, 2792 134 B3
Haiku HI, 6578 153 D1
Hailey ID, 6200 22 C4
Haileyville OK, 891 116 A2
Haines AK, 1811 155 D3
Haines OR, 426 21 F2
Haines City FL, 13174 141 D2
Halaula HI, 495 153 E2
Halawa HI, 13891 152 C3
Hale Ctr. TX, 2263 58 A1
Hale Co. AL, 15760 127 E2
Hale Co. TX, 36602 58 A1
Haledon NJ, 8252 148 B3
Haleiwa HI, 2225 152 A2
Hales Corners WI, 7765 74 C3
Haleyville AL, 4182 119 E3
Halfmoon NY, 2300 188 E1
Half Moon NC, 6645 115 D4
Half Moon Bay CA, 11842 36 B4
Halfway MD, 10065 144 A1
Halfway OR, 337 22 A2
Halifax MA, 1000 151 D2
Halifax NC, 344 113 E3
Halifax PA, 875 93 D4
Halifax VA, 1389 112 C2
Halifax Co. NC, 57370 113 E4
Halifax Co. VA, 37355 112 C2
Haliimaile HI, 895 153 D1
Hallam PA, 1532 103 E1
Hallandale Beach FL, 34282 143 F2
Hall Co. GA, 139277 121 D3
Hall Co. NE, 53534 35 D4
Hall Co. TX, 3782 50 B4
Hallettsville TX, 2345 61 F3
Halliday ND, 227 18 A3
Hallock MN, 1196 19 E1
Hallowell ME, 2467 82 C2
Halls TN, 2311 108 C4
Hallsburg TX, 518 59 F4
Halls Crossroads TN, 2100 110 C4
Halls Gap KY, 450 110 B1
Hallstead PA, 1216 93 F1
Hallsville MO, 978 97 E2
Hallsville TX, 2772 124 B2
Halsey OR, 724 20 B3
Halstad MN, 622 19 F3
Halstead KS, 1873 43 E3
Haltom City TX, 39018 207 B2
Hamblen Co. TN, 58128 111 D3
Hamburg AR, 3039 125 F1
Hamburg IA, 1240 86 A3
Hamburg MN, 538 66 C4
Hamburg NJ, 3105 148 A2
Hamburg NY, 10116 78 B4
Hamburg PA, 4114 146 A1
Hamden CT, 56913 149 D2
Hamden OH, 871 101 D2
Hamel IL, 570 98 B3
Hamilton AL, 6786 119 D3
Hamilton GA, 307 128 C2
Hamilton IL, 3029 87 F4
Hamilton IN, 1233 90 A2
Hamilton MI, 1300 75 F4
Hamilton MO, 1813 96 C1
Hamilton MT, 3705 23 D1
Hamilton NY, 3509 79 E3
Hamilton NC, 516 113 E4
Hamilton OH, 60690 100 B2
Hamilton RI, 2500 150 C4
Hamilton TX, 2977 59 E4
Hamilton VA, 562 144 A2
Hamilton City CA, 1903 36 B1
Hamilton Co. FL, 13327 138 C2
Hamilton Co. IL, 8621 98 C4
Hamilton Co. IN, 182740 99 F1
Hamilton Co. IA, 16438 72 C4
Hamilton Co. KS, 2670 42 A3
Hamilton Co. NE, 9403 35 E4
Hamilton Co. NY, 5379 79 F2
Hamilton Co. OH, 845303 100 B2
Hamilton Co. TN, 307896 120 B1
Hamilton Co. TX, 8229 59 D4
Hamilton Square NJ, 26419 147 D2
Ham Lake MN, 12710 67 D3
Hamler OH, 650 90 B2
Hamlet IN, 820 89 E2
Hamlet NC, 6018 122 C2
Hamlin TX, 2248 58 C2
Hamlin WV, 1119 101 E4
Hamlin Co. SD, 5540 27 E3
Hammon OK, 469 50 C3
Hammond IL, 518 98 C1
Hammond IN, 83048 89 D2
Hammond LA, 17639 134 B2
Hammond WI, 1153 67 E4
Hammondsport NY, 731 78 C4
Hammondville AL, 486 120 A2
Hammonton NJ, 12604 147 D4
Hamorton PA, 1400 146 B3
Hampden ME, 4126 83 D1
Hampden Co. MA, 456228 150 A2
Hampden Sydney VA, 1264 113 D2
Hampshire IL, 2900 88 C1
Hampshire Co. MA, 152251 94 C2
Hampshire Co. WV, 20203 102 C2
Hampstead MD, 5060 144 B1
Hampstead NH, 1100 95 E1
Hampton AR, 1579 117 E4
Hampton FL, 431 138 C3
Hampton GA, 3857 129 D1
Hampton IL, 1626 208 C1
Hampton IA, 4218 73 D4
Hampton MD, 5004 193 C1
Hampton NE, 439 35 E4
Hampton NH, 9126 95 E1
Hampton NJ, 1546 104 C1
Hampton PA, 6433 103 E1
Hampton SC, 2837 130 B2
Hampton TN, 1300 111 E3
Hampton VA, 146437 113 F2
Hampton Bays NY, 12236 149 E3
Hampton Beach NH, 1800 95 E1
Hampton Co. SC, 21386 130 B2
Hampton Park NY, 950 149 E3
Hamtramck MI, 22976 210 C3
Hana HI, 709 153 E1
Hanahan SC, 12937 131 D1
Hanamaulu HI, 3272 152 B1
Hanapepe HI, 2153 152 B1
Hanceville AL, 2951 119 F3
Hancock MD, 1725 102 C1
Hancock MI, 4323 65 F3
Hancock MN, 717 66 A3
Hancock NH, 375 81 E4
Hancock NY, 1189 93 F1
Hancock Co. GA, 10076 129 E1
Hancock Co. IL, 20121 87 F4
Hancock Co. IN, 55391 100 A1
Hancock Co. IA, 12100 72 C3
Hancock Co. KY, 8392 109 F1
Hancock Co. ME, 51791 83 D1
Hancock Co. MS, 42967 134 C2
Hancock Co. OH, 71295 90 B3
Hancock Co. TN, 6786 111 D3
Hancock Co. WV, 32667 91 F4
Hand Co. SD, 3741 27 D3
Hanford CA, 41686 45 D3
Hankinson ND, 1058 27 F1
Hanley Hills MO, 2124 256 B2
Hanna WY, 873 33 D2
Hanna City IL, 1013 88 B3
Hannibal MO, 17757 97 F1
Hannibal NY, 542 79 D3
Hanover CT, 700 149 F1
Hanover IL, 836 74 A4
Hanover IN, 2834 100 A3
Hanover KS, 653 43 F1
Hanover MA, 2200 151 E2
Hanover MN, 1355 66 C3
Hanover NH, 8162 81 E3
Hanover NJ, 11500 148 A3
Hanover OH, 885 91 D4
Hanover PA, 14535 103 E1
Hanover VA, 225 113 E1
Hanover Co. VA, 86320 103 D4
Hanover Park IL, 38278 203 B3
Hansen ID, 970 30 C1
Hansford Co. TX, 5369 50 B2
Hanson KY, 625 109 E1
Hanson MA, 2044 151 D2
Hanson Co. SD, 3139 27 E4
Hapeville GA, 6180 190 D5
Happy TX, 647 50 A4
Happy Camp CA, 800 28 B2
Happy Valley OR, 4519 251 D2
Harahan LA, 9885 239 B2
Haralson Co. GA, 25690 120 B4
Harbert MI, 1619 89 E1
Harbeson DE, 375 145 F4
Harbor OR, 2622 28 A2
Harbor Beach MI, 1837 76 C2
Harbor Bluffs FL, 2807 266 A2
Harbor Hills NY, 563 241 G2
Harbor Hills OH, 1303 101 D1
Harbor Sprs. MI, 1567 70 B3
Harbour Hts. FL, 2873 140 C4
Hardee Co. FL, 26938 140 C3
Hardeeville SC, 1793 130 B3
Hardeman Co. TN, 28105 118 C1
Hardeman Co. TX, 4724 50 C4
Hardin IL, 959 98 A2
Hardin KY, 564 109 D2
Hardin MO, 614 96 C2
Hardin MT, 3384 24 C1
Hardin TX, 755 132 B2
Hardin Co. IL, 4800 109 D1
Hardin Co. IA, 18812 73 D4
Hardin Co. KY, 94174 110 A1
Hardin Co. OH, 31945 90 C3
Hardin Co. TN, 25578 119 D1
Hardin Co. TX, 48073 132 C2
Harding Co. NM, 810 49 E2
Harding Co. SD, 1353 25 F1
Hardinsburg KY, 2345 109 F1
Hardwick GA, 5135 129 E1
Hardwick VT, 1100 81 E2
Hardy AR, 578 107 F3
Hardy Co. WV, 12669 102 C2
Harewood Park MD, 3400 145 D1
Harford Co. MD, 218590 144 C1
Hargill TX, 900 63 E4
Harker Hts. TX, 17308 59 E4
Harkers Island NC, 1525 115 E4
Harlan IA, 5282 86 A2
Harlan KY, 2081 111 D2
Harlan Co. KY, 33202 111 D2
Harlan Co. NE, 3786 35 D4
Harlem FL, 2730 141 D4
Harlem GA, 1814 129 F1
Harlem MT, 848 16 C2
Harleysville PA, 8795 146 C2
Harleyville SC, 594 130 C1
Harlingen TX, 57564 63 F4
Harlowton MT, 1062 16 B4
Harmon Co. OK, 3283 50 C4
Harmony IN, 589 99 E1
Harmony MN, 1080 73 E2
Harmony NC, 526 112 A4
Harmony PA, 937 92 A3
Harmony RI, 850 150 C3
Harnett Co. NC, 91025 123 D1
Harney Co. OR, 7609 21 E4
Harold KY, 1400 111 E1
Harper KS, 1567 43 E4
Harper TX, 1006 60 C1
Harper Co. KS, 6536 43 E4
Harper Co. OK, 3562 50 C1
Harpersville AL, 1620 128 A1
Harper Woods MI, 14254 210 D2
Harrah OK, 4719 51 E3
Harrah WA, 542 13 D4
Harriman NY, 2252 148 B2
Harriman TN, 6744 110 B4
Harrington DE, 3174 145 E3

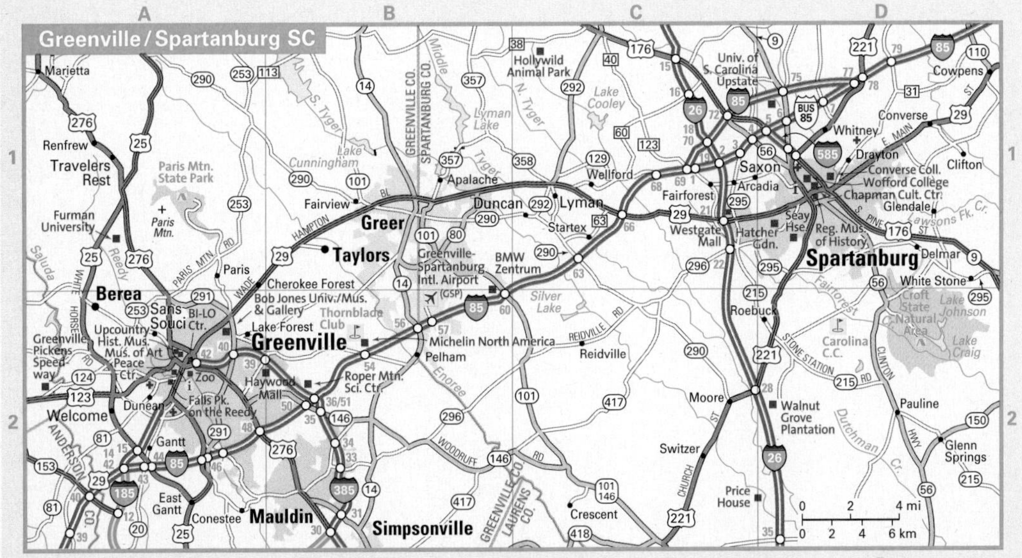

Apalache B1
Arcadia C1
Berea A2
Cherokee Forest A1
Clifton D1
Conestee A2
Converse D1
Cowpens D1
Crescent C2
Delmar D1
Drayton D1
Duncan C1
Dunean A2
E. Gantt A2
Fairforest C1
Fairview B1
Gantt A2
Glendale D1
Glenn Sprs. D2
Greenville A2
Greer B1
Lake Forest A2
Lyman C1
Marietta A1
Mauldin B2
Moore C2
Paris A1
Pauline D2
Pelham B2
Reidville C2
Renfrew A1
Roebuck D2
Sans Souci A2
Saxon C1
Simpsonville B2
Spartanburg D1
Startex C1
Switzer C2
Taylors B1
Travelers Rest A1
Welcome A2
Wellford C1
White Stone D1
Whitney D1

218
Harrington–Henry County

Figures after entries indicate population, page number, and grid reference.

Harrington ME, *425* **83** E2
Harrington WA, *426* **13** F3
Harris MN, *1121* **67** D3
Harrisburg AR, *2192* **118** A1
Harrisburg IL, *9860* **109** D1
Harrisburg NE, *75* **33** F3
Harrisburg NC, *4493* **122** B1
Harrisburg OR, *2795* **20** B3
Harrisburg PA, *48950* 93 D4
Harrisburg SD, *958* **27** F4
Harris Co. GA, *23695* **128** C2
Harris Co. TX, *3400578* **132** A3
Harrison AR, *12152* **107** D3
Harrison GA, *509* **129** F2
Harrison ID, *267* **14** B3
Harrison ME, *375* **82** B2
Harrison MI, *2108* **76** A1
Harrison NE, *279* **33** F1
Harrison NJ, *14424* **148** B4
Harrison NY, *24154* **148** C3

Bressler . . . C2	Fair Acres . . . B2	Marsh Run . . . C2	Penbrook . . . B1	Summerdale . . . A1
Camp Hill . . . A2	Good Hope . . . A1	Mechanicsburg . . . A2	Progress . . . B1	W. Enola . . . A1
Colonial Park . . . C1	Green Lane Farms . . . B2	New Cumberland . . . B2	Reesers Summit . . . B2	W. Fairview . . . A1
Eberlys Mill . . . B2	Harrisburg . . . B1	Oakleigh . . . C2	Rossmoyne . . . A2	White Hill . . . A2
Edgemont . . . B1	Highland Park . . . B2	Oberlin . . . C2	Rossmoyne Manor . . A2	Wormleysburg . . . B2
Enhaut . . . C2	Highspire . . . C2	Paxtang . . . B1	Rutherford Hts. . . . C1	
Enola . . . A1	Lawnton . . . C1	Paxtang Manor . . . C1	Shiremanstown . . . A2	
Estherton . . . B1	Lemoyne . . . B2	Paxtonia . . . C1	Steelton . . . B2	

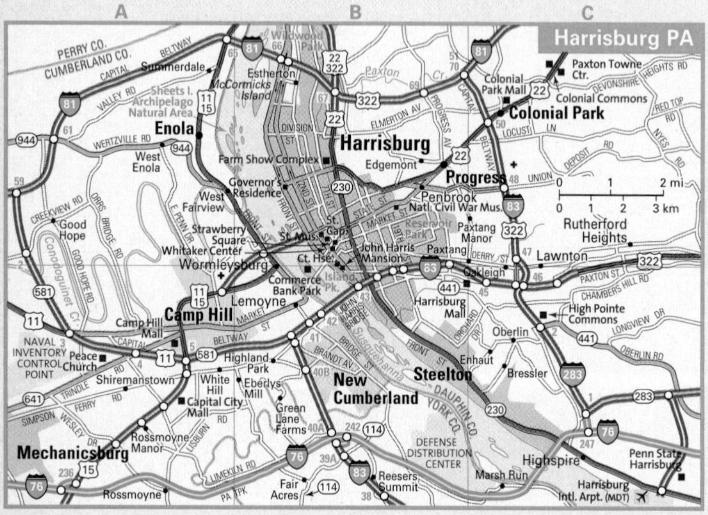
Harrisburg PA
Harrisburg
Enola
Colonial Park
Progress
Camp Hill
Lemoyne
Wormleysburg
New Cumberland
Steelton
Mechanicsburg
Highspire
Penbrook
Rutherford Heights
Lawnton
Oberlin
Shiremanstown
Rossmoyne
Harrisburg Intl. Arpt. (MDT)

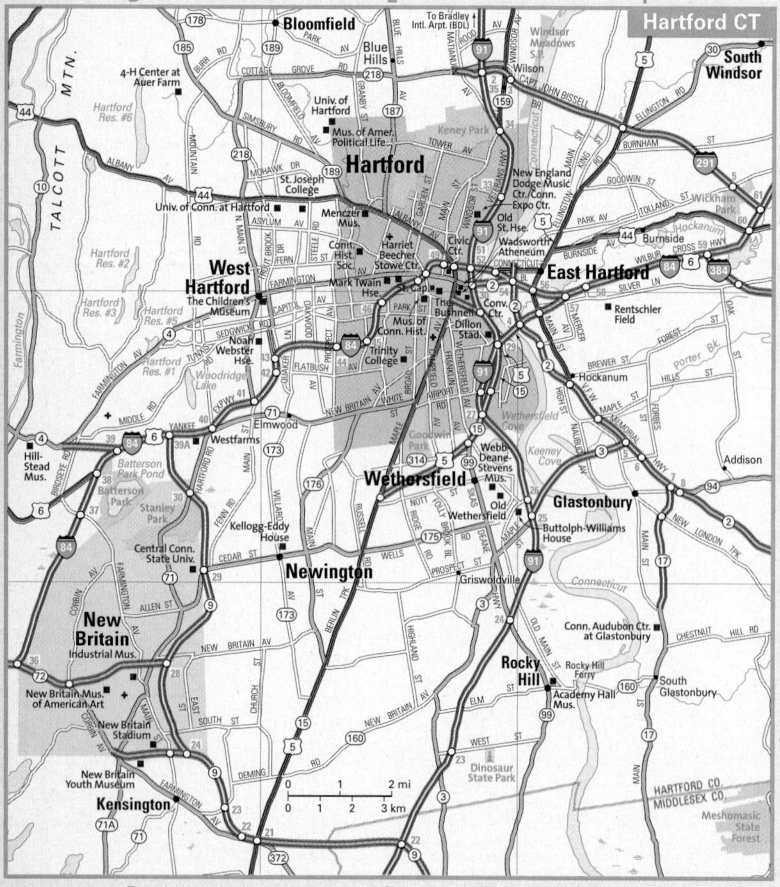
Hartford CT
Hartford
West Hartford
East Hartford
Bloomfield
Wethersfield
Glastonbury
Newington
New Britain
Rocky Hill
Kensington
South Windsor
South Glastonbury

Addison . . . F2	E. Hartford . . . F1	Hartford . . . E1	Newington . . . E2	W. Hartford . . . D2
Bloomfield . . . E1	Elmwood . . . E2	Hockanum . . . F2	Rocky Hill . . . F3	Wethersfield . . . E2
Blue Hills . . . E1	Glastonbury . . . E2	Kensington . . . D3	S. Glastonbury . . . F3	Wilson . . . E1
Burnside . . . F1	Griswoldville . . . E2	New Britain . . . D3	S. Windsor . . . F1	

Harrison OH, *7487* **100** B2
Harrison TN, *7630* **120** B1
Harrisonburg LA, *746* **125** F3
Harrisonburg VA, *40468* **102** C3
Harrison Co. IN, *34325* **99** F4
Harrison Co. IA, *15666* **86** A1
Harrison Co. KY, *17983* **100** B3
Harrison Co. MS, *189601* **134** C2
Harrison Co. MO, *8850* **86** C4
Harrison Co. OH, *15856* **91** E4
Harrison Co. TX, *62110* **124** B2
Harrison Co. WV, *68652* **102** A2
Harrisonville MO, *8946* **96** B3
Harristown IL, *1338* **98** C1
Harrisville MD, *600* **146** A4
Harrisville MI, *514* **71** D4
Harrisville NH, *400* **95** D1
Harrisville NY, *653* **79** E1
Harrisville PA, *883* **92** A3
Harrisville RI, *1561* **150** C2
Harrisville UT, *3645* **31** E3
Harrisville WV, *1842* **101** F2
Harrodsburg KY, *8014* **110** B1
Harrogate TN, *4052* **110** C3
Harrold SD, *209* **27** D3
Hart MI, *1950* **75** E2
Hart TX, *1198* **50** A4
Hart Co. GA, *22997* **121** E3
Hart Co. KY, *17445* **110** A2
Hartford AL, *2369* **136** C1
Hartford AR, *772* **116** C2
Hartford CT, *121578* 150 A3
Hartford IL, *1545* **98** A3
Hartford IA, *759* **86** C2
Hartford KS, *500* **43** F3
Hartford KY, *2571* **109** E1
Hartford MI, *2476* **89** F1
Hartford SD, *1844* **27** F4
Hartford WV, *519* **101** E2
Hartford WI, *10905* **74** C3
Hartford City IN, *6928* **90** A4
Hartford Co. CT, *857183* **150** A3
Hartington NE, *1640* **35** E1
Hartland ME, *872* **82** C1
Hartland VT, *500* **81** E3
Hartland WI, *7905* **74** C3
Hartley IA, *1733* **72** A3
Hartley Co. TX, *5537* **50** A2
Hartly DE, *78* **145** E2
Hartman AR, *596* **116** C1
Harts WV, *2361* **101** E4
Hartselle AL, *12019* **119** F3
Hartshorne OK, *2102* **116** A2
Hartsville SC, *7556* **122** B3
Hartsville TN, *7354* **109** F3
Hartville MO, *607* **107** E2
Hartville OH, *2174* **91** E3
Hartwell GA, *4188* **121** E3
Harvard IL, *7996* **74** C4
Harvard MA, *800* **150** C1
Harvard NE, *998* **35** E4
Harvest AL, *3054* **119** F2
Harvey IL, *30000* **203** E6
Harvey LA, *22226* **239** C2
Harvey MI, *1321* **69** D1
Harvey ND, *1989* **18** C3
Harvey Co. KS, *32869* **43** E3
Harveysburg OH, *563* **100** C2
Harveys Lake PA, *2888* **93** E2
Harwich MA, *1832* **151** F3
Harwich Port MA, *1809* **151** F3
Harwinton CT, *3242* **94** C3
Harwood ND, *607* **19** F4
Harwood Hts. IL, *8297* **203** D3
Hasbrouck Hts. NJ, *11662* **240** C1
Haskell AR, *2645* **117** E3
Haskell OK, *1765* **106** A4
Haskell TX, *3106* **58** C2
Haskell Co. KS, *4307* **42** B4
Haskell Co. OK, *11792* **116** B1
Haskell Co. TX, *6093* **58** C2
Haskins OH, *638* **90** C2
Haslet TX, *1134* **207** A1
Haslett MI, *11283* **76** A4
Hastings FL, *521* **139** D3
Hastings MI, *7095* **75** F4
Hastings MN, *18204* **67** D4
Hastings NE, *24064* **35** E4
Hastings PA, *1398* **92** B3
Hatboro PA, *7393* **146** C2
Hatch NM, *1673* **56** B2
Hatfield AR, *402* **116** C3
Hatfield IN, *1000* **99** E4
Hatfield MA, *1298* **150** A1
Hatfield PA, *2605* **146** C2
Hatley MS, *476* **119** D4
Hatteras NC, *650* **115** F3
Hattiesburg MS, *44779* **126** C4
Hatton ND, *707* **19** E3
Haubstadt IN, *1529* **99** D4
Haughton LA, *2792* **125** D2
Hauppauge NY, *20100* **149** D3
Hauser ID, *668* **14** B3
Hauula HI, *3651* **152** A2
Havana FL, *1713* **137** E2
Havana IL, *3577* **88** A4
Havelock NC, *22442* **115** D4
Haven KS, *1175* **43** E4
Haverhill FL, *1454* **143** F1
Haverhill MA, *58969* **95** E1
Haverhill NH, *500* **81** E3
Haverstraw NY, *10117* **148** B2
Havertown PA, *22300* **248** B3
Haviland KS, *612* **43** D4
Havre MT, *9621* **16** B2
Havre de Grace MD, *11331* **145** D1
Hawaiian Gardens CA, *14779* **228** E4
Hawaii Co. HI, *148677* **153** E2
Hawarden IA, *2478* **35** F1
Hawesville KY, *971* **99** E4
Hawi HI, *938* **153** E2
Hawkins TX, *1331* **124** B2
Hawkins Co. TN, *53563* **111** D3
Hawkinsville GA, *3280* **129** E3
Hawley MN, *1882* **19** F4
Hawley PA, *1303* **93** F2
Hawley TX, *646* **58** C2
Hawleyville CT, *800* **148** C1
Haw River NC, *1908* **112** C4
Hawthorn PA, *587* **92** B3
Hawthorne CA, *84112* **228** C3
Hawthorne FL, *1415* **138** C3
Hawthorne NV, *3311* **37** E3
Hawthorne NJ, *18218* **148** B3
Hawthorne NY, *5083* **148** B3
Hawthorn Woods IL, *6002* **203** B1
Haxtun CO, *982* **34** A4
Hayden AL, *470* **119** F4
Hayden AZ, *892* **55** D2
Hayden CO, *1634* **32** C4
Hayden ID, *9159* **14** B3
Hayden Lake ID, *494* **14** B3
Haydenville MA, *700* **150** A1
Hayes LA, *750* **133** E2
Hayes Ctr. NE, *240* **34** B4
Hayes Co. NE, *1068* **34** B4
Hayesville NC, *297* **121** D2
Hayesville OR, *18222* **20** B2
Hayfield MN, *1325* **73** D2
Hayfork CA, *2315* **28** B4
Haymarket VA, *879* **144** A3
Haynesville LA, *2679* **125** D1
Haynesville VA, *550* **103** E4
Hayneville AL, *1177* **128** A3
Hays KS, *20013* **43** D2
Hays MT, *702* **16** C2
Hays NC, *1731* **112** A3
Hays Co. TX, *97589* **61** D2
Hay Sprs. NE, *652* **34** A1
Haysville KS, *8502* **43** E4
Hayti MO, *3207* **108** B3
Hayti SD, *367* **27** F3
Hayti Hts. MO, *771* **108** B3
Hayward CA, *140030* **36** B4
Hayward WI, *2129* **67** F2
Haywood Co. NC, *54033* **111** D4
Haywood Co. TN, *19797* **108** C4
Hazard KY, *4806* **111** D2
Hazardville CT, *4900* **150** A2
Hazel KY, *440* **109** D3
Hazel Crest IL, *14816* **203** E6
Hazel Green AL, *3805* **119** F2
Hazel Green WI, *1183* **74** A4
Hazel Park MI, *18963* **210** C2
Hazelton ID, *687* **31** D1
Hazelton ND, *237* **18** C4
Hazelwood MO, *26206* **256** B1
Hazen AR, *1637* **117** F2
Hazen ND, *2457* **18** B3
Hazlehurst GA, *3787* **129** F3
Hazlehurst MS, *4400* **126** B3
Hazleton IA, *950* **73** E4
Hazleton PA, *23329* **93** E3
Hazlettville DE, *450* **145** E2
Headland AL, *3523* **128** B4
Head of the Harbor NY, *1447* **149** D3
Healdsburg CA, *10722* **36** B3
Healdton OK, *2786* **51** E4
Healy AK, *1000* **154** C2
Heard Co. GA, *11012* **128** B1
Hearne TX, *4690* **61** F1
Heart Butte MT, *698* **15** E2
Heath OH, *8527* **101** D1
Heathcote NJ, *4755* **147** D1
Heath Sprs. SC, *864* **122** B2
Heathsville VA, *30* **103** E4
Heavener OK, *3201* **116** B2
Hebbronville TX, *4498* **63** E2
Hebbville MD, *10900* **193** A2
Heber AZ, *2722* **47** E4
Heber CA, *2988* **53** E4
Heber City UT, *7291* **31** F4
Heber Sprs. AR, *6432* **117** E1
Hebron CT, *1200* **149** E1
Hebron IL, *1038* **74** C4
Hebron IN, *3596* **89** E2
Hebron KY, *1300* **100** B2
Hebron MD, *807* **103** F3
Hebron NE, *1565* **43** E1
Hebron ND, *803* **18** B4
Hebron OH, *2034* **101** D1
Hebron Estates KY, *1104* **100** A4
Hecla SD, *314* **27** E1
Hector AR, *506* **117** D1
Hector MN, *1166* **66** B4
Hedrick IA, *837* **87** E2
Hedwig Vil. TX, *2334* **220** B2
Heeia HI, *4944* **152** A3
Heflin AL, *3002* **120** A4
Heidelberg MS, *840* **127** D3
Heidelberg PA, *1225* **250** A3
Heilwood PA, *786* **92** B3
Helena AL, *10296* **127** F1
Helena AR, *6323* **118** A2
Helena GA, *2307* **129** E3
Helena MS, *778* **195** C1
Helena MT, *25780* 15 E4
Helena OK, *443* **51** D1
Helenwood TN, *846* **110** B3
Hellertown PA, *5606* **146** C1
Helmetta NJ, *1825* **147** E1
Helotes TX, *4285* **61** D2
Helper UT, *2025* **39** F1
Hemet CA, *58812* **53** D3
Hemingford NE, *993* **34** A2
Hemingway SC, *573* **122** C4
Hemlock MI, *1585* **76** B2
Hemphill TX, *1106* **124** C4
Hemphill Co. TX, *3351* **50** C2
Hempstead NY, *56554* **148** C4
Hempstead TX, *4691* **61** F2
Hempstead Co. AR, *23587* **116** C4
Henagar AL, *2400* **120** A2
Henderson KY, *27373* **109** E1
Henderson LA, *1531* **133** F2
Henderson MN, *910* **66** C4
Henderson NE, *986* **35** E4
Henderson NV, *175381* **46** B2
Henderson NC, *16095* **113** D3
Henderson TN, *5670* **119** D1
Henderson TX, *11273* **124** B3
Henderson Co. IL, *8213* **87** F3
Henderson Co. KY, *44829* **109** E1
Henderson Co. NC, *89173* **121** E1
Henderson Co. TN, *25522* **109** D4
Henderson Co. TX, *73277* **124** A2
Hendersonville NC, *10420* **121** E1
Hendersonville TN, *40620* **109** F3
Hendricks MN, *725* **27** F3
Hendricks Co. IN, *104093* **99** F1
Hendron KY, *4239* **108** C2
Hendry Co. FL, *36210* **143** D1
Henefer UT, *684* **31** F3
Henlopen Acres DE, *139* **145** F4
Hennepin IL, *707* **88** B2
Hennepin Co. MN, *1116200* **66** C4
Hennessey OK, *2058* **51** E2
Henniker NH, *1627* **81** F4
Henning MN, *719* **64** A4
Henning TN, *970* **108** B4
Henrico Co. VA, *262300* **113** E1
Henrietta NY, *6600* **78** C3
Henrietta TX, *3264* **59** D1
Henry IL, *2540* **88** B3
Henry SD, *268* **27** E2
Henry TN, *520* **109** D3
Henry Co. AL, *16310* **128** B4
Henry Co. GA, *119341* **129** D1
Henry Co. IL, *51020* **88** A2
Henry Co. IN, *48508* **100** A1
Henry Co. IA, *20336* **87** F3
Henry Co. KY, *15060* **100** A3
Henry Co. MO, *21997* **96** C4
Henry Co. OH, *29210* **90** B2
Henry Co. TN, *31115* **109** D3

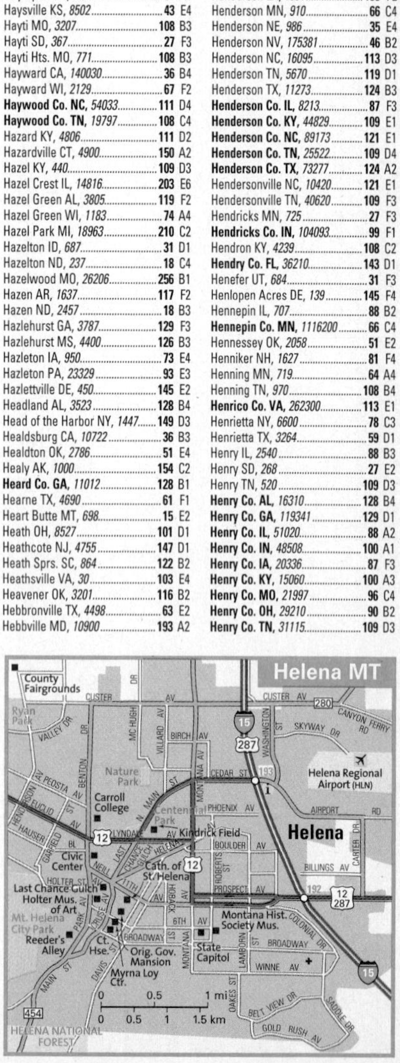
Helena MT
Helena
County Fairgrounds
Carroll College
Helena Regional Airport (HLN)
Kindrick Field
Civic Center
Cath. of St. Helena
Last Chance Gulch
Holter Mus. of Art
Montana Hist. Society Mus.
State Capitol
Orig. Gov. Mansion
Myrna Loy Ctr.
Reeder's Alley
Mt. Helena City Park
HELENA NATIONAL FOREST

219
Henry County–Hopkins County

Entries in **bold black** indicate counties or parishes.
Entries in **bold color** indicate cities with detailed inset maps.

Henry Co. VA, *57930* 112 B2
Henryetta OK, *6096* 51 F3
Henryville IN, *1545* 100 A3
Hephzibah GA, *3880* 129 F1
Heppner OR, *1395* 21 E2
Herculaneum MO, *2805* 98 A4
Hercules CA, *19488* 259 C1
Hereford PA, *1400* 146 B1
Hereford TX, *14597* 50 A4
Herington KS, *2563* 43 F3
Herkimer NY, *7498* 79 F3
Herkimer Co. NY, *64427* 79 F2
Hermann MO, *2674* 97 F3
Hermantown MN, *7448* 64 C4
Herminie PA, *856* 92 A4
Hermiston OR, *13154* 21 E1
Hermitage AR, *769* 117 E4
Hermitage MO, *406* 97 D4
Hermitage PA, *16157* 91 F2
Hermon ME, *750* 83 D1
Hermosa CO, *700* 40 B4
Hermosa SD, *315* 26 A4
Hermosa Beach CA, *18566* 228 C4
Hernandez NM, *600* 48 C2
Hernando FL, *8253* 140 C1
Hernando MS, *6812* 118 B2
Hernando Beach FL, *2185* 140 B1
Hernando Co. FL, *130802* 140 B1
Herndon VA, *21655* 144 A3
Heron Lake MN, *768* 72 A2
Herreid SD, *482* 26 C1
Herricks NY, *4076* 241 G3
Herriman UT, *1523* 31 E4
Herrin IL, *11298* 108 C1
Herscher IL, *1523* 89 D3
Hershey NE, *572* 34 B3
Hershey PA, *12771* 93 E4
Hertford NC, *2070* 113 F3
Hertford Co. NC, *22601* 113 F3
Hesperia CA, *62582* 53 D2
Hesperia MI, *954* 75 E2
Hessmer LA, *642* 133 F1
Hesston KS, *3509* 43 E3
Hettinger ND, *1307* 26 A1
Hettinger Co. ND, *2715* 18 A4
Heuvelton NY, *804* 80 B2
Hewitt TX, *11085* 59 E4
Hewitt WI, *670* 68 A4
Hewlett NY, *7060* 241 G4
Hewlett Harbor NY, *1271* 241 G5
Hewlett Neck NY, *504* 241 G5
Heyburn ID, *2899* 31 D1
Heyworth IL, *2431* 88 C4
Hialeah FL, *226419* 143 E2
Hialeah Gardens FL, *19297* 143 E2
Hiawassee GA, *808* 121 D2
Hiawatha IA, *6480* 87 E1
Hiawatha KS, *3417* 96 A1
Hibbing MN, *17071* 64 B3
Hickman KY, *2560* 108 C3
Hickman NE, *1084* 35 F4
Hickman Co. KY, *5262* 108 C3
Hickman Co. TN, *22295* 109 E4
Hickory MS, *499* 126 C2
Hickory NC, *37222* 111 F4
Hickory Co. MO, *8940* 97 D4
Hickory Flat MS, *565* 118 C2
Hickory Hills IL, *13926* 203 D5
Hickory Withe TN, *2574* 118 C1
Hicksville NY, *41260* 148 C4
Hicksville OH, *3649* 90 A2
Hico TX, *1341* 59 E3
Hidalgo TX, *7322* 63 E4
Hidalgo Co. NM, *5932* 55 F4
Hidalgo Co. TX, *569463* 63 E3
Hidden Hills CA, *1875* 228 A2
Hiddenite NC, *650* 112 A4
Hideaway TX, *2672* 124 A2
Higbee MO, *623* 97 E2
Higganum CT, *1671* 149 E1
Higginsville MO, *4682* 96 C2
High Bridge NJ, *3776* 104 C1
Highgate Ctr. VT, *600* 81 D1
Highgrove CA, *3445* 229 J3
Highland AR, *986* 107 F3
Highland CA, *44605* 229 K2
Highland IL, *8438* 98 B3
Highland IN, *23546* 89 D2
Highland KS, *976* 96 A1
Highland MD, *800* 144 B2
Highland NY, *5060* 94 B3
Highland UT, *8172* 31 F4
Highland WI, *855* 74 A3
Highland Beach FL, *3775* 143 F1
Highland City FL, *2051* 140 C2
Highland Co. OH, *40875* 100 C2
Highland Co. VA, *2536* 102 B4
Highland Falls NY, *3678* 148 B2
Highland Hts. KY, *6554* 204 B3
Highland Hts. OH, *8082* 204 G1
Highland Hills OH, *1618* 204 G2
Highland Lakes NJ, *5051* 148 A2
Highland Mills NY, *3468* 148 B2
Highland Park IL, *31365* 89 D1
Highland Park MI, *16746* 210 C3
Highland Park NJ, *13999* 147 E1
Highland Park PA, *4900* 218 B2
Highland Park TX, *8842* 207 D2
Highlands NJ, *5097* 147 F1
Highlands NC, *909* 121 D2
Highlands TX, *7089* 132 B3
Highlands Co. FL, *87366* 141 D4
Highland Sprs. VA, *15137* 254 C2
Highlands Ranch CO, *70931* 209 C4
Highlandville MO, *872* 107 D2
Highmore SD, *851* 27 D3
High Pt. FL, *5800* 266 B2
High Pt. NC, *85839* 112 B4
High Ridge MO, *4236* 98 A3
High Rolls NM, *425* 56 C2
High Shoals NC, *729* 122 A1
Highspire PA, *2720* 218 C2
High Sprs. FL, *3863* 138 C3
Hightstown NJ, *5216* 147 D2
Hightsville NC, *759* 275 A1
Highwood IL, *4143* 203 D1
Hiland Park FL, *999* 136 C2
Hilbert WI, *1089* 74 C1
Hilda SC, *436* 130 B1
Hildale UT, *1895* 46 C1
Hiles WI, *404* 68 B2
Hillandale MD, *3054* 270 E1
Hillburn NY, *881* 148 B2
Hill City KS, *1604* 42 C2
Hill City MN, *479* 64 B4
Hill City SD, *780* 25 F4
Hill Country Vil. TX, *1028* 257 E1
Hill Co. MT, *16673* 16 A1
Hill Co. TX, *32321* 59 E3
Hillcrest IL, *1158* 88 B1
Hillcrest NY, *7106* 148 B2
Hillcrest TX, *722* 132 B4
Hillcrest Hts. MD, *16359* 144 B3
Hilliard FL, *2702* 139 D1
Hilliard OH, *24230* 101 D1
Hillman MI, *685* 70 C3
Hills IA, *679* 87 F2
Hills MN, *565* 27 F4
Hillsboro AL, *608* 119 E2
Hillsboro IL, *4359* 98 B2
Hillsboro IN, *489* 89 E4
Hillsboro KS, *2854* 43 E3
Hillsboro MO, *1675* 98 A4
Hillsboro ND, *1563* 19 E3
Hillsboro OH, *6368* 100 C2
Hillsboro OR, *70186* 20 B2
Hillsboro TX, *8232* 59 E3
Hillsboro WI, *1302* 74 A2
Hillsboro Beach FL, *2163* 143 F1
Hillsborough CA, *10825* 259 B4
Hillsborough NH, *1842* 81 E4
Hillsborough NC, *5446* 112 C4
Hillsborough Co. FL, *998948* 140 C3
Hillsborough Co. NH, *380841* 81 F4
Hillsdale IL, *588* 88 A2
Hillsdale MI, *8233* 90 B1
Hillsdale MO, *1477* 256 B2
Hillsdale NJ, *10087* 148 B3
Hillsdale Co. MI, *46527* 90 B1
Hillside IL, *8155* 203 C4
Hillside NJ, *21747* 148 A4
Hillside Lake NY, *2022* 148 B1
Hillsville VA, *2607* 112 A2
Hilltop MN, *766* 235 C1
Hillview KY, *7037* 100 A4
Hilmar CA, *4807* 36 C4
Hilo HI, *40759* 153 F3
Hilshire Vil. TX, *720* 220 B2
Hilton NY, *5856* 78 C3
Hilton Head Island SC, *33862* 130 C3
Hinckley IL, *1994* 88 C1
Hinckley MN, *1291* 67 D2
Hinckley UT, *698* 39 D2
Hindman KY, *787* 111 D1
Hinds Co. MS, *250800* 126 B3
Hines OR, *1623* 21 E4
Hinesburg VT, *900* 81 D2
Hinesville GA, *30392* 130 B3
Hingham MA, *5352* 151 D1
Hinsdale IL, *17349* 203 C5
Hinsdale MA, *750* 94 C1
Hinsdale NH, *1713* 94 C1
Hinsdale Co. CO, *790* 40 C4
Hinson FL, *750* 137 E2
Hinton IA, *808* 35 F1
Hinton OK, *2175* 51 D3
Hinton WV, *2880* 112 A1
Hiram GA, *1361* 120 C4
Hiram OH, *1242* 91 E2
Hitchcock TX, *6386* 132 B4
Hitchcock Co. NE, *3111* 34 B4
Hitchins KY, *475* 101 D4
Hobart IN, *25363* 89 D2
Hobart OK, *3997* 51 D3
Hobart WA, *6251* 12 C3
Hobbs NM, *28657* 57 F2
Hobe Sound FL, *11376* 141 F4
Hoboken NJ, *38577* 148 B4
Hobson MT, *244* 16 B4
Hockessin DE, *12902* 146 B3
Hocking Co. OH, *28241* 101 D1
Hockley Co. TX, *22716* 58 A1
Hodge LA, *492* 125 E3
Hodgeman Co. KS, *2085* 42 C3
Hodgenville KY, *2874* 110 A1
Hodgkins IL, *2134* 203 C5
Hoffman MN, *672* 66 A2
Hoffman NC, *624* 122 C2
Hoffman Estates IL, *49495* 203 B3
Hogansville GA, *2774* 128 C1
Hohenwald TN, *3754* 119 E1
Hoisington KS, *2975* 43 D3
Hokah MN, *614* 73 F2
Hoke Co. NC, *33646* 123 D2
Hokendauqua PA, *3411* 189 A1
Hokes Bluff AL, *4149* 120 A3
Holbrook AZ, *4917* 47 F3
Holbrook MA, *10785* 151 D2
Holbrook NY, *27512* 149 D4
Holcomb KS, *2026* 42 B3
Holcomb MO, *696* 108 B3
Holden MA, *4200* 150 B1
Holden MO, *2510* 96 C3
Holden UT, *400* 39 E2
Holden WV, *1105* 111 E1
Holden Beach NC, *787* 123 E4
Holdenville OK, *4732* 51 F3
Holdingford MN, *736* 66 B2
Holdrege NE, *5636* 35 D4
Holgate OH, *1194* 90 B2
Holiday FL, *21904* 140 B2
Holiday Hills IL, *831* 203 A1
Holiday Lakes TX, *1095* 132 A4
Holladay UT, *14561* 257 B2
Holland AR, *577* 117 E1
Holland IN, *695* 99 E4
Holland MA, *1444* 150 B2
Holland MI, *35048* 75 E4
Holland NY, *1261* 78 B4
Holland OH, *1306* 90 C2
Holland TX, *1102* 61 E1
Hollandale MS, *3437* 126 A1
Holley FL, *650* 135 F2
Holley NY, *1802* 78 B3
Holliday TX, *1632* 59 D1
Hollidaysburg PA, *5368* 92 C4
Hollins VA, *14309* 112 B1
Hollis NH, *550* 95 D1
Hollis OK, *2264* 50 C4
Hollis Ctr. ME, *450* 82 B3
Hollister CA, *34413* 44 B2
Hollister MO, *3867* 107 D3
Hollister NC, *600* 113 D3
Holliston MA, *3400* 150 C2
Hollow Creek KY, *815* 230 E3
Hollow Rock TN, *963* 109 D4
Holly CO, *1048* 42 A3
Holly MI, *6135* 76 B4
Holly Grove AR, *722* 117 F2
Holly Hill FL, *12119* 139 E4
Holly Hill SC, *1281* 130 C1
Holly Park NJ, *2200* 147 E3
Holly Pond AL, *645* 119 F3
Holly Ridge NC, *831* 115 C4
Holly Sprs. GA, *3195* 120 C3
Holly Sprs. MS, *7957* 118 C2
Holly Sprs. NC, *9192* 112 C4
Hollyvilla KY, *481* 100 A4
Hollywood AL, *950* 120 A2
Hollywood FL, *139357* 143 F2
Hollywood MD, *650* 103 E4
Hollywood SC, *3946* 131 D2
Hollywood Park TX, *2983* 61 D2
Holmdel NJ, *1200* 147 E2
Holmen WI, *6200* 73 F1
Holmes Beach FL, *4966* 140 B3
Holmes Co. FL, *18564* 136 C1
Holmes Co. MS, *21609* 126 B1
Holmes Co. OH, *38943* 91 D4
Holstein IA, *1470* 72 A4
Holt AL, *4103* 127 E1
Holt MI, *11315* 76 A4
Holt Co. MO, *5351* 86 A4
Holt Co. NE, *11551* 35 D1
Holton KS, *3353* 96 A2
Holts Summit MO, *2935* 97 E3
Holtville CA, *5612* 53 E4
Holualoa HI, *6107* 153 E3
Holyoke CO, *2261* 34 A4
Holyoke MA, *39838* 150 A2
Holyrood KS, *464* 43 D3
Homecroft IN, *751* 99 F1
Homedale ID, *2528* 22 A4
Home Gardens CA, *9461* 229 H4
Homeland CA, *3710* 229 K4
Homeland GA, *765* 139 D1
Homeland Park SC, *6337* 121 E3
Homer AK, *3946* 154 C3
Homer GA, *950* 121 D3
Homer IL, *1200* 99 D1
Homer LA, *3788* 125 D2
Homer MI, *1851* 90 A1
Homer NE, *590* 35 F2
Homer NY, *3368* 79 D4
Homer City PA, *1844* 92 B4
Homer Glen IL, *22899* 203 C6
Homerville GA, *2803* 138 C1
Homestead FL, *31909* 143 E3
Homestead PA, *3569* 250 C2
Homestead Valley CA, *10691* 259 A2
Hometown IL, *4467* 203 D5
Hometown PA, *1399* 93 E3
Hometown WV, *750* 101 E3
Homewood AL, *25043* 119 F4
Hominy OK, *2584* 51 F1
Homosassa FL, *2294* 140 B1
Homosassa Sprs. FL, *12458* 140 B1
Honaker VA, *945* 111 E2
Honalo HI, *1987* 153 E3
Honaunau HI, *2414* 153 E3
Hondo TX, *7897* 60 C3
Honea Path SC, *3504* 121 E3
Honeoye NY, *800* 78 C4
Honeoye Falls NY, *2595* 78 C3
Honesdale PA, *4874* 93 F2
Honey Brook PA, *1287* 146 B2
Honey Grove TX, *1746* 59 F1
Honeyville UT, *1214* 31 E3
Honokaa HI, *2233* 153 E2
Honokowai HI, *6788* 153 D1
Honolulu HI, *371657* 152 A3
Honolulu Co. HI, *876156* 152 A3
Honomu HI, *541* 153 F3
Hood Co. TX, *41100* 59 E3
Hood River OR, *5831* 21 D1
Hood River Co. OR, *20411* 20 C2
Hooker OK, *1788* 50 B1
Hooker Co. NE, *783* 34 B2
Hooks TX, *2973* 116 C4
Hooksett NH, *3609* 81 F4
Hoonah AK, *860* 155 D4
Hooper NE, *827* 35 F3
Hooper UT, *4026* 244 A2
Hooper Bay AK, *1014* 154 B3
Hoopeston IL, *5965* 89 D4
Hoople ND, *292* 19 E2
Hoosick Falls NY, *3436* 94 B1
Hoover AL, *62742* 127 F1
Hooverson Hts. WV, *2909* 91 F4
Hooversville PA, *779* 92 B4
Hopatcong NJ, *15888* 148 A3
Hope AR, *10616* 117 D4
Hope IN, *2140* 99 F2
Hope ND, *303* 19 E3
Hope RI, *1900* 150 C3
Hopedale IL, *929* 88 B4
Hopedale MA, *4158* 150 C2
Hopedale OH, *984* 91 F4
Hope Mills NC, *11237* 123 D2
Hope Valley RI, *1649* 150 C4
Hopewell NJ, *2035* 147 D1
Hopewell TN, *1815* 120 B1
Hopewell VA, *22354* 113 E1
Hopewell Jct. NY, *2610* 148 B1
Hopkins MI, *592* 75 F4
Hopkins MN, *17145* 235 A3
Hopkins MO, *579* 86 B4
Hopkins Co. KY, *46519* 109 E2

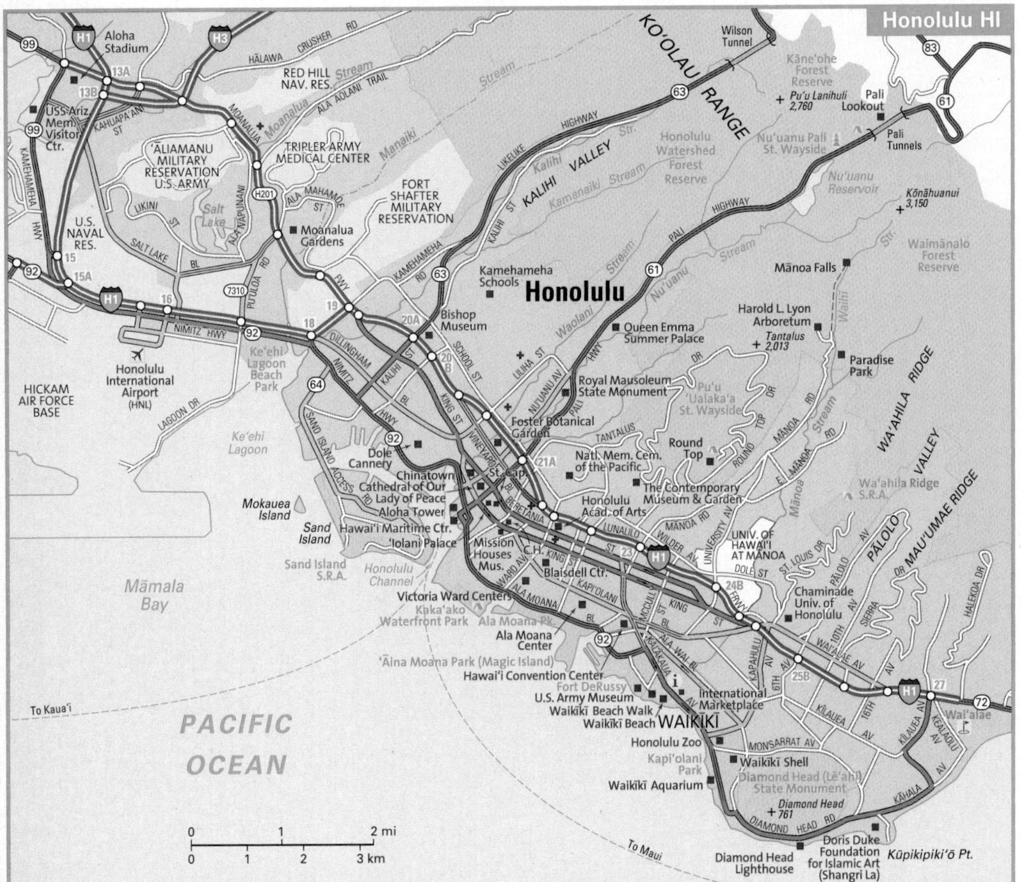
Honolulu HI
Honolulu
KO'OLAU RANGE
Aloha Stadium
RED HILL NAV. RES.
USS Ariz. Mem. Visitor Ctr.
'ALIAMANU MILITARY RESERVATION U.S. ARMY
TRIPLER ARMY MEDICAL CENTER
FORT SHAFTER MILITARY RESERVATION
U.S. NAVAL RES.
Moanalua Gardens
KALIHI VALLEY
Wilson Tunnel
Kāne'ohe Forest Reserve
Pu'u Lanihuli 2,760
Pali Lookout
Pali Tunnels
Nu'uanu Pali St. Wayside
Honolulu Watershed Forest Reserve
Nu'uanu Reservoir
Kōnāhuanui 3,150
Waimānalo Forest Reserve
Mānoa Falls
Kamehameha Schools
Bishop Museum
Harold L. Lyon Arboretum
Tantalus 2,013
Queen Emma Summer Palace
Paradise Park
HICKAM AIR FORCE BASE
Honolulu International Airport (HNL)
Ke'ehi Lagoon Beach Park
Ke'ehi Lagoon
Royal Mausoleum State Monument
Pu'u 'Ualaka'a St. Wayside
Foster Botanical Garden
Round Top
WA'AHILA RIDGE
Dole Cannery
Natl. Mem. Cem. of the Pacific
Chinatown
Cathedral of Our Lady of Peace
Aloha Tower
The Contemporary Museum & Garden
Wa'ahila Ridge S.R.A.
Mokauea Island
Sand Island
Hawai'i Maritime Ctr.
'Iolani Palace
Honolulu Acad. of Arts
UNIV. OF HAWAI'I AT MĀNOA
PĀLOLO VALLEY
MAU'UMAE RIDGE
Sand Island S.R.A.
Honolulu Channel
Mission Houses Mus.
Blaisdell Ctr.
Mālama Bay
Victoria Ward Centers
Kaka'ako Waterfront Park
Ala Moana Pk.
Ala Moana Center
Chaminade Univ. of Honolulu
'Āina Moana Park (Magic Island)
Hawai'i Convention Center
Fort DeRussy
U.S. Army Museum
Waikīkī Beach Walk
Waikīkī Beach
WAIKĪKĪ
International Marketplace
To Kaua'i
PACIFIC OCEAN
Honolulu Zoo
Kapi'olani Park
Waikīkī Shell
Waikīkī Aquarium
Diamond Head (Lē'ahi) State Monument
Diamond Head 761
Wai'alae
Diamond Head Lighthouse
Doris Duke Foundation for Islamic Art (Shangri La)
Kūpikipiki'ō Pt.
To Maui
0 1 2 mi
0 1 2 3 km

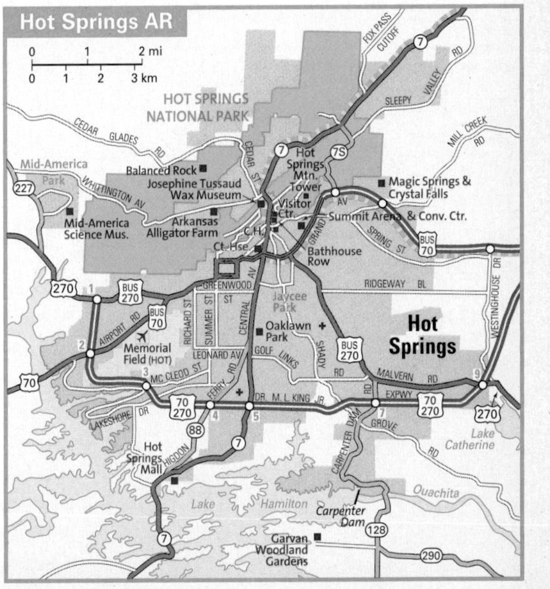
Hot Springs AR
0 1 2 mi
0 1 2 3 km
HOT SPRINGS NATIONAL PARK
FOX PASS CUTOFF
SLEEPY VALLEY RD
MILL CREEK RD
CEDAR GLADES RD
Mid-America Park
Balanced Rock
Josephine Tussaud Wax Museum
Hot Springs Mtn. Tower
Magic Springs & Crystal Falls
Mid-America Science Mus.
Arkansas Alligator Farm
Visitor Ctr.
Summit Arena & Conv. Ctr.
C.H.
Ct. Hse.
Bathhouse Row
RIDGEWAY BL
GREENWOOD
Jaycee Park
Oaklawn Park
Memorial Field (HOT)
Hot Springs
MALVERN RD
EXPWY
GROVE
Lake Catherine
Quachita
Hot Springs Mall
Lake Hamilton
Carpenter Dam
Garvan Woodland Gardens

220
Hopkins County–Humboldt County

Figures after entries indicate population, page number, and grid reference.

Aldine C1
Barrett.............D1
Beaumont Place ...D2
Bellaire............B3
Booth..............A4
Brookside Vil.......C2
Bunker Hill Vil......B2

Channelview D2
Cloverleaf.........D2
Crabb.............A4
Crosby............D1
Cypress...........A1
Deer Park.........D3
Four Corners A3

Fresno B4
Friendswood......D4
Galena Park.......C3
Hedwig Vil.........B2
Highlands.........D2
Hilshire Vil........B2
Houmont Park.....D2

Houston...........C2
Humble............C1
Hunters Creek Vil...B2
Jacinto City........C2
Jersey Vil..........A1
La Porte...........D3
League City........D4

Lynchburg.........D2
Magnolia Gardens..D1
Meadows Place....A3
Mission Bend......A3
Missouri City......B4
Nassau Bay........D4
N. Houston........B1

Pasadena..........D3
Pearland...........C4
Piney Pt. Vil........B2
Satsuma...........A1
Sheldon...........D2
S. Houston.........C3
Southside Place....B3

Spring Valley B2
Stafford...........B4
Sugar Land.........A3
Webster...........D4
W. University Place ...B3

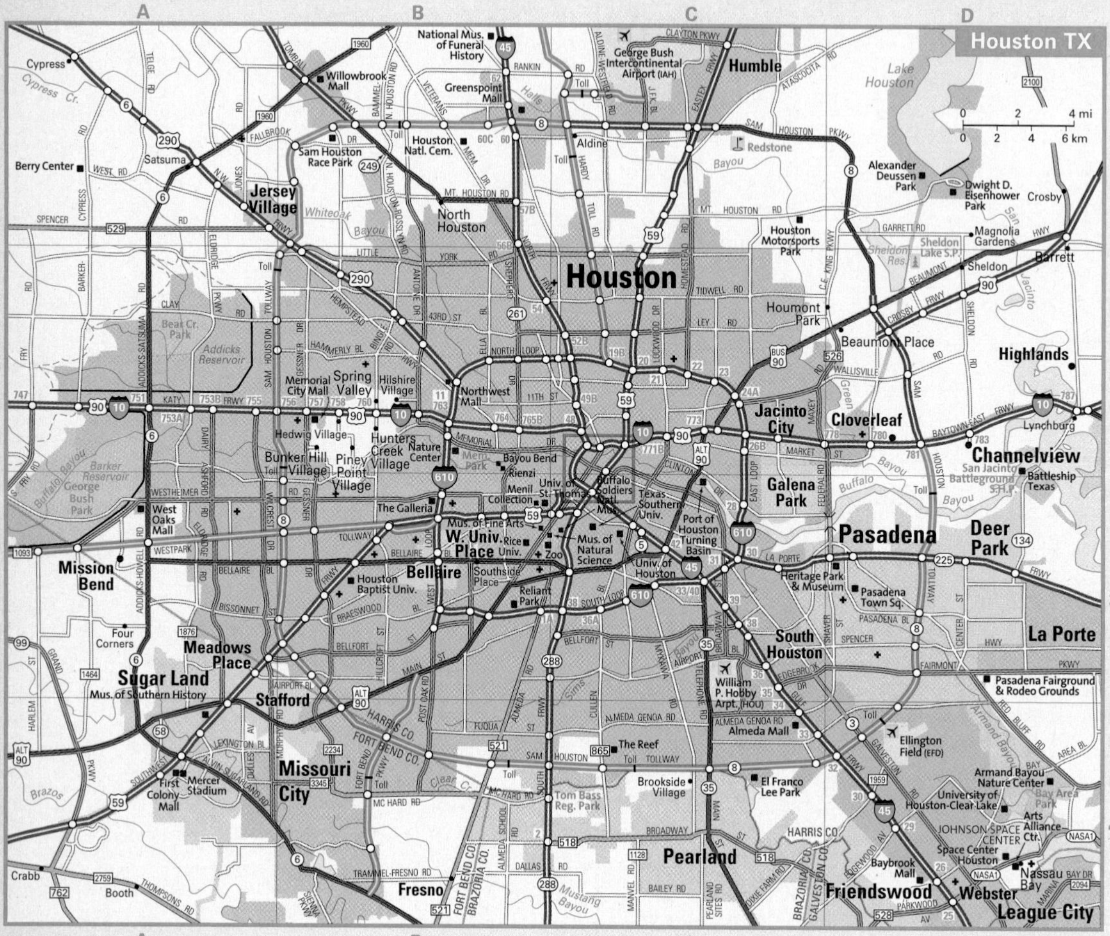

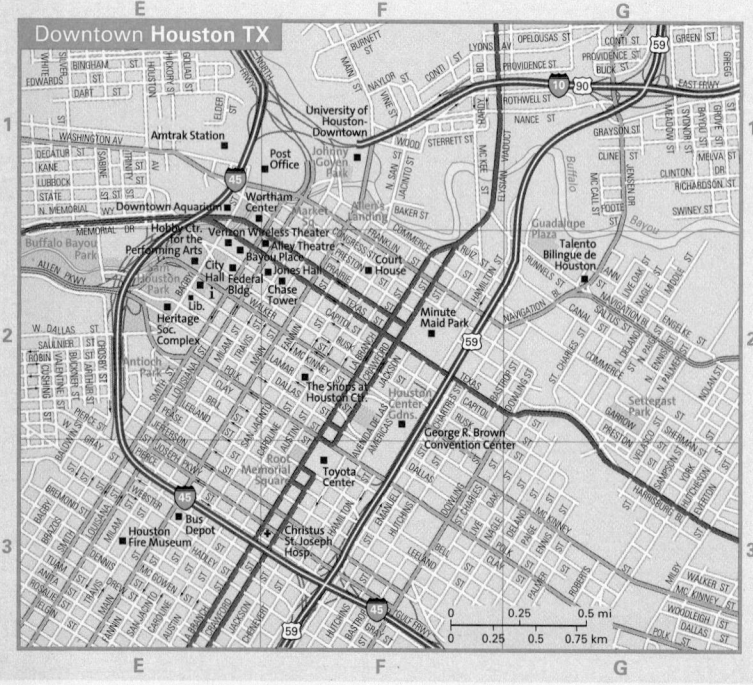

Houston TX

Downtown Houston TX

POINTS OF INTEREST

Allen's Landing F1
Alley Theatre F2
Amtrak Station.....................E1
Bayou Place F2
Bus Depot.........................E3
Chase Tower F2
City Hall F2
Court House F2
Downtown Aquarium E1
Federal Building F2
George R. Brown Convention Center ...F2
Heritage Society Complex E2
Hobby Center for the Performing Arts ...E2
Houston Fire Museum E3
Jones Hall F2
Library............................E2
Minute Maid Park...................F1
Post Office F1
The Shops at Houston Center.......F2
Talento Bilingue de Houston G2
Toyota Center......................F3
Univ. of Houston-Downtown........F1
Verizon Wireless Theater E2
Wortham Center....................E1

Entries in **bold black** indicate counties or parishes.
Entries in **bold color** indicate cities with detailed inset maps.

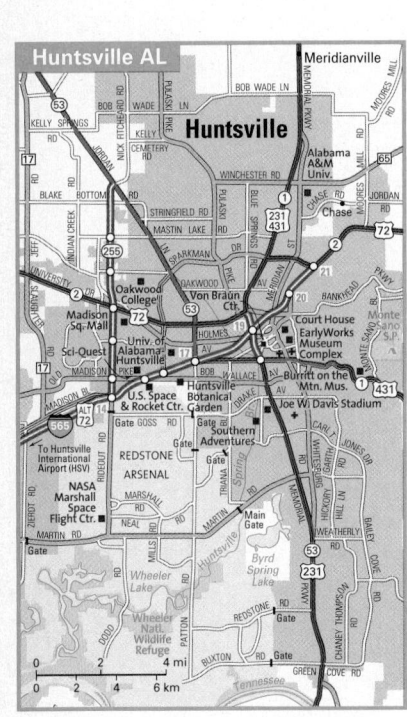

Huntington WV

Huntsville AL

Idaho Falls ID

Indianapolis IN

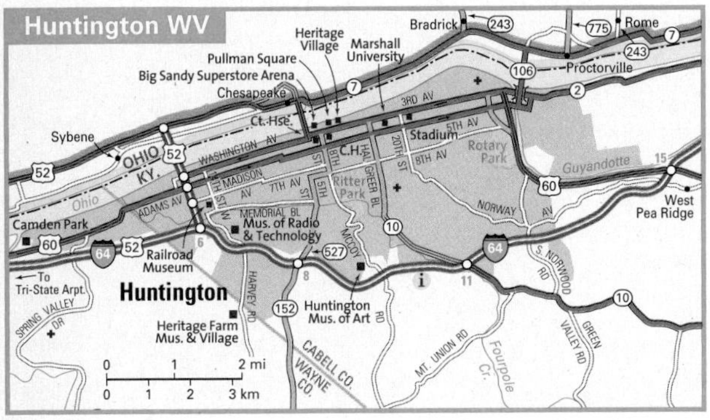

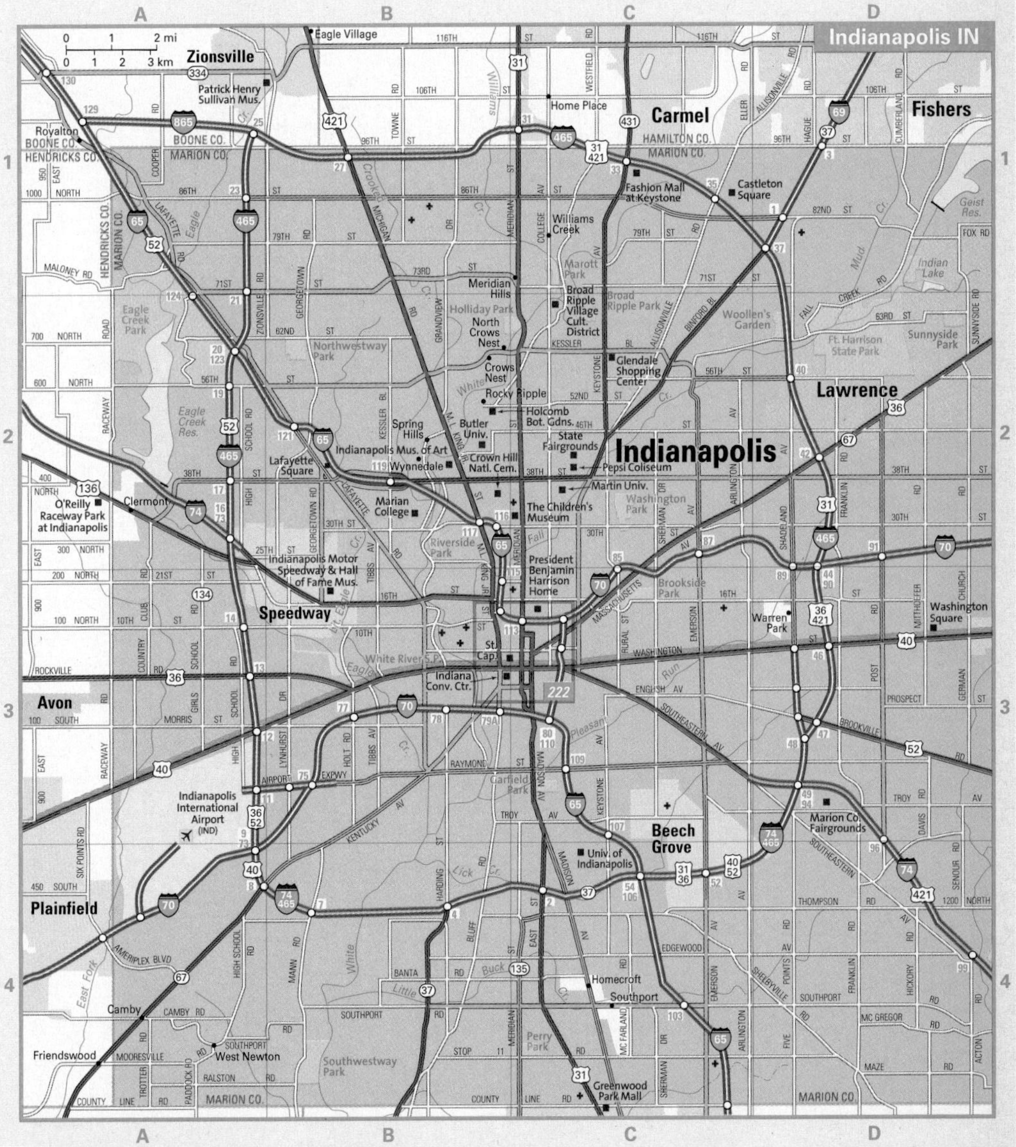

Figures after entries indicate population, page number, and grid reference.

POINTS OF INTEREST

American Legion National Headquarters.. A1
Artsgarden A2
Canal & State Park Cultural District A2
Circle Centre A2
City Market. A2
Conseco Fieldhouse B2
Eiteljorg Museum A2
Herron School of Art A2
Indiana Avenue Cultural District A1
Indiana Convention Center. A2
Indiana State Museum. A2
Indiana Univ./Purdue Univ. Indianapolis .. A1
Indiana War Memorial. A1

James Whitcomb Riley Home B1
Lucas Oil Stadium........................... A2
Madame Walker Theatre Center........ A1
Massachusetts Avenue Cultural District .. B1
Morris-Butler House B1
Murat Center B1
NCAA Hall of Champions................... A2
President Benjamin Harrison Home B1
Scottish Rite Cathedral A1
Soldiers & Sailors Monument A2
State Capitol A2
Victory Field A2
White River State Park A2
Zoo.. A2

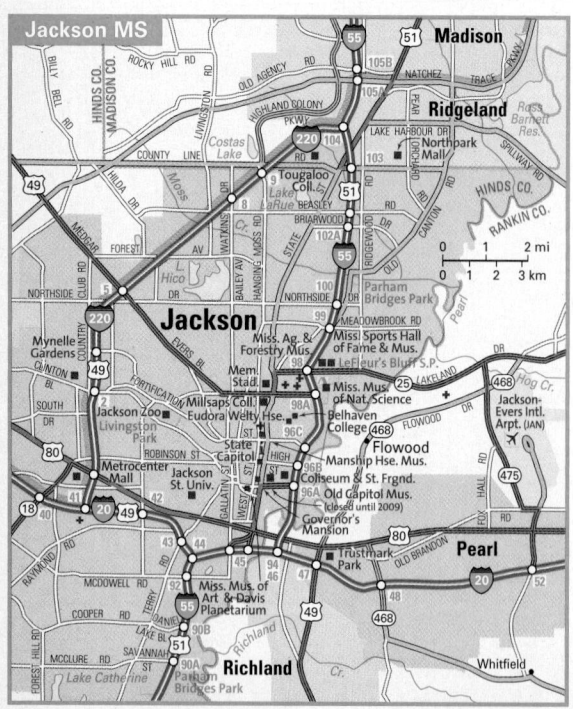

Jackson MS

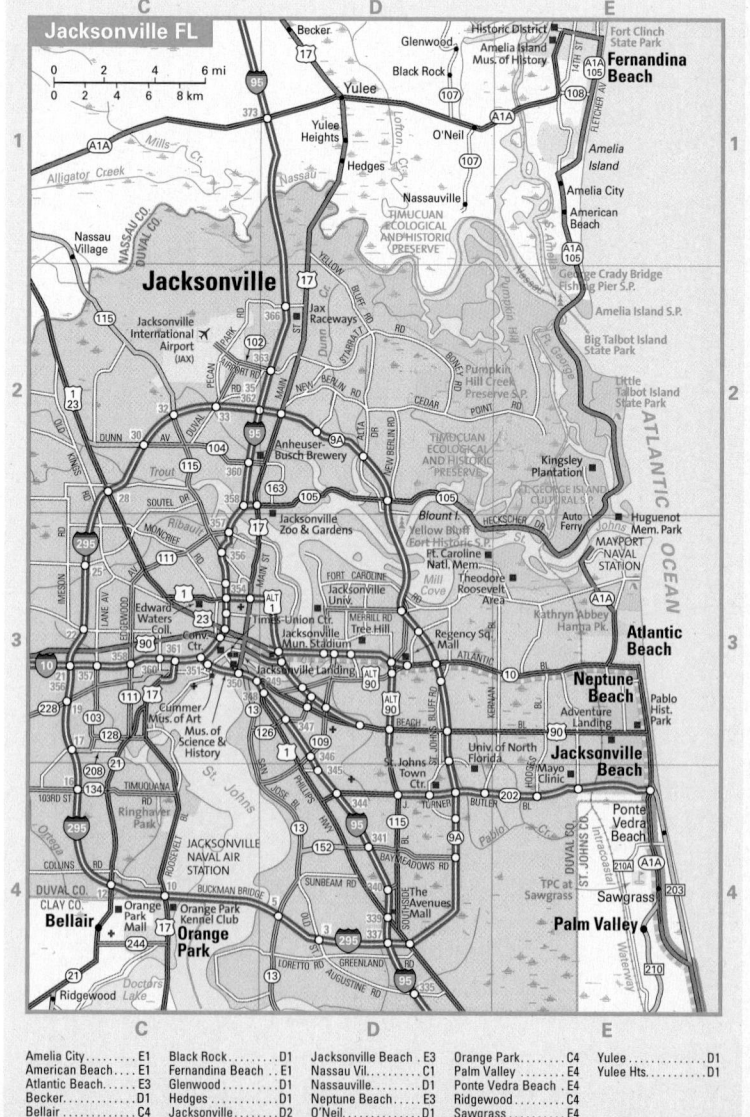

Jacksonville FL

Entries in **bold black** indicate counties or parishes.
Entries in **bold color** indicate cities with detailed inset maps.

Jefferson City MO

Juneau AK

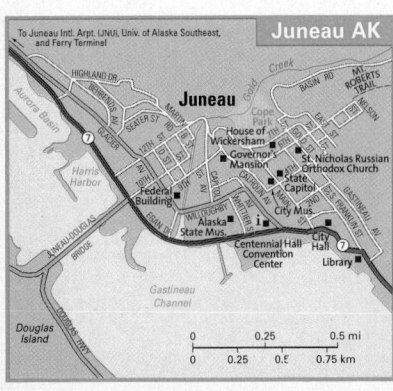

Kalamazoo MI

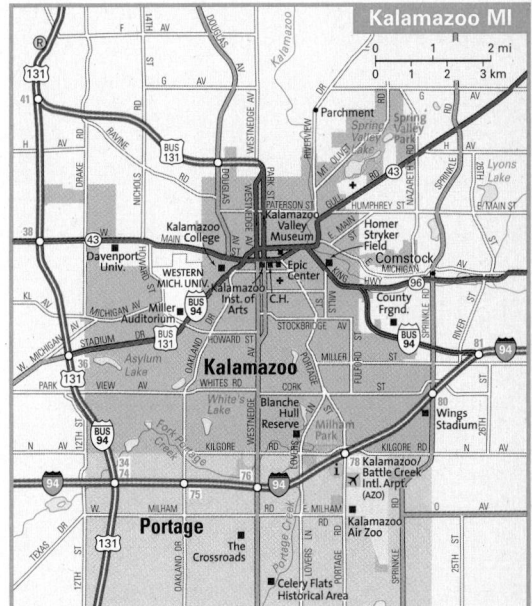

Figures after entries indicate population, page number, and grid reference.

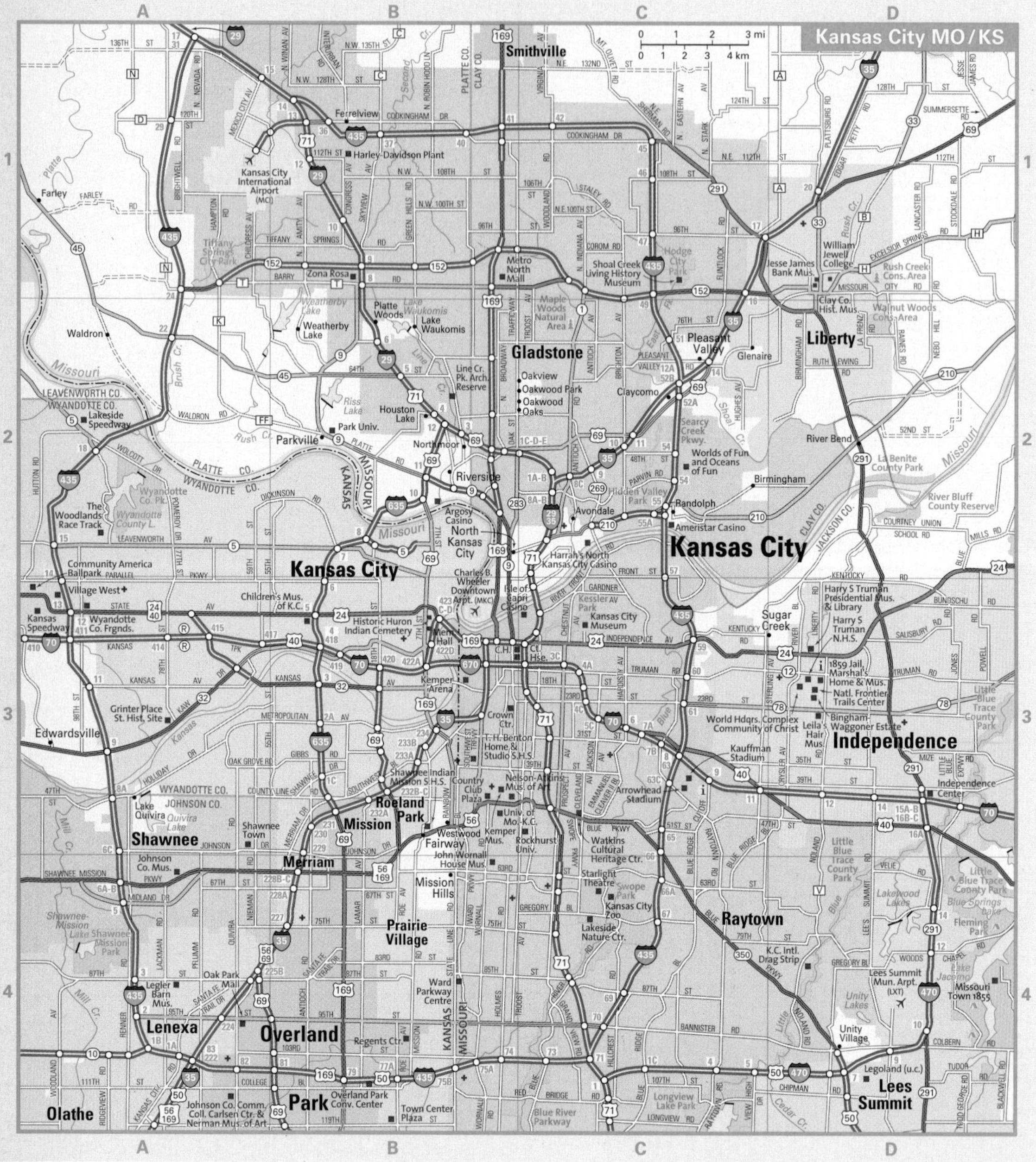

Kansas City MO/KS

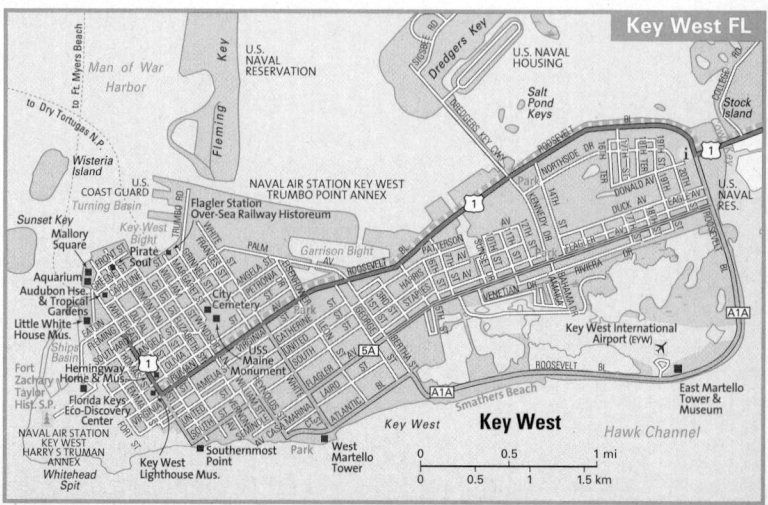

Key West FL

Entries in **bold black** indicate counties or parishes.
Entries in **bold color** indicate cities with detailed inset maps.

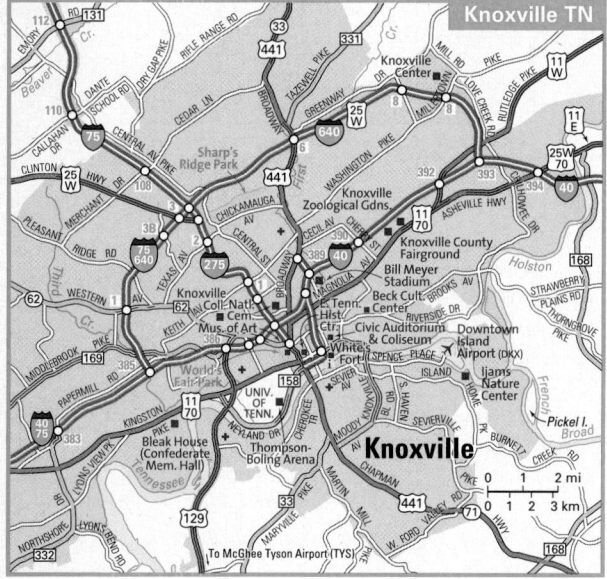

Knoxville TN

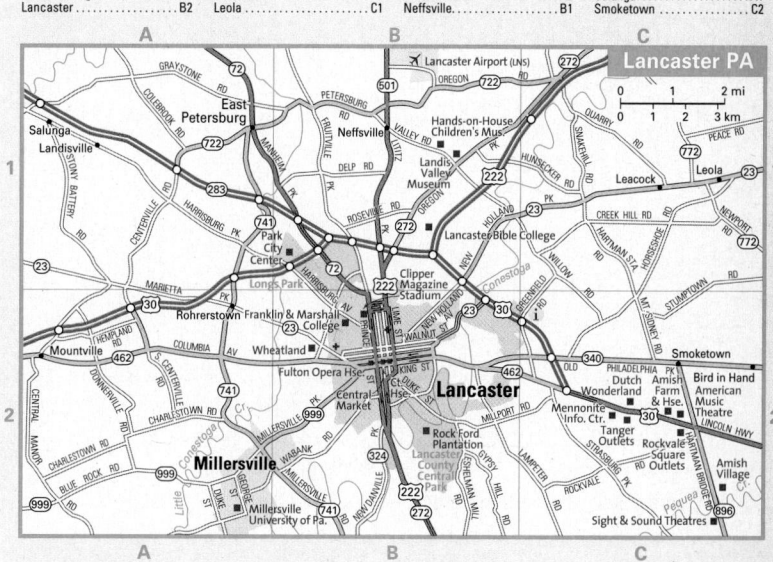

Lancaster PA

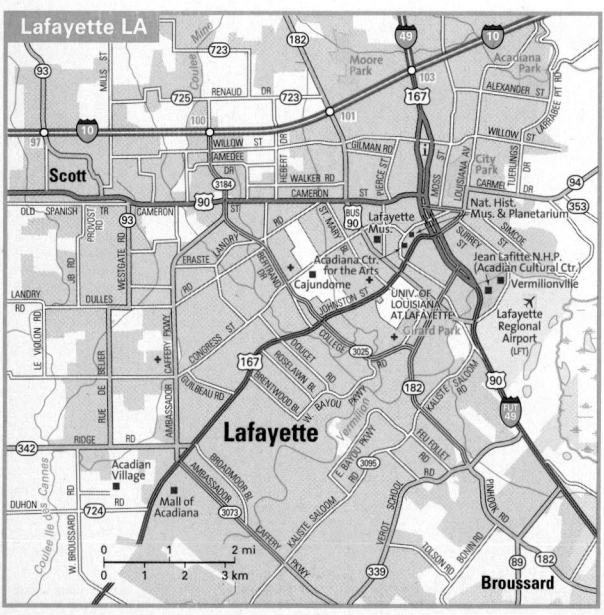

Lafayette LA

Lansing MI

Figures after entries indicate population, page number, and grid reference.

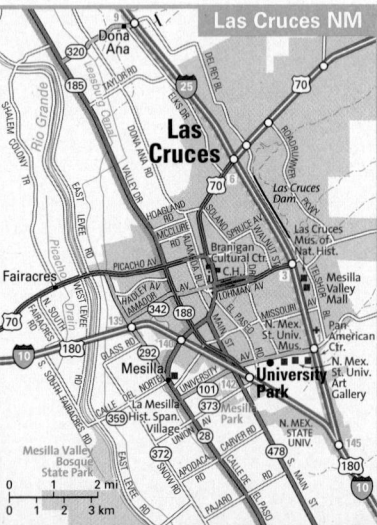

POINTS OF INTEREST

Atomic Testing Museum B2	MGM Grand A3
Bally's Las Vegas A2	The Mirage A2
Bellagio A2	Monte Carlo A3
Caesars Palace A2	New York-New York A3
Circus Circus A1	Palace Station A1
Excalibur A3	The Palazzo A2
Fashion Show Mall A2	Paris-Las Vegas A3
Flamingo Las Vegas A2	Planet Hollywood A3
Hard Rock B3	Riviera A1
Harrah's Las Vegas A2	Sahara B1
Imperial Palace A2	Showcase Mall A3
Las Vegas Convention Center B1	Stratosphere B1
Las Vegas Hilton B1	Treasure Island A2
Las Vegas Plaza (u.c.) B1	Tropicana A3
Luxor Las Vegas A3	Univ. of Nevada, Las Vegas B3
Mandalay Bay A3	The Venetian A2
	Wynn Las Vegas A2

Entries in **bold black** indicate counties or parishes.
Entries in **bold color** indicate cities with detailed inset maps.

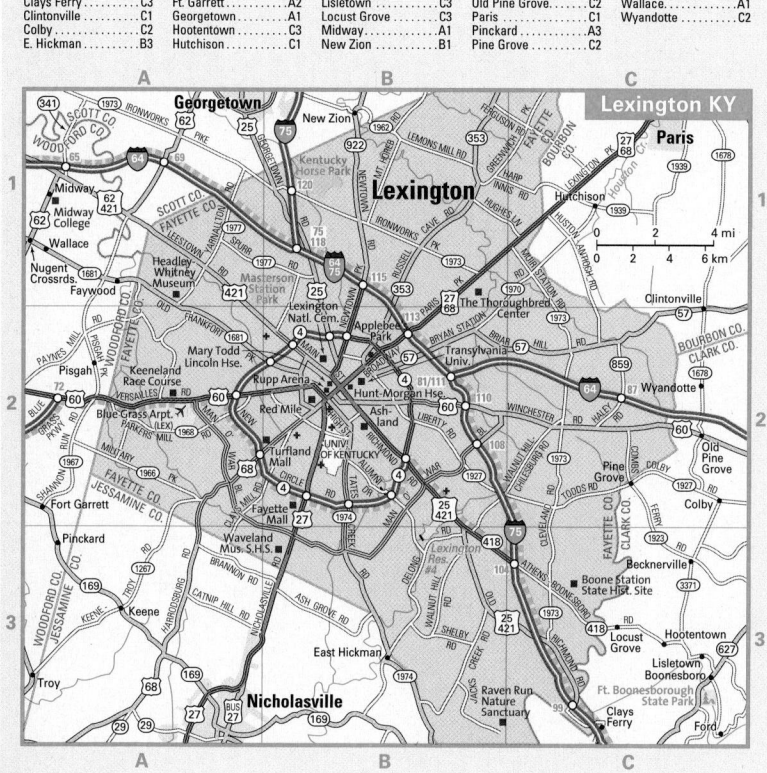

Georgetown

Lexington

Paris

Lexington KY

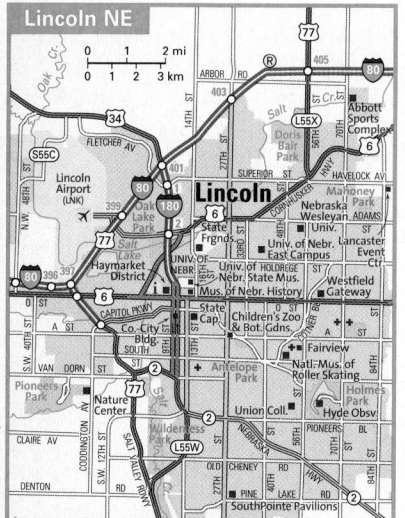

Lincoln NE

Lincoln

Little Rock AR

Maumelle

Sherwood

Jacksonville

North Little Rock

Little Rock

Figures after entries indicate population, page number, and grid reference.

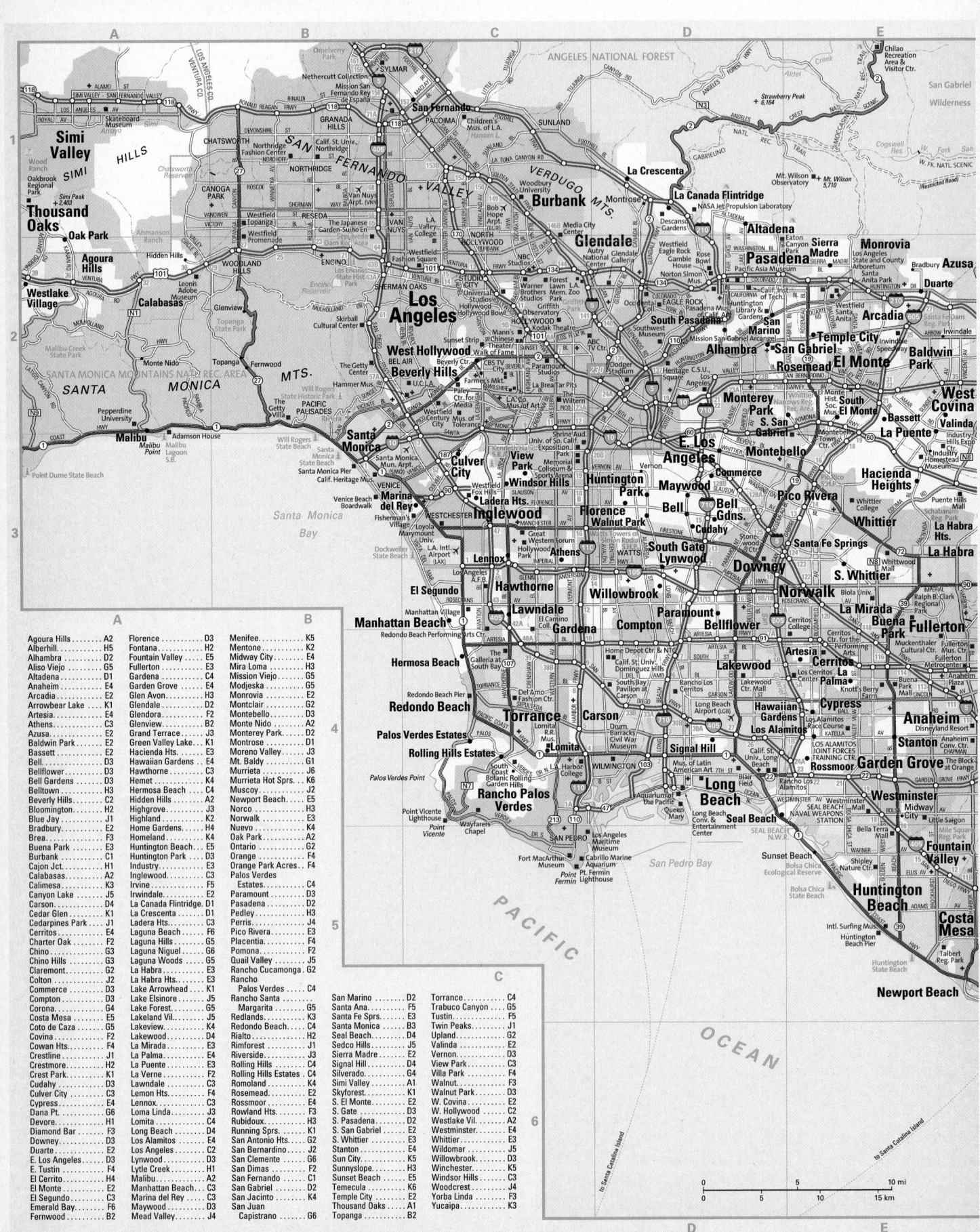

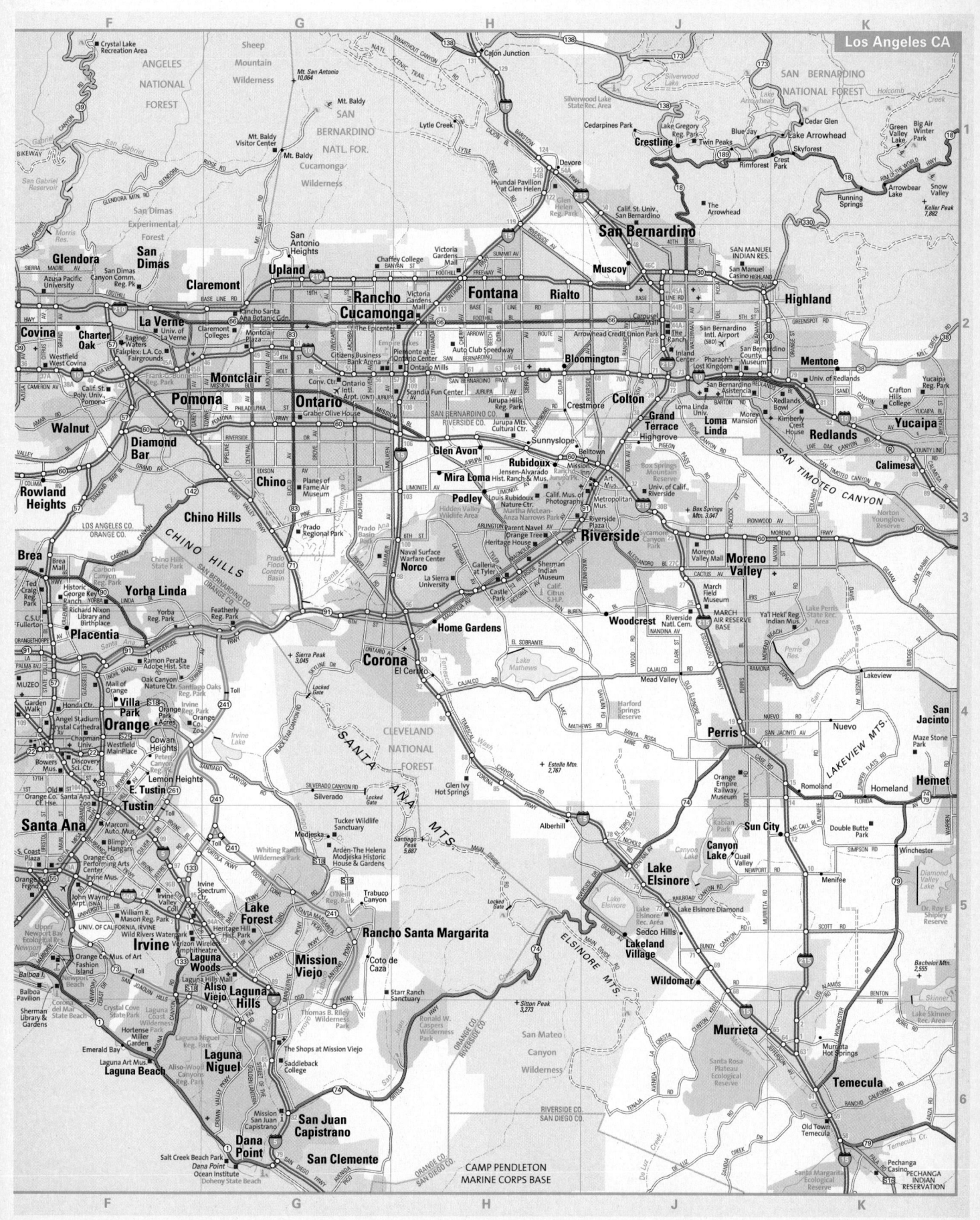

Los Angeles CA

230
Lexington–Lodi

Figures after entries indicate population, page number, and grid reference.

POINTS OF INTEREST

Angels Flight	A1
Bradbury Building	A1
Bus Terminal	B2
California Plaza	A1
Cathedral of Our Lady of the Angels	B1
Chinese American Museum	B1
City Hall	B1
Convention Center	A2
Court House	A1
Dodger Stadium	B1
El Pueblo de Los Angeles Hist. Mon.	B1
Flower District	A2
Japanese American Natl. Museum	B1
Jewelry District	A2
L.A. Center Studios	A1
L.A. Live	A2
Library	A1
MOCA at the Geffen Contemporary	B1
Mt. St. Mary's College	A2
Museum of Contemporary Art (MOCA)	A1
Museum of Neon Art	A2
Music Center	A1
NOKIA Theatre	A2
Olvera Street	B1
Post Office	B1
STAPLES Center	A2
Union Station	B1
Walt Disney Concert Hall	A1

Downtown Los Angeles CA

Lincoln Hts. OH, 4113	204	B1
Lincolnia VA, 15788	270	B4
Lincoln Par. LA, 42509	125	E2
Lincoln Park CA, 3904	41	E3
Lincoln Park MI, 40008	90	C1
Lincoln Park NJ, 10930	148	A3
Lincolnton GA, 1595	121	E4
Lincolnton NC, 9965	122	A1
Lincoln Vil. OH, 9482	206	A3
Lincolnville SC, 904	131	D1
Lincolnville Ctr. ME, 325	82	C2
Lincolnwood IL, 12359	203	D3
Lind WA, 582	13	F4
Linda CA, 13474	36	C2
Lindale GA, 4088	120	B3
Lindale TX, 2954	124	A2
Lindcove CA, 650	45	D3
Linden AL, 2424	127	E2
Linden CA, 1103	36	C3
Linden IN, 700	89	E4
Linden MI, 2861	76	B3
Linden NJ, 39394	147	E1
Linden TN, 1015	119	E1
Linden TX, 2256	124	C1
Linden WI, 615	74	A3
Lindenhurst IL, 12539	74	C4
Lindenhurst NY, 27819	148	C4
Lindenwold NJ, 17414	146	C3
Lindon UT, 8363	31	F4
Lindsay CA, 10297	45	D3
Lindsay OK, 2889	51	E4
Lindsay TX, 788	59	F1
Lindsborg KS, 3321	43	E3
Lindstrom MN, 3015	67	D3
Linesville PA, 1155	91	F2
Lineville AL, 2401	128	B1
Lingle WY, 510	33	F2
Linglestown PA, 6414	93	E4
Linn KS, 425	43	F1
Linn MO, 1354	97	E3
Linn TX, 958	63	E3
Linn Co. IA, 191701	87	E1
Linn Co. KS, 9570	96	B4
Linn Co. MO, 13754	97	D1
Linn Co. OR, 103069	20	C3
Linneus MO, 369	97	D1
Linn Valley KS, 562	96	B4
Lino Lakes MN, 16791	235	D7
Linthicum MD, 7539	193	C4
Linton IN, 5774	99	E2
Linton ND, 1321	26	C1
Linwood IN, 700	89	F4
Linwood KS, 374	96	B2
Linwood MI, 1200	76	B2
Linwood NJ, 7172	147	F4

Lionville PA, 6298	146	B3
Lipscomb AL, 2458	195	D2
Lipscomb TX, 44	50	C2
Lipscomb Co. TX, 3057	50	C2
Lisbon IA, 1898	87	F1
Lisbon ME, 1800	82	B3
Lisbon NH, 1070	81	E2
Lisbon ND, 2292	19	E4
Lisbon OH, 2788	91	F3
Lisbon Falls ME, 4420	82	B3
Lisle IL, 21182	203	B5
Lisman AL, 653	127	D3
Litchfield CT, 1378	94	B2
Litchfield IL, 6815	98	B2
Litchfield ME, 325	82	B2
Litchfield MN, 6562	66	B3
Litchfield Park AZ, 3810	249	A2
Lithia Sprs. GA, 2072	120	C4
Lithonia GA, 2187	120	C4
Lithopolis OH, 600	101	D1
Lititz PA, 9029	146	A2
Little Canada MN, 9771	235	D2
Little Chute WI, 10476	74	C1
Little Compton RI, 400	151	D4
Little Creek DE, 195	145	E2
Little Cypress TX, 1800	132	C2
Little Eagle SD, 370	26	C1
Little Elm TX, 3646	59	F2
Little Falls MN, 7719	66	C2
Little Falls NJ, 10855	148	A3
Little Falls NY, 5188	79	F3
Little Ferry NJ, 10800	240	C2
Littlefield TX, 6507	58	A1
Little Flock AR, 2585	106	C3
Littlefork MN, 680	64	B2
Little Heaven DE, 1400	145	E3
Little River KS, 536	43	E3
Little River SC, 7027	123	D4
Little River-Academy TX, 1645	61	E1
Little River Co. AR, 13628	116	C4
Little Rock AR, 183133	117	E2
Littlerock CA, 1402	52	C2
Little Silver NJ, 6170	147	E2
Littlestown PA, 3947	103	E1
Littleton CO, 40340	41	E1
Littleton NH, 4431	81	F2
Littleton NC, 692	113	D3
Little Valley NY, 1130	92	B1
Littleville AL, 978	119	E2
Live Oak CA, 6229	36	C2
Live Oak FL, 16628	236	D1
Live Oak FL, 6480	138	B2
Live Oak TX, 9156	61	D2
Live Oak Co. TX, 12309	61	D4
Livermore CA, 73345	36	B4

Livermore KY, 1482	109	E1
Livermore Falls ME, 1626	82	B2
Liverpool NY, 2505	265	A1
Liverpool PA, 876	93	D4
Livingston AL, 3297	127	D2
Livingston CA, 10473	36	C4
Livingston IL, 825	98	B2
Livingston LA, 1342	134	A2
Livingston MT, 6851	23	F1
Livingston NJ, 27391	148	A4
Livingston TN, 3498	110	A3
Livingston TX, 5433	132	B1
Livingston WI, 597	74	A3
Livingston Co. IL, 39678	88	C3
Livingston Co. KY, 9804	109	D2
Livingston Co. MI, 156951	76	B4
Livingston Co. MO, 14558	96	C1
Livingston Co. NY, 64328	78	C4
Livingston Manor NY, 1355	94	A2
Livingston Par. LA, 91814	134	B2
Livonia LA, 1339	133	F2
Livonia MI, 100545	76	B4
Livonia NY, 1373	78	C3
Llangollen Estates DE, 5600	145	E1
Llano TX, 3325	61	D1
Llano Co. TX, 17044	61	D1
Lloyd Harbor NY, 3675	148	C3
Loa UT, 525	39	E3
Loami IL, 804	98	B1
Lobelville TN, 915	109	D4
Lochbuie CO, 2049	209	D1
Lochearn MD, 25269	144	C2
Loch Lynn Hts. MD, 469	102	B2
Loch Sheldrake NY, 800	94	A3
Lockeford CA, 3179	36	C3
Lockesburg AR, 711	116	C4
Lockhart AL, 548	136	B1
Lockhart FL, 12944	246	B1
Lockhart TX, 11615	61	E2
Lock Haven PA, 9149	93	D3
Lockland OH, 3707	204	B1
Lockney TX, 2056	50	B4
Lockport IL, 15191	89	D2
Lockport LA, 2624	134	B3
Lockport NY, 22279	78	B3
Lockwood MO, 989	106	C1
Locust NC, 2416	122	B1
Locust Fork AL, 1016	119	F4
Locust Grove GA, 2322	129	D1
Locust Grove OK, 1366	106	B3
Locust Valley NY, 3521	148	C3
Lodge Grass MT, 510	24	C2
Lodgepole MT, 214	16	C2
Lodi CA, 56999	36	C3
Lodi NJ, 23971	240	C1
Lodi OH, 3061	91	D3
Lodi WI, 2882	74	B3

Lexington IL, 1912	88	C3
Lexington KY, 260512	100	B4
Lexington MA, 30355	151	D1
Lexington MI, 1104	76	C3
Lexington MN, 2214	235	C1
Lexington MS, 2025	126	B1
Lexington MO, 4453	96	C2
Lexington NE, 10011	34	C4
Lexington NC, 19953	112	B4
Lexington OH, 4165	91	D3
Lexington OK, 2086	51	E3
Lexington SC, 9793	122	A3
Lexington TN, 7393	109	D4
Lexington TX, 1178	61	E1
Lexington VA, 6867	112	C1
Lexington Co. SC, 216014	122	A4
Lexington Park MD, 11021	103	F4
Libby MT, 2626	14	C2
Liberal KS, 19666	50	B1
Liberal MO, 779	106	B1
Liberty IL, 519	97	F1
Liberty IN, 2061	100	B1
Liberty KY, 1850	110	B1
Liberty ME, 300	82	C2
Liberty MS, 633	134	A1
Liberty MO, 26232	96	B2
Liberty NY, 3975	94	A3
Liberty NC, 2661	112	B4
Liberty PA, 2670	250	C3
Liberty SC, 3009	121	E2
Liberty TN, 367	110	A4
Liberty TX, 8033	132	B3
Liberty Ctr. OH, 1109	90	B2
Liberty City TX, 1935	124	B2
Liberty Corner NJ, 1207	147	D1
Liberty Co. FL, 7021	137	D2
Liberty Co. GA, 61610	130	B3
Liberty Co. MT, 2158	15	F1
Liberty Co. TX, 70154	132	B2
Liberty Hill TX, 1409	61	E1
Liberty Lake WA, 3076	14	B3
Libertyville IL, 20742	74	C4
Licking MO, 1471	107	F1
Licking Co. OH, 145491	91	D4
Lidgerwood ND, 738	27	F1
Lido Beach NY, 2825	147	F1
Lighthouse Pt. FL, 10767	143	F1
Ligonier IN, 4357	89	F2
Ligonier PA, 1695	92	B4
Lihue HI, 5674	152	B1
Lilbourn MO, 1303	108	B3
Lilburn GA, 11307	120	C4
Lillington NC, 2915	123	D1
Lilly PA, 948	92	B4
Lily KY, 1200	110	C2

Lilydale MN, 552	235	D3
Lily Lake IL, 825	88	C1
Lima MT, 242	23	E3
Lima NY, 2459	78	C3
Lima OH, 40081	90	B3
Lima PA, 3225	248	A4
Lime Lake NY, 1422	78	B4
Limeport PA, 1100	146	C1
Limerick ME, 425	82	A3
Limerick PA, 850	146	B2
Limestone ME, 1453	85	E1
Limestone Co. AL, 65676	119	F2
Limestone Co. TX, 22051	59	F4
Lincoln AL, 4577	120	A4
Lincoln AR, 1752	106	B4
Lincoln CA, 11205	36	C2
Lincoln DE, 950	145	E3
Lincoln ID, 2800	23	E4
Lincoln IL, 15369	88	B4
Lincoln KS, 1349	43	E2
Lincoln ME, 2933	85	D4
Lincoln MA, 650	197	A1
Lincoln MO, 1026	97	D4
Lincoln MT, 1100	15	E4
Lincoln NE, 225581	35	F4
Lincoln NH, 750	81	F3
Lincoln ND, 1730	18	C4
Lincoln Beach OR, 2078	20	B2
Lincoln City OR, 7437	20	B2
Lincoln Co. AR, 14492	117	F3
Lincoln Co. CO, 6087	41	F2
Lincoln Co. GA, 8348	121	E4
Lincoln Co. ID, 4044	31	D1
Lincoln Co. KS, 3578	43	E2
Lincoln Co. KY, 23361	110	B1
Lincoln Co. ME, 33616	82	C2
Lincoln Co. MN, 6429	27	F3
Lincoln Co. MS, 33166	126	B4
Lincoln Co. MO, 38944	97	F2
Lincoln Co. MT, 18837	14	C2
Lincoln Co. NE, 34632	34	C3
Lincoln Co. NV, 4165	38	B4
Lincoln Co. NM, 63780	122	A1
Lincoln Co. OK, 32080	51	F2
Lincoln Co. OR, 44479	20	B3
Lincoln Co. SD, 24131	35	F1
Lincoln Co. TN, 31340	119	F1
Lincoln Co. WA, 10184	13	F3
Lincoln Co. WV, 22108	101	E4
Lincoln Co. WI, 29641	68	A3
Lincoln Co. WY, 14573	32	A2
Lincolndale NY, 2018	148	C2

Louisville KY

Bancroft	F1	Crossgate	E1	Hurstbourne
Barbourmeade	F1	Douglass Hills	F2	Hurstbourne Acres
Beechwood Vil.	E1	Fincastle	E1	Indian Hills
Bellemeade	F2	Forest Hills	E2	Jeffersontown
Bellewood	E1	Glenview	E1	Jeffersonville
Blue Ridge Manor	E1	Glenview Hills	E1	Langdon Place
Briarwood	E1	Graymoor-Devondale	E1	Louisville
Broeck Pointe	E1	Hickory Hill	F2	Lyndon
Brownsboro Vil.	E1	Hills and Dales	E1	Lynnview
Clarksville	D1	Hollow Creek	E3	Manor Creek
Creekside	F1	Houston Acres	F1	Meadow Vale

Hurstbourne	F2	Middletown	F1	Rolling Fields	E1
Hurstbourne Acres	F2	Mockingbird Valley	E1	Rolling Hills	E1
Indian Hills	E1	Moorland	E1	St. Matthews	E1
Jeffersontown	F2	Murray Hill	F1	St. Regis Park	E2
Jeffersonville	D1	New Albany	C1	Seneca Gardens	E2
Langdon Place	E1	Northfield	E1	Shively	C3
Louisville		Norwood	E1	Spring Mill	E2
Lyndon	F1	Parkway Vil.	D2	Spring Valley	F1
Lynnview	D3	Plantation	E1	Strathmoor Vil.	E2
Manor Creek	F1	Poplar Hills	E3	Sycamore	F2
Meadow Vale	F1	Riverwood	E1	Thornhill	E1

Watterson Park	E2
Wellington	E2
W. Buechel	E2
Wildwood	E1
Windy Hills	E1
Woodlawn Park	E1

Entries in **bold black** indicate counties or parishes.
Entries in **bold color** indicate cities with detailed inset maps.

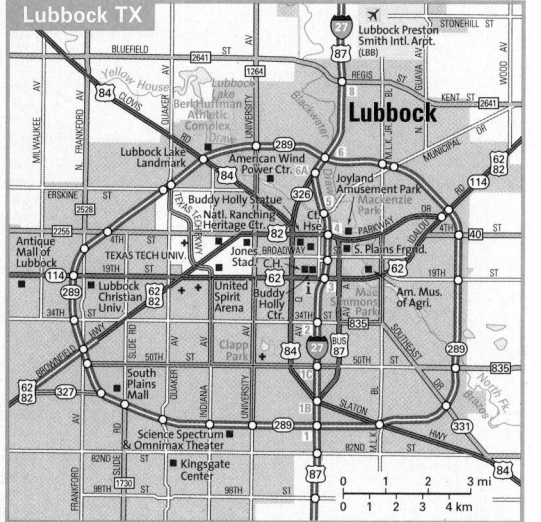

Lubbock TX

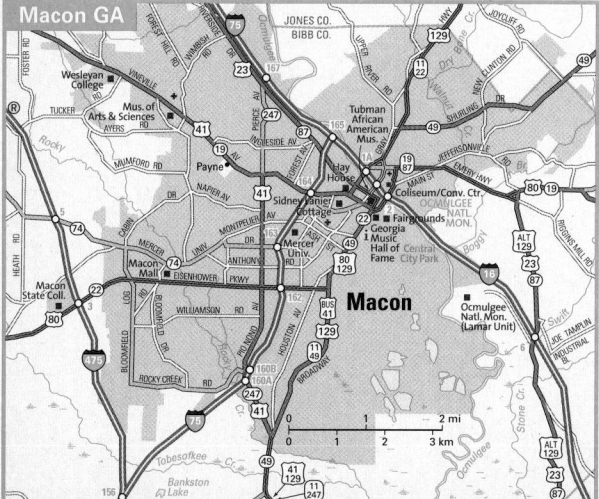

Macon GA

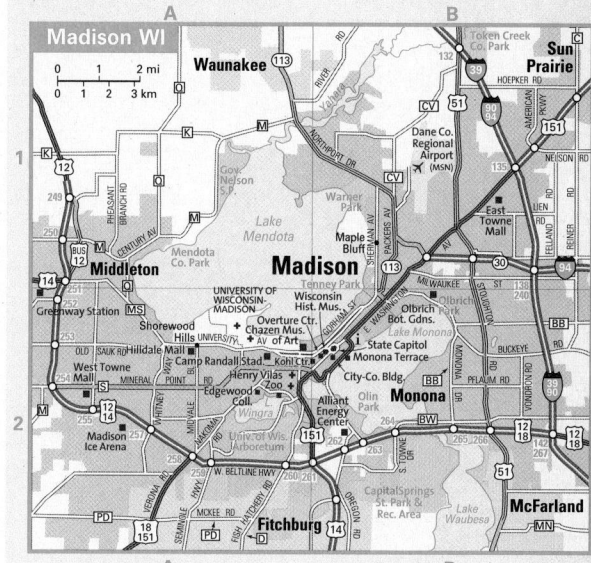

Madison WI

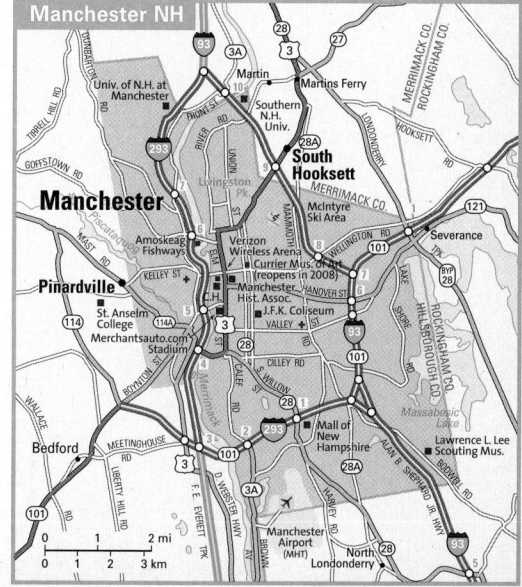

Manchester NH

232

Macon County–Many Farms

Figures after entries indicate population, page number, and grid reference.

Macon Co. AL, 24105	128 B3
Macon Co. GA, 14074	129 D2
Macon Co. IL, 114706	98 C1
Macon Co. MO, 15762	97 D1
Macon Co. NC, 29811	121 D1
Macon Co. TN, 20386	110 A3
Macoupin Co. IL, 49019	98 B2
Macungie PA, 3039	146 B1
Macy NE, 956	35 F2
Madawaska ME, 3326	85 D1
Maddock ND, 498	19 D2
Madeira OH, 8923	204 C2
Madeira Beach FL, 4511	140 B3
Madelia MN, 2340	72 B1
Madera CA, 43207	44 C2
Madera Co. CA, 123109	44 C2
Madill OK, 3410	51 F4
Madison AL, 29329	119 F2
Madison AR, 987	118 A2
Madison CT, 2222	149 E2
Madison FL, 3061	137 F2
Madison GA, 3636	121 D4
Madison IN, 12004	100 A3
Madison KS, 857	43 F3
Madison ME, 2733	82 B1
Madison MN, 1768	27 F2
Madison MS, 14692	126 B2
Madison MO, 586	97 E2
Madison NE, 2367	35 E2
Madison NJ, 16530	148 A4
Madison NC, 2262	112 B3
Madison OH, 2921	91 F1
Madison SD, 6540	27 F3
Madison VA, 210	102 C4
Madison WV, 2677	101 E4
Madison WI, 208054	74 B3
Madison Co. AL, 276700	119 F2
Madison Co. AR, 14243	106 C4
Madison Co. FL, 18733	137 F2
Madison Co. GA, 25730	121 E3
Madison Co. ID, 27467	23 F4
Madison Co. IL, 258941	98 B3
Madison Co. IN, 133358	89 F4
Madison Co. IA, 14019	86 C2
Madison Co. KY, 70872	110 C1
Madison Co. MS, 74674	126 B2
Madison Co. MO, 11800	108 A1
Madison Co. MT, 6851	23 E2
Madison Co. NE, 35226	35 E2
Madison Co. NY, 69441	79 E4
Madison Co. NC, 19635	111 E4
Madison Co. OH, 40213	100 C1
Madison Co. TN, 91837	108 C4
Madison Co. TX, 12940	61 F1
Madison Co. VA, 12520	102 C3
Madison Hts. MI, 31101	210 C2
Madison Hts. VA, 11584	112 C1
Madison Lake MN, 837	72 C1
Madisonville KY, 19307	109 E1
Madisonville LA, 677	134 B2
Madisonville TN, 3939	120 C1
Madisonville TX, 4159	61 F1
Madras OR, 5078	21 D3
Madrid IA, 2264	86 C1
Madrid NY, 650	80 B1
Maeser UT, 2855	32 A4
Magalia CA, 10569	36 C1
Magazine AR, 915	116 C1
Magdalena NM, 913	48 B4
Magee MS, 4200	126 C3
Maggie Valley NC, 607	121 E1
Magna UT, 22770	257 A2
Magnolia DE, 226	145 E2
Magnolia MS, 2071	134 B1
Magnolia NJ, 4409	248 D4
Magnolia NC, 932	123 E2
Magnolia OH, 931	91 E3
Magnolia TX, 1111	132 A2
Magoffin Co. KY, 13332	111 D1
Mahanoy City PA, 4647	93 E3
Mahaska Co. IA, 22335	87 D2
Mahnomen MN, 1202	19 F3
Mahnomen Co. MN, 5190	19 F3
Mahomet IL, 4877	88 C4
Mahopac NY, 8478	148 C2
Mahtomedi MN, 7563	235 E1
Mahwah NJ, 5200	148 B3
Maiden NC, 3282	122 A1
Maili HI, 5943	152 A3
Maine NY, 1000	93 E1
Maineville OH, 885	100 B3
Maitland FL, 12019	141 D1
Maize KS, 1868	43 E4
Majestic KY, 600	111 E1
Major Co. OK, 7545	51 D2
Makaha HI, 7753	152 A3
Makakilo City HI, 13156	152 A3
Makawao HI, 6327	153 D1
Makena HI, 5671	153 D1
Malabar FL, 2622	141 E2
Malad City ID, 2158	31 E2
Malaga CA, 1400	44 C3
Malaga NJ, 1400	145 F1
Malakoff TX, 2257	59 F3
Malcolm NE, 413	35 F4
Malden MA, 56340	151 D1
Malden MO, 4782	108 B3
Malden WV, 750	200 B2
Malheur Co. OR, 31615	22 A4
Malibu CA, 12575	52 B2
Malin OR, 638	29 D2
Mallory WV, 1143	111 F1
Malone FL, 2007	137 D1
Malone NY, 6075	80 C1
Malta ID, 177	31 D2
Malta IL, 969	88 C1
Malta MT, 2120	16 C2
Malta NY, 2100	80 B2
Malta OH, 696	101 E1
Maltby WA, 8267	262 B2
Malvern AL, 1215	136 C1
Malvern AR, 9021	117 D3
Malvern IA, 1256	86 A3
Malvern OH, 1218	91 E3
Malvern PA, 3059	146 B3
Malverne NY, 8934	241 G4
Mamaroneck NY, 18752	148 C3
Mammoth AZ, 1762	55 D2
Mammoth Hot Sprs. WY, 275	23 F2
Mammoth Lakes CA, 7093	37 E4
Mammoth Spr. AR, 1147	107 F3
Mamou LA, 3566	133 E2
Man WV, 770	111 F1
Manahawkin NJ, 2004	147 E4
Manasquan NJ, 6310	147 E2
Manassa CO, 1042	41 D4
Manassas VA, 35135	144 A4
Manassas Park VA, 10290	144 A3
Manatee Co. FL, 264002	140 C3
Manawa WI, 1330	74 B1
Mancelona MI, 1408	70 B4
Manchaca TX, 1200	61 E2
Manchaug MA, 850	150 C2
Manchester CT, 30585	150 A3
Manchester GA, 3988	128 C2
Manchester IA, 5257	73 F4
Manchester KY, 1738	110 C2
Manchester ME, 600	82 B2
Manchester MD, 3329	103 E1
Manchester MI, 2160	90 B1
Manchester MO, 19161	256 A3
Manchester NH, 107006	81 F4
Manchester NY, 1475	78 C3
Manchester OH, 2043	100 C3
Manchester PA, 2350	93 E4
Manchester TN, 8294	120 A1
Manchester VT, 602	81 D4
Manchester WA, 4958	262 A3
Manchester-by-the-Sea MA, 3600	151 E1
Manchester Ctr. VT, 2065	81 D4
Mancos CO, 1119	40 B4
Mandan ND, 16718	18 C4
Mandaree ND, 558	18 A3
Manderson SD, 626	26 A4
Mandeville AR, 700	116 C4
Mandeville LA, 10489	134 B2
Mangham LA, 595	125 F2
Mango FL, 8842	266 C2
Mangonia Park FL, 1283	141 F4
Mangum OK, 2924	50 C3
Manhasset NY, 8362	148 C4
Manhasset Hills NY, 3661	241 G3
Manhattan KS, 44831	43 F2
Manhattan MT, 1396	23 F1
Manhattan Beach CA, 33852	228 C3
Manheim PA, 4784	93 E4
Manila AR, 3055	108 B4
Manila UT, 308	32 A3
Manila IA, 839	86 A1
Manistee MI, 6586	75 E1
Manistee Co. MI, 24527	70 A4
Manistique MI, 3583	69 E2
Manito IL, 1733	88 B4
Manitou Beach MI, 2080	90 B1
Manitou Sprs. CO, 4980	41 E2
Manitowoc WI, 34053	75 D1
Manitowoc Co. WI, 82887	75 D1
Mankato KS, 976	43 E1
Mankato MN, 32427	72 C1
Manlius NY, 4819	79 E3
Manly IA, 1342	73 D3
Mannford OK, 2095	51 F2
Manning IA, 1490	86 B1
Manning ND, 30	18 A3
Manning SC, 4025	122 B4
Mannington WV, 2124	102 A1
Mannsville OK, 587	51 F4
Manokotak AK, 399	154 B3
Manomet MA, 2900	151 E3
Manor PA, 2796	92 A4
Manor TX, 1204	61 E1
Manorhaven NY, 6138	241 G2
Manorville NY, 11131	149 D3
Mansfield AR, 1097	116 C2
Mansfield IL, 949	88 C4
Mansfield LA, 5582	124 C3
Mansfield MA, 7320	151 D2
Mansfield OH, 49346	91 D3
Mansfield PA, 3411	93 D1
Mansfield TX, 28031	59 E3
Mansfield Ctr. CT, 973	150 B3
Mansfield Four Corners CT, 700	150 B3
Manson IA, 1893	72 B4
Manson WA, 900	13 E2
Mansura LA, 1573	133 F1
Mantachie MS, 1107	119 D3
Manteca CA, 49258	36 C4
Manteno IL, 6414	89 D2
Manteo NC, 1052	115 F2
Manti UT, 3040	39 E2
Manton MI, 1221	75 F1
Mantorville MN, 1054	73 D1
Mantua OH, 1046	91 E2
Mantua UT, 791	31 E3
Mantua VA, 7485	270 A4
Manvel ND, 370	19 E2
Manvel TX, 3046	132 A4
Manville RI, 3800	150 C2
Manville NJ, 10343	147 D1
Many LA, 2889	125 D4
Many Farms AZ, 1548	47 F2

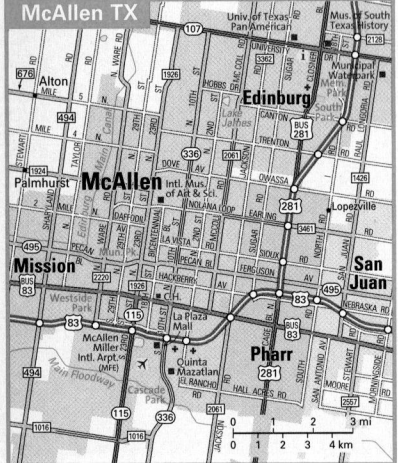

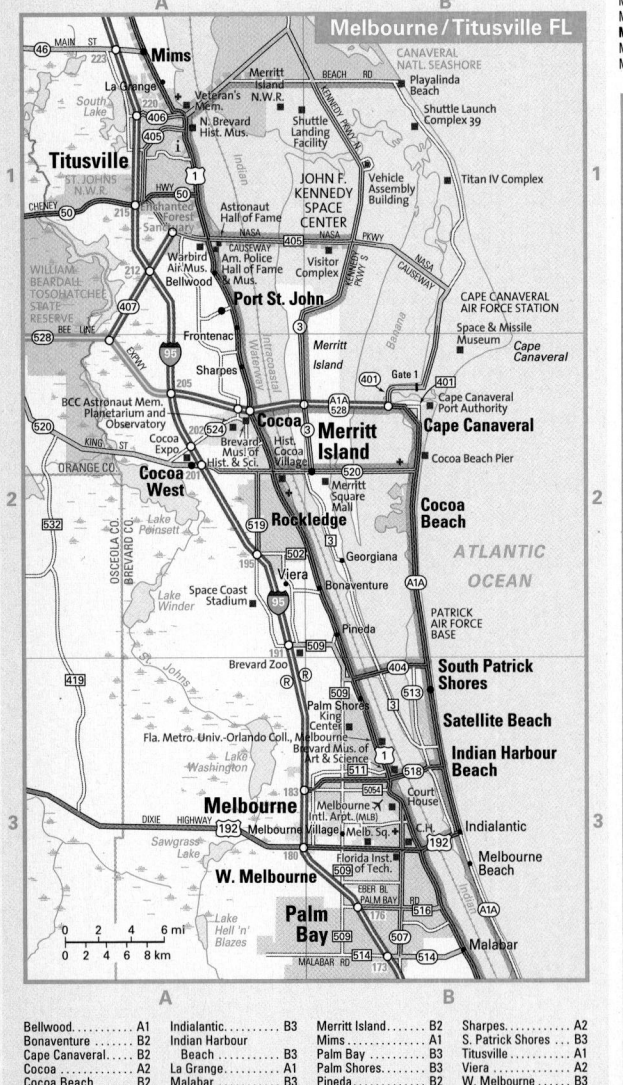

Bellwood	A1	Indialantic	B3
Bonaventure	B2	Indian Harbour Beach	B3
Cape Canaveral	B2	La Grange	A1
Cocoa	A2	Malabar	B3
Cocoa Beach	B2	Melbourne	A3
Cocoa West	A2	Melbourne Beach	B3
Frontenac	A1	Melbourne Vil.	B3
Georgiana	B2	Merritt Island	B2
Mims	A1	Sharpes	A2
Palm Bay	B3	S. Patrick Shores	B3
Palm Shores	B3	Titusville	A1
Pineda	B2	Viera	A2
Port St. John	A1	W. Melbourne	B3
Rockledge	A2		
Satellite Beach	B3		

Entries in **bold black** indicate counties or parishes.
Entries in **bold color** indicate cities with detailed inset maps.

Miami / Fort Lauderdale FL

Downtown Miami FL

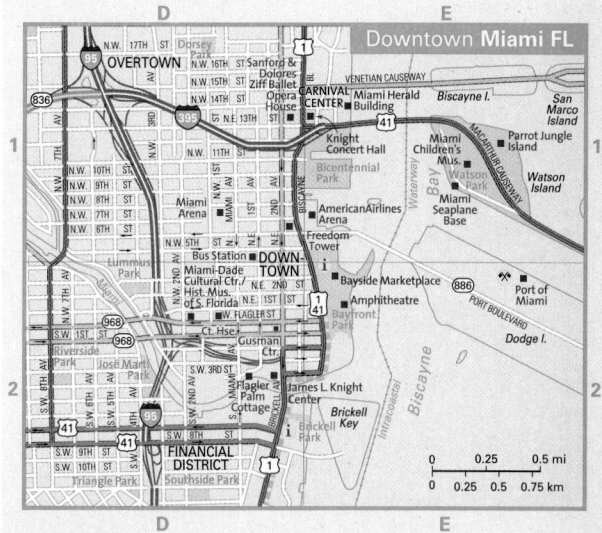

POINTS OF INTEREST

234

Marysvale–Medina County

Figures after entries indicate population, page number, and grid reference.

Milwaukee WI

POINTS OF INTEREST

Downtown Milwaukee WI

Entries in **bold black** indicate counties or parishes.
Entries in **bold color** indicate cities with detailed inset maps.

Minneapolis / St Paul MN

Figures after entries indicate population, page number, and grid reference.

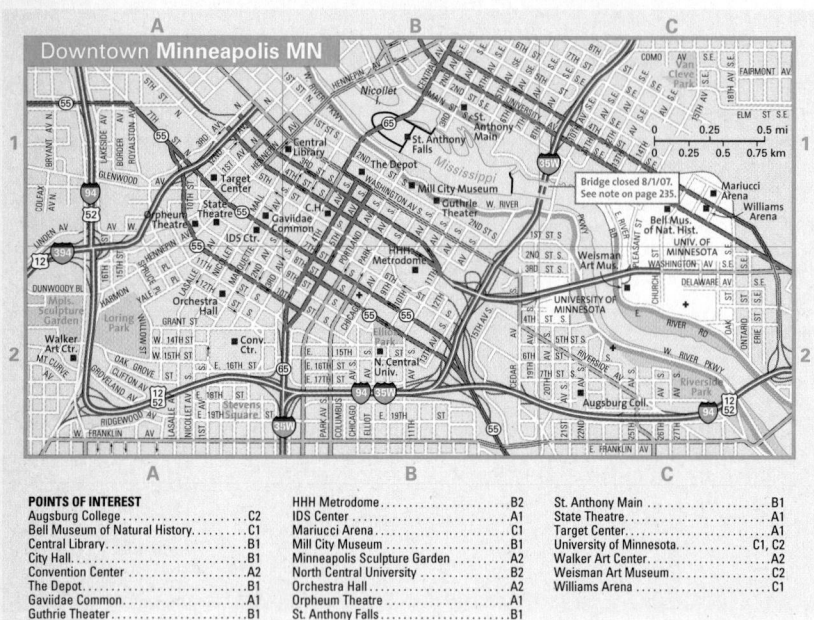

Downtown Minneapolis MN

POINTS OF INTEREST

Augsburg College	C2
Bell Museum of Natural History	C1
Central Library	B1
City Hall	B1
Convention Center	A2
The Depot	B1
Gaviidae Common	A1
Guthrie Theater	B1
HHH Metrodome	B2
IDS Center	A1
Mariucci Arena	C1
Mill City Museum	B1
Minneapolis Sculpture Garden	A2
North Central University	B2
Orchestra Hall	A1
Orpheum Theatre	A1
St. Anthony Falls	B1
St. Anthony Main	B1
State Theatre	A1
Target Center	A1
University of Minnesota	C1, C2
Walker Art Center	A2
Weisman Art Museum	C2
Williams Arena	C1

Missoula MT

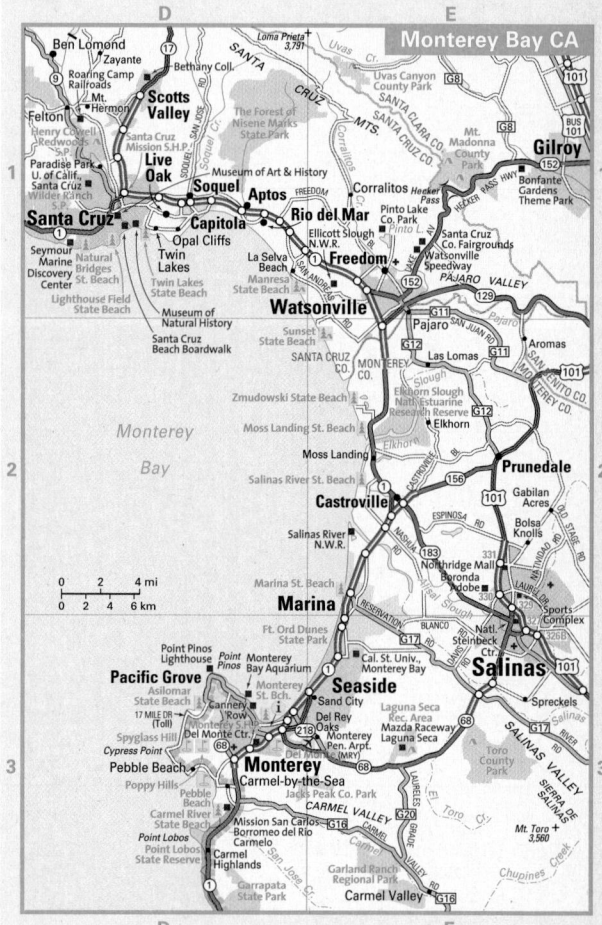

Monterey Bay CA

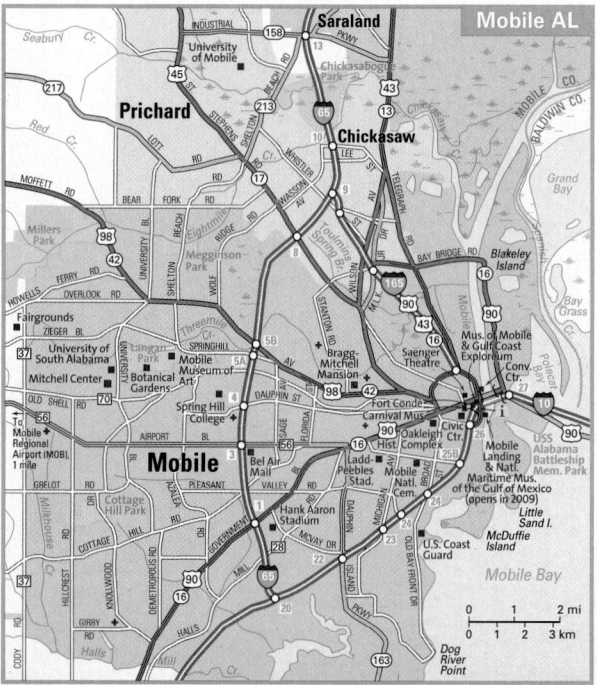

Mobile AL

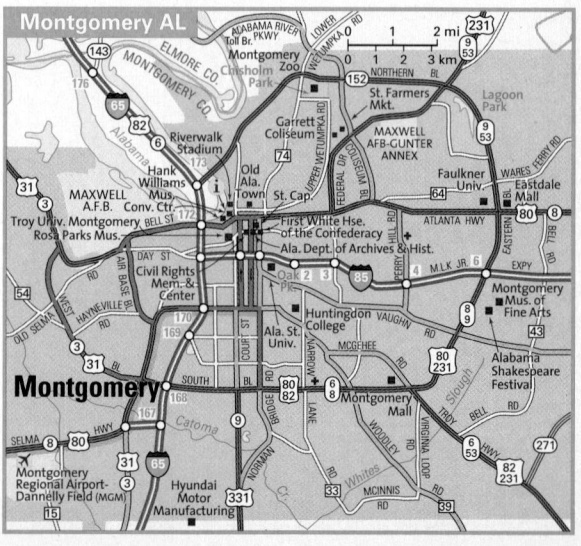

Montgomery AL

Entries in **bold black** indicate counties or parishes.
Entries in **bold color** indicate cities with detailed inset maps.

Miles City MT, 8487...17 E4
Milford CT, 52305...149 D2
Milford DE, 6732...145 F3
Milford IL, 1369...89 D3
Milford IN, 1550...89 F2
Milford IA, 2474...72 A3
Milford KS, 502...43 F2
Milford ME, 2197...83 D1
Milford MD, 26527...193 B2
Milford MA, 24230...150 C2
Milford MI, 6272...76 B4
Milford NE, 2070...35 F4
Milford NH, 8293...95 D1
Milford NJ, 1195...146 C1
Milford NY, 511...79 F4
Milford OH, 6284...100 B2
Milford TX, 685...59 F3
Milford UT, 1451...39 D3
Milford Ctr. OH, 626...90 C4
Milford Square PA, 1100...146 C1

Mililani Town HI, 28608...152 A3
Millard Co. UT, 12405...39 D2
Millbourne PA, 943...248 B3
Millbrae CA, 20718...259 B4
Millbrook AL, 10386...128 C4
Millbrook NY, 1429...94 B3
Millburn NJ, 19765...240 A3
Millbury MA, 4700...150 C2
Millbury OH, 1161...90 C2
Mill City NV, 300...29 F4
Mill City OR, 1537...20 C3
Mill Creek WA, 11525...12 C3
Mill Creek WV, 662...102 A3
Milledgeville GA, 18757...129 E1
Milledgeville IL, 1016...88 B1
Mille Lacs Co. MN, 22330...66 C2
Millen GA, 3492...129 F2
Miller MO, 754...106 C2
Miller SD, 1530...27 D3
Miller Co. AR, 40443...124 C1
Miller Co. GA, 6383...128 C4

Miller Co. MO, 23564...97 E4
Miller Place NY, 10580...149 D3
Millersburg IN, 868...89 F2
Millersburg KY, 842...100 B4
Millersburg OH, 3326...91 E4
Millersburg OR, 651...20 B3
Millersburg PA, 2562...93 D4
Millers Creek NC, 2071...111 F3
Millers Falls MA, 1072...94 C1
Millersport OH, 963...101 D1
Millerstown PA, 679...93 D4
Millersville PA, 7774...146 A3
Millersville TN, 5308...109 F3
Millerton NY, 925...94 B2
Mill Hall PA, 1568...93 D3
Milliken CO, 2888...33 E4
Millington MI, 1137...76 B3
Millington NJ, 3500...148 A4
Millington TN, 10433...118 B1
Millinocket ME, 5190...85 D4
Millis MA, 4607...150 C2
Mill Neck NY, 825...148 C3
Millport AL, 1160...119 D4
Millry AL, 615...127 D4
Mills WY, 2591...33 D1
Millsboro DE, 2360...145 F4
Mills Co. IA, 14547...86 A3
Mills Co. TX, 5151...59 D4
Millstadt IL, 2794...98 A3
Millstone KY, 650...111 E2
Milltown IN, 932...99 F4
Milltown NJ, 7000...147 E1
Milltown WI, 888...67 E3
Millvale PA, 3800...250 B1
Millville CA, 600...28 C4
Millville DE, 259...145 F4
Millville NJ, 26847...145 F1
Millville OH, 817...100 B2
Millville PA, 991...93 E3
Millville UT, 1507...31 E3
Millwood NY, 2300...148 B2
Millwood WA, 1649...14 A3
Milner GA, 522...129 D3
Milnor ND, 711...27 E1
Milo IA, 839...86 C2
Milo ME, 1898...84 C4
Milpitas CA, 62698...36 B4
Milroy IN, 800...100 A2
Milroy PA, 1386...93 D3
Milton DE, 1657...145 F3
Milton FL, 7045...135 F1
Milton IN, 611...100 A1
Milton IA, 550...87 E3
Milton KY, 525...100 A3
Milton MA, 26062...151 D1

Milton NH, 950...81 F4
Milton NY, 1251...148 B1
Milton PA, 6650...93 D3
Milton VT, 1537...81 D1
Milton WA, 5795...262 B5
Milton WV, 2206...101 E3
Milton WI, 5132...74 B4
Milton-Freewater OR, 6470...21 F1
Miltonvale KS, 523...43 E2
Milwaukee WI, 596974...74 C3
Milwaukee Co. WI, 940164...75 D3
Milwaukie OR, 20490...251 D2
Mimosa Park LA, 4500...239 A2
Mims FL, 9147...141 E1
Mina NV, 275...37 F3
Minatare NE, 810...33 F2
Minco OK, 1672...51 E3
Minden IA, 564...86 A2
Minden LA, 13027...125 D2
Minden NV, 2836...37 D2
Mineola NY, 19234...148 C4
Mineola TX, 4550...124 A4
Mineral VA, 424...103 D4
Mineral Co. CO, 831...40 C4
Mineral Co. MT, 3884...14 C3
Mineral Co. NV, 5071...37 E3
Mineral Co. WV, 27078...102 C2
Mineral Pt. WI, 2617...74 A3
Mineral Ridge OH, 3900...276 B2
Mineral Sprs. AR, 1264...116 C4
Mineral Sprs. NC, 1370...122 B2
Mineral Wells TX, 16946...59 E2
Mineral Wells WV, 1860...101 E2
Minersville PA, 4552...93 E3
Minersville UT, 817...39 D3
Minerva OH, 3934...91 F3
Minerva Park OH, 1288...206 B1
Minetto NY, 1086...79 D2
Mineville NY, 1747...81 E1
Mingo Co. WV, 28253...101 E4
Mingo Jct. OH, 3631...91 F4
Minidoka Co. ID, 20174...31 D1
Minier IL, 1244...88 B4
Minneapolis KS, 2046...43 E2
Minneapolis MN, 382618...67 D4
Minneola FL, 5435...140 C1
Minneola KS, 717...42 C4
Minneota MN, 1449...27 F3
Minnesota Lake MN, 681...72 C2
Minnetonka MN, 51301...235 A3
Minnewaukan ND, 318...19 D2

Minoa NY, 3348...79 E3
Minocqua WI, 750...68 B2
Minong WI, 531...67 E2
Minonk IL, 2168...88 B3
Minooka IL, 3971...88 C2
Minor Hill TN, 437...119 E2
Minot ME, 400...82 B3
Minot MA, 1100...151 E2
Minot ND, 36567...18 B2
Minster OH, 2794...90 B4
Mint Hill NC, 14922...122 B1
Minto ND, 657...19 E2
Minturn CO, 1068...41 D1
Mio MI, 2016...70 C4
Mira Loma CA, 15717...229 H3
Miramar FL, 72739...143 E2
Miramar Beach FL, 2435...136 B2
Misenheimer NC, 750...122 B1
Mishawaka IN, 46557...89 F2
Mishicot WI, 1422...75 D1
Missaukee Co. MI, 14478...75 F1
Mission KS, 9727...224 B3
Mission SD, 904...26 C4
Mission TX, 45408...60 C4
Mission Bend TX, 30831...220 A3
Mission Hills KS, 3593...224 B4
Mission Viejo CA, 93102...52 C3
Mississippi Co. AR, 51979...108 B4
Mississippi Co. MO, 13427...108 C2
Mississippi State MS, 3500...119 D4
Missoula Co. MT, 95802...15 D4
Missouri City TX, 52913...132 A3
Missouri Valley IA, 2992...86 A2
Mitchell IN, 4567...99 F3
Mitchell NE, 1831...33 F2
Mitchell SD, 15408...27 E4
Mitchell Co. GA, 23932...137 E1
Mitchell Co. IA, 10874...73 D2
Mitchell Co. KS, 6932...43 E2
Mitchell Co. NC, 15687...111 E4
Mono Co. CA, 12853...37 E4
Mitchellville AR, 497...117 F4
Mitchellville IA, 1715...87 D2
Mi-Wuk Vil. CA, 1485...37 D3
Moab UT, 4779...40 A3
Moapa NV, 928...46 B1
Mobeetie TX, 107...50 A4
Moberly MO, 11945...97 E2
Mobile Co. AL, 399843...135 E1
Mobridge SD, 3574...26 C2
Mocksville NC, 4178...112 A4
Moclips WA, 615...12 B3
Modena NY, 1100...148 B1
Modena PA, 610...146 B3

Modesto CA, 188856...36 C4
Modoc Co. CA, 9449...29 D3
Moffat Co. CO, 13184...32 B4
Mogadore OH, 3893...188 B2
Mohall ND, 812...18 B1
Mohave Co. AZ, 155032...46 B3
Mohave Valley AZ, 13694...46 B3
Mohawk NY, 2660...79 F3
Mohegan CT, 3500...149 F1
Mohegan Lake NY, 5700...148 B3
Mohnton PA, 2963...146 A2
Mohrsville PA, 800...146 A1
Mojave CA, 3836...52 C1
Mokelumne Hill CA, 774...36 C3
Mokuleia HI, 1839...152 A2
Molalla OR, 5647...20 C2
Molena GA, 475...128 C1
Moline IL, 43768...88 A2
Moline KS, 457...43 F4
Moline Acres MO, 2662...256 C1
Molino FL, 1312...135 F1
Momence IL, 3171...89 D2
Mona UT, 850...39 E1
Monaca PA, 6286...91 F3
Monahans TX, 6821...57 F4
Monarch Mills SC, 1930...121 F2
Moncks Corner SC, 5952...131 D1
Mondovi WI, 2634...67 E4
Monee IL, 2924...89 D2
Monessen PA, 8669...92 A4
Monett MO, 7396...106 C2
Monette AR, 1179...108 A4
Monfort Hts. OH, 3880...204 A2
Moniteau Co. MO, 14827...97 D3
Monmouth IL, 9841...88 A3
Monmouth ME, 500...82 B2
Monmouth OR, 9741...20 B2
Monmouth Beach NJ, 3595...147 E2
Monmouth Co. NJ, 615301...147 E2
Monmouth Jct. NJ, 2721...147 D1
Mono Co. CA, 12853...37 E4
Monon IN, 1733...89 E3
Monona IA, 1533...73 F3
Monona WI, 8018...74 B4
Monona Co. IA, 10020...86 A1
Monongah WV, 939...102 A2
Monongahela PA, 4761...92 A4
Monongalia Co. WV, 81866...102 A1
Monponsett MA, 1700...151 E2
Monroe CT, 3000...149 D2
Monroe GA, 11407...121 D4
Monroe IN, 734...90 A3
Monroe IA, 1808...87 D2
Monroe LA, 53107...125 E2

Monroe MI, 22076...90 C1
Monroe NY, 7780...148 B2
Monroe NC, 26228...122 B2
Monroe OH, 7133...100 B2
Monroe OR, 607...20 B3
Monroe UT, 1845...39 E3
Monroe WA, 13795...12 C3
Monroe WI, 10843...74 B4
Monroe City IN, 548...99 E3
Monroe City MO, 2588...97 E1
Monroe Co. AL, 24324...127 F4
Monroe Co. AR, 10254...118 A2
Monroe Co. FL, 79589...143 D3
Monroe Co. GA, 26424...128 C1
Monroe Co. IL, 27619...98 A4
Monroe Co. IN, 120563...99 F2
Monroe Co. IA, 8016...87 D3
Monroe Co. KY, 11756...110 A2
Monroe Co. MI, 145945...90 C1
Monroe Co. MS, 38014...119 D4
Monroe Co. MO, 9311...97 E1
Monroe Co. NY, 735343...78 C3
Monroe Co. OH, 15180...101 F1
Monroe Co. PA, 138687...93 F3
Monroe Co. TN, 38961...120 C1
Monroe Co. WV, 13502...112 A1
Monroe Co. WI, 40899...73 F1
Monroeville AL, 6862...127 E4
Monroeville IN, 1236...90 A3
Monroeville OH, 1433...91 D2
Monroeville PA, 28386...92 A4
Monrovia CA, 36929...228 E2
Monrovia IN, 1063...99 F1
Monsey NY, 14504...148 B3
Monson MA, 2103...150 B2
Montague CA, 1456...28 C3
Montague MA, 800...94 C1
Montague MI, 2407...75 E2
Montague TX, 225...59 E1
Montague Co. TX, 19117...59 E1
Mont Alto PA, 1357...103 D1
Montana City MT, 2094...15 E4
Montara CA, 2950...259 A4
Montauk NY, 3851...149 F3
Mont Belvieu TX, 2324...132 B3
Montcalm WV, 885...111 F1
Montcalm Co. MI, 61266...75 F2
Montclair CA, 33049...229 G2
Montclair NJ, 38971...148 A3
Mont Clare PA, 1900...146 B2
Monteagle TN, 1200...120 A1
Monte Alto TX, 1611...63 E4
Montebello CA, 62150...228 D3
Montecito CA, 10000...52 B2
Montegut LA, 1803...134 B4

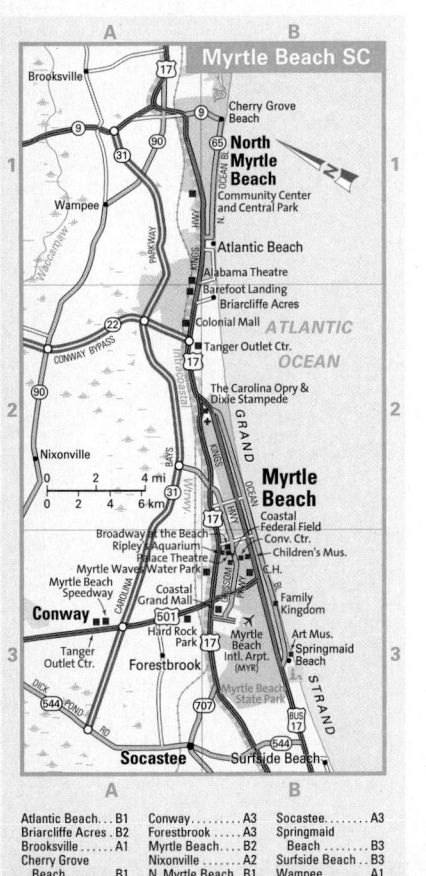

Montpelier VT

Myrtle Beach SC

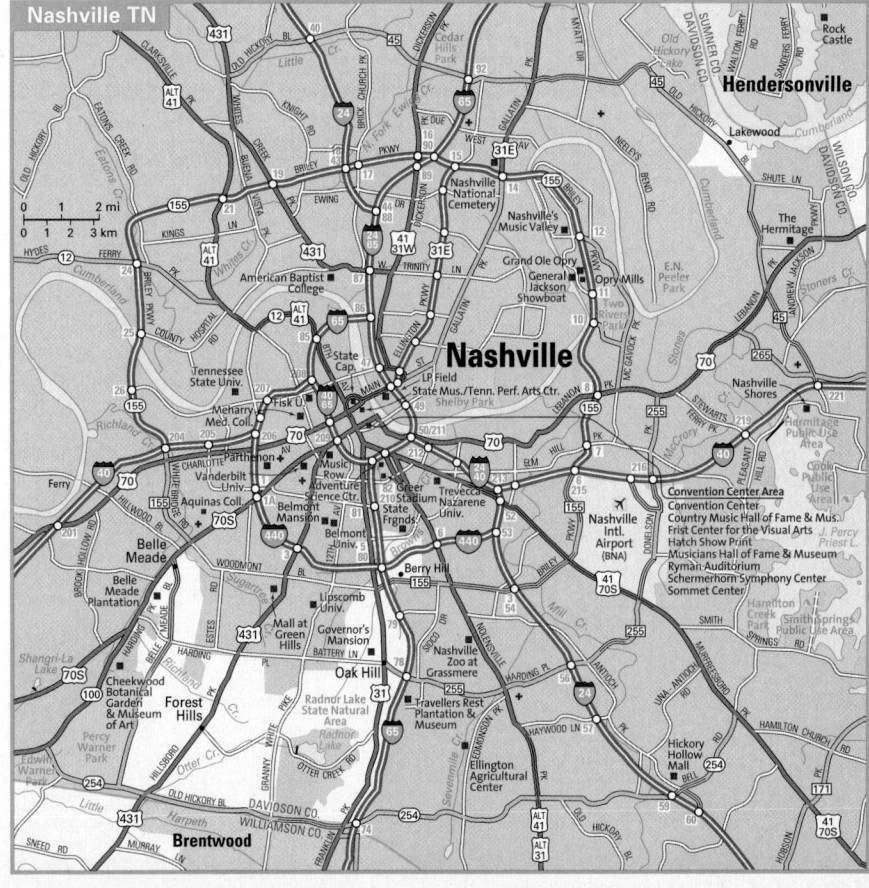

Nashville TN

Figures after entries indicate population, page number, and grid reference.

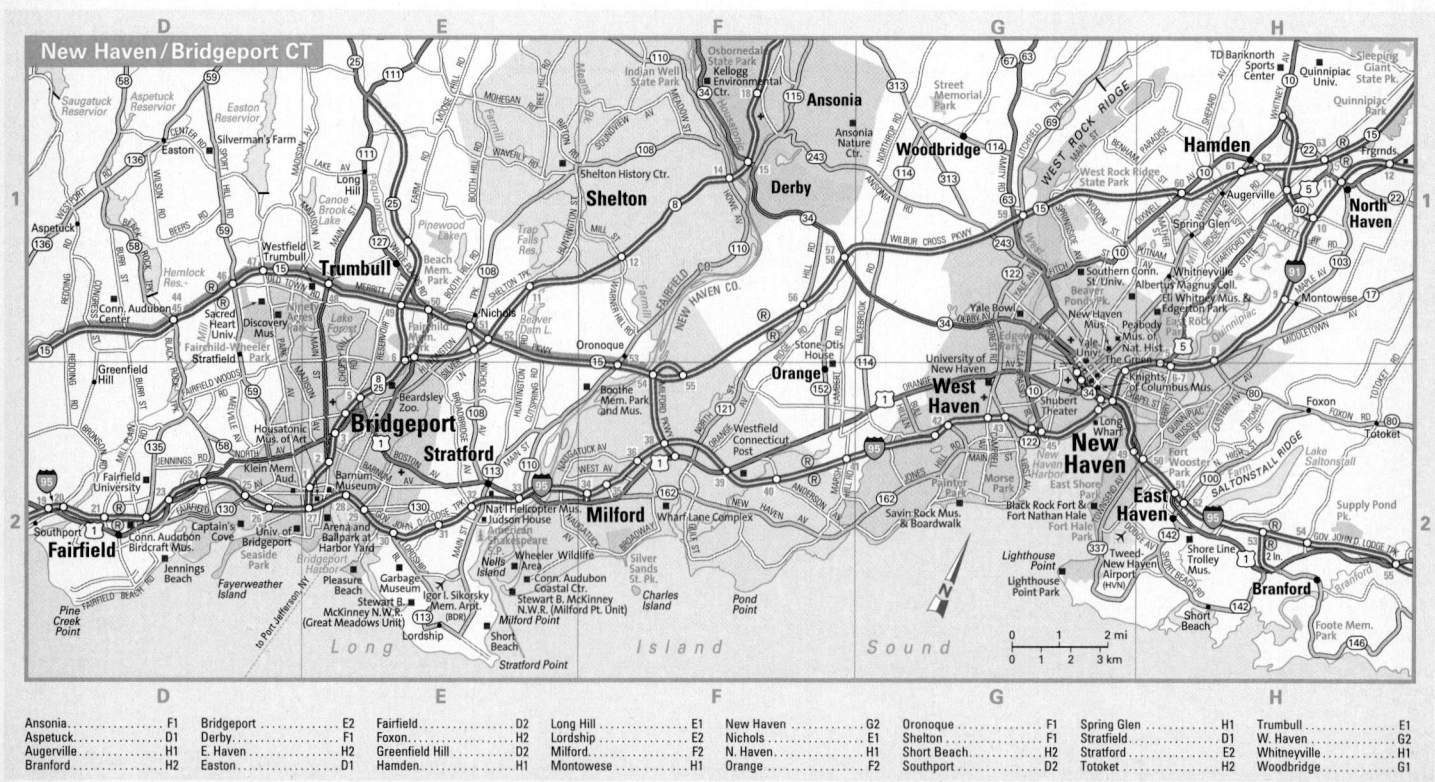

New Bedford/Fall River MA

New Haven/Bridgeport CT

Entries in **bold black** indicate counties or parishes.
Entries in **bold color** indicate cities with detailed inset maps.

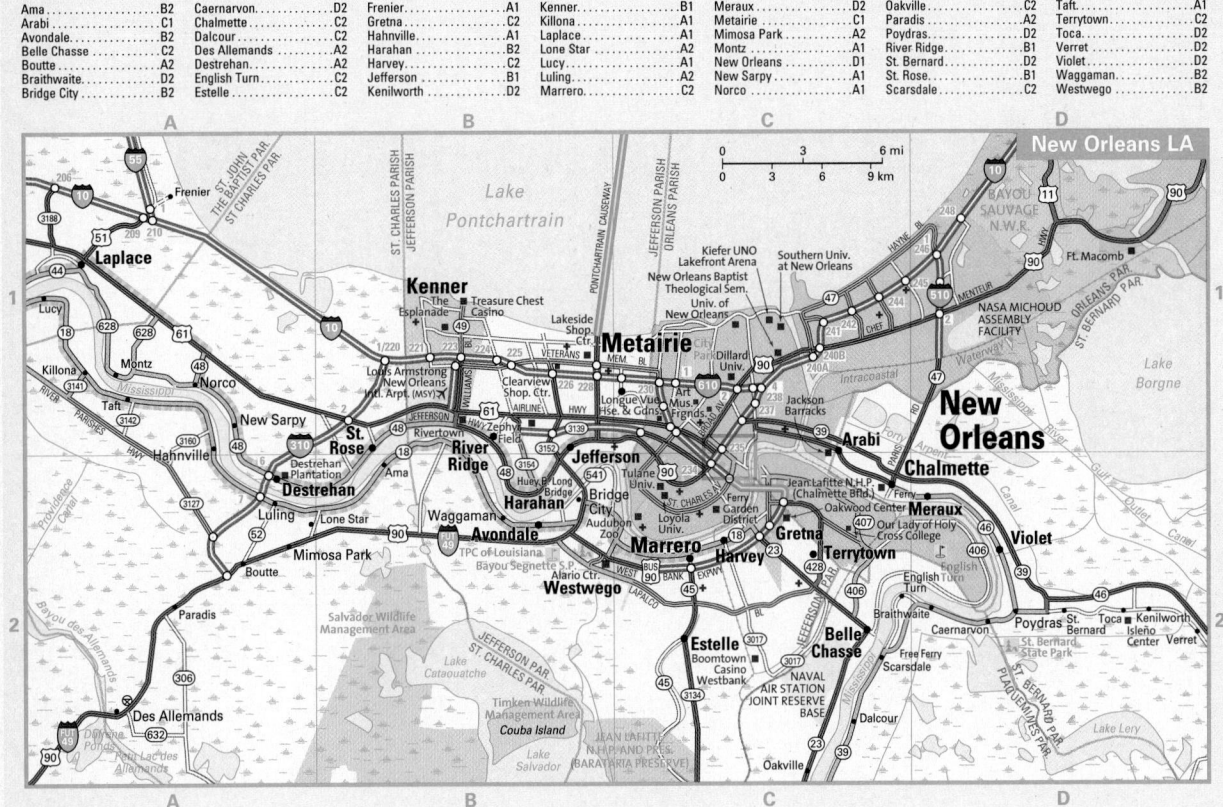

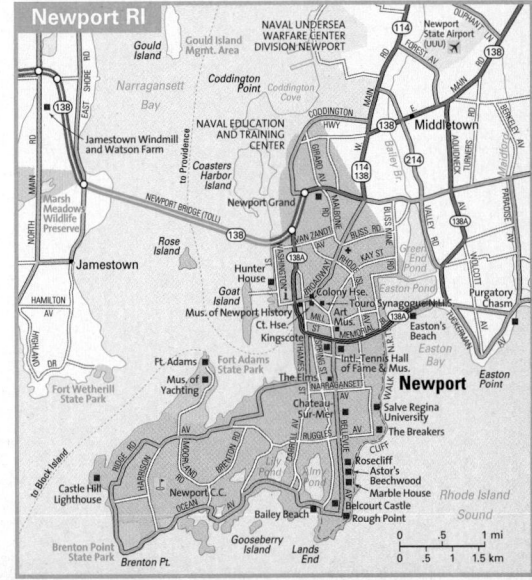

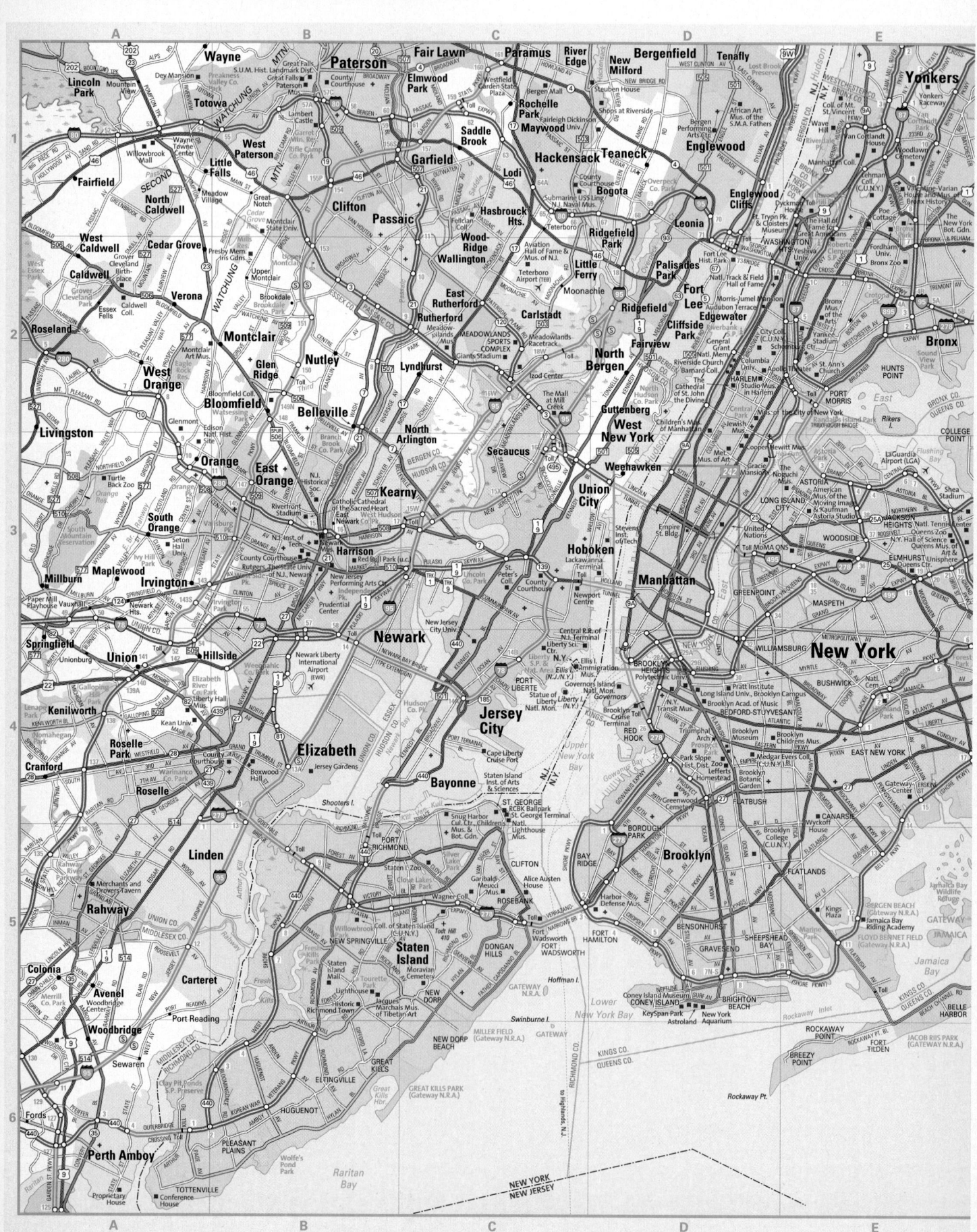

Entries in **bold black** indicate counties or parishes.
Entries in **bold color** indicate cities with detailed inset maps.

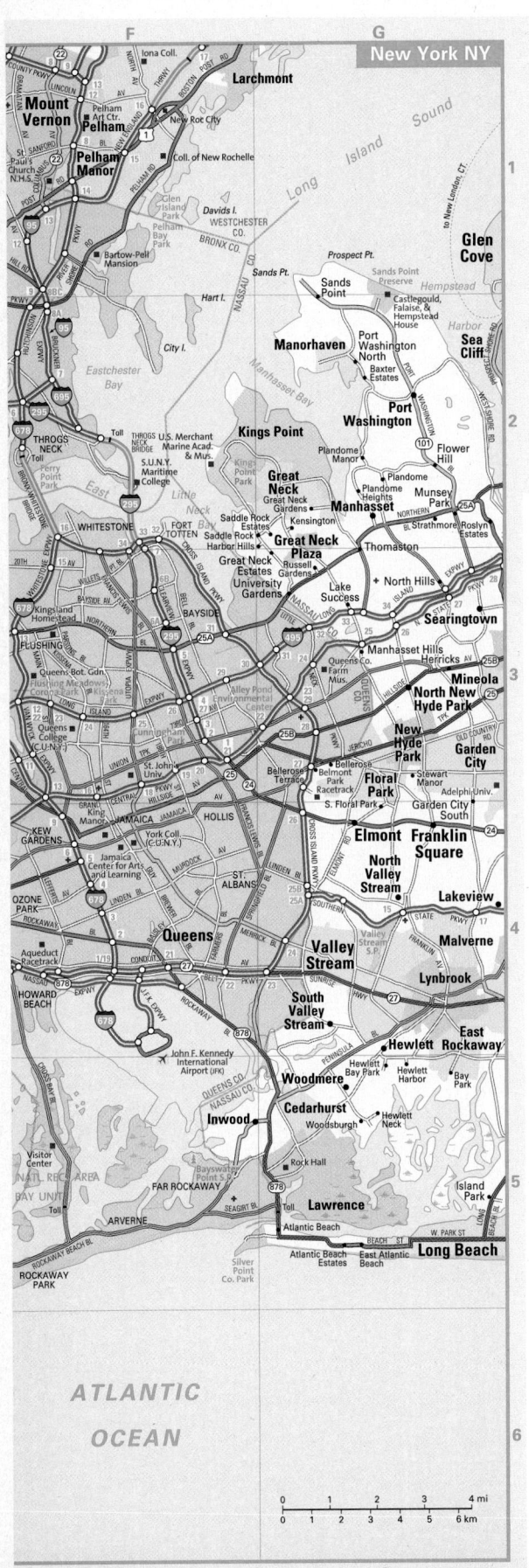

New York NY

Figures after entries indicate population, page number, and grid reference.

POINTS OF INTEREST

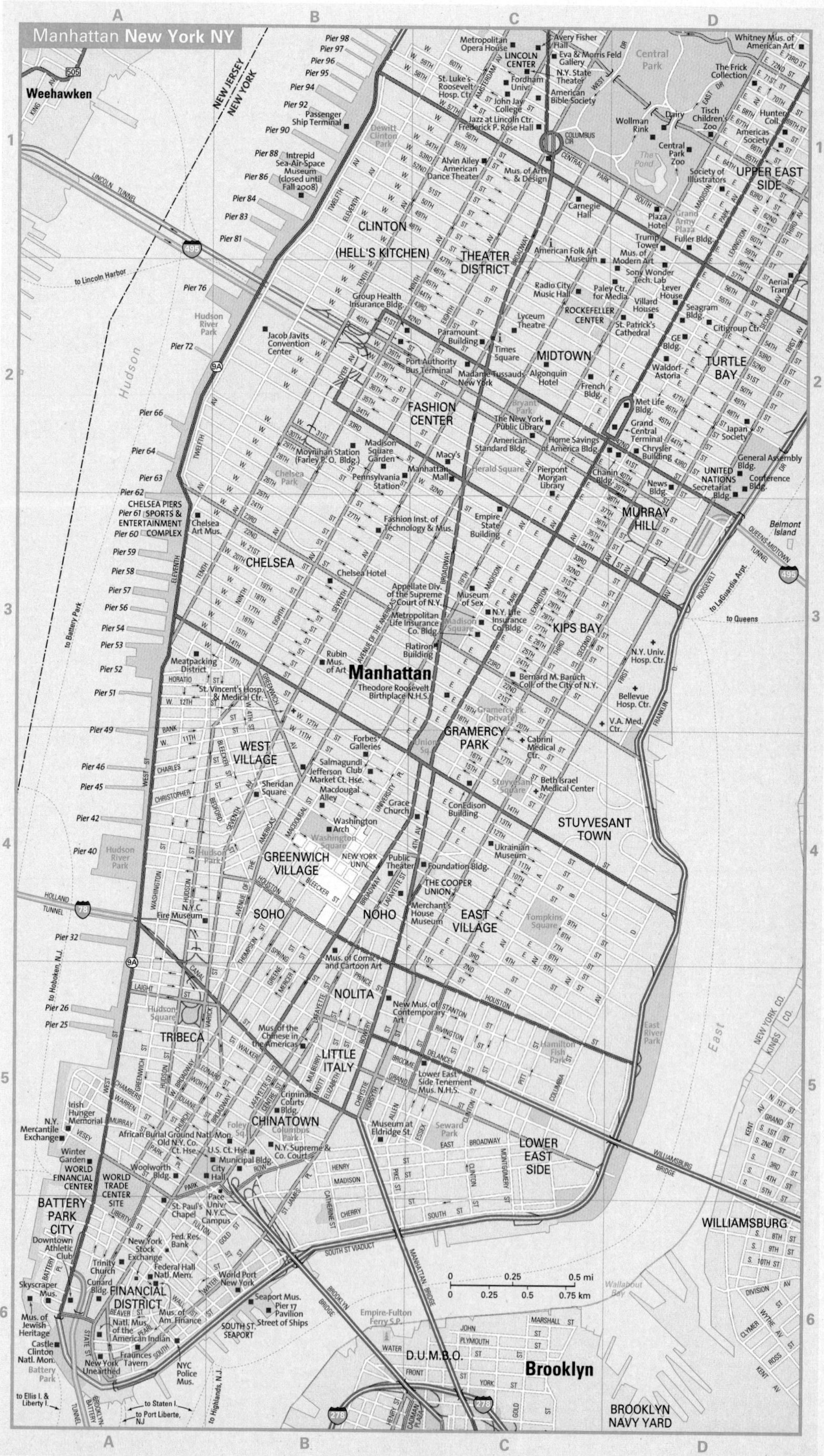
Manhattan New York NY
Weehawken
NEW JERSEY
NEW YORK
Hudson
LINCOLN TUNNEL
HOLLAND TUNNEL
CLINTON
(HELL'S KITCHEN)
THEATER DISTRICT
MIDTOWN
TURTLE BAY
UPPER EAST SIDE
FASHION CENTER
MURRAY HILL
CHELSEA
KIPS BAY
Manhattan
GRAMERCY PARK
WEST VILLAGE
STUYVESANT TOWN
GREENWICH VILLAGE
SOHO
NOHO
EAST VILLAGE
NOLITA
TRIBECA
LITTLE ITALY
CHINATOWN
LOWER EAST SIDE
BATTERY PARK CITY
FINANCIAL DISTRICT
D.U.M.B.O.
Brooklyn
WILLIAMSBURG
BROOKLYN NAVY YARD
Central Park
East
WILLIAMSBURG BRIDGE
BROOKLYN BRIDGE
MANHATTAN BRIDGE
Belmont Island
to LaGuardia Arpt.
to Queens
to Lincoln Harbor
to Battery Park
to Hoboken, N.J.
to Ellis I. & Liberty I.
to Staten I.
to Port Liberte, NJ
to Highlands, N.J.
0 0.25 0.5 mi
0 0.25 0.5 0.75 km

Entries in **bold black** indicate counties or parishes.
Entries in **bold color** indicate cities with detailed inset maps.

Figures after entries indicate population, page number, and grid reference.

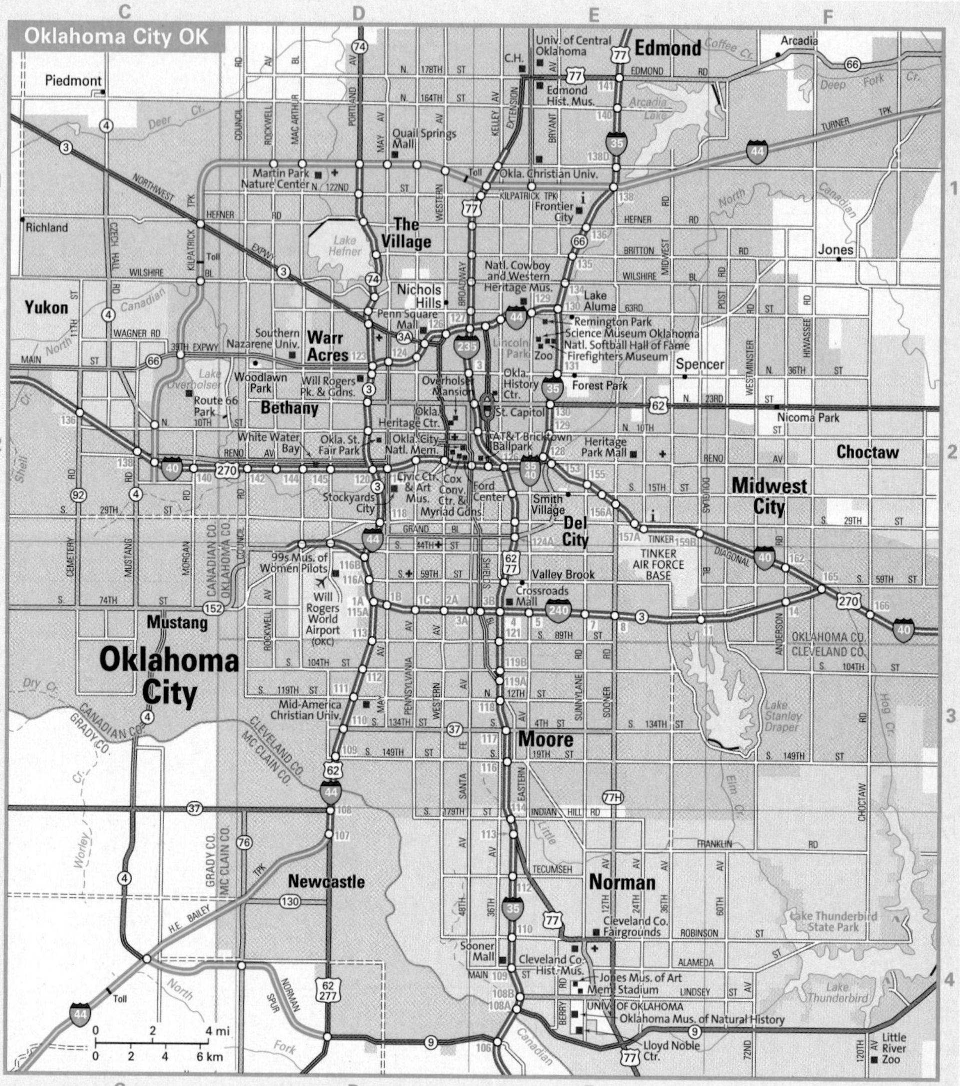

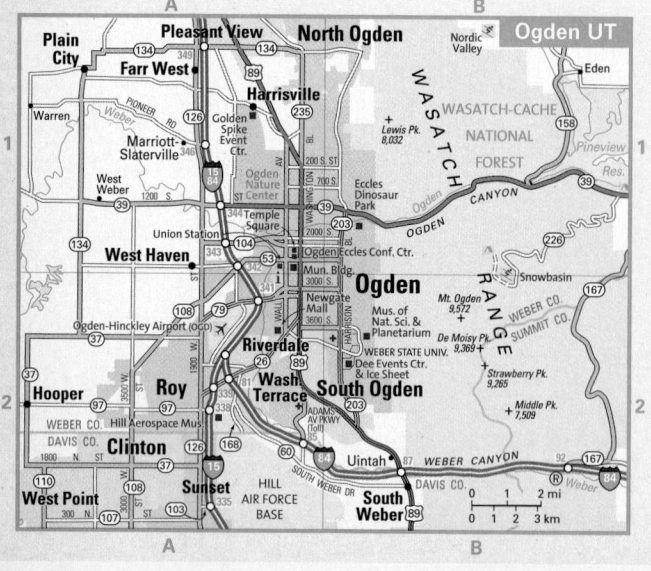

245
Northwood–Ossining

Entries in **bold black** indicate counties or parishes.
Entries in **bold color** indicate cities with detailed inset maps.

Northwood NH, 500 ... 81 F4
Northwood ND, 959 ... 19 E3
Northwood OH, 5471 ... 90 C2
Northwoods MO, 4643 ... 256 B2
N. Woodstock NH, 750 ... 81 F3
Northwye MO, 550 ... 97 E4
N. York PA, 1689 ... 275 E1
Norton KS, 3012 ... 42 C1
Norton MA, 2618 ... 151 D2
Norton OH, 11523 ... 91 E3
Norton VA, 3904 ... 111 E2
Norton Co. KS, 5953 ... 42 C1
Norton Shores MI, 22527 ... 75 E3
Nortonville KS, 620 ... 96 A2
Nortonville KY, 1264 ... 109 E2
Norwalk CA, 103298 ... 52 C3
Norwalk CT, 82951 ... 148 C2
Norwalk IA, 6884 ... 86 C2
Norwalk OH, 16238 ... 91 D2
Norwalk WI, 653 ... 73 F2
Norway IA, 601 ... 87 E1
Norway ME, 2623 ... 82 B2
Norway MI, 2959 ... 69 D2
Norwell MA, 1300 ... 151 E2
Norwich CT, 36117 ... 149 F1
Norwich KS, 551 ... 43 E4
Norwich NY, 7355 ... 79 E4
Norwich VT, 1200 ... 81 E3
Norwood CO, 438 ... 40 B3
Norwood KY, 395 ... 230 F1
Norwood MA, 28587 ... 151 D2
Norwood MO, 552 ... 107 E2
Norwood NY, 1685 ... 80 B1
Norwood NC, 2216 ... 122 B1
Norwood OH, 21675 ... 100 B2
Norwood PA, 5985 ... 248 B4
Norwood Young America MN, 3108 ... 66 C4
Notasulga AL, 916 ... 128 B2
Nottingham NH, 550 ... 81 F4
Nottoway VA, 100 ... 113 D2
Nottoway Co. VA, 15725 ... 113 D2
Notus ID, 458 ... 22 B4
Novato CA, 47630 ... 36 B3
Novi MI, 47386 ... 76 B4
Novinger MO, 534 ... 87 D4
Nowata OK, 3971 ... 106 A3
Nowata Co. OK, 10569 ... 106 A2
Noxapater MS, 419 ... 126 C1
Noxon MT, 230 ... 14 C2
Noxubee Co. MS, 12548 ... 127 D1
Noyack NY, 2696 ... 149 E3
Nuangola PA, 671 ... 93 E3
Nuckolls Co. NE, 5057 ... 35 E4
Nucla CO, 734 ... 40 B3
Nueces Co. TX, 313645 ... 63 F2
Nuevo CA, 4135 ... 53 D3
Nuiqsut AK, 433 ... 154 C1
Nunda NY, 1330 ... 78 B4
Nunn CO, 471 ... 33 E4
Nutley NJ, 27362 ... 148 B3
Nutter Fort WV, 1686 ... 102 A2
Nyack NY, 6737 ... 148 B3
Nye Co. NV, 32485 ... 37 F3
Nyssa OR, 3163 ... 22 A4

O

Oacoma SD, 390 ... 27 D4
Oak Bluffs MA, 1700 ... 151 E4
Oakboro NC, 1198 ... 122 B1
Oak Brook IL, 8702 ... 203 C4
Oakbrook Terrace IL, 2300 ... 203 C4
Oak City UT, 650 ... 39 D2
Oak Creek CO, 849 ... 32 C4
Oak Creek WI, 28456 ... 74 C3
Oakdale CA, 15503 ... 36 C4
Oakdale CT, 1100 ... 149 F1
Oakdale KY, 4937 ... 109 D2
Oakdale LA, 8137 ... 133 E1
Oakdale MA, 1100 ... 150 C1
Oakdale MN, 26653 ... 235 E2
Oakdale NY, 8075 ... 149 D4
Oakdale PA, 1551 ... 92 A4
Oakes ND, 1979 ... 27 E1
Oakesdale WA, 420 ... 14 A3
Oakfield ME, 475 ... 85 D3
Oakfield NY, 1805 ... 78 B3
Oakfield WI, 1012 ... 74 C2
Oak Forest IL, 28051 ... 89 D2
Oak Grove AL, 457 ... 128 A1
Oak Grove IL, 1318 ... 88 A2
Oak Grove KY, 7064 ... 109 E3
Oak Grove LA, 2174 ... 125 F1
Oak Grove MI, 700 ... 70 C4
Oak Grove MN, 6903 ... 67 D3
Oak Grove MS, 1400 ... 126 C4
Oak Grove MO, 5535 ... 96 C2
Oak Grove OR, 12808 ... 251 D3
Oak Grove SC, 8183 ... 122 A3
Oak Grove TN, 4072 ... 111 E3
Oak Grove Hts. AR, 727 ... 108 A4
Oak Harbor OH, 2841 ... 90 C2
Oak Harbor WA, 19795 ... 12 C2
Oak Hill FL, 1378 ... 141 E1
Oak Hill OH, 1685 ... 101 D3
Oak Hill WV, 7589 ... 101 F4
Oak Hills IL, 2400 ... 256 D2
Oakhurst CA, 2868 ... 37 D4
Oakhurst NJ, 4152 ... 147 F2
Oakhurst OK, 2731 ... 51 F2
Oak Island NC, 6571 ... 123 E4
Oakland CA, 399484 ... 36 B4
Oakland FL, 936 ... 141 D1
Oakland IL, 996 ... 99 D1
Oakland IA, 1487 ... 86 A2
Oakland ME, 2758 ... 82 C2
Oakland MD, 1930 ... 102 B2
Oakland MD, 2100 ... 144 B1
Oakland MS, 586 ... 118 B3
Oakland MO, 1540 ... 256 B3
Oakland NE, 1367 ... 35 F2
Oakland NJ, 12466 ... 148 A3
Oakland OK, 674 ... 51 F4
Oakland OR, 954 ... 20 B4
Oakland PA, 622 ... 93 F1
Oakland TN, 1279 ... 118 C1
Oakland City IN, 2588 ... 99 E4
Oakland Co. MI, 1194156 ... 76 B4
Oakland Park FL, 30966 ... 143 F1
Oak Lawn IL, 55245 ... 89 D1
Oakley ID, 668 ... 31 D2
Oakley KS, 2173 ... 42 B2
Oakley UT, 948 ... 31 F4
Oaklyn NJ, 4188 ... 248 D4
Oakman AL, 944 ... 119 E4
Oakmont PA, 6911 ... 92 A4
Oak Orchard DE, 750 ... 145 F4
Oak Park CA, 2320 ... 228 A2
Oak Park IL, 52524 ... 89 D1
Oak Park MI, 29793 ... 76 C4
Oak Park Hts. MN, 3957 ... 67 D3
Oak Ridge NJ, 750 ... 148 A3
Oak Ridge NC, 3988 ... 112 B4
Oakridge OR, 3148 ... 20 C4
Oak Ridge TN, 27387 ... 110 C4
Oak Ridge North TX, 2991 ... 132 A2
Oak Shade NJ, 1500 ... 147 D3
Oakton VA, 29348 ... 144 A3
Oaktown IN, 633 ... 99 E3
Oak Trail Shores TX, 2475 ... 59 E3
Oak View CA, 4199 ... 52 B2
Oakville CT, 8618 ... 149 D1
Oakville MO, 35309 ... 98 A3
Oakville WA, 675 ... 12 B4
Oakwood GA, 2689 ... 121 D3
Oakwood IL, 1502 ... 89 D4
Oakwood OH, 607 ... 90 B3
Oakwood OH, 3667 ... 204 G3
Oakwood OH, 9215 ... 208 E2
Oakwood Beach NJ, 700 ... 145 E1
Oakwood Hills IL, 2194 ... 203 A1
Oasis NV, 200 ... 30 C3
Oberlin KS, 1994 ... 42 C1
Oberlin LA, 1853 ... 133 E2
Oberlin OH, 8195 ... 91 D2
Oberlin PA, 2809 ... 218 C2
Obetz OH, 3977 ... 206 B3
Obion TN, 1134 ... 108 C3
Obion Co. TN, 32450 ... 108 C3
Oblong IL, 1580 ... 99 D2
O'Brien Co. IA, 15102 ... 72 A3
Ocala FL, 45943 ... 138 C4
Occidental CA, 1272 ... 36 A3
Occoquan VA, 759 ... 144 B4
Oceana WV, 1550 ... 111 F1
Oceana Co. MI, 26873 ... 75 E2
Ocean Bluff MA, 5100 ... 151 E2
Ocean Breeze Park FL, 463 ... 141 E4
Ocean City FL, 5594 ... 136 B2
Ocean City MD, 7173 ... 114 C1
Ocean City NJ, 15378 ... 147 F4
Ocean Co. NJ, 510916 ... 147 E3
Ocean Gate NJ, 2076 ... 147 E3
Ocean Grove MA, 3012 ... 151 D3
Ocean Grove NJ, 4256 ... 147 F2
Oceano CA, 7260 ... 52 A1
Ocean Park WA, 1459 ... 12 B4
Ocean Pines MD, 10496 ... 114 C1
Oceanport NJ, 5807 ... 147 F2
Ocean Reef Club FL, 1000 ... 143 E3
Ocean Ridge FL, 1636 ... 143 F1
Ocean Shores WA, 3836 ... 12 B4
Oceanside CA, 161029 ... 53 D3
Oceanside NY, 32733 ... 147 F1
Oceanside OR, 326 ... 20 B2
Ocean Sprs. MS, 17225 ... 135 D2
Ocean View DE, 1006 ... 145 F4
Ochelata OK, 494 ... 51 F1
Ocheyedan IA, 536 ... 72 A2
Ochiltree Co. TX, 9006 ... 50 B2
Ochlocknee GA, 605 ... 137 E1
Ocilla GA, 3270 ... 129 E4
Ocoee FL, 24391 ... 141 D1
Oconee Co. GA, 26225 ... 121 D4
Oconee Co. SC, 66215 ... 121 E2
Oconomowoc WI, 12382 ... 74 C3
Oconto WI, 4708 ... 69 D4
Oconto Co. WI, 35634 ... 68 C4
Oconto Falls WI, 2843 ... 68 C4
Ocracoke NC, 769 ... 115 E3
Odebolt IA, 1153 ... 72 A4
Odell IL, 1014 ... 88 C3
Odell OR, 1849 ... 20 C1
Odem TX, 2499 ... 61 E4
Odenton MD, 20534 ... 144 C2
Odenville AL, 1131 ... 119 F4
Odessa DE, 286 ... 145 E1
Odessa FL, 3173 ... 140 B2
Odessa MO, 4818 ... 96 C2
Odessa NY, 617 ... 79 D4
Odessa TX, 90943 ... 58 A3
Odessa WA, 957 ... 13 F3
Odin IL, 1122 ... 98 C3
Odon IN, 1376 ... 99 E3
O'Donnell TX, 1011 ... 58 A2
Oelwein IA, 6692 ... 73 E4
O'Fallon IL, 21910 ... 98 B3
O'Fallon MO, 46169 ... 98 A3
Ogallala NE, 4930 ... 34 B3
Ogden IL, 743 ... 89 D4
Ogden IA, 2023 ... 86 C1
Ogden KS, 1762 ... 43 F2
Ogden NC, 5481 ... 123 E3
Ogden UT, 77226 ... 31 E3
Ogden Dunes IN, 1313 ... 89 E2
Ogdensburg NJ, 2638 ... 148 A3
Ogdensburg NY, 12364 ... 80 B1
Ogemaw Co. MI, 21645 ... 76 B1
Oglala SD, 1229 ... 34 A1
Ogle Co. IL, 53497 ... 88 B1
Oglesby IL, 3647 ... 88 B2
Oglethorpe GA, 1200 ... 129 D3
Oglethorpe Co. GA, 12635 ... 121 E4
Ogunquit ME, 800 ... 82 B4
Ohatchee AL, 1215 ... 120 A4
Ohio City OH, 784 ... 90 B3
Ohio Co. IN, 5623 ... 100 A2
Ohio Co. KY, 22916 ... 109 F1
Ohio Co. WV, 47427 ... 91 F4
Ohioville PA, 3759 ... 91 F3
Oil City LA, 1219 ... 124 C2
Oil City PA, 11504 ... 92 A2
Oildale CA, 27885 ... 45 D4
Oilton OK, 1099 ... 51 F2
Ojai CA, 7862 ... 52 B2
Okaloosa Co. FL, 170498 ... 136 B2
Okanogan WA, 2484 ... 13 E2
Okanogan Co. WA, 39564 ... 13 E1
Okarche OK, 1110 ... 51 E2
Okauchee WI, 2100 ... 74 C3
Okawville IL, 1355 ... 98 B3
Okay OK, 597 ... 106 A4
Okeechobee FL, 5376 ... 141 E4
Okeechobee Co. FL, 35910 ... 141 E3
Okeene OK, 1240 ... 51 D2
Okemah OK, 3038 ... 51 F3
Okemos MI, 22805 ... 76 A4
Okfuskee Co. OK, 11814 ... 51 F3
Oklahoma City OK, 506132 ... 51 E3
Oklahoma Co. OK, 660448 ... 51 E2
Okmulgee OK, 13022 ... 51 F2
Okmulgee Co. OK, 39685 ... 51 F2
Okoboji IA, 820 ... 72 A2
Okolona MS, 3056 ... 119 D3
Oktibbeha Co. MS, 42902 ... 118 C4
Ola AR, 1204 ... 117 D2
Olanta SC, 613 ... 122 C4
Olathe CO, 1573 ... 40 B3
Olathe KS, 92962 ... 96 B3
Olcott NY, 1156 ... 78 B3
Old Bennington VT, 232 ... 94 C1
Old Bridge NJ, 22833 ... 147 E1
Oldenburg IN, 647 ... 100 A2
Old Field NY, 947 ... 149 D3
Old Forge NY, 800 ... 79 F2
Old Forge PA, 8798 ... 93 F2
Old Fort NC, 963 ... 111 E4
Oldham SD, 206 ... 27 E3
Oldham Co. KY, 46178 ... 100 A4
Oldham Co. TX, 2185 ... 49 F3
Old Lyme CT, 850 ... 149 E2
Old Mystic CT, 3205 ... 149 F2
Old Orchard Beach ME, 8856 ... 82 B4
Old River-Winfree TX, 1364 ... 132 B3
Old Saybrook CT, 1962 ... 149 E2
Oldsmar FL, 11910 ... 140 B2
Old Town ID, 190 ... 14 B2
Old Town ME, 8130 ... 83 D1
Old Zionsville PA, 950 ... 146 B1
Olean NY, 15347 ... 92 C1
Oley PA, 1100 ... 146 B1
Olin IA, 716 ... 87 F1
Olive Branch MS, 21054 ... 118 B2
Olive Hill KY, 1813 ... 101 D4
Olivehurst CA, 11061 ... 36 C2
Oliver PA, 2925 ... 102 B1
Oliver Co. ND, 2065 ... 18 B4
Oliver Sprs. TN, 3303 ... 110 C4
Olivet MI, 1758 ... 76 A4
Olivet NJ, 1420 ... 145 F1
Olivet SD, 70 ... 35 E1
Olivette MO, 7438 ... 256 B2
Olivia MN, 2570 ... 66 B4
Olla LA, 1417 ... 125 E3
Olmos Park TX, 2343 ... 257 E2
Olmsted Co. MN, 124277 ... 73 E1
Olmsted Falls OH, 7962 ... 204 D3
Olney IL, 8631 ... 99 D3
Olney MD, 31438 ... 144 B2
Olney TX, 3396 ... 59 D1
Olney Sprs. CO, 389 ... 41 F3
Olpe KS, 504 ... 43 F3
Olton TX, 2288 ... 50 A4
Olustee OK, 680 ... 50 C4
Olympia WA, 42514 ... 12 B4
Olympian Vil. MO, 669 ... 98 A4
Olyphant PA, 4978 ... 261 E2
Omaha NE, 390007 ... 86 A2
Omaha TX, 999 ... 124 B1
Omak WA, 4721 ... 13 E2
Omao HI, 1221 ... 152 B1
Omega GA, 1340 ... 129 D4
Omro WI, 3177 ... 74 C1
Onaga KS, 704 ... 43 F1
Onalaska TX, 1174 ... 132 B1
Onalaska WI, 14839 ... 73 F2
Onamia MN, 847 ... 66 C2
Onancock VA, 1525 ... 114 C3
Onarga IL, 1438 ... 89 D3
Onawa IA, 3091 ... 35 F2
Onaway ID, 230 ... 14 B4
Onaway MI, 993 ... 70 C3
Oneco FL, 7500 ... 140 B3
Oneida IL, 752 ... 88 A3
Oneida NY, 10987 ... 79 E3
Oneida TN, 3615 ... 110 B3
Oneida Co. ID, 4125 ... 31 E2
Oneida Co. NY, 235469 ... 79 E2
Oneida Co. WI, 35776 ... 68 B2
O'Neill NE, 3733 ... 35 D2
Onekama MI, 647 ... 75 E1
Oneonta AL, 6576 ... 119 F4
Oneonta NY, 13292 ... 79 F4
Onida SD, 740 ... 26 C3
Onley VA, 496 ... 114 C3
Onondaga Co. NY, 458336 ... 79 E3
Onset MA, 1292 ... 151 E3
Onslow Co. NC, 150355 ... 115 D4
Onsted MI, 813 ... 90 B1
Ontario CA, 158007 ... 52 C2
Ontario OH, 5303 ... 91 D3
Ontario OR, 10985 ... 22 A4
Ontario Co. NY, 100224 ... 78 C4
Ontonagon MI, 1494 ... 65 E4
Ontonagon Co. MI, 7818 ... 65 E4
Onyx CA, 476 ... 45 E4
Oolitic IN, 1152 ... 99 F3
Oologah OK, 883 ... 106 A3
Ooltewah TN, 687 ... 120 B2
Oostburg WI, 2660 ... 75 D2
Opal Cliffs CA, 6458 ... 236 D1
Opa-Locka FL, 14951 ... 143 E2
Opelika AL, 23498 ... 128 B2
Opelousas LA, 22860 ... 133 F2
Opp AL, 6607 ... 128 A4
Oppelo AR, 725 ... 117 E1
Oquawka IL, 1539 ... 87 F3
Oracle AZ, 3563 ... 55 D2
Oracle Jct. AZ, 550 ... 55 D3
Oradell NJ, 8047 ... 148 B3
Oran MO, 1264 ... 108 B2
Orange CA, 128821 ... 52 C3
Orange CT, 13233 ... 149 D2
Orange MA, 3945 ... 95 D1
Orange NJ, 32868 ... 240 A3
Orange OH, 3236 ... 204 G2
Orange TX, 18643 ... 132 C2
Orange VA, 4123 ... 103 D4
Orange Beach AL, 3784 ... 135 F2
Orangeburg NY, 3388 ... 148 B3
Orangeburg SC, 12765 ... 122 A4
Orangeburg Co. SC, 91582 ... 122 A4
Orange City FL, 6604 ... 141 D1
Orange City IA, 5582 ... 35 F1
Orange Co. CA, 2846289 ... 52 C3
Orange Co. FL, 896344 ... 141 D1
Orange Co. IN, 19306 ... 99 F3
Orange Co. NY, 341367 ... 148 A2
Orange Co. NC, 118227 ... 112 C4
Orange Co. TX, 84966 ... 132 C2
Orange Co. VT, 28226 ... 81 E3
Orange Co. VA, 25881 ... 103 D4
Orange Cove CA, 7722 ... 45 D3
Orange Grove TX, 1288 ... 61 E4
Orange Lake FL, 650 ... 138 C4
Orange Lake NY, 6085 ... 148 B1
Orange Park FL, 9081 ... 139 D2
Orangeville IL, 751 ... 74 B4
Orangeville UT, 1398 ... 39 F2
Orchard Beach MD, 4400 ... 193 D5
Orchard City CO, 2880 ... 40 B2
Orchard Lake MI, 2215 ... 210 A1
Orchard Mesa CO, 6456 ... 40 B2
Orchard Park NY, 3294 ... 78 B4
Orchards WA, 17852 ... 20 C1
Orcutt CA, 28830 ... 52 A1
Ord NE, 2269 ... 35 D3
Orderville UT, 596 ... 39 D4
Ordway CO, 1248 ... 41 F3
Oreana IL, 892 ... 98 C1
Ore City TX, 1106 ... 124 B2
Orefield PA, 1600 ... 146 B1
Oregon IL, 4060 ... 88 B1
Oregon MO, 935 ... 96 B1
Oregon OH, 19355 ... 90 C2
Oregon WI, 7514 ... 74 B3
Oregon City OR, 25754 ... 20 C2
Oregon Co. MO, 10344 ... 107 F3
Oreland PA, 5509 ... 248 C1
Orem UT, 84324 ... 31 F4
Orfordville WI, 1272 ... 74 B4
Orient NY, 709 ... 149 F2
Oriental NC, 875 ... 115 E3
Orient Park FL, 5703 ... 266 C2
Orinda CA, 17599 ... 259 C2
Orion IL, 1713 ... 88 A2
Oriskany NY, 1459 ... 79 E3
Oriskany Falls NY, 698 ... 79 E3
Orland CA, 6281 ... 36 B1
Orland ME, 500 ... 83 D2
Orland Hills IL, 6779 ... 203 C6
Orlando FL, 185951 ... 141 D1
Orland Park IL, 51077 ... 89 D2
Orleans IN, 2273 ... 99 F3
Orleans IA, 583 ... 72 B2
Orleans MA, 1716 ... 151 F3
Orleans NE, 425 ... 43 D1
Orleans VT, 826 ... 81 E1
Orleans Co. NY, 44171 ... 78 B3
Orleans Co. VT, 26277 ... 81 E1
Orleans Par. LA, 484674 ... 134 B2
Orlinda TN, 594 ... 109 F3
Orlovista FL, 6047 ... 246 B2
Ormond Beach FL, 36301 ... 139 E4
Ormond-by-the-Sea FL, 8430 ... 139 E4
Orofino ID, 3247 ... 14 B4
Orono ME, 8253 ... 83 D1
Orono MN, 7538 ... 66 C4
Oronoco MN, 883 ... 73 D1
Oronogo MO, 976 ... 106 B2
Orosi CA, 8770 ... 45 D3
Oro Valley AZ, 29700 ... 55 D3
Oroville CA, 13004 ... 36 C1
Oroville WA, 1653 ... 13 E1
Orrick MO, 889 ... 96 C2
Orrington ME, 325 ... 83 D1
Orrs Island ME, 550 ... 82 B3
Orrville OH, 8551 ... 91 E3
Orting WA, 3760 ... 12 C3
Ortonville MI, 1535 ... 76 B3
Ortonville MN, 2158 ... 27 F2
Orwell OH, 1519 ... 91 F2
Orwigsburg PA, 3106 ... 146 A1
Osage IA, 3451 ... 73 D3
Osage WY, 215 ... 25 F4
Osage Beach MO, 3662 ... 97 D4
Osage City KS, 3034 ... 96 A3
Osage Co. KS, 16712 ... 96 A3
Osage Co. MO, 13062 ... 97 F4
Osage Co. OK, 44437 ... 51 F1
Osakis MN, 1567 ... 66 B2
Osawatomie KS, 4645 ... 96 B3
Osborne KS, 1607 ... 43 D2
Osborne PA, 566 ... 250 A1
Osborne Co. KS, 4452 ... 43 D2
Osburn ID, 1545 ... 14 B3
Oscawana Corners NY, 1500 ... 148 B2
Osceola AR, 8875 ... 108 B4
Osceola IN, 1859 ... 89 F2
Osceola IA, 4659 ... 86 C3
Osceola MO, 835 ... 96 C4
Osceola NE, 921 ... 35 E3
Osceola WI, 2421 ... 67 D3
Osceola Co. FL, 172493 ... 141 D2
Osceola Co. IA, 7003 ... 72 A2
Osceola Co. MI, 23197 ... 75 F1
Osceola Mills PA, 1249 ... 92 C3
Oscoda MI, 992 ... 76 C1
Oscoda Co. MI, 9418 ... 70 C4
Osgood IN, 1624 ... 100 A2
Oshkosh NE, 887 ... 34 A3
Oshkosh WI, 62916 ... 74 C1
Oskaloosa IA, 10938 ... 87 D2
Oskaloosa KS, 1165 ... 96 A2
Oslo FL, 1900 ... 141 E3
Osmond NE, 796 ... 35 E2
Osprey FL, 4143 ... 140 B4
Osseo MN, 2434 ... 235 A1
Osseo WI, 1669 ... 67 F4
Ossian IN, 2943 ... 90 A3
Ossian IA, 853 ... 73 E3
Ossineke MI, 1059 ... 71 D4
Ossining NY, 24010 ... 148 B2

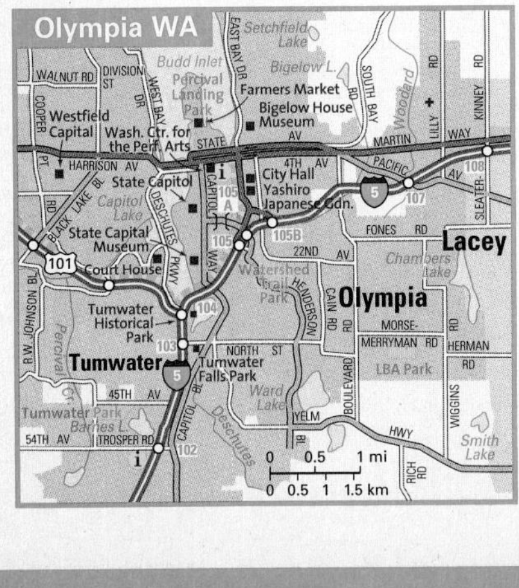
Olympia WA
Budd Inlet
Percival Landing Park
Farmers Market
Bigelow House Museum
Westfield Capital
Wash. Ctr. for the Perf. Arts
State Capitol
Capitol Lake
City Hall
Yashiro Japanese Gdn.
State Capital Museum
Court House
Tumwater Historical Park
Tumwater
Tumwater Falls Park
Olympia
Lacey
Chambers Lake
Ward Lake
LBA Park
Smith Lake
0 0.5 1 mi
0 0.5 1 1.5 km

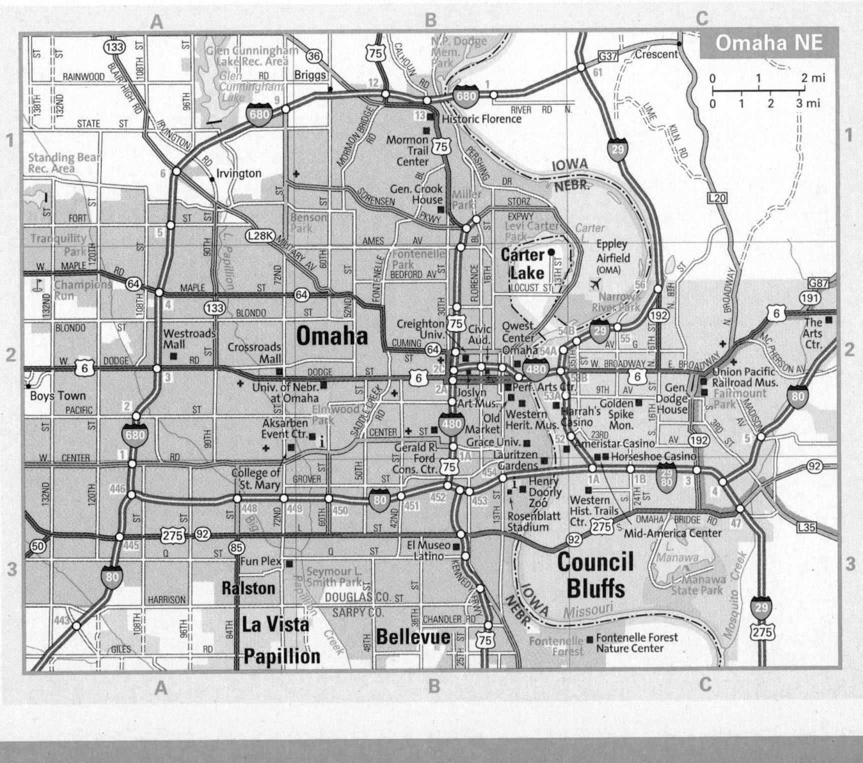
Omaha NE
Glen Cunningham Lake Rec. Area
N.P. Dodge Mem. Park
Crescent
Briggs
Historic Florence
Mormon Trail Center
Irvington
Standing Bear Rec. Area
Gen. Crook House
Miller Park
Benson Park
Tranquility Park
Fontenelle Park
Carter Lake
Eppley Airfield (OMA)
Champions Run
Westroads Mall
Crossroads Mall
Omaha
Creighton Univ.
Civic Aud.
Qwest Center Omaha
Boys Town
Univ. of Nebr. at Omaha
Joslyn Art Mus.
Perf. Arts Ctr.
Old Market
Western Herit. Mus.
Harrah's Casino
Golden Spike Mon.
Ameristar Casino
Horseshoe Casino
Gen. Dodge House
Union Pacific Railroad Mus.
Fairmount Park
The Arts Ctr.
Aksarben Event Ctr.
Elmwood Park
Gerald R. Ford Cons. Ctr.
Lauritzen Gardens
Henry Doorly Zoo
Rosenblatt Stadium
College of St. Mary
Western Hist. Trails Ctr.
Mid-America Center
Lake Manawa State Park
Council Bluffs
Fun Plex
Seymour L. Smith Park
Ralston
La Vista
Papillion
Bellevue
El Museo Latino
Fontenelle Forest Nature Center
IOWA
NEBR.
Missouri
0 1 2 mi
0 1 2 3 mi

Bellevue ... B3
Boys Town ... A2
Briggs ... B1
Carter Lake ... B2
Council Bluffs ... C3
Crescent ... C1
Irvington ... A1
La Vista ... A3
Omaha ... B2
Papillion ... A3
Ralston ... A3

Figures after entries indicate population, page number, and grid reference.

Orlando FL

Entries in **bold black** indicate counties or parishes.
Entries in **bold color** indicate cities with detailed inset maps.

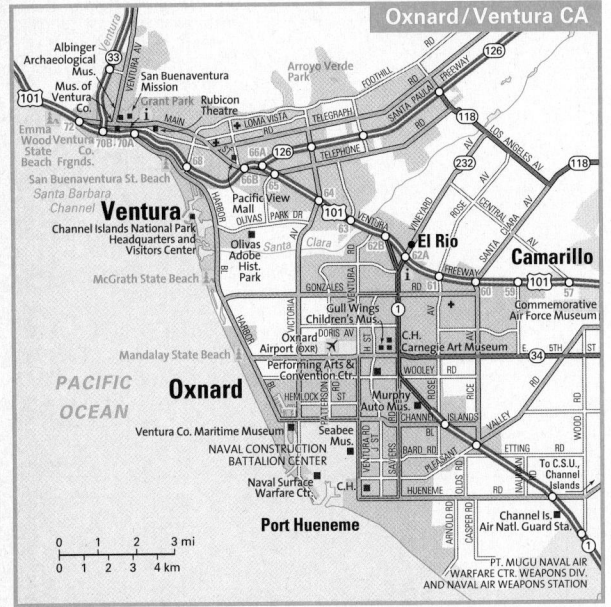

Oxnard/Ventura CA

Palm Springs CA

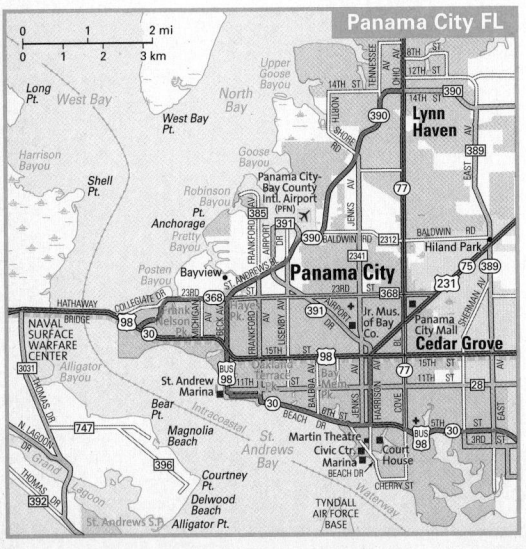

Panama City FL

Pensacola FL

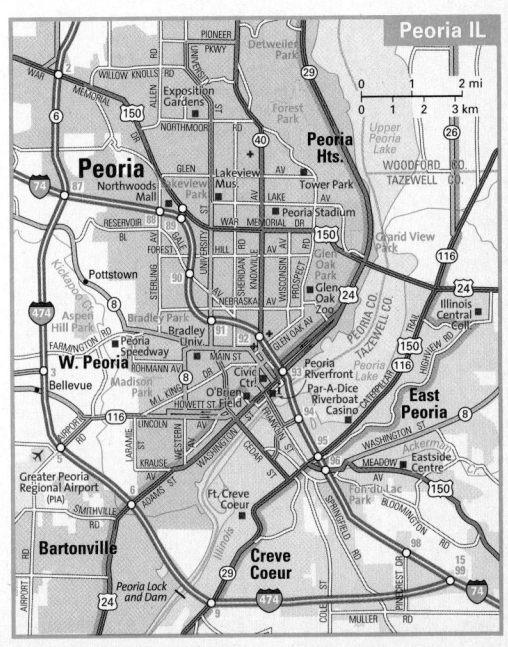

Peoria IL

Figures after entries indicate population, page number, and grid reference.

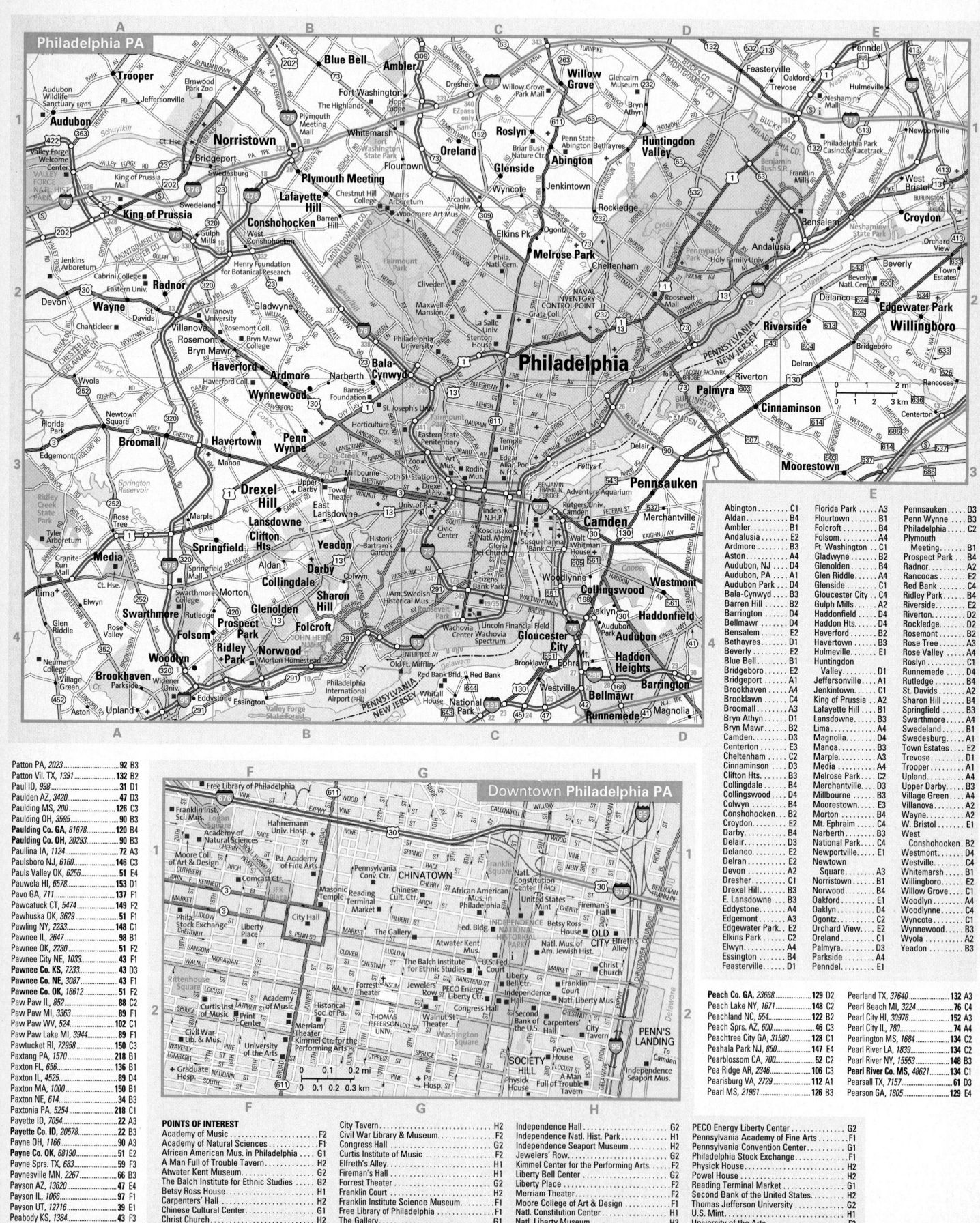

Philadelphia PA

Downtown Philadelphia PA

POINTS OF INTEREST

Academy of Music F2
Academy of Natural Sciences F1
African American Mus. in Philadelphia G1
A Man Full of Trouble Tavern H2
Atwater Kent Museum G2
The Balch Institute for Ethnic Studies G2
Betsy Ross House H1
Carpenters' Hall H2
Chinese Cultural Center G1
Christ Church H2
City Hall F1

City Tavern H2
Civil War Library & Museum F2
Congress Hall G2
Curtis Institute of Music F2
Elfreth's Alley H1
Fireman's Hall H1
Forrest Theater F2
Franklin Court H2
Franklin Institute Science Museum F1
Free Library of Philadelphia F1
The Gallery G2
Historical Society of Pennsylvania F2

Independence Hall G2
Independence Natl. Hist. Park H1
Independence Seaport Museum H2
Jewelers' Row G2
Kimmel Center for the Performing Arts F2
Liberty Bell Center G2
Liberty Place F2
Merriam Theater F2
Moore College of Art & Design F1
Natl. Constitution Center H1
Natl. Liberty Museum H2
Natl. Mus. of American Jewish History H2

PECO Energy Liberty Center G2
Pennsylvania Academy of Fine Arts F1
Pennsylvania Convention Center G1
Philadelphia Stock Exchange F1
Physick House H2
Powel House H2
Reading Terminal Market G1
Second Bank of the United States H2
Thomas Jefferson University G2
U.S. Mint H1
University of the Arts F2
Walnut Street Theater G2

Entries in **bold black** indicate counties or parishes.
Entries in **bold color** indicate cities with detailed inset maps.

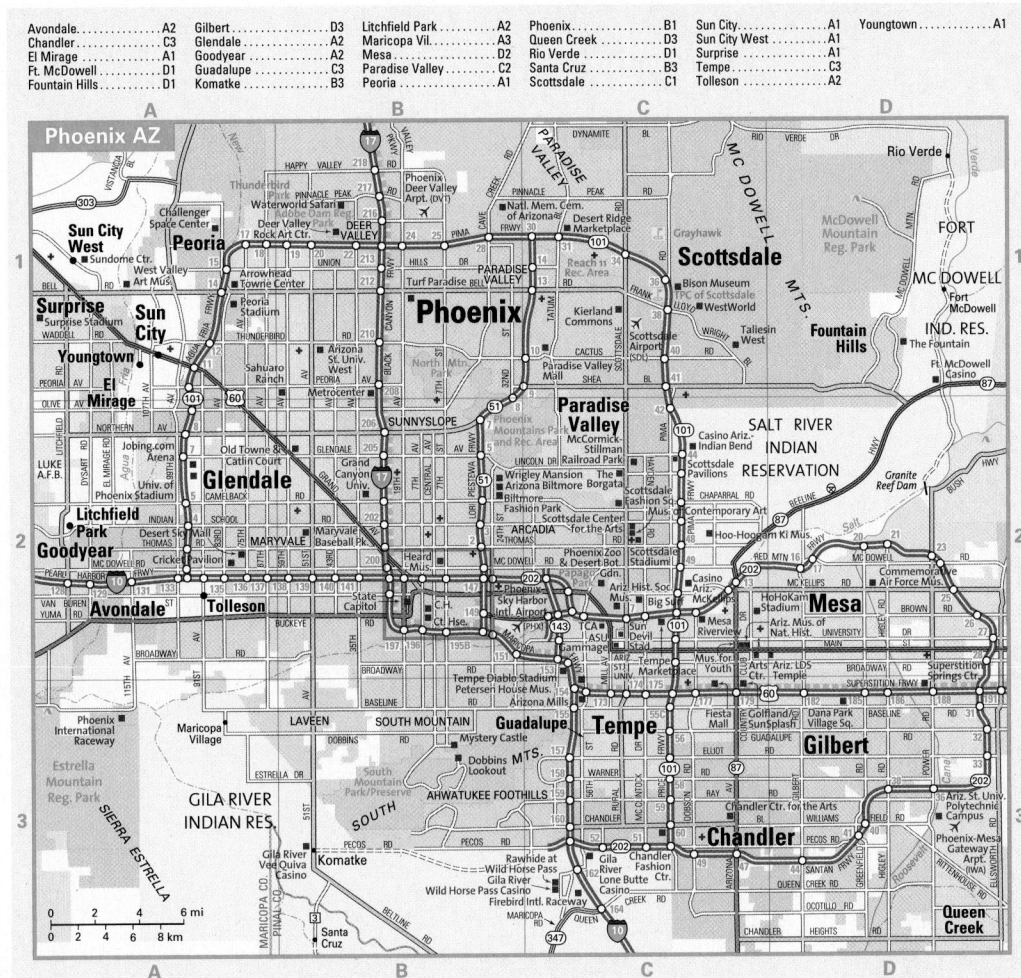

Phoenix AZ

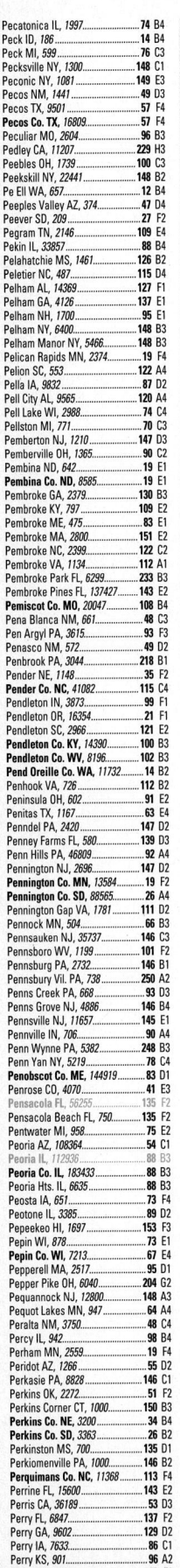

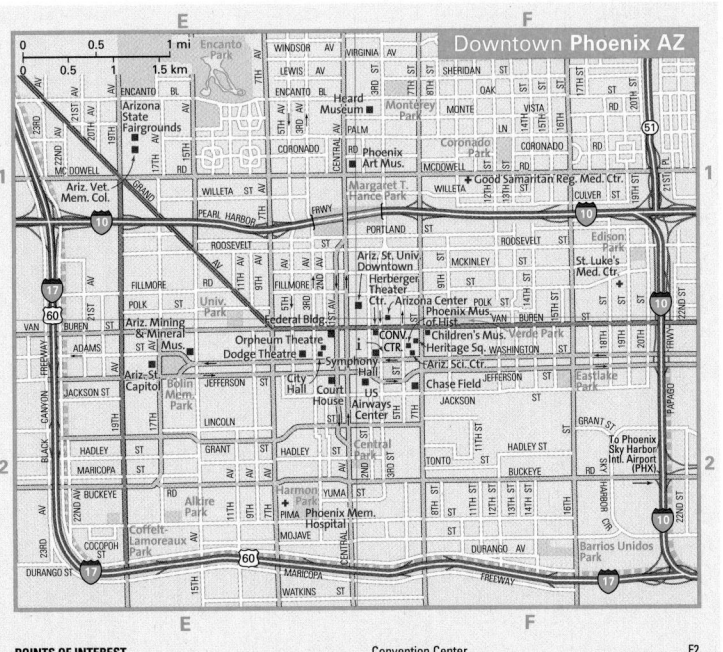

Downtown Phoenix AZ

POINTS OF INTEREST

Arizona Center......F1
Arizona Mining & Mineral Museum......E2
Arizona Science Center......F2
Arizona State Capitol......E2
Arizona State Fairgrounds......E1
Arizona Veterans Memorial Coliseum......E1
Chase Field......F2
Children's Museum......E2
City Hall......E2
Convention Center......F2
Dodge Theatre......F1
Heard Museum......F1
Herberger Theater Center......F1
Heritage Square......F2
Orpheum Theatre......E1
Phoenix Art Museum......F1
Phoenix Museum of History......F2
Symphony Hall......F2
US Airways Center......F2

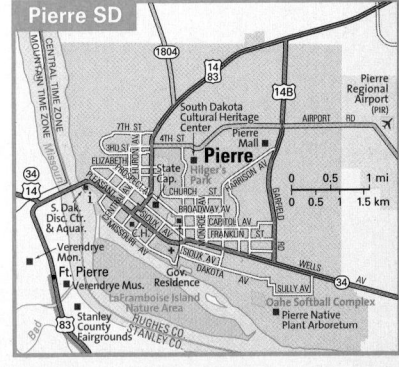

Pierre SD

Figures after entries indicate population, page number, and grid reference.

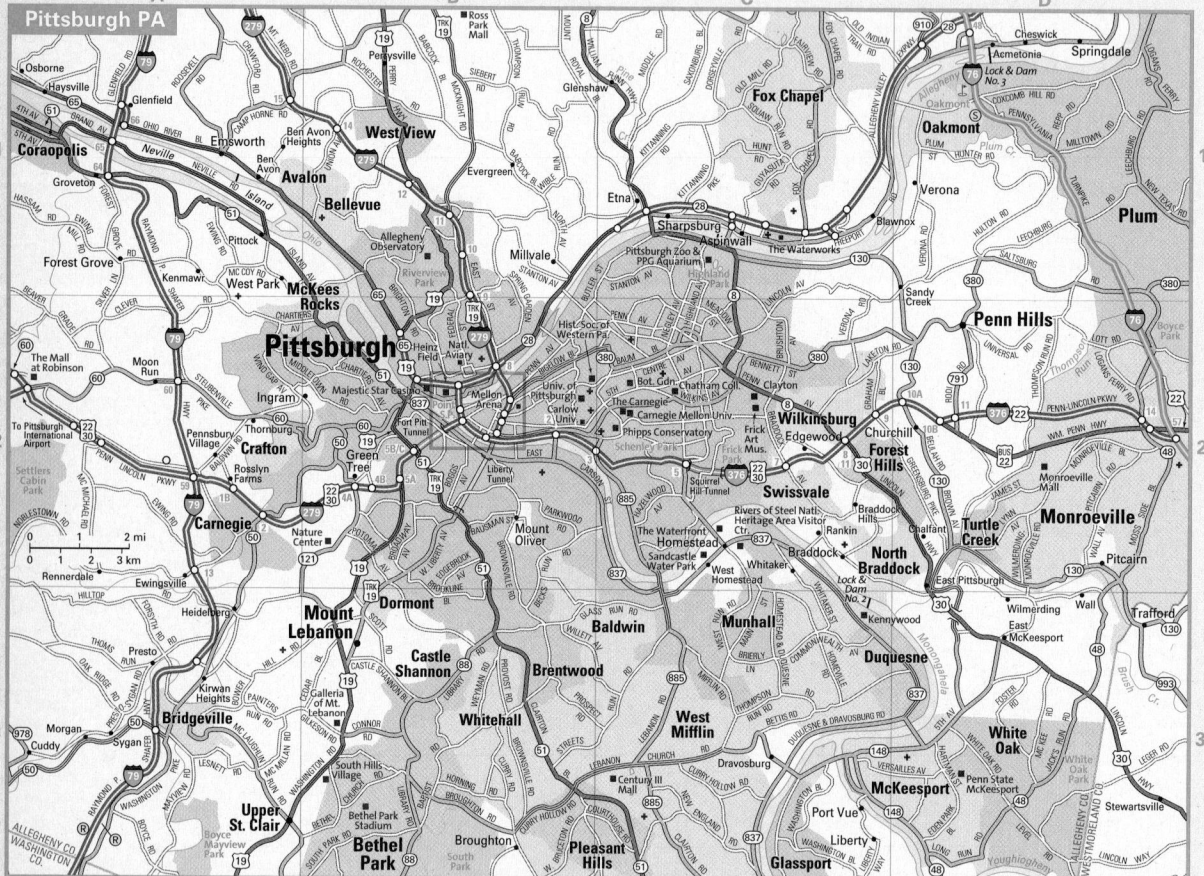

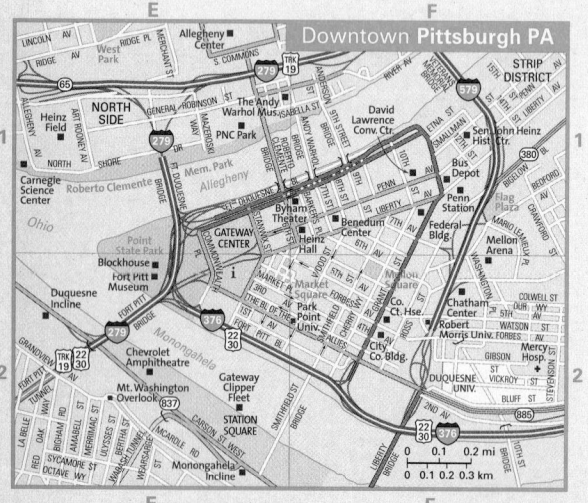

POINTS OF INTEREST

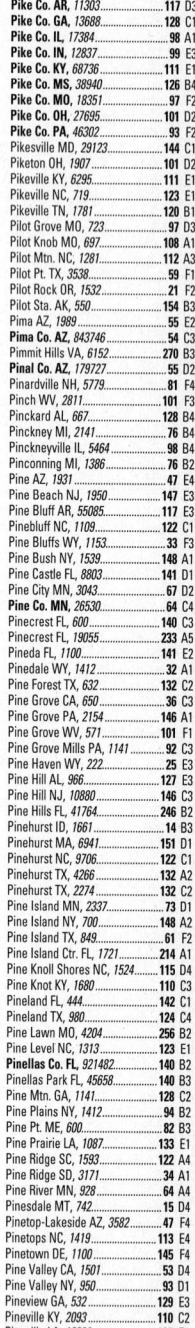

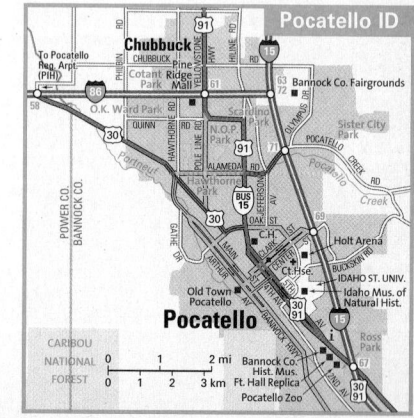

Entries in **bold black** indicate counties or parishes.
Entries in **bold color** indicate cities with detailed inset maps.

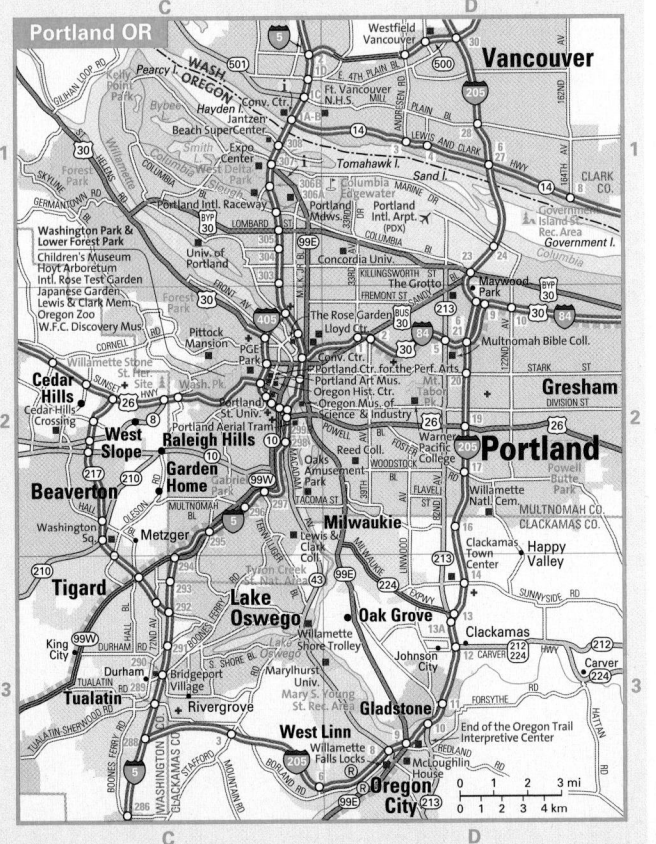

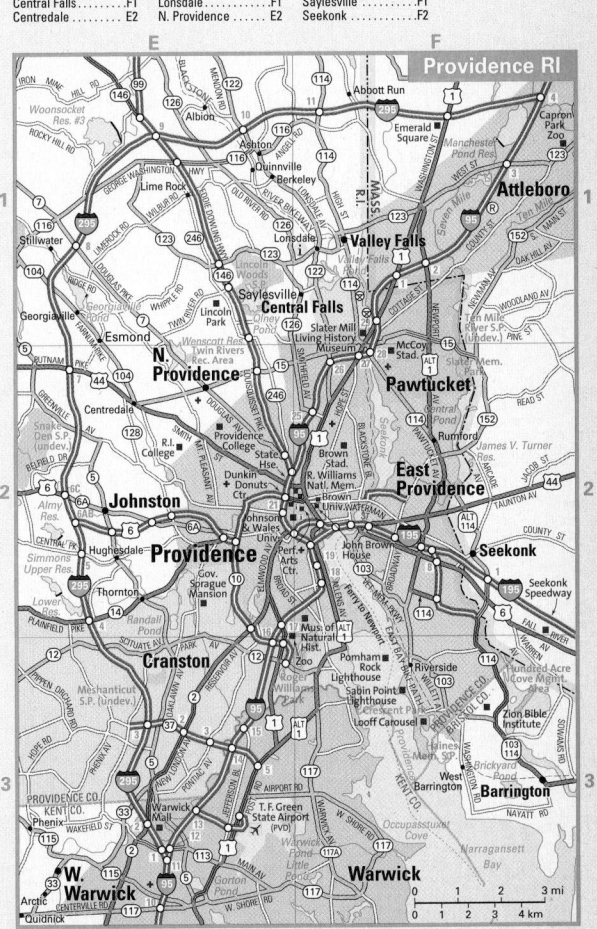

252
Point Pleasant – Quincy

Figures after entries indicate population, page number, and grid reference.

Pt. Pleasant NJ, *19306* 147 E2
Pt. Pleasant WV, *4637* 101 E3
Pt. Pleasant Beach NJ, *5314* 147 E2
Pt. Reyes Sta. CA, *818* 36 B3
Poipu HI, *1075* 152 B1
Pojoaque NM, *1261* 49 D2
Polacca AZ, *1100* 47 F2
Poland OH, *2866* 276 C3
Polk PA, *1031* 92 A2
Polk City FL, *1516* 140 C2
Polk City IA, *2344* 86 C1
Polk Co. AR, *20229* 116 C3
Polk Co. FL, *483924* 140 C3
Polk Co. GA, *38127* 120 B4
Polk Co. IA, *374601* 86 C1
Polk Co. MN, *31369* 19 F2
Polk Co. MO, *26992* 107 D1
Polk Co. NE, *5639* 35 E3
Polk Co. NC, *18324* 121 F1
Polk Co. OR, *62380* 20 B2
Polk Co. TN, *16050* 120 C1
Polk Co. TX, *41133* 132 B1
Polk Co. WI, *41319* 67 E3
Polkton NC, *1195* 122 B2
Polkville NC, *535* 121 F1
Pollock SD, *339* 26 C1
Pollock Pines CA, *4728* 36 C2
Polo IL, *2477* 88 B1
Polo MO, *582* 96 C1
Polson MT, *4041* 15 D3
Pomeroy IA, *710* 72 B4
Pomeroy OH, *1966* 101 E2
Pomeroy WA, *1517* 13 F4
Pomona CA, *149473* 52 C2
Pomona KS, *923* 96 A3
Pomona NJ, *4019* 105 D3
Pomona NY, *2726* 148 B2
Pomona Park FL, *789* 139 D4
Pomonkey MD, *750* 144 B4
Pompano Beach FL, *78191* 143 F1
Pompton Lakes NJ, *10640* 148 A3
Pompton Plains NJ, *6500* 148 A3
Ponca NE, *1062* 35 F1
Ponca City OK, *25919* 51 E1
Ponce de Leon FL, *457* 136 C1
Ponce Inlet FL, *2513* 139 E4
Poncha Sprs. CO, *466* 41 D3
Ponchatoula LA, *5180* 134 B2
Pond Creek OK, *896* 51 E1
Pondera Co. MT, *6424* 15 E2
Ponderay ID, *638* 14 B2
Ponderosa NM, *310* 48 C2
Ponemah MN, *874* 64 A2
Ponte Vedra Beach FL, *1100* 139 D2
Pontiac IL, *11864* 88 C3
Pontiac MI, *66337* 76 C4
Pontoon Beach IL, *5620* 256 D1
Pontotoc MS, *5253* 118 C3
Pontotoc Co. MS, *26726* 118 C3
Pontotoc Co. OK, *35143* 51 F4
Pooler GA, *6239* 130 B3
Poolesville MD, *5151* 144 A2
Pope Co. AR, *54469* 117 D1
Pope Co. IL, *4413* 109 D1
Pope Co. MN, *11236* 66 A3
Poplar CA, *1496* 45 D3
Poplar MT, *971* 17 E2
Poplar WI, *552* 64 C4
Poplar Bluff MO, *16651* 108 A2
Poplar Grove IL, *1368* 74 B4
Poplar Hills KY, *396* 230 E3
Poplarville MS, *2601* 134 C1
Poquetanuck CT, *1100* 149 F1
Poquonock CT, *2200* 150 A3
Poquonock Bridge CT, *1592* 149 F2
Poquoson VA, *11566* 113 F2
Poquott NY, *975* 149 D3
Porcupine SD, *407* 26 B4
Portage IN, *33496* 89 E2
Portage MI, *44897* 89 F1
Portage PA, *2837* 92 B4
Portage WI, *9728* 74 B2
Portage Co. OH, *152061* 91 E3
Portage Co. WI, *67182* 74 B1
Portage Lakes OH, *9870* 188 A2
Portageville MO, *3295* 108 B3
Portal GA, *597* 129 F2
Portales NM, *11131* 49 F4
Port Allegany PA, *2355* 92 C1
Port Allen LA, *5278* 134 A2
Port Angeles WA, *18397* 12 B2
Port Aransas TX, *3370* 63 F2
Port Arthur TX, *57755* 132 C3
Port Austin MI, *737* 76 C1
Port Barre LA, *2287* 133 F2
Port Barrington IL, *788* 203 A1
Port Byron IL, *1535* 88 A2
Port Byron NY, *1297* 79 D3
Port Carbon PA, *2019* 93 E3
Port Charlotte FL, *46451* 140 C4
Port Chester NY, *27867* 148 C3
Port Clinton OH, *6391* 90 C2
Port Deposit MD, *676* 145 D1
Port Edwards WI, *1944* 74 A1
Porter IN, *4972* 89 E2
Porter OK, *574* 106 A4
Porter WA, *473* 12 B4
Porter Corners NY, *800* 80 C4
Porter Co. IN, *146798* 89 E2
Porterdale GA, *1281* 121 D4
Porter Hts. TX, *1490* 132 A2
Porterville CA, *39615* 45 D3
Port Ewen NY, *3650* 94 B2
Port Gibson MS, *1840* 126 A3
Port Hadlock WA, *3476* 12 C2
Port Henry NY, *1152* 81 D3
Port Hueneme CA, *21845* 52 B2
Port Huron MI, *32338* 77 D3
Portia AR, *483* 107 F4
Port Isabel TX, *4865* 63 F4
Port Jefferson NY, *7837* 149 D3
Port Jefferson Sta. NY, *7527* 149 D3
Port Jervis NY, *8860* 148 A2
Port La Belle FL, *3050* 141 D4
Portland AR, *552* 125 F1
Portland CT, *5534* 149 E1
Portland IN, *6437* 90 A4
Portland ME, *64249* 82 B3
Portland MI, *3789* 76 A3
Portland ND, *604* 19 E3
Portland OR, *529121* 20 C2
Portland PA, *579* 93 F3
Portland TN, *8458* 109 F3
Portland TX, *14827* 63 F2
Port Lavaca TX, *12035* 61 F4
Port Leyden NY, *665* 79 E2
Port Ludlow WA, *1968* 12 C2
Port Matilda PA, *638* 92 C3
Port Monmouth NJ, *3742* 147 E1
Port Neches TX, *13601* 132 C3
Port Norris NJ, *1507* 145 F2
Portola CA, *2227* 37 D1
Portola Valley CA, *4462* 259 C6
Port Orange FL, *45823* 139 E4
Port Orchard WA, *7693* 12 C3
Port Orford OR, *1153* 28 A1
Port Reading NJ, *3829* 240 A5
Port Republic NJ, *1037* 147 E4
Port Richey FL, *3021* 140 B2
Port Royal PA, *977* 93 D4
Port Royal SC, *3950* 130 C2
Port St. Joe FL, *3644* 137 D3
Port St. John FL, *12112* 141 E1
Port St. Lucie FL, *88769* 141 E4
Port Salerno FL, *10141* 141 E4
Port Sanilac MI, *658* 76 C2
Portsmouth NH, *20784* 82 A4
Portsmouth OH, *20909* 101 D3
Portsmouth RI, *2700* 151 D4
Portsmouth VA, *100565* 113 F2
Port Sulphur LA, *3115* 134 C4
Port Townsend WA, *8334* 12 C2
Portville NY, *1024* 92 C1
Port Vincent LA, *463* 134 A2
Port Vue PA, *4228* 250 C3
Port Washington NY, *15215* 148 C3
Port Washington WI, *10467* 75 D2
Port Washington North NY, *2700* 241 G2
Port Wentworth GA, *3276* 130 B3
Porum OK, *725* 116 A1
Posen IL, *4730* 203 D6
Posey Co. IN, *27061* 99 D4
Poseyville IN, *1187* 99 D4
Post TX, *3708* 58 B2
Post Falls ID, *17247* 14 B3
Poston AZ, *389* 53 F2
Postville IA, *2273* 73 E3
Poteau OK, *7939* 116 B2
Poteet TX, *3305* 61 D3
Poth TX, *1850* 61 D3
Potlatch ID, *791* 14 B4
Potomac IL, *681* 89 D4
Potomac MD, *44822* 144 B3
Potomac Hts. MD, *1154* 144 B4
Potosi MO, *2662* 98 A4
Potosi TX, *1664* 58 C3
Potosi WI, *711* 73 F4
Potsdam NY, *9425* 80 B1
Pottawatomie Co. KS, *18209* 43 F2
Pottawatomie Co. OK, *65521* 51 F3
Pottawattamie Co. IA, *87704* 86 A2
Potter Co. PA, *18080* 92 C2
Potter Co. SD, *2693* 27 D2
Potter Co. TX, *113546* 50 A3
Pottersville NY, *750* 80 C3
Potter Valley CA, *650* 36 A2
Potterville MI, *2168* 76 A4
Pottsboro TX, *1579* 59 F1
Potts Camp MS, *494* 118 C2
Pottstown PA, *21859* 146 B2
Pottsville AR, *1271* 117 D1
Pottsville PA, *15549* 93 E3
Potwin KS, *457* 43 F3
Poughkeepsie NY, *29871* 148 B1
Poughquag NY, *900* 148 C1
Poulan GA, *946* 129 D4
Poulsbo WA, *6813* 12 C3
Poultney VT, *1575* 81 D4
Pound VA, *1089* 111 E2
Pound Ridge NY, *800* 148 C2
Poway CA, *48044* 53 D4
Powderly KY, *846* 109 E2
Powder River Co. MT, *1858* 25 E2
Powder Sprs. GA, *12481* 120 C4
Powell AL, *926* 120 A2
Powell OH, *6247* 90 C4
Powell TN, *7500* 110 C4
Powell WY, *5373* 24 B3
Powell Co. KY, *13237* 100 C4
Powell Co. MT, *7180* 15 D3
Powells Crossroads TN, *1286* 120 B1
Powellton WV, *1796* 101 F4
Power Co. ID, *7538* 31 E1
Powers OR, *734* 28 A1
Powers Lake ND, *309* 18 A2
Powers Lake WI, *1500* 74 C4
Poweshiek Co. IA, *18815* 87 D1
Powhatan VA, *550* 113 D1
Powhatan Co. VA, *22377* 113 E1
Powhatan Pt. OH, *1744* 101 F1
Pownal VT, *700* 94 C1
Poydras LA, *3886* 134 C3
Poynette WI, *2266* 74 B2
Prague OK, *2138* 51 F3
Prairie City IA, *1365* 87 D2
Prairie City OR, *1080* 21 F3
Prairie Co. AR, *9539* 117 F2
Prairie Co. MT, *1199* 17 E4
Prairie Creek AR, *1849* 106 C3
Prairie du Chien WI, *6018* 73 F3
Prairie du Rocher IL, *613* 98 A4
Prairie du Sac WI, *3231* 74 A3
Prairie Grove AR, *2540* 106 C4
Prairie Grove IL, *960* 203 A1
Prairie View TX, *4410* 61 F2
Prairie Vil. KS, *22072* 224 B4
Prairieville LA, *950* 134 A2
Pratt KS, *6570* 43 D4
Pratt WV, *551* 101 F4
Pratt Co. KS, *9647* 43 D4
Prattsburgh NY, *650* 78 C4
Prattville AL, *24303* 128 A2
Preble Co. OH, *42337* 100 B1
Premont TX, *2772* 63 E2
Prentice WI, *626* 68 A3
Prentiss MS, *1158* 126 B4
Prentiss Co. MS, *25556* 119 D2
Prescott AZ, *33938* 47 D4
Prescott AR, *3686* 117 D4
Prescott WI, *3764* 67 D4
Prescott Valley AZ, *23535* 47 D4
Presho SD, *588* 26 C4
Presidential Lakes Estates NJ, *2332* 147 D3
Presidio TX, *4167* 62 B4
Presidio Co. TX, *7304* 62 B3
Presque Isle ME, *9511* 85 D2
Presque Isle Co. MI, *14411* 70 C3
Preston GA, *453* 128 C3
Preston ID, *4682* 31 E2
Preston IA, *949* 88 A1
Preston MD, *566* 145 E4
Preston MN, *1426* 73 E2
Preston Co. WV, *29334* 102 B2
Prestonsburg KY, *3612* 111 E1
Pretty Prairie KS, *615* 43 E4
Price UT, *8402* 39 F1
Price Co. WI, *15822* 68 A2
Priceville AL, *1631* 119 F3
Prichard AL, *28633* 135 E1
Priest River ID, *1754* 14 B2
Primghar IA, *891* 72 A3
Prince Edward Co. VA, *19720* 113 D2
Prince Frederick MD, *1432* 144 C4
Prince George VA, *750* 113 E2
Prince George Co. VA, *33047* 113 E2
Prince George's Co. MD, *801515* 144 C3
Princes Lakes IN, *1506* 99 F2
Princess Anne MD, *2313* 103 F4
Princeton FL, *10090* 143 E3
Princeton IL, *7501* 88 B2
Princeton IN, *8175* 99 D4
Princeton IA, *946* 88 A2
Princeton KY, *6536* 109 D2
Princeton MN, *3933* 66 C3
Princeton MO, *1047* 86 C4
Princeton NJ, *14203* 147 D2
Princeton NC, *1066* 123 E1
Princeton TX, *3477* 59 F2
Princeton WV, *6347* 111 F1
Princeton WI, *1504* 74 B2
Princeton Jct. NJ, *2382* 147 D2
Princeville HI, *1698* 152 B1
Princeville IL, *1621* 88 B3
Princeville NC, *940* 113 E4
Prince William Co. VA, *280813* 144 A4
Prineville OR, *7356* 21 D3
Pringle PA, *991* 261 B1
Prior Lake MN, *15917* 67 D4
Proctor MN, *2852* 64 C4
Proctor VT, *1700* 81 D3
Proctorville OH, *620* 101 E3
Progreso TX, *4851* 63 E4
Progress PA, *9647* 218 B1
Progress Vil. FL, *2482* 266 C2
Prophetstown IL, *2023* 88 A2
Prospect CT, *2200* 149 D1
Prospect KY, *4657* 100 A4
Prospect OH, *1191* 90 C4
Prospect PA, *1234* 92 A3
Prospect Hts. IL, *17081* 203 C2
Prospect Park PA, *6594* 248 B4
Prosper TX, *2097* 59 F2
Prosperity SC, *1047* 122 A3
Prosser WA, *4838* 21 E1
Protection KS, *558* 43 D4
Provencal LA, *708* 125 D4
Providence FL, *1100* 140 C2
Providence KY, *3611* 109 D1
Providence RI, *173618* 150 C3
Providence UT, *4377* 31 E3
Providence Co. RI, *621602* 150 C3
Provincetown MA, *3192* 151 F2
Provo UT, *105166* 31 F4
Prowers Co. CO, *14483* 42 A3
Prudenville MI, *1737* 76 A1
Prue OK, *433* 51 F2
Prunedale CA, *16432* 44 B2
Pruntytown WV, *600* 102 A2
Pryor MT, *628* 24 C2
Pryor OK, *8659* 106 A3
Pueblo CO, *102121* 41 E3
Pueblo Co. CO, *141472* 41 E3
Pueblo Pintado NM, *247* 48 B2
Pueblo West CO, *16899* 41 E3
Puhi HI, *1186* 152 B1
Pukalani HI, *7380* 153 D1
Pukwana SD, *287* 27 D4
Pulaski NY, *2398* 79 D2
Pulaski TN, *7871* 119 F1
Pulaski VA, *9473* 112 A2
Pulaski WI, *3060* 68 C4
Pulaski Co. AR, *361474* 117 E2
Pulaski Co. GA, *9588* 129 E3
Pulaski Co. IL, *7348* 108 C2
Pulaski Co. IN, *13755* 89 E3
Pulaski Co. KY, *56217* 110 B2
Pulaski Co. MO, *41165* 97 E4
Pulaski Co. VA, *35127* 112 A2
Pullman MI, *700* 75 E4
Pullman WA, *24675* 14 B4
Pumphrey MD, *5317* 193 C4
Pumpkin Ctr. CA, *700* 45 D4
Pumpkin Ctr. NC, *2228* 115 D4
Punaluu HI, *881* 152 A2
Punta Gorda FL, *14344* 140 C4
Punta Rassa FL, *1731* 142 C1
Punxsutawney PA, *6271* 92 B3
Pupukea HI, *4250* 152 A2
Purcell OK, *5571* 51 E3
Purcellville VA, *3584* 144 A2
Purdy MO, *1103* 106 C2
Purdys NY, *1200* 148 C2
Purvis MS, *2164* 134 C1
Puryear TN, *667* 109 D3
Pushmataha Co. OK, *11667* 116 A3
Putnam CT, *6746* 150 B3
Putnam Co. FL, *70423* 139 D3
Putnam Co. GA, *18812* 129 E1
Putnam Co. IL, *6086* 88 B2
Putnam Co. IN, *36019* 99 E1
Putnam Co. MO, *5223* 87 D4
Putnam Co. NY, *95745* 148 B2
Putnam Co. OH, *34726* 90 B3
Putnam Co. TN, *62315* 110 A3
Putnam Co. WV, *51589* 101 E3
Putnam Lake NY, *3855* 148 C1
Putney GA, *2998* 129 D4
Putney KY, *600* 111 D2
Putney VT, *800* 81 E4
Puxico MO, *1145* 108 B2
Puyallup WA, *33011* 12 C3
Pyatt AR, *253* 107 D3

Q

Quail Valley CA, *1639* 229 J5
Quaker City OH, *563* 101 F1
Quaker Hill CT, *4200* 149 F2
Quakertown PA, *8931* 146 C1
Quanah TX, *3022* 50 C4
Quantico VA, *561* 144 A4
Quapaw OK, *984* 106 B2
Quarryville CT, *2500* 150 A3
Quarryville PA, *1994* 146 A3
Quartz Hill CA, *9890* 52 C2
Quartzsite AZ, *3354* 54 A1
Quasqueton IA, *574* 73 E4
Quay Co. NM, *10155* 49 F3
Quechee VT, *550* 81 E3
Queen Anne's Co. MD, *40563* 145 D3
Queen City MO, *638* 87 D4
Queen City TX, *1613* 124 C1
Queen Creek AZ, *4316* 54 C2
Queens Co. NY, *2229379* 148 B4
Queenstown MD, *617* 145 D3
Quenemo KS, *468* 96 A3
Questa NM, *1864* 49 D1
Quidnessett RI, *3600* 150 C4
Quidnick RI, *6300* 150 C3
Quilcene WA, *591* 12 C3
Quimby IA, *368* 72 A4
Quinby SC, *842* 122 C3
Quince Orchard MD, *23044* 144 B2
Quincy CA, *1879* 36 C1
Quincy FL, *6982* 137 D2
Quincy IL, *40366* 97 F1
Quincy MA, *88025* 151 D1
Quincy MI, *1701* 90 A1
Quincy OH, *734* 90 B4

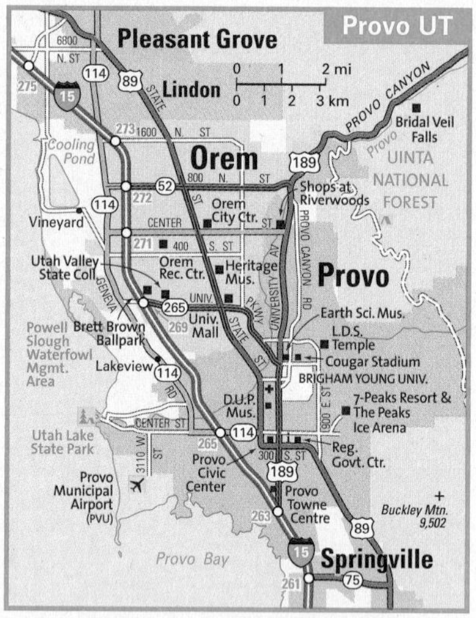
Provo UT
Pleasant Grove
Lindon
Orem
Provo
Springville
Vineyard
UINTA NATIONAL FOREST
PROVO CANYON
Bridal Veil Falls
Shops at Riverwoods
Orem City Ctr.
Orem Rec. Ctr.
Heritage Mus.
Utah Valley State Coll.
Univ. Mall
Earth Sci. Mus.
L.D.S. Temple
Cougar Stadium
BRIGHAM YOUNG UNIV.
Powell Slough Waterfowl Mgmt. Area
Brett Brown Ballpark
Lakeview
D.U.P. Mus.
7-Peaks Resort & The Peaks Ice Arena
Utah Lake State Park
Provo Civic Center
Reg. Govt. Ctr.
Provo Municipal Airport (PVU)
Provo Towne Centre
Buckley Mtn. 9,502
Provo Bay
Cooling Pond

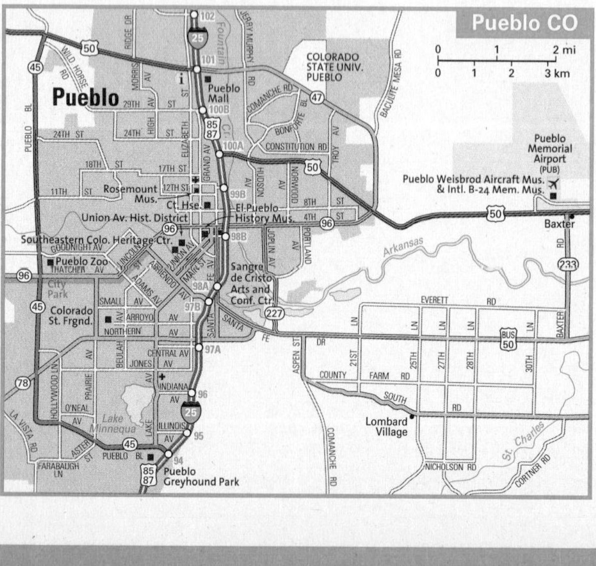
Pueblo CO
Pueblo
Fountain
COLORADO STATE UNIV. PUEBLO
Pueblo Mall
Pueblo Memorial Airport (PUB)
Pueblo Weisbrod Aircraft Mus. & Intl. B-24 Mem. Mus.
Rosemount Mus.
City Hall
Ct. Hse.
Union Av. Hist. District
El Pueblo History Mus.
Southeastern Colo. Heritage Ctr.
Pueblo Zoo
City Park
Sangre de Cristo Arts and Conf. Ctr.
Colorado St. Frgnd.
Arkansas
Lake Minnequa
Baxter
Lombard Village
Pueblo Greyhound Park
St. Charles

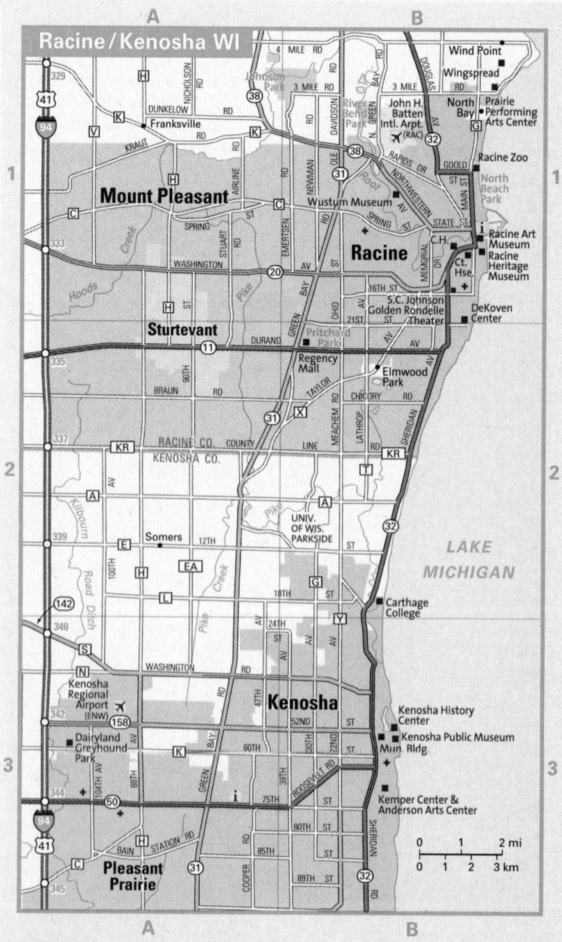
Racine / Kenosha WI
Wind Point
Wingspread
Franksville
John H. Batten Intl. Arpt. (RAC)
North Bay
Prairie Performing Arts Center
Racine Zoo
North Beach Park
Mount Pleasant
Wustum Museum
Racine
Racine Art Museum
Racine Heritage Museum
S.C. Johnson Golden Rondelle Theater
DeKoven Center
Sturtevant
Regency Mall
Elmwood Park
RACINE CO.
KENOSHA CO.
Somers
UNIV. OF WIS. PARKSIDE
LAKE MICHIGAN
Carthage College
Kenosha Regional Airport (ENW)
Dairyland Greyhound Park
Kenosha
Kenosha History Center
Kenosha Public Museum
Kemper Center & Anderson Arts Center
Pleasant Prairie

Elmwood Park B2
Franksville A1
Kenosha A3
Mount Pleasant A1
N. Bay B1
Pleasant Prairie A3
Racine B1
Sturtevant A2
Wind Pt. B1

Entries in **bold black** indicate counties or parishes.
Entries in **bold color** indicate cities with detailed inset maps.

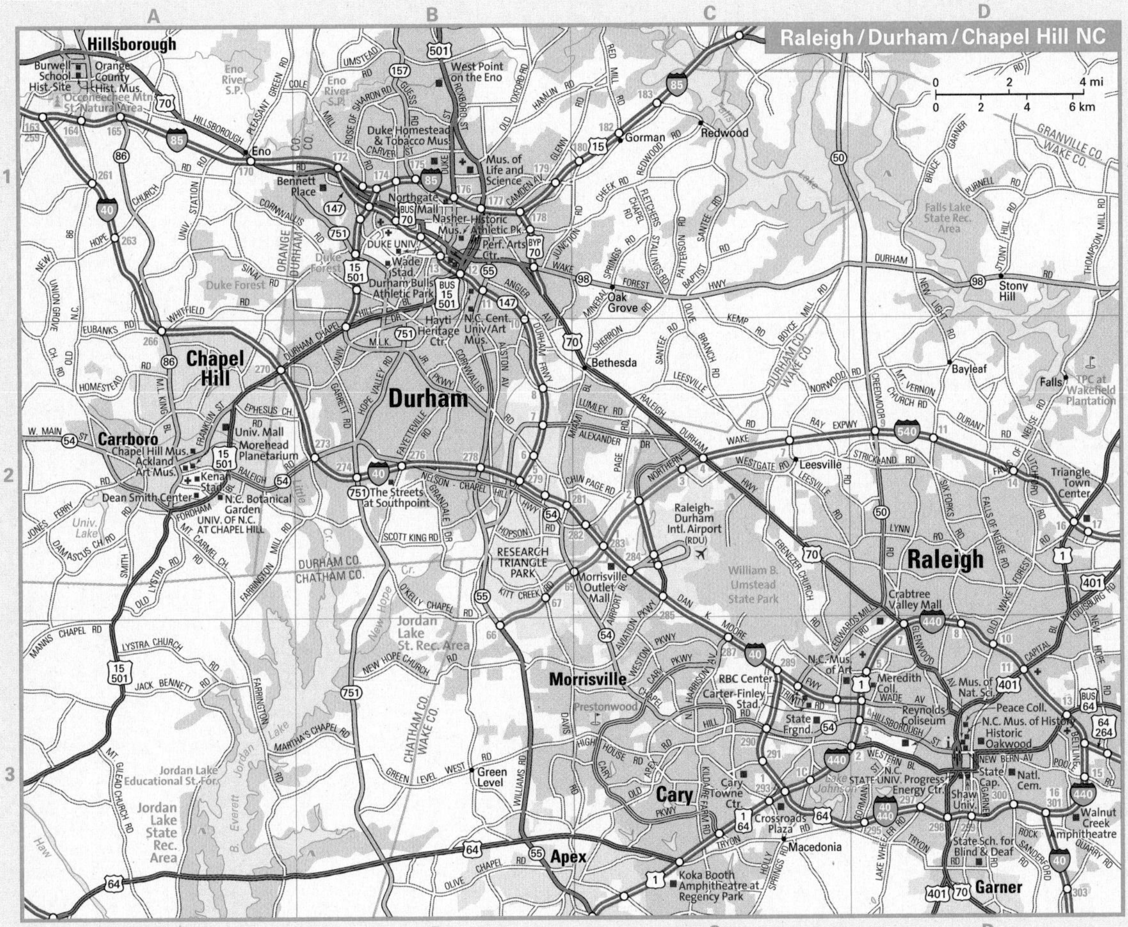
Raleigh/Durham/Chapel Hill NC
Hillsborough
Durham
Chapel Hill
Carrboro
Raleigh
Morrisville
Cary
Apex
Garner
Raleigh-Durham Intl. Airport (RDU)
Research Triangle Park
Jordan Lake St. Rec. Area
Falls Lake State Rec. Area
William B. Umstead State Park
Duke Forest
Eno
Gorman
Redwood
Bethesda
Leesville
Bayleaf
Stony Hill
Oak Grove
Green Level
Macedonia
Falls

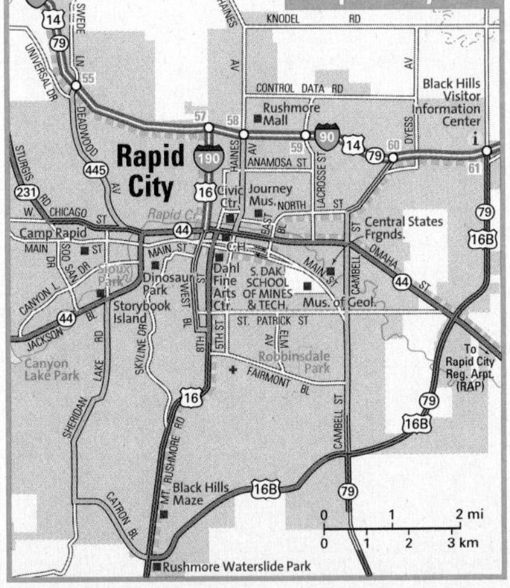
Rapid City SD
Rapid City
Rushmore Mall
Black Hills Visitor Information Center
Central States Frgnds.
Dinosaur Park
Storybook Island
Canyon Lake Park
Black Hills Maze
Rushmore Waterslide Park

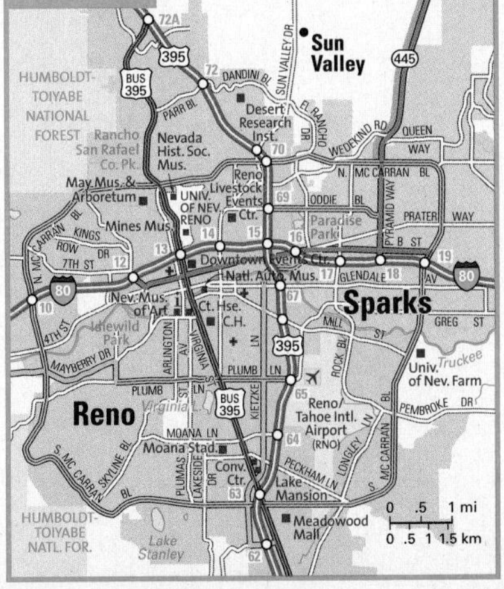
Reno NV
Sun Valley
Sparks
Reno
Humboldt-Toiyabe National Forest
Reno/Tahoe Intl. Airport (RNO)
Desert Research Inst.
Meadowood Mall

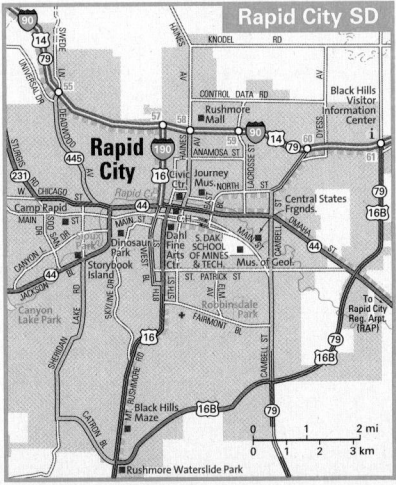

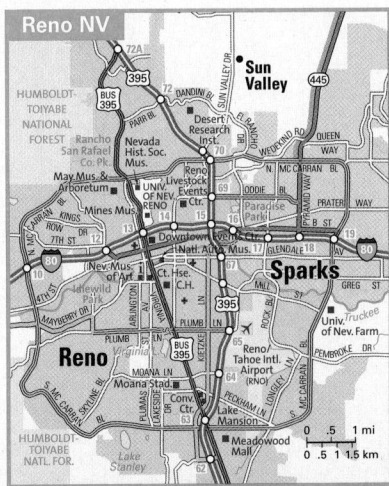

Figures after entries indicate population, page number, and grid reference.

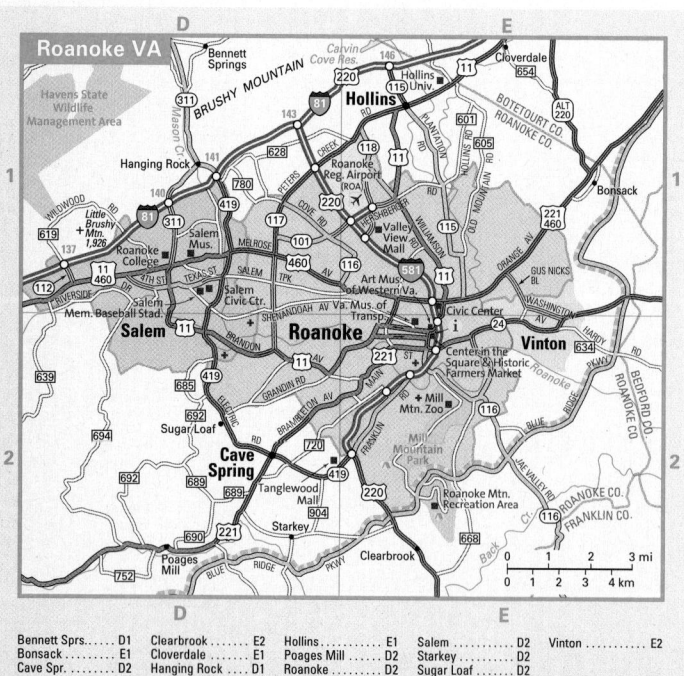

Richmond VA

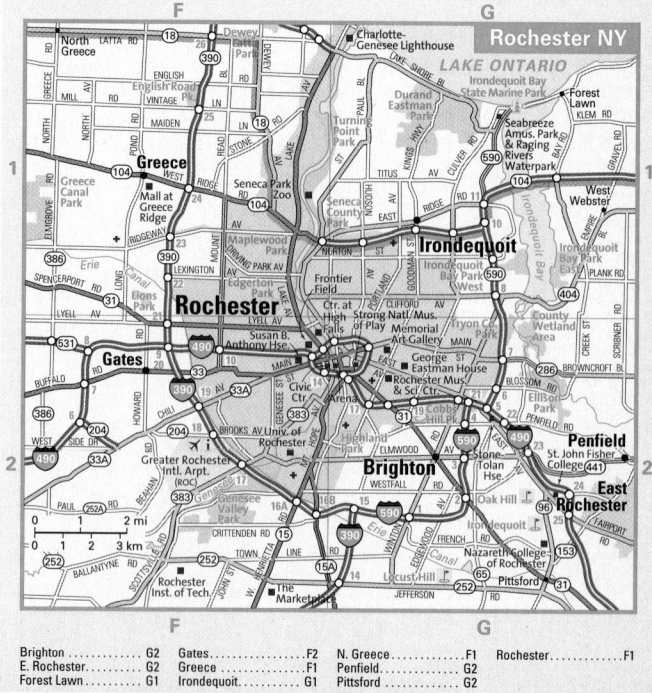

Roanoke VA

Rochester NY

255
River Edge–Rusk

Entries in **bold black** indicate counties or parishes.
Entries in **bold color** indicate cities with detailed inset maps.

River Edge NJ, 10946 240 C1
River Falls AL, 616 128 A4
River Falls WI, 12560 67 D4
River Forest IL, 11635 203 D4
River Grove IL, 10668 203 D4
Rivergrove OR, 324 251 C3
Riverhead NY, 10513 149 E3
River Hills WI, 1631 234 D1
River Oaks TX, 6985 207 A2
River Ridge LA, 14588 239 B1
River Rouge MI, 9917 210 C4
Riverside AL, 1564 120 A4
Riverside CA, 255166 53 D2
Riverside IL, 8895 203 D4
Riverside IA, 928 87 F2
Riverside MO, 2979 224 B2
Riverside NJ, 8000 147 D3
Riverside NY, 2875 149 E3
Riverside OH, 23545 100 C1
Riverside PA, 1861 93 E3
Riverside Co. CA, 1545387 53 E3
Riverton IL, 3048 98 B1
Riverton KS, 850 106 B2
Riverton NJ, 2759 146 C3
Riverton UT, 25011 31 E4
Riverton WY, 9310 32 B1
Riverview FL, 12035 140 C2
Riverview MO, 3146 256 C1
Riverwood KY, 469 230 E1
Riverwoods IL, 3843 203 C2
Rives Jct. MI, 650 76 A4
Rivesville WV, 913 102 A1
Riviera Beach FL, 29884 141 F4
Riviera Beach MD, 12695 144 C2
Roachdale IN, 975 99 E1
Roaming Shores OH, 1239 91 F2
Roane Co. TN, 51910 110 B4
Roane Co. WV, 15446 101 F3
Roan Mtn. TN, 1160 111 E3
Roanoke AL, 6563 128 B1
Roanoke IL, 1994 88 B3
Roanoke IN, 1495 90 A3
Roanoke TX, 2810 207 B1
Roanoke VA, 94911 112 B2
Roanoke Co. VA, 85778 112 B1
Roanoke Rapids NC, 16957 113 E3
Roaring Spr. PA, 2418 92 C4
Robards KY, 564 109 E1
Robbins IL, 6635 203 D6
Robbins NC, 1195 122 C1
Robbinsdale MN, 14123 235 B2
Robbinsville NJ, 1900 147 D2
Robbinsville NC, 747 121 D1
Robersonville NC, 1731 113 E4
Roberta GA, 808 129 D2
Robert Lee TX, 1171 58 B3
Roberts ID, 647 23 E4
Roberts WI, 969 67 E4
Roberts Co. SD, 10016 27 F1
Roberts Co. TX, 887 50 B2
Robertsdale AL, 3782 135 E2
Robertson Co. KY, 2266 100 C3
Robertson Co. TN, 54433 109 F3
Robertson Co. TX, 16000 61 F1
Robertsville NJ, 9800 147 E2
Robeson Co. NC, 123339 123 D2
Robesonia PA, 2036 146 A2
Robins IA, 1806 87 E1
Robinson IL, 6822 99 D2
Robinson TX, 7845 59 E4
Robstown TX, 12727 63 F2
Roby TX, 673 58 B2
Rochdale MA, 1400 150 B2
Rochelle GA, 1415 129 E3
Rochelle IL, 9424 88 B1
Rochelle Park NJ, 5528 240 C1
Rochester IL, 2893 98 B1
Rochester IN, 6414 89 F3
Rochester MN, 85806 73 D1
Rochester NH, 28461 81 F4
Rochester NY, 219773 78 C3
Rochester PA, 4014 91 F3
Rochester VT, 300 81 D3
Rochester WA, 1829 12 B4
Rochester WI, 1149 74 C4
Rochester Hills MI, 68825 76 C4
Rock MA, 850 151 D3
Rockaway NJ, 6473 148 A3
Rockaway Beach MO, 577 107 D3
Rockaway Beach OR, 1267 20 B1
Rockbridge Co. VA, 20808 102 B4
Rockcastle Co. KY, 16582 110 C2
Rock Co. MN, 9721 27 F4
Rock Co. NE, 1756 35 D2
Rock Co. WI, 152307 74 B4
Rock Creek MN, 1119 67 D2
Rock Creek OH, 584 91 F2
Rockdale MD, 16100 144 C2
Rockdale TX, 5439 61 E1
Rockdale Co. GA, 70111 120 C4
Rockfall CT, 1500 149 E1
Rock Falls IL, 9580 88 B1
Rockford AL, 428 128 A1
Rockford IL, 150115 74 B4
Rockford IA, 907 73 D3
Rockford MI, 4626 75 F3
Rockford MN, 3484 66 C3
Rockford OH, 1126 90 A3
Rockford TN, 798 110 C4
Rockford WA, 413 14 B3
Rock Hall MD, 1396 145 D2
Rock Hill MO, 4765 256 B2
Rock Hill NY, 1056 148 A1
Rock Hill SC, 49765 122 A2
Rockingham NC, 9672 122 C2
Rockingham Co. NH, 277359 81 F4
Rockingham Co. NC, 91928 112 B3
Rockingham Co. VA, 67725 102 C3
Rock Island IL, 39684 88 A2
Rock Island OK, 709 116 B1
Rock Island WA, 863 13 E3
Rock Island Co. IL, 149374 88 A2
Rockland ID, 316 31 E1
Rockland ME, 7609 82 C2
Rockland MA, 17670 151 D2
Rockland WI, 628 73 F1
Rockland Co. NY, 286753 148 B2
Rockledge AL, 600 120 A3
Rockledge FL, 20170 141 E2
Rockledge PA, 2577 248 D2
Rocklin CA, 36330 36 C2
Rockmart GA, 3870 120 B3
Rock Mills AL, 676 128 B1
Rock Pt. AZ, 724 47 F1
Rockport AR, 792 117 D3
Rockport IN, 2160 99 E4
Rockport KY, 334 109 E1
Rockport ME, 900 82 C2
Rockport MA, 5606 151 F1
Rock Port MO, 1395 86 A4
Rockport TX, 7385 61 E4
Rock Rapids IA, 2573 27 F4
Rock River WY, 235 33 D2
Rocksprings TX, 1285 60 B2
Rock Sprs. WY, 18708 32 B3
Rockton IL, 5296 74 B4
Rockvale CO, 426 41 E3
Rock Valley IA, 2702 35 F1
Rockville CT, 7708 150 A3
Rockville IN, 2765 99 E1
Rockville MD, 47388 144 B2
Rockville MN, 749 66 C3
Rockville RI, 425 150 C4
Rockwall TX, 17976 59 F2
Rockwall Co. TX, 43080 59 F2
Rockwell AR, 3024 117 D3
Rockwell IA, 989 73 D3
Rockwell NC, 1971 122 B1
Rockwell City IA, 2264 72 B4
Rockwood MI, 3442 90 C1
Rockwood PA, 954 102 B1
Rockwood TN, 5774 110 B4
Rocky Ford CO, 4286 41 F3
Rocky Hill CT, 17966 149 E1
Rocky Hill NJ, 662 147 D1
Rocky Mount NC, 55893 113 E4
Rocky Mount VA, 4066 112 B2
Rocky Pt. NY, 10185 149 D3
Rocky Ridge UT, 403 39 E1
Rocky Ripple IN, 712 221 B2
Rocky River OH, 20735 204 E2
Rodarte NM, 350 49 D2
Rodeo CA, 8717 259 C1
Roebuck SC, 1725 121 F2
Roeland Park KS, 6817 224 B3
Roessleville NY, 10800 188 D2
Roff OK, 734 51 F4
Roger Mills Co. OK, 3436 50 C2
Rogers AR, 38829 106 C3
Rogers MN, 3588 66 C3
Rogers TX, 1117 61 E1
Rogers City MI, 3322 71 D3
Rogers Co. OK, 70641 106 A3
Rogersville AL, 1199 119 E2
Rogersville MO, 1508 107 D2
Rogersville TN, 4240 111 D3
Rogue River OR, 1847 28 B2
Rohnert Park CA, 42236 36 B3
Roland IA, 1324 86 C1
Roland OK, 2842 116 B1
Rolesville NC, 907 113 D4
Rolette ND, 538 18 C1
Rolette Co. ND, 13674 18 C1
Rolfe IA, 675 72 B3
Rolla KS, 482 50 B1
Rolla MO, 16367 97 F4
Rolla ND, 1417 18 C1
Rolling Fields KY, 648 230 E1
Rolling Fork MS, 2486 126 A1
Rolling Hills CA, 1871 228 C4
Rolling Hills KY, 907 230 F1
Rolling Hills WY, 449 33 D1
Rolling Hills Estates CA, 7676 228 C4
Rolling Meadows IL, 24604 203 B3
Rolling Prairie IN, 800 89 E2
Rollingstone MN, 697 73 E1
Rollinsford NH, 1500 82 A4
Roma TX, 9617 63 D4
Romancoke MD, 800 145 D3
Roman Forest TX, 1279 132 B2
Rome GA, 34980 120 B3
Rome IL, 1776 88 B3
Rome NY, 34950 79 E3
Rome City IN, 1615 90 A2
Romeo CO, 375 41 D4
Romeo MI, 3721 76 C4
Romeoville IL, 21153 89 D2
Romney WV, 1940 102 C2
Romoland CA, 2764 229 K4
Romulus MI, 22979 90 C1
Ronan MT, 1812 15 D3
Ronceverte WV, 1557 112 A1
Ronkonkoma NY, 20029 149 D3
Roodhouse IL, 2214 98 A2
Rooks Co. KS, 5685 43 D2
Roosevelt NJ, 933 147 E2
Roosevelt UT, 4299 32 A4
Roosevelt Co. MT, 10620 17 E2
Roosevelt Co. NM, 18018 49 F4
Roosevelt Park MI, 3890 75 E3
Roper NC, 613 113 F4
Ropesville TX, 517 58 A1
Rosalia WA, 648 14 A3
Rosamond CA, 14349 52 C1
Rosaryville MD, 12322 144 C4
Rosburg WA, 40 12 B4
Roscoe IL, 6244 74 B4
Roscoe NY, 597 94 A2
Roscoe SD, 324 27 D2
Roscoe TX, 1378 58 B3
Roscommon MI, 1133 70 C4
Roscommon Co. MI, 25469 76 A1
Roseau MN, 2756 19 F1
Roseau Co. MN, 16338 19 F1
Roseboro NC, 1267 123 D2
Rose Bud AR, 429 117 E1
Rosebud SD, 1557 34 C1
Rosebud TX, 1493 59 F4
Rosebud Co. MT, 9383 17 D4
Roseburg OR, 20017 28 B1
Rose City MI, 721 76 B1
Rose City TX, 519 132 C2
Rosedale IN, 750 99 E1
Rosedale LA, 753 133 F2
Rosedale MD, 19199 144 C2
Rosedale MS, 2414 118 A4
Rosedale Beach DE, 750 145 F4
Rose Haven MD, 1400 144 C4
Rose Hill KS, 3432 43 F4
Rose Hill NC, 1330 123 E2
Rose Hill VA, 714 111 D3
Rose Hill VA, 15058 270 C5
Roseland FL, 1775 141 E3
Roseland LA, 1162 134 B1
Roseland NJ, 5298 240 A2
Roselawn IN, 3933 89 D2
Roselle IL, 23115 203 B3
Roselle NJ, 21274 147 E1
Roselle Park NJ, 13281 147 E1
Rose Lodge OR, 1708 20 B2
Rosemead CA, 53505 228 E2
Rosemont CA, 22904 255 C3
Rosemont IL, 4224 203 C3
Rosemount MN, 14619 235 D4
Rosemount OH, 2043 101 D3
Rosenberg TX, 24043 132 A3
Rosendale NY, 1374 94 B3
Rosendale WI, 923 74 C2
Rosenhayn NJ, 1099 145 F1
Rosepine LA, 1390 133 D1
Roseto PA, 1653 93 F3
Rose Valley PA, 944 248 A4
Roseville CA, 79921 36 C2
Roseville IL, 1083 88 A3
Roseville MI, 48129 210 D2
Roseville MN, 33690 235 C2
Roseville OH, 1936 101 E1
Roseville Park DE, 6200 146 B4
Rosholt SD, 419 27 F1
Rosiclare IL, 1213 109 D1
Roslyn PA, 16900 248 C1
Roslyn SD, 225 27 E2
Roslyn WA, 1017 13 D3
Roslyn Estates NY, 1210 241 G2
Rosman NC, 490 121 E1
Ross CA, 2329 259 A1
Ross OH, 1971 100 B2
Ross Co. OH, 73345 101 D2
Rossford OH, 6406 267 B2
Rossiter PA, 670 92 B3
Rossmoor CA, 10298 228 E4
Rossmoor NJ, 3129 147 E2
Rossville GA, 3511 120 B2
Rossville IL, 1217 89 D4
Rossville IN, 1513 89 E4
Rossville KS, 1014 43 F2
Rossville MD, 11515 193 E2
Roswell GA, 79334 120 C3
Roswell NM, 45293 57 E1
Rotan TX, 1611 58 B2
Rothsay MN, 497 19 F4
Rothschild WI, 4970 68 B4
Rothsville PA, 3017 146 A2
Rotonda FL, 6574 140 C4
Rotterdam NY, 20536 94 B1
Rotterdam Jct. NY, 918 94 B1
Rougemont NC, 600 112 C3
Rough Rock AZ, 469 47 F1
Round Hill VA, 500 103 D2
Round Lake NY, 604 94 B1
Round Mtn. NV, 550 37 F2
Round Pond ME, 325 82 C3
Round Rock AZ, 601 47 F1
Round Rock TX, 61136 61 E1
Roundup MT, 1931 16 C4
Rouses Pt. NY, 2277 81 D1
Routt Co. CO, 19690 32 C4
Rouzerville PA, 862 103 D1
Rowan Co. KY, 22094 100 C4
Rowan Co. NC, 130340 112 A4
Rowland NC, 1146 122 C3
Rowland Hts. CA, 48553 229 F3
Rowlesburg WV, 613 102 B2
Rowlett TX, 44503 207 E1
Rowley MA, 1434 151 F1
Roxana DE, 375 145 F4
Roxboro NC, 8696 112 C3
Roxie MS, 569 126 A4
Roxton TX, 694 116 A4
Roy NM, 304 49 E2
Roy UT, 32885 31 E3
Royal Ctr. IN, 832 89 E3
Royal City WA, 1823 13 E4
Royal Oak MD, 750 145 D4
Royal Oak MI, 60062 76 C4
Royal Palm Beach FL, 21523 143 E1
Royal Pines NC, 5334 121 E1
Royalton IL, 1130 98 C4
Royalton MN, 816 66 C2
Royersford PA, 4246 146 B2
Royse City TX, 2957 59 F2
Royston GA, 2493 121 E3
Rubidoux CA, 29180 229 H3
Rubonia FL, 1700 266 B4
Ruch OR, 700 28 B2
Rudyard MT, 275 15 F2
Rugby ND, 2939 18 C2
Ruidoso NM, 7698 57 D2
Ruidoso Downs NM, 1824 57 D2
Rule TX, 698 58 C2
Ruleville MS, 3234 118 A4
Rumford ME, 4795 82 B2
Rumson NJ, 7137 147 F2
Runaway Bay TX, 1104 59 E2
Runge TX, 1080 61 E3
Runnels Co. TX, 11495 58 C3
Runnemede NJ, 8533 146 C3
Running Sprs. CA, 5125 229 K1
Rupert ID, 5645 31 D1
Rupert WV, 940 102 A4
Rural Hall NC, 2464 112 B3
Rural Retreat VA, 1350 111 F2
Rural Valley PA, 922 92 B3
Rush City MN, 2102 67 D2
Rush Co. IN, 18261 100 A1
Rush Co. KS, 3551 43 D3
Rushford MN, 1696 73 E2
Rushford Vil. MN, 714 73 E2
Rushmere VA, 1083 113 F2
Rush Sprs. OK, 1278 51 E4
Rush Valley UT, 453 31 E4
Rushville IL, 3212 88 A4
Rushville IN, 5995 100 A1
Rushville NE, 999 34 A1
Rushville NY, 621 78 C4
Rusk TX, 5085 124 B3

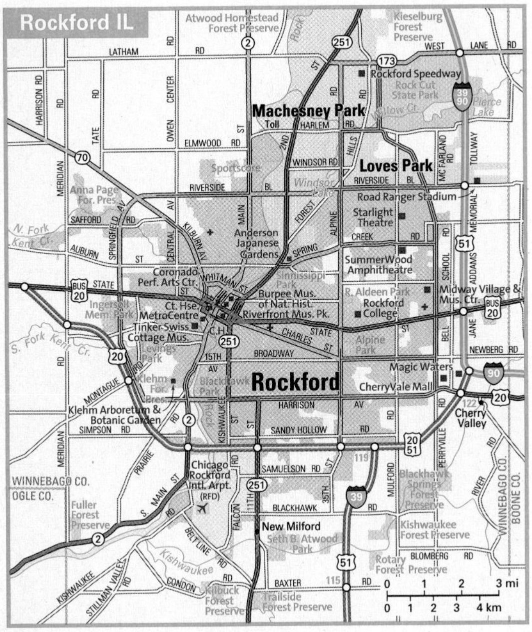
Rockford IL
Machesney Park
Loves Park
Rockford
Cherry Valley
New Milford
Rockford Speedway
Road Ranger Stadium
Starlight Theatre
Anderson Japanese Gardens
Sinnissippi Park
SummerWood Amphitheatre
Burpee Mus. of Nat. Hist.
Riverfront Mus. Pk.
Coronado Perf. Arts Ctr.
MetroCentre
Tinker Swiss Cottage Mus.
R. Aldeen Park
Rockford College
Midway Village & Mus. Ctr.
Magic Waters
CherryVale Mall
Klehm Arboretum & Botanic Garden
Chicago Rockford Intl. Arpt. (RFD)
WINNEBAGO CO.
OGLE CO.
WINNEBAGO CO.
BOONE CO.
Atwood Homestead Forest Preserve
Kieselburg Forest Preserve
Fuller Forest Preserve
Seth B. Atwood Park
Kishwaukee Forest Preserve
Blackhawk Springs Forest Preserve
Rotary Forest Preserve
Trailside Forest Preserve
Kilbuck Forest Preserve
0 1 2 3 mi
0 1 2 3 4 km

Sacramento CA
Sacramento
West Sacramento
Rio Linda
North Highlands
Citrus Hts.
Foothill Farms
Fair Oaks
Carmichael
Arcade
Arden
Rancho Cordova
Rosemont
Florin
Sacramento Intl. Airport (SMF)
Aerospace Museum of California
Discovery Mus. Sci. & Space Ctr./Challenger Learning Ctr.
ARCO Arena
Old Sacramento
B.F. Hastings Bldg./Visitor Center
Big Four Bldg.
Calif. St. Military Museum
Calif. St. Railroad Museum
Discovery Mus. Gold Rush History Ctr.
Wells Fargo History Museum
California Highway Patrol Academy
Crocker Art Mus.
Raley Field
State Capitol
Towe Auto Mus.
Port of Sacramento
Sacramento Zoo
Cal Expo & Raging Waters
California State Univ., Sacramento
Arden Fair Mall
Country Club Plaza Mall
Sunrise Mall
Del Paso Park
Mather Regional Park
Goethe Park
Ancil Hoffman Park
American River Parkway
Jedediah Smith Natl. Rec. Trail
YOLO CO.
SACRAMENTO CO.
0 1 2 mi
0 1 2 3 km

Arcade B2
Arden B2
Carmichael C2
Citrus Hts. C1
Fair Oaks C1
Florin B3
Foothill Farms C1
N. Highlands B1
Rancho Cordova C2
Rio Linda B1
Rosemont C3
Sacramento A2
W. Sacramento A3

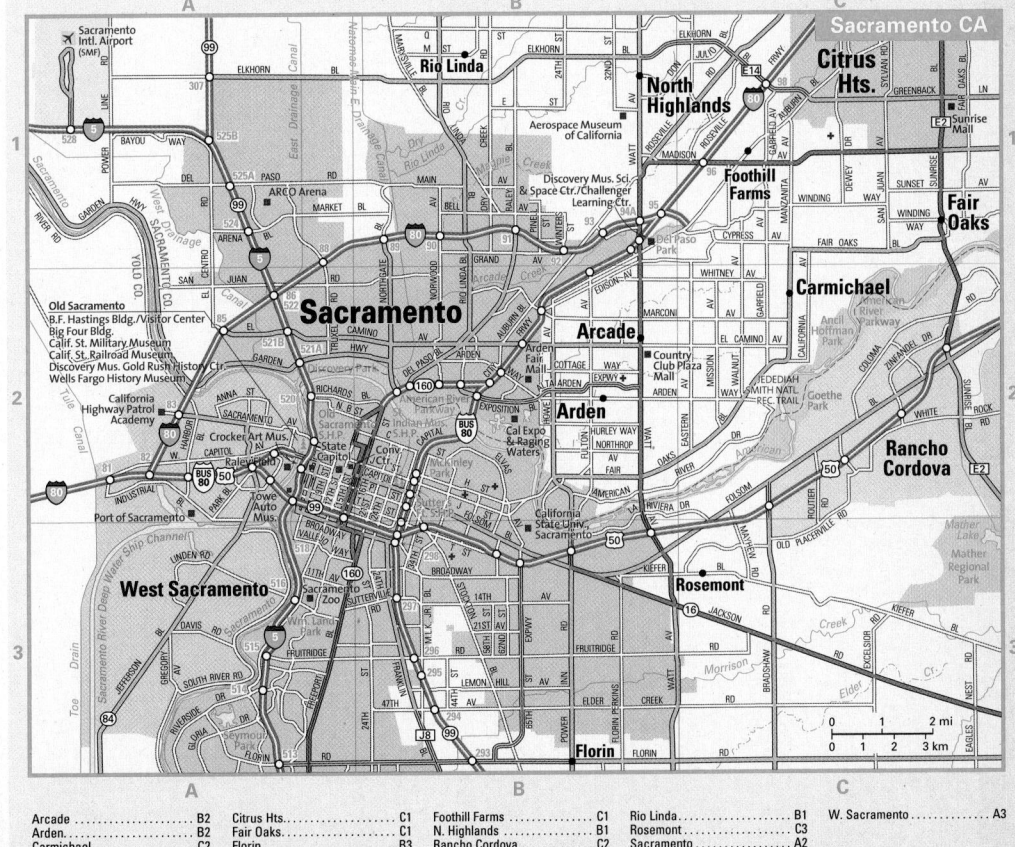

Figures after entries indicate population, page number, and grid reference.

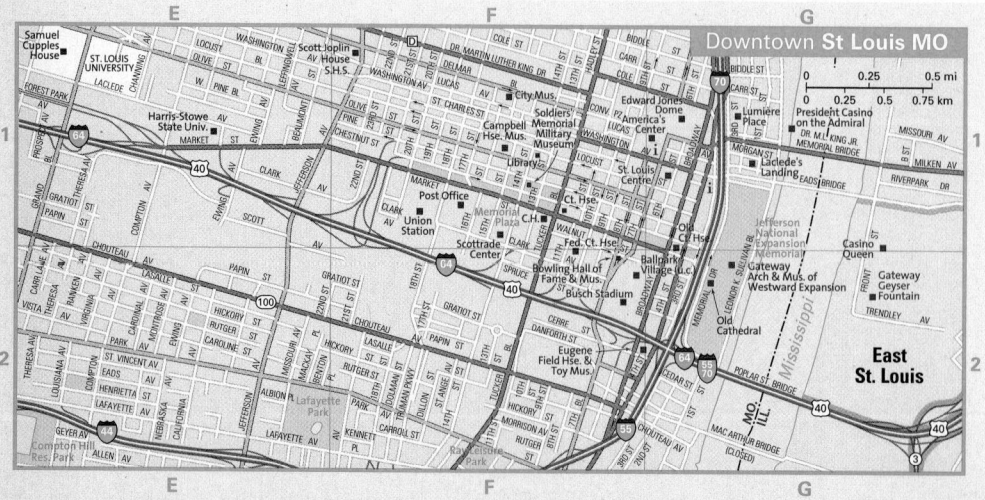

St Louis MO

Downtown St Louis MO

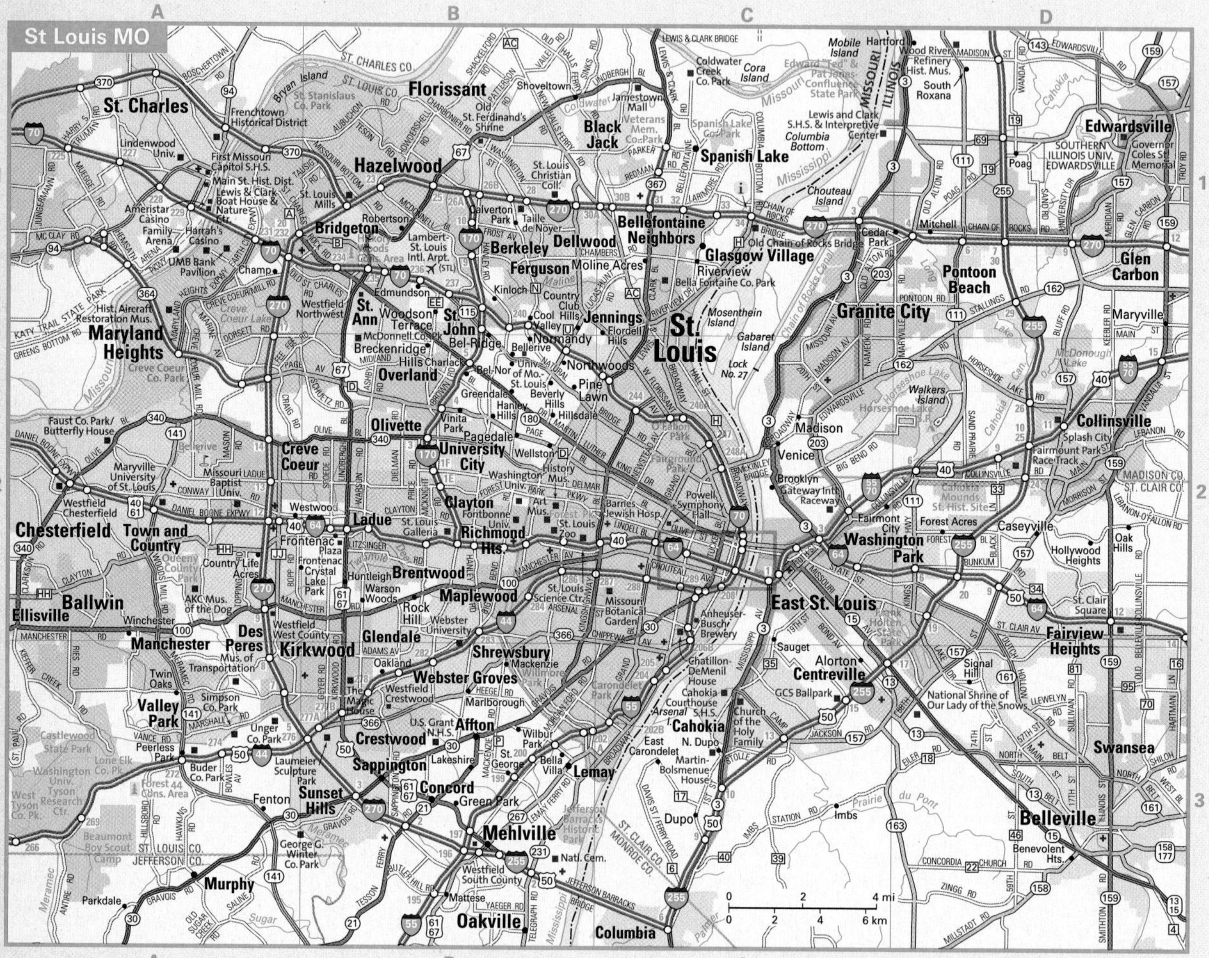

POINTS OF INTEREST

America's Center	G1
Ballpark Village	F2
Bowling Hall of Fame & Museum	F2
Busch Stadium	F2
Campbell House Museum	F1
Casino Queen	G1
City Hall	F1
City Museum	F1
Court House	F1
Edward Jones Dome	F1
Eugene Field House & Toy Museum	F2
Federal Court House	F1
Gateway Arch & Mus. of Westward Expansion	G2
Gateway Geyser Fountain	G2
Harris-Stowe State University	E1
Jefferson Natl. Expansion Memorial	G1
Laclede's Landing	G1
Library	F1
Lumière Place	G1
Old Cathedral	G2
Old Court House	F1
Post Office	F1
President Casino on the Admiral	G1
St. Louis Centre	F1
St. Louis University	E1
Samuel Cupples House	E1
Scott Joplin House State Hist. Site	F1
Scottrade Center	F1
Soldiers' Memorial Military Museum	F1
Union Station	F1

Entries in **bold black** indicate counties or parishes.
Entries in **bold color** indicate cities with detailed inset maps.

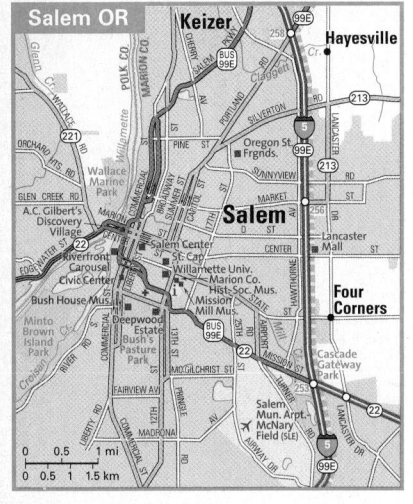

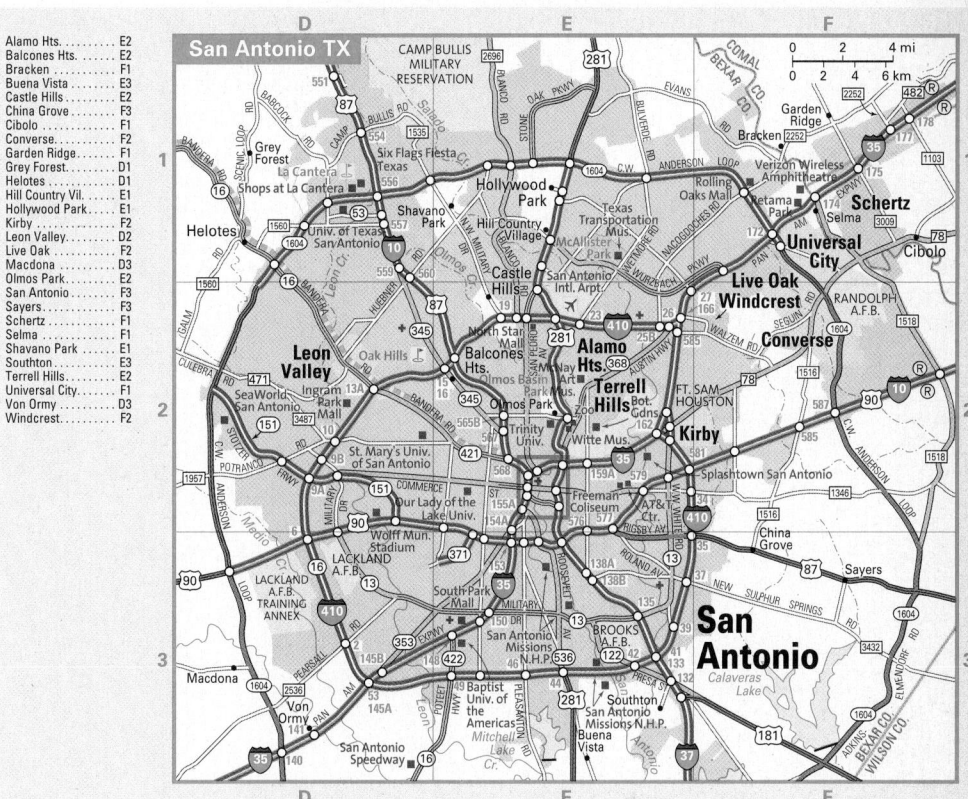

San Antonio TX

Salem OR

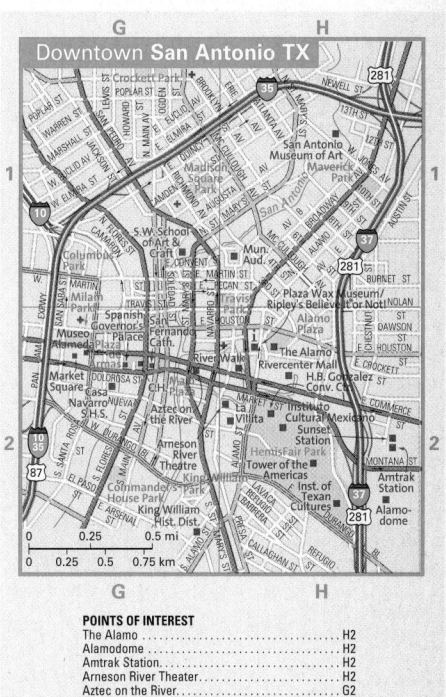

Downtown **San Antonio** TX

Salt Lake City UT

Figures after entries indicate population, page number, and grid reference.

Bonita C2	El Cajon C1	La Mesa C2	San Diego C2	Sunnyside C2
Chula Vista B3	Imperial Beach B3	Lemon Grove C2	Santee C1	Tijuana, MX C3
Coronado A2	Lakeside C1	National City B2	Spring Valley C2	

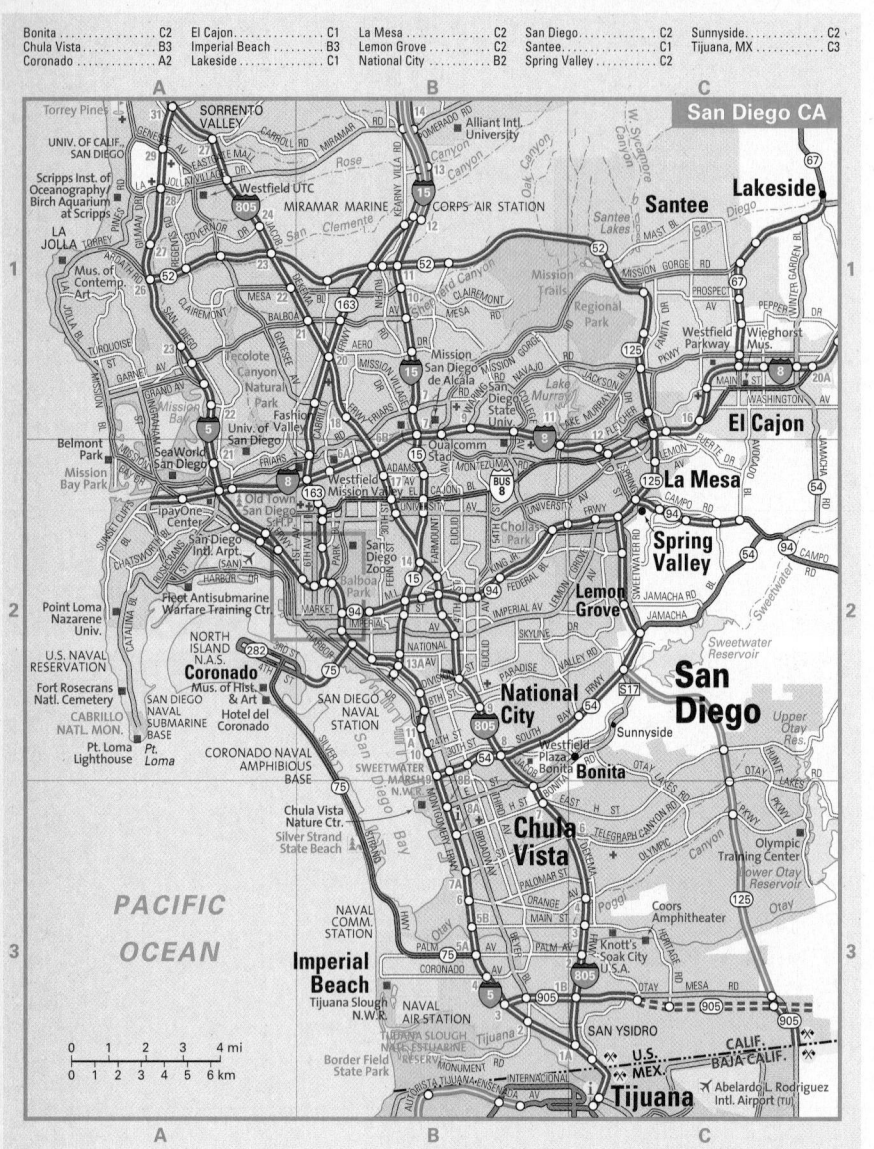

San Diego CA

POINTS OF INTEREST

Automotive Museum E1	San Diego Aircraft Carrier Museum D2
Balboa Park E1	San Diego Convention Center D2
Balboa Stadium E2	San Diego Hall of Champions E1
Casa del Prado E1	San Diego International Airport D1
Children's Museum D2	San Diego Museum of Art E1
Civic Center D2	San Diego Museum of Man E1
Copley Symphony Hall E2	San Diego Natural History Museum E1
County Court House D2	San Diego Zoo E1
Firehouse Museum D2	Santa Fe Depot D2
Gaslamp Quarter & W. H. Davis House . . . E2	Seaport Village D2
The Globe Theatres E1	Spanish Village Art Center E1
House of Hospitality E1	Spreckels Organ Pavilion E2
Maritime Museum D2	Spreckels Theatre D2
Museum of Contemporary Art, San Diego . D2	Starlight Bowl E1
PETCO Park E2	Timken Museum of Art E1
Reuben H. Fleet Science Center E1	Veterans Museum & Memorial Center E2
San Diego Aerospace Museum E1	Villa Montezuma E2
	Westfield Horton Plaza D2

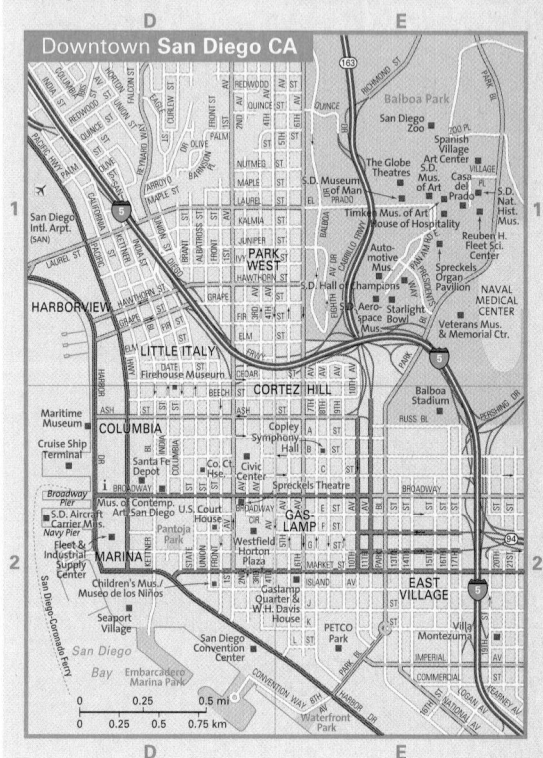

Downtown **San Diego CA**

Entries in **bold black** indicate counties or parishes.
Entries in **bold color** indicate cities with detailed inset maps.

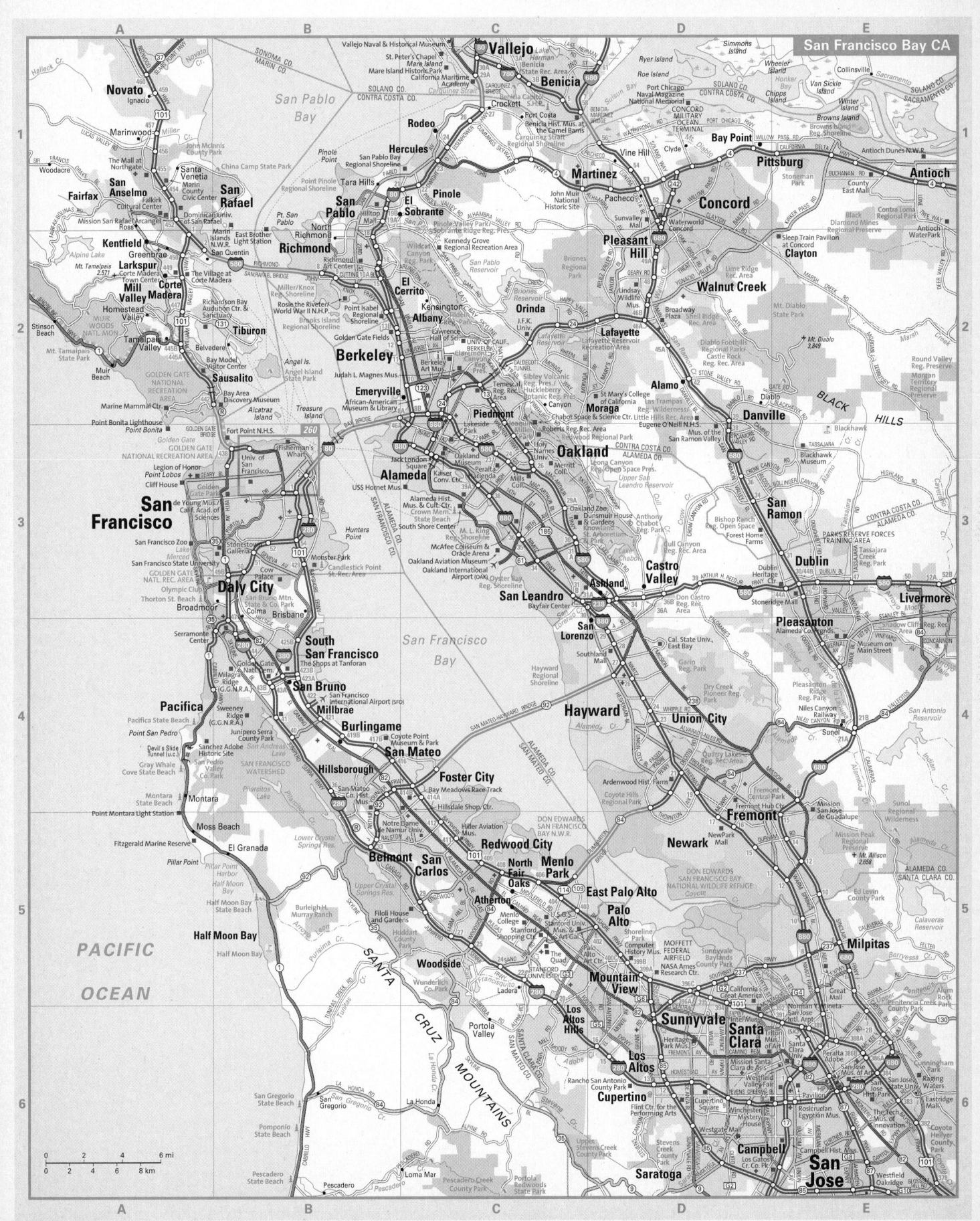

San Francisco Bay CA

PACIFIC OCEAN

Figures after entries indicate population, page number, and grid reference.

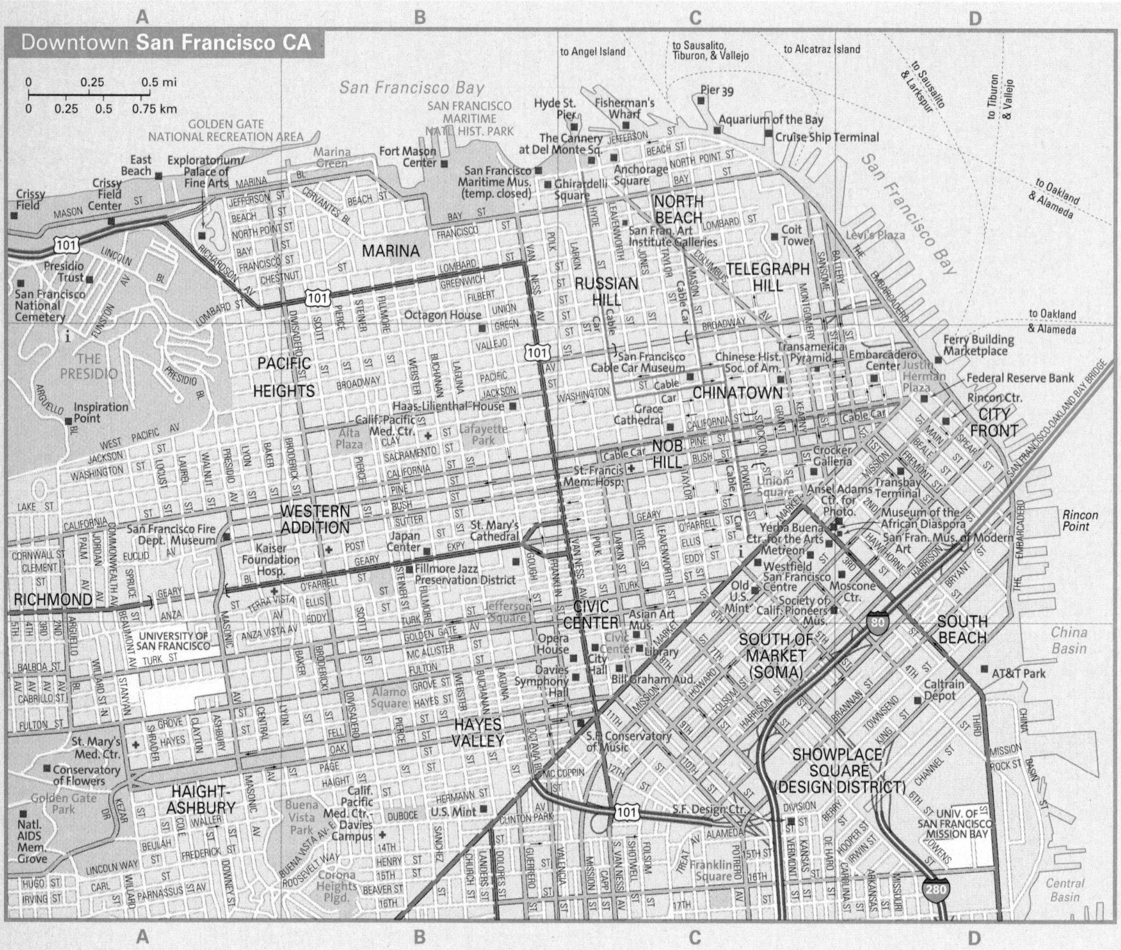

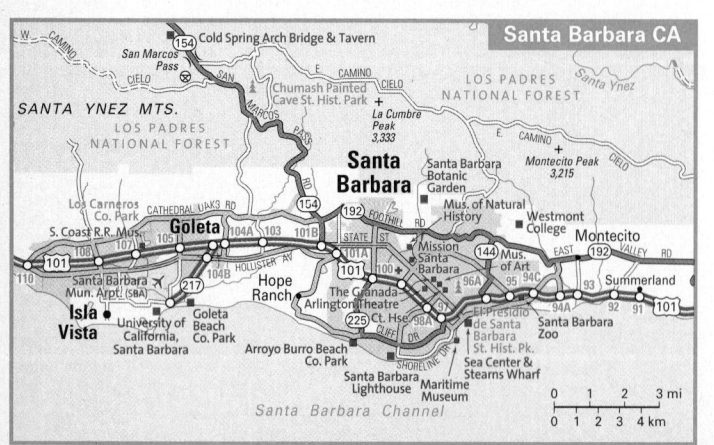

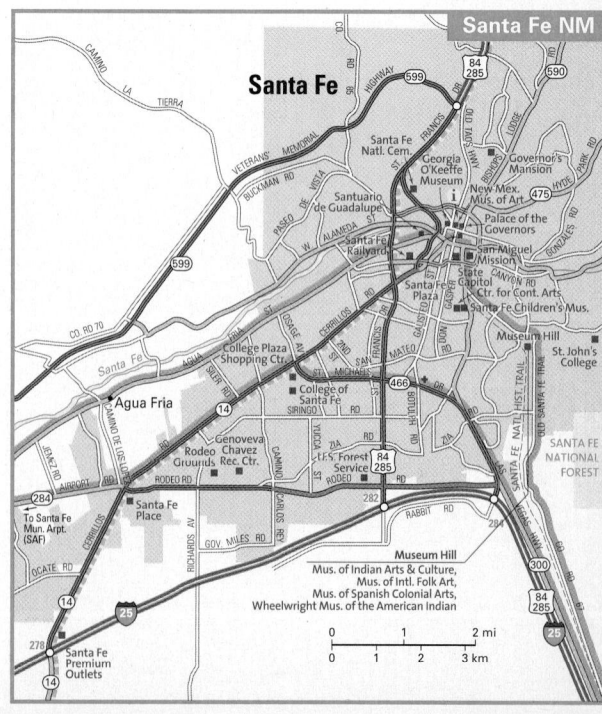

Downtown San Francisco CA

POINTS OF INTEREST

Anchorage Square C1
Ansel Adams Center
  for Photography D2
Aquarium of the Bay C1
Asian Art Museum C3
AT&T Park D3
Bill Graham Auditorium C3
Caltrain Depot D3
The Cannery
  at Del Monte Square C1
Chinese Historical
  Society of America C2
City Hall C3
Coit Tower C1
Conservatory of Flowers A3
Crissy Field A1
Crissy Field Center A1
Crocker Galleria C2
Cruise Ship Terminal C1
Davies Symphony Hall C3
East Beach A1
Embarcadero Center D2
Exploratorium/
  Palace of Fine Arts A1

Fillmore Jazz Preservation
  District B2
Ferry Building Marketplace . . . D2
Fisherman's Wharf C1
Fort Mason Center B1
Ghirardelli Square B1
Golden Gate Natl. Rec. Area . . . A1
Golden Gate Park A3
Grace Cathedral C2
Haas-Lilienthal House B2
Hyde Street Pier B1
Inspiration Point A2
Japan Center B2
Levi's Plaza D1
Library C3
Metreon C3
Moscone Center D2
Museum of the African
  Diaspora D2
National AIDS Memorial Grove . A3
Octagon House B2
Old U.S. Mint C3
Opera House C3
Pier 39 . . . . C1
The Presidio A2
Presidio Trust A1

Rincon Center D2
St. Mary's Cathedral B2
San Francisco Art Institute
  Galleries C1
San Francisco Cable Car Mus. . . . C2
San Francisco Conservatory
  of Music C3
San Francisco Design Center C3
San Francisco Fire Dept. Mus. . . . A2
San Francisco Maritime Mus. B1
San Francisco Maritime
  Natl. Hist. Park B1
San Francisco Museum of
  Modern Art D2
San Francisco Natl. Cemetery . . . A1
Soc. of Calif. Pioneers Mus. C2
Transamerica Pyramid C2
Transbay Terminal D2
U.S. Mint B3
Univ. of San Francisco A3
Univ. of San Francisco-
  Mission Bay D3
Westfield San Francisco
  Centre C2
Yerba Buena
  Center for the Arts C2

Santa Barbara CA

Santa Fe NM

Entries in **bold black** indicate counties or parishes.
Entries in **bold color** indicate cities with detailed inset maps.

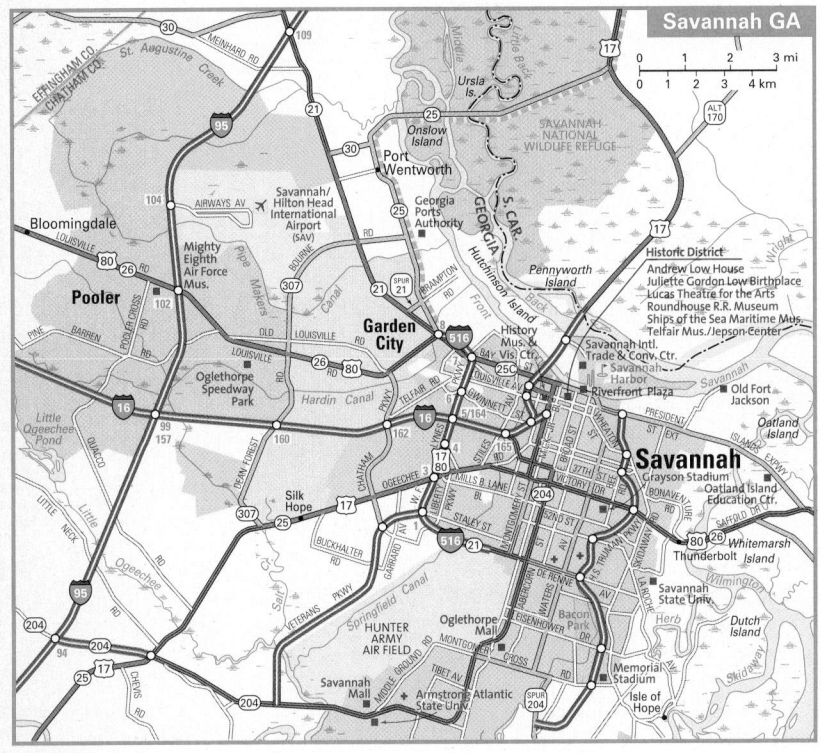

Savannah GA

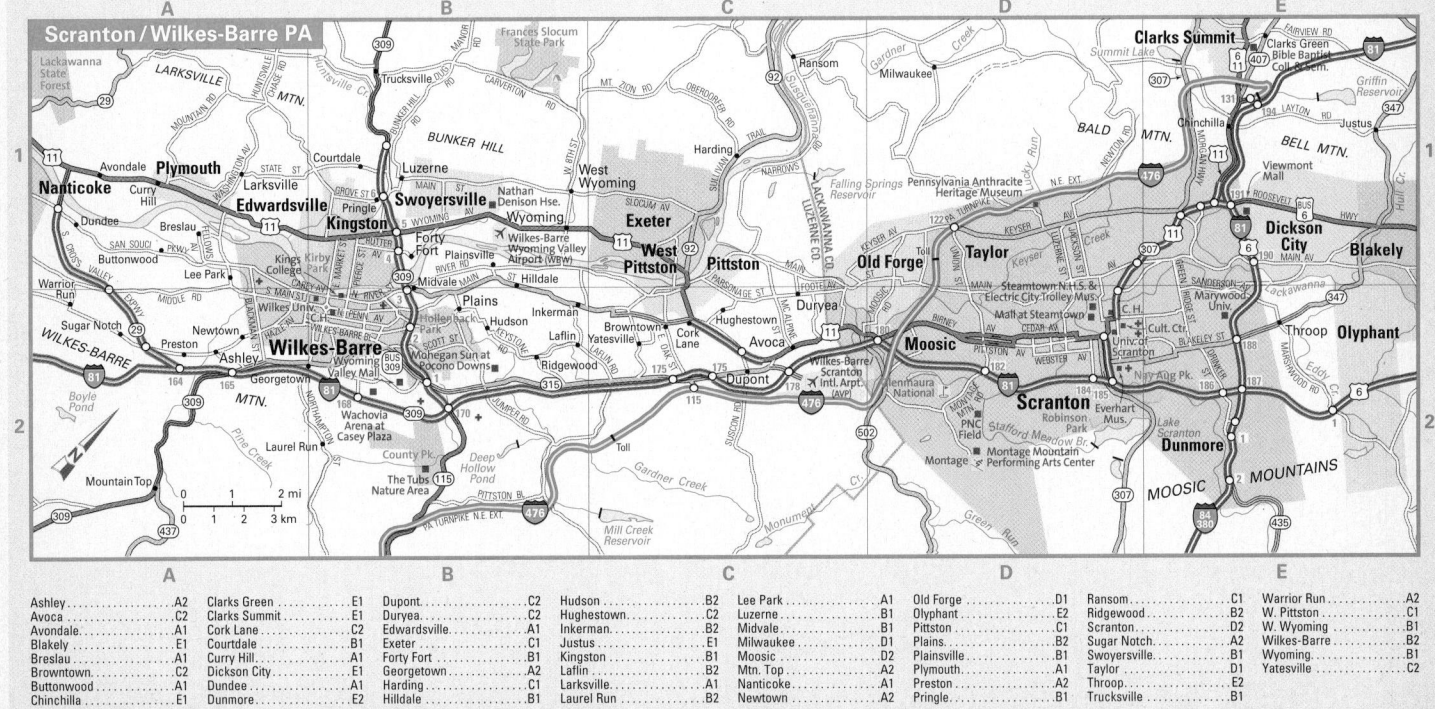

Scranton / Wilkes-Barre PA

Figures after entries indicate population, page number, and grid reference.

Seattle / Tacoma WA

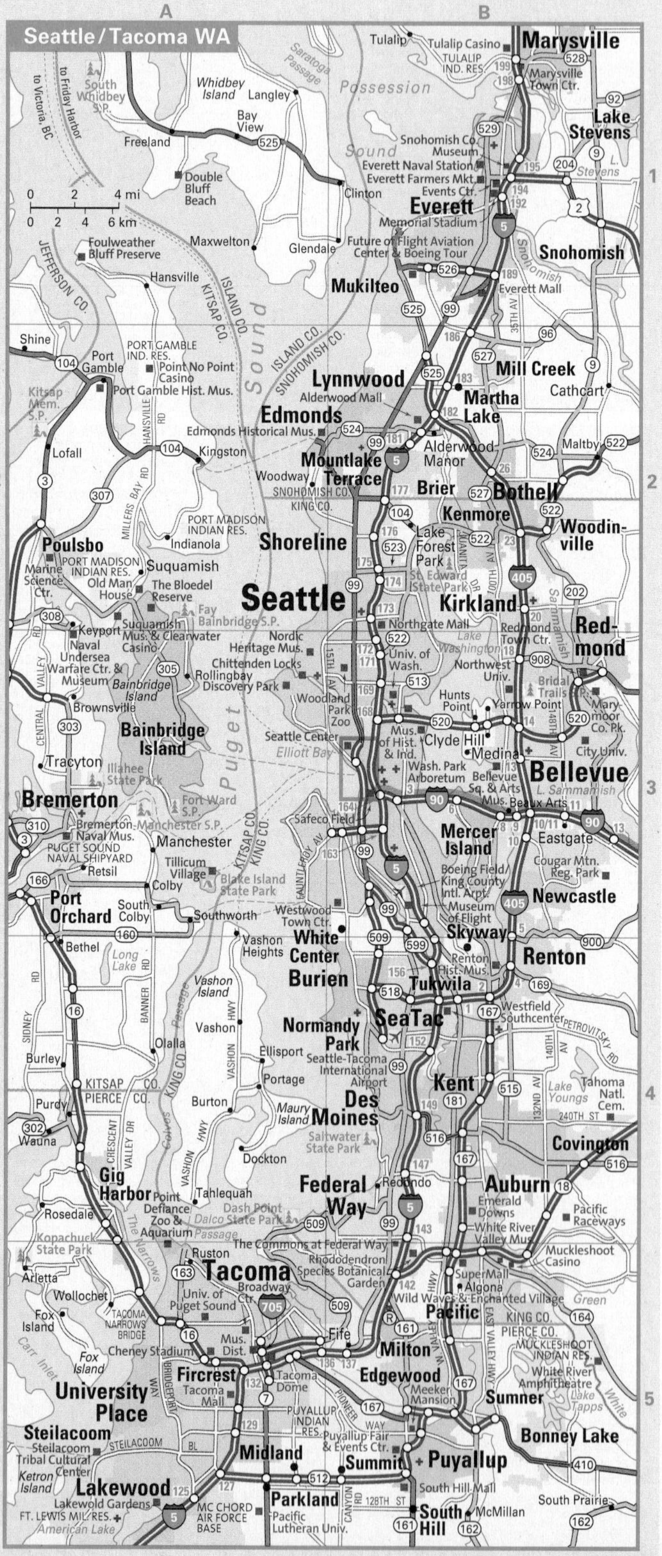

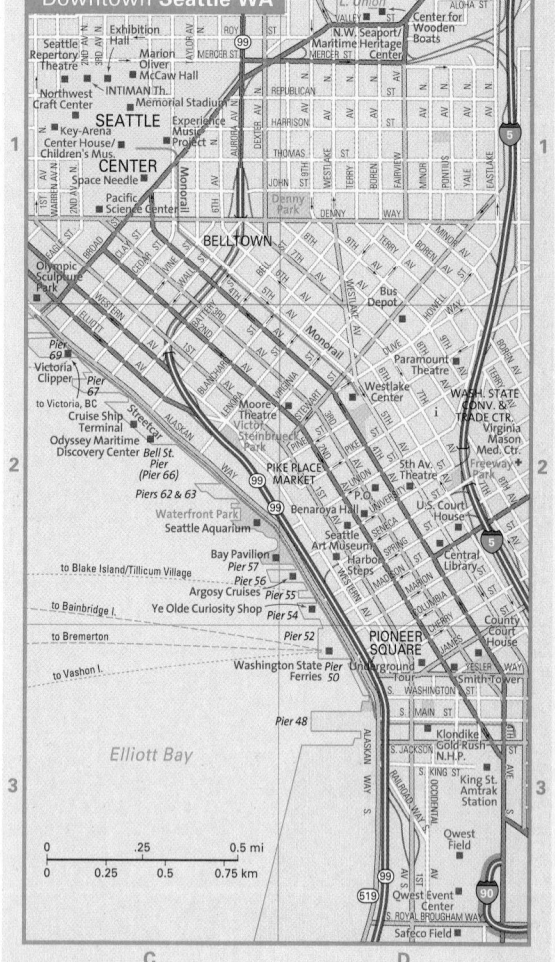

Downtown Seattle WA

Entries in **bold black** indicate counties or parishes.
Entries in **bold color** indicate cities with detailed inset maps.

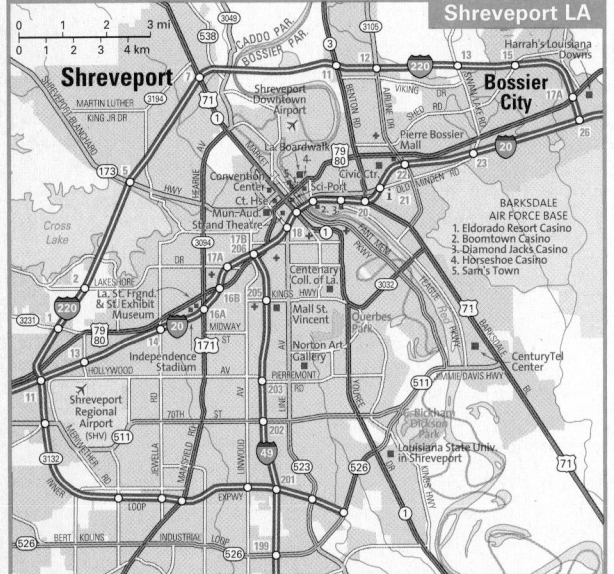

Shreveport LA

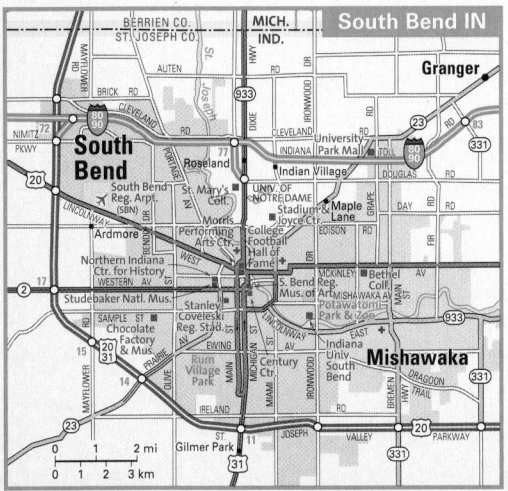

South Bend IN

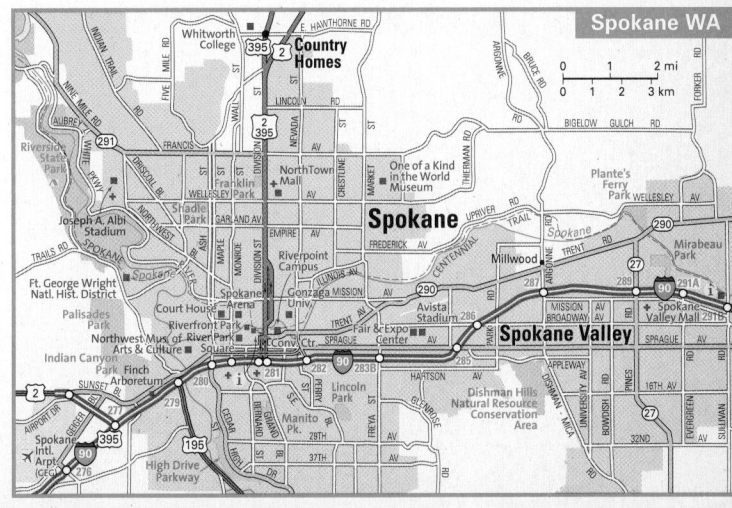

Spokane WA

Figures after entries indicate population, page number, and grid reference.

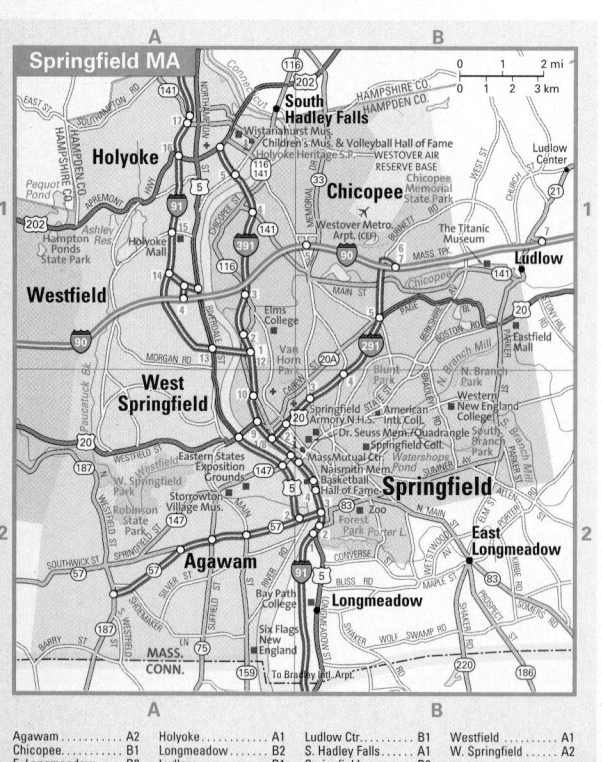

Springfield IL

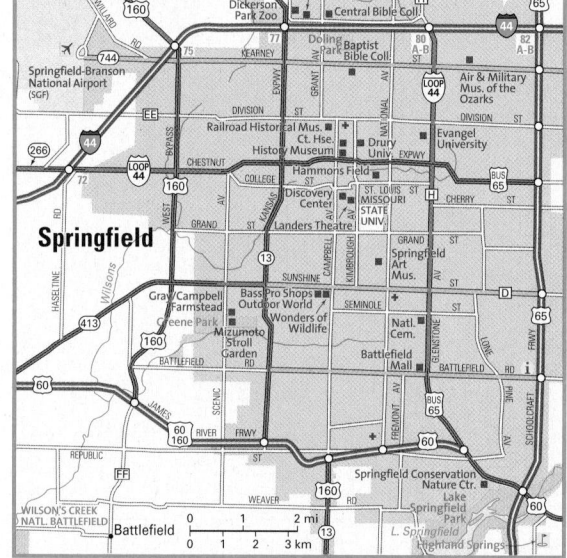

Springfield MO

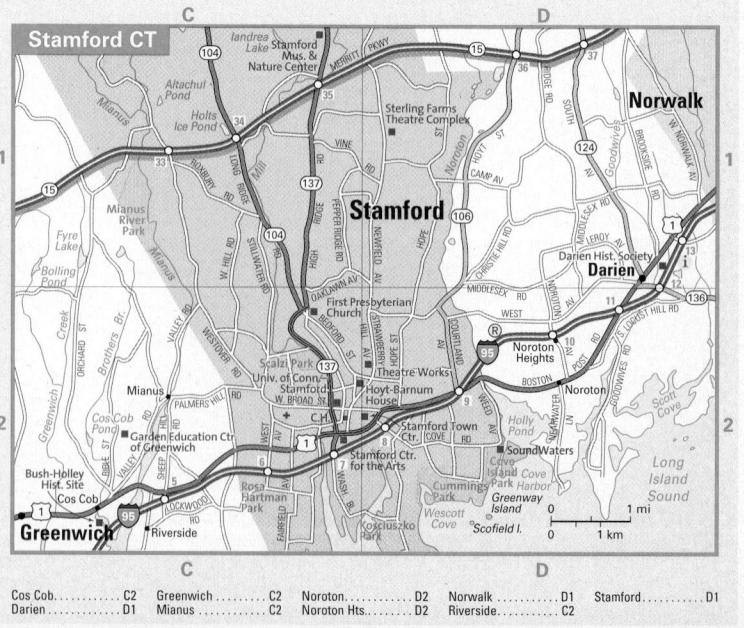

Stamford CT

Entries in **bold black** indicate counties or parishes.
Entries in **bold color** indicate cities with detailed inset maps.

Bayberry.....A1	Galeville.....A1	Nedrow.....A2	Taunton.....A2
Collamer.....B1	Jamesville.....B2	N. Syracuse.....B1	Westvale.....A2
DeWitt.....B2	Lakeland.....A1	Onondaga Hill.....A2	
E. Syracuse.....A2	Liverpool.....B1	Solvay.....A2	
Fairmount.....A2	Lyndon.....B2	Split Rock.....A2	
Franklin Park.....B1	Mattydale.....B1	Syracuse.....A2	

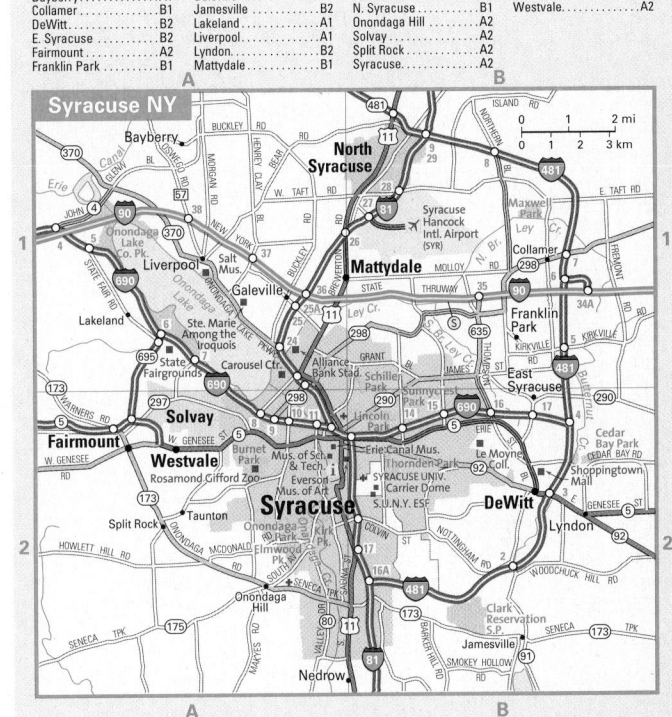

Syracuse NY

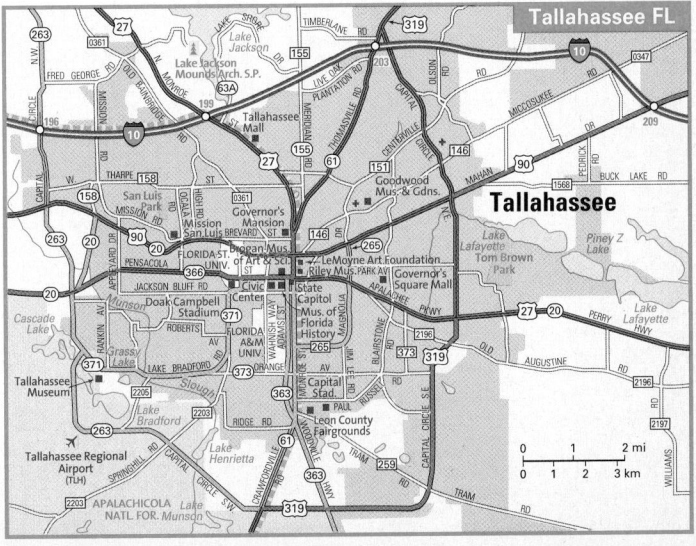

Stockton CA

Tallahassee FL

Figures after entries indicate population, page number, and grid reference.

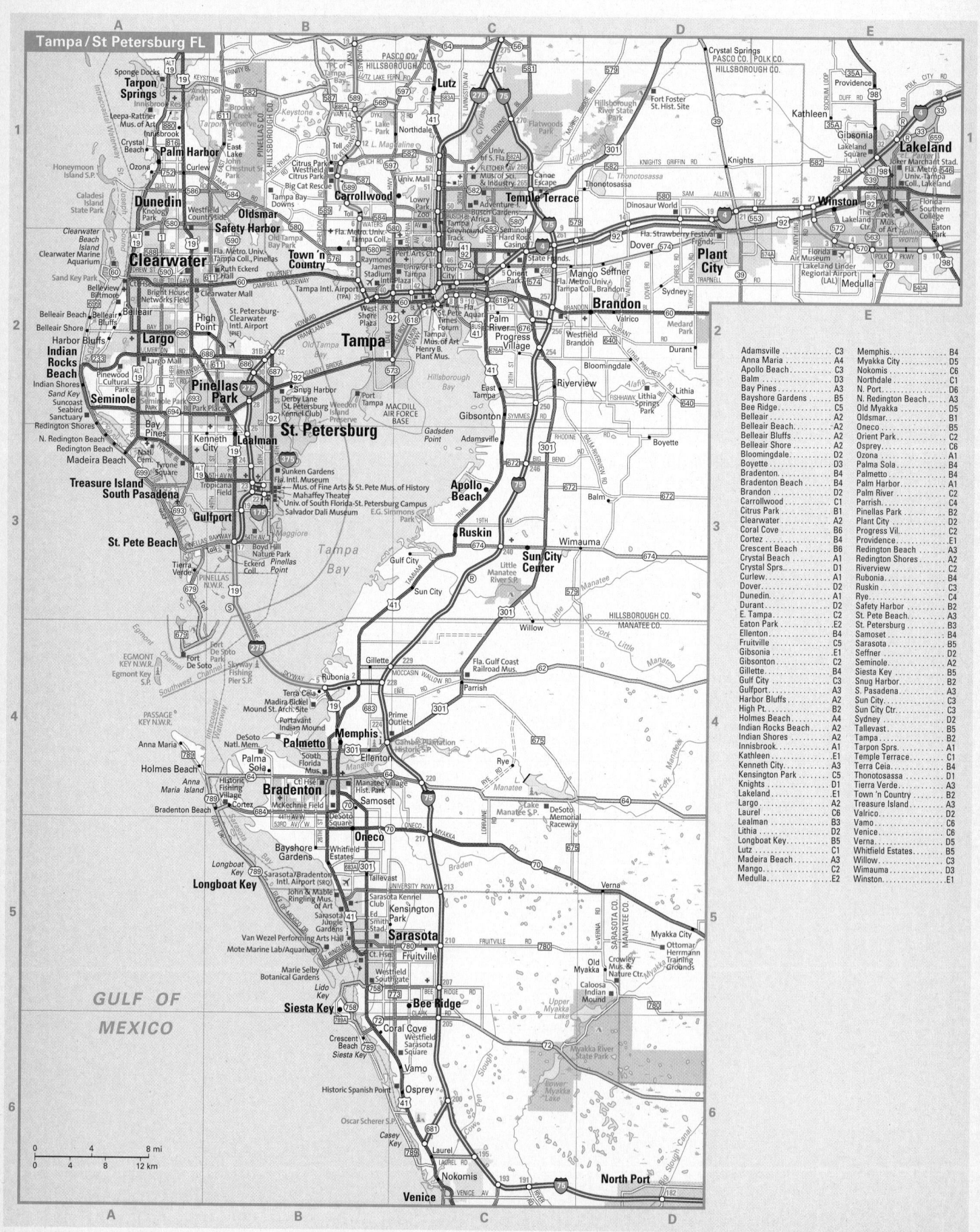

Tampa/St Petersburg FL

Entries in **bold black** indicate counties or parishes.
Entries in **bold color** indicate cities with detailed inset maps.

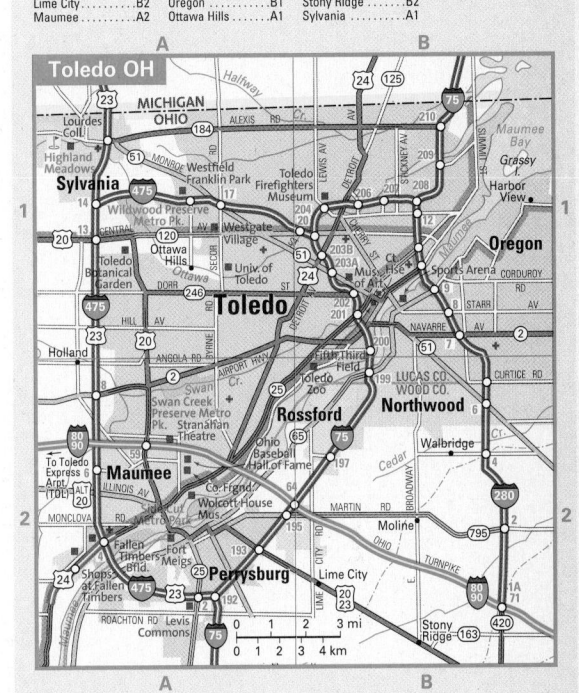

Toledo OH inset map index:
Harbor View.........B1
Holland.............A2
Lime City..........B2
Maumee.............A2
Moline.............B2
Northwood..........B2
Oregon.............B1
Ottawa Hills.......A1
Perrysburg.........A2
Rossford...........B2
Stony Ridge........B2
Sylvania...........A1
Toledo.............A1
Walbridge..........B2

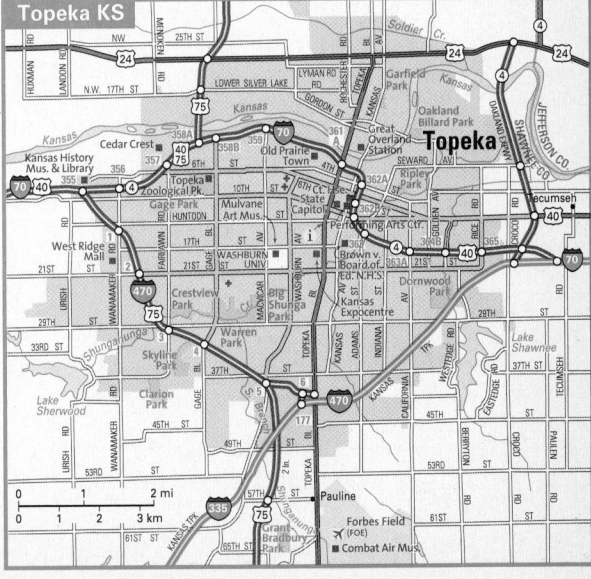

Topeka KS

Figures after entries indicate population, page number, and grid reference.

Bakersville B1	Fallsington A2	Mercerville B1	Trenton B2
Ewing A1	Lawrenceville B1	Morrisville A2	W. Trenton A1
Ewingville A1	Lewisville B1	Slackwood B1	White Horse........ B2

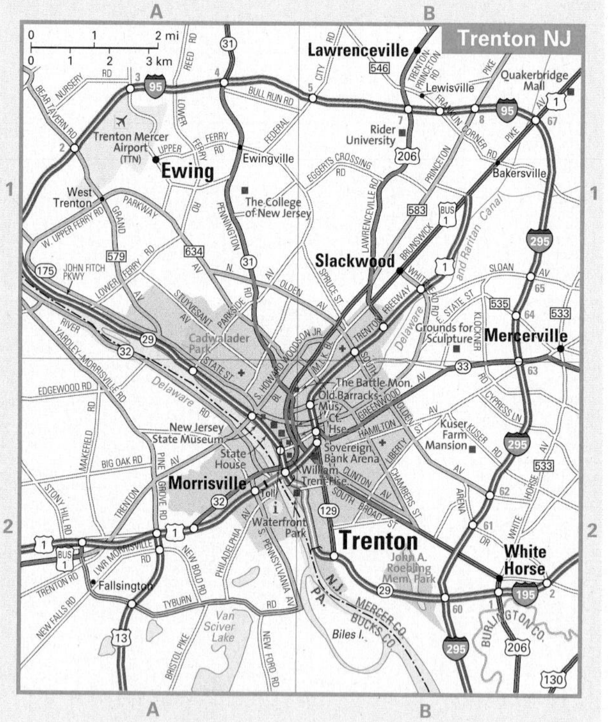

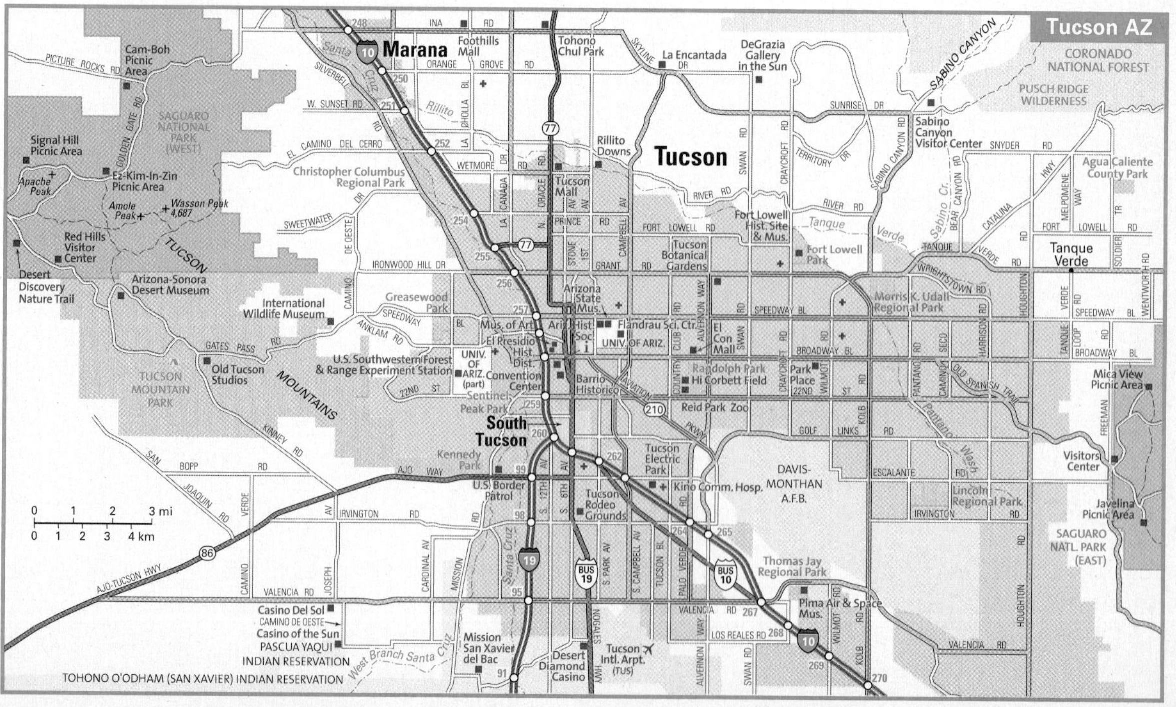

269
Troy–Vermilion County

Entries in **bold black** indicate counties or parishes.
Entries in **bold color** indicate cities with detailed inset maps.

Troy ID, 798 ... 14 B4
Troy IL, 8524 ... 98 B3
Troy KS, 1054 ... 96 B1
Troy MI, 80959 ... 76 C4
Troy MO, 6737 ... 97 F2
Troy MT, 957 ... 14 C2
Troy NH, 1300 ... 95 D1
Troy NY, 49170 ... 94 B1
Troy NC, 3430 ... 122 C1
Troy OH, 21999 ... 100 B1
Troy PA, 1508 ... 93 D1
Troy TN, 1273 ... 108 C3
Troy TX, 1378 ... 59 E4
Troy VT, 375 ... 81 E1
Truckee CA, 13864 ... 37 D2
Truman MN, 1259 ... 72 B2
Trumann AR, 6889 ... 108 A4
Trumansburg NY, 1581 ... 79 D4
Trumbauersville PA, 1059 ... 146 C1
Trumbull CT, 34243 ... 149 D2
Trumbull Co. OH, 225116 ... 91 F2
Trussville AL, 12924 ... 119 F4
Truth or Consequences NM, 7289 ... 56 B2
Tryon NE, 100 ... 34 B3
Tryon NC, 1760 ... 121 F1
Tryon OK, 448 ... 51 F2
Tsaile AZ, 1078 ... 48 A2
Tualatin OR, 22791 ... 20 C2
Tubac AZ, 949 ... 55 D4
Tuba City AZ, 8225 ... 47 E2
Tuckahoe NY, 1741 ... 149 E3
Tucker MS, 534 ... 126 C2
Tucker Co. WV, 7321 ... 102 B2
Tuckerman AR, 1757 ... 107 F4
Tuckerton NJ, 3517 ... 147 E4
Tucson AZ, 486699 ... 55 D3
Tucumcari NM, 5989 ... 49 F3
Tukwila WA, 17181 ... 262 B4
Tulalip WA, 1561 ... 262 B1
Tulare CA, 43994 ... 45 D3
Tulare SD, 221 ... 27 E3
Tulare Co. CA, 368021 ... 45 D3
Tularosa NM, 2864 ... 56 C2
Tulelake CA, 1020 ... 29 D2
Tulia TX, 5117 ... 50 A4
Tullahoma TN, 17994 ... 120 A1
Tullos LA, 419 ... 125 E3
Tully NY, 924 ... 79 E4
Tullytown PA, 2031 ... 147 D2
Tulsa OK, 393049 ... 51 F2
Tulsa Co. OK, 563299 ... 106 A4
Tuluksak AK, 428 ... 154 B3
Tumacacori AZ, 569 ... 55 D4
Tunica MS, 1132 ... 118 B2
Tunica Co. MS, 9227 ... 118 B2
Tunkhannock PA, 1911 ... 93 E2
Tunnel Hill GA, 1209 ... 120 B2
Tuolumne CA, 1865 ... 37 D3
Tuolumne Co. CA, 54501 ... 37 D3
Tupelo MS, 34211 ... 119 D3
Tupper Lake NY, 3935 ... 79 F1
Turbeville SC, 602 ... 122 B4
Turbotville PA, 691 ... 93 D3
Turley NM, 425 ... 48 B1
Turley OK, 3231 ... 51 F2
Turlock CA, 55810 ... 36 C4
Turner ME, 550 ... 82 B2
Turner OR, 1199 ... 20 B2
Turner Co. GA, 9504 ... 129 D4
Turner Co. SD, 8849 ... 27 F4
Turners Falls MA, 4441 ... 94 C1
Turnersville NJ, 3867 ... 146 C4
Turon KS, 436 ... 43 D4
Turpin Hills OH, 4960 ... 204 C3
Turrell AR, 957 ... 118 B1
Turtle Creek PA, 6076 ... 250 D2
Turtle Lake ND, 580 ... 18 C3
Turtle Lake WI, 1065 ... 67 E3
Tusayan AZ, 562 ... 47 D2
Tuscaloosa AL, 77906 ... 127 E1
Tuscaloosa Co. AL, 164875 ... 119 E4
Tuscarawas OH, 934 ... 91 E4
Tuscarawas Co. OH, 90914 ... 91 E4
Tuscarora PA, 939 ... 93 E3
Tuscola IL, 4448 ... 99 D1
Tuscola TX, 714 ... 58 C3
Tuscola Co. MI, 58266 ... 76 C2
Tusculum TN, 2004 ... 111 E4
Tuscumbia AL, 7856 ... 119 E2
Tuscumbia MO, 218 ... 97 E4
Tuskegee AL, 11846 ... 128 B2
Tustin CA, 67504 ... 229 F5
Tuttle OK, 4294 ... 51 E3
Tutwiler MS, 1364 ... 118 A3
Tuxedo Park NY, 731 ... 148 B2
Twain Harte CA, 2586 ... 37 D3
Twentynine Palms CA, 14764 ... 46 A4
Twiggs Co. GA, 10590 ... 129 E2
Twin Bridges MT, 400 ... 23 E2
Twin City GA, 1752 ... 129 F2
Twin Falls ID, 34469 ... 30 C1
Twin Falls Co. ID, 64284 ... 30 C2
Twin Lake MI, 1613 ... 75 E2
Twin Lakes CA, 5533 ... 236 D1
Twin Lakes GA, 750 ... 137 F1
Twin Lakes NM, 1069 ... 48 A2
Twin Lakes WI, 5124 ... 74 C4
Twin Rivers NJ, 7422 ... 147 E2
Twinsburg OH, 17006 ... 91 E2
Twin Valley MN, 865 ... 19 F3
Twisp WA, 938 ... 13 E2
Two Harbors MN, 3613 ... 64 C4
Two Rivers WI, 12639 ... 75 D1
Tybee Island GA, 3392 ... 130 C3
Tye TX, 1158 ... 58 C3
Tyler MN, 1218 ... 27 F3
Tyler TX, 83650 ... 124 A2
Tyler Co. TX, 20871 ... 132 C1
Tyler Co. WV, 9592 ... 101 F2
Tylersport PA, 950 ... 146 C2
Tylertown MS, 1910 ... 134 B1
Tyndall SD, 1239 ... 35 E1
Tyrone GA, 3916 ... 120 C4
Tyrone NM, 500 ... 55 F2
Tyrone OK, 880 ... 50 B1
Tyrone PA, 5528 ... 92 C3
Tyronza AR, 918 ... 118 B1
Tyrrell Co. NC, 4149 ... 113 F4
Tysons Corner VA, 18540 ... 270 A3
Ty Ty GA, 716 ... 129 D4

U

Ubly MI, 873 ... 76 C2
Ucon ID, 943 ... 23 E4
Udall KS, 794 ... 43 F4
Uhrichsville OH, 5662 ... 91 E4
Uinta Co. WY, 19742 ... 31 F3
Uintah UT, 1127 ... 244 B2
Uintah Co. UT, 25224 ... 32 A4
Ukiah CA, 15497 ... 36 A2
Ulah NC, 800 ... 122 C1
Uledi PA, 1100 ... 102 B1
Ulen MN, 532 ... 19 F3
Ullin IL, 779 ... 108 C2
Ulm MT, 750 ... 15 F3
Ulster Co. NY, 177749 ... 148 A1
Ulysses KS, 5960 ... 42 B4
Ulysses PA, 684 ... 92 C1
Umatilla FL, 2214 ... 141 D1
Umatilla OR, 4978 ... 21 E1
Umatilla Co. OR, 70548 ... 21 E2
Unadilla GA, 2772 ... 129 D3
Unadilla NY, 1127 ... 79 E4
Unalakleet AK, 747 ... 154 B2
Unalaska AK, 4283 ... 154 A4
Uncasville CT, 1500 ... 149 F1
Underhill VT, 1200 ... 81 D2
Underwood IA, 688 ... 86 A2
Underwood ND, 812 ... 18 B3
Unicoi TN, 3519 ... 111 E4
Unicoi Co. TN, 17667 ... 111 E4
Union IL, 576 ... 88 C1
Union KY, 2893 ... 100 B3
Union ME, 475 ... 82 C2
Union MS, 2021 ... 126 C2
Union MO, 7757 ... 97 F3
Union NH, 425 ... 81 F4
Union NJ, 54405 ... 148 A4
Union OH, 5574 ... 100 B1
Union OR, 1926 ... 21 F2
Union SC, 8793 ... 121 F2
Union WV, 548 ... 112 A1
Union Beach NJ, 6649 ... 147 E1
Union Bridge MD, 989 ... 144 B1
Union City CA, 66869 ... 259 D4
Union City GA, 11621 ... 120 C4
Union City IN, 3622 ... 90 A4
Union City MI, 1804 ... 90 A1
Union City NJ, 67088 ... 148 B4
Union City OH, 1767 ... 90 A4
Union City OK, 1375 ... 51 E3
Union City PA, 3463 ... 92 A1
Union City TN, 10876 ... 108 C3
Union Co. AR, 45629 ... 125 E1
Union Co. FL, 13442 ... 138 C3
Union Co. GA, 17289 ... 120 C2
Union Co. IL, 18293 ... 108 C1
Union Co. IN, 7349 ... 100 B1
Union Co. IA, 12309 ... 86 B3
Union Co. KY, 15637 ... 109 D1
Union Co. MS, 25362 ... 118 C3
Union Co. NJ, 522541 ... 147 E1
Union Co. NM, 4174 ... 49 F1
Union Co. NC, 123677 ... 122 B2
Union Co. OH, 40909 ... 90 C4
Union Co. OR, 24530 ... 21 F2
Union Co. PA, 41624 ... 93 D3
Union Co. SC, 29881 ... 121 F2
Union Co. SD, 12584 ... 35 F1
Union Co. TN, 17808 ... 110 C3
Union Gap WA, 5621 ... 13 D4
Union Grove WI, 4322 ... 74 C4
Union Hall VA, 957 ... 112 B2
Union Lake MI, 2500 ... 210 A1
Union Par. LA, 22803 ... 125 E1
Union Park FL, 10191 ... 246 D2
Union Pt. GA, 1669 ... 121 E4
Union Sprs. AL, 3670 ... 128 B3
Union Sprs. NY, 1074 ... 79 D3
Uniontown AL, 1636 ... 127 E2
Uniontown KY, 1064 ... 109 D1
Uniontown OH, 2802 ... 91 E3
Uniontown PA, 12422 ... 102 B1
Unionville CT, 5100 ... 94 C3
Unionville GA, 2074 ... 129 E4
Unionville MI, 605 ... 76 B2
Unionville MO, 2041 ... 87 D4
Unionville NV, 250 ... 29 F4
Unionville NY, 536 ... 148 A2
Unionville NC, 4797 ... 122 B1
Unionville PA, 1200 ... 146 B3
Unity ME, 486 ... 82 C2
Universal City TX, 14849 ... 61 D2
University City MO, 37428 ... 256 B2
University Gardens NY, 4138 ... 241 G3
University Hts. OH, 14146 ... 204 G2
University Park IA, 536 ... 87 D2
University Park MD, 2318 ... 270 E2
University Park NM, 2732 ... 56 C3
University Park TX, 23324 ... 207 D2
University Place WA, 29933 ... 12 C3
Upland CA, 68393 ... 229 G2
Upland IN, 3803 ... 89 F4
Upland PA, 2977 ... 248 A4
Upper Arlington OH, 33686 ... 101 D1
Upper Darby PA, 1900 ... 248 B3
Upper Lake CA, 989 ... 36 A2
Upper Marlboro MD, 648 ... 144 C3
Upper Saddle River NJ, 7741 ... 148 B3
Upper Sandusky OH, 6533 ... 90 C3
Upshur Co. TX, 35291 ... 124 B2
Upshur Co. WV, 23404 ... 102 A3
Upson Co. GA, 27597 ... 129 D2
Upton KY, 654 ... 110 A1
Upton MA, 2326 ... 150 C2
Upton WY, 872 ... 25 F3
Upton Co. TX, 3404 ... 58 A4
Urania LA, 700 ... 125 E3
Urbana IL, 36395 ... 88 C4
Urbana IA, 1019 ... 87 E1
Urbana OH, 11613 ... 90 B4
Urbancrest OH, 868 ... 206 A3
Urbandale IA, 29072 ... 86 C2
Urbanna VA, 543 ... 113 F1
Urich MO, 499 ... 96 C3
Ursa IL, 595 ... 87 F4
Usquepaug RI, 350 ... 150 C4
Utah Co. UT, 368536 ... 39 E1
Utica IN, 591 ... 100 A4
Utica MI, 4577 ... 210 C1
Utica MS, 966 ... 126 A3
Utica NE, 844 ... 35 E4
Utica NY, 60651 ... 79 E3
Utica OH, 2130 ... 91 D4
Utica SC, 1322 ... 121 E2
Uvalda GA, 530 ... 129 F3
Uvalde TX, 14929 ... 60 C3
Uvalde Co. TX, 25926 ... 60 C3
Uxbridge MA, 3300 ... 150 C2

V

Vacaville CA, 88625 ... 36 B3
Vader WA, 590 ... 12 B4
Vadito NM, 242 ... 49 D2
Vadnais Hts. MN, 13069 ... 235 D1
Vado NM, 3003 ... 56 C3
Vaiden MS, 840 ... 126 C1
Vail AZ, 2484 ... 55 D3
Vail CO, 4531 ... 41 D1
Vails Gate NY, 3319 ... 148 B1
Valatie NY, 1712 ... 94 B2
Valders WI, 948 ... 74 C1
Valdese NC, 4485 ... 111 F4
Valdez AK, 4036 ... 154 C3
Valdosta GA, 43724 ... 137 F1
Vale OR, 1976 ... 22 A4
Valencia NM, 4500 ... 48 C4
Valencia Co. NM, 66152 ... 48 C4
Valentine NE, 2820 ... 34 C1
Valhalla NY, 5379 ... 148 B3
Valier IL, 662 ... 98 C4
Valier MT, 498 ... 15 E2
Valinda CA, 21776 ... 228 E2
Vallejo CA, 116760 ... 36 B3
Vallersville MA, 2000 ... 151 E3
Valley AL, 9198 ... 128 B2
Valley NE, 1788 ... 35 F3
Valley Brook OK, 817 ... 244 E3
Valley Ctr. CA, 7323 ... 53 D3
Valley Ctr. KS, 4883 ... 43 E4
Valley City ND, 6826 ... 19 E4
Valley Cottage NY, 9269 ... 148 B2
Valley Co. ID, 7651 ... 22 C2
Valley Co. MT, 7675 ... 17 D2
Valley Co. NE, 4647 ... 35 D3
Valley Falls KS, 1254 ... 96 A2
Valley Falls RI, 11599 ... 150 C3
Valley Farms AZ, 300 ... 54 C2
Valley Forge PA, 1200 ... 146 B2
Valley Grove WV, 405 ... 91 F4
Valley Head AL, 611 ... 120 A2
Valley Mills TX, 1123 ... 59 E4
Valley Park MO, 6518 ... 256 A3
Valley Sprs. CA, 2560 ... 36 C3
Valley Sprs. SD, 792 ... 27 F4
Valley Stream NY, 36368 ... 148 C4
Valley View OH, 2179 ... 204 F3
Valleyview OH, 601 ... 206 A2
Valley View PA, 1677 ... 93 E3
Valley View TX, 737 ... 59 E1
Valliant OK, 771 ... 116 B3
Valmeyer IL, 608 ... 98 A4
Valparaiso FL, 6408 ... 136 B2
Valparaiso IN, 27428 ... 89 E2
Valparaiso NE, 563 ... 35 F3
Valrico FL, 6582 ... 266 D2
Val Verde Co. TX, 44856 ... 60 B2
Val Verde Park CA, 1472 ... 52 C2
Vamo FL, 5285 ... 140 B4
Van TX, 2362 ... 124 A2
Van Alstyne TX, 2502 ... 59 F1
Van Buren AR, 18986 ... 116 C1
Van Buren IN, 935 ... 89 F3
Van Buren ME, 2369 ... 85 E1
Van Buren MO, 845 ... 107 F2
Van Buren Co. AR, 16192 ... 117 E1
Van Buren Co. IA, 7809 ... 87 E3
Van Buren Co. MI, 76263 ... 75 F4
Van Buren Co. TN, 5508 ... 110 A4
Vance AL, 500 ... 127 F1
Vanceboro NC, 898 ... 115 D3
Vanceburg KY, 1731 ... 100 C3
Vance Co. NC, 42954 ... 113 D3
Vancleave MS, 4910 ... 135 D2
Vancouver WA, 143560 ... 20 C1
Vandalia IL, 6975 ... 98 C3
Vandalia MO, 2529 ... 97 F2
Vandalia OH, 14603 ... 100 B1
Vandenberg Vil. CA, 5802 ... 52 A1
Vander NC, 1204 ... 123 D2
Vanderbilt MI, 587 ... 70 C3
Vanderburgh Co. IN, 171922 ... 99 D4
Vandercook Lake MI, 4809 ... 90 B1
Vandergrift PA, 5455 ... 92 A4
Vandling PA, 738 ... 93 F2
Van Etten NY, 581 ... 93 E1
Vanhiseville NJ, 700 ... 147 E2
Van Horn TX, 2435 ... 57 D4
Van Horne IA, 716 ... 87 E1
Van Lear KY, 1100 ... 111 E1
Vanlue OH, 371 ... 90 C3
Van Meter IA, 866 ... 86 C2
Vansant VA, 989 ... 111 E2
Van Vleck TX, 1411 ... 132 A4
Van Wert OH, 10690 ... 90 B3
Van Wert Co. OH, 29659 ... 90 B3
Van Zandt Co. TX, 48140 ... 124 A2
Vardaman MS, 1065 ... 118 C4
Varnamtown NC, 481 ... 123 E4
Varnell GA, 1491 ... 120 B2
Varnville SC, 2074 ... 130 B2
Vashon WA, 10123 ... 262 A4
Vashon Hts. WA, 1100 ... 262 A3
Vass NC, 750 ... 122 C1
Vassalboro ME, 350 ... 82 C2
Vassar MI, 2823 ... 76 B3
Vaughn MT, 701 ... 15 F3
Vaughn NM, 539 ... 49 D4
Veazie ME, 1500 ... 83 D1
Veblen SD, 281 ... 27 E1
Veedersburg IN, 2299 ... 89 D4
Vega TX, 936 ... 50 A3
Velma OK, 664 ... 51 E4
Velva ND, 1049 ... 18 B2
Venango Co. PA, 57565 ... 92 A2
Veneta OR, 2755 ... 20 B3
Venice FL, 17764 ... 140 B4
Venice IL, 2528 ... 256 C2
Venice LA, 2220 ... 134 C4
Venice Gardens FL, 7466 ... 140 C4
Ventnor City NJ, 12910 ... 147 F4
Ventura CA, 100916 ... 52 B2
Ventura IA, 670 ... 72 C3
Ventura Co. CA, 753197 ... 52 B2
Venus TX, 910 ... 59 E3
Verden OK, 659 ... 51 E3
Verdi NV, 2949 ... 37 D1
Verdigre NE, 519 ... 35 E1
Vergennes VT, 2741 ... 81 D2
Vermilion OH, 10927 ... 91 D2
Vermilion Co. IL, 83919 ... 89 D4

Bixby ... C3
Bowden ... A3
Broken Arrow ... C3
Catoosa ... C1
Jenks ... B3
Oakhurst ... A3
Sand Sprs. ... A2
Sapulpa ... A3
Tiger ... C1
Tulsa ... B2

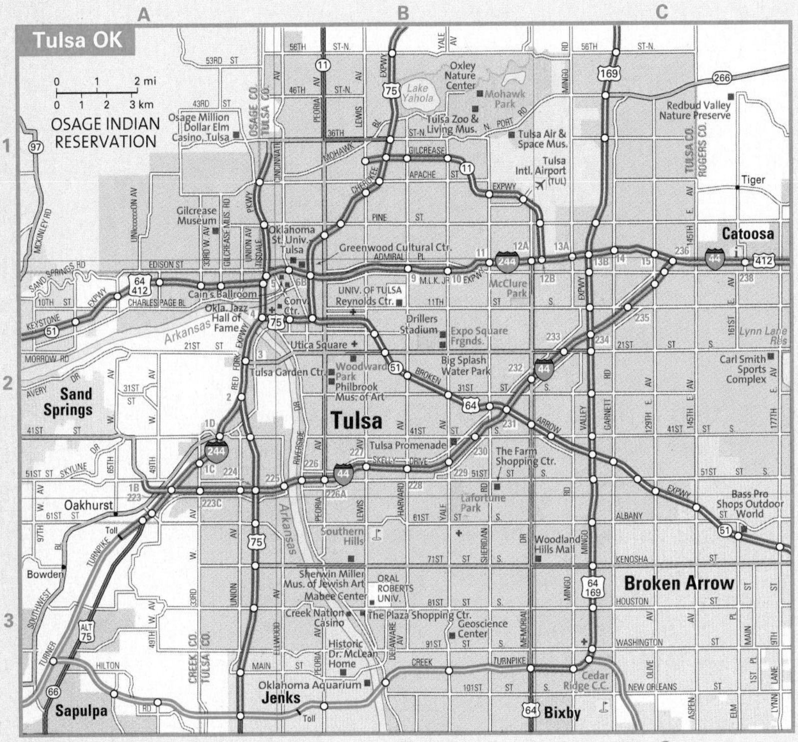
Tulsa OK
A
B
C
1
2
3
OSAGE INDIAN RESERVATION
Osage Million Dollar Elm Casino, Tulsa
Gilcrease Museum
Oxley Nature Center
Mohawk Park
Lake Yahola
Tulsa Zoo & Living Mus.
Tulsa Air & Space Mus.
Tulsa Intl. Airport (TUL)
Redbud Valley Nature Preserve
Tiger
Catoosa
Oklahoma St. Univ. Tulsa
Greenwood Cultural Ctr.
Cain's Ballroom
Okla. Jazz Hall of Fame
UNIV. OF TULSA
Reynolds Ctr.
McClure Park
Drillers Stadium
Expo Square Frgnds.
Utica Square
Big Splash Water Park
Carl Smith Sports Complex
Lynn Lane Res.
Tulsa Garden Ctr.
Woodward Park
Philbrook Mus. of Art
Sand Springs
Tulsa
Tulsa Promenade
The Farm Shopping Ctr.
Lafortune Park
Oakhurst
Bass Pro Shops Outdoor World
Southern Hills
Woodland Hills Mall
Bowden
Sherwin Miller Mus. of Jewish Art
Mabee Center
ORAL ROBERTS UNIV.
Broken Arrow
Creek Nation Casino
The Plaza Shopping Ctr.
Geoscience Center
Historic Dr. McLean Home
Oklahoma Aquarium
Cedar Ridge C.C.
Sapulpa
Jenks
Bixby
Arkansas
Toll

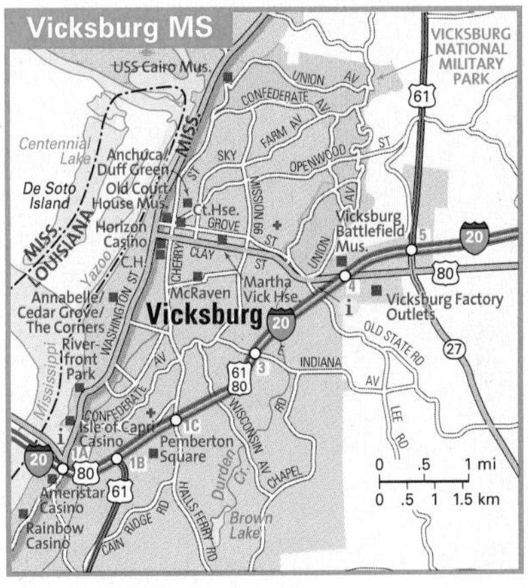
Vicksburg MS
VICKSBURG NATIONAL MILITARY PARK
USS Cairo Mus.
Centennial Lake
De Soto Island
Anchuca/ Duff Green
Old Court House Mus.
Horizon Casino
Ct. Hse.
Vicksburg Battlefield Mus.
Martha Vick Hse.
Vicksburg Factory Outlets
McRaven
Annabelle/ Cedar Grove/ The Corners
River-front Park
Vicksburg
Isle of Capri Casino
Pemberton Square
Ameristar Casino
Rainbow Casino
Brown Lake
MISSISSIPPI
LOUISIANA
0 .5 1 mi
0 .5 1 1.5 km

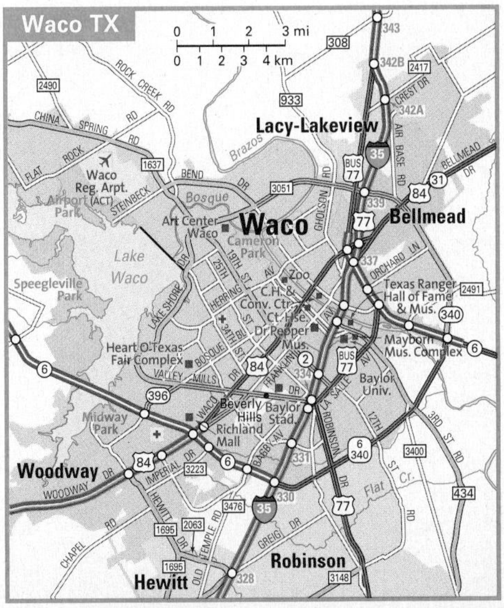
Waco TX
0 1 2 3 mi
0 1 2 3 4 km
Lacy-Lakeview
Bellmead
Waco Reg. Arpt. (ACT)
Airport Park
Art Center Waco
Cameron Park
Waco
Lake Waco
Speegleville Park
Zoo
C.H. & Conv. Ctr.
Ct. Hse.
Dr Pepper Mus.
Texas Ranger Hall of Fame & Mus.
Mayborn Mus. Complex
Heart O' Texas Fair Complex
Baylor Univ.
Beverly Hills
Baylor Stad.
Richland Mall
Midway Park
Woodway
Hewitt
Robinson
Brazos
Bosque

Figures after entries indicate population, page number, and grid reference.

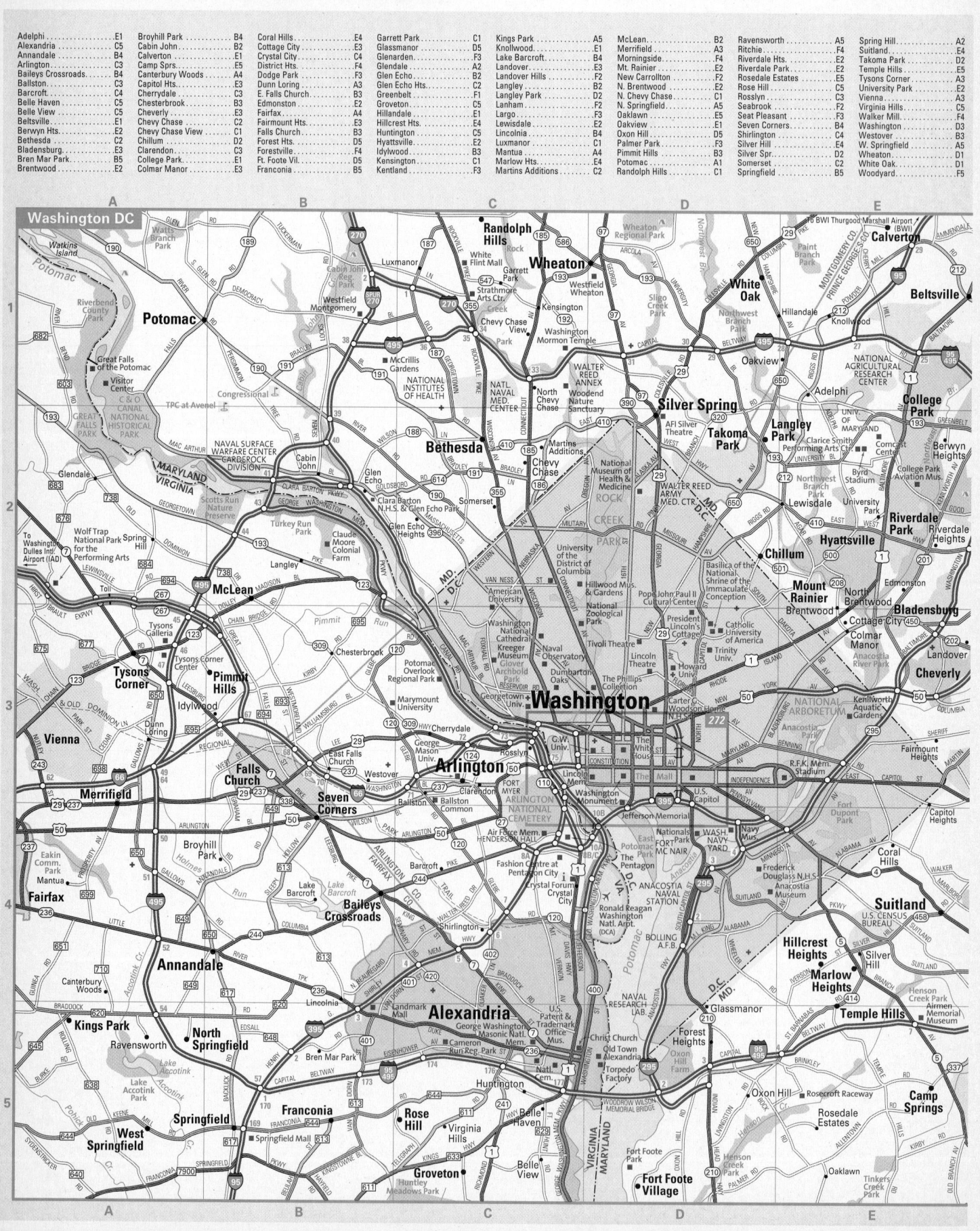

Washington DC

Entries in **bold black** indicate counties or parishes.
Entries in **bold color** indicate cities with detailed inset maps.

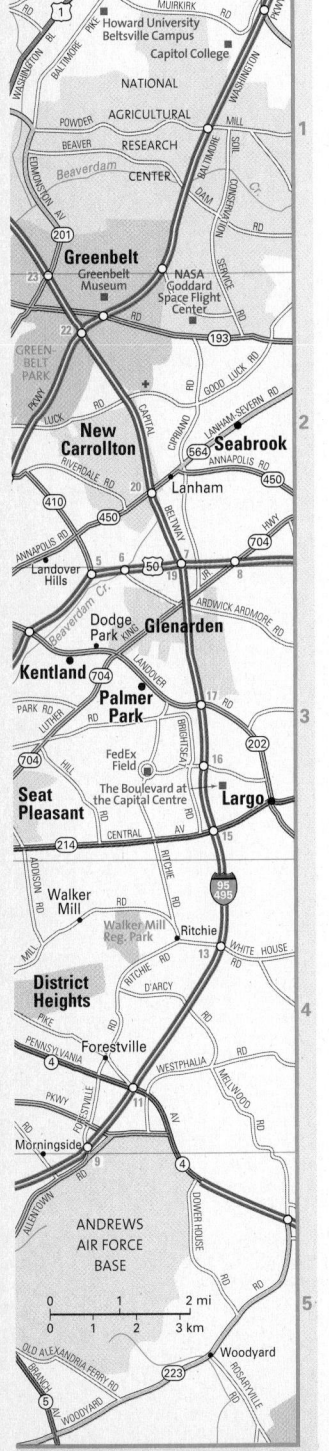

Figures after entries indicate population, page number, and grid reference.

POINTS OF INTEREST

Entries in **bold black** indicate counties or parishes.
Entries in **bold color** indicate cities with detailed inset maps.

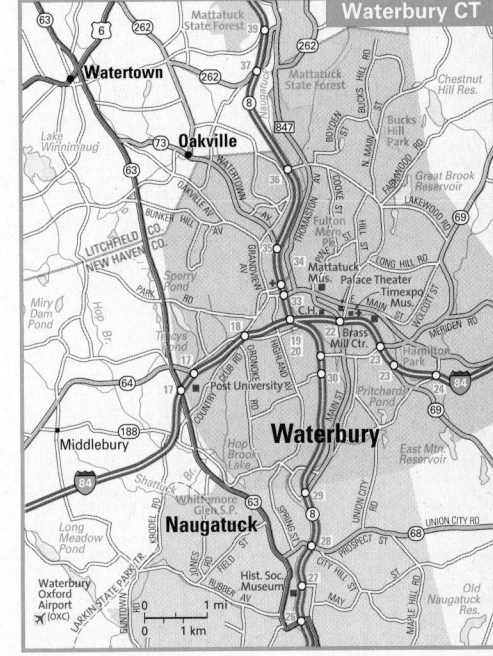

Waterbury CT

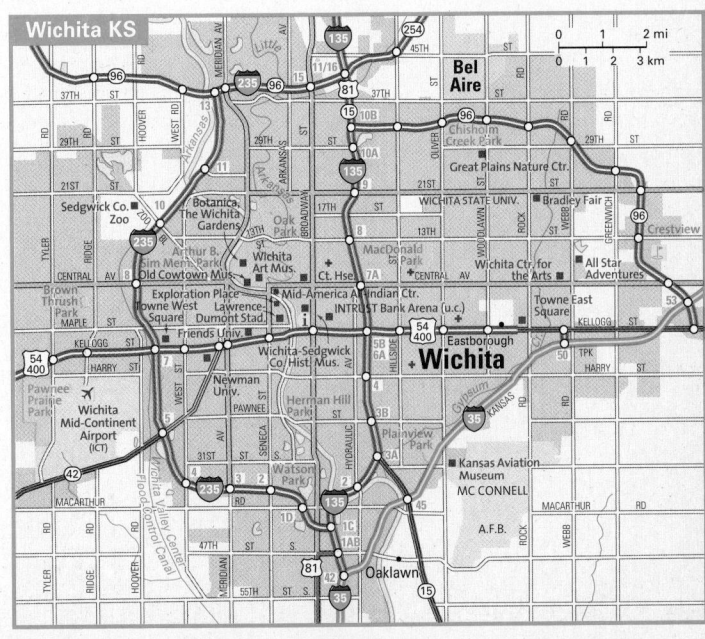

Wichita KS

Downtown Washington DC

274
Wewahitchka–Winnebago County

Figures after entries indicate population, page number, and grid reference.

Wewahitchka FL, *1722* 137 D2
Wewoka OK, *3562* 51 F3
Wexford Co. MI, *30484* 69 F4
Weyauwega WI, *1806* 74 B1
Weyers Cave VA, *1225* 102 C4
Weymouth MA, *53988* 151 D2
Wharton NJ, *6298* 148 A3
Wharton OH, *409* 90 C3
Wharton TX, *9237* 61 F3
Wharton Co. TX, *41188* 61 F3
What Cheer IA, *678* 87 E2
Whatcom Co. WA, *166814* 12 C1
Whately MA, *425* 150 A1
Wheatfield IN, *772* 89 E2
White Hall VA, *300* 103 D2
Whitehall PA, *14444* 250 B3
Whitehall WV, *595* 102 A2
Whitehall WI, *1651* 73 F1
White Haven PA, *1182* 93 F3
White Horse NJ, *9373* 147 D2
White Horse PA, *475* 146 A3
White Horse Beach MA, *2300* 151 E3
Whitehouse OH, *2733* 90 B2
White House TN, *7220* 109 F3
Whitehouse TX, *5346* 124 B3
White House Sta. NJ, *1951* 147 D1
White Island Shores MA, *2133* 151 E3
White Lake NY, *475* 94 A3
Whitney TX, *1833* 59 E3
Whitney Pt. NY, *965* 79 E4
Whitsett NC, *686* 112 B4
Whittemore IA, *530* 72 B3
Whittemore MI, *476* 76 B1
Whittier CA, *83680* 52 C2
Whitwell TN, *1660* 120 B1
Why AZ, *225* 54 B3
Wibaux MT, *567* 17 F4
Wibaux Co. MT, *1068* 17 F4
Wichita KS, *344284* 43 E4
Wichita Co. KS, *2531* 42 B3
Wichita Co. TX, *131664* 59 D1
Wichita Falls TX, *104197* 59 D1
Williamsburg CO, *714* 41 E3
Williamsburg FL, *6736* 246 B4
Williamsburg IA, *2622* 87 E2
Williamsburg KS, *351* 96 A3
Williamsburg KY, *5143* 110 C3
Williamsburg MA, *550* 150 A1
Williamsburg NM, *527* 56 B2
Williamsburg OH, *2358* 100 C2
Williamsburg PA, *1345* 92 C4
Williamsburg VA, *11998* 113 F2
Williamsburg Co. SC, *37217* 122 C4
Williams Co. ND, *19761* 17 F2
Williams Co. OH, *39188* 90 A2
Williams Creek IN, *413* 221 C1
Wilmar AR, *571* 117 F4
Wilmer AL, *500* 135 E1
Wilmer TX, *3393* 207 E3
Wilmerding PA, *2145* 250 D3
Wilmette IL, *27651* 89 D1
Wilmington DE, *72664* 146 B4
Wilmington IL, *5134* 88 C2
Wilmington NC, *75838* 123 E3
Wilmington OH, *11921* 100 C2
Wilmington VT, *800* 94 C1
Wilmington Island GA, *14213* 130 C3
Wilmington Manor DE, *8262* 274 D3
Wilmore KY, *5905* 100 B4
Wilmot AR, *786* 125 F1
Wilmot SD, *543* 27 F2
Wilsall MT, *237* 23 F1
Wilson AR, *939* 118 B1
Wilson KS, *799* 43 D2
Wilson LA, *668* 134 A1
Wilson NY, *1213* 78 B3
Wilson NC, *44405* 113 D4
Wilson OK, *1584* 51 E4
Wilson PA, *7682* 93 F3
Wilson TX, *532* 58 A2
Wilson WY, *1294* 23 F4
Wilson Co. KS, *10332* 106 A1
Wilson Co. NC, *73814* 113 E4
Wilson Co. TN, *88809* 109 F3
Wilson Co. TX, *32408* 61 E3
Wilson's Mills NC, *1291* 123 D1
Wilsonville AL, *1551* 128 A1
Wilsonville IL, *604* 98 B2
Wilsonville OR, *13991* 20 C2
Wilton AL, *580* 127 F1
Wilton AR, *439* 116 C4
Wilton CA, *4551* 36 C3
Wilton CT, *2000* 148 C2
Wilton IA, *2829* 87 F2
Wilton ME, *2290* 82 B2
Wilton NH, *1236* 95 D1
Wilton NY, *600* 80 C4
Wilton ND, *807* 18 C3
Wilton WI, *519* 73 F2
Wilton Manors FL, *12697* 233 C2
Wimauma FL, *4246* 140 C3
Wimberley TX, *2685* 61 D2
Wimbledon ND, *237* 19 D3
Winamac IN, *2418* 89 E3
Winchendon MA, *4246* 95 D1
Winchester CA, *2155* 53 D3
Winchester ID, *308* 22 B1
Winchester IL, *1650* 98 A1
Winchester IN, *5037* 90 A4
Winchester KS, *579* 96 A2
Winchester KY, *16724* 100 B4
Winchester MA, *20810* 151 D1
Winchester MO, *1651* 256 A2
Winchester NH, *1832* 94 C1
Winchester OH, *1025* 100 C3
Winchester OK, *424* 51 F2
Winchester OH, *1025* 100 C3
Winchester TN, *7329* 120 A1
Winchester VA, *23585* 103 D2
Winchester Bay OR, *488* 20 A4
Windber PA, *4395* 92 B4
Windcrest TX, *5105* 61 D2
Winder GA, *10201* 121 D3
Windermere FL, *1897* 141 D1
Windfall IN, *712* 89 F4
Wind Gap PA, *2812* 93 F3
Windham CT, *1000* 149 F1
Windham NH, *1600* 95 E1
Windham OH, *2806* 91 F2
Windham Co. CT, *109091* 150 B3
Windham Co. VT, *44216* 81 E4
Wind Lake WI, *5202* 74 C3
Windom MN, *4490* 72 B2
Window Rock AZ, *3059* 48 A2
Wind Pt. WI, *1853* 75 D4
Windsor CA, *22744* 36 B3
Windsor CO, *9896* 33 E4
Windsor CT, *3600* 150 A3
Windsor IL, *1125* 98 C2
Windsor MO, *3087* 96 C3
Windsor NY, *901* 93 F1
Windsor NC, *2283* 113 F4
Windsor PA, *1331* 103 E1
Windsor VT, *2200* 81 E4
Windsor VA, *916* 113 F2
Windsor WI, *2533* 74 B3
Windsor Co. VT, *57418* 81 E3
Windsor Hts. WV, *431* 91 F4
Windsor Hills CA, *10958* 228 C3
Windsor Locks CT, *12043* 150 A2
Windthorst TX, *440* 59 D1
Windy Hills KY, *2480* 230 E1
Winfall NC, *554* 113 F3
Winfield AL, *4540* 119 E4
Winfield IL, *8718* 203 B4
Winfield IN, *2298* 89 D2
Winfield IA, *1131* 87 F3
Winfield KS, *12206* 43 F4
Winfield MO, *723* 98 A2
Winfield TN, *911* 110 C3
Winfield TX, *499* 124 B1
Winfield WV, *1858* 101 E3
Wingate NC, *2406* 122 B2
Wingdale NY, *1500* 148 C1
Wingo KY, *581* 108 C3
Winifred MT, *156* 16 B3
Wink TX, *919* 57 F4
Winkelman AZ, *443* 55 D2
Winkler Co. TX, *7173* 57 F3
Winlock WA, *1166* 12 B4
Winnebago IL, *2958* 74 B4
Winnebago MN, *1487* 72 C2
Winnebago NE, *768* 35 F2
Winnebago Co. IL, *278418* 74 B4

Five Forks A1
Gloucester Pt. C2
Hayes C1
Lackey C2
Newport News C2
Scotland A2
Wicomico C1
Williamsburg A1
Yorktown C2

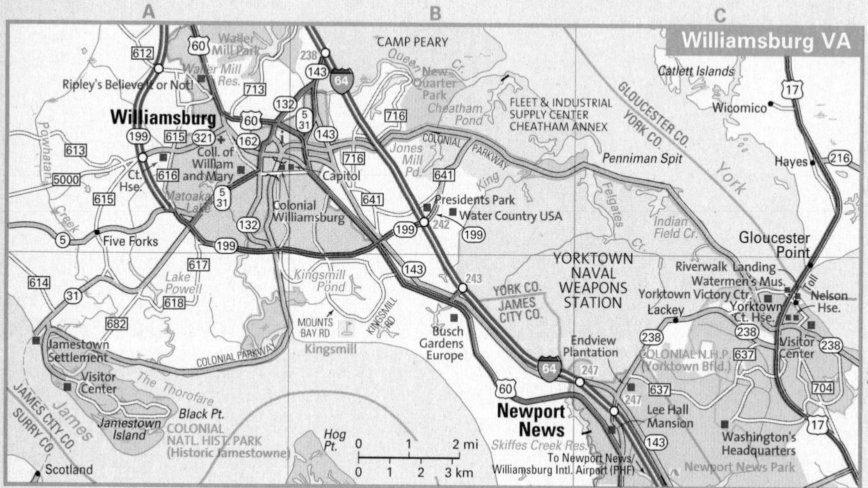

Wheatland CA, *2275* 36 C2
Wheatland IN, *504* 99 E3
Wheatland IA, *772* 87 F1
Wheatland WY, *3548* 33 E2
Wheatland Co. MT, *2259* 16 B4
Wheatley AR, *372* 118 A2
Wheaton IL, *55416* 89 D1
Wheaton MD, *57694* 144 B3
Wheaton MN, *1619* 27 F1
Wheaton MO, *721* 106 C2
Wheat Ridge CO, *32913* 209 B3
Wheeler MS, *300* 119 D2
Wheeler OR, *391* 20 B1
Wheeler TX, *1378* 50 C3
Wheeler Co. GA, *6179* 129 E3
Wheeler Co. NE, *886* 35 D2
Wheeler Co. OR, *1547* 21 E3
Wheeler Co. TX, *5284* 50 C3
Wheelersburg OH, *6471* 101 D3
Wheeling IL, *34496* 89 D1
Wheeling WV, *31419* 91 F4
Wheelwright KY, *1042* 111 E1
Wheelwright MA, *425* 150 B1
Whigham GA, *631* 137 E1
Whippany NJ, *3800* 148 A3
Whispering Pines NC, *2090* 122 C1
Whitaker PA, *1338* 250 C2
Whitakers NC, *799* 113 E4
White GA, *693* 120 C3
White SD, *530* 27 F3
White Bear Lake MN, *24325* 235 D1
White Bird ID, *106* 22 B1
White Bluff TN, *2142* 109 E4
White Castle LA, *1946* 134 A2
White Ctr. WA, *20975* 262 B4
White City FL, *4221* 141 E3
White City KS, *518* 43 F2
White City OR, *5466* 28 B2
White Cloud MI, *1420* 75 F2
White Co. AR, *67165* 117 F1
White Co. GA, *19944* 121 D2
White Co. IL, *15371* 99 D4
White Co. IN, *25267* 89 E3
White Co. TN, *23102* 110 A4
White Deer TX, *1060* 50 B3
White Earth MN, *424* 19 F3
Whiteface TX, *465* 57 F1
Whitefield NH, *1089* 81 F2
Whitefish MT, *5032* 15 D2
Whitefish Bay WI, *14163* 234 D1
Whiteford MD, *700* 146 A4
White Hall AL, *1014* 127 F2
White Hall AR, *4732* 117 E3
White Hall IL, *2629* 98 A2
Whitehall MI, *2884* 75 E2
Whitehall MT, *1044* 23 E1
Whitehall NY, *2667* 81 D3
Whitehall OH, *19201* 206 C2
Whitehall PA, *14268* 146 B1
Whitehall VA, *250* 102 C4
White Lake NC, *529* 123 D2
White Lake SD, *405* 27 D4
Whiteland IN, *3958* 99 F1
Whitelaw WI, *757* 75 D1
White Marsh MD, *8485* 193 E2
White Marsh VA, *600* 113 F1
White Oak MD, *20973* 270 D1
White Oak OH, *13277* 204 A2
White Oak PA, *8437* 92 A4
White Oak TX, *5624* 124 B2
White Pigeon MI, *1627* 89 F1
White Pine MI, *700* 65 E4
White Pine TN, *1997* 111 D4
White Pine Co. NV, *9181* 38 B1
White Plains KY, *800* 109 E2
White Plains MD, *3600* 144 B4
White Plains NY, *53077* 148 B3
White Plains NC, *1049* 112 A3
Whiteriver AZ, *5220* 55 E1
White River SD, *598* 26 C4
White River Jct. VT, *2569* 81 E3
White Rock NM, *6045* 48 C2
Whiterocks UT, *341* 32 A4
White Salmon WA, *2193* 21 D1
Whitesboro NY, *3943* 79 E3
Whitesboro TX, *3760* 59 F1
Whitesburg GA, *596* 120 B4
Whitesburg KY, *1600* 111 E2
White Settlement TX, *14831* 207 A2
White Shield ND, *348* 18 B3
Whiteside Co. IL, *60653* 88 A1
White Sprs. FL, *819* 138 C2
White Stone VA, *358* 113 F1
White Sulphur Sprs. MT, *984* 15 F4
White Sulphur Sprs. WV, *2315* 112 B1
Whitesville KY, *632* 109 F1
Whitesville NY, *400* 92 C1
Whitesville WV, *520* 101 F4
White Swan WA, *3033* 13 D4
Whiteville NC, *5148* 123 D3
Whiteville TN, *3148* 118 C1
Whitewater KS, *653* 43 E3
Whitewater WI, *13437* 74 C3
Whitewood SD, *844* 25 F3
Whitewright TX, *1740* 59 F1
Whitfield Co. GA, *83525* 120 B2
Whitfield Estates FL, *4200* 140 B3
Whiting IN, *5137* 89 D2
Whiting IA, *707* 35 F2
Whiting NJ, *1800* 147 E3
Whiting WI, *1760* 68 B4
Whitinsville MA, *6340* 150 C2
Whitley City KY, *1111* 110 C3
Whitley Co. IN, *30707* 89 F3
Whitley Co. KY, *35865* 110 C2
Whitman MA, *13882* 151 D2
Whitman Co. WA, *40740* 14 A4
Whitmire SC, *1512* 121 F3
Whitmore Lake MI, *6574* 76 B4
Whitmore Vil. HI, *4057* 152 A2
Wickenburg AZ, *5082* 54 B1
Wickes AR, *675* 116 C3
Wickett TX, *455* 57 F4
Wickford RI, *1900* 150 C4
Wickliffe KY, *794* 108 C2
Wickliffe OH, *13484* 91 E2
Wicomico Church VA, *250* 113 F1
Wicomico Co. MD, *84644* 114 C1
Widefield CO, *29845* 205 D2
Wiggins CO, *838* 33 F4
Wiggins MS, *3849* 135 D1
Wilbarger Co. TX, *14676* 58 C1
Wilber NE, *1761* 35 F4
Wilberforce OH, *1579* 100 C1
Wilbraham MA, *3544* 150 A2
Wilbur WA, *914* 13 F3
Wilbur Park MO, *475* 256 B3
Wilburton OK, *2972* 116 A2
Wilcox NE, *360* 35 D4
Wilcox PA, *500* 92 B2
Wilcox Co. AL, *13183* 127 F3
Wilcox Co. GA, *8577* 129 E3
Wilder ID, *1462* 22 A4
Wilder KY, *2624* 204 B3
Wilder VT, *1636* 81 E3
Wilderness VA, *300* 103 D4
Wildomar CA, *14064* 53 D3
Wild Rose WI, *765* 74 B1
Wildwood FL, *3924* 140 C1
Wildwood MO, *32884* 98 A3
Wildwood NJ, *5436* 104 C4
Wildwood TX, *550* 132 C2
Wildwood Crest NJ, *3980* 104 C4
Wiley CO, *483* 42 A3
Wilhoit AZ, *664* 47 D4
Wilkes-Barre PA, *43123* 93 E2
Wilkesboro NC, *3159* 111 F4
Wilkes Co. GA, *10687* 121 E4
Wilkes Co. NC, *65632* 112 A3
Wilkeson WA, *395* 12 C3
Wilkin Co. MN, *7138* 19 F4
Wilkinsburg PA, *19196* 250 C2
Wilkinson Co. GA, *10220* 129 E2
Wilkinson Co. MS, *10312* 125 F4
Willacoochee GA, *1434* 129 E4
Willacy Co. TX, *20082* 63 F3
Willamina OR, *1844* 20 B2
Willard MO, *3193* 107 D2
Willard NM, *240* 49 D4
Willard OH, *6806* 91 D3
Willard UT, *1630* 31 E3
Willards MD, *938* 114 C1
Will Co. IL, *502266* 89 D2
Willcox AZ, *3733* 55 E3
Willernie MN, *549* 235 E1
Williams AZ, *2842* 47 D3
Williams CA, *3670* 36 B2
Williams IA, *427* 72 C4
Williams OR, *200* 28 B2
Williams Bay WI, *2415* 74 C4
Williamsfield IL, *620* 88 A3
Williamson NY, *2100* 78 C3
Williamson WV, *3414* 111 E1
Williamson Co. IL, *61296* 108 C1
Williamson Co. TN, *126638* 109 F4
Williamson Co. TX, *249967* 61 E1
Williamsport IN, *1935* 89 D4
Williamsport MD, *1868* 103 D1
Williamsport OH, *1002* 101 D1
Williamsport PA, *30706* 93 D2
Williamston MI, *3441* 76 A4
Williamston NC, *5843* 113 E4
Williamston SC, *3791* 121 E2
Williamstown KY, *3227* 100 B3
Williamstown MA, *4754* 94 C1
Williamstown NJ, *11812* 146 C4
Williamstown NY, *475* 79 E2
Williamstown PA, *1433* 93 E4
Williamstown VT, *850* 81 E2
Williamstown WV, *2996* 101 F2
Williamsville DE, *350* 114 C1
Williamsville IL, *1439* 98 B1
Williamsville MS, *400* 126 C1
Williamsville NY, *5573* 198 C2
Willimantic CT, *15823* 150 B3
Willingboro NJ, *36300* 147 D3
Willis TX, *3985* 132 A2
Willisburg KY, *304* 110 B1
Williston FL, *2297* 138 C4
Williston MD, *425* 145 E3
Williston ND, *12512* 17 F2
Williston OH, *800* 90 C2
Williston SC, *3307* 130 B1
Williston TN, *341* 118 C1
Williston VT, *500* 81 D2
Willisville IL, *694* 98 B4
Willis Wharf VA, *475* 114 B3
Willits CA, *5073* 36 A2
Willmar MN, *18351* 66 B3
Willoughby OH, *22621* 91 E2
Willoughby Hills OH, *8595* 204 G1
Willow AK, *1658* 154 C3
Willowbrook CA, *34138* 228 D3
Willowbrook IL, *8967* 203 C5
Willow City ND, *221* 18 C2
Willow Creek CA, *1743* 28 B4
Willow Creek MT, *209* 23 E1
Willow Grove PA, *16234* 146 C2
Willowick OH, *14361* 91 E2
Willow Lake SD, *294* 27 E3
Willow Park TX, *2849* 59 E2
Willows CA, *6220* 36 B1
Willows MD, *900* 144 C4
Willow Sprs. IL, *5027* 203 C5
Willow Sprs. MO, *2147* 107 E2
Willow Street PA, *7258* 146 A3
Willsboro NY, *600* 81 D2
Willshire OH, *463* 90 A3
Wills Pt. TX, *3496* 59 F2
Willwood WY, *100* 24 B3

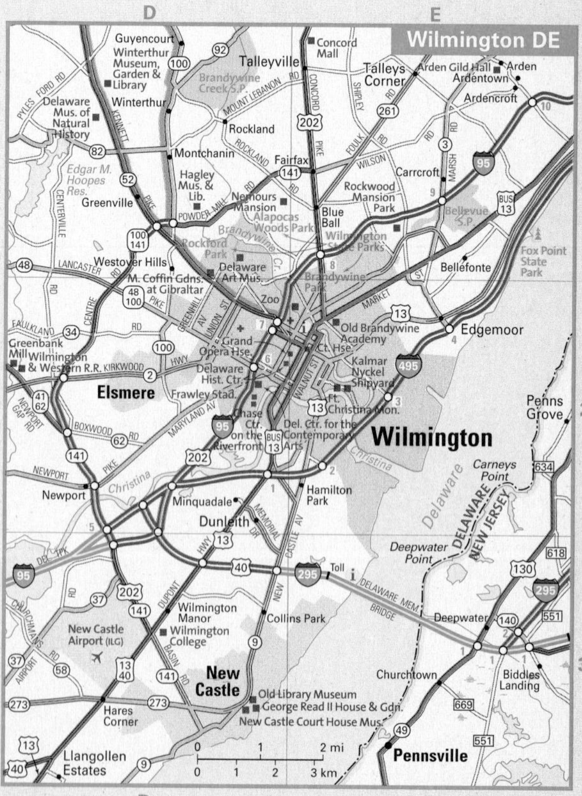

Arden E1
Ardencroft E1
Ardentown E1
Bellefonte E1
Biddles Landing E3
Blue Ball E1
Carrcroft E1
Churchtown E3
Collins Park D3
Deepwater E3
Dunleith D2
Edgemoor E2
Elsmere D2
Fairfax E1
Greenville D1
Guyencourt D1
Hamilton Park E2
Hares Corner D3
Llangollen Estates D3
Minquadale D2
Montchanin D1
New Castle D3
Newport D2
Penns Grove E2
Pennsville E3
Rockland D1
Talleys Corner E1
Talleyville E1
Westover Hills D1
Wilmington E2
Wilmington Manor D3
Winterthur D1

Entries in **bold black** indicate counties or parishes.
Entries in **bold color** indicate cities with detailed inset maps.

Worcester MA

Yakima WA

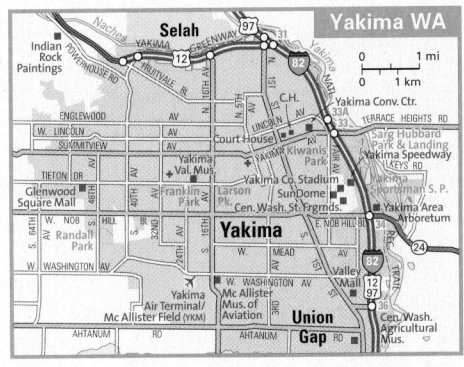

Wilmington NC

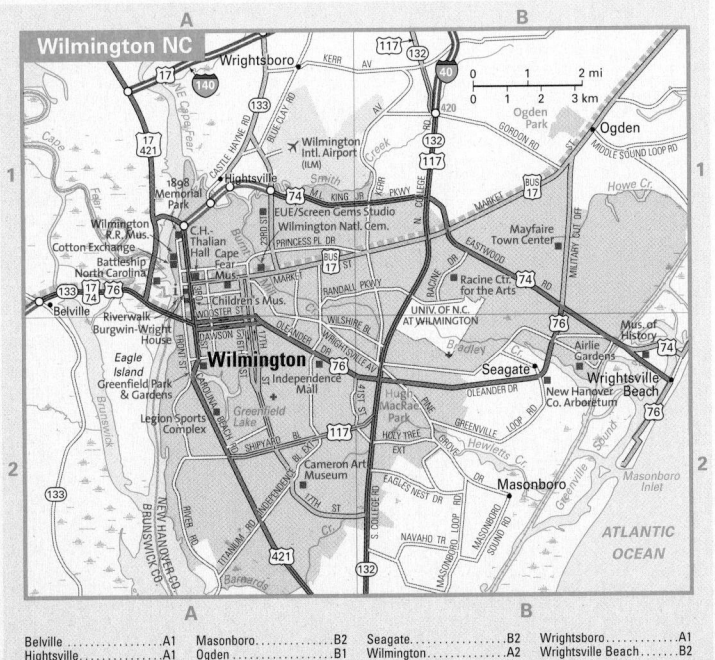

York PA

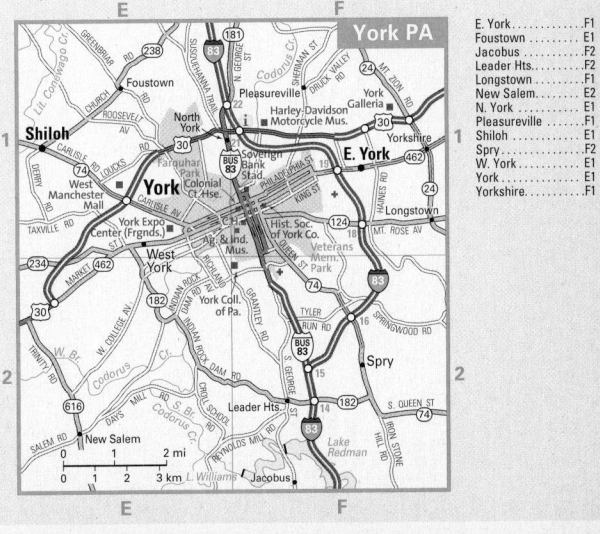

276
Wycombe–Yaurel

Figures after entries indicate population, page number, and grid reference.

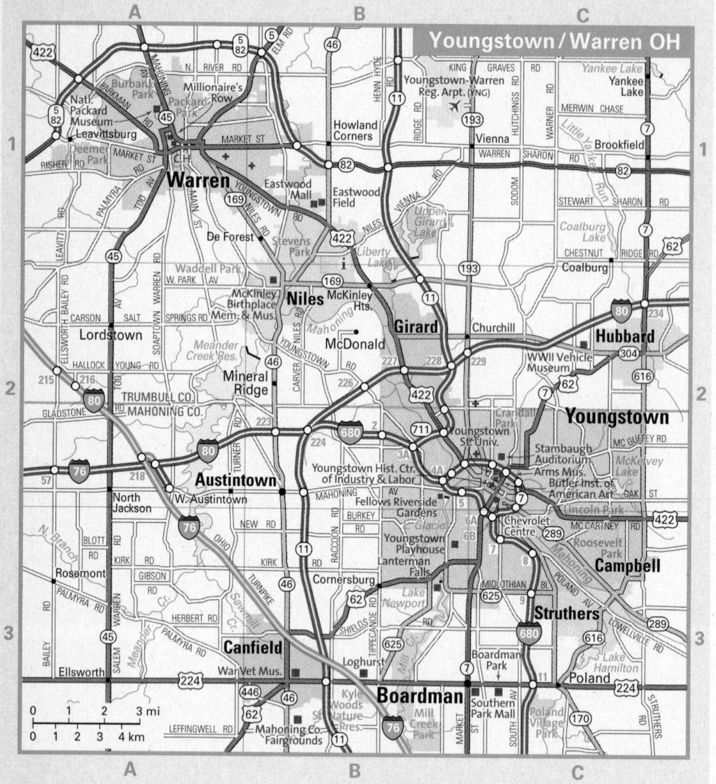

Austintown . . . B2
Boardman . . . B3
Brookfield . . . C1
Campbell . . . C3
Canfield . . . B3
Churchill . . . C2
Coalburg . . . C1
Cornersburg . . . B3
De Forest . . . B1
Ellsworth . . . A3
Girard . . . B2
Howland Corners . . . B1
Hubbard . . . C2
Leavittsburg . . . A1
Lordstown . . . A2
McDonald . . . B2
McKinley Hts. . . . B2
Mineral Ridge . . . B2
Niles . . . B2
N. Jackson . . . A2
Poland . . . C3
Rosemont . . . A3
Struthers . . . C3
Vienna . . . C1
Warren . . . A1
W. Austintown . . . A2
Yankee Lake . . . C1
Youngstown . . . C2

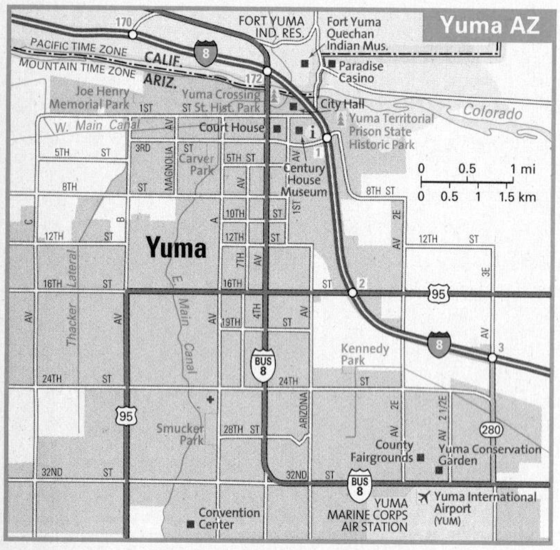

Wycombe PA, *650* **146** C2
Wykoff MN, *460* **73** E2
Wylie TX, *15132* **59** F2
Wymore NE, *1656* **43** F1
Wynantskill NY, *3018* **188** E2
Wyncote PA, *3046* **248** C1
Wyndmere ND, *533* **27** F1
Wynne AR, *8615* **118** A1
Wynnewood OK, *2367* **51** E4
Wynona OK, *531* **51** F1
Wyocena WI, *668* **74** B2
Wyodak WY, *125* **25** E3
Wyola MT, *186* **24** C2
Wyoming DE, *1141* **145** E2
Wyoming IL, *1424* **88** B3
Wyoming IA, *626* **87** F1
Wyoming MI, *69368* **75** F3
Wyoming MN, *3048* **67** D3
Wyoming NY, *513* **78** B3
Wyoming OH, *8261* **204** B1
Wyoming PA, *3221* **261** B1
Wyoming RI, *475* **150** C4
Wyoming Co. NY, *43424* **78** B4
Wyoming Co. PA, *28080* **93** E2
Wyoming Co. WV, *25708* **111** F1
Wyomissing PA, *11155* **146** A2
Wythe Co. VA, *27599* **112** A2
Wytheville VA, *7804* **112** A2

X

Xenia IL, *407* **98** C3
Xenia OH, *24164* **100** C1

Y

Yachats OR, *617* **20** B3
Yacolt WA, *1055* **20** C1
Yadkin Co. NC, *36348* **112** A3
Yadkinville NC, *2818* **112** A4
Yah-Tah-Hey NM, *580* **48** A2
Yakima WA, *71845* **13** D4
Yakima Co. WA, *222581* **13** D4
Yakutat AK, *680* **155** D3
Yalaha FL, *1175* **140** C1
Yale MI, *2063* **76** C3
Yale OK, *1342* **51** F2
Yalesville CT, *3600* **149** D1
Yalobusha Co. MS, *13051* **118** B3
Yamhill OR, *794* **20** B2
Yamhill Co. OR, *84992* **20** B2
Yampa CO, *443* **40** C1
Yancey Co. NC, *17774* **111** E4
Yanceyville NC, *2091* **112** C3
Yankeetown FL, *629* **138** C4
Yankton SD, *13528* **35** E1
Yankton Co. SD, *21652* **35** E1
Yaphank NY, *5025* **149** D3
Yardley PA, *2498* **147** D2
Yardville NJ, *9208* **147** D2
Yarmouth ME, *3560* **82** B3
Yarmouth MA, *2100* **151** F3
Yarmouth Port MA, *5395* **151** F3
Yarnell AZ, *645* **47** D4
Yarrow Pt. WA, *1008* **262** B3
Yates Ctr. KS, *1599* **96** A4
Yates City IL, *725* **88** A3
Yates Co. NY, *24621* **78** C4
Yatesville GA, *408* **129** D1
Yatesville PA, *649* **261** C2
Yavapai Co. AZ, *167517* **47** D4
Yazoo City MS, *14550* **126** B2
Yazoo Co. MS, *28149* **126** B2
Yeadon PA, *11762* **146** C3
Yeagertown PA, *1035* **93** D3
Yell Co. AR, *21139* **117** D2
Yellow House PA, 475 **146** B2
Yellow Medicine Co. MN, *11080* **66** A4
Yellow Sprs. MD, *1100* **144** A1
Yellow Sprs. OH, *3761* **100** C1
Yellowstone Co. MT, *129352* **24** C1
Yellville AR, *1312* **107** E3
Yelm WA, *3289* **12** C4
Yemassee SC, *807* **130** C2
Yerington NV, *2883* **37** E2
Yerkes KY, *500* **111** D2
Yermo CA, *900* **53** D1
Yoakum TX, *5731* **61** E3
Yoakum Co. TX, *7322* **57** F2
Yoder WY, *169* **33** F2
Yoe PA, *1022* **103** E1
Yolo CA, *550* **36** B2
Yolo Co. CA, *168660* **36** B2
Yoncalla OR, *1052* **20** B4
Yonkers NY, *196086* **148** B3
Yorba Linda CA, *58918* **229** F3
York AL, *2854* **127** D2
York NE, *8081* **35** E4
York NY, *450* **78** C3
York PA, *40862* **103** E1
York SC, *6985* **122** A2
York Beach ME, *1400* **82** B4
York Co. ME, *186742* **82** B4
York Co. NE, *14598* **35** E4
York Co. PA, *381751* **103** E1
York Co. SC, *164614* **122** A2
York Co. VA, *56297* **113** F2
York Harbor ME, *3321* **82** B4
York Haven PA, *809* **93** E4
Yorkshire NY, *1403* **78** B4
Yorkshire VA, *6732* **144** A3
York Sprs. PA, *574* **103** E1
Yorktown IN, *4785* **89** F4
Yorktown NY, *14891* **148** B2
Yorktown TX, *2271* **61** E3
Yorktown VA, *203* **113** F2
Yorktown Hts. NY, *7972* **148** B2
York Vil. ME, *2000* **82** B4
Yorkville IL, *6189* **88** C2
Yorkville OH, *1230* **91** F4
Young AZ, *561* **47** E4
Young Co. TX, *17943* **59** D2
Young Harris GA, *604* **121** D2
Youngstown NY, *1957* **78** A3
Youngstown OH, *82026* **91** F3
Youngstown PA, *400* **92** B4
Youngsville LA, *3992* **133** F2
Youngsville NC, *651* **113** D4
Youngsville PA, *1834* **92** B1
Youngtown AZ, *3010* **249** A1
Youngwood PA, *4138* **92** A4
Yountville CA, *2916* **36** B3
Ypsilanti MI, *22362* **90** C1
Yreka CA, *7290* **28** C2
Yuba City CA, *36758* **36** C2
Yuba Co. CA, *60219* **36** C2
Yucaipa CA, *41207* **53** D2
Yucca Valley CA, *16865* **53** E2
Yukon OK, *21043* **51** E3
Yulee FL, *8392* **139** D2
Yuma AZ, *77515* **53** F4
Yuma CO, *3285* **42** A1
Yuma Co. AZ, *160026* **54** A2
Yuma Co. CO, *9841* **34** A4
Yutan NE, *1216* **35** F3

Z

Zacata VA, *450* **103** E4
Zachary LA, *11275* **134** A1
Zanesville IN, *602* **90** A3
Zanesville OH, *25586* **101** E1
Zap ND, *231* **18** B3
Zapata TX, *4856* **63** D3
Zapata Co. TX, *12182* **63** D3
Zavala Co. TX, *11600* **60** C3
Zavalla TX, *647* **132** C1
Zearing IA, *617* **87** D1
Zeb OK, *498* **106** B4
Zebulon GA, *1181* **128** C1
Zebulon KY, *700* **111** E1
Zebulon NC, *4046* **113** D4
Zeeland MI, *5805* **75** F3
Zeigler IL, *1669* **98** C4
Zelienople PA, *4123* **92** A3
Zephyr Cove NV, *1649* **37** D2
Zephyrhills FL, *10833* **140** C2
Zia Pueblo NM, *646* **48** C3
Ziebach Co. SD, *2519* **26** B2
Zillah WA, *2198* **13** E4
Zimmerman MN, *2851* **66** C3
Zion IL, *22866* **75** D4
Zion KY, *550* **109** E1
Zion PA, *2054* **92** C3
Zion Crossroads VA, 375 **102** C4
Zionsville IN, *8775* **99** F1
Zolfo Sprs. FL, *1641* **140** C3
Zumbrota MN, *2789* **73** D1
Zuni Pueblo NM, *6367* **48** A3
Zwolle LA, *1783* **125** D4

PUERTO RICO

Aceitunas PR, *1688* **187** D1
Adjuntas PR, *4980* **187** D1
Aguada PR, *3871* **187** D1
Aguadilla PR, *16776* **187** D1
Aguas Buenas PR, *4368* **187** E1
Aguilita PR, *4922* **187** E1
Aibonito PR, *9269* **187** E1
Añasco PR, *5880* **187** D1
Arecibo PR, *9318* **187** E1
Arroyo PR, *7244* **187** E1
Bajadero PR, *3877* **187** E1
Barceloneta PR, *4253* **187** E1
Barranquitas PR, *2910* **187** E1
Bayamón PR, *203499* **187** E1
Betances PR, *835* **187** D1
Boquerón PR, *1218* **187** D1
Cabo Rojo PR, *10610* **187** D1
Caguas PR, *88680* **187** E1
Camuy PR, *4013* **187** D1
Canóvanas PR, *8069* **187** F1
Carolina PR, *168164* **187** F1
Cataño PR, *30071* **187** E1
Cayey PR, *19940* **187** E1
Cayuco PR, *1284* **187** D1
Ceiba PR, *6277* **187** E1
Ceiba PR, *3698* **187** E1
Ciales PR, *3082* **187** E1
Cidra PR, *4881* **187** E1
Coamo PR, *12356* **187** E1
Coco PR, *5803* **187** E1
Comerío PR, *4478* **187** E1
Comunas PR, *2027* **187** F1
Coquí PR, *3590* **187** E1
Corazón PR, *2925* **187** E1
Corozal PR, *11444* **187** E1
Coto Norte PR, *1381* **187** E1
Daguao PR, *1488* **187** F1
Dorado PR, *12747* **187** E1
Duque PR, *1529* **187** F1
El Mangó PR, *1979* **187** F1
Esperanza PR, *1092* **187** F1
Fajardo PR, *33286* **187** F1
Florida PR, *5652* **187** E1
Guánica PR, *9247* **187** D1
Guayabal PR, *2377* **187** E1
Guayama PR, *21624* **187** E1
Guayanilla PR, *5110* **187** D1
Guaynabo PR, *78806* **187** E1
Gurabo PR, *9046* **187** F1
Hatillo PR, *5321* **187** D1
Hormigueros PR, *12444* **187** D1
Humacao PR, *20682* **187** F1
Isabela PR, *12818* **187** D1
Jagual PR, *1402* **187** E1
Jayuya PR, *3516* **187** E1
Jobos PR, *3475* **187** E1
Juana Diaz PR, *9505* **187** E1
Juncos PR, *8978* **187** F1
Lajas PR, *5036* **187** D1
La Parguera PR, *1141* **187** D1
La Plena PR, *1036* **187** E1
Lares PR, *7042* **187** D1
Las Marías PR, *1823* **187** D1
Las Marías PR, *988* **187** D1
Las Piedras PR, *6352* **187** F1
Levittown PR, *30140* **187** E1
Loíza PR, *4123* **187** F1
Los Llanos PR, *2301* **187** E1
Luquillo PR, *7947* **187** F1
Manatí PR, *16173* **187** E1
Maricao PR, *1123* **187** D1
Maunabo PR, *2075* **187** F1
Mayagüez PR, *78647* **187** D1
Moca PR, *4757* **187** D1
Mora PR, *1857* **187** D1
Morovis PR, *2285* **187** E1
Naguabo PR, *4432* **187** F1
Naranjito PR, *1931* **187** E1
Orocovis PR, *909* **187** E1
Palmarejo PR, *1087* **187** D1
Palomas PR, *1742* **187** D1
Patillas PR, *4091* **187** E1
Peñuelas PR, *6712* **187** D1
Playita PR, *2192* **187** F1
Pole Ojea PR, *1829* **187** D1
Ponce PR, *155038* **187** E1
Potala Pastillo PR, *3819* **187** E1
Puerto Real PR, *6166* **187** D1
Punta Santiago PR, *5803* **187** F1
Quebrada PR, *1130* **187** D1
Quebradillas PR, *5319* **187** D1
Rafael Capó PR, *1863* **187** D1
Rincón PR, *1436* **187** D1
Río Grande PR, *13467* **187** F1
Sabana Eneas PR, *1847* **187** D1
Sabana Grande PR, *8784* **187** D1
Sabana Hoyos PR, *1823* **187** E1
Salinas PR, *6141* **187** E1
San Antonio PR, *6456* **187** D1
San Antonio PR, *2300* **187** D1
San Germán PR, *12033* **187** D1
San Isidro PR, *8071* **187** F1
San Juan PR, *421958* **187** E1
San Lorenzo PR, *8947* **187** F1
San Sebastián PR, *11598* **187** D1
Santa Isabel PR, *6993* **187** E1
Santo Domingo PR, *3633* **187** D1
Tallaboa PR, *1150* **187** D1
Toa Alta PR, *4368* **187** E1
Trujillo Alto PR, *50841* **187** E1
Utuado PR, *9887* **187** E1
Vázquez PR, *2297* **187** E1
Vega Alta PR, *11755* **187** E1
Vega Baja PR, *28811* **187** E1
Vieques PR, *4325* **187** F1
Villalba PR, *4388* **187** E1
Yabucoa PR, *6636* **187** F1
Yauco PR, *19609* **187** D1
Yaurel PR, *1468* **187** E1

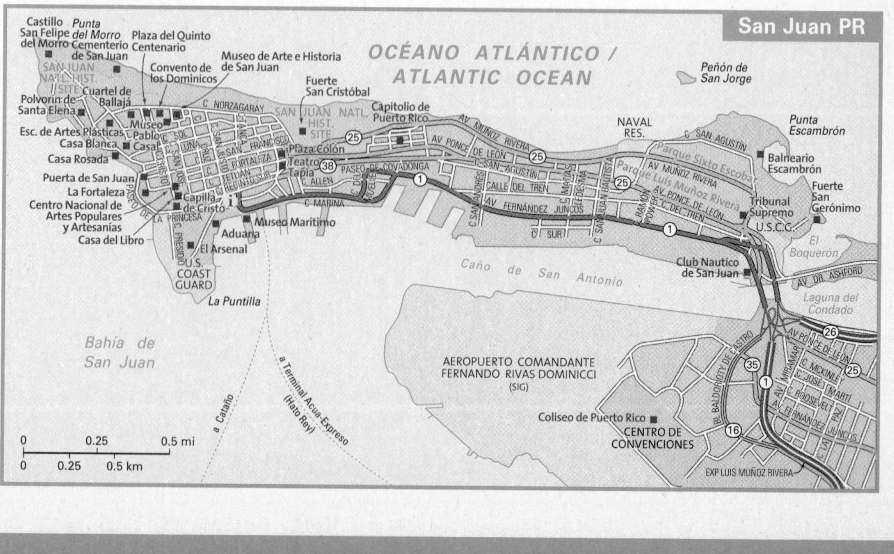

Entries in **bold color** indicate cities with detailed inset maps.

CANADA

Abbotsford BC, 115463.........**163** D3
Aberdeen SK, 534.........**165** F1
Acton ON, 7767.........172 C2
Acton Vale QC, 7299.........175 D3
Adstock QC, 1629.........175 E2
Airdrie AB, 20382.........164 C2
Air Ronge SK, 955.........160 B3

Beauharnois QC, 6387.........174 C3
Beaumont AB, 7006.........159 D4
Beaumont QC, 2153.........175 E1
Beaupré QC, 2761.........175 E1
Beauséjour MB, 2772.........167 F3
Beauval SK, 843.........159 F2
Beaverlodge AB, 2110.........157 F1
Beaverton ON, 3065.........173 D1
Bécancour QC, 11051.........175 D2

Blanc-Sablon QC, 1201.........183 D1
Blenheim ON, 4795.........172 B4
Blind Bay BC, 2464.........163 F1
Blind River ON, 3969.........170 B3
Blue Mts. ON, 6116.........172 C1
Brooklin ON, 5789.........173 D2
Bluewater ON, 6919.........172 B2
Blyth ON, 987.........172 B2
Bobcaygeon ON, 2854.........173 E1
Bois-Blanc NB, 857.........179 D2

Broadview SK, 669.........166 C3
Brochet MB, 226.........161 D1
Brockville ON, 21375.........174 B4
Bromont QC, 4808.........175 D3
Bromptonville QC, 5571.........175 E3
Brooklin ON, 5789.........173 D2
Brooklyn NS, 1078.........180 C4
Brooks AB, 11604.........165 D3
Brookside NS, 1286.........181 D3
Brownsburg-Chatham QC, 6770.174 C3
Bruderheim AB, 1202.........159 D4
Bruno SK, 571.........166 B2
Brussels ON, 1143.........172 B2
Buchans NL, 877.........183 D3
Buckingham QC, 11668.........174 B3
Buffalo Creek BC, 701.........157 F4
Buffalo Lake AB, 1571.........157 E4
Buffalo Narrows SK, 1137.........159 F2
Burford ON, 1841.........172 C3
Burgeo NL, 1782.........182 C4
Burin NL, 2470.........183 E4
Burk's Falls ON, 940.........171 D4
Burlington ON, 150836.........173 D3
Burnaby BC, 193954.........163 D3
Burns Lake BC, 1942.........157 D2
Burnt Islands NL, 801.........182 C4
Bury QC, 1171.........175 E3
Cabano QC, 3213.........178 A2
Cache Creek BC, 1056.........163 E1
Caledon ON, 50595.........172 C2
Caledon East ON, 1974.........172 C2
Caledonia ON, 8582.........172 C3
Caledon Vil. ON, 1651.........172 C2
Calgary AB, 878866.........164 C3
Calmar AB, 1902.........159 D4
Cambridge NS, 723.........180 C2
Cambridge ON, 110372.........172 C3
Cambridge-Narrows NB, 654.....180 B1
Campbellford ON, 3675.........173 E1
Campbell River BC, 28456.........162 B2
Campbellton NB, 7798.........178 C2
Camperville MB, 524.........167 D2
Camrose AB, 14854.........159 D4
Canal Flats BC, 709.........164 B3
Candle Lake SK, 503.........160 B4
Canmore AB, 10792.........164 B3
Canning NS, 811.........180 C2
Cannington ON, 2007.........173 D1
Canora SK, 2200.........166 C2
Canso NS, 992.........181 F2
Cantley QC, 5898.........174 B3
Cap-aux-Meules QC, 1659.........179 E4
Cap-Chat QC, 2913.........178 C1
Cap-de-la-Madeleine QC, 32534.175 D2
Cape Breton Reg. Mun. NS,
105968.........181 F1
Cape St. George NL, 926.........182 C3
Caplan QC, 2010.........179 D2
Cap-Pele NB, 2266.........179 D4
Capreol ON, 3471.........170 C3
Cap-St-Ignace QC, 3204.........175 E1
Cap-Santé QC, 2571.........175 E1
Caraquet NB, 4442.........179 D4
Carberry MB, 1513.........167 D4
Carbonear NL, 4759.........183 E4
Cardigan PE, 382.........179 E4
Cardinal ON, 1739.........174 B4
Cardston AB, 3475.........164 C4
Carleton Place ON, 9083.........174 A3
Carleton-St-Omer QC, 4010.......178 C2
Carlisle ON, 2180.........172 C2
Carlyle SK, 1260.........166 C4
Carman MB, 2831.........167 E4
Carmanville NL, 798.........183 E2
Carnduff SK, 1017.........166 C4
Caronport SK, 1007.........166 A3
Carrot River SK, 1017.........160 C4
Carseland AB, 662.........164 C3
Carstairs AB, 2254.........164 C3
Cartwright MB, 304.........167 D4
Cartwright NL, 629.........183 E1
Casselman ON, 2910.........174 B3
Cassidy BC, 978.........162 C3
Castlegar BC, 7002.........164 A4
Castor AB, 935.........165 D2
Catalina NL, 995.........183 E3
Causapscal QC, 2432.........178 B1
Cavendish PE, 267.........179 E4
Cawston BC, 1013.........163 F3
Cayuga ON, 1643.........172 C3
Cedar BC, 4440.........162 C3
Central Saanich BC, 15348.......163 D4
Centreville NS, 1047.........180 C2
Centreville-Wareham-Trinity NL,
1146.........183 E3
Chalk River ON, 1071.........171 E4
Chambly QC, 20342.........175 D3
Chambord QC, 1693.........176 B3
Champlain QC, 1863.........175 D2
Chandler QC, 2817.........179 D1
Channel-Port aux-Basques NL,
4637.........182 C4
Chapais QC, 1795.........176 A2
Chapleau ON, 2832.........170 B2
Charlesbourg QC, 70310.........175 E1
Charlie Lake BC, 1727.........158 A3
Charlo NB, 1449.........178 C2
Charlottetown PE, 32245.........179 E4
Charny QC, 10507.........175 E1
Chase BC, 2460.........163 F1
Châteauguay QC, 41003.........174 C3
Château-Richer QC, 3442.........175 E1

Chatham ON, 44156.........172 B4
Chatham-Kent ON, 107341.........172 A4
Chemainus BC, 2706.........163 D3
Chertsey QC, 4112.........174 C2
Chesley ON, 1880.........172 B1
Chester NS, 1590.........180 C3
Chestermere AB, 3414.........164 C3
Chesterville ON, 1498.........174 B4
Chéticamp NS.........181 E1
Chetwynd BC, 2591.........157 E1
Chibougamau QC, 7922.........176 A2
Chicoutimi QC, 60008.........176 C3
Chilliwack BC, 62927.........163 E3
Chipman NB, 1432.........178 C4
Christina Lake BC, 1035.........164 A4
Churchbridge SK, 796.........166 C3
Chute-aux-Outardes QC, 1968...177 D2
Clair NB, 863.........178 A3

Clairmont AB, 1481.........157 F1
Clarence-Rockland ON, 19612...174 B3
Clarenville NL, 5104.........183 E3
Claresholm AB, 3622.........164 C4
Clarington ON, 69834.........173 D2
Clarke's Beach NL, 1257.........183 E4
Clark's Hbr. NS, 944.........180 B4
Clermont QC, 3078.........176 C4
Clinton ON, 3117.........172 B2

Calgary AB

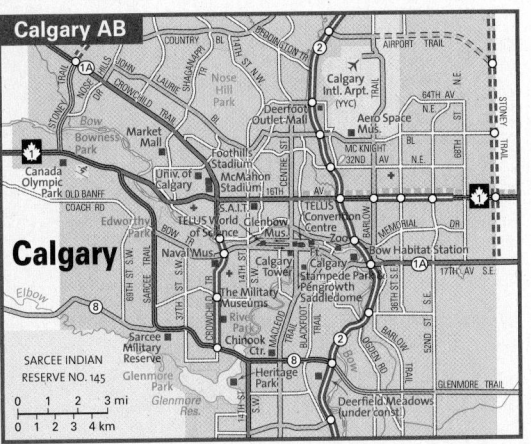

Edmonton AB

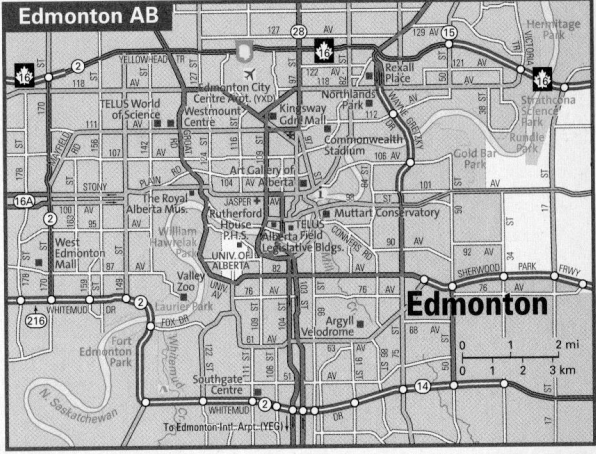

Ajax ON, 73753.........173 D2
Aklavik NT, 632.........155 D1
Alban ON, 1084.........170 C3
Albanel QC, 2455.........176 B3
Alberta Beach AB, 762.........158 C4
Alberton PE, 1115.........179 E3
Aldergrove BC, 11910.........163 D3
Alexandria ON, 3369.........174 B3
Alfred ON, 1348.........174 B3
Alix AB, 825.........164 C2
Allan SK, 679.........165 F3
Alliston ON, 9679.........172 C1
Alma QC, 25918.........176 C3
Almonte ON, 4659.........174 A3
Altona MB, 3434.........167 E4
Amherst NS, 9470.........180 C1
Amherstburg ON, 20339.........172 A4
Amos QC, 13044.........171 E1
Amqui QC, 6473.........178 B1
Ange-Gardien QC, 1994.........175 D3
Angus ON, 9722.........172 C1
Annapolis Royal NS, 550.........180 B3
Antigonish NS, 4754.........181 E1
Arborg MB, 959.........167 E3
Arcola SK, 532.........166 C4
Armagh QC, 1603.........175 F1
Armstrong BC, 4256.........164 A3
Arnold's Cove NL, 1024.........183 E4
Arnprior ON, 7192.........174 A3
Arthur ON, 2284.........172 C2
Asbestos QC, 6580.........175 E3
Ascot Corner QC, 2342.........175 E3
Ashcroft BC, 1788.........163 E1
Asquith SK, 574.........165 F2
Assiniboia SK, 2483.........166 A4
Athabasca AB, 2415.........159 D3
Athens ON, 1026.........174 A4
Atholville NB, 1381.........178 C2
Atikokan ON, 3560.........168 C4
Aurora ON, 40167.........173 D2
Austin QC, 1201.........175 D3
Avondale NL, 701.........183 E4
Ayer's Cliff QC, 1102.........175 D3
Aylesford NS, 807.........180 C2
Aylmer ON, 7126.........172 C3
Aylmer QC, 36085.........174 B3
Ayr ON, 3636.........172 C3
Baddeck NS, 907.........181 F1
Badger NL, 906.........183 D3
Baie-Comeau QC, 23079.........177 D2
Baie-du-Febvre QC, 1135.........175 D2
Baie-Ste-Anne NB, 1600.........179 D3
Baie-St-Paul QC, 7290.........176 C4
Baie Verte NL, 1492.........183 D2
Balcarres SK, 622.........166 B3
Balgonie SK, 1239.........166 B3
Balmoral NB, 1836.........178 C2
Bancroft ON, 4089.........171 E4
Banff AB, 7135.........164 B3
Barraute QC, 2010.........171 E2
Barrhead AB, 4213.........158 C4
Barrie ON, 103710.........173 D1
Barry's Bay ON, 1259.........171 E4
Bas-Caraquet NB, 1689.........179 D2
Bashaw AB, 825.........164 C1
Bassano AB, 1320.........165 D3
Bathurst NB, 12924.........179 D2
Battleford SK, 3820.........159 F4
Bay Bulls NL, 1014.........183 E4
Bayfield ON, 909.........172 B2
Bay Roberts NL, 5237.........183 E4
Beachburg ON, 870.........171 E4
Beamsville ON, 9047.........173 D3
Beauceville QC, 6261.........175 E2

Bedford NS.........181 D3
Bedford QC, 2667.........175 D3
Beechville NS, 2312.........181 D3
Beeton ON, 3822.........172 D2
Behchokò NT, 1894.........155 F2
Beiseker AB, 838.........164 C2
Bella Bella BC, 1253.........156 C4
Belledune NB, 1923.........178 C2
Bellefeuille QC, 14066.........174 C3
Bethwell ON, 1002.........172 B3
Belleville ON, 45986.........173 E1
Belmont ON, 1819.........172 B3
Beloeil QC, 19053.........175 D3
Benito MB, 415.........166 C2
Bentley AB, 1035.........164 C2
Beresford NB, 4414.........179 D2
Berthierville QC, 3939.........175 D2
Bertrand NB, 1269.........179 D2
Berwick NS, 2282.........180 C2
Betsiamites QC, 1625.........178 A1
Bible Hill NS, 5741.........180 C2
Bienfait SK, 786.........166 C4
Big River SK, 741.........159 F3
Binscarth MB, 445.........166 C3
Birch Hills SK, 957.........160 B4
Birch Bay NL, 612.........183 E2
Birtle MB, 715.........167 D3
Bishop's Falls NL, 3688.........183 D3
Black Diamond AB, 1866.........164 C3
Blackfalds AB, 3042.........164 C2
Black Lake QC, 4109.........175 E2
Blacks Hbr. NB, 1082.........180 A2
Blackville NB, 1015.........178 C4
Blaine Lake SK, 508.........160 B4
Blainville QC, 36029.........174 C3
Blairmore AB, 1993.........164 C4

Boischatel QC, 4303.........175 E1
Boissevain MB, 1495.........167 D4
Bolton ON, 20553.........173 D2
Bon Accord AB, 1532.........159 D4
Bonaventure QC, 2756.........179 D2
Bonavista NL, 4021.........183 E3
Bonnyville AB, 5709.........159 E3
Borden-Carleton PE, 798.........179 E4
Bothwell ON, 1002.........172 B3
Botwood NL, 3221.........183 D2
Bouctouche NB, 2426.........179 D4
Bourget ON, 1005.........174 B3
Bowden AB, 1174.........164 C2
Bowen Island BC, 2957.........163 D3
Bow Island AB, 1704.........165 D4
Bowmanville ON, 32556.........173 D2
Bowser BC, 1307.........162 C3
Bowsman MB, 320.........166 C2
Boyle AB, 836.........159 D3
Bracebridge ON, 13751.........171 D4
Bradford ON, 16978.........173 D2
Bradford-W. Gwillimbury ON,
22228.........173 D1
Bragg Creek AB, 678.........164 C3
Brampton ON, 325428.........173 D2
Brandon MB, 39716.........167 D4
Brant ON, 31669.........172 C3
Brantford ON, 86417.........172 C3
Brantville NB, 1153.........179 D3
Bridgenorth ON, 2279.........173 E1
Bridgetown NS, 1035.........180 B3
Bridgewater NS, 7621.........180 C3
Brigham QC, 2250.........175 D3
Brighton ON, 9449.........173 E2
Brigus NL, 784.........183 E4
Bristol QC, 719.........178 B4

Fredericton NB

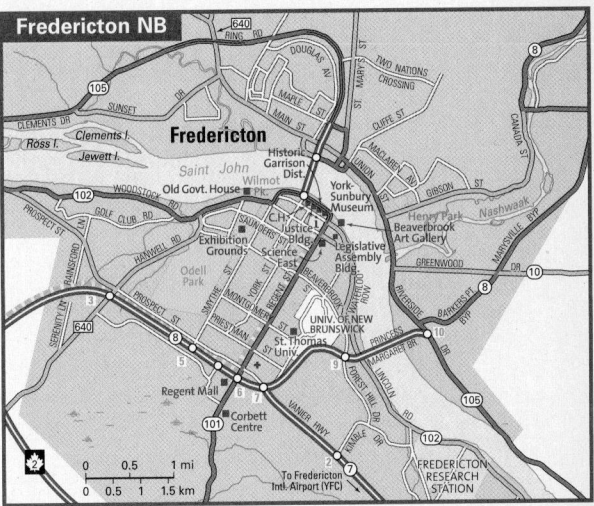

Charlottetown PE

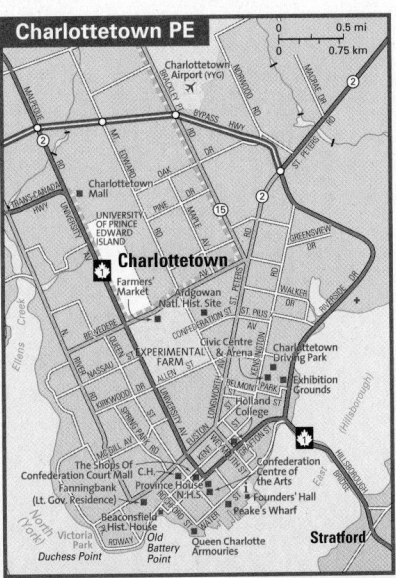

Halifax NS

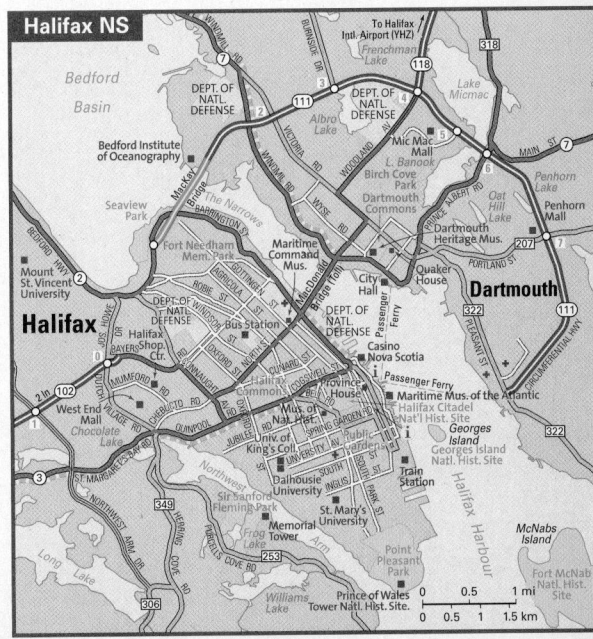

278
Clyde River–L'Islet

Figures after entries indicate population, page number, and grid reference.

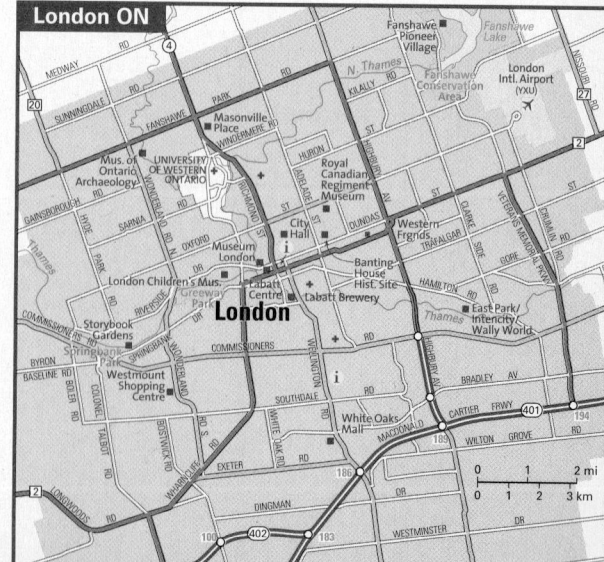

Entries in **bold color** indicate cities with detailed inset maps.

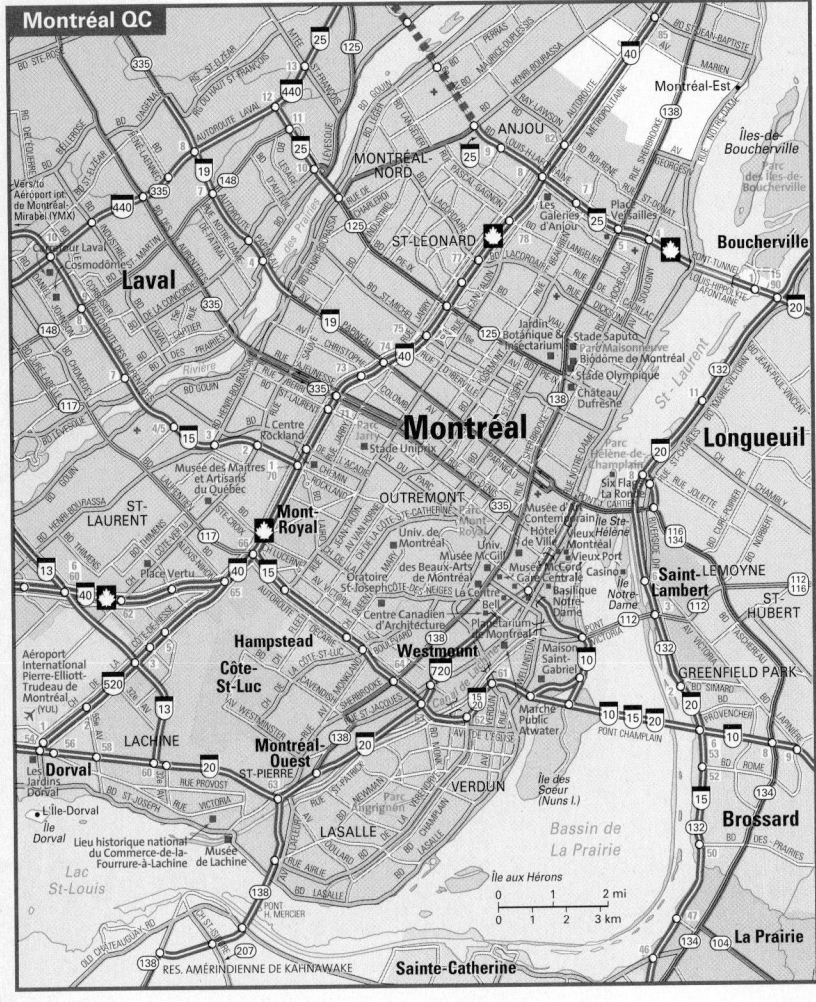

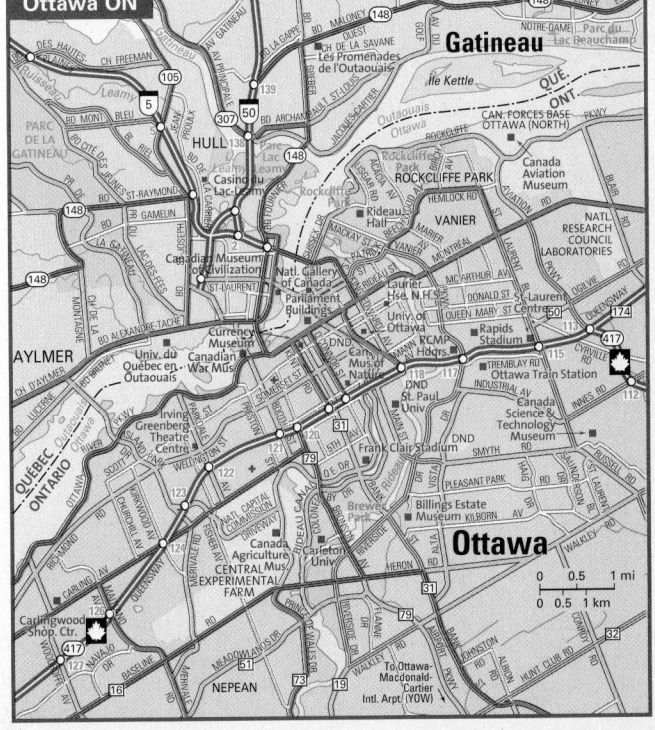

Figures after entries indicate population, page number, and grid reference.

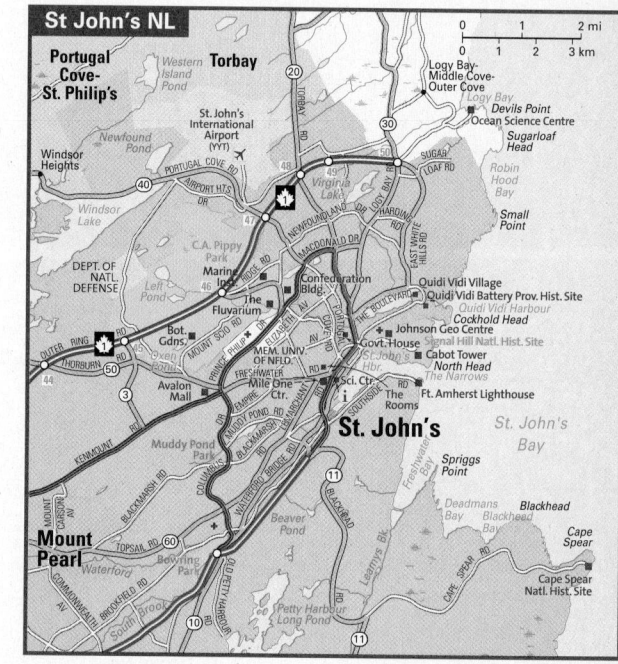

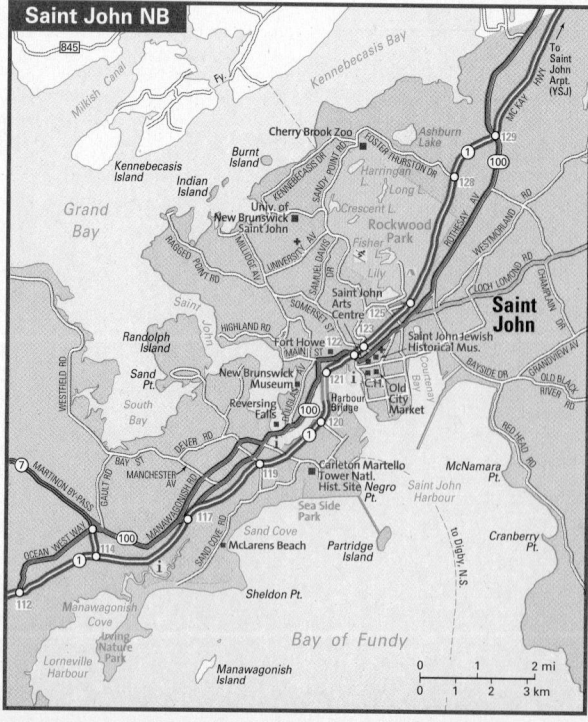

Entries in **bold color** indicate cities with detailed inset maps.

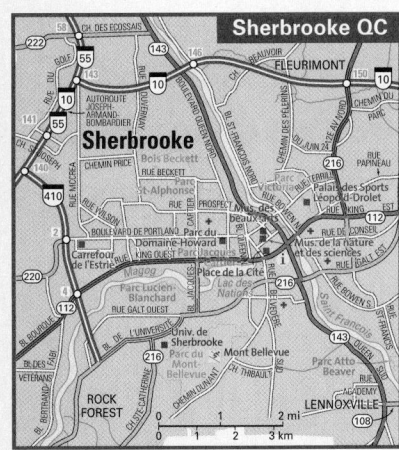

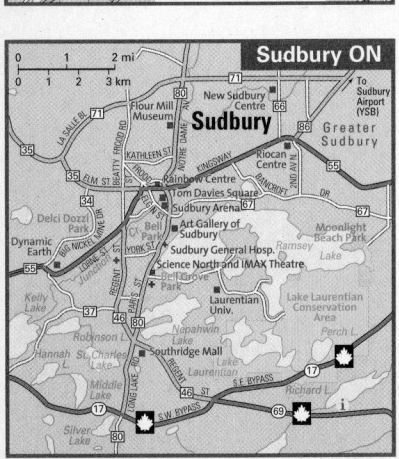

POINTS OF INTEREST

Air Canada Centre B2
Art Gallery of Ontario...........A1
CBC Broadcast Center.............A2
CN Tower A2
Eaton Centre B1
Four Seasons Centre
  for the Performing Arts A1
The Grange A1

Harbourfront Centre A2
Hockey Hall of Fame..............B2
MacKenzie House..................B1
Metro Convention Center A2
Old City Hall B1
Princess of Wales Theatre A1
Queen's Quay Terminal A2
Redpath Sugar Museum B2
Rogers Centre A2

Royal Alexandra Theatre..........A1
Ryerson Polytechnic University ..B1
Roy Thomson Hall.................A2
Saint Lawrence Centre B2
Saint Lawrence Market............B2
Sony Centre for the Perf. Arts ..B2
Textile Museum of Canada A1
Toronto Island Ferry Terminal ...B2
Toronto Stock Exchange...........A1

Figures after entries indicate population, page number, and grid reference.

St-Stanislas QC, *1076* **175** D2
St. Stephen NB, *4667* **180** A2
St-Théodore-d'Acton QC, *1544* **175** D3
St. Thomas ON, *33236* **172** B3
St-Timothée QC, *8299* **174** C3
St-Tite QC, *3845* **175** D1
St-Tite-des-Caps QC, *1426* **175** E1
St-Ubalde QC, *1460* **175** D1
St-Ulric QC, *1649* **178** B1
St-Urbain QC, *1430* **176** C4
St-Valère QC, *1308* **175** D2
St-Victor QC, *2460* **175** E2
St. Walburg SK, *672* **159** F4
St-Wenceslas QC, *1132* **175** D2
St-Zacharie QC, *2100* **175** F2
St-Zénon QC, *1180* **174** C2
St-Zotique QC, *4158* **174** C3
Salaberry-de-Valleyfield QC, *26170* **174** C3
Salisbury NB, *1954* **180** C1
Salmo BC, *1120* **164** B4
Salmon Arm BC, *15210* **163** F1
Salmon Cove NL, *746* **183** E4
Salmon River NS, *2259* **180** B4
Sandy Bay SK, *1092* **160** C2
Saratoga Beach BC, *1627* **162** B2
Sarnia ON, *70876* **172** A3
Saskatoon SK, *196811* **165** F2
Saugeen Shores ON, *11388* **172** B1
Sault Ste. Marie ON, *74566* **170** B3
Sayabec QC, *1999* **178** B1
Schomberg ON, *1216* **173** D2
Scott QC, *1705* **175** E2
Scoudouc NB, *1047* **179** D4
Seaforth ON, *2692* **172** B2
Sechelt BC, *7775* **162** C3
Sedgewick AB, *865* **165** D1
Selkirk MB, *9752* **167** E3
Senneterre QC, *3275* **171** E2
Sept-Îles QC, *23791* **177** E2
Sexsmith AB, *1653* **157** F1
Shannon QC, *3668* **175** E1
Shaunavon SK, *1775* **165** F4
Shawinigan QC, *17535* **175** D2
Shawinigan-Sud QC, *11544* **175** D2
Shawville QC, *1582* **174** A3
Shediac NB, *4892* **179** D4
Shediac Bridge NB, *950* **179** D4
Shediac Cape NB, *787* **179** D4
Shelburne NS, *2013* **180** B4
Shelburne ON, *4122* **172** C2
Shellbrook SK, *1276* **160** B4
Sherbrooke QC, *75916* **175** E3
Sherwood Park AB, *47645* **164** C1
Shippagan NB, *2872* **179** D2
Shoal Lake MB, *801* **167** D3
Shubenacadie NS, *906* **181** D2
Sicamous BC, *2720* **164** A3
Sidney BC, *10929* **163** D4
Silver Creek BC, *1062* **163** F1
Simcoe ON, *14175* **172** C3
Sioux Lookout ON, *5336* **168** C2
Slave Lake AB, *6600* **158** C3
Smithers BC, *5414* **156** C2
Smiths Falls ON, *9140* **174** A4
Smithville ON, *3317* **173** D3
Smoky Lake AB, *1011* **159** D3
Smooth Rock Falls ON, *1830* **170** C1
Snow Lake MB, *1207* **161** D3
Somerset MB, *459* **167** E4
Sooke BC, *8735* **162** C4
Sorel-Tracy QC, *34194* **175** D2
Sorrento BC, *1197* **163** F1
Souris MB, *1683* **167** D4
Souris PE, *1248* **179** F4
Southampton ON, *3360* **172** B1
S. Bruce Peninsula ON, *8090* **172** B1
Southey SK, *693* **166** B3
S. Huron ON, *10019* **172** B3
S. Indian Lake MB, *808* **161** E1
S. River ON, *1040* **171** D4
Spallumcheen BC, *5134* **164** A3
Spaniard's Bay NL, *2694* **183** E4
Sparwood BC, *3812* **164** C4
Spirit River AB, *1100* **157** F1
Spiritwood SK, *907* **159** F4
Springdale NL, *3045* **183** D2
Springhill NS, *4091* **180** C1
Springside SK, *525* **166** C2
Sproat Lake BC, *1888* **162** C3
Spruce Grove AB, *15983* **159** D4
Squamish BC, *14247* **163** D2
Stanstead QC, *2995* **175** D4
Stayner ON, *3885* **172** C1
Steinbach MB, *9227* **167** E4
Stellarton NS, *4809* **181** D2
Stephenville NL, *7109* **182** C3
Stephenville Crossing NL, *1993* **182** C3
Stettler AB, *5215* **165** D2
Stewiacke NS, *1388* **181** D2
Stirling AB, *877* **165** D4
Stirling ON, *2149* **173** E1
Stoke QC, *2475* **175** E3
Stonewall MB, *4012* **167** E3
Stoney Pt. ON, *1316* **172** A4
Stony Mtn. MB, *1700* **167** E3
Stony Plain AB, *9589* **159** D4
Stouffville ON, *11073* **173** D2
Stoughton SK, *720* **166** C4
Strasbourg SK, *760* **166** B3
Stratford ON, *29676* **172** C2
Strathmore AB, *7621* **164** C3
Strathroy ON, *12805* **172** B3
Sturgeon Falls ON, *5978* **171** D3
Sturgis SK, *627* **166** C2
Sudbury ON, *103879* **170** C3
Summerford NL, *1010* **183** E2
Summerland BC, *10713* **163** F2
Summerside PE, *14654* **179** E4
Sundre AB, *2267* **164** C2
Sundridge ON, *983* **171** D4
Sunny Corner NB, *910* **178** C3
Surrey BC, *347825* **163** D3
Sussex NB, *4182* **180** B1
Sussex Corner NB, *1321* **180** B1
Sutton ON, *6324* **173** D1
Sutton QC, *1631* **175** D4
Swan Hills AB, *1807* **158** C3
Swan River MB, *4032* **166** C2
Swift Current SK, *14821* **165** F3
Sydney NS, *33913* **181** F1
Sydney Mines NS, *16068* **181** F1
Sydney River NS, *4496* **181** F1
Sylvan Lake AB, *7493* **164** C2
Taber AB, *7671* **165** D4
Tabusintac NB, *893* **179** D3
Tappen BC, *788* **163** F1
Tara ON, *905* **172** B1
Tatamagouche NS, *738* **181** D1
Tavistock ON, *2513* **172** C3
Taylor BC, *1143* **158** A2
Tecumseh ON, *25105* **172** A4
Teeswater ON, *1109* **172** B2
Telkwa BC, *1371* **156** C2
Temagami ON, *893* **171** D3
Témiscaming QC, *2903* **171** D3
Terrace BC, *12109* **156** C2
Terrace Bay ON, *1950* **169** E4
Terrebonne QC, *43149* **174** C3
Teulon MB, *1058* **167** E3
Thamesford ON, *1748* **172** C3
Thamesville ON, *928* **172** B4
The Pas MB, *5795* **161** D4
Thessalon ON, *1386* **170** B3
Thetford Mines QC, *16628* **175** E2
Thompson MB, *13256* **161** E2
Thornbury ON, *1865* **172** C1
Thorold ON, *18048* **173** D3
Thorsby AB, *799* **159** D4
Three Hills AB, *2902* **164** C2
Thunder Bay ON, *109016* **169** D4
Thurso QC, *2436* **174** B3
Tide Head NB, *1149* **178** C2
Tignish PE, *831* **179** E3
Tilbury ON, *4599* **172** A4
Tillsonburg ON, *14052* **172** C3
Timberlea NS, *4781* **181** D3
Timmins ON, *43686* **170** C1
Tisdale SK, *3063* **160** C4
Tofield AB, *1818* **159** D4
Tofino BC, *1466* **162** B3
Torbay NL, *5474* **183** F4
Toronto ON, *2481494* **173** D2
Tottenham ON, *4829* **173** D2
Tracadie-Sheila NB, *4724* **179** D3
Trail BC, *7575* **164** A4
Treherne MB, *644* **167** E4
Trent Hills ON, *12569* **173** E1
Trenton NS, *2798* **181** D2
Trenton ON **173** E2
Trepassey NL, *889* **183** E4
Tring-Jonction QC, *1333* **175** E2
Triton NL, *1102* **183** D2
Trochu AB, *1033* **164** C2
Trois-Pistoles QC, *3635* **178** A2
Trois-Rivières QC, *46264* **175** D2
Truro NS, *11457* **181** D2
Tuktoyaktuk NT, *930* **155** D1
Tumbler Ridge BC, *1851* **157** F1
Turner Valley AB, *1608* **164** C3
Tweed ON, *1539* **173** E1
Twillingate NL, *2611* **183** E2
Two Hills AB, *1091* **159** E4
Ucluelet BC, *1559* **162** B3
Union Bay BC, *1167* **162** C3
Unity SK, *2243* **165** E2
Upton QC, *1986* **175** D3
Uxbridge ON, *8540* **173** D2
Val-Comeau NB, *823* **179** D3
Valcourt QC, *2411* **175** D3
Val-David QC, *3819* **174** C2
Val-des-Monts QC, *7842* **174** B3
Val-d'Or QC, *22748* **171** E2
Valemount BC, *1195* **157** F3
Val-Joli QC, *1532* **175** E3
Vallée-Jonction QC, *1882* **175** E2
Valleyview AB, *1856* **158** B3
Val-Morin QC, *2216* **174** C2
Val-Senneville QC, *2479* **171** E2
Vancouver BC, *545671* **163** D3
Vanderhoof BC, *4390* **157** D2
Vankleek Hill ON, *2022* **174** B3
Varennes QC, *19653* **174** C3
Vaudreuil-Dorion QC, *19920* **174** C3
Vauxhall AB, *1112* **165** D4
Vegreville AB, *5376* **159** D4
Venise-en-Québec QC, *1243* **175** D4
Verchères QC, *4782* **174** C3
Verdun QC, *60564* **174** C3
Vermilion AB, *3948* **159** E4
Vernon BC, *33494* **164** A3
Victoria BC, *74125* **163** D4
Victoria NL, *1798* **183** E4
Victoriaville QC, *38841* **175** E2
Viking AB, *1052* **159** E4
Ville-Marie QC, *2770* **171** D2
Virden MB, *3109* **167** D4
Vulcan AB, *1762* **164** C3
Wabana NL, *2679* **183** F4
Wabasca AB, *1114* **159** D2
Wabowden MB, *497* **161** E3
Wabush NL, *1894* **183** E1
Wadena SK, *1412* **166** B2
Wainwright AB, *5117* **159** E4
Wakaw SK, *884* **165** F1
Waldheim SK, *889* **165** F1
Walkerton ON, *4970* **172** B1
Wallaceburg ON, *11114* **172** A3
Warfield BC, *1739* **164** A4
Warman SK, *3481* **165** F2
Warwick QC, *4874* **175** E2
Wasaga Beach ON, *12419* **172** C1
Waterford ON, *2871* **172** C3
Waterloo ON, *86543* **172** C2
Waterloo QC, *3993* **175** D3
Waterville NS, *808* **180** C2
Waterville QC, *1824* **175** E3
Watford ON, *1625* **172** B3
Watrous SK, *1808* **166** B2
Watson SK, *794* **166** B2
Watson Lake YT, *912* **155** E3
Waverley NS, *934* **181** D3
Wawa ON, *3279* **169** F4
Wawanesa MB, *516* **167** D4
Wawota SK, *538* **166** C4
Wedgeport NS, *1217* **180** B4
Weedon QC, *2646* **175** E3
Welland ON, *48402* **173** D3
Wellesley ON, *1666* **172** C2
Wellington ON, *1943* **173** E2
Wellington PE, *382* **179** E4
Wembley AB, *1497* **157** F1
Wentworth-Nord QC, *1121* **174** C3
Westbank BC, *15700* **163** F2
Western Shore NS, *1015* **180** C3
Westlock AB, *4819* **159** D3
W. Lorne ON, *1458* **172** B4
W. Nipissing ON, *13114* **171** D3
W. Vancouver BC, *41421* **163** D3
Westville NS, *3879* **181** D2
Wetaskiwin AB, *11154* **159** D4
Weyburn SK, *9534* **166** B4
Wheatley ON, *1920* **172** A4
Whistler BC, *8896* **163** D2
Whitbourne NL, *930* **183** E4
Whitby ON, *87413* **173** D2
Whitchurch-Stouffville ON, *22008* **173** D2
White City SK, *1013* **166** B3
Whitecourt AB, *8334* **158** C3
Whitehorse YT, *19058* **155** D3
White Rock BC, *18250* **163** D3
Whitewood SK, *947* **166** C3
Wiarton ON, *2349* **172** B1
Wickham QC, *2516* **175** D3
Wikwemikong ON, *1352* **170** C4
Wilkie SK, *1282* **165** E2
Williams Lake BC, *11153* **157** E4
Winchester ON, *2427* **174** B4
Windermere BC, *1060* **164** B3
Windsor NS, *3778* **180** C2
Windsor ON, *208402* **172** A4
Windsor QC, *5321* **175** E3
Wingham ON, *2885* **172** B2
Winkler MB, *7943* **167** E4
Winnipeg MB, *619544* **167** E4
Winnipeg Beach MB, *801* **167** E3
Winnipegosis MB, *621* **167** D2
Witless Bay NL, *1056* **183** F4
Wolfville NS, *3658* **180** C2
Wolseley SK, *766* **166** C3
Wood Buffalo AB, *41466* **159** E1
Woodstock NB, *5198* **178** B4
Woodstock ON, *33061* **172** C3
Woodville ON, *871* **173** D1
Wotton QC, *1568* **175** E3
Wright QC, *1137* **174** A2
Wynyard SK, *1919* **166** B2
Wyoming ON, *2200* **172** B3
Yamachiche QC, *2631* **175** D2
Yarmouth NS, *7561* **180** B4
Yellowknife NT, *16541* **155** F2
Yorkton SK, *15107* **166** C3
Youbou BC, *727* **162** C3

Anmore D1
Belcarra D1
Burnaby D2
Coquitlam D2
New Westminster D2
N. Vancouver B1
N. Vancouver (DM) C1
Port Moody D1
Richmond C2
Surrey D2
Vancouver B2
W. Vancouver A1

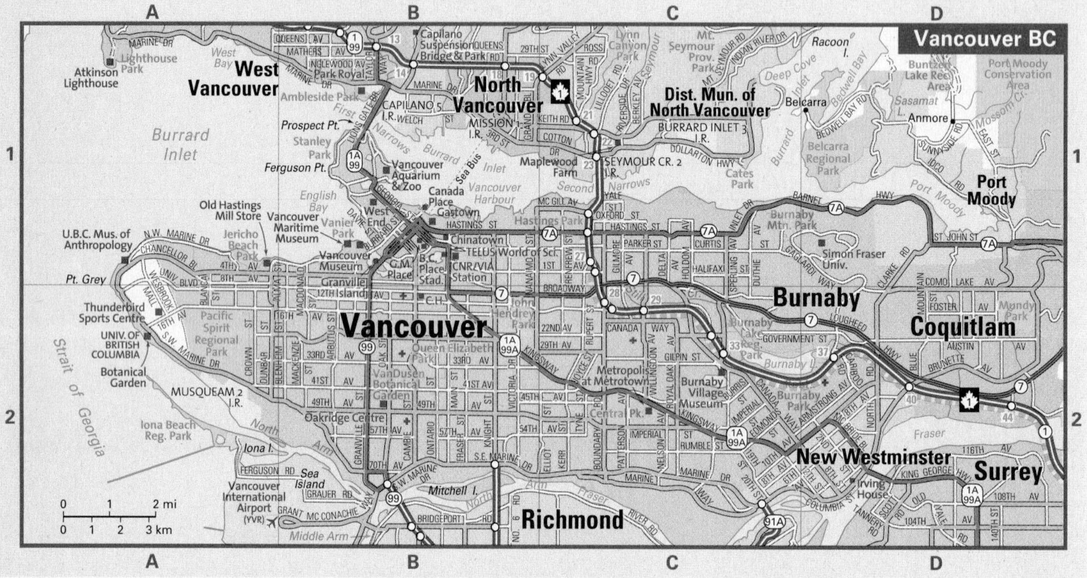
Vancouver BC
A
B
C
D
1
2
West Vancouver
North Vancouver
Dist. Mun. of North Vancouver
Burrard Inlet
Atkinson Lighthouse
Lighthouse Park
Ambleside Park
Prospect Pt.
Stanley Park
Ferguson Pt.
Vancouver Aquarium & Zoo
Canada Place
Gastown
Vancouver Harbour
Old Hastings Mill Store
Vancouver Maritime Museum
U.B.C. Mus. of Anthropology
Pt. Grey
Jericho Beach Park
Vancouver Museum
Chinatown
TELUS World of Sci.
B.C. Place Stad.
CNR/VIA Station
Granville Island
Thunderbird Sports Centre
Pacific Spirit Regional Park
UNIV. OF BRITISH COLUMBIA
Botanical Garden
Vancouver
Queen Elizabeth Park
VanDusen Botanical Garden
Strait of Georgia
MUSQUEAM 2 I.R.
Iona Beach Reg. Park
Iona I.
Sea Island
Oakridge Centre
Vancouver International Airport (YVR)
Middle Arm
Mitchell I.
Richmond
Burnaby
Coquitlam
Metropolis at Metrotown
Burnaby Village Museum
Central Pk.
Burnaby Lake Park
Simon Fraser Univ.
Burnaby Mtn. Park
New Westminster
Surrey
Irving House
Fraser
Port Moody
Anmore
Belcarra
Belcarra Regional Park
Buntzen Lake Rec. Area
Port Moody Conservation Area
Racoon I.
Sasamat L.
Deep Cove
Mt. Seymour Prov. Park
Lynn Canyon Park
Capilano Suspension Bridge & Park
Park Royal
CAPILANO 5 I.R.
MISSION 1 I.R.
BURRARD INLET 3 I.R.
SEYMOUR CR. 2 I.R.
Maplewood Farm
Cates Park
Second Narrows
First Narrows
Sea Bus
Hastings Park
0 1 2 mi
0 1 2 3 km

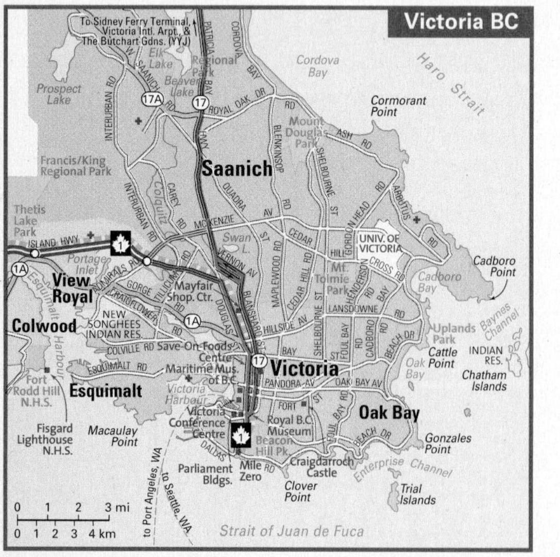
Victoria BC
To Sidney Ferry Terminal, Victoria Intl. Arpt., & The Butchart Gdns. (YYJ)
Elk Lake
Beaver Lake
Regional Park
Prospect Lake
Cordova Bay
Haro Strait
Cormorant Point
Mount Douglas Park
Saanich
Francis/King Regional Park
Thetis Lake Park
Swan L.
UNIV. OF VICTORIA
Mt. Tolmie Park
Cadboro Bay
Cadboro Point
View Royal
Colwood
Mayfair Shop. Ctr.
NEW SONGHEES INDIAN RES.
Save-On-Foods Centre
Maritime Mus. of B.C.
Victoria
Esquimalt
Fort Rodd Hill N.H.S.
Fisgard Lighthouse N.H.S.
Macaulay Point
Victoria Conference Centre
Royal B.C. Museum
Beacon Hill Pk.
Parliament Bldgs.
Mile Zero
Craigdarroch Castle
Clover Point
Oak Bay
Uplands Park
Cattle Point
INDIAN RES.
Chatham Islands
Gonzales Point
Trial Islands
Enterprise Channel
Strait of Juan de Fuca
to Port Angeles, WA
to Seattle, WA
0 1 2 3 mi
0 1 2 3 4 km

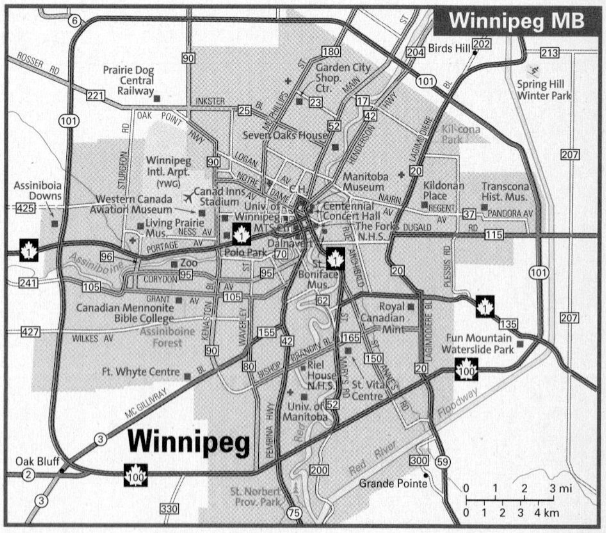
Winnipeg MB
Birds Hill
Spring Hill Winter Park
Prairie Dog Central Railway
Garden City Shop. Ctr.
Seven Oaks House
Kil-cona Park
Winnipeg Intl. Arpt. (YWG)
Manitoba Museum
Kildonan Place
Transcona Hist. Mus.
Assiniboia Downs
Western Canada Aviation Museum
Canad Inns Stadium
Univ. of Winnipeg
Centennial Concert Hall
The Forks N.H.S.
Living Prairie Mus.
Polo Park
Zoo
St. Boniface Mus.
Canadian Mennonite Bible College
Assiniboine Forest
Royal Canadian Mint
Fun Mountain Waterslide Park
Ft. Whyte Centre
Riel House N.H.S.
St. Vital Centre
Univ. of Manitoba
Winnipeg
Oak Bluff
St. Norbert Prov. Park
Grande Pointe
Red River
Floodway
0 1 2 3 mi
0 1 2 3 4 km

Entries in **bold color** indicate cities with detailed inset maps.

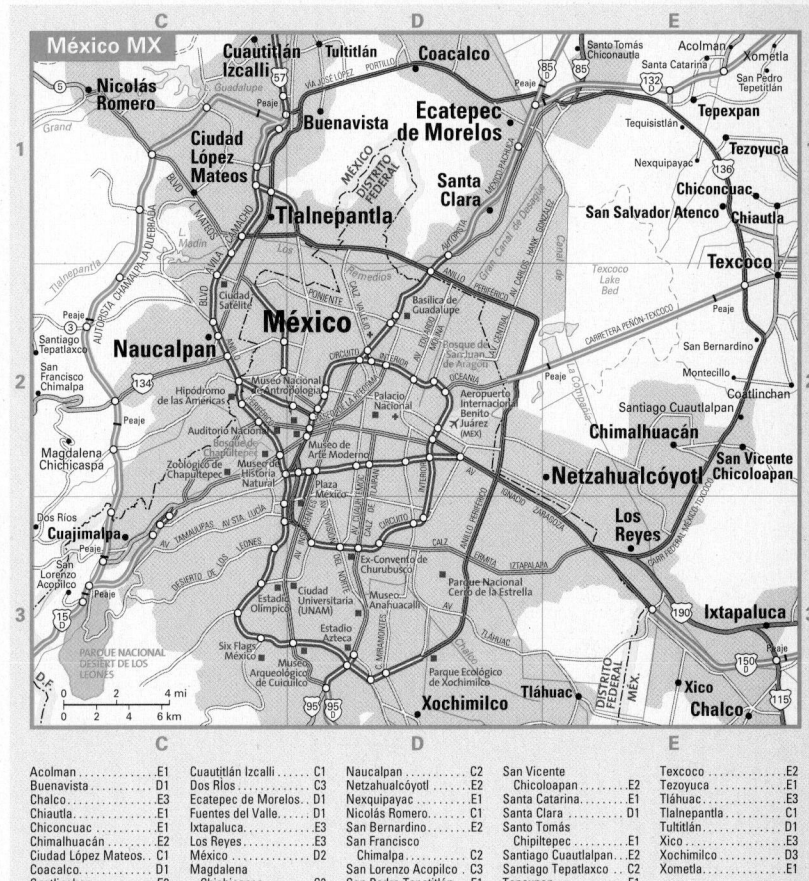

México MX

Cancún MX

Guadalajara MX

Monterrey MX

Miles

Diagonal city labels (top-left to bottom-right):

Albany, NY · Albuquerque, NM · Amarillo, TX · Anchorage, AK · Atlanta, GA · Baltimore, MD · Billings, MT · Birmingham, AL · Bismarck, ND · Boise, ID · Boston, MA · Buffalo, NY · Calgary, AB · Charleston, SC · Charleston, WV · Charlotte, NC · Cheyenne, WY · Chicago, IL · Cincinnati, OH · Cleveland, OH · Columbus, OH · Dallas, TX · Denver, CO · Des Moines, IA · Detroit, MI · El Paso, TX · Halifax, NS · Houston, TX · Indianapolis, IN · Jackson, MS · Jacksonville, FL · Kansas City, MO · Las Vegas, NV · Little Rock, AR · Los Angeles, CA · Louisville, KY

Upper-triangle rows (miles), by origin city:

Albany, NY: 2095 1811 4421 1010 333 2083 1093 1675 2526 172 292 2512 913 634 771 1789 832 730 484 621 1680 1833 1155 571 2326 877 1768 795 1331 1094 1282 2586 1354 2859 832
Albuquerque, NM: 286 3563 1490 1902 991 1274 1333 966 2240 1808 1498 1793 1568 1649 538 1352 1409 1619 1476 754 438 1091 1608 263 2945 994 1298 1157 1837 894 578 900 806 1320
Amarillo, TX: 3734 1206 1618 988 991 1398 1266 1957 1524 1669 1510 1285 1365 534 1069 1126 1335 1192 470 434 808 1324 438 2662 711 1014 874 1517 610 864 617 1092 1036
Anchorage, AK: 4304 4297 2601 4253 2724 2745 4592 4133 2065 4495 4093 4348 3056 3584 3890 3935 3946 4087 3300 3421 3872 4002 4821 4328 3872 4294 4652 3356 3929 3403 3886
Atlanta, GA: 679 1889 150 1559 2218 1100 910 2395 317 503 238 1482 717 476 726 577 792 1403 967 735 1437 1805 800 531 386 344 801 2067 528 2237 419
Baltimore, MD: 1959 795 1551 2401 422 370 2388 583 352 441 1665 708 521 377 420 1399 1690 1031 532 2045 1128 1470 600 1032 763 1087 2445 1072 2705 602
Billings, MT: 1839 413 626 2254 1796 536 2157 1755 2012 455 1246 1552 1597 1608 1433 554 1007 1534 1255 2806 1673 1432 1836 2237 1088 965 1530 1239 1547
Birmingham, AL: 1509 2170 1215 909 2346 466 578 389 1434 667 475 725 576 647 1356 919 734 1292 678 481 241 494 753 1852 381 2092 369
Bismarck, ND: 1039 1846 1388 794 1749 1347 1604 594 838 1144 1189 1200 1342 693 675 1126 1597 2398 1582 1024 1548 1906 801 1378 1183 1702 1193
Boise, ID: 2697 2239 735 2520 2182 2375 737 1708 1969 2040 2036 1711 833 1369 1977 1206 3249 1952 1852 2115 2566 1376 760 1808 1033 1933
Boston, MA: 462 2683 1003 741 861 1961 1003 862 654 760 1819 2004 1326 741 2465 714 1890 940 1453 1184 1427 2757 1493 3046 964
Buffalo, NY: 2224 899 431 695 1502 545 442 197 333 1393 1546 868 277 2039 1167 1513 508 1134 1080 995 2299 1066 2572 545
Calgary, AB: 2586 2184 2441 991 1675 1981 2026 2037 2114 1234 1512 1963 2912 2355 1862 2385 2743 1638 1291 2020 1565 1718
Charleston, SC: 204 1783 907 622 724 637 1109 1205 1204 879 1754 1708 1110 721 703 238 1102 2371 900 2554 610
Charleston, WV: 468 265 1445 506 209 255 168 1072 1367 802 410 1718 1446 1192 320 816 649 764 2122 745 2374 251
Charlotte, NC: 265 1637 761 476 520 433 1031 1559 1057 675 1677 1566 1041 575 625 385 956 2225 754 2453 464
Cheyenne, WY: 972 1233 1304 1300 979 100 633 1247 801 2513 1220 1382 1829 640 843 1076 1116 1197
Chicago, IL: 302 346 359 936 1015 337 283 1543 1555 1108 184 750 1065 532 1768 662 2042 299
Cincinnati, OH: 253 105 958 1200 599 261 1605 1567 1079 116 700 803 597 1955 632 2215 106
Cleveland, OH: 144 1208 1347 669 171 1854 1359 1328 319 950 904 806 2100 882 2374 356
Columbus, OH: 1059 1266 665 192 1706 1465 1179 176 801 818 663 2021 733 2281 207
Dallas, TX: 887 752 1218 647 2524 241 913 406 1049 554 1331 327 1446 852
Denver, CO: 676 1284 701 2556 1127 1088 1290 1751 603 756 984 1029 1118
Des Moines, IA: 606 1283 1878 992 481 931 1315 194 1429 567 1703 595
Detroit, MI: 1799 1278 1338 318 960 1060 795 2037 891 2310 366
El Paso, TX: 3171 758 1489 1051 1642 1895 717 974 801 1499
Halifax, NS: 2595 1646 2158 1889 2133 3309 2198 3583 1669
Houston, TX: 839 445 884 795 1474 447 1558 972
Indianapolis, IN: 675 879 485 1843 587 2104 112
Jackson, MS: 598 747 1735 269 1851 594
Jacksonville, FL: 1148 2415 873 2441 766
Kansas City, MO: 1358 382 1632 516
Las Vegas, NV: 1478 274 1874
Little Rock, AR: 1706 526
Los Angeles, CA: 2126

First-column (Albany, km) values for the lower labeled rows and labeled rows (kilometers):

Memphis, TN: 1953 1662 1207 6570 626 1501 2615 388 2151 3144 2177 1492 3498 1223 975 988 1958 867 793 1194 956 750 1796 1158 1210 1789 3311 943 747 339 1179 862 2592 225 2959 621
México, MX: 4520 2352 2051 8061 3821 3899 3641 2624 3952 3985 4574 4058 4737 3319 3541 3208 2911 3421 3360 3760 3522 1815 2750 3002 3776 1926 5709 1535 3287 2249 2956 2684 2846 2344 2981 3187
Miami, FL: 2315 3847 2951 7997 1064 1784 4109 1307 3578 4639 2460 2293 4925 938 1599 1175 3455 2224 1836 2011 1811 2200 3329 2626 2254 3152 3595 1932 1924 1472 555 2359 4397 1915 4439 1744
Milwaukee, WI: 1495 2294 1837 5651 1308 1295 1891 1228 1234 2813 1770 1033 2579 1614 967 1379 628 143 640 713 730 1625 1697 608 611 2602 2658 1920 449 1344 1866 922 2909 3350 634
Minneapolis, MN: 2003 2154 1697 5110 1817 1804 1350 1736 693 2357 2280 1541 2039 2122 1477 1887 1418 658 1149 1223 1241 1607 1487 396 1121 2462 3168 1995 959 1852 2376 710 2698 1310 3139 1144
Mobile, AL: 2162 2162 1780 7258 534 1630 3249 415 2840 3704 2306 1874 4187 1033 1347 920 2526 1485 1176 1578 1339 1028 2378 1794 1595 1981 1981 761 1186 301 660 1496 3092 735 3268 1006
Montréal, QC: 370 3495 3038 6607 1997 907 3368 2074 2711 4079 504 633 3535 1842 1323 1616 2895 1353 1311 946 1167 2851 2965 1874 907 3802 1150 3044 1403 2436 2132 2187 4616 1480
Nashville, TN: 1614 2008 1553 6534 389 1152 2652 312 2116 3179 1828 1152 3463 874 636 639 1995 763 452 854 615 1096 1870 1167 870 2137 2962 1289 462 681 948 899 2938 571 3305 282
New Orleans, LA: 2317 2053 1598 7207 761 1837 3146 565 2790 3595 2515 2018 4135 1260 1490 1147 2417 1504 1319 1722 1482 845 2267 1797 1736 1799 3649 579 1329 298 895 1500 2983 732 3084 1149
New York, NY: 243 3242 2785 7062 1398 309 3297 1585 2640 4008 346 644 3990 1244 829 1015 2824 1282 1023 750 861 2557 2895 1804 1001 3596 1480 2671 1150 1968 1533 1934 4106 2031 4537 1189
Oklahoma City, OK: 2492 879 422 6245 1519 2179 1974 1173 2828 2423 2726 2031 3070 2008 1444 1773 1249 1298 1373 1244 1298 1726 1496 336 1096 879 1709 1186 985 2077 560 1809 571 2175 1245
Omaha, NE: 2079 1168 5409 1591 1819 1455 1514 991 1986 2354 1617 2338 2076 1532 1841 800 769 1184 1297 1290 1076 870 219 1195 1989 2662 1464 994 1504 2150 302 2082 917 2521 1133
Orlando, FL: 1987 3112 2595 7641 708 1455 3754 951 3223 4283 2130 1965 4570 610 1271 845 3099 1868 1480 1681 1541 1844 2972 2270 1899 2796 3266 1577 1569 1117 227 2003 4042 1559 4084 1389
Ottawa, ON: 486 3392 2936 6455 1866 842 3265 1971 2608 3977 665 536 3384 1780 1221 1483 2793 1252 1208 845 1064 2748 2862 1772 805 3701 1324 2941 1302 2333 2069 2085 4074 2224 4515 1377
Philadelphia, PA: 359 3144 2689 7010 1258 167 3249 1463 2592 3961 516 466 3939 1102 730 874 2776 1236 927 703 763 2415 2806 1755 953 3455 1561 2529 1054 1863 1393 1891 4441 1091
Phoenix, AZ: 4121 750 1212 5776 3006 3821 1929 2772 2674 1598 4354 3659 2454 3514 3274 3390 1615 2927 3018 3325 3125 1733 1455 2507 3337 695 5490 1911 2838 2385 3334 2188 459 2200 594 2874
Pittsburgh, PA: 780 2687 2230 6526 1088 396 2766 1228 2109 3477 953 349 3455 1033 349 705 2293 751 470 219 306 2005 2349 1273 470 3046 2087 2198 595 1590 1323 1379 3564 1480 3984 634
Portland, ME: 434 3762 3305 7546 1926 837 3784 2113 3128 4497 172 901 4475 1772 1350 1543 3313 1772 1545 1208 1381 3084 3382 2291 1348 4124 872 3199 1670 2494 2061 2454 4594 2558 5059 1709
Portland, OR: 4753 2245 2727 3902 4259 4553 1430 4182 2093 695 5030 4291 1371 4743 4199 4508 1876 3438 3858 3973 3965 3443 2029 2893 3870 2643 5918 3831 3669 4093 4817 2904 1013 3599 1562 3800
Québec, QC: 582 3734 3279 6846 2209 1120 3607 2314 2951 4320 624 879 3775 2055 1564 1763 3136 1595 1441 1406 1301 3091 3205 2114 1147 4043 940 3284 1644 2428 2417 2366 4858 1720
Raleigh, NC: 1028 2867 2412 7157 637 497 3395 880 2739 4014 1173 1033 4085 449 504 254 2829 1385 840 914 776 1913 2703 1862 1165 2951 2307 1928 1028 1260 740 1733 3797 1430 4164 907
Rapid City, SD: 2816 1353 1347 4795 2431 2616 610 2354 515 1496 3091 2354 1472 2935 2288 2700 491 1469 1961 2034 2051 1733 650 1012 1932 1778 3979 2121 1772 2346 2991 1142 1665 1759 2106 1955
Reno, NV: 4420 1641 2101 4843 3926 4220 1545 3849 2208 692 4697 3958 2069 4410 3866 4175 1543 3105 3525 3640 3632 3110 1696 2560 3537 2116 5585 3334 3335 3760 4484 2571 711 3266 835 3467
Richmond, VA: 776 3018 2563 7065 848 245 3303 1091 2647 4016 920 787 3994 689 518 465 2832 1290 853 758 832 2106 2716 1812 1009 3146 1812 2140 1031 1471 980 1746 3932 1582 4315 920
St. Louis, MO: 1667 1691 1234 6113 883 1353 2158 806 1424 2619 1900 1205 3001 1368 824 1133 1435 473 563 901 671 1022 1376 702 883 1998 3036 1389 385 813 1442 405 2590 669 2986 425
Salt Lake City, UT: 3578 1004 1551 4729 3083 3379 882 3006 1545 550 3854 3115 1406 3569 3025 3334 702 2262 2682 2796 2790 2269 854 1717 2695 1390 4742 2655 2492 2917 3643 1728 671 2425 1112 2624
San Antonio, TX: 3142 1316 825 6833 1609 2689 2414 1413 2573 2833 3366 2679 3511 2108 2162 1997 1683 2043 1981 2383 204 436 1522 1623 2397 895 4500 322 1908 1036 1744 1307 2047 965 2182 1810
San Diego, CA: 4697 1327 1788 5673 3494 4383 2095 3252 2814 1763 4932 4307 1892 3977 3986 4721 2619 3995 3860 3897 3387 3551 3921 3701 2212 1757 2841 3818 1175 5890 2386 2393 3414 2864 3813 619 3817
San Francisco, CA: 4769 1788 2248 4940 4212 4506 1892 3977 2409 1039 5044 4307 2409 4721 4216 4439 1892 3453 3873 3987 3981 3553 2138 2932 3781 3128 5828 3940 3619 4203 4911 3012 2021 3709 1847 3804
Seattle, WA: 4664 2354 2837 3623 4352 4465 1313 4275 1977 805 4940 4203 1093 4784 4137 4549 1986 3318 3810 3883 3900 3553 2138 2932 3781 3128 5828 3940 3619 4203 4911 3012 2021 3709 1847 3804
Tampa, FL: 2076 3136 2619 7664 732 1545 3778 975 3247 4307 2220 2053 4592 698 1360 935 3123 1892 1504 1772 1667 1868 2996 2294 1921 2821 3355 1601 1593 1141 315 2026 4064 1583 4108 1413
Toronto, ON: 644 2962 2505 6595 1541 909 2835 1541 2179 3546 917 171 3524 1619 864 1290 2362 821 779 188 708 2319 2633 1342 375 3524 1512 2870 1903 1910 1656 1794 4084 948 ...
Vancouver, BC: 4878 2570 3052 3430 4566 4591 1527 4491 2191 1018 5155 4417 2191 4998 4352 4763 2201 3533 4024 4098 4116 3768 2354 3147 3995 3358 6043 4156 3834 4418 5126 3229 2237 3924 2077 4018
Washington, DC: 594 3051 2594 6903 1023 61 3142 1220 2486 3854 737 618 3831 867 557 639 2669 1128 832 595 669 2191 2713 1649 846 3231 1873 2306 959 1603 1158 1743 3928 1667 4348 959
Wichita, KS: 2367 1138 681 5921 1591 2053 1717 1348 1503 2166 2600 1905 2814 2077 1533 1842 986 1171 1263 1601 1371 591 838 628 1583 1445 3736 978 1084 1241 2151 309 2053 747 2434 1134
Winnipeg, MB: 2730 2587 2285 4385 2542 2531 1324 2463 668 2336 3006 2269 1313 2850 2203 2615 1821 1384 1876 1948 1966 2193 1892 1121 1847 3010 3361 2581 1685 2526 3102 1324 3012 1939 3453 1870

Louisville, KY (diagonal, lower-right corner).

Milles

	Memphis, TN	México, MX	Miami, FL	Milwaukee, WI	Minneapolis, MN	Mobile, AL	Montréal, QC	Nashville, TN	New Orleans, LA	New York, NY	Oklahoma City, OK	Omaha, NE	Orlando, FL	Ottawa, ON	Philadelphia, PA	Phoenix, AZ	Pittsburgh, PA	Portland, ME	Portland, OR	Québec, QC	Raleigh, NC	Rapid City, SD	Reno, NV	Richmond, VA	St. Louis, MO	Salt Lake City, UT	San Antonio, TX	San Diego, CA	San Francisco, CA	Seattle, WA	Tampa, FL	Toronto, ON	Vancouver, BC	Washington, DC	Wichita, KS	Winnipeg, MB
Albany, NY	1214	2809	1439	929	1245	1344	230	1003	1440	151	1549	1292	1235	302	223	2561	485	270	2954	362	639	1750	2747	482	1036	2224	1953	2919	2964	2899	1290	400	3032	369	1471	1697
Albuquerque, NM	1033	1462	2155	1426	1339	1344	2172	1248	1276	2015	546	973	1934	2108	1954	466	1670	2338	1395	2321	1782	841	1020	1876	1051	624	818	825	1111	1463	1949	1841	1597	1896	707	1608
Amarillo, TX	750	1275	1834	1142	1055	1106	1888	965	993	1731	262	726	1613	1825	1671	753	1386	2054	1695	2038	1499	837	1306	1593	767	964	513	1111	1397	1763	1628	1557	1897	1612	423	1420
Anchorage, AK	4083	5010	4970	3512	3176	4511	4106	4061	4479	4389	3881	3362	4749	4012	4357	3590	4056	4690	2425	4255	4448	2980	3010	4391	3799	2939	4247	3526	3070	2252	4763	4099	2132	4290	3680	2725
Atlanta, GA	389	1753	661	813	1129	332	1241	242	473	869	944	989	440	1160	782	1868	676	1197	2647	1373	396	1511	2440	527	549	1916	1000	2166	2618	2705	455	958	2838	636	989	1580
Baltimore, MD	933	2423	1109	805	1121	1013	564	716	1142	192	1354	1168	904	523	104	2366	246	520	2830	696	309	1626	2623	152	841	2100	1671	2724	2840	2775	960	565	2908	38	1276	1573
Billings, MT	1625	2263	2554	1175	839	2019	2093	1648	1955	2049	1227	904	2333	2029	2019	1199	1719	2352	889	2242	2110	379	960	2053	1341	548	1500	1302	1176	816	2348	1762	949	1953	1067	823
Birmingham, AL	241	1631	812	763	1079	258	1289	194	351	985	729	941	591	1225	897	1723	763	1313	2599	1438	547	1463	2392	678	501	1868	878	2021	2472	2657	606	958	2791	758	838	1531
Bismarck, ND	1337	2456	2224	767	431	1765	1685	1315	1734	1641	1136	616	2003	1621	1611	1662	1311	1944	1301	1834	1702	320	1372	1645	1053	960	1599	1765	1749	1229	2018	1354	1362	1545	934	415
Boise, ID	1954	2477	2883	1748	1465	2302	2535	1976	2234	2491	1506	1234	2662	2472	2462	993	2161	2795	432	2685	2495	930	430	2496	1628	342	1761	1096	646	500	2677	2204	633	2395	1346	1452
Boston, MA	1353	2843	1529	1100	1417	1433	313	1136	1563	215	1694	1463	1324	413	321	2706	592	107	3126	388	729	1921	2919	572	1181	2395	2092	3065	3135	3070	1380	570	3204	458	1616	1868
Buffalo, NY	927	2522	1425	642	958	1165	397	716	1254	400	1262	1005	1221	333	414	2274	217	560	2667	546	642	1463	2460	485	749	1936	1665	2632	2677	2612	1276	106	2745	384	1184	1410
Calgary, AB	2174	2944	3061	1603	1267	2602	2197	2152	2570	2480	1908	1453	2840	2103	2448	1525	2147	2781	852	2346	2539	915	1286	2482	1890	874	2182	1628	1497	679	2854	2190	559	2381	1749	816
Charleston, SC	760	2063	583	1003	1319	642	1145	543	783	773	1248	1290	379	1106	685	2184	642	1101	2948	1277	279	1824	2741	428	850	2218	1310	2483	2934	2973	434	1006	3106	539	1291	1771
Charleston, WV	606	2201	994	601	918	837	822	395	926	515	1022	952	790	759	454	2035	217	839	2610	972	313	1422	2403	322	512	1880	1344	2393	2620	2571	845	537	2705	346	953	1369
Charlotte, NC	614	1994	730	857	1173	572	1003	397	713	631	1102	1144	525	922	543	2107	438	959	2802	1135	158	1678	2595	289	704	2072	1241	2405	2759	2827	581	802	2960	397	1145	1625
Cheyenne, WY	1217	1809	2147	1012	881	1570	1799	1240	1502	1755	773	497	1926	1736	1725	1004	1425	2059	1166	1949	1758	305	959	1760	892	436	1046	1179	1176	1234	1941	1468	1368	1659	613	1132
Chicago, IL	539	2126	1382	89	409	923	841	474	935	797	807	474	1161	778	768	1819	467	1101	2137	991	861	913	1930	802	294	1406	1270	2105	2146	2062	1176	510	2196	701	728	860
Cincinnati, OH	493	2088	1141	398	714	731	815	281	820	636	863	736	920	751	576	1876	292	960	2398	972	522	1219	2191	530	350	1667	1231	2234	2407	2368	935	484	2501	517	785	1166
Cleveland, OH	742	2337	1250	443	760	981	588	531	1070	466	1073	806	1045	525	437	2085	136	751	2469	738	568	1264	2262	471	560	1738	1481	2437	2478	2413	1101	303	2547	370	995	1211
Columbus, OH	594	2189	1163	454	771	832	725	382	921	535	930	802	958	661	474	1942	190	858	2464	874	482	1275	2257	517	417	1734	1332	2300	2474	2424	1036	440	2558	416	852	1222
Dallas, TX	466	1128	1367	1010	999	639	1772	681	525	1589	209	669	1146	1708	1501	1077	1246	1917	2140	1921	1189	1077	1933	1309	635	1410	271	1375	1827	2208	1161	1441	2342	1362	367	1363
Denver, CO	1116	1709	2069	1055	924	1478	1843	1162	1409	1799	681	541	1847	1779	1744	904	1460	2102	1261	1992	1680	404	1054	1688	855	531	946	1092	1271	1329	1862	1512	1463	1686	521	1176
Des Moines, IA	720	1866	1632	378	246	1115	1165	725	1117	1121	546	136	1411	1101	1091	1558	791	1424	1798	1314	1157	629	1591	1126	436	1067	1009	1766	1807	1822	1426	834	1956	1025	390	697
Detroit, MI	752	2347	1401	380	697	991	564	541	1079	622	1062	743	1180	500	592	2074	292	838	2405	713	724	1201	2198	627	549	1675	1490	2373	2415	2350	1194	233	2483	526	984	1148
El Paso, TX	1112	1197	1959	1617	1530	1231	2363	1328	1118	2235	737	1236	1738	2300	2147	432	1893	2563	1767	2513	1834	1105	1315	1955	1242	864	556	730	1181	1944	1753	2032	2087	2008	898	1871
Halifax, NS	2058	3548	2234	1652	1969	1231	715	1841	2268	920	2400	2015	2030	823	1026	3412	1297	542	3678	584	1434	2473	3471	1277	1887	2947	2797	3646	3687	3622	2085	1045	3756	1164	2322	2089
Houston, TX	586	954	1201	1193	1240	473	1892	801	360	1660	449	910	980	1828	1572	1188	1366	1988	2381	2041	1198	1318	2072	1330	863	1650	200	1487	1938	2449	995	1561	2583	1433	608	1604
Indianapolis, IN	464	2043	1196	279	596	737	872	287	826	715	752	618	975	809	655	1764	370	1038	2280	1022	639	1101	2073	641	239	1549	1186	2122	2290	2249	990	541	2383	596	674	1047
Jackson, MS	211	1398	915	835	1151	187	1514	423	185	1223	612	935	694	1450	1135	1482	988	1550	2544	1663	783	1458	2337	914	505	1813	644	1780	2232	2612	709	1183	2746	996	771	1570
Jacksonville, FL	733	1837	345	1160	1477	410	1325	589	556	953	1291	1336	141	1286	866	2072	822	1281	2994	1457	460	1859	2787	609	896	2264	1084	2370	2822	3052	196	1187	3186	720	1337	1928
Kansas City, MO	536	1668	1466	573	441	930	1359	559	932	1202	348	188	1245	1296	1141	1360	857	1525	1805	1509	1077	710	1598	1085	252	1074	812	1695	1814	1872	1259	1028	2007	1083	192	823
Las Vegas, NV	1611	1769	2733	1808	1677	1922	2596	1826	1854	2552	1124	1294	2512	2532	2500	285	2215	2855	1188	2745	2360	1035	442	2444	1610	417	1272	337	575	1256	2526	2265	1390	2441	1276	1872
Little Rock, AR	140	1457	1190	747	814	457	1446	355	455	1262	355	570	969	1382	1175	1367	920	1590	2237	1595	889	1093	2030	983	416	1507	600	1703	2012	2305	984	1115	2439	1036	464	1205
Los Angeles, CA	1839	1853	2759	2082	1951	2031	2869	2054	1917	2820	1352	1567	2538	2806	2760	369	2476	3144	971	3019	2588	1309	519	2682	1856	691	1356	124	385	1148	2553	2538	1291	2702	1513	2146
Louisville, KY	386	1981	1084	394	711	625	920	175	714	739	774	704	863	856	678	1786	394	1062	2362	1069	564	1215	2155	572	264	1631	1125	2144	2372	2364	878	589	2497	596	705	1162
Memphis, TN		1595	1051	624	940	395	1306	215	396	1123	487	724	830	1243	1035	1500	780	1451	2382	1456	749	1247	2175	843	294	1652	739	1841	2144	2440	845	975	2574	896	597	1359
México, MX			2154	2200	2113	1426	2900	1810	1313	2619	1323	1783	1933	2838	2525	1484	2375	2941	2819	3051	2151	2365	2367	2283	1825	2135	853	1683	2233	2996	1948	2570	3139	2386	1481	2477
Miami, FL				1478	1794	727	1671	907	874	1299	1609	1654	232	1631	1211	2390	1167	1627	3312	1803	805	2176	3105	954	1214	2581	1401	2688	3140	3370	274	1532	3504	1065	1655	2246
Milwaukee, WI					337	1019	939	569	1020	894	880	514	1257	875	865	1892	564	1198	2063	1088	956	842	1970	899	367	1446	1343	2145	2186	1991	1272	607	2124	799	769	789
Minneapolis, MN						1335	1255	886	1337	1211	793	383	1573	1192	1181	1805	881	1515	1727	1405	1273	606	1839	1216	621	1315	1257	2014	2055	1654	1588	924	1788	1115	637	452
Mobile, AL							1575	450	146	1203	799	1119	506	1481	1115	1662	1019	1531	2731	1707	730	1641	2545	861	688	2000	673	1960	2411	2799	521	1214	2933	970	958	1787
Montréal, QC								1094	1632	383	1625	1300	1466	121	454	2637	607	282	2963	155	871	1758	2756	714	1112	2232	2043	2931	2972	2907	1522	330	3041	600	1547	1374
Nashville, TN									539	906	703	747	686	1031	818	1715	569	1234	2405	1244	532	1269	2198	626	307	1675	954	2056	2360	2463	701	764	2597	679	748	1337
New Orleans, LA										1332	731	1121	653	1570	1245	1548	1108	1660	2663	1783	871	1643	2431	1002	690	1932	560	1846	2298	2731	668	1302	2865	1106	890	1755
New York, NY											1469	1258	1094	439	91	2481	367	313	2920	515	499	1716	2713	342	956	2189	1861	2839	2929	2864	1150	507	2998	228	1391	1665
Oklahoma City, OK												463	1388	1563	1408	1012	1124	1792	1934	1776	1237	871	1727	1331	505	1204	466	1370	1657	2002	1403	1295	2136	1350	161	1158
Omaha, NE													1433	1238	1228	1440	928	1561	1662	1451	1265	525	1455	1263	440	932	927	1630	1672	1719	1448	971	1853	1162	307	638
Orlando, FL														1427	1006	2169	963	1422	3091	1598	601	1955	2884	750	993	2360	1180	2467	2918	3149	82	1327	3283	860	1434	2025
Ottawa, ON															451	2575	545	382	2901	257	831	1696	2694	675	1050	2170	1981	2869	2910	2845	1483	268	2978	562	1485	1280
Philadelphia, PA																2420	306	419	2890	586	411	1686	2683	254	895	2160	1774	2779	2900	2835	1062	522	2968	140	1330	1633
Phoenix, AZ																	2136	2804	1335	2788	2249	1308	883	2343	1517	651	987	358	750	1513	2184	2307	1655	2362	1173	2075
Pittsburgh, PA																		690	2590	758	497	1386	2383	341	611	1859	1519	2494	2599	2534	1019	321	2668	240	1046	1332
Portland, ME																			3223	264	827	2019	3016	670	1279	2493	2189	3162	3233	3168	1478	668	3301	556	1714	1966
Portland, OR																				3114	2923	1268	578	2925	2057	771	2322	1093	638	170	3106	2633	313	2824	1775	1463
Québec, QC																					1003	1908	2905	846	1261	2381	2193	3080	3122	3057	1654	479	3190	732	1696	1523
Raleigh, NC																						1777	2716	157	825	2193	1398	2563	2894	2926	656	820	3060	265	1266	1724
Rapid City, SD																							1151	1720	963	628	1335	1372	1368	1195	1970	1429	1328	1620	712	792
Reno, NV																								2718	1850	524	1870	642	217	755	2899	2426	898	2617	1568	1867
Richmond, VA																									834	2194	1530	2684	2934	2869	805	660	3003	108	1274	1667
St. Louis, MO																										1326	968	1875	2066	2125	1008	782	2259	837	441	1075
Salt Lake City, UT																											1419	754	740	839	2375	1902	973	2094	1044	1455
San Antonio, TX																												1285	1737	2275	1195	1714	2410	1635	624	1621
San Diego, CA																													508	1271	2481	2601	1414	2720	1531	2209
San Francisco, CA																														816	2933	2643	958	2834	1784	2193
Seattle, WA																															3164	2577	140	2769	1843	1390
Tampa, FL																																1383	3297	916	1448	2039
Toronto, ON																																	2711	563	1217	1375
Vancouver, BC																																		2902	1977	1375
Washington, DC																																			1272	1566
Wichita, KS																																				956

	Memphis, TN	México, MX	Miami, FL	Milwaukee, WI	Minneapolis, MN	Mobile, AL	Montréal, QC	Nashville, TN	New Orleans, LA	New York, NY	Oklahoma City, OK	Omaha, NE	Orlando, FL	Ottawa, ON	Philadelphia, PA	Phoenix, AZ	Pittsburgh, PA	Portland, ME	Portland, OR	Québec, QC	Raleigh, NC	Rapid City, SD	Reno, NV	Richmond, VA	St. Louis, MO	Salt Lake City, UT	San Antonio, TX	San Diego, CA	San Francisco, CA	Seattle, WA	Tampa, FL	Toronto, ON	Vancouver, BC	Washington, DC	Wichita, KS
México, MX	2566																																		
Miami, FL	1691	3466																																	
Milwaukee, WI	1004	3540	2378																																
Minneapolis, MN	1512	3400	2887	542																															
Mobile, AL	636	2294	1170	1640	2148																														
Montréal, QC	2101	4666	2689	1511	2019	2534																													
Nashville, TN	346	2912	1459	916	1426	724	1760																												
New Orleans, LA	637	2113	1406	1641	2151	235	2626	867																											
New York, NY	1807	4214	2090	1438	1948	1936	616	1458	2143																										
Oklahoma City, OK	784	2129	2589	1416	1276	1286	2615	1131	1176	2364																									
Omaha, NE	1165	2869	2661	827	616	1800	2092	1202	1804	2024	745																								
Orlando, FL	1335	3110	373	2023	2531	814	2359	1104	1051	1760	2233	2306																							
Ottawa, ON	2000	4566	2624	1408	1918	2383	194	1659	2526	706	2515	1992	2296																						
Philadelphia, PA	1665	4063	1948	1392	1900	1794	730	1316	2003	146	2265	1976	1619	726																					
Phoenix, AZ	2414	2388	3846	3044	2904	2674	4243	2759	2491	3992	1628	2317	3490	4143	3894																				
Pittsburgh, PA	1255	3821	1878	907	1418	1640	977	916	1783	591	1809	1493	1549	877	492	3437																			
Portland, ME	2335	4732	2618	1928	2438	2463	454	1986	2671	504	2883	2512	2288	615	674	4512	1110																		
Portland, OR	3833	4536	5329	3319	2779	4394	4767	3870	4285	4698	3112	2674	4973	4668	4650	2148	4167	5186																	
Québec, QC	2343	4909	2901	1751	2261	2747	249	2002	2869	829	2858	2335	2571	414	943	4486	1220	425	5010																
Raleigh, NC	1205	3461	1295	1538	2048	1175	1401	856	1401	803	1990	2035	967	1337	661	3619	800	1331	4703	1614															
Rapid City, SD	2006	3805	3501	1355	975	2640	2829	2042	2644	2761	1401	845	3146	2729	2713	2105	2230	3249	2040	3070	2859														
Reno, NV	3500	3809	4996	3170	2959	4095	4434	3537	3911	4365	2779	2341	4640	4335	4317	1421	3834	4853	930	4674	4370	1852													
Richmond, VA	1356	3673	1535	1446	1957	1385	1149	1007	1612	550	2142	2032	1207	1086	409	3770	549	1078	4706	1361	253	2767	4373												
St. Louis, MO	473	2936	1953	591	999	1107	1789	494	1110	1538	813	708	1598	1689	1440	2441	983	2058	3310	2029	1327	1549	2977	1342											
Salt Lake City, UT	2658	3435	4153	2327	2116	3218	3591	2695	3109	3522	1937	1500	3797	3492	3475	1047	2991	4011	1241	3831	3529	1010	843	3530	2134										
San Antonio, TX	1189	1372	2254	2161	2023	1083	3287	1535	901	2994	750	1492	1899	3187	2854	1588	2444	3522	3736	3529	2249	2148	3009	2462	1558	2283									
San Diego, CA	2962	2708	4325	3451	3241	3154	4716	3308	2970	4568	2204	2623	3969	4616	4471	576	4013	5088	1759	4956	4124	2208	1033	4319	3017	1213	2068								
San Francisco, CA	3450	3593	5052	3517	3306	3879	4782	3797	3697	4713	2666	2690	4695	4682	4666	1207	4182	5202	1027	5023	4656	2201	349	4721	3324	1191	2795	817							
Seattle, WA	3926	4821	5422	3204	2661	4504	4677	3963	4394	4608	3221	2766	5067	4578	4562	2434	4077	5097	274	4919	4708	1923	1215	4616	3419	1350	3660	2045	1313						
Tampa, FL	1360	3134	441	2047	2555	838	2449	1128	1075	1850	2257	2330	132	2386	1709	3514	1640	2378	4998	2661	1056	3170	4664	1295	1622	3821	1923	3992	4719	5091					
Toronto, ON	1569	4135	2465	977	1487	1953	531	1229	2095	816	2084	1562	2135	431	840	3712	516	1075	4236	771	1319	2299	3903	1062	1258	3060	2758	4185	4253	4146	2225				
Vancouver, BC	4142	5051	5638	3418	2877	4719	4893	4179	4610	4824	3437	2981	5282	4792	4776	2663	4293	5311	504	5133	4924	2137	1445	4832	3635	1566	3878	2275	1541	225	5305	4362			
Washington, DC	1442	3839	1714	1286	1794	1561	965	1093	1780	367	2172	1870	1384	904	225	3800	386	895	4544	1178	426	2607	4211	174	1347	3369	2631	4376	4560	4455	1474	906	4669		
Wichita, KS	961	2383	2663	1237	1025	1541	2489	1204	1432	2238	259	494	2307	2389	2140	1887	1683	2758	2856	2729	2037	1146	2523	2050	710	1680	1004	2463	2870	2965	2330	1958	3181	2047	
Winnipeg, MB	2187	3985	3614	1270	727	2875	2211	2151	2824	2679	1863	1027	3258	2060	2627	3339	2143	3163	2354	2451	2774	1274	3004	2682	1730	2341	2608	3554	3529	2237	3281	2212	2212	2520	1538

Kilomètres

°F	°C	°C	°F
110	43.3	40	104
100	37.8	35	95
90	32.2	30	86
80	26.7	25	77
70	21.1	20	68
60	15.6	15	59
50	10.0	10	50
40	4.4	5	41
32	0	0	32
30	-1.1	-5	23
20	-6.7	-10	14
10	-12.2	-15	5
0	-17.8	-20	-4
-10	-23.3	-25	-13
-20	-28.9	-30	-22
-30	-34.4	-35	-31
-40	-40.0	-40	-40
-50	-45.6	-45	-49

TEMPERATURE CONVERSIONS

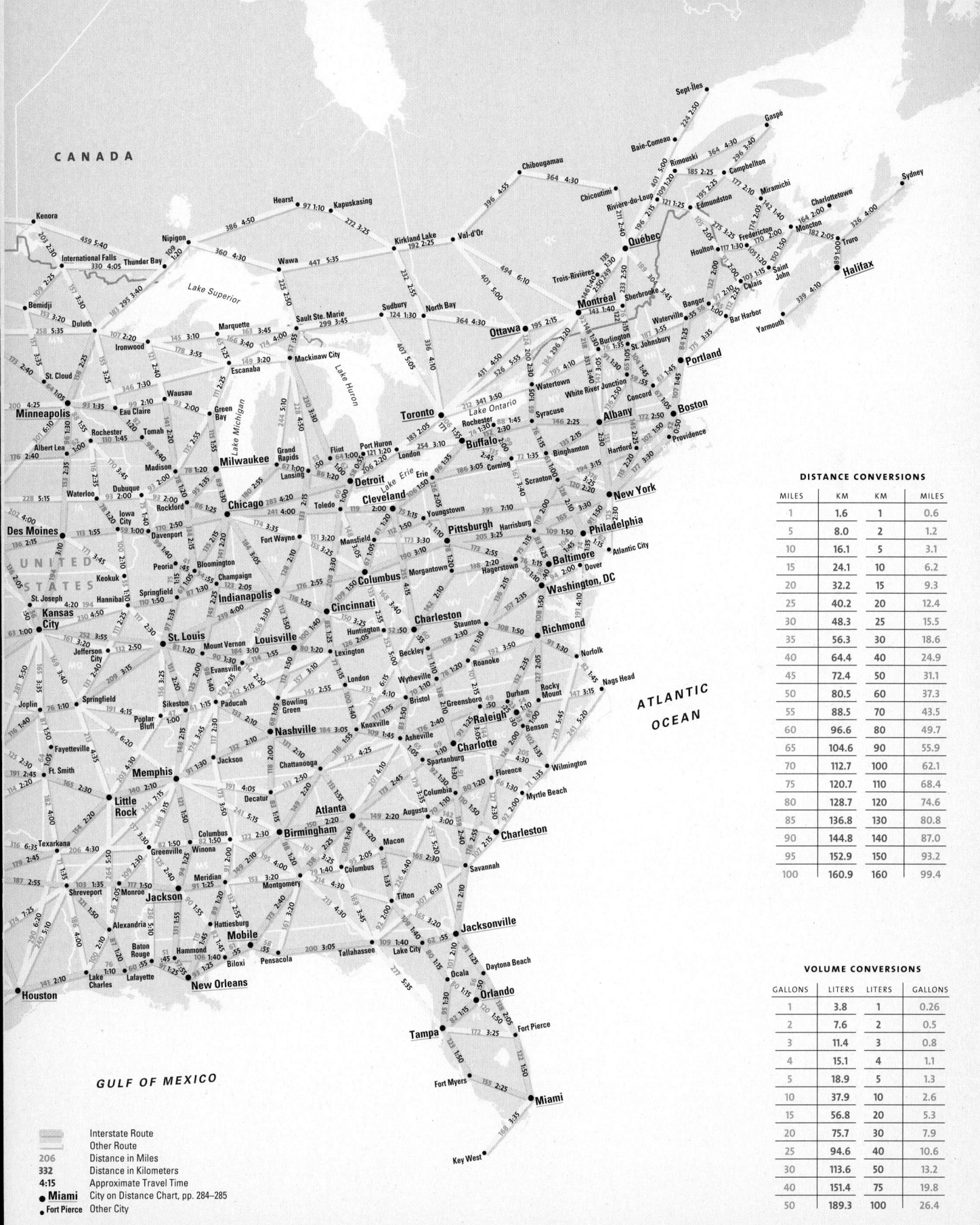

DISTANCE CONVERSIONS

MILES	KM	KM	MILES
1	1.6	1	0.6
5	8.0	2	1.2
10	16.1	5	3.1
15	24.1	10	6.2
20	32.2	15	9.3
25	40.2	20	12.4
30	48.3	25	15.5
35	56.3	30	18.6
40	64.4	40	24.9
45	72.4	50	31.1
50	80.5	60	37.3
55	88.5	70	43.5
60	96.6	80	49.7
65	104.6	90	55.9
70	112.7	100	62.1
75	120.7	110	68.4
80	128.7	120	74.6
85	136.8	130	80.8
90	144.8	140	87.0
95	152.9	150	93.2
100	160.9	160	99.4

VOLUME CONVERSIONS

GALLONS	LITERS	LITERS	GALLONS
1	3.8	1	0.26
2	7.6	2	0.5
3	11.4	3	0.8
4	15.1	4	1.1
5	18.9	5	1.3
10	37.9	10	2.6
15	56.8	20	5.3
20	75.7	30	7.9
25	94.6	40	10.6
30	113.6	50	13.2
40	151.4	75	19.8
50	189.3	100	26.4

Interstate Route
Other Route
206 Distance in Miles
332 Distance in Kilometers
4:15 Approximate Travel Time
● **Miami** City on Distance Chart, pp. 284–285
● Fort Pierce Other City

Distances and driving times may vary depending on actual
route traveled and driving conditions.

TOURISM INFORMATION

UNITED STATES

Alabama
Alabama Bureau of Tourism & Travel
800.252.2262, 334.242.4169
www.800alabama.org

Alaska
Alaska Travel Industry Association
www.travelalaska.com

Arizona
Arizona Office of Tourism
866.275.5816, 602.364.3700
www.arizonaguide.com

Arkansas
Arkansas Dept. of Parks & Tourism
800.628.8725, 501.682.7777
www.1800natural.com

California
California Tourism
800.862.2543, 916.444.4429
www.visitcalifornia.com

Colorado
Colorado Tourism Office
800.265.6723, 303.892.3885
www.colorado.com

Connecticut
Connecticut Commission on
Culture & Tourism
888.288.4748, 860.256.2800
www.ctvisit.com

Delaware
Delaware Tourism Office
866.284.7483
www.visitdelaware.com

District of Columbia
DC Convention and Tourism Corp.
800.422.8644, 202.789.7000 or 7030
www.washington.org

Florida
Visit Florida
850.488.5607, 888.735.2872
www.visitflorida.com

Georgia
Georgia Dept. of Industry, Trade & Tourism
800.847.4842
www.georgia.org/travel

Hawaii
Hawaii Visitors & Conv. Bureau
800.464.2924, 808.923.1811
www.gohawaii.com

Idaho
Idaho Div. of Tourism Development
800.847.4843, 208.334.2470
www.visitidaho.org

Illinois
Illinois Bureau of Tourism
800.406.6418
www.enjoyillinois.com

Indiana
Indiana Office of Tourism Development
800.677.9800, 317.232.8860
www.enjoyindiana.com

Iowa
Iowa Division of Tourism
888.472.6035, 515.242.4705
www.traveliowa.com

Kansas
Kansas Travel & Tourism
800.252.6727, 785.296.2009
www.travelks.com

Kentucky
Kentucky Department of Tourism
800.225.8747, 502.564.4930
www.kentuckytourism.com

Louisiana
Louisiana Office of Tourism
225.342.8100, 800.334.8626
www.louisianatravel.com

Maine
Maine Office of Tourism
888.624.6345, 207.624.7483
www.visitmaine.com

Maryland
Maryland Office of Tourism
866.639.3526
www.mdisfun.org

Massachusetts
Mass. Office of Travel & Tourism
800.227.6277, 617.973.8500
www.massvacation.com

Michigan
Travel Michigan
800.644.2489
www.michigan.org

Minnesota
Explore Minnesota Tourism
888.868.7476, 651.296.5029
www.exploreminnesota.com

Mississippi
Mississippi Div. of Tourism Development
866.733.6477, 601.359.3297
www.visitmississippi.org

Missouri
Missouri Division of Tourism
800.519.2100, 573.751.4133
www.visitmo.com

Montana
Travel Montana
800.847.4868, 406.841.2870
www.visitmt.com

Nebraska
Nebraska Travel & Tourism
877.632.7275, 402.471.3796
www.visitnebraska.org

Nevada
Nevada Commission on Tourism
800.638.2328, 775.687.4322
www.travelnevada.com

New Hampshire
New Hampshire Division of Travel &
  Tourism Development
800.386.4664, 603.271.2665
www.visitnh.gov

New Jersey
New Jersey Tourism Commission
800.847.4865, 609.777.0885
www.visitnj.org

New Mexico
New Mexico Tourism Department
800.545.2070, 505.827.7400
www.newmexico.org

New York
New York State Division of Tourism
800.225.5697, 518.474.4116
www.iloveny.com

North Carolina
North Carolina Division of Tourism,
  Film & Sports Development
800.847.4862, 919.733.4171
www.visitnc.com

North Dakota
North Dakota Tourism Division
800.435.5663, 701.328.2525
www.ndtourism.com

Ohio
Ohio Division of Travel & Tourism
800.282.5393, 614.466.8844
www.discoverohio.com

Oklahoma
Oklahoma Dept. of Tourism & Rec.
800.652.6552, 405.230.8400
www.travelok.com

Oregon
Oregon Tourism Commission
800.547.7842, 503.378.8850
www.traveloregon.com

Pennsylvania
Pennsylvania Tourism Office
800.847.4872, 717.787.5453
www.visitpa.com

Rhode Island
Rhode Island Tourism Division
800.556.2484
www.visitrhodeisland.com

South Carolina
S.C. Dept. of Parks, Rec. & Tourism
866.224.9339, 803.734.1700
www.discoversouthcarolina.com

South Dakota
South Dakota Department of Tourism
800.732.5682, 605.773.3301
www.travelsd.com

Tennessee
Tenn. Dept. of Tourist Development
800.462.8366, 615.741.2159
www.tnvacation.com

Texas
Texas Dept. of Econ. Dev., Tourism Div.
800.888.8839
www.traveltex.com

Utah
Utah Office of Tourism
800.882.4386, 801.538.1900
www.utah.com

Vermont
Vermont Dept. of Tourism & Marketing
800.837.6668, 802.828.3237
www.vermontvacation.com

Virginia
Virginia Tourism Corporation
800.847.4882, 804.545.5500
www.virginia.org

Washington
Washington State Tourism Division
800.544.1800
www.experiencewashington.com

West Virginia
West Virginia Division of Tourism
800.225.5982, 304.558.2200
www.wvtourism.com

Wisconsin
Wisconsin Department of Tourism
800.432.8747, 608.266.2161
www.travelwisconsin.com

Wyoming
Wyoming Travel & Tourism
800.225.5996, 307.777.7777
www.wyomingtourism.org

Puerto Rico
Puerto Rico Tourism Company
800.866.7827, 787.721.2400
www.gotopuertorico.com

CANADA

Alberta
Travel Alberta Canada
800.252.3782, 780.427.4321
www.travelalberta.com

British Columbia
Tourism British Columbia
800.435.5622, 250.356.6363
www.hellobc.com

Manitoba
Travel Manitoba
800.665.0040
www.travelmanitoba.com

New Brunswick
Tourism Communication Center
800.561.0123
www.tourismnewbrunswick.ca

Newfoundland & Labrador
Newfoundland & Labrador Tourism
800.563.6353, 709.729.2830
www.gov.nl.ca/tourism

Nova Scotia
Tourism Nova Scotia
800.565.0000, 902.425.5781
www.novascotia.com

Ontario
Ontario Tourism
800.668.2746, 905.282.1721
www.ontariotravel.net

Prince Edward Island
Tourism PEI
800.463.4734, 902.368.4444
www.gov.pe.ca/visitorsguide

Québec
Tourisme Québec
877.266.5687, 514.873.2015
www.bonjourquebec.com

Saskatchewan
Tourism Saskatchewan
877.237.2273, 306.787.9600
www.sasktourism.com

MEXICO

Mexico Ministry of Tourism
800.446.3942
www.visitmexico.com

BORDER CROSSING INFORMATION

TRAVEL ADVISORY

All travelers journeying to or from Canada, Mexico, Central and South America, and the Caribbean by air are now required to have a valid passport. Travelers to or from these countries by land or sea (including ferries) will soon be required to have a valid passport. Implementation of this requirement will occur on June 1, 2009. U.S. citizens traveling directly to or from Puerto Rico and the U.S. Virgin Islands are not required to have a passport. For more detailed information and updated schedules, please see http://travel.state.gov.

CANADA

New air travel regulations are in effect (see Travel Advisory). For land and sea travel, the old regulations remain in effect (temporarily), requiring U.S citizens to present either a passport or other proof of U.S. citizenship accompa nied by photo identification. U.S. citizens entering from a third country must have a valid passport. Naturalized citizens and alien permanent residents should carry the appropriate official documentation. Individuals under the age of 18 traveling alone, with one parent, or with other adults must carry notarized parental/legal guardian authorization.

U.S. driver's licenses are valid in Canada. Drivers should be prepared to present proof of their vehicle's registration, ownership, and insurance.

UNITED STATES (FROM CANADA)

New air travel regulations are in effect (see Travel Advisory). For land and sea travel, the old regulations remain in effect (temporarily), requiring Canadian citizens to present either a passport or other proof of citizenship accompanied by photo identification. Visas are not required for customary tourist travel. Individuals under the age of 18 traveling alone, with one parent, or with other adults must carry notarized parental/legal guardian authorization.

Canadian driver's licenses are valid in the U.S. for one year. Drivers should be prepared to present proof of their vehicle's registration, ownership, and insurance.

MEXICO

New air travel regulations are in effect (see Travel Advisory). For land and sea travel, the old regulations remain in effect (temporarily), requiring U.S. citizens to present either a passport or other proof of U.S. citizenship accompanied by photo identification. Passports are strongly recommended. Visas are not required for stays of up to 180 days. Naturalized citizens and alien permanent residents should carry the appropriate official documentation. Individuals under the age of 18 traveling alone, with one parent, or with other adults must carry notarized parental/legal guardian authorization. All U.S. citizens visiting for up to 180 days must also procure a tourist card, obtainable from Mexican consulates, tourism offices, border crossing points, and airlines serving Mexico. However, tourist cards are not needed for visits shorter than 72 hours to areas within the Border Zone (extending approximately 25 km into Mexico).

U.S. driver's licenses are valid in Mexico. Visitors who wish to drive beyond the Baja California Peninsula or the Border Zone must obtain a temporary import permit for their vehicles. To acquire a permit, one must submit evidence of citizenship and of the vehicle's title and registration, as well as a valid driver's license. A processing fee must be paid. Permits are available at any Mexican Army Bank (Banjercito) located at border crossings or selected Mexican consulates. Mexican law also requires the posting of a refundable bond, via credit card or cash, at the Banjercito to guarantee the departure of the vehicle. Do not deal with any individual operating outside of official channels.

All visitors driving in Mexico should be aware that U.S. auto insurance policies are not valid and that buying short-term tourist insurance is mandatory. Many U.S. insurance companies sell Mexican auto insurance. American Automobile Association (for members only) and Sanborn's Mexico Insurance (800.638.9423) are popular companies with offices at most U.S. border crossings.

COMMON ABBREVIATIONS

Arch.	Archaeological
Bfld.	Battlefield
Cons.	Conservation
Ent.	Entrance
Hist.	Historic(al)
Mem.	Memorial
Mon.	Monument
Mtn.	Mountain
Mts.	Mountains
Mus.	Museum
Natl.	National
Nat.	Natural
N.H.S.	National Historic Site
N.H.P.	National Historical Park
N.M.P.	National Military Park
N.R.A.	National Recreation Area
Pk. Hqtrs.	Park Headquarters
Pres.	Preserve
Prov.	Provincial
Rec.	Recreation(al)
Res.	Reservation–Reserve
S.H.S.	State Historic Site
S.P.	State Park
Sta.	Station
Vis. Ctr.	Visitor Center

ALABAMA

ALABAMA	PAGE	GRID	LATITUDE LONGITUDE
National Park & Rec. Areas			
Horseshoe Bend N.M.P.-Main Road	128	B1	32.977130 -85.739600
Horseshoe Bend N.M.P.-Vis. Ctr.	128	B1	32.977130 -85.739600
Russell Cave Natl. Mon.-Main Road	120	A2	34.980220 -85.809650
Russell Cave Natl. Mon.-Vis. Ctr.	120	A2	34.980400 -85.809800
Tuskegee Airmen N.H.S.	128	B2	32.424942 -85.691052
Tuskegee Airmen N.H.S.-Pk. Hqtrs.	128	B2	32.428600 -85.708500
Tuskegee Institute N.H.S.	128	B2	32.428751 -85.704120
Tuskegee Institute N.H.S.-Pk. Hqtrs.	128	B2	32.428600 -85.708500
State Park & Rec. Areas			
Bladon Springs S.P.	127	E4	31.730920 -88.195580
Blue Springs S.P.	128	B4	31.661990 -85.508150
Bucks Pocket S.P.	120	A3	34.469560 -86.049080
Cathedral Caverns S.P.	120	A2	34.572299 -86.221499
Cheaha S.P.	120	A4	33.474490 -85.807260
Chewacla S.P.	128	B2	32.554520 -85.481920
Chickasaw S.P.	127	E2	32.361770 -87.779780
Desoto S.P.	120	A3	34.495460 -85.618860
Florala S.P.	136	B1	30.998590 -86.329980
Frank Jackson S.P.	128	A4	31.291400 -86.255900
Gulf S.P.	135	F2	30.270490 -87.582130
Joe Wheeler S.P.	119	E2	34.793020 -87.379950
Lake Guntersville S.P.	120	A3	34.367530 -86.222850
Lake Lurleen S.P.	127	E1	33.295880 -87.676870
Lakepoint Resort S.P.	128	C3	31.990320 -85.114970
Meaher S.P.	135	E1	30.669720 -87.936030
Monte Sano S.P.	119	F2	34.745220 -86.511650
Oak Mtn. S.P.	127	F1	33.324710 -86.758740
Paul M. Grist S.P.	127	F2	32.595380 -86.996080
Rickwood Caverns S.P.	119	F4	33.876870 -86.867230
Roland Cooper S.P.	127	F3	32.055350 -87.245330
Wind Creek S.P.	128	A1	32.856820 -85.946540

ALASKA

ALASKA	PAGE	GRID	LATITUDE LONGITUDE
National Park & Rec. Areas			
Admiralty Island Natl. Mon.	155	E4	57.618060 -134.161110
Aleutian WWII Natl. Hist. Area	154	A4	53.888889 -166.527222
Aniakchak Natl. Mon. & Pres.	154	B4	56.833333 -158.250556
Bering Land Bridge Natl. Pres.	154	B2	65.595320 -164.301800
Cape Krusenstern Natl. Mon.	154	B1	67.471630 -163.312300
Denali Natl. Park & Pres.-Denali Vis. Ctr.	154	C2	63.737000 -148.895000
Denali Natl. Park & Pres.-Eielson Vis. Ctr.	154	C2	63.440900 -150.239000
Gates of the Arctic Natl. Park & Pres.-Anaktuvuk Pass Ranger Sta.	154	C1	68.139900 -151.735400
Gates of the Arctic Natl. Park & Pres.-Arctic Interagency Vis. Ctr.	154	C1	67.253700 -150.187000
Gates of the Arctic Natl. Park & Pres.-Bettles Ranger Sta.	154	C1	66.912500 -151.667100
Gates of the Arctic Natl. Park & Pres.-Coldfoot Ranger Sta.	154	C1	67.253700 -150.187000
Glacier Bay Natl. Park & Pres.-Glacier Bay Lodge & Vis. Ctr.	155	D3	58.454900 -135.882600
Katmai Natl. Park & Pres.	154	C3	58.667030 -156.524600
Kenai Fjords Natl. Park-Vis. Ctr.	154	C3	60.105300 -149.435000
Klondike Gold Rush N.H.P.	155	D3	60.113550 -149.441342
Kobuk Valley Natl. Park	154	B1	67.073230 -159.839500
Lake Clark Natl. Park & Pres.	154	C3	60.471450 -154.576390
Misty Fiords Natl. Mon.	155	E4	55.472600 -130.429700
Noatak Natl. Pres.	154	C1	67.320740 -162.646370
White Mts. N.R.A.	154	C2	65.524300 -147.156400
Wrangell-Saint Elias Natl. Park & Pres.-Kennecott Vis. Ctr.	155	D3	61.485600 -142.881100
Wrangell-Saint Elias Natl. Park & Pres.-Wrangell-Saint Elias Vis. Ctr.	155	D3	61.964300 -145.317900
Yukon-Charley Rivers Natl. Pres.	155	D2	65.341680 -143.120650
State Park & Rec. Areas			
Afognak Island S.P.	154	C4	58.227100 -152.067300
Chilkat S.P.	155	D3	59.211111 -135.398056
Chugach S.P.	154	C3	61.037440 -149.780830
Denali S.P.	154	C3	62.734600 -150.199600
Point Bridget S.P.	155	E3	58.671225 -134.958801
Shuyak Island S.P.	154	C4	58.533100 -152.486100
Wood-Tikchik S.P.	154	B3	59.909600 -158.672000

ARIZONA

ARIZONA	PAGE	GRID	LATITUDE LONGITUDE
National Park & Rec. Areas			
Agua Fria Natl. Mon.	47	D4	34.276490 -112.114350
Canyon de Chelly Natl. Mon.-Vis. Ctr.	48	A2	36.153200 -109.539000
Casa Grande Ruins Natl. Mon.-Ent. Sta.	54	C2	32.994700 -111.537000
Chiricahua Natl. Mon.-Main Road	55	E3	32.009250 -109.382230
Chiricahua Natl. Mon.-Ent. Sta.	55	E3	32.007500 -109.388900
Coronado Natl. Mem.-Vis. Ctr.	55	E4	31.346300 -110.254000
Fort Bowie N.H.S.-Vis. Ctr.	55	E3	32.146600 -109.435000
Glen Canyon N.R.A.-Ent. Sta.	47	E1	36.943300 -111.493600
Grand Canyon Natl. Park-East Ent.	47	D2	36.038800 -111.828000
Grand Canyon Natl. Park-North Ent.	47	D2	36.334900 -112.116000
Grand Canyon Natl. Park-South Ent.	47	D2	36.000100 -112.121600
Grand Canyon-Parashant Natl. Mon.	46	C2	36.452170 -113.724367
Ironwood Forest Natl. Mon.	54	C3	32.478380 -111.530220
Lake Mead N.R.A.-Boulder City Ent.	46	C2	36.020800 -114.796000
Lake Mead N.R.A.-Henderson Ent.	46	C2	36.105400 -114.901020
Lake Mead N.R.A.-Las Vegas–Rt 147 Ent.	46	C2	36.161000 -114.905100
Lake Mead N.R.A.-South Ent.	46	C2	35.225600 -114.551000
Montezuma Castle Natl. Mon.-Vis. Ctr.	47	D4	34.611600 -111.839000
Navajo Natl. Mon.-Betatakin Ruin	47	E1	36.683500 -110.541470
Navajo Natl. Mon.-Inscription House Ruin-Closed To Public	47	E1	36.661250 -110.775940
Navajo Natl. Mon.-Keet Seel Ruin	47	E1	36.683500 -110.541470
Navajo Natl. Mon.-Vis. Ctr.	47	E1	36.678200 -110.541000
Organ Pipe Cactus Natl. Mon.-Vis. Ctr.	54	B3	31.954800 -112.801000
Petrified Forest Natl. Park-North Ent.	47	F3	35.069600 -109.778000
Petrified Forest Natl. Park-South Ent.	47	F3	34.799600 -109.885000
Pipe Spring Natl. Mon.-Vis. Ctr.	47	D1	36.862500 -112.737000
Saguaro Natl. Park-East	55	D3	32.178430 -110.737990
Saguaro Natl. Park-Vis. Ctr.	55	D3	32.180200 -110.736000
Saguaro Natl. Park-West	55	D3	32.251660 -111.191660
Sonoran Desert Natl. Mon.	54	C2	33.001730 -112.421220
Sunset Crater Volcano Natl. Mon.-Vis. Ctr.	47	E3	35.368800 -111.543000
Tonto Natl. Mon.-Vis. Ctr.	55	D1	33.645200 -111.113000
Tumacácori N.H.P.-Vis. Ctr.	55	D4	31.567800 -111.051000
Tuzigoot Natl. Mon.-Pk. Hqtrs.	47	D4	34.561000 -111.853000
Vermilion Cliffs Natl. Mon.	47	D1	36.806389 -111.741111
Walnut Canyon Natl. Mon.-Walnut Canyon Vis. Ctr.	47	E3	35.171700 -111.509000
Wupatki Natl. Mon.-Vis. Ctr.	47	E3	35.520300 -111.372000
State Park & Rec. Areas			
Alamo Lake S.P.	46	C4	34.234270 -113.553220
Boyce Thmpson Arbrtum S.P.	55	D2	33.311150 -111.055790
Buckskin Mtn. S.P.	46	B4	34.255000 -114.134070
Catalina S.P.	55	D3	32.416760 -110.937500
Cattail Cove S.P.	46	B4	34.355075 -114.165877
Dead Horse Ranch S.P.	47	D4	34.748490 -112.022930
Homolovi Ruins S.P.	47	E3	35.023940 -110.630120
Kartchner Caverns S.P.	55	D3	31.840770 -110.342710
Lake Havasu S.P.	46	B4	34.473970 -114.345850
Lost Dutchman S.P.	54	C1	33.464920 -111.481350
Lyman Lake S.P.	48	A4	34.362870 -109.375370
Oracle S.P.	55	D2	32.610239 -110.740619
Patagonia Lake S.P.	55	D4	31.488970 -110.853790
Picacho Peak S.P.	54	C2	32.646340 -111.398090
Red Rock S.P.	47	D4	34.818920 -111.836700
Roper Lake S.P.	55	E2	32.758710 -109.709520
Slide Rock S.P.	47	D3	34.944340 -111.752810
Tonto Nat. Bridge S.P.	47	E4	34.323400 -111.449460

ARKANSAS

ARKANSAS	PAGE	GRID	LATITUDE LONGITUDE
National Park & Rec. Areas			
Fort Smith N.H.S.-Main Road	116	B1	35.387480 -94.429660
Fort Smith N.H.S.-Vis. Ctr.	116	B1	35.385800 -94.429800
Hot Springs Natl. Park-Main Road	117	D2	34.511660 -93.053980
Hot Springs Natl. Park-Vis. Ctr.	117	D2	34.513800 -93.053400
Pea Ridge N.M.P.-Main Road	106	C3	36.442600 -94.025980
Pea Ridge N.M.P.-Vis. Ctr.	106	C3	36.443800 -94.025900
State Park & Rec. Areas			
Bull Shoals-White River S.P.	107	E3	36.365590 -92.557490
Conway Cemetery S.P.	124	C1	33.101909 -93.683161
Crater of Diamonds S.P.	116	C3	34.038610 -93.667630
Crowley's Ridge S.P.	108	A4	36.044840 -90.666770
Degray Lake Resort S.P.-North Ent.	117	D3	34.248870 -93.116880
Degray Lake Resort S.P.-South Ent.	117	D3	34.217390 -93.085820
Hampson Arch. Mus. S.P.	118	B1	35.568990 -90.041060
Historic Washington S.P.	116	C4	33.774005 -93.683235
Hobbs S.P.-Cons. Area	106	C3	36.244880 -93.972640
Jacksonport S.P.	107	F4	35.641440 -91.305350
Jenkins' Ferry S.P.	117	E3	34.212070 -92.547490
Lake Charles S.P.	107	F4	36.066870 -91.132700
Lake Chicot S.P.	126	A1	33.373070 -91.194940
Lake Dardanelle S.P.	117	D1	35.251690 -93.213380
Lake Fort Smith S.P.	106	C4	35.654040 -94.150140
Lake Frierson S.P.	108	A4	35.988570 -90.717540
Lake Ouachita S.P.	117	D2	34.610990 -93.165520
Lake Poinsett S.P.	118	A1	35.535510 -90.688700
Louisiana Purchase S.P.	118	A2	35.150340 -90.734990
Lower White River Mus. S.P.	117	F2	34.977035 -91.495131
Mammoth Spring S.P.	107	F3	36.496010 -91.535960
Marks' Mills S.P.	117	E4	33.781085 -92.256427
Moro Bay S.P.	125	E1	33.298890 -92.348940
Mount Magazine S.P.	116	C1	35.149900 -93.563600
Mount Nebo S.P.	117	D1	35.224870 -93.229930
Ozark Folk Center S.P.	107	E4	35.883480 -92.116340
Parkin Arch. S.P.	118	A1	35.268607 -90.554809
Petit Jean S.P.	117	D1	35.128320 -92.898530
Poison Spring S.P.	117	D4	33.638340 -93.005250
Powhatan Hist. S.P.	107	F4	36.083234 -91.117858
Prairie Grove Bfld. S.P.	106	C4	35.983120 -94.305590
Toltec Mounds Arch. S.P.	117	E2	34.647370 -92.058510
Village Creek S.P.	118	A1	35.199650 -90.724540
White Oak Lake S.P.	117	D4	33.687490 -93.117240
Withrow Springs S.P.	106	C4	36.203800 -93.578200
Woolly Hollow S.P.	117	E1	35.286402 -92.285646

CALIFORNIA

CALIFORNIA	PAGE	GRID	LATITUDE LONGITUDE
National Park & Rec. Areas			
Amboy Crater Natl. Nat. Landmark	53	E2	34.542196 -115.790920
Carrizo Plain Natl. Mon.	52	B1	35.191000 -119.792000
Channel Islands Natl. Park	52	B2	34.248500 -119.267000
Death Valley Natl. Park-Furnace Creek Vis. Ctr.	45	F3	36.461800 -116.867000
Devils Postpile Natl. Mon.	37	E4	37.630330 -119.084300
Giant Sequoia Natl. Mon.-North Unit	45	D2	36.705501 -118.824821
Giant Sequoia Natl. Mon.-South Unit	45	E3	36.062389 -118.317784
Golden Gate N.R.A.-Marin Headlands	36	B4	37.830900 -122.525000
Golden Gate N.R.A.-Mott Vis. Ctr.	36	B4	37.799800 -122.460000
Joshua Tree Natl. Park-Indian Cove	53	E3	34.120000 -116.156000
Joshua Tree Natl. Park-North Ent.	53	E3	34.078300 -116.037000
Joshua Tree Natl. Park-West Ent.	53	E3	34.093600 -116.266000
Kings Canyon Natl. Park-East Ent.	45	D2	36.715870 -118.940420
Kings Canyon Natl. Park-West Ent.	45	D2	36.723720 -118.956490
Lassen Volcanic Natl. Park-Ent.	29	D4	40.537900 -121.571000
Lava Beds Natl. Mon.-Vis. Ctr.	29	D2	41.713900 -121.509000
Manzanar N.H.S.	45	E3	36.732260 -118.148500
Pinnacles Natl. Mon.-East Ent.	44	B3	36.483200 -121.162000
Pinnacles Natl. Mon.-West Ent.	44	B3	36.473300 -121.224400
Point Reyes Natl. Seashore-Bear Valley Vis. Ctr.	36	A3	38.043100 -122.799000
Point Reyes Natl. Seashore-Kenneth C. Patrick Vis. Ctr.	36	A3	38.027800 -122.961000
Point Reyes Natl. Seashore-Vis. Ctr.	36	A3	37.996500 -123.021000
Redwood Natl. Park-Kuchel Vis. Ctr.	28	A3	41.286800 -124.090900
Redwood Natl. Park-Prairie Creek Vis. Ctr.	28	A3	41.365300 -124.022000
Santa Monica Mts. N.R.A.-Vis. Ctr.	52	B2	34.188600 -118.887000
Santa Rosa & San Jacinto Mts. Natl. Mon.	53	E3	33.755173 -116.729736
Sequoia Natl. Park-North Ent.	45	D3	36.647900 -118.826370
Sequoia Natl. Park-South Ent.	45	D3	36.487130 -118.836810
Shasta-Trinity N.R.A.	28	C4	40.633204 -122.601127
Trona Pinnacles Natl. Nature Landmark	45	F4	35.611944 -117.369444
Whiskeytown-N.R.A.	28	C4	40.751500 -122.320580
Yosemite Natl. Park-Arch Rock Ent.	37	D3	37.687500 -119.730000
Yosemite Natl. Park-Big Oak Flat Ent.	37	D3	37.800800 -119.874000
Yosemite Natl. Park-Hetch Hetchy Ent.	37	D3	37.893500 -119.842000
Yosemite Natl. Park-South Ent.	37	D3	37.507000 -119.632000
Yosemite Natl. Park-Tioga Pass Ent.	37	D3	37.910700 -119.258000
State Park & Rec. Areas			
Ahjumawi Lava Springs S.P.	29	D3	41.107140 -121.468600
Anza-Borrego Desert S.P.	53	E4	33.256550 -116.399340
Big Basin Redwoods S.P.	44	A2	37.168380 -122.221530
Bothe-Napa Valley S.P.	36	B3	38.553410 -122.525640
Butano S.P.	44	A2	37.200660 -122.344140
Carlsbad State Beach	53	D3	33.147530 -117.345280
Castle Crags S.P.	28	C3	41.149280 -122.317480
Caswell Mem. S.P.	36	C4	37.702660 -121.181770
China Camp S.P.	36	B3	38.003990 -122.466480
Clear Lake S.P.	36	B2	39.009780 -122.805400
Cuyamaca Rancho S.P.	53	D4	32.933790 -116.562560
Del Norte Coast Redwoods S.P.-North Ent.	28	A3	41.712860 -124.130310
Del Norte Coast Redwoods S.P.-South Ent.	28	A3	41.603280 -124.100130
Doheny State Beach	52	C3	33.463820 -117.688830
Donner Mem. S.P.	37	D2	39.323880 -120.228370
Ed Z'Berg-Sugar Pine Point S.P.	37	D2	39.056290 -120.119200
Emerald Bay S.P.	37	D2	38.956710 -120.108850
Fremont Peak S.P.	44	B3	36.760340 -121.502670
Garrapata S.P.	44	B3	36.475310 -121.936280
Gaviota S.P.	52	A2	34.475250 -120.228590
Grizzly Creek Redwoods S.P.	28	B4	40.486630 -123.903520
Grover Hot Springs S.P.	37	D3	38.695230 -119.836760
Henry Cowell Redwoods S.P.	44	A2	37.044020 -122.070990
Henry W. Coe S.P.	44	B2	37.085600 -121.467340
Humboldt Lagoons S.P.	28	A3	41.284330 -124.089720
Humboldt Redwoods S.P.	28	A4	40.284740 -124.056950
Jedediah Smith Redwoods S.P.	28	A2	41.798190 -124.084030
Julia Pfeiffer Burns S.P.	44	B3	36.160700 -121.668210
Limekiln S.P.	44	B3	36.013380 -121.526870
Little River State Beach	28	A3	41.013580 -124.109680
Los Osos Oaks State Rec.	52	A1	35.310200 -120.835300
Manchester S.P.	36	A2	38.980450 -123.703020
Marina State Beach	44	B3	36.683030 -121.809440
McGrath State Beach	52	B2	34.227270 -119.256460
Mendocino Headlands S.P.	36	A2	39.307570 -123.798910
Morro Bay S.P.	44	B4	35.354020 -120.843800
Morro Strand State Beach	44	B4	35.435390 -120.888060
Mount Diablo S.P.	36	B4	37.844210 -121.950200
Mount Tamalpais S.P.	36	B3	37.904290 -122.604040

	PAGE	GRID	LATITUDE LONGITUDE
Navarro River Redwoods S.P.	36	A2	39.175000 -123.676390
Pacheco S.P.	44	B2	37.055650 -121.016250
Palomar Mtn. S.P.	53	D3	33.325340 -116.893330
Patrick's Point S.P.	28	A3	41.135690 -124.150500
Pfeiffer Big Sur S.P.	44	B3	36.250930 -121.786550
Placerita Canyon S.P.	52	C2	34.377530 -118.470290
Plumas-Eureka S.P.	36	C1	39.758360 -120.695360
Point Dume State Beach	52	B2	34.003110 -118.807250
Point Sal State Beach	52	A1	34.897760 -120.642760
Prairie Creek Redwoods S.P.	28	A3	41.355490 -124.073670
Red Rock Canyon S.P.	52	C1	35.359734 -117.978351
Russian Gulch S.P.	36	A2	39.330990 -123.805050
Saddleback Butte S.P.	52	C2	34.689820 -117.824340
Samuel P. Taylor S.P.	36	B3	38.004660 -122.708400
San Gregorio State Beach	36	B4	37.321490 -122.401640
San Onofre State Beach	53	D3	33.383380 -117.580790
Sonoma Coast State Beach	36	A3	38.441060 -123.122970
Sunset State Beach	44	B2	36.897780 -121.835450
The Forest of Nisene Marks S.P.	44	B2	37.042024 -121.856231
Tolowa Dunes S.P.	28	A2	41.825800 -124.187500
Trinidad State Beach	28	A3	41.061090 -124.142290
Van Damme S.P.	36	A2	39.273990 -123.790490
Westport-Union Landing State Beach	36	A1	39.658350 -123.784930
Wilder Ranch S.P.	44	A2	36.962160 -122.080850
Zmudowski State Beach	44	B2	36.845580 -121.804300

COLORADO	PAGE	GRID	LATITUDE LONGITUDE
National Park & Rec. Areas			
Arapaho N.R.A.	41	D1	40.197870 -105.869440
Bent's Old Fort N.H.S.	41	F3	38.045980 -103.431440
Black Canyon-Gunnison Natl. Park-North Ent.	40	C3	38.586890 -107.695940
Black Canyon-Gunnison Natl. Park-South Ent.	40	C3	38.553980 -107.686390
Canyons of the Ancients Natl. Mon.	40	A4	37.587880 -108.916890
Colorado Natl. Mon.-Northwest Ent.	40	B2	39.117620 -108.730910
Colorado Natl. Mon.-Southeast Ent.	40	B2	39.032860 -108.631460
Colorado Natl. Mon.-South Ent.	40	B2	39.021100 -108.659540
Colorado Natl. Mon.-Southwest Ent.	40	B2	39.055070 -108.742500
Curecanti N.R.A.-East Ent.	40	C3	38.515010 -107.020560
Curecanti N.R.A.-North Ent.	40	C3	38.463380 -107.419580
Curecanti N.R.A.-South Ent.	40	C3	38.473160 -107.076450
Curecanti N.R.A.-West Ent.	40	C3	38.444680 -107.341980
Dinosaur Natl. Mon.-East Ent.	32	B4	40.443120 -108.517790
Dinosaur Natl. Mon.-South Ent.	32	B4	40.243920 -108.973750
Florissant Fossil Beds Natl. Mon.	41	E2	38.937440 -105.283400
Great Sand Dunes Natl. Park-Ent. Sta.	41	D4	37.725000 -105.519000
Hovenweep Natl. Mon.-Cutthroat	40	A4	37.413000 -108.720240
Hovenweep Natl. Mon.-Hackberry	40	A4	37.398890 -109.036680
Hovenweep Natl. Mon.-Holly	40	A4	37.398890 -109.036680
Hovenweep Natl. Mon.-Horseshoe	40	A4	37.464610 -108.974680
Mesa Verde Natl. Park-Ent. Sta.	40	B4	37.331100 -108.416000
Rocky Mtn. Natl. Park-Beaver Meadows Ent.	33	E4	40.367300 -105.578000
Rocky Mtn. Natl. Park-Fall River Ent.	33	E4	40.404000 -105.590000
Rocky Mtn. Natl. Park-Grand Lake Ent.	33	E4	40.267300 -105.833000
Rocky Mtn. Natl. Park-Wild Basin Ent.	33	E4	40.219000 -105.534000
Sand Creek Massacre N.H.S.	42	A3	38.541250 -102.505910
Yucca House Natl. Mon.	40	B4	37.251678 -108.684911
State Park & Rec. Areas			
Barr Lake S.P.	41	E1	39.938160 -104.733470
Bonny Lake S.P.	42	A1	39.601030 -102.245640
Boyd Lake S.P.	33	E4	40.428990 -105.045400
Castlewood Canyon S.P.	41	E2	39.325860 -104.737640
Crawford S.P.	40	C3	38.708000 -107.617550
Eleven Mile S.P.	41	D2	38.948570 -105.526450
Golden Gate Canyon S.P.	41	D1	39.875560 -105.453650
Harvey Gap S.P.	40	C1	39.606210 -107.659010
Highline Lake S.P.	40	B2	39.270910 -108.835930
Jackson Lake S.P.	33	F4	40.409110 -104.070130
James M. Robb-Colorado River S.P.-Corn Lake	40	B2	39.062709 -108.455110
James M. Robb-Colorado River S.P.-Island Acres	40	B2	39.165709 -108.300610
John Martin Reservoir S.P.	42	A3	38.065390 -102.927110
Lake Pueblo S.P.	41	E3	38.258130 -104.719160
Lathrop S.P.	41	E4	37.602830 -104.833740
Lone Mesa S.P.	40	B4	37.699890 -108.466750
Lory S.P.	33	E4	40.593143 -105.185413
Mancos S.P.	40	B4	37.399890 -108.266750
Mueller S.P.	41	E2	38.884940 -105.157710
Navajo S.P.	48	B1	37.067800 -107.407599
North Sterling S.P.	34	A4	40.787740 -103.264990
Paonia S.P.	40	C2	38.980440 -107.342900
Pearl Lake S.P.	33	D4	40.790160 -106.894610
Ridgway S.P.	40	B3	38.229710 -107.729410
Rifle Falls S.P.	40	B1	39.695290 -107.701090
Rifle Gap S.P.	40	B1	39.627460 -107.762520
Roxborough S.P.	41	E2	39.451300 -105.070200
San Luis S.P.	41	D4	37.663130 -105.734480
Spinney Mtn. S.P.	41	D2	39.014760 -105.625880
Stagecoach S.P.	33	D4	40.286100 -106.866920
Steamboat Lake S.P.	32	C4	40.805240 -106.943600
Sweitzer Lake S.P.	40	B2	38.712050 -108.042640
Sylvan Lake S.P.	40	C1	39.516710 -106.753170
Trinidad Lake S.P.	49	E1	37.149700 -104.563650
Vega S.P.	40	B2	39.226890 -107.810250
Yampa River S.P.	32	C4	40.533190 -107.444483

CONNECTICUT	PAGE	GRID	LATITUDE LONGITUDE
National Park & Rec. Areas			
Weir Farm N.H.S.	148	C2	41.255890 -73.455980
State Park & Rec. Areas			
Bigelow Hollow S.P.	150	B2	41.991600 -72.134840
Bluff Point S.P.	149	F2	41.335800 -72.033520
Chatfield Hollow S.P.	150	A4	41.361400 -72.580190
Day Pond S.P.	150	A4	41.553432 -72.418419
Devil's Hopyard S.P.	150	A4	41.486529 -72.342462
Gay City S.P.	150	A3	41.716100 -72.434470
Gillette Castle S.P.	150	A4	41.430670 -72.427990
Hammonasset Beach S.P.	149	E2	41.273640 -72.562350
Haystack Mtn. S.P.	94	C2	42.002010 -73.209960
Horseguard S.P.	94	C3	41.807100 -72.848300
Hurd S.P.	150	A4	41.530650 -72.537650
John A. Minetto S.P.	94	C2	41.884020 -73.170280
Lake Waramaug S.P.	148	C1	41.706290 -73.382460
Mashamoquet Brook S.P.	150	B3	41.860320 -71.987230
Mount Riga S.P.	94	B2	42.028830 -73.428620
Putnam Mem. S.P.	148	C2	41.344200 -73.381500
Rocky Neck S.P.	149	F2	41.316920 -72.242690
Selden Neck S.P.	150	A4	41.287500 -72.331100
Silver Sands S.P.	149	D2	41.198410 -73.076180
Southford Falls S.P.	149	D1	41.455700 -73.166150
Squantz Pond S.P.	148	C1	41.508580 -73.471040
Stoddard Hill S.P.	150	B4	41.461900 -72.065500
Wadsworth Falls S.P.	150	A4	41.536080 -72.687380
West Rock Ridge S.P.	149	D2	41.347810 -72.968260

DELAWARE	PAGE	GRID	LATITUDE LONGITUDE
State Park & Rec. Areas			
Cape Henlopen S.P.	145	F3	38.782360 -75.103010
Delaware Seashore S.P.	145	F4	38.614420 -75.071540
Fenwick Island S.P.	145	F4	38.469740 -75.051550
Fort Delaware S.P.	145	E1	39.578700 -75.588320
Fort Dupont S.P.	145	E1	39.568930 -75.588590
Holts Landing S.P.	145	F4	38.584080 -75.128380
Killens Pond S.P.	145	E3	38.990320 -75.544920
Lums Pond S.P.	145	E1	39.570520 -75.733490
Trap Pond S.P.	145	E4	38.525860 -75.483170
White Clay Creek S.P.	146	B4	39.709810 -75.776560

FLORIDA	PAGE	GRID	LATITUDE LONGITUDE
National Park & Rec. Areas			
Biscayne Natl. Park-Dante Fascell Vis. Ctr.	143	F3	25.464400 -80.334900
Canaveral Natl. Seashore	141	E1	28.611410 -80.808390
Castillo de San Marcos Natl. Mon.	139	D3	29.897747 -81.311461
Dry Tortugas Natl. Park-Vis. Ctr.	142	B4	24.628500 -82.873400
Everglades Natl. Park-Ent.	143	E3	25.394400 -80.589300
Fort Matanzas Natl. Mon.	139	E3	29.715660 -81.234190
Gulf Islands Natl. Seashore	135	F2	30.362880 -87.139630
State Park & Rec. Areas			
Alafia River S.P.	140	C3	27.789920 -82.120830
Amelia Island S.P.	139	D2	30.543900 -81.449700
Anastasia S.P.	139	E3	29.874740 -81.285030
Anclote Key Pres. S.P.	140	B2	28.193070 -82.850660
Avalon S.P.	141	E3	27.542840 -80.318060
Bahia Honda S.P.	143	D4	24.659540 -81.277810
Bald Point S.P.	138	A3	29.902700 -84.408600
Big Lagoon S.P.	135	F2	30.322290 -87.401170
Big Shoals S.P.	138	C2	30.339115 -82.683182
Big Talbot Island S.P.	139	D2	30.460500 -81.421950
Blue Spring S.P.	141	D1	28.952270 -81.331300
Bulow Creek S.P.	139	E4	29.388000 -81.132399
Bulow Plantation Ruins Hist. S.P.	139	E4	29.433590 -81.144590
Caladesi Island S.P.	140	B2	28.059890 -82.813780
Cedar Key Mus. S.P.	138	B4	29.151172 -83.048299
Charlotte Harbor Pres. S.P.	140	C4	26.850691 -82.022026
Collier-Seminole S.P.	143	D2	25.991630 -81.591700
Crystal River Pres. S.P. & Arch. S.P.	140	B1	28.909530 -82.628680
Curry Hammock S.P.	143	E4	24.742640 -80.984793
Dade Btfd. Hist. S.P.	140	C1	28.654430 -82.124970
Deleon Springs S.P.	139	D4	29.131920 -81.360400
Delnor-Wiggins Pass S.P.	142	C1	26.272500 -81.826900
Dudley Farm Hist. S.P.	138	C3	29.649617 -82.630738
Eden Gardens S.P.	136	B2	30.361530 -86.125010
Egmont Key S.P.	140	B3	27.723490 -82.679390
Fakahatchee Strand Pres. S.P.	143	D2	25.961900 -81.364200
Faver-Dykes S.P.	139	E3	29.668050 -81.268030
Florida Caverns S.P.	137	D1	30.809160 -85.212270
Fort Clinch S.P.	139	D1	30.668010 -81.434300
Fort Cooper S.P.	140	C1	28.801300 -82.309200
Fort Pierce Inlet S.P.-East Ent.	141	E3	27.485160 -80.299430
Fort Pierce Inlet S.P.-West Ent.	141	E3	27.475930 -80.316980
Gasparilla Island S.P.	140	C4	26.718200 -82.261400
Grayton Beach S.P.	136	B2	30.328930 -86.155790
Henderson Beach S.P.	136	B2	30.387000 -86.447499
Highlands Hammock S.P.	141	D3	27.476554 -81.557148
Hontoon Island S.P.	141	D1	28.976680 -81.357690
Hugh Taylor Birch S.P.	143	F1	26.138220 -80.104450
Indian Key Hist. S.P.	143	E4	24.888056 -80.678056
John Gorrie Mus. S.P.	137	D3	29.725768 -84.983244
John Pennekamp Coral Reef S.P.	143	E3	25.127620 -80.409650
Jonathan Dickinson S.P.	141	F4	27.002920 -80.099980
Kissimmee Prairie Pres. S.P.	141	D3	27.538826 -81.022945
Lafayette Blue Springs S.P.	138	B2	30.115136 -83.229417
Lake Griffin S.P.	140	C1	28.857450 -81.902240
Lake Kissimmee S.P.	141	D2	27.971930 -81.380220
Lake Louisa S.P.	140	C1	28.460070 -81.751620
Lake Manatee S.P.	140	C3	27.475140 -82.336800
Little Talbot Island S.P.	139	D2	30.460500 -81.421950
Long Key S.P.	143	E4	24.821580 -80.819510
Lovers Key S.P.	142	C1	26.391000 -81.877800
Manatee Springs S.P.	138	B4	29.496230 -82.958630
Myakka River S.P.	140	C4	27.242670 -82.332240
Natural Bridge Btfd. Hist. S.P.	138	A2	30.284730 -84.152260
Navarre Beach S.P.	135	F2	30.401370 -86.864790
O'Leno S.P.	138	C3	29.809100 -82.550700
Olustee Btfd. Hist. S.P.	138	C2	30.214650 -82.428960
Oscar Scherer S.P.	140	B4	27.168840 -82.477360
Paynes Prairie Pres. S.P.	138	C3	29.520720 -82.300400
Perdido Key S.P.	135	F2	30.291480 -87.465360
Ponce De Leon Springs S.P.	136	C1	30.713260 -85.922490
Rainbow Springs S.P.	138	C4	29.103818 -82.438782
Ravine Gardens S.P.	139	D3	29.637490 -81.646830
River Rise Pres. S.P.	138	C3	29.859961 -82.605395
Saint Sebastian River Pres. S.P.	141	E3	27.815241 -80.513820
San Marcos de Apalache Hist. S.P.	138	A2	30.152890 -84.210030
Savannas Pres. S.P.	141	E3	27.245960 -80.250270
Sebastian Inlet S.P.	141	E2	27.870200 -80.453599
Silver River S.P.	139	D4	29.202550 -82.053610
Suwannee River S.P.	138	B2	30.389610 -83.157850
Three Rivers S.P.	137	D1	30.736800 -84.936500
Tomoka S.P.	139	E4	29.342210 -81.086200
Torreya S.P.	137	D2	30.553530 -84.946740
Troy Spring S.P.	138	B3	29.918000 -82.893300
Waccasassa Bay Pres. S.P.	138	B4	29.188100 -82.925500
Washington Oaks Gardens S.P.	139	E3	29.634670 -81.205500
Wekiwa Springs S.P.	141	D1	28.710490 -81.462810
Windley Key Fossil Reef Geological S.P.	143	E4	24.914100 -80.642800
Yulee Sugar Mill Ruins Hist. S.P.	140	B1	28.784730 -82.607370

GEORGIA	PAGE	GRID	LATITUDE LONGITUDE
National Park & Rec. Areas			
Chattahoochee River N.R.A.	120	C3	34.002910 -84.349180
Chickamauga & Chattanooga N.M.P.	120	B2	34.941430 -85.258790
Cumberland Island Natl. Seashore	139	D1	30.720300 -81.548760
Ed Jenkins N.R.A.	120	C2	34.682900 -84.198200
Fort Frederica Natl. Mon.	130	B4	31.219790 -81.386570
Fort Pulaski Natl. Mon.	130	C3	32.016520 -80.891680
Jimmy Carter N.H.S.	128	C3	32.034090 -84.401600
Kennesaw Mtn. Natl. Battlefied Park-Vis. Ctr.	120	C3	33.983000 -84.577900
Ocmulgee Natl. Mon.	129	D2	32.848560 -83.602140
State Park & Rec. Areas			
Amicalola Falls S.P.	120	C2	34.558940 -84.248890
Black Rock Mtn. S.P.	121	D2	34.918150 -83.400310
Bobby Brown S.P.	121	E3	33.979030 -82.588960
Cloudland Canyon S.P.	120	B2	34.830430 -85.482040
Crooked River S.P.	139	D1	30.844840 -81.559350
Elijah Clark S.P.	121	E4	33.854210 -82.391913
Florence Marina S.P.	128	C3	32.090988 -85.043263
Fort Mtn. S.P.	120	C2	34.763090 -84.689330
Fort Yargo S.P.	121	D4	33.984940 -83.733580
Franklin D. Roosevelt S.P.	128	C2	32.848670 -84.793230
General Coffee S.P.	129	E4	31.511490 -82.745360
George L. Smith S.P.	130	A2	32.570310 -82.103760
George T. Bagby S.P.	128	C4	31.739940 -85.074820
Georgia Veterans S.P.	129	D3	31.957951 -83.903787
Gordonia-Alatamaha S.P.	130	A3	32.081900 -82.123550
Hamburg S.P.	129	E1	33.208800 -82.774870
Hard Labor Creek S.P.	121	D4	33.677820 -83.593840
Hart S.P.	121	E3	34.376040 -82.910260
High Falls S.P.	129	D1	33.176590 -84.020280
Indian Springs S.P.	129	D1	33.247480 -83.921190
James H. "Sloppy" Floyd S.P.	120	B3	34.440260 -85.347580
John Tanner S.P.	120	B4	33.602750 -85.167070
Laura S. Walker S.P.	138	C1	31.143130 -82.212920
Little Ocmulgee S.P.	129	E3	32.100590 -82.886360
Magnolia Springs S.P.	130	A1	32.875460 -81.962560
Mistletoe S.P.	121	E4	33.638770 -82.390540
Moccasin Creek S.P.	121	D2	34.845160 -83.589140
Panola Mtn. S.P.	120	C4	33.622042 -84.173078
Providence Canyon S.P.	128	C3	32.068270 -84.929150
Red Top Mtn. S.P.	120	C3	34.145950 -84.720190
Reed Bingham S.P.	137	F1	31.161310 -83.538880
Richard B. Russell S.P.	121	E3	34.166778 -82.745691
Seminole S.P.	137	D1	30.811420 -84.873570
Skidaway Island S.P.	130	C3	31.947720 -81.052550

Sprewell Bluff S.P.	128	C2	32.857269 -84.482657
Stephen C. Foster S.P.	138	C1	30.827020 -82.361310
Tallulah Gorge S.P.	121	D2	34.736350 -83.391950
Tugaloo S.P.	121	E3	34.501940 -83.082320
Unicoi S.P.	121	D2	34.724620 -83.728170
Victoria Bryant S.P.	121	E3	34.299380 -83.158770
Vogel S.P.	121	D2	34.766190 -83.922000
Watson Mill Bridge S.P.	121	E3	34.041140 -83.126990

HAWAII	PAGE	GRID	LATITUDE LONGITUDE
National Park & Rec. Areas			
Haleakala Natl. Park-Main Road	153	D1	20.769130 -156.242850
Haleakala Natl. Park-Kipahulu Ent.	153	D1	20.662000 -156.045600
Haleakala Natl. Park-North Ent.	153	D1	20.769000 -156.243000
Hawaii Volcanoes Natl. Park-Ent.	153	F4	19.428700 -155.254500
Kalaupapa N.H.P.	152	C3	21.174110 -157.002830
State Park & Rec. Areas			
Ahupuaa O Kahana S.P.	152	A2	21.555210 -157.873260
Haena S.P.	152	B1	22.220930 -159.579600
Kaena Point S.P.	152	A2	21.551270 -158.244180
Kaumahina State Wayside Park	153	D1	20.871610 -156.170310
Kokee S.P.	152	B1	22.112580 -159.671050
Makena S.P.	153	D1	20.634030 -156.444180
Manuka State Wayside	153	E4	19.107990 -155.824610
Palaau S.P.	152	C3	21.174110 -157.002830
Polihale S.P.	152	B1	22.084480 -159.756700
Puaa Kaa State Wayside	153	D1	20.817560 -156.125800
Waianapanapa S.P.	153	E1	20.786230 -156.003010
Wailua River S.P.	152	B1	22.044180 -159.337250
Wailua Valley State Wayside	153	D1	20.840110 -156.139980
Wailuku River S.P.	153	F3	19.713340 -155.130490
Waimea Canyon S.P.	152	B1	22.031990 -159.671100

IDAHO	PAGE	GRID	LATITUDE LONGITUDE
National Park & Rec. Areas			
City of Rocks Natl. Res.	31	D2	42.078950 -113.677650
Craters of the Moon Natl. Mon.	23	D4	43.462030 -113.559930
Hagerman Fossil Beds Natl. Mon.	30	C1	42.760980 -114.928220
Minidoka Internment Natl. Mon.	31	D1	42.636944 -114.232222
Nez Perce N.H.P.-Clearwater Bfld.	22	B1	46.072600 -115.975400
Nez Perce N.H.P.-East Kamiah Site	22	B1	46.216600 -115.992400
Nez Perce N.H.P.-Vis. Ctr.	22	B1	46.446500 -116.817000
Nez Perce N.H.P.-White Bird Bfld.	22	B1	45.794400 -116.282000
Sawtooth N.R.A.	22	C3	44.211000 -114.946000
State Park & Rec. Areas			
Bear Lake S.P.	31	F2	42.026180 -111.257690
Bruneau Dunes S.P.	30	B1	42.910940 -115.713890
Castle Rocks S.P.	31	D2	42.135400 -113.670000
Dworshak S.P.	14	B4	46.577610 -116.327310
Eagle Island S.P.	22	B4	43.684510 -116.400300
Farragut S.P.	14	B2	47.952790 -116.602170
Harriman S.P.	23	F3	44.321000 -111.471200
Hells Gate S.P.	14	B4	46.380500 -117.044780
Henrys Lake S.P.	23	F3	44.620000 -111.373060
Heyburn S.P.	14	B3	47.353840 -116.748770
Lake Cascade S.P.	22	B3	44.520686 -116.046685
Lake Walcott S.P.	31	D1	42.674850 -113.482570
Land of the Yankee Fork S.P.	22	C3	44.475190 -114.208860
Lucky Peak S.P.	22	B4	43.530880 -116.055160
Massacre Rocks S.P.	31	D1	42.672200 -112.990800
McCroskey S.P.	14	B4	47.721080 -116.826310
Old Mission S.P.	14	B3	47.549420 -116.356940
Ponderosa S.P.	22	B2	44.926810 -116.083860
Priest Lake S.P.	14	B1	48.622082 -116.827798
Round Lake S.P.	14	B2	48.166110 -116.634230
Thousand Springs S.P.-Box Canyon	30	C1	42.709800 -114.791900
Thousand Springs S.P.-Malad Gorge	30	C1	42.864400 -114.854600
Thousand Springs S.P.-Niagara Springs	30	C1	42.662800 -114.672400
Three Island Crossing S.P.	30	C1	42.945280 -115.314850
Winchester Lake S.P.	22	B1	46.232280 -116.635570

ILLINOIS	PAGE	GRID	LATITUDE LONGITUDE
National Park & Rec. Areas			
Lincoln Home N.H.S.	98	B1	39.798120 -89.645150
Ronald Reagan Boyhood Home N.H.S.	88	B1	41.836700 -89.481100
State Park & Rec. Areas			
Apple River Canyon S.P.	74	A4	42.443990 -90.053280
Argyle Lake S.P.	87	F4	40.450680 -90.805080
Banner Marsh State Fish & Wildlife Area	88	B4	40.539600 -89.864450
Beall Woods S.P.	99	D4	38.351540 -87.836380
Beaver Dam S.P.	98	B2	39.214390 -89.959390
Big Bend State Fish & Wildlife Area	88	A2	41.634900 -90.044600
Buffalo Rock S.P.	88	C2	41.329720 -88.913090
Carlyle Lake State Fish & Wildlife Area	98	C3	38.768500 -89.193900
Castle Rock S.P.	88	B1	41.978230 -89.357040
Cave-In-Rock S.P.	109	D1	37.468010 -88.159950
Chain O'Lakes S.P.	74	C4	42.458390 -88.211950
Channahon S.P.	88	C2	41.415826 -88.223133
Coffeen Lake State Fish & Wildlife Area	98	B2	39.057000 -89.412400
Crawford County State Fish & Wildlife Area	99	D2	39.099800 -87.713100
Delabar S.P.	87	F3	40.957830 -90.939460
Des Plaines State Fish & Wildlife Area	88	C2	41.376600 -88.207400
Dixon Springs S.P.	108	C1	37.383600 -88.672830
Donnelley–Depue State Fish & Wildlife Area	88	B2	41.324000 -89.314100
Edward R. Madigan S.P.	88	B4	40.115280 -89.402240
Eldon Hazlet S.P.	98	B3	38.667610 -89.327200
Ferne Clyffe S.P.	108	C1	37.532550 -88.966430
Fort Massac S.P.	108	C2	37.161720 -88.693850
Fox Ridge S.P.	99	D2	39.406020 -88.134810
Gebhard Woods S.P.	88	C2	41.357350 -88.440210
Giant City S.P.	108	C1	37.612250 -89.181790
Green River State Wildlife Area	88	B2	41.631600 -89.516500
Hamilton County State Fish & Wildlife Area	98	C4	38.065100 -88.404700
Hazel & Bill Rutherford Wildlife Prairie S.P.	88	B3	40.734180 -89.747270
Henderson County State Fish & Wildlife Area	87	F3	40.857505 -90.975005
Horseshoe Lake State Fish & Wildlife Area	108	C2	37.130465 -89.338505
Illini S.P.	88	C2	41.318770 -88.711070
Illinois Beach S.P.	75	D4	42.429920 -87.820150
Iroquois County State Wildlife Area	89	D3	40.994300 -87.598700
Jim Edgar Panther Creek State Fish & Wildlife Area	98	B1	40.011700 -90.177005
Johnson-Sauk Trail S.P.	88	A2	41.327510 -89.904850
Jubilee College S.P.	88	B3	40.844580 -89.827260
Kankakee River S.P.	89	D2	41.203400 -88.001880
Kaskaskia River State Fish & Wildlife Area	98	B4	38.229700 -89.879500
Kickapoo S.P.	89	D4	40.138290 -87.737770
Lake Le Aqua-Na S.P.	74	A4	42.422800 -89.823900
Lake Murphysboro S.P.	108	C1	37.771800 -89.382670
Lasalle Lake State Fish & Wildlife Area	88	C2	41.238400 -88.655550
Lincoln Trail S.P.	99	D2	39.346480 -87.696460
Lowden S.P.	88	B1	42.034860 -89.324950
Mackinaw River State Fish & Wildlife Area	88	B4	40.545801 -89.294301
Marshall State Fish & Wildlife Area	88	B3	41.007900 -89.410100
Matthiessen S.P.	88	C2	41.285010 -89.010050
Mautino State Fish & Wildlife Area	88	B2	41.323100 -89.718900
Middle Fork State Fish & Wildlife Area	89	D4	40.258300 -87.795900
Mississippi Palisades S.P.	88	A1	42.135820 -90.163300
Mississippi River State Fish & Wildlife Area	98	A2	38.991900 -90.542100
Morrison-Rockwood S.P.	88	A1	41.856350 -89.950120
Nauvoo S.P.	87	F4	40.543590 -91.386650
Newton Lake State Fish & Wildlife Area	99	D2	38.922400 -88.306700
Pere Marquette S.P.	98	A2	38.968110 -90.497430
Prophetstown S.P.	88	B2	41.672090 -89.920310
Pyramid S.P.	98	B4	38.004110 -89.425680
Ray Norbut State Fish & Wildlife Area	98	A1	39.685000 -90.648500
Red Hills S.P.	99	D3	38.728850 -87.838660
Rend Lake State Fish & Wildlife Area	98	C4	38.043800 -88.988900
Rice Lake State Fish & Wildlife Area	88	A4	40.476785 -89.949205
Saline County State Fish & Wildlife Area	109	D1	37.691300 -88.379100
Sam Dale Lake State Fish & Wildlife Area	98	C3	38.536005 -88.565605
Sam Parr State Fish & Wildlife Area	99	D2	39.011022 -88.126955
Sanganois State Fish & Wildlife Area	88	A4	40.091605 -90.283205
Sangchris Lake S.P.	98	B1	39.656830 -89.487940
Shabbona Lake S.P.	88	C1	41.732250 -88.864930
Shelbyville State Fish & Wildlife Area	98	C2	39.566300 -88.566200
Siloam Springs S.P.	97	F1	39.899340 -90.955050
Silver Springs S.P.	88	C2	41.627500 -88.518550
Snakeden Hollow State Fish & Wildlife Area	88	A3	41.030200 -90.080100
South Shore S.P.	98	B3	38.610250 -89.314570
Starved Rock S.P.	88	C2	41.321750 -89.010850
Stephen A. Forbes S.P.	98	C3	38.718140 -88.743250
Ten Mile Creek State Fish & Wildlife Area	98	C4	38.081200 -88.594200
Turkey Bluffs State Fish & Wildlife Area	98	B4	37.877200 -89.771100
Walnut Point S.P.	99	D1	39.705150 -88.030390
Wayne Fitzgerrell S.P.	98	C4	38.089250 -88.937010
Weinberg-King S.P.	87	F4	40.226830 -90.899700
Weldon Springs S.P.	88	C4	40.125080 -88.921400
White Pines Forest S.P.	88	B1	41.988730 -89.461590
Wolf Creek S.P.	98	C2	39.488310 -88.680370
Woodford State Fish & Wildlife Area	88	B3	40.878900 -89.444800

INDIANA	PAGE	GRID	LATITUDE LONGITUDE
National Park & Rec. Areas			
George Rodgers Clark N.H.P.	99	D3	38.677880 -87.535350
Indiana Dunes Natl. Lakeshore	89	D1	41.653160 -87.062630
Lincoln Boyhood Natl. Mem.	99	E4	38.116800 -86.997860
State Park & Rec. Areas			
Bass Lake State Beach	89	E2	41.220100 -86.580200
Brown County S.P.	99	F2	39.197170 -86.215830
Chain O' Lakes S.P.	90	A2	41.336000 -85.422950
Charlestown S.P.	100	A3	38.448300 -85.644700
Clifty Falls S.P.	100	A3	38.761220 -85.420720
Fort Harrison S.P.	99	F1	39.871921 -86.018859
Harmonie S.P.	99	D4	38.089210 -87.934080
Indiana Dunes S.P.	89	E2	41.651470 -87.062620
Lincoln S.P.	99	E4	38.118370 -86.980080
McCormick's Creek S.P.	99	E2	39.283340 -86.724680
O'Bannon Woods S.P.	99	F4	38.200600 -86.254678
Ouabache S.P.	90	A3	40.728090 -85.111060
Pokagon S.P.	90	A1	41.707960 -85.029320
Potato Creek S.P.	89	E2	41.534950 -86.360290
Prophetstown S.P.	89	E4	40.500211 -86.829548
Shades S.P.	99	E1	39.941630 -87.057670
Shakamak S.P.	99	E2	39.181800 -87.232200
Spring Mill S.P.	99	F3	38.723330 -86.418460
Summit Lake S.P.	100	A1	40.018680 -85.302720
Tippecanoe River S.P.	89	E3	41.117330 -86.602750
Turkey Run S.P.	99	E1	39.882010 -87.200550
Versailles S.P.	100	A2	39.063900 -85.205330
Whitewater Mem. S.P.	100	B1	39.611300 -84.942300

IOWA	PAGE	GRID	LATITUDE LONGITUDE
National Park & Rec. Areas			
Effigy Mounds Natl. Mon.	73	F3	43.089310 -91.192350
Herbert Hoover N.H.S.	87	F1	41.671390 -91.346640
State Park & Rec. Areas			
Ambrose A. Call S.P.	72	B3	43.049650 -94.243430
Backbone S.P.	73	E4	42.600730 -91.532700
Beed's Lake S.P.	73	D4	42.767209 -93.241705
Bellevue S.P.	88	A1	42.247870 -90.416920
Black Hawk S.P.	72	B4	42.302700 -95.048680
Bobwhite S.P.	86	C3	40.710200 -93.393850
Cold Springs S.P.	86	B2	41.289540 -95.083810
Crystal Lake S.P.	72	C3	43.224895 -93.792925
Echo Valley S.P.	73	E3	42.944040 -91.776880
Elk Rock S.P.	87	D2	41.400470 -93.063050
Fort Defiance S.P.	72	B2	43.393260 -94.851290
George Wyth Mem. S.P.	73	E4	42.536980 -92.394210
Green Valley S.P.	86	B3	41.114490 -94.377270
Heery Woods S.P.	73	D4	42.766450 -92.675250
Honey Creek S.P.	87	D3	40.863940 -92.939050
Lake Ahquabi S.P.	86	C2	41.286710 -93.572690
Lake Anita S.P.	86	B2	41.434150 -94.762470
Lake Icaria S.P.	86	B3	41.053380 -94.756990
Lake Keomah S.P.	87	D2	41.286570 -92.541660
Lake Macbride S.P.	87	F1	41.803090 -91.570950
Lake Wapello S.P.	87	D3	40.824890 -92.570530
Ledges S.P.	86	C1	41.998970 -93.896110
Maquoketa Caves S.P.	87	F1	42.119890 -90.770950
McIntosh Woods S.P.	72	C3	43.132580 -93.457580
Mini-Wakan S.P.	72	B2	43.498460 -95.102320
Nine Eagles S.P.	86	C3	40.591250 -93.765130
Oakland Mills S.P.	87	E3	40.935400 -91.619370
Palisades-Kepler S.P.	87	F1	41.916880 -91.497050
Pammel S.P.	86	C2	41.295590 -94.073150
Pikes Point S.P.	72	A2	43.415320 -95.162860
Pilot Knob S.P.	72	C3	43.255470 -93.574840
Prairie Rose S.P.	86	A2	41.601590 -95.210660
Preparation Canyon S.P.	86	A1	41.901570 -95.911670
Rice Lake S.P.	72	C2	43.401350 -93.502490
Rock Creek S.P.	87	D1	41.760580 -92.835410
Spring Lake S.P.	86	B1	42.070600 -94.291500
Stone S.P.	35	F1	42.555460 -96.476050
Trappers Bay S.P.	72	A2	43.453630 -95.335510
Twin Lakes S.P.	72	B4	42.480180 -94.629860
Viking Lake S.P.	86	B3	40.973170 -95.053710
Wanata S.P.	72	A3	42.911340 -95.338080
Waubonsie S.P.	86	A3	40.677770 -95.683680
Wildcat Den S.P.	87	F2	41.467700 -90.869330

KANSAS	PAGE	GRID	LATITUDE LONGITUDE
National Park & Rec. Areas			
Fort Larned N.H.S.	43	D3	38.188740 -99.220620
Fort Scott N.H.S.	106	B1	37.843350 -94.704840
Monument Rocks Natl. Landmark	42	B2	38.790569 -100.762366
Nicodemus N.H.S.	42	C2	39.390833 -99.617500
State Park & Rec. Areas			
Atchison State Fishing Lake	96	B1	39.639010 -95.171830
Bourbon State Fishing Lake	106	B1	37.793450 -95.069690
Brown State Fishing Lake	96	A1	39.847020 -95.373860
Cedar Bluff S.P.	42	C2	38.798230 -99.715060
Chase State Fishing Lake	43	F3	38.368480 -96.588000
Cheney S.P.	43	E4	37.732700 -97.844350
Clark State Fishing Lake	42	C4	37.391670 -99.784720
Clinton S.P.	96	A3	38.941970 -95.353960
Cowley State Fishing Lake	51	F1	37.104040 -96.795000
Crawford S.P.	106	B1	37.634320 -94.809820
Cross Timbers S.P.	106	A1	37.774514 -95.943431
Douglas State Fishing Lake	96	B3	38.796030 -95.165150
Eisenhower S.P.	96	A3	38.535720 -95.744270
El Dorado S.P.	43	F4	37.861420 -96.749460
Elk City S.P.	106	A2	37.251130 -95.774090
Fallriver S.P.	43	F4	37.653550 -96.043600
Glen Elder S.P.	43	D1	39.512160 -98.339140
Hain State Fishing Lake	42	C4	37.854250 -99.858020
Hamilton State Fishing Lake	42	B3	38.039090 -101.816940
Hillsdale S.P.	96	B3	38.660700 -94.894000
Kanopolis S.P.	43	E3	38.600340 -97.979500
Kingman State Fishing Lake	43	E4	37.651390 -98.306940
Kiowa State Fishing Lake	43	D4	37.854720 -99.299000
Leavenworth State Fishing Lake	96	B2	39.126970 -95.141700
Logan State Fishing Lake	42	B2	38.940280 -101.236940
Lovewell S.P.	43	E1	39.903310 -98.043090
Lyon State Fishing Lake	43	F3	38.546520 -96.058050
McPherson State Fishing Lake	43	E3	38.478667 -97.468267

	PAGE	GRID	LATITUDE LONGITUDE
Meade S.P.	42	C4	37.172220 -100.450000
Miami State Fishing Lake	96	B3	38.422220 -94.785280
Milford S.P.	43	F2	39.104290 -96.895520
Mushroom Rock S.P.	43	E2	38.722222 -98.032222
Nebo State Fishing Lake	96	A2	39.447220 -95.595830
Neosho State Fishing Lake	106	B1	37.430570 -95.202550
Ottawa State Fishing Lake	43	E2	39.103040 -97.573060
Perry S.P.	96	A2	39.140210 -95.492480
Pomona S.P.	96	A3	38.652400 -95.600800
Pottawatomie State Fishing Lake No. 1	43	F1	39.470370 -96.407510
Pottawatomie State Fishing Lake No. 2	43	F2	39.228100 -96.533660
Prairie Dog S.P.	42	C1	39.811810 -99.963920
Prairie Spirit Trail S.P.	96	A4	38.280278 -95.242222
Rooks State Fishing Lake	43	D2	39.398290 -99.315020
Saline State Fishing Lake	43	E2	38.903159 -97.657510
Sand Hills S.P.	43	E3	38.116667 -97.833333
Scott S.P.	42	B2	38.684867 -100.922500
Shawnee State Fishing Lake	96	A2	39.206940 -95.804170
Tuttle Creek S.P.	43	F2	39.255560 -96.583330
Washington State Fishing Lake	43	E1	39.929780 -97.118830
Webster S.P.	43	D2	39.407840 -99.454550
Wilson State Fishing Lake	106	A1	38.910450 -98.497950
Wilson S.P.	43	D2	38.915000 -98.500000

KENTUCKY	PAGE	GRID	LATITUDE LONGITUDE
National Park & Rec. Areas			
Abraham Lincoln Birthplace N.H.S.	110	A1	37.532280 -85.733570
Land Between the Lakes N.R.A.	109	D2	36.776912 -88.059988
Mammoth Cave Natl. Park-Vis. Ctr.	109	F2	37.186800 -86.101300
State Park & Rec. Areas			
Barren River Lake State Resort Park	110	A2	36.853220 -86.053850
Ben Hawes S.P.	109	E1	37.797034 -87.188186
Blue Licks Bfld. State Resort Park	100	C3	38.434960 -83.991340
Buckhorn Lake State Resort Park	111	D1	37.312890 -83.423040
Carter Caves State Resort Park	101	D4	38.371470 -83.108510
Columbus-Belmont S.P.	108	C2	36.761990 -89.107000
Cumberland Falls State Resort Park	110	C2	36.834390 -84.350170
Fishtrap Lake S.P.	111	E1	37.432048 -82.417926
Fort Boonesborough S.P.	110	C1	37.899345 -84.270040
General Butler State Resort Park	100	A3	38.669950 -85.146050
Grayson Lake S.P.	101	D4	38.208630 -83.014910
Greenbo Lake State Resort Park	101	D3	38.479130 -82.867630
Green River Lake S.P.	110	A2	37.277440 -85.338730
Jenny Wiley State Resort Park-East Ent.	111	E1	37.730120 -82.740990
Jenny Wiley State Resort Park-South Ent.	111	E1	37.687680 -82.725690
Jenny Wiley State Resort Park-West Ent.	111	E1	37.727250 -82.745880
John James Audubon S.P.	99	D4	37.889250 -87.556510
Kentucky Dam Village State Resort Park	109	D2	36.996880 -88.285716
Kingdom Come S.P.	111	D2	36.981850 -82.982210
Lake Barkley State Resort Park	109	D2	36.809190 -87.928310
Lake Cumberland State Resort Park	110	B2	36.930320 -85.040960
Levi Jackson S.P.	110	C2	37.085250 -84.059250
Lincoln Homestead S.P.	110	B1	37.760080 -85.215930
My Old Kentucky Home S.P.	110	A1	37.808140 -85.458840
Natural Bridge State Resort Park	110	C1	37.777470 -83.676310
Nolin Lake S.P.	109	F1	37.297641 -86.212624
Old Fort Harrod S.P.	110	B1	37.762130 -84.845670
Pennyrile Forest State Resort Park	109	E2	37.057410 -87.649390
Pine Mtn. State Resort Park	110	C3	36.735270 -83.700790
Rough River State Resort Park	109	F1	37.615410 -86.504410
Taylorsville Lake S.P.	100	A4	37.993990 -85.227813
Yatesville Lake S.P.	101	D4	38.093300 -82.617800

LOUISIANA	PAGE	GRID	LATITUDE LONGITUDE
National Park & Rec. Areas			
Cane River Creole N.H.P.	125	D4	31.739690 -93.083080
Jean Lafitte N.H.P. & Pres.-Chalmette Vis. Ctr.	134	A3	29.942100 -89.994400
Jean Lafitte N.H.P. & Pres.-French Quarter Vis. Ctr.	134	A3	29.954600 -90.065100
Jean Lafitte N.H.P.-Wetlands Acadian Cultural Center	134	A3	29.795969 -90.824480
Poverty Point Natl. Mon. & S.H.S.	125	F2	32.633370 -91.403880
State Park & Rec. Areas			
Bayou Segnette S.P.	134	B3	29.902720 -90.153800
Chemin-A-Haut S.P.	125	F1	32.913460 -91.847550
Chicot S.P.	133	E1	30.829870 -92.276180
Cypremort Point S.P.	133	F3	29.731960 -91.840740
Fairview-Riverside S.P.	134	B2	30.408730 -90.140360
Fontainebleau S.P.	134	B2	30.345470 -90.022850
Grand Isle S.P.-Temp. Closed	134	B4	29.256640 -89.958480
Hodges Gardens S.P.	125	D4	31.369280 -93.424860
Jimmie Davis S.P.	125	E3	32.265000 -92.540300
Lake Bistineau S.P.	125	D2	32.440250 -93.395910
Lake Bruin S.P.	126	A3	31.955370 -91.198080
Lake Claiborne S.P.	125	D2	32.713000 -92.923360
Lake D'Arbonne S.P.	125	E2	32.784850 -92.490310
Lake Fausse Pointe S.P.	133	F3	30.067820 -91.615790
North Toledo Bend S.P.	124	C4	31.558910 -93.732060
Poverty Point Reservoir S.P.	125	F2	32.540446 -91.421356
Saint Bernard S.P.	134	C3	29.864460 -89.899190
South Toledo Bend S.P.	125	D4	31.213889 -93.575000
Tickfaw S.P.	134	B2	30.382180 -90.631150

MAINE	PAGE	GRID	LATITUDE LONGITUDE
National Park & Rec. Areas			
Acadia Natl. Park-Cadillac Mtn. Ent.	83	D2	44.384400 -68.229800
Acadia Natl. Park-Park Loop Road	83	D2	44.338700 -68.183200
Acadia Natl. Park-Sieur de Monts Ent.	83	D2	44.360000 -68.205200
Acadia Natl. Park-Stanley Brook Ent.	83	D2	44.296300 -68.242000
State Park & Rec. Areas			
Aroostook S.P.	85	E2	46.612720 -68.005840
Baxter S.P.	84	C3	45.950290 -69.049080
Camden Hills S.P.	82	C2	44.232050 -69.046530
Cobscook Bay S.P.	83	E1	44.855290 -67.171680
Damariscotta Lake S.P.	82	C2	44.200070 -69.452900
Ferry Beach S.P.	82	B4	43.482410 -70.391520
Lake Saint George S.P.	82	C2	44.398950 -69.345710
Lamoine S.P.	83	D2	44.456000 -68.298520
Mount Blue S.P.	82	B1	44.721780 -70.417080
Peaks-Kenny S.P.	84	C4	45.256680 -69.254600
Popham Beach S.P.	82	C3	43.738740 -69.795830
Rangeley Lake S.P.	82	B1	44.919550 -70.696950
Range Ponds S.P.	82	B3	44.033540 -70.345080
Roque Bluffs S.P.	83	E2	44.614680 -67.479300
Saint Croix Island International Hist. Site	83	E1	45.128333 -67.133333
Sebago Lake S.P.	82	B3	43.916590 -70.570190
Shackford Head S.P.	83	F1	44.906191 -66.989979
Swan Lake S.P.	82	C2	44.568860 -68.981070
Vaughan Woods S.P.	82	A4	43.212680 -70.809320
Warren Island S.P.	82	C2	44.260445 -68.952255
Wolfe's Neck Woods S.P.	82	B3	43.827190 -70.084460

MARYLAND	PAGE	GRID	LATITUDE LONGITUDE
National Park & Rec. Areas			
Assateague Island Natl. Seashore	114	C2	38.239580 -75.140410
Thomas Stone N.H.S.	144	B4	38.529700 -77.032370
State Park & Rec. Areas			
Assateague S.P.	114	C2	38.250170 -75.156270
Big Run S.P.	102	B1	39.545090 -79.137254
Catoctin Mtn. Park-Vis. Ctr.	144	A1	39.633100 -77.449700
Cunningham Falls S.P.	144	A1	39.625040 -77.458130
Deep Creek Lake S.P.	102	B1	39.512110 -79.300150
Elk Neck S.P.	145	D1	39.482890 -75.983630
Fort Frederick S.P.	103	D1	39.616050 -78.007060
Gambrill S.P.	144	A1	39.468330 -77.495730
Greenwell S.P.	103	E4	38.364930 -76.525260
Gunpowder Falls S.P.	144	C1	39.536710 -76.502800
Hart-Miller Island S.P.	144	C2	39.251219 -76.376903
Janes Island S.P.	103	F4	38.009810 -75.846380
Martinak S.P.	145	E3	38.862920 -75.837790
North Point S.P.	144	C2	39.221910 -76.431600
Patapsco Valley S.P.	144	B2	39.296580 -76.781500
Patuxent River S.P.	144	B2	39.280790 -77.129620
Pocomoke River S.P.	114	C2	38.135410 -75.494870
Point Lookout S.P.	103	F4	38.066190 -76.336550
Purse S.P.	103	E3	38.430540 -77.252030
Rocks S.P.	144	C1	39.630140 -76.418120
Rocky Gap S.P.	102	C1	39.698430 -78.651150
Rosaryville S.P.	144	C3	38.778450 -76.799260
Saint Clement's Island S.P.	103	E4	38.225200 -76.749690
Saint Mary's River S.P.	103	E4	38.262940 -76.525640
Sandy Point S.P.	144	C3	39.021750 -76.420280
Seneca Creek S.P.	144	A2	39.152200 -77.247710
Smallwood S.P.	144	B4	38.556509 -77.185257
South Mtn. S.P.	144	A1	39.540058 -77.607422
Susquehanna S.P.	145	D1	39.599840 -76.154590
Swallow Falls S.P.	102	B1	39.506550 -79.448750
Tuckahoe S.P.	145	D3	38.967120 -75.943410
Washington Mon. S.P.	144	A1	39.499810 -77.631890
Wye Oak S.P.	145	D3	38.939150 -76.080230

MASSACHUSETTS	PAGE	GRID	LATITUDE LONGITUDE
National Park & Rec. Areas			
Adams N.H.P.-Vis. Ctr.	151	D1	42.257000 -71.011200
Boston Harbor Island N.R.A.	151	D1	42.319705 -70.928555
Cape Cod Natl. Seashore	151	F2	41.835890 -69.973730
Lowell N.H.P.-Market Mills Vis. Ctr.	95	E1	42.644400 -71.312800
Minute Man N.H.P.-Minute Man Vis. Ctr.	151	D1	42.449000 -71.268700
Minute Man N.H.P.-North Bridge Vis. Ctr.	151	D1	42.470800 -71.352600
New Bedford Whaling N.H.P.	151	D4	41.635570 -70.924250
Salem Maritime N.H.S.	151	D1	42.521490 -70.886980
Saugus Iron Works N.H.S.	151	D1	42.468230 -71.009110
Waquoit Bay Natl. Estuarine Research Res.	151	E4	41.581300 -70.524800
State Park & Rec. Areas			
Ames-Nowell S.P.	151	D2	42.113140 -70.975230
Ashland S.P.	150	C2	42.246380 -71.475560
Blackstone River & Canal Heritage S.P.	150	C2	42.099500 -71.618780
Borderland S.P.	151	D2	42.058560 -71.166330
Bradley Palmer S.P.	151	F1	42.652180 -70.911000
Callahan S.P.	150	C1	42.315140 -71.367710
Demarest Lloyd S.P.	151	D4	41.525790 -70.990530
Dighton Rock S.P.	151	D3	41.811230 -71.098440
Halibut Point S.P.	151	F1	42.686100 -70.631070
Hampton Ponds S.P.	150	A2	42.178350 -72.690030
Holyoke Range S.P.	150	A1	42.297270 -72.530890
Joseph Sylvia State Beach	151	E4	41.424140 -70.553870
Lake Wyola S.P.-Carroll Holmes Rec. Area	150	A1	42.500366 -72.430642
Moore S.P.	150	B1	42.312354 -71.954269
Nickerson S.P.	151	F3	41.775550 -70.028290
Pilgrim Mem. (Plymouth Rock) S.P.	151	E2	41.958850 -70.662870
Red Bridge S.P.	150	A2	42.175500 -72.406600
Robinson S.P.	150	A2	42.081680 -72.658650
Rutland S.P.	150	B1	42.371470 -71.997680
Savoy Mtn. State Forest	94	C1	42.626540 -73.015580
Skinner S.P.	150	A1	42.304220 -72.598790
South Cape Beach S.P.	151	E4	41.554582 -70.508194
Wahconah Falls S.P.	94	C1	42.491430 -73.120790
Watson Pond S.P.	151	D2	41.956260 -71.116090
Wells S.P.	150	B2	42.142290 -72.042400
Whitehall S.P.	150	C2	42.227210 -71.584330
Wompatuck S.P.	151	D2	42.218770 -70.866600

MICHIGAN	PAGE	GRID	LATITUDE LONGITUDE
National Park & Rec. Areas			
Father Marquette Natl. Mem.	70	C2	45.853912 -84.728874
Grand Island N.R.A.	70	A1	46.500405 -86.657605
Isle Royale Natl. Park-Rock Harbor Vis. Ctr.	65	F2	48.145530 -88.482220
Isle Royale Natl. Park-Windigo Vis. Ctr.	65	F2	47.912700 -89.156990
Keweenaw N.H.P.	65	F3	47.242160 -88.448020
Pictured Rocks Natl. Lakeshore-East Ent.	70	A1	46.657450 -86.021160
Pictured Rocks Natl. Lakeshore-West Ent.	70	A1	46.474000 -86.553000
Sleeping Bear Dunes Natl. Lakeshore	70	A4	44.785210 -86.049690
State Park & Rec. Areas			
Albert E. Sleeper S.P.	76	C2	43.972880 -83.205530
Algonac S.P.	76	C4	42.654760 -82.514510
Aloha S.P.	70	C3	45.525850 -84.464390
Baraga S.P.	65	F4	46.762070 -88.499320
Bewabic S.P.	68	C2	46.094260 -88.422290
Brimley S.P.	70	C1	46.412970 -84.555040
Burt Lake S.P.	70	C3	45.401305 -84.619505
Cambridge Junction Hist. S.P.	90	B1	42.066990 -84.225550
Charles Mears S.P.	75	E2	43.781980 -86.439670
Cheboygan S.P.	70	C2	45.644860 -84.420440
Clear Lake S.P.	70	C3	45.127390 -84.173910
Coldwater Lake S.P.	90	A1	43.665975 -84.948703
Craig Lake S.P.	68	C1	46.538810 -88.127700
Duck Lake S.P.	75	E3	43.354880 -86.397560
F.J. Mclain S.P.	65	F3	47.239400 -88.587190
Fayette Hist. S.P.	70	A2	45.717200 -86.664600
Fisherman's Island S.P.	70	B3	45.307550 -85.301540
Fort Wilkins Hist. S.P.	65	F3	47.466780 -87.878240
Grand Haven S.P.	75	E3	43.056100 -86.245990
Grand Mere S.P.	89	E1	41.995190 -86.538790
Harrisville S.P.	71	D4	44.649800 -83.293920
Hart-Montague Trail S.P.	75	E2	43.688800 -86.371900
Hartwick Pines S.P.	70	C4	44.744180 -84.648340
Holland S.P.	75	E4	42.780310 -86.201410
Indian Lake S.P.	70	A2	45.960420 -86.364400
Interlochen S.P.	70	B4	44.631370 -85.766630
J.W. Wells S.P.	69	D3	45.389070 -87.371360
Kal-Haven Trail S.P.	75	E4	42.324698 -85.667739
Lake Gogebic S.P.	68	B1	46.459950 -89.573110
Lakelands Trail S.P.	76	B4	42.408249 -83.964043
Lakeport S.P.	76	C3	43.129120 -82.501820
Leelanau S.P.	70	B3	45.209320 -85.546220
Ludington S.P.	75	E1	44.031100 -86.505460
Mackinac Island S.P.	70	C2	45.849880 -84.617650
Muskallonge Lake S.P.	70	B1	46.677100 -85.625210
Muskegon S.P.	75	E3	43.247900 -86.341480
Negwegon S.P.	71	D4	44.855020 -83.329240
Newaygo S.P.	75	F2	43.500600 -85.582260
North Higgins Lake S.P.	70	C4	44.515030 -84.753980
Onaway S.P.	70	C3	45.430530 -84.229020
Orchard Beach S.P.	75	E1	44.278860 -86.314480
Otsego Lake S.P.	70	C4	44.927770 -84.688980
P.H. Hoeft S.P.	70	C3	45.463700 -83.883560
P.J. Hoffmaster S.P.	75	E3	43.132870 -86.265460
Palms Book S.P.	70	A2	46.003280 -86.385130
Petoskey S.P.	70	B3	45.407950 -84.902160
Porcupine Mts. Wilderness S.P.	65	E4	46.816070 -89.621850
Port Crescent S.P.	76	C1	44.007570 -83.051290
Sanilac Petroglyphs Hist. S.P.	76	C2	43.649367 -83.018016
Saugatuck Dunes S.P.	75	E4	42.695990 -86.186840
Seven Lakes S.P.	76	B3	42.816750 -83.648120
Silver Lake S.P.	75	E2	43.663650 -86.492660
Sleepy Hollow S.P.	76	A3	42.925020 -84.408620
South Higgins Lake S.P.	76	A1	44.432818 -84.670299
Sterling S.P.	90	C1	41.921490 -83.342680
Straits S.P.	70	C2	45.858090 -84.720200
Tahquamenon Falls S.P.-East Ent.	70	B1	46.598030 -85.147890
Tahquamenon Falls S.P.-West Ent.	70	B1	46.564190 -85.292530
Tawas Point S.P.	76	B1	44.255820 -83.443050
Thompson's Harbor S.P.	71	D3	45.346705 -83.567431
Traverse City S.P.	70	B4	44.748050 -85.553800
Twin Lakes S.P.	65	E4	46.892210 -88.856560
Van Buren S.P.	75	E4	42.333830 -86.304830

Van Buren Trail S.P.	89	F1	42.211405 -86.171105
Van Riper S.P.	68	C1	46.525260 -87.991150
W.C. Wetzel S.P.	76	C4	42.596720 -82.825140
Walter J. Hayes S.P.	90	B1	42.072830 -84.137820
Warren Dunes S.P.	89	E1	41.900980 -86.595260
Warren Woods S.P.	89	E1	41.840680 -86.631290
White Pine Trail S.P.	75	F2	44.222900 -85.426700
Wilderness S.P.-East Ent.	70	B2	45.748160 -84.853500
Wilderness S.P.-West Ent.	70	B2	45.679360 -84.964170
William Mitchell S.P.	75	F1	44.236880 -85.453990
Wilson S.P.	76	A1	44.029620 -84.806070
Young S.P.	70	B3	45.235240 -85.041450

MINNESOTA

MINNESOTA	PAGE	GRID	LATITUDE LONGITUDE
National Park & Rec. Areas			
Grand Portage Natl. Mon.	65	E2	47.996274 -89.734256
Pipestone Natl. Mon.	27	F3	44.013150 -96.325360
Voyageurs Natl. Park-Ash River Vis. Ctr.	64	C2	48.435600 -92.850300
Voyageurs Natl. Park-Kabetogama Lake Vis. Ctr.	64	C2	48.446100 -93.030100
Voyageurs Natl. Park-Rainy Lake Vis. Ctr.	64	C2	48.584400 -93.161500
State Park & Rec. Areas			
Afton S.P.	67	D4	44.847930 -92.791020
Banning S.P.	67	D2	46.179730 -92.855170
Bear Head Lake S.P.	64	C3	47.792720 -92.083720
Beaver Creek Valley S.P.	73	E2	43.636790 -91.573190
Blue Mounds S.P.	27	F4	43.714340 -96.183100
Buffalo River S.P.	19	F4	46.866260 -96.469980
Camden S.P.	27	F3	44.362880 -95.917480
Caribou Falls State Wayside	65	D3	47.463890 -91.030660
Carley S.P.	73	E1	44.116790 -92.169320
Cascade River S.P.	65	D3	47.712950 -90.497930
Charles A. Lindbergh S.P.	66	C2	45.959410 -94.387640
Cross River State Wayside	65	D3	47.543420 -90.897770
Crow Wing S.P.	66	C1	46.272630 -94.316400
Father Hennepin S.P.	66	C1	46.144520 -93.484260
Flandrau S.P.	72	B1	44.294360 -94.482020
Flood Bay State Wayside	64	C4	47.038500 -91.642540
Forestville Mystery Cave S.P.	73	E2	43.637520 -92.220270
Fort Ridgely S.P.	72	B1	44.454810 -94.718310
Franz Jevne S.P.	64	B2	48.641140 -94.058260
Frontenac S.P.	67	E4	44.525200 -92.338730
George H. Crosby Manitou S.P.	65	D3	47.478990 -91.123070
Glacial Lakes S.P.	66	A3	45.540550 -95.529600
Glendalough S.P.	19	F4	46.313314 -95.679290
Gooseberry Falls S.P.	65	D3	47.145430 -91.462380
Grand Portage S.P.	65	E2	47.999150 -89.598690
Great River Bluffs S.P.	73	E1	43.939100 -91.430050
Hayes Lake S.P.	19	F1	48.641070 -95.570600
Hill Annex Mine S.P.	64	B3	47.327490 -93.277520
Inspiration Peak State Wayside	66	A1	46.136880 -95.578650
Itasca S.P.	64	A3	47.194490 -95.166740
Jay Cooke S.P.	64	C4	46.658790 -92.349200
John A. Latsch S.P.	73	E1	44.164720 -91.823860
Joseph R. Brown State Wayside	66	B4	44.750328 -95.324425
Judge C.R. Magney S.P.	65	E3	47.818090 -90.051230
Kilen Woods S.P.	72	B2	43.732140 -95.072220
Kodonce River State Wayside	65	E3	47.793930 -90.154140
Lac Qui Parle S.P.	27	F2	45.024680 -95.896580
Lake Bemidji S.P.	64	A3	47.536890 -94.832320
Lake Bronson S.P.	19	F1	48.730940 -96.630720
Lake Carlos S.P.	66	B2	46.000540 -95.334430
Lake Louise S.P.	73	D2	43.532620 -92.509250
Lake Maria S.P.	66	C3	45.304810 -93.935570
Lake Shetek S.P.	72	A1	44.105740 -95.699730
Maplewood S.P.	19	F4	46.549910 -95.966720
McCarthy Beach S.P.	64	B3	47.674110 -93.027350
Mille Lacs Kathio S.P.	66	C2	46.160740 -93.758020
Minneopa S.P.	72	C1	44.162190 -94.110310
Monson Lake S.P.	66	B3	45.321300 -95.270470
Moose Lake S.P.	64	C4	46.436360 -92.743090
Myre-Big Island S.P.	73	D2	43.623847 -93.289096
Nerstrand Big Woods S.P.	73	D1	44.327040 -93.111210
Old Mill S.P.	19	F2	48.369790 -96.569420
Ray Berglund State Wayside	65	D3	47.608200 -90.771930
Rice Lake S.P.	73	D1	44.095380 -93.063940
Rush River State Wayside	66	C4	44.507240 -93.931409
Saint Croix S.P.	67	D2	45.960615 -92.611630
Sakatah Lake S.P.	72	C1	44.218000 -93.509970
Sam Brown Mon. State Wayside	27	F1	45.596160 -96.841410
Savanna Portage S.P.	64	B4	46.819130 -93.176040
Scenic S.P.	64	B3	47.702450 -93.564710
Schoolcraft S.P.	64	B3	47.223040 -93.805320
Sibley S.P.	66	B3	45.318990 -95.011930
Soudan Underground Mine S.P.	64	C2	47.818130 -92.246090
Split Rock Creek S.P.	27	F4	43.907240 -96.367970
Split Rock Lighthouse S.P.	65	D3	47.189800 -91.395010
Temperance River S.P.	65	D3	47.558780 -90.867930
Tettegouche S.P.	65	D3	47.337210 -91.200670
Upper Sioux Agency S.P.	66	B4	44.734540 -95.456460
Whitewater S.P.	73	E1	44.068880 -92.040100
Wild River S.P.	67	D3	45.524100 -92.754500
William O'Brien S.P.	67	D3	45.223900 -92.763500
Zippel Bay S.P.	64	A1	48.840630 -94.849950

MISSISSIPPI

MISSISSIPPI	PAGE	GRID	LATITUDE LONGITUDE
National Park & Rec. Areas			
Gulf Islands Natl. Seashore	135	D2	30.407200 -88.749220
Natchez N.H.P.-Vis. Reception Ctr.	125	F4	31.553900 -91.412400
State Park & Rec. Areas			
Bogue Homa State Fishing Lake	127	D4	31.703200 -89.026400
Clarkco S.P.	127	D3	32.108500 -88.693970
Columbia State Fishing Lake	134	C1	31.183500 -89.738400
Dockery State Fishing Lake	126	B3	32.197100 -90.265100
Florewood S.P.	118	B4	33.525120 -90.250362
George Payne Cossar S.P.	118	B3	34.122710 -89.882100
Golden Mem. S.P.	126	C2	32.568560 -89.407640
Great River Road S.P.	118	A4	33.851733 -91.027574
Hugh White S.P.	118	B4	33.796080 -89.743010
J.P. Coleman S.P.	119	D2	34.924254 -88.171706
Jeff Davis State Fishing Lake	126	B4	31.567700 -89.839800
Kemper County State Fishing Lake	127	D2	32.804167 -88.730556
Lakeland Park State Fishing Lake	127	D4	31.681225 -88.599550
Lake Lincoln S.P.	126	B4	31.684354 -90.337142
Legion S.P.	127	D1	33.148690 -89.042460
Leroy Percy S.P.	126	A1	33.160500 -90.938250
Mary Crawford State Fishing Lake	126	B4	31.574900 -90.154000
Monroe State Fishing Lake	119	D4	33.941500 -88.568700
Natchez S.P.	126	A4	31.589580 -91.220350
Neshoba County State Fishing Lake	126	C2	32.706200 -89.010500
Oktibbeha County State Fishing Lake	118	C4	33.505700 -88.933400
Paul B. Johnson S.P.	134	C1	31.133800 -89.233910
Percy Quin S.P.	134	B1	31.189020 -90.510660
Perry State Fishing Lake	135	D1	31.132400 -88.899800
Roosevelt S.P.	126	C2	32.321920 -89.664980
Ross Barnett State Fishing Lake	126	C3	31.833200 -89.589500
Simpson County State Fishing Lake	126	C3	31.913500 -89.794500
Tippah County State Fishing Lake	118	C2	34.794290 -88.950660
Tishomingo S.P.	119	D2	34.615670 -88.183390
Tom Bailey State Fishing Lake	127	D2	32.425030 -88.523069
Tombigbee S.P.	119	D3	34.231870 -88.628870
Trace S.P.	118	C3	34.260020 -88.886560
Wall Doxey S.P.	118	C2	34.660270 -89.459290

MISSOURI

MISSOURI	PAGE	GRID	LATITUDE LONGITUDE
National Park & Rec. Areas			
George Washington Carver Natl. Mon.	106	C2	36.986160 -94.351890
Ozark Natl. Scenic Riverways	107	F2	37.281400 -91.408000
State Park & Rec. Areas			
Bennett Spring S.P.	107	D1	37.725440 -92.856390
Big Lake S.P.	86	A4	40.092090 -95.347300
Big Oak Tree S.P.	108	C3	36.641990 -89.290180
Big Sugar Creek S.P.	106	C3	36.584106 -93.819122
Crowder S.P.	86	C4	40.082140 -93.669310
Cuivre River S.P.	97	F2	39.062380 -90.938640
Elephant Rocks S.P.	108	A1	37.652150 -90.690810
Finger Lakes S.P.	97	E2	39.075400 -92.314750
Graham Cave S.P.	97	F3	38.908850 -91.576090
Grand Gulf S.P.	107	F3	36.544100 -91.636370
Ha Ha Tonka S.P.	97	D4	37.975410 -92.762230
Harry S. Truman S.P.	97	D4	38.274650 -93.442390
Hawn S.P.	108	B1	37.833660 -90.241610
Johnson's Shut-Ins S.P.	108	A1	37.547920 -90.853020
Katy Trail S.P.	97	E3	38.975190 -92.750160
Knob Noster S.P.	96	C3	38.753020 -93.577440
Lake of the Ozarks S.P.	97	E4	38.133990 -92.564260
Lake Wappapello S.P.	108	A2	36.942210 -90.344400
Lewis & Clark S.P.	96	B1	39.538900 -95.052900
Long Branch S.P.	97	E1	39.767610 -92.526480
Mark Twain S.P.	97	E2	39.485270 -91.795340
Meramec S.P.	97	F4	38.215350 -91.123070
Montauk S.P.	107	F1	37.454710 -91.690970
Morris S.P.	108	B3	36.554166 -90.043220
Onondaga Cave S.P.	97	F4	38.064310 -91.230140
Pershing S.P.	97	D1	39.776270 -93.211130
Pomme de Terre S.P.	107	D1	37.874380 -93.318700
Prairie S.P.	106	B1	37.518510 -94.571280
Roaring River S.P.	106	C3	36.590110 -93.834420
Robertsville S.P.	98	A3	38.429120 -90.818110
Rock Bridge Mem. S.P.	97	E3	38.883350 -92.331890
Saint Francois S.P.	98	A4	37.972900 -90.536210
Saint Joe S.P.	108	A1	37.824990 -90.537480
Sam A. Baker S.P.	108	A2	37.254530 -90.505080
Stockton S.P.	106	C1	37.622470 -93.753070
Table Rock S.P.	107	D3	36.583440 -93.309150
Taum Sauk Mtn. S.P.	108	A1	37.669500 -90.673400
Thousand Hills S.P.	87	D4	40.185160 -92.643070
Trail of Tears S.P.	108	B1	37.452880 -89.490760
Van Meter S.P.	97	D2	39.262590 -93.267210
Wakonda S.P.	97	F1	40.004250 -91.526060
Wallace S.P.	96	C1	39.660760 -94.213290
Washington S.P.	98	A4	38.085600 -90.685650
Watkins Mill S.P.	96	C2	39.383920 -94.265130
Weston Bend S.P.	96	B2	39.392960 -94.863430

MONTANA

MONTANA	PAGE	GRID	LATITUDE LONGITUDE
National Park & Rec. Areas			
Bighorn Canyon N.R.A.	24	C2	45.330090 -107.871650
Fort Benton Natl. Hist. Landmark	16	A2	47.823210 -110.661910
Glacier Natl. Park-Many Glacier Ent.	15	D1	48.827150 -113.551540
Glacier Natl. Park-St Mary Ent.	15	D1	48.747120 -113.439650
Glacier Natl. Park-Two Medicine Ent.	15	D1	48.494210 -113.262250
Glacier Natl. Park-West Ent.	15	D1	48.499890 -113.987190
Grant-Kohrs Ranch N.H.S.	15	E4	46.398900 -112.736680
Little Bighorn Bfld. Natl. Mon.	24	C1	45.570080 -107.434710
Natl. Bison Range	15	D3	47.371674 -114.262066
Rattlesnake N.R.A.	15	D4	47.040775 -113.933333
State Park & Rec. Areas			
Ackley Lake S.P.	16	B4	46.947220 -109.936110
Anaconda Smoke Stack S.P.	23	D1	46.111037 -112.969599
Bannack S.P.	23	D2	45.159170 -112.997780
Beaverhead Rock S.P.	23	E2	45.383330 -112.458330
Beavertail Hill S.P.	15	D4	46.721660 -113.576420
Big Arm S.P.	15	D3	47.815360 -114.307930
Black Sandy S.P.	15	E4	46.756940 -111.888890
Brush Lake S.P.	17	F1	48.603000 -104.113000
Chief Plenty Coups S.P.	24	B2	45.429700 -108.532500
Clark's Lookout S.P.	23	E2	45.236110 -112.630560
Cooney S.P.	24	B2	45.435050 -109.225330
Council Grove S.P.	15	D4	46.912500 -114.150000
Finley Point S.P.	15	D3	47.763830 -114.078723
Fort Owen S.P.	15	D4	46.519440 -114.095830
Frenchtown Pond S.P.	15	D3	47.039530 -114.259220
Granite Ghost Town S.P.	23	D1	46.319000 -113.257000
Greycliff Prairie Dog Town S.P.	24	B1	45.767600 -109.794180
Hell Creek S.P.	17	D3	47.620290 -106.884510
Lake Elmo S.P.	24	C1	45.845280 -108.481310
Lake Mary Ronan S.P.	15	D2	48.204020 -114.330340
Lewis & Clark Caverns S.P.	23	E1	45.821840 -111.858510
Logan S.P.	14	C2	48.204020 -114.330340
Lone Pine S.P.	15	D2	48.175580 -114.339560
Lost Creek S.P.	23	D1	46.203020 -112.993810
Madison Buffalo Jump S.P.	23	F1	45.665140 -111.062770
Makoshika S.P.	17	F4	47.090240 -104.709970
Medicine Rocks S.P.	25	F1	46.046460 -104.456740
Missouri Headwaters S.P.	23	F1	45.909129 -111.497411
Painted Rocks S.P.	22	C1	45.706650 -114.282530
Pictograph Cave S.P.	24	C1	45.737500 -108.430830
Pirogue Island S.P.	17	E4	46.440560 -105.816670
Placid Lake S.P.	15	D3	47.138040 -113.524960
Rosebud Bfld. S.P.	25	D2	45.208270 -106.944460
Salmon Lake S.P.	15	D4	47.042270 -113.390390
Sluice Boxes S.P.	16	A3	47.211400 -110.939660
Smith River S.P.	16	A4	46.721219 -111.173819
Spring Meadow Lake S.P.	15	E4	46.612220 -112.075000
Thompson Falls S.P.	14	C3	47.618060 -115.387500
Tongue River Reservoir S.P.	25	D2	45.093520 -106.804670
Tower Rock S.P.	15	E3	47.181000 -111.816000
Travelers' Rest S.P.	15	D4	46.751240 -114.089000
Ulm Pishkun S.P.	16	A3	47.494887 -111.525201
Wayfarers S.P.	15	D2	48.057400 -114.079550
West Shore S.P.	15	D2	47.948780 -114.189160
Whitefish Lake S.P.	15	D2	48.204020 -114.330340
Wild Horse Island S.P.	15	D3	47.844640 -114.279970
Yellow Bay S.P.	15	D2	47.874500 -114.027080

NEBRASKA

NEBRASKA	PAGE	GRID	LATITUDE LONGITUDE
National Park & Rec. Areas			
Agate Fossil Beds Natl. Mon.	33	F2	42.423860 -103.791120
Chimney Rock N.H.S.	33	F3	41.719650 -103.336070
Pine Ridge N.R.A.	33	F1	42.625880 -103.205570
Scotts Bluff Natl. Mon.	33	F2	41.832380 -103.717550
State Park & Rec. Areas			
Chadron S.P.	34	A1	42.711540 -103.008500
Eugene T. Mahoney S.P.	35	F3	41.026387 -96.314180
Fort Robinson S.P.	33	F1	42.654050 -103.492100
Indian Cave S.P.	86	A4	40.263280 -95.586630
Niobrara S.P.	35	E1	42.747450 -98.051850
Platte River S.P.	35	F3	40.986840 -96.219290
Ponca S.P.	35	F1	42.600360 -96.714940
Smith Falls S.P.	34	C1	42.891670 -100.316670

NEVADA

NEVADA	PAGE	GRID	LATITUDE LONGITUDE
National Park & Rec. Areas			
Devils Hole (Death Valley Natl. Park)	45	F3	36.423889 -116.305833
Great Basin Natl. Park-Vis. Ctr.	38	C2	39.005600 -114.220000
Lake Mead N.R.A.-North Ent.	46	B2	36.161180 -114.905200
Lake Mead N.R.A.-South Ent.	46	B2	36.021230 -114.796340
Lake Mead N.R.A.-West Ent.	46	B2	36.105980 -114.900940
Spring Mts. N.R.A.	46	A1	36.245200 -115.233910
State Park & Rec. Areas			
Beaver Dam S.P.	38	C4	37.529130 -114.107930
Berlin-Ichthyosaur S.P.	37	F2	38.880300 -117.607930
Big Bend of the Colorado State Rec. Area	53	F1	35.116730 -114.640820
Cathedral Gorge S.P.-North Ent.	38	C4	37.850890 -114.415120
Cathedral Gorge S.P.-South Ent.	38	C4	37.820280 -114.407890

	Page	Grid	Latitude Longitude
Dayton S.P.-North Ent.	37	D2	39.253540 -119.587190
Dayton S.P.-South Ent.	37	D2	39.250650 -119.588020
Echo Canyon S.P.	38	C4	38.195000 -114.512900
Floyd Lamb S.P.	46	A2	36.321240 -115.269900
Kershaw-Ryan S.P.	38	C4	37.586380 -114.533260
Lake Tahoe-Nevada S.P.	37	D2	39.213670 -119.928300
Spring Mtn. Ranch S.P.	46	A2	36.073830 -115.443710
Spring Valley S.P.	38	C3	38.003920 -114.207570
Valley of Fire S.P.	46	B1	36.429710 -114.513590
Wild Horse State Rec. Area	30	B3	41.670739 -115.799805

NEW HAMPSHIRE	PAGE	GRID	LATITUDE LONGITUDE
National Park & Rec. Areas			
Saint-Gaudens N.H.S.	81	E4	43.501570 -72.362510
State Park & Rec. Areas			
Bear Brook S.P.	81	F4	43.133800 -71.366040
Cardigan S.P.	81	E3	43.647990 -71.949570
Crawford Notch S.P.	81	F2	44.181760 -71.398780
Echo Lake S.P.	81	F3	44.067430 -71.166000
Forest Lake S.P.	81	F2	44.354490 -71.673180
Hampton Beach S.P.	95	E1	42.898333 -70.812778
Kingston S.P.	95	E1	42.929020 -71.054680
Lake Tarleton S.P.	81	E3	43.975833 -71.963333
Miller S.P.	95	D1	42.861630 -71.878750
Monadnock S.P.	95	D1	42.845440 -72.086590
Mount Sunapee S.P.	81	E4	43.332120 -72.079800
Pawtuckaway S.P.	81	F4	43.082150 -71.152130
Pillsbury S.P.	81	E4	43.236860 -72.122830
Pisgah S.P.	94	C1	42.810310 -72.408340
Umbagog Lake S.P.	81	F1	44.712990 -71.072700
Wellington S.P.	81	F3	43.641280 -71.782980
Wentworth S.P.	81	F3	43.603056 -71.136389
White Lake S.P.	81	F3	43.830880 -71.218220
Winslow S.P.	81	E4	43.391730 -71.869540

NEW JERSEY	PAGE	GRID	LATITUDE LONGITUDE
National Park & Rec. Areas			
Delaware Water Gap N.R.A.	94	A4	40.970390 -75.128100
Gateway N.R.A.	147	F1	40.396420 -73.981160
Morristown N.H.P.	148	A4	40.744670 -74.565290
State Park & Rec. Areas			
Allaire S.P.	147	E2	40.153470 -74.111390
Allamuchy Mtn. S.P.	104	C1	40.921244 -74.782222
Barnegat Lighthouse S.P.	147	E4	39.762750 -74.107950
Cape May Point S.P.	104	C4	38.932950 -74.961010
Corson's Inlet S.P.	105	D4	39.216340 -74.647070
Delaware & Raritan Canal S.P.	147	D1	40.473230 -74.571100
Double Trouble S.P.	147	E3	39.900550 -74.225120
Farny S.P.	148	A3	40.997170 -74.459060
Forked River State Marina	147	E3	39.834886 -74.195019
Fortescue State Marina	145	F2	39.243178 -75.176636
Fort Mott S.P.	146	B4	39.612100 -75.543430
Hacklebarney S.P.	105	D1	40.751170 -74.736590
High Point S.P.	148	A2	41.304800 -74.669650
Hopatcong S.P.	148	A3	40.911780 -74.667000
Island Beach S.P.	147	E3	39.905240 -74.081510
Liberty S.P.	148	B4	40.697330 -74.063870
Long Pond Ironworks S.P.	148	A2	41.140986 -74.309228
Monmouth Bfld. S.P.	147	E2	40.269340 -74.302800
Parvin S.P.	146	C4	39.524490 -75.160460
Pigeon Swamp S.P.	147	E1	40.394420 -74.487150
Princeton Bfld. S.P.	147	D2	40.332490 -74.675650
Rancocas S.P.	147	D3	39.990420 -74.837480
Ringwood S.P.	148	A2	41.127600 -74.260130
Swartswood S.P.	94	A4	41.081680 -74.813620
Voorhees S.P.	104	C1	40.695060 -74.887030
Washington Crossing S.P.	147	D2	40.296920 -74.866420
Washington Rock S.P.	148	A4	40.613580 -74.472860
Wawayanda S.P.	148	A2	41.199240 -74.392440

NEW MEXICO	PAGE	GRID	LATITUDE LONGITUDE
National Park & Rec. Areas			
Aztec Ruins Natl. Mon.	48	B1	36.833920 -108.000570
Bandelier Natl. Mon.	48	C2	35.780130 -106.264830
Capulin Mtn. Natl. Mon.	49	E1	36.781990 -103.986110
Carlsbad Caverns Natl. Park-Vis. Ctr.	57	E3	32.175400 -104.444000
Chaco Culture N.H.P.	48	B2	36.016190 -107.924060
Datil Well N.R.A.	48	B4	34.154130 -107.852610
El Malpais Natl. Cons. Area	48	B4	35.059720 -107.876400
El Morro Natl. Mon.	48	B3	35.043480 -108.346250
Fort Union Natl. Mon.	49	D2	35.904230 -105.010740
Gila Cliff Dwellings Natl. Mon.	56	A2	33.229540 -108.264630
Kasha-Katuwe Tent Rocks Natl. Mon.	48	C2	35.663200 -106.410800
Pecos N.H.P.	49	D3	35.578750 -105.762400
Petroglyph Natl. Mon.	48	C3	35.139490 -106.709670
Salinas Pueblo Missions Natl. Mon.	48	C4	34.520370 -106.241250
Salinas Pueblo Missions Natl. Mon.-Gran Quivira	49	D4	34.260000 -106.091000
White Sands Natl. Mon.	56	C2	32.820130 -106.272980
State Park & Rec. Areas			
Bluewater Lake S.P.	48	B3	35.302730 -108.106930
Bottomless Lakes S.P.	57	E2	33.316630 -104.332880
Brantley Lake S.P.	57	E3	32.571390 -104.366210
Caballo Lake S.P.	56	B2	32.911370 -107.313580
Cimarron Canyon S.P.	49	D1	36.537600 -105.221130
City of Rocks S.P.	56	A2	32.594860 -107.973850
Clayton Lake S.P.	49	F1	36.573070 -103.300690
Conchas Lake S.P.	49	E3	35.394760 -104.181790
Coronado S.P.	48	C3	35.329130 -106.557870
Coyote Creek S.P.	49	D2	36.188020 -105.233260
Eagle Nest S.P.	49	D1	36.542100 -105.261300
Elephant Butte Res. S.P.-South Ent.	56	B1	33.176180 -107.207460
El Vado Lake S.P.	48	C1	36.593710 -106.735790
Fenton Lake S.P.	48	C2	35.887230 -106.723170
Heron Lake S.P.	48	C1	36.693840 -106.654230
Hyde Mem. S.P.	49	D2	35.737890 -105.836540
Leasburg Dam S.P.	56	B3	32.492680 -106.922380
Living Desert Zoo & Gardens S.P.	57	E3	32.449839 -104.286341
Manzano Mtn. S.P.	48	C4	34.603880 -106.360960
Morphy Lake S.P.	49	D2	35.968660 -105.366600
Navajo Lake S.P.	48	B1	36.831950 -107.586950
Oasis S.P.	49	F4	34.259740 -103.334280
Oliver Lee Mem. S.P.	56	C2	32.744640 -105.934520
Pancho Villa S.P.	56	B4	31.828050 -107.641200
Percha Dam S.P.	56	B2	32.873610 -107.308100
Red Rock S.P.	48	A3	35.537910 -108.605900
Rock Hound S.P.	56	B3	32.185550 -107.613090
Santa Rosa Lake S.P.	49	E3	34.987930 -104.658750
Smokey Bear Hist. S.P.	57	D1	33.545620 -105.573170
Spring Canyon Rec. Area-Rockhound S.P.	56	B3	32.125550 -107.589990
Storrie Lake S.P.	49	D2	35.655720 -105.231840
Sugarite Canyon S.P.	49	E1	36.944191 -104.381651
Sumner Lake S.P.	49	E4	34.607520 -104.389050
Ute Lake S.P.	49	F3	35.340630 -103.442500
Villanueva S.P.	49	D3	35.259530 -105.368970

NEW YORK	PAGE	GRID	LATITUDE LONGITUDE
National Park & Rec. Areas			
Eleanor Roosevelt N.H.S.	94	B3	41.763170 -73.902960
Fire Island Natl. Seashore	149	D4	40.735320 -72.866620
Fort Stanwix Natl. Mon.	79	E3	43.211930 -75.454740
Gateway N.R.A.	148	B4	40.581100 -73.887790
Home of F.D.R. N.H.S.	94	B3	41.767038 -73.938193
Sagamore Hill N.H.S.	148	C3	40.882480 -73.505550
Saratoga N.H.P.	81	D4	43.002690 -73.612110
Statue of Liberty Natl. Mon.	148	B4	40.689547 -74.044029
Thomas Cole N.H.S.	94	B2	42.225900 -73.861600
Van Buren N.H.S.	94	B2	42.370610 -73.701010
Vanderbilt Mansion N.H.S.	94	B3	41.796482 -73.942359
Women's Rights N.H.P.	79	D3	42.910580 -76.800260
State Park & Rec. Areas			
Adirondack Park	80	C2	43.455590 -73.695930
Allegany S.P.	92	B1	42.106480 -78.765940
Battle Island S.P.	79	D3	43.362780 -76.442150
Bear Mtn. S.P.	148	B2	41.278350 -73.970290
Beaver Island S.P.	78	A3	42.968170 -78.969560
Blauvelt S.P.	148	B3	41.069460 -73.949370
Bowman Lake S.P.	79	E4	42.516970 -75.670400
Buttermilk Falls S.P.	79	D4	42.347410 -76.489130
Caleb Smith S.P. Pres.	149	D3	40.854190 -73.221190
Canandaigua Lake State Marine Park	78	C3	42.875964 -77.275600
Captree S.P.	149	D4	40.636640 -73.263210
Catskill Park	94	A2	42.050290 -74.288840
Cedar Point S.P.	79	D1	44.200670 -76.191000
Chenango Valley S.P.	93	E1	42.215040 -75.818020
Chittenango Falls S.P.	79	E3	42.981520 -75.845030
Clarence Fahnestock S.P.	148	B1	41.423620 -73.799560
Cold Spring Harbor S.P.	148	C3	40.867450 -73.461900
Connetquot River S.P. Pres.	149	D4	40.748070 -73.153510
Cumberland Bay S.P.	81	D1	44.725090 -73.421450
Darien Lakes S.P.	78	B3	42.908460 -78.433300
Delta Lake S.P.	79	E3	43.290030 -75.414910
Evangola S.P.	78	A4	42.604460 -79.105610
Fair Haven Beach S.P.	79	D3	43.320570 -76.696210
Fort Niagara S.P.	78	A3	43.261790 -79.061460
Four Mile Creek S.P.	78	A3	43.272530 -78.996270
Golden Hill S.P.	78	B2	43.365250 -78.489310
Goosepond Mtn. S.P.	148	A2	41.354460 -74.254470
Gov. Alfred E. Smith/Sunken Meadow S.P.	149	D3	40.911970 -73.262940
Green Lakes S.P.	79	E3	43.060000 -75.969030
Hamlin Beach S.P.	78	C2	43.361130 -77.944460
Harriman S.P.	148	B2	41.293010 -74.026560
Heckscher S.P.	149	D4	40.712860 -73.168480
Highland Lakes S.P.	148	A1	41.489806 -74.325085
Hither Hills S.P.	149	F3	41.007700 -72.014500
Hudson Highlands S.P.	148	B2	41.428060 -73.966740
Hudson River Islands S.P.	94	B2	42.318574 -73.778343
Hunt's Pond S.P.	79	E4	42.594020 -75.378140
James Baird S.P.	148	B1	41.689100 -73.799390
Jones Beach S.P.	148	C4	40.595000 -73.521070
Keewaydin S.P.	79	E1	44.322390 -75.925740
Keuka Lake S.P.	78	C4	42.594280 -77.130360
Lake Erie S.P.	78	A4	42.419070 -79.434430
Lakeside Beach S.P.	78	B2	43.367090 -78.236040
Lake Superior S.P.	94	A3	41.658590 -74.869280
Letchworth S.P.	78	B4	42.693530 -77.961210
Lodi Point S.P.	79	D4	42.619210 -76.863980
Long Point S.P.	79	D1	44.026130 -76.219650
Mark Twain S.P.	93	D1	42.205200 -76.823799
Mary Island S.P.	79	E1	44.350460 -75.930400
Max V. Shaul S.P.	79	F4	42.546790 -74.410370
Mexico Point S.P.	79	D2	43.523050 -76.258733
Minnewaska S.P. Pres.	148	A1	41.745910 -74.268370
Montauk Point S.P.	149	F3	41.065020 -71.886700
Moreau Lake S.P.	80	C4	43.226370 -73.707710
Oquaga Creek S.P.	93	F1	42.172320 -75.442840
Orient Beach S.P.	149	F2	41.154580 -72.245600
Pinnacle S.P.	93	D1	42.098100 -77.220180
Pixley Falls S.P.	79	E2	43.401100 -75.345960
Point Au Roche S.P.	81	D1	44.779990 -73.411090
Robert Moses S.P.	148	C4	40.624930 -73.261900
Saratoga Spa S.P.	80	C4	43.056950 -73.801490
Selkirk Shores S.P.	79	D2	43.544300 -76.191510
Seneca Lake S.P.	79	D3	42.873410 -76.960940
Southwick Beach S.P.	79	D2	43.767270 -76.196230
Sterling Forest S.P.	148	A2	41.220200 -74.187210
Storm King S.P.	148	B2	41.432560 -73.987020
Taconic S.P.	94	B2	42.007680 -73.508400
Tallman Mtn. S.P.	148	B3	41.037270 -73.915920
Verona Beach S.P.	79	E3	43.179070 -75.725090
Waterson Point S.P.	79	E1	44.339030 -76.010580
Wellesley Island S.P.	79	E1	44.315970 -76.019480
Whetstone Gulf S.P.	79	E2	43.702310 -75.459120
Wildwood S.P.	149	D3	40.954230 -72.788470
Wilson-Tuscarora S.P.	78	B3	43.307080 -78.854500

NORTH CAROLINA	PAGE	GRID	LATITUDE LONGITUDE
National Park & Rec. Areas			
Cape Hatteras Natl. Seashore	115	F3	35.766700 -75.526640
Cape Lookout Natl. Seashore	115	E4	34.886110 -76.331220
Carl Sandburg Home N.H.S.	121	E1	35.270000 -82.450000
Fort Raleigh N.H.S.	115	F2	35.932360 -75.708500
Great Smoky Mts. Natl. Park-Cades Cove Vis. Ctr.	121	D1	35.585300 -83.842900
Great Smoky Mts. Natl. Park-Oconaluftee Vis. Ctr.	121	D1	35.515300 -83.305300
Great Smoky Mts. Natl. Park-Sugarlands Vis. Ctr.	121	D1	35.685600 -83.536700
State Park & Rec. Areas			
Carolina Beach S.P.	123	E3	34.045240 -77.903430
Cliffs of the Neuse S.P.	123	E1	35.232900 -77.898390
Crowders Mtn. S.P.	122	A1	35.212350 -81.292920
Dismal Swamp S.P.	113	F3	36.517470 -76.360720
Fort Macon S.P.	115	E4	34.697750 -76.699580
Goose Creek S.P.	123	F1	35.483140 -76.902290
Gorges S.P.	121	E1	35.108400 -82.943900
Hammocks Beach S.P.	123	F2	34.671810 -77.138720
Hanging Rock S.P.	112	B3	36.413030 -80.253950
Jockey's Ridge S.P.	115	F2	35.961820 -75.626970
Jones Lake S.P.	123	D2	34.698900 -78.624990
Lake James S.P.	111	F4	35.728064 -81.901980
Lake Norman S.P.	112	A4	35.665780 -80.938410
Lake Waccamaw S.P.	123	D3	34.272650 -78.466040
Lumber River S.P.	123	D3	34.390831 -79.004145
Medoc Mtn. S.P.	113	D3	36.280410 -77.877820
Merchants Millpond S.P.	113	F3	36.450601 -76.692978
Morrow Mtn. S.P.	122	B1	35.370390 -80.102410
Mount Mitchell S.P.	111	E4	35.814600 -82.146100
Pettigrew S.P.	113	F4	35.789580 -76.406980
Pilot Mtn. S.P.	112	A3	36.345530 -80.478390
Raven Rock S.P.	123	D1	35.461520 -78.912660
Singletary Lake S.P.	123	D2	34.581570 -78.452070
South Mts. S.P.	121	F1	35.601190 -81.626700
Stone Mtn. S.P.	112	A3	36.374390 -81.018010
The Summit at Haw River S.P.	112	B3	36.249719 -79.755971

NORTH DAKOTA	PAGE	GRID	LATITUDE LONGITUDE
National Park & Rec. Areas			
Fort Union N.H.S.	17	F2	48.002390 -104.043560
Knife River N.H.S.	18	B3	47.336680 -101.387450
Theodore Roosevelt Natl. Park-Elkhorn Site	17	F3	47.226950 -103.622310
Theodore Roosevelt Natl. Park-North Unit	18	A3	47.600300 -103.261000
Theodore Roosevelt Natl. Park-South Unit	18	A4	46.915500 -103.527000
State Park & Rec. Areas			
Beaver Lake S.P.	18	C4	46.401260 -99.615860
Cross Ranch S.P.	18	B3	47.213530 -101.000180
Doyle Mem. S.P.	27	D1	46.204880 -99.482150
Fort Abercrombie S.P.	19	F4	46.444530 -96.718800
Fort Lincoln S.P.	18	B4	46.769420 -100.847860
Fort Ransom S.P.	19	E4	46.544100 -97.925570
Fort Stevenson S.P.	18	B3	47.596890 -101.420530
Grahams Island S.P.	19	D2	48.052500 -99.068300
Icelandic S.P.	19	E1	48.772620 -97.736990
Lake Metigoshe S.P.	18	C1	48.980640 -100.326710
Lake Sakakawea S.P.	18	B3	47.511020 -101.449350
Lewis & Clark S.P.	18	A2	48.115350 -103.241490
Little Missouri Bay S.P.	18	A3	47.550030 -102.738240

Pembina S.P.	19	E1	48.964720 -97.240500
Turtle River S.P.	19	E2	47.931660 -97.505390
Whitestone Btld. S.P.	27	D1	46.169190 -98.857330

OHIO	PAGE	GRID	LATITUDE LONGITUDE
National Park & Rec. Areas			
Cuyahoga Valley Natl. Park-Canal Vis. Ctr.	91	E2	41.372600 -81.613700
Cuyahoga Valley Natl. Park-Hunt Farm Vis. Info. Ctr.	91	E2	41.200900 -81.573100
Hopewell Culture N.H.P.	101	D2	39.298360 -82.917810
James A. Garfield N.H.S.	91	E2	41.663600 -81.351260
State Park & Rec. Areas			
A.W. Marion S.P.	101	D1	39.633730 -82.885720
Adams Lake S.P.	100	C3	38.812900 -83.519400
Alum Creek S.P.	90	C4	40.226870 -82.981320
Barkcamp S.P.	101	F1	40.047030 -81.031710
Beaver Creek S.P.	91	F3	40.726220 -80.613590
Blue Rock S.P.	101	E1	39.832780 -81.858370
Buck Creek S.P.	100	C1	39.946410 -83.729550
Buckeye Lake S.P.	101	D1	39.906540 -82.526270
Burr Oak S.P.	101	E1	39.527740 -82.023260
Caesar Creek S.P.	100	C1	39.515730 -84.041070
Catawba Island S.P.	91	D2	41.573530 -82.855780
Cowan Lake S.P.	100	C2	39.387600 -83.882970
Crane Creek S.P.	90	C2	41.603770 -83.192910
Deer Creek S.P.	101	D1	39.649260 -83.246340
Delaware S.P.	90	C4	40.377690 -83.071590
Dillon S.P.	101	E1	40.023600 -82.111910
East Fork S.P.	100	C2	39.002050 -84.151210
East Harbor S.P.	91	D2	41.540930 -82.820830
Findley S.P.	91	D3	41.122990 -82.219390
Forked Run S.P.	101	E2	39.085000 -81.770460
Geneva S.P.	91	F1	41.852760 -80.963280
Grand Lake Saint Marys S.P.	90	B4	40.549240 -84.436500
Great Seal S.P.	101	D2	39.401930 -82.946050
Guilford Lake S.P.	91	F3	40.796100 -80.893760
Harrison Lake S.P.	90	B2	41.637190 -84.361760
Headlands Beach S.P.	91	E1	41.752140 -81.294480
Hocking Hills S.P.	101	D2	39.494180 -82.611910
Hueston Woods S.P.	100	B1	39.573820 -84.715380
Independence Dam S.P.	90	B2	41.282470 -84.313500
Indian Lake S.P.	90	B4	40.510360 -83.842980
Jackson Lake S.P.	101	D3	38.902850 -82.596780
Jefferson Lake S.P.	91	F4	40.472050 -80.808930
John Bryan S.P.	100	C1	39.791020 -83.867790
Kelleys Island S.P.	91	D2	41.614080 -82.712110
Kiser Lake S.P.	90	B4	40.197650 -83.981740
Lake Alma S.P.	101	D2	39.153450 -82.516810
Lake Hope S.P.	101	E2	39.318500 -82.354920
Lake Logan S.P.	101	D1	39.536400 -82.460590
Lake Loramie S.P.	90	B4	40.359750 -84.359390
Lake White S.P.	101	D2	39.109160 -83.040330
Madison Lake S.P.	100	C1	39.866250 -83.374930
Malabar Farm S.P.	91	D3	40.649590 -82.398390
Mary Jane Thurston S.P.	90	B2	41.409630 -83.881320
Maumee Bay S.P.	90	C2	41.678020 -83.353360
Mohican S.P.	91	D4	40.609510 -82.257600
Mosquito Lake S.P.	91	F2	41.301940 -80.767990
Mount Gilead S.P.	91	D4	40.547820 -82.816770
Muskingum River S.P.	101	E1	40.044140 -81.978260
Nelson-Kennedy Ledges S.P.	91	F2	41.330090 -81.040190
Paint Creek S.P.	100	C2	39.228360 -83.374450
Pike Lake S.P.	101	D2	39.158270 -83.220950
Portage Lakes S.P.	91	E3	40.966260 -81.565190
Punderson S.P.	91	E2	41.461540 -81.219590
Pymatuning S.P.	91	F2	41.580110 -80.541530
Quail Hollow S.P.	91	E3	40.970200 -81.325100
Rocky Fork S.P.	100	C2	39.188310 -83.529730
Salt Fork S.P.	91	E4	40.081830 -81.460400
Scioto Trail S.P.	101	D2	39.223620 -82.931210
Shawnee S.P.	101	D3	38.747670 -83.211220
South Bass Island S.P.	91	D2	41.644690 -82.835950
Stonelick S.P.	100	C2	39.226160 -84.057210
Strouds Run S.P.	101	E2	39.334320 -82.017690
Sycamore S.P.	100	B1	39.803410 -84.373470
Tar Hollow S.P.	101	D2	39.353790 -82.780200
Tinker's Creek S.P.	91	E2	41.276180 -81.368910
Van Buren S.P.	90	C3	41.138290 -83.644940
West Branch S.P.	91	E3	41.133310 -81.189660
Wolf Run S.P.	101	F1	39.789770 -81.540180

OKLAHOMA	PAGE	GRID	LATITUDE LONGITUDE
National Park & Rec. Areas			
Chickasaw N.R.A.	51	F4	34.497390 -96.970110
Winding Stair Mtn. N.R.A.	116	B2	34.749705 -94.793055
State Park & Rec. Areas			
Adair S.P.	106	B4	35.832230 -94.624100
Alabaster Caverns S.P.	51	D1	36.697490 -99.149430
Arrowhead S.P.	116	A1	35.168240 -95.639970
Beaver Dunes S.P.	50	B1	36.841129 -100.514988
Bernice S.P.	106	B3	36.626670 -94.901670
Black Mesa S.P.	49	F1	36.855620 -102.885680
Boggy Depot S.P.	51	F4	34.321747 -96.311302
Boiling Springs S.P.	51	D1	36.452950 -99.298900
Brushy Lake S.P.	116	B1	35.543680 -94.817676
Cherokee Landing S.P.	106	B4	35.758890 -94.908610
Cherokee S.P.	106	B3	36.480280 -95.050560
Clayton Lake S.P.	116	A2	34.549420 -95.308330
Dripping Springs S.P.	51	F3	35.611437 -96.068911
Fort Cobb S.P.	51	D3	35.203720 -98.464990
Foss S.P.	51	D3	35.578510 -99.186830
Gloss Mtn. S.P.	51	D2	36.367190 -98.576460
Great Plains S.P.	51	D4	34.730340 -98.985690
Great Salt Plains S.P.	51	E1	36.753170 -98.149930
Greenleaf S.P.	106	A4	35.623260 -95.180950
Hochatown S.P.	116	B3	34.197390 -94.766300
Honey Creek S.P.	106	B3	36.574060 -94.784370
Hugo Lake S.P.	116	A3	34.016384 -95.375061
Keystone S.P.	51	F2	36.137440 -96.264340
Lake Eucha S.P.	106	B3	36.353930 -94.824000
Lake Eufaula S.P.	116	A1	35.427900 -95.546100
Lake Murray S.P.	51	F4	34.154880 -97.120950
Lake Texoma S.P.	59	F1	33.997590 -96.651310
Lake Thunderbird S.P.	51	E3	35.232320 -97.247550
Lake Wister S.P.	116	B2	34.948700 -94.710400
Little Blue-Disney S.P.	106	B3	36.480260 -95.009130
Little Sahara S.P.	51	D1	36.532900 -98.890870
McGee Creek S.P.	116	A3	34.302927 -95.875467
Natural Falls S.P.	106	B4	36.151900 -94.673300
Okmulgee S.P.	51	F2	35.621900 -96.067700
Osage Hills S.P.	51	F1	36.757360 -96.176220
Raymond Gary S.P.	116	A3	33.997580 -95.253860
Red Rock Canyon S.P.	51	D3	35.456350 -98.358310
Sequoyah Bay S.P.	106	A4	35.886000 -95.276000
Sequoyah S.P.	106	A4	35.932960 -95.230650
Snowdale S.P.	106	A3	36.307710 -95.199040
Spavinaw S.P.	106	B3	36.385890 -95.053290
Talimena S.P.	116	B2	34.788290 -94.950690
Tenkiller S.P.	116	B1	35.598000 -95.031100
Twin Bridges S.P.	106	B2	36.804320 -94.757920
Wah-Sha-She S.P.	51	F1	36.926000 -96.091000
Walnut Creek S.P.	51	F2	36.251210 -96.280130

OREGON	PAGE	GRID	LATITUDE LONGITUDE
National Park & Rec. Areas			
Cascade-Siskiyou Natl. Mon.	28	C2	42.068300 -122.399940
Crater Lake Natl. Park-Annie Spring Ent. Sta.	28	C1	42.868700 -122.169000
Crater Lake Natl. Park-North Ent. Sta.	28	C1	43.086900 -122.116000
Hells Canyon N.R.A.-East Ent.	22	B1	45.500680 -116.806560
Hells Canyon N.R.A.-South Ent.	22	B1	44.903300 -116.957080
Hells Canyon N.R.A.-West Ent.	22	B1	45.176360 -117.040740
John Day Fossil Beds Natl. Mon.-Clarno Unit	21	D2	44.911250 -120.431780
John Day Fossil Beds Natl. Mon.-Painted Hills Unit	21	D3	44.661170 -120.254750
John Day Fossil Beds Natl. Mon.-Sheep Rock Unit	21	E3	44.555480 -119.645010
Lewis & Clark N.H.P.-Fort Clatsop	20	B1	46.138260 -123.876670
Lewis & Clark N.H.P.-Salt Works	20	B1	46.134551 -123.880420
Lewis & Clark N.H.P.-Sunset Beach	20	B1	46.099430 -123.936390
Newberry Natl. Volcanic Mon.	21	D4	43.716800 -121.376960
Oregon Caves Natl. Mon.	28	B2	42.103910 -123.414300
Oregon Dunes N.R.A.-North Ent.	20	A4	43.885610 -124.120860
Oregon Dunes N.R.A.-South Ent.	20	A4	43.579470 -124.186490
State Park & Rec. Areas			
Ainsworth S.P.	20	C2	45.595720 -122.052980
Alfred A. Loeb S.P.	28	A2	42.113180 -124.188520
Beverly Beach S.P.	20	B3	44.726250 -124.057290
Bullards Beach S.P.	28	A1	43.150990 -124.395480
Cape Arago S.P.	20	A4	43.326140 -124.381770
Cape Blanco S.P.	28	A1	42.826660 -124.524640
Cape Lookout S.P.	20	B2	45.367667 -123.961127
Carl G. Washburne Mem. S.P.	20	A3	44.141990 -124.117490
Cascadia S.P.	20	C3	44.397100 -122.477480
Catherine Creek S.P.	22	A2	45.148890 -117.733990
Collier Mem. S.P.	28	C1	42.641810 -121.880630
Ecola S.P.	20	B1	45.916550 -123.967430
Elijah Bristow S.P.	20	C4	43.935470 -122.844270
Fort Columbia S.P.	20	B1	46.252580 -123.921500
Fort Stevens S.P.	20	B1	46.183200 -123.959940
Harris Beach S.P.	28	A2	42.067930 -124.305860
Hat Rock S.P.	21	E1	45.908260 -119.164510
Hilgard Junction S.P.	21	F2	45.342060 -118.236470
Humbug Mtn. S.P.	28	A1	42.686870 -124.445970
Illinois River Forks S.P.	28	B2	42.154870 -123.649870
Jessie M. Honeyman Mem. S.P.	20	A4	43.933440 -124.106440
Lake Owyhee S.P.	22	A4	43.638380 -117.229090
Lapine S.P.	21	D4	43.768452 -121.513399
Maryhill S.P.	21	D1	45.683060 -120.825830
Mayer S.P.	21	D1	45.682780 -121.301080
Milo Mciver S.P.	20	C2	45.306110 -122.372220
Molalla River S.P.	20	C2	45.294840 -122.696400
Nehalem Bay S.P.	20	B1	45.710000 -123.931470
Ona Beach S.P.	20	B3	44.518060 -124.075960
Oswald West S.P.	20	B1	45.770000 -123.958610
Port Orford Heads S.P.	28	A1	42.739470 -124.509730
Prineville Reservoir S.P.	21	D3	44.144660 -120.737770
Robert Straub S.P.	20	B2	45.183160 -123.965116
Rooster Rock S.P.	20	C2	45.546320 -122.236500
Shore Acres S.P.	20	A4	43.329940 -124.376510
Silver Falls S.P.	20	C2	44.853752 -122.662258
Smith Rock S.P.	21	D3	44.360540 -121.138400
South Beach S.P.	20	B3	44.598450 -124.059350
Starvation Creek S.P.	20	C1	45.688550 -121.690180
Stub Stewart S.P.	20	B1	45.739050 -123.199461
Sunset Bay S.P.	20	A4	43.339010 -124.353990
The Cove Palisades S.P.	21	D3	44.557460 -121.262110
Tumalo S.P.	21	D3	44.086760 -121.308730
Umpqua Lighthouse S.P.	20	A4	43.669610 -124.182830
Valley of the Rogue S.P.	28	B1	42.410770 -123.129310
Viento S.P.	20	C1	45.697240 -121.668310
Wallowa Lake S.P.	22	A2	45.280690 -117.208230
White River Falls S.P.	21	D2	45.166870 -121.087420
Willamette Mission S.P.	20	B2	45.080740 -123.031510
William M. Tugman S.P.	20	A4	43.623640 -124.181910

PENNSYLVANIA	PAGE	GRID	LATITUDE LONGITUDE
National Park & Rec. Areas			
Allegheny N.R.A	92	B1	41.943055 -78.867025
Allegheny Portage Railroad N.H.S.	92	B4	40.377020 -78.835870
Eisenhower N.H.S.	103	E1	39.818000 -77.232610
Flight 93 Natl. Mem.	92	B4	40.055200 -78.900900
Fort Necessity Natl. Btld.	102	B1	39.816340 -79.584310
Friendship Hill N.H.S.	102	B1	39.777778 -79.929167
Gettysburg N.M.P.	103	E1	39.811600 -77.226100
Hopewell Furnace N.H.S.	146	B2	40.206760 -75.773570
Johnstown Flood Natl. Mem.	92	B4	40.350710 -78.772480
Valley Forge N.H.P.	146	C2	40.102240 -75.422960
State Park & Rec. Areas			
Bald Eagle S.P.	92	C3	41.041960 -77.642780
Big Spring S.P.	92	C4	40.266850 -77.654410
Black Moshannon S.P.	92	C3	40.915190 -78.058570
Blue Knob S.P.	92	B4	40.265800 -78.584480
Buchanan's Birthplace S.P.	103	D1	39.872660 -77.953190
Caledonia S.P.	103	D1	39.905610 -77.478880
Canoe Creek S.P.	92	C4	40.475070 -78.277290
Chapman S.P.	92	B1	41.757850 -79.170350
Cherry Springs S.P.	92	C2	41.662778 -77.823056
Codorus S.P.	103	E1	39.783180 -76.908920
Colonel Denning S.P.	93	D4	40.281820 -77.416630
Colton Point S.P.	93	D2	41.711180 -77.465430
Cook Forest S.P.	92	B2	41.333790 -79.210440
Cowans Gap S.P.	103	D1	39.997980 -77.921530
Delaware Canal S.P.	146	C1	40.545565 -75.087831
Elk S.P.	92	B2	41.606100 -78.564780
Erie Bluffs S.P.	91	F1	42.008333 -80.410833
Evansburg S.P.	146	C2	40.197510 -75.407080
Frances Slocum S.P.	93	E2	41.347380 -75.893760
French Creek S.P.	146	B2	40.236580 -75.795660
Gouldsboro S.P.	93	F2	41.232250 -75.495730
Greenwood Furnace S.P.	92	C3	40.649610 -77.756090
Hickory Run S.P.	93	F3	41.035170 -75.736220
Hills Creek S.P.	93	D1	41.805190 -77.187600
Hyner Run S.P.	92	C2	41.359150 -77.623850
Kettle Creek S.P.	92	C2	41.377120 -77.930130
Keystone S.P.	92	A4	40.374250 -79.377830
Lackawanna S.P.	93	F2	41.575030 -75.711520
Laurel Hill S.P.	102	B1	39.984470 -79.234840
Laurel Mtn. S.P.	92	B4	40.179670 -79.131530
Laurel Ridge S.P.	92	B4	39.958400 -79.360160
Lehigh Gorge S.P.	93	F3	40.971900 -75.761840
Leonard Harrison S.P.	93	D2	41.698420 -77.450810
Little Buffalo S.P.	93	D4	40.454420 -77.169170
Little Pine S.P.	93	D2	41.371240 -77.360310
Lyman Run S.P.	92	C1	41.723650 -77.768470
Marsh Creek S.P.	146	B3	40.069360 -75.717320
Maurice K. Goddard S.P.	92	A2	41.428380 -80.145140
McConnells Mill S.P.	92	A3	40.963530 -80.168810
Memorial Lake S.P.	93	E4	40.424760 -76.590540
Mont Alto S.P.	103	D1	39.839130 -77.540630
Moraine S.P.	92	A3	40.940280 -80.098520
Nescopeck S.P.	93	E3	41.067100 -75.925300
Nockamixon S.P.	146	C1	40.463630 -75.242010
Ohiopyle S.P.	102	B1	39.865030 -79.504310
Oil Creek S.P.-East Ent.	92	A2	41.512130 -79.661810
Ole Bull S.P.	92	C2	41.543590 -77.709430
Parker Dam S.P.	92	C2	41.205140 -78.504310
Penn-Roosevelt S.P.	92	C3	40.726389 -77.702500
Pine Grove Furnace S.P.	103	D1	40.032910 -77.305070
Poe Paddy S.P.	93	D3	40.834150 -77.417380
Presque Isle S.P.	92	A1	42.114200 -80.153590
Prince Gallitzin S.P.	92	B3	40.669760 -78.575650
Promised Land S.P.	93	F2	41.313560 -75.210370
Pymatuning S.P.	91	F2	41.605440 -80.387840
Raccoon Creek S.P.	91	F4	40.503160 -80.424460
Ralph Stover S.P.	146	C1	40.440420 -75.106050

Raymond B. Winter S.P.	93	D3	40.992340 -77.200450
Ricketts Glen S.P.	93	E2	41.336190 -76.300420
Ryerson Station S.P.	102	A1	39.892310 -80.450030
S.B. Elliott S.P.	92	C3	41.112740 -78.526100
Salt Springs S.P.	93	E1	41.911090 -75.868720
Samuel S. Lewis S.P.	103	E1	39.996580 -76.550410
Shawnee S.P.	102	C1	40.038060 -78.645850
Shikellamy S.P.	93	D3	40.879390 -76.802950
Sinnemahoning S.P.	92	C2	41.450650 -78.055090
Susquehannock S.P.	146	A3	39.805770 -76.283410
Swatara S.P.	93	E4	40.481480 -76.551350
Tobyhanna S.P.	93	F2	41.214130 -75.384030
Trough Creek S.P.	92	C4	40.311620 -78.131820
Tyler S.P.	146	C2	40.233330 -74.951170
Upper Pine Bottom S.P.	93	D2	41.325071 -77.394699
Warriors Path S.P.	92	C4	40.193330 -78.249880
Whipple Dam S.P.	92	C3	40.682250 -77.868410
Worlds End S.P.	93	E2	41.471880 -76.587060
Yellow Creek S.P.	92	B4	40.575830 -79.004420

RHODE ISLAND

RHODE ISLAND	PAGE	GRID	LATITUDE LONGITUDE
State Park & Rec. Areas			
Beavertail S.P.	150	C4	41.457030 -71.396950
Block Island State Beach	95	D4	41.180850 -71.566460
Brenton Point S.P.	150	C4	41.450430 -71.355870
Burlingame S.P.	150	C4	41.361610 -71.701370
Casimir Pulaski Mem. S.P.	150	C3	41.950000 -71.766670
Colt S.P.	151	D3	41.684590 -71.288860
Diamond Hill S.P.	150	C2	42.009620 -71.431630
East Matunuck State Beach	150	C4	41.378350 -71.525630
Fishermen's Mem. S.P.	150	C4	41.380630 -71.488000
Fort Adams S.P.	150	C4	41.469150 -71.339990
Goddard Mem. S.P.	150	C3	41.651030 -71.442040
Haines Mem. S.P.	150	C3	41.752960 -71.348600
Misquamicut State Beach	95	D4	41.324510 -71.800670
R.W. Wheeler State Beach	150	C4	41.372620 -71.495530
Scarborough State Beach	150	C4	41.389770 -71.474260

SOUTH CAROLINA

SOUTH CAROLINA	PAGE	GRID	LATITUDE LONGITUDE
National Park & Rec. Areas			
Charles Pinckney N.H.S.	131	D2	32.847150 -79.824090
Congaree Natl. Park	122	A4	33.836100 -80.827660
Kings Mtn. N.M.P.	122	A1	35.140120 -81.386890
Ninety Six N.H.S.	121	F3	34.162740 -82.010980
State Park & Rec. Areas			
Andrew Jackson S.P.	122	B2	34.839560 -80.810110
Barnwell S.P.	130	B1	33.329250 -81.300400
Calhoun Falls S.P.	121	E3	34.106792 -82.604200
Cheraw S.P.	122	C2	34.642370 -79.927640
Colleton S.P.	130	C1	33.063520 -80.613440
Devils Fork S.P.	121	E2	34.952527 -82.946085
Edisto Beach S.P.	130	C2	32.505410 -80.310310
Givhans Ferry S.P.	130	C1	33.031640 -80.382150
Hickory Knob State Resort Park	121	E4	33.884250 -82.416010
Huntington Beach S.P.	123	D4	33.502650 -79.081200
Jones Gap S.P.	121	E1	35.126360 -82.558350
Kings Mtn. S.P.	122	A1	35.113030 -81.394040
Lake Warren S.P.	130	B2	32.844830 -81.165070
Little Pee Dee S.P.	122	C3	34.331020 -79.282170
Myrtle Beach S.P.	123	D4	33.649210 -78.938600
N.R. Goodale S.P.	122	B3	34.281580 -80.525150
Oconee S.P.	121	E2	34.867297 -83.106098
Paris Mtn. S.P.	121	E2	34.924970 -82.365540
Poinsett S.P.	122	B4	33.804360 -80.544920
Santee S.P.	122	B4	33.500200 -80.489820
Table Rock S.P.	121	E2	35.022050 -82.710700

SOUTH DAKOTA

SOUTH DAKOTA	PAGE	GRID	LATITUDE LONGITUDE
National Park & Rec. Areas			
Badlands Natl. Park-Interior Ent.	26	B4	43.741900 -101.957000
Badlands Natl. Park-Northeast Ent.	26	B4	43.792400 -101.906000
Badlands Natl. Park-Pinnacles Ent.	26	B4	43.885500 -102.238000
Jewel Cave Natl. Mon.	25	F4	43.736500 -103.819940
Minuteman Missile N.H.S.	26	B4	43.833931 -101.899685
Mount Rushmore Natl. Mem.	26	A4	43.886730 -103.440610
Wind Cave Natl. Park-Vis. Ctr.	26	A4	43.556100 -103.478000
State Park & Rec. Areas			
Bear Butte S.P.	26	A3	44.460580 -103.433750
Custer S.P.	26	A4	43.770310 -103.440130
Fisher Grove S.P.	27	E2	44.883340 -98.356660
Hartford Beach S.P.	27	F2	45.398870 -96.665260
Lake Herman S.P.	27	F4	43.993120 -97.159790
Newton Hills S.P.	35	F1	43.218860 -96.569700
Oakwood Lakes S.P.	27	F3	44.454310 -96.989490
Palisades S.P.	27	F4	43.687970 -96.511470
Roy Lake S.P.	27	E1	45.703360 -97.419650
Sica Hollow S.P.	27	E1	45.740690 -97.229150
Union Grove S.P.	35	F1	42.922630 -96.785530

TENNESSEE

TENNESSEE	PAGE	GRID	LATITUDE LONGITUDE
National Park & Rec. Areas			
Andrew Johnson N.H.S.	111	D4	36.157710 -82.836880
Big South Fork Natl. River & Rec. Area	110	B3	36.475400 -84.752100
State Park & Rec. Areas			
Big Hill Pond S.P.	119	D1	35.078890 -88.718860
Big Ridge S.P.	110	C3	36.241600 -83.929280
Bledsoe Creek S.P.	109	F3	36.378050 -86.356660
Cedars of Lebanon S.P. & Forest	109	F4	36.093930 -86.335620
Chickasaw S.P.	119	D1	35.393241 -88.772298
Cove Lake S.P.	110	C3	36.305830 -84.210750
Cumberland Mtn. S.P.	110	B4	35.898460 -84.995130
David Crockett S.P.	119	E1	35.242690 -87.354850
Davy Crockett Birthplace S.P.	111	E3	36.221980 -82.662770
Edgar Evins S.P.	110	A4	36.086050 -85.812460
Fall Creek Falls S.P.	120	B1	35.622200 -85.208000
Frozen Head S.P. & Nat. Area-North Ent.	110	B4	36.122550 -84.433320
Frozen Head S.P. & Nat. Area-South Ent.	110	B4	36.102180 -84.446970
Harpeth River S.P.	109	E4	36.079240 -86.956920
Harrison Bay S.P.	120	B1	35.175850 -85.115350
Henry Horton S.P.	119	F1	35.596510 -86.698690
Hiwassee–Ocoee Scenic Rivers S.P.	120	C1	35.224557 -84.504269
Indian Mtn. S.P.	110	C3	36.583050 -84.139900
Long Hunter S.P.	109	F4	36.094340 -86.557330
Meeman-Shelby Forest S.P.	118	B1	35.336800 -90.029010
Montgomery Bell S.P.	109	E4	36.106750 -87.268690
Mousetail Landing S.P.	109	D4	35.581900 -87.859100
Natchez Trace S.P.	109	D4	35.839580 -88.252820
Nathan Bedford Forrest S.P.	109	D4	36.087900 -87.979750
Norris Dam S.P.	110	C3	36.234560 -84.127020
Old Stone Fort State Arch. Park	120	A1	35.487270 -86.101330
Panther Creek S.P.	111	D3	36.212760 -83.412420
Paris Landing State Resort Park	109	D3	36.441760 -88.090180
Pickett S.P.	110	B3	36.537374 -84.802126
Pickwick Landing S.P.	119	D2	35.051790 -88.224650
Pinson Mounds State Arch. Park	119	D1	35.504130 -88.683020
Reelfoot Lake S.P.	108	B3	36.414410 -89.426880
Roan Mtn. S.P.	111	E4	36.161110 -82.097000
Rock Island S.P.	110	A4	35.810000 -85.641550
Standing Stone S.P.	110	A3	36.458910 -85.437690
T.O. Fuller S.P.	118	B2	35.057810 -90.113650
Tims Ford S.P.	120	A1	35.220999 -86.255889
Warriors Path S.P.	111	E5	36.504610 -82.481090

TEXAS

TEXAS	PAGE	GRID	LATITUDE LONGITUDE
National Park & Rec. Areas			
Alibates Flint Quarries Natl. Mon.	50	A3	35.571900 -101.633880
Amistad N.R.A.	60	B2	29.449920 -101.053170
Big Bend Natl. Park-North Ent.	62	C4	29.680900 -103.167000
Big Bend Natl. Park-West Ent.	62	C4	29.306600 -103.523000
Fort Davis N.H.S.	62	B2	30.604120 -103.886010
Guadalupe Mts. Natl. Park-Vis. Ctr.	57	D3	31.894300 -104.822000
Lyndon B. Johnson N.H.P.	61	D2	30.276020 -98.411990
Padre Island Natl. Seashore	63	F3	27.553470 -97.248370
Palo Alto Btld. N.H.S.	63	F4	26.011630 -97.481570
State Park & Rec. Areas			
Abilene S.P.	58	C3	32.241360 -99.879230
Atlanta S.P.	124	C1	33.229500 -94.249300
Balmorhea S.P.	62	B2	30.946270 -103.784890
Bastrop S.P.	61	E2	30.098960 -97.229090
Bentsen-Rio Grande Valley S.P.	63	E4	26.182530 -98.382360
Big Bend Ranch S.P.	62	B4	29.265070 -103.791910
Big Spring S.P.	58	A3	32.229650 -101.483090
Blanco S.P.	61	D2	30.093240 -98.423420
Bonham S.P.	59	F1	33.543100 -96.149640
Brazos Bend S.P.	132	A4	29.371480 -95.631890
Buescher S.P.	61	E2	30.073570 -97.176140
Caddo Lake S.P.	124	C2	32.684230 -94.177070
Caprock Canyons S.P.	50	B4	34.406440 -101.048830
Choke Canyon S.P.-Calliham Unit	61	D4	28.460970 -98.356380
Choke Canyon S.P.-South Shore Unit	61	D4	28.467610 -98.239550
Cleburne S.P.	59	E3	32.265180 -97.560680
Colorado Bend S.P.	61	D1	31.062510 -98.504250
Cooper Lake S.P.	124	A1	33.305282 -95.648346
Copper Breaks S.P.	50	C4	34.113660 -99.747800
Daingerfield S.P.	124	B1	33.028720 -94.714510
Davis Mts. S.P.	62	B2	30.599520 -103.929220
Dinosaur Valley S.P.	59	E3	32.250020 -97.814620
Eisenhower S.P.	59	F1	33.822670 -96.612020
Fairfield Lake S.P.	59	F3	31.765910 -96.076220
Falcon S.P.	63	D3	26.583500 -99.144790
Fort Boggy S.P.	124	A4	31.189627 -95.986069
Fort Griffin S.P. & Hist. Site	58	C2	32.924690 -99.219370
Fort Parker S.P.	59	F4	31.592650 -96.524370
Fort Richardson S.P. & Hist. Site	59	D2	33.206060 -98.164810
Franklin Mts. S.P.	56	C3	31.912060 -106.517140
Galveston Island S.P.	132	B4	29.196240 -94.956210
Garner S.P.	60	C2	29.600900 -99.744220
Goliad S.P.	61	E4	28.655190 -97.383580
Goose Island S.P.	61	F4	28.134060 -96.984350
Guadalupe River S.P.	61	D2	29.849890 -98.509590
Huntsville S.P.	132	A2	30.638130 -95.511370
Inks Lake S.P.	61	D1	30.738290 -98.366450
Kerrville-Schreiner S.P.	60	C2	30.007930 -99.117640
Lake Arrowhead S.P.	59	D1	33.759300 -98.396610
Lake Bob Sandlin S.P.	124	B1	33.054090 -95.101250
Lake Brownwood S.P.	59	D3	31.857370 -99.021280
Lake Casa Blanca International S.P.	63	D2	27.536739 -99.432449
Lake Colorado City S.P.	58	B3	32.313460 -100.924080
Lake Corpus Christi S.P.	61	E4	28.060360 -97.867690
Lake Livingston S.P.	132	B1	30.671300 -95.008200
Lake Mineral Wells S.P.	59	E2	32.814570 -98.042270
Lake Somerville S.P.	61	F1	30.315760 -96.625080
Lake Tawakoni S.P.	59	F2	32.841610 -95.990710
Lake Texana S.P.	61	F3	28.953610 -96.567190
Lake Whitney S.P.	59	E3	31.924780 -97.356280
Lockhart S.P.	61	E2	29.857610 -97.697400
Longhorn Cavern S.P.	61	D1	30.686610 -98.351380
Lyndon B. Johnson S.P. & Hist. Site-Ranch Unit	61	D2	30.235180 -98.629100
Martin Creek Lake S.P.	124	B3	32.283090 -94.583470
Martin Dies Junior S.P.	132	C1	30.848980 -94.164720
Meridian S.P.	59	E3	31.892440 -97.695670
Mission Tejas S.P.	124	A4	31.546110 -95.234720
Monahans Sandhills S.P.	57	F4	31.634940 -102.814850
Mother Neff S.P.	59	E4	31.319150 -97.474210
Mustang Island S.P.	63	F2	27.677020 -97.173730
Palmetto S.P.	61	E2	29.597280 -97.584640
Palo Duro Canyon S.P.	50	B3	34.985710 -101.703190
Pedernales Falls S.P.	61	D1	30.273110 -98.256830
Possum Kingdom S.P.	59	D2	32.878970 -98.561740
Purtis Creek S.P.	124	A2	32.373340 -95.974530
Ray Roberts Lake S.P.	59	F1	33.444050 -96.925860
Rusk–Palestine S.P.-East	124	B3	31.803560 -95.194880
Rusk–Palestine S.P.-West	124	A4	31.739260 -95.570450
Sabine Pass Battleground S.P. & Hist. Site	132	C3	29.726520 -93.878280
San Angelo S.P.	58	B4	31.491919 -100.547148
Sea Rim S.P.	132	C3	29.677900 -94.039900
Seminole Canyon S.P. & Hist. Site	60	A2	29.709000 -101.298480
South Llano River S.P.	60	C1	30.445430 -99.804610
Stephen F. Austin S.P.	61	F2	29.812030 -96.108200
Texas State Railroad S.P.	124	B3	31.805820 -95.194550
Tyler S.P.	124	A2	32.481750 -95.281760

UTAH

UTAH	PAGE	GRID	LATITUDE LONGITUDE
National Park & Rec. Areas			
Arches Natl. Park	40	A2	38.615570 -109.616920
Bryce Canyon Natl. Park	39	E4	37.641700 -112.168000
Canyonlands Natl. Park-East Ent.	40	A3	38.168510 -109.750980
Canyonlands Natl. Park-Horseshoe Canyon Unit	39	F3	38.497740 -110.205960
Canyonlands Natl. Park-North Ent.	40	A3	38.490150 -109.807930
Canyonlands Natl. Park-West Ent.	40	A3	38.255440 -110.180050
Capitol Reef Natl. Park	39	E3	38.291020 -111.261410
Cedar Breaks Natl. Mon.-East Ent.	39	D4	37.655230 -112.811350
Cedar Breaks Natl. Mon.-North Ent.	39	D4	37.665730 -112.838130
Cedar Breaks Natl. Mon.-South Ent.	39	D4	37.598730 -112.850080
Glen Canyon N.R.A.	39	F4	38.255440 -110.180050
Golden Spike N.H.S.	31	E3	41.620482 -112.547471
Grand Staircase-Escalante Natl. Mon.	39	E4	37.420000 -111.550000
Natural Bridges Natl. Mon.	39	F4	37.608120 -109.966280
Rainbow Bridge Natl. Mon.	47	F1	37.110810 -110.406050
Zion Natl. Park-East Ent.	39	D4	37.235370 -112.864470
Zion Natl. Park-Main Ent.	39	D4	37.201970 -112.988380
State Park & Rec. Areas			
Anasazi S.P. Mus.	39	E3	37.922399 -111.425743
Antelope Island S.P.	31	E4	41.089290 -112.116490
Bear Lake (Rendezvous Beach) S.P.	31	F2	41.962200 -111.400320
Bear Lake S.P.	31	F2	41.965360 -111.399480
Camp Floyd– Stagecoach Inn S.P.	31	E4	40.258360 -112.097270
Coral Pink Sand Dunes S.P.-North Ent.	47	D1	37.065540 -112.705530
Coral Pink Sand Dunes S.P.-West Ent.	47	D1	37.034580 -112.741260
Dead Horse Point S.P.	40	A3	38.510220 -109.729460
Deer Creek S.P.	31	F4	40.452620 -111.477820
Edge of the Cedars S.P.	40	A4	37.629760 -109.491730
Escalante S.P.	39	E4	37.783820 -111.630220
Fremont Indian S.P.	39	D3	38.579537 -112.314773
Goblin Valley S.P.	39	F3	38.580620 -110.712580
Goosenecks S.P.	40	A4	37.174730 -109.926950
Green River S.P.	39	F2	38.995500 -110.156910
Gunlock S.P.-North Ent.	38	C4	37.275970 -113.768780
Gunlock S.P.-South Ent.	38	C4	37.251490 -113.772820
Huntington S.P.	39	F2	39.315200 -110.977100
Hyrum S.P.	31	E3	41.626220 -111.872170
Iron Mission S.P.	39	D4	37.688349 -113.061896
Kodachrome Basin S.P.	39	E4	37.501670 -111.993610
Millsite S.P.	39	E2	39.099020 -111.184240
Otter Creek S.P.	39	E3	38.167430 -112.021570
Palisade S.P.	39	E2	39.195800 -111.691600
Piute S.P.	39	E3	38.322530 -112.204200
Quail Creek S.P.	39	D4	37.105000 -113.576600
Red Fleet S.P.	32	B4	40.553300 -109.518472
Rockport S.P.	31	F4	40.751890 -111.367410
Sand Hollow S.P.	46	C1	37.144830 -113.382139
Scofield S.P.	39	E1	39.708600 -110.921000
Snow Canyon S.P.-East Ent.	38	C4	37.212120 -113.630870
Snow Canyon S.P.-North Ent.	38	C4	37.256790 -113.632990
Snow Canyon S.P.-South Ent.	38	C4	37.183380 -113.645010

	PAGE	GRID	LATITUDE LONGITUDE
Starvation S.P.	32	A4	40.104100 -110.330900
Steinaker S.P.-North Ent.	32	A4	40.534870 -109.522440
Steinaker S.P.-South Ent.	32	A4	40.504850 -109.528870
Territorial Statehouse S.P.	39	D2	38.985880 -112.353530
Wasatch Mtn. S.P.	31	F4	40.477770 -111.519990
Willard Bay S.P.-North Ent.	31	E3	41.418810 -112.052390
Willard Bay S.P.-South Ent.	31	E3	41.350610 -112.069060
Yuba S.P.	39	E2	39.381240 -112.028360

VERMONT

VERMONT	PAGE	GRID	LATITUDE LONGITUDE
National Park & Rec. Areas			
Marsh-Billings-Rockefeller N.H.P.	81	E3	43.635833 -72.538333
State Park & Rec. Areas			
Allis S.P.	81	E3	44.051150 -72.626440
Branbury S.P.	81	D3	43.904250 -73.065370
Burton Island S.P.	81	D1	44.779660 -73.180050
Camp Plymouth S.P.	81	E4	43.475810 -72.694987
D.A.R. S.P.	81	D3	44.058850 -73.409210
Emerald Lake S.P.	81	D4	43.283790 -73.002250
Gifford Woods S.P.	81	D3	43.676500 -72.810860
Half Moon S.P.	81	D3	43.699720 -73.223220
Kingsland Bay S.P.	81	D2	44.226230 -73.277660
Lake Saint Catherine S.P.	81	D4	43.483000 -73.202580
Little River S.P.	81	D2	44.388940 -72.768360
Molly Stark S.P.	94	C1	42.854920 -72.813790
North Hero S.P.	81	D1	44.908210 -73.235110
Ricker Pond S.P.	81	E2	44.251467 -72.247550
Stillwater S.P.	81	E2	44.280200 -72.275060
Townshend S.P.	81	E4	43.041920 -72.691600
Underhill S.P.	81	D2	44.528880 -72.843920
Woodford S.P.	94	C1	42.894450 -73.037790
Woods Island S.P.	81	D1	44.802500 -73.209283

VIRGINIA

VIRGINIA	PAGE	GRID	LATITUDE LONGITUDE
National Park & Rec. Areas			
Appomattox Court House N.H.P.	112	C1	37.377367 -78.795290
Booker T. Washington Natl. Mon.	112	B2	37.120500 -79.733340
Cedar Creek & Belle Grove N.H.P.	102	C2	39.023500 -78.289000
Colonial N.H.P.	114	A4	37.211390 -76.776730
Cumberland Gap N.H.P.-Vis. Ctr.	111	D3	36.602600 -83.695400
Fredericksburg & Spotsylvania N.M.P.	103	D4	38.254300 -77.451890
George Washington Birthplace Natl. Mon.	114	A2	38.192353 -76.927192
Manassas Natl. Bfld. Park	144	A3	38.806030 -77.572810
Mount Rogers N.R.A.	111	F2	36.811360 -81.420130
Shenandoah Natl. Park-Front Royal North Ent.	102	C3	38.903300 -78.192400
Shenandoah Natl. Park-Rockfish Gap South Ent.	102	C3	38.033900 -78.858900
Shenandoah Natl. Park-Swift Run Gap Ent.	102	C3	38.359100 -78.546700
Shenandoah Natl. Park-Thornton Gap Ent.	102	C3	38.662300 -78.320600
State Park & Rec. Areas			
Bear Creek Lake S.P.	113	D1	37.532970 -78.274890
Belle Isle S.P.	114	B2	37.774526 -76.599222
Chippokes Plantation S.P.	114	A4	37.140400 -76.748590
Claytor Lake S.P.	112	A2	37.057620 -80.622140
Douthat S.P.	102	B4	37.914520 -79.796740
Fairy Stone S.P.	112	B2	36.791790 -80.117890
False Cape S.P.	115	F1	36.691370 -75.924410
First Landing S.P.	114	B4	36.915601 -76.057000
Grayson Highlands S.P.	111	F3	36.611920 -81.489900
Holliday Lake S.P.	113	D1	37.404610 -78.644920
Hungry Mother S.P.	111	F2	36.880860 -81.525750
James River S.P.	112	C1	37.540400 -78.839300
Kiptopeke S.P.	114	B4	37.169292 -75.982919
Lake Anna S.P.	103	D4	38.125850 -77.821690
Leesylvania S.P.	103	E3	38.591200 -77.248400
Mason Neck S.P.	103	E3	38.640740 -77.194400
Natural Tunnel S.P.	111	E3	36.707520 -82.744090
New River Trail S.P.	112	A2	36.870180 -80.868550
Occoneechee S.P.	113	D3	36.633330 -78.525420
Pocahontas S.P.	113	E1	37.366240 -77.573870
Sailor's Creek Bfld. Hist. S.P.	113	D1	37.298470 -78.229470
Smith Mtn. Lake S.P.	112	B2	37.091110 -79.592110
Twin Lakes S.P.	113	D2	37.336900 -77.934100
Westmoreland S.P.	103	E4	38.158690 -76.870120
Wilderness Road S.P.	111	D3	36.621300 -83.512900
York River S.P.	113	F1	37.414190 -76.713650

WASHINGTON

WASHINGTON	PAGE	GRID	LATITUDE LONGITUDE
National Park & Rec. Areas			
Columbia River Gorge Natl. Scenic Area	21	D1	45.715322 -121.818667
Fort Vancouver N.H.S.	20	C1	45.626940 -122.656310
Hanford Reach Natl. Mon.	13	E4	46.483333 -119.533333
Lake Chelan N.R.A.	13	D2	48.309080 -120.657730
Lake Roosevelt N.R.A.	13	F2	47.972680 -118.970580
Lewis & Clark N.H.P.-Discovery Trail	12	B4	46.370033 -124.053503
Lewis & Clark N.H.P.-Dismal Nitch	20	B1	46.249033 -123.862903
Lewis & Clark N.H.P.-Sta. Camp	20	B1	46.263111 -123.932571
Mount Baker N.R.A.	12	C1	48.714167 -121.805900
Mount Rainier Natl. Park-Carbon River Ent.	12	C6	46.994810 -121.918090
Mount Rainier Natl. Park-Nisqually Ent.	12	C5	46.741400 -121.919040
Mount Rainier Natl. Park-Stevens Canyon Ent.	12	C7	46.754730 -121.557010
Mount Rainier Natl. Park-White River Ent.	12	C8	46.902040 -121.554340
Mount Saint Helens Natl. Mon.	12	C4	46.277590 -122.218820
North Cascades Natl. Park-Golden West	13	D1	48.308200 -120.655000
North Cascades Natl. Park-Northern Cascades Vis. Ctr.	13	D1	48.666100 -121.264000
Olympic Natl. Park-Vis. Ctr.	12	B2	48.096700 -123.428000
Olympic Natl. Park-Vis. Ctr.-Hoh Rain Forest	12	B2	47.860700 -123.935000
Olympic Natl. Park-Vis. Ctr.-Hurricane Ridge	12	B2	47.969200 -123.498000
Ross Lake N.R.A.	13	D1	48.674250 -121.244730
San Juan Island N.H.P.	12	B2	48.534580 -123.016250
Whitman Mission N.H.S.	21	F1	46.040910 -118.468110
State Park & Rec. Areas			
Alta Lake S.P.	13	E2	48.031990 -119.934710
Anderson Lake S.P.	12	C2	48.014590 -122.810680
Belfair S.P.	12	C3	47.430630 -122.881400
Birch Bay S.P.	12	C1	48.903210 -122.757880
Bogachiel S.P.	12	A2	47.894790 -124.362820
Brooks Mem. S.P.	21	D1	45.950590 -120.664200
Camano Island S.P.	12	C2	48.131680 -122.503240
Cape Disappointment S.P.	20	B1	46.294210 -124.053610
Columbia Hills S.P.	21	D1	45.643030 -121.106410
Crawford S.P.	14	A1	48.992070 -117.370370
Curlew Lake S.P.	13	F1	48.719280 -118.661740
Damon Point S.P.	12	B4	46.945300 -124.132100
Deception Pass S.P.	12	C2	48.390970 -122.646880
Dosewallips S.P.	12	C3	47.687570 -122.899860
Fields Spring S.P.	22	A1	46.087520 -117.173650
Flaming Geyser S.P.	12	C3	47.280230 -122.041870
Fort Casey S.P.	12	C2	48.159760 -122.672410
Fort Okanogan S.P.	13	E2	48.102370 -119.678720
Fort Simcoe S.P.	13	D4	46.345340 -120.823460
Ginkgo Petrified Forest S.P.	13	E4	46.949010 -119.997490
Goldendale Observatory S.P.	21	D1	45.837090 -120.815890
Griffiths-Priday S.P.	12	B3	47.125100 -124.179900
Ike Kinswa S.P.	12	C4	46.555780 -122.536570
Jarrell Cove S.P.	12	B3	47.285940 -122.881080
Joseph Whidbey S.P.	12	C2	48.308370 -122.713170
Kitsap Mem. S.P.	12	C3	47.816580 -122.646840
Lake Chelan S.P.	13	D2	47.869430 -120.191110
Lake Easton S.P.	13	D3	47.249380 -121.190920
Lake Wenatchee S.P.	13	D3	47.816340 -120.729780
Larrabee S.P.	12	C2	48.650620 -122.489810
Lewis & Clark S.P.	12	C4	46.525850 -122.817910
Lewis & Clark Trail S.P.	13	F4	46.287600 -118.073340
Lincoln Rock S.P.	13	D3	47.535490 -120.282280
Millersylvania S.P.	12	B4	46.909610 -122.905950
Moran S.P.	12	C1	48.657700 -122.859630
Mount Spokane S.P.	14	B2	47.899290 -117.124350
Nolte S.P.	12	C3	47.267320 -121.943420
Ocean City S.P.	12	B4	47.038520 -124.158130
Old Fort Townsend S.P.	12	C2	48.078260 -122.805690
Osoyoos S.P.	13	E1	48.950060 -119.434350
Pacific Beach S.P.	12	A3	47.205980 -124.202220
Pacific Pines S.P.	12	B4	46.507610 -124.049150
Palouse Falls S.P.	13	F4	46.664030 -118.228660
Peace Arch S.P.	12	C1	49.000980 -122.751580
Pearrygin Lake S.P.	13	E2	48.496720 -120.146950
Peshastin Pinnacles S.P.	13	D3	47.578810 -120.613860
Potholes S.P.	13	E4	46.970780 -119.351180
Potlatch S.P.	12	B3	47.363000 -123.158140
Rainbow Falls S.P.	12	B4	46.631010 -123.237350
Rockport S.P.	12	C2	48.487920 -121.601870
Sacajawea S.P.	21	F1	46.210140 -119.046050
Scenic Beach S.P.	12	C3	47.649250 -122.845470
Seaquest S.P.	12	C4	46.295880 -122.820860
Sequim Bay S.P.	12	B2	48.040750 -123.030920
Shine Tidelands S.P.	12	C2	47.867990 -122.638700
Steamboat Rock S.P.	13	E2	47.828650 -119.134340
Sun Lakes S.P.	13	E3	47.596540 -119.387760
Triton Cove S.P.	12	B3	47.609112 -122.986526
Twenty-Five Mile Creek S.P.	13	D2	47.992520 -120.263610
Twin Harbors S.P.	12	B4	46.858850 -124.104210
Wallace Falls S.P.	12	C2	47.865610 -121.680050
Wanapum S.P.	13	E4	46.924760 -119.991690
Westport Light S.P.	12	B4	46.891700 -124.111630

WEST VIRGINIA

WEST VIRGINIA	PAGE	GRID	LATITUDE LONGITUDE
National Park & Rec. Areas			
Bluestone Natl. Scenic River	112	A1	37.584300 -80.957900
Gauley River N.R.A.	101	F4	38.191800 -81.001920
Harpers Ferry N.H.P.	103	D2	39.318820 -77.759060
New River Gorge Natl. River	101	F4	37.875670 -81.077598
Spruce Knob Seneca Rocks N.R.A.	102	B3	38.681180 -79.544480
State Park & Rec. Areas			
Audra S.P.	102	A2	39.041110 -80.067500
Beartown S.P.	102	A4	38.051750 -80.275420
Blennerhassett Island Hist. S.P.	101	E2	39.273300 -81.644800
Bluestone S.P.	112	A1	37.623050 -80.934710
Cacapon Resort S.P.	102	C1	39.502980 -78.291330
Camp Creek S.P.	111	F1	37.508173 -81.132873
Carnifex Ferry Bfld. S.P.	101	F4	38.211290 -80.941850
Cass Scenic Railroad S.P.	102	A3	38.396520 -79.914280
Cedar Creek S.P.	101	F3	38.880780 -80.849420
Droop Mtn. Bfld. S.P.	102	A4	38.113200 -80.271670
Holly River S.P.	102	A3	38.653140 -80.382620
Little Beaver S.P.	112	A1	37.756570 -81.079780
Moncove Lake S.P.	112	B1	37.616950 -80.354730
Pinnacle Rock S.P.	111	F1	37.308190 -81.291430
Prickett's Fort S.P.	102	A1	39.514090 -80.099960
Tomlinson Run S.P.	91	F4	40.550660 -80.595950
Tygart Lake S.P.	102	A2	39.248160 -80.021060
Valley Falls S.P.	102	A2	39.392900 -80.070480
Watoga S.P.	102	A4	38.122510 -80.155660
Watters Smith Mem. S.P.	102	A2	39.174520 -80.414260

WISCONSIN

WISCONSIN	PAGE	GRID	LATITUDE LONGITUDE
National Park & Rec. Areas			
Apostle Islands Natl. Lakeshore	65	D4	46.812210 -90.820780
Saint Croix Natl. Scenic Riverway	67	E2	45.415700 -92.646270
State Park & Rec. Areas			
Amnicon Falls S.P.	64	C4	46.608210 -91.887850
Aztalan S.P.	74	B3	43.068310 -88.863750
Belmont Mound S.P.	74	A4	42.768611 -90.349444
Big Bay S.P.	65	D4	46.811030 -90.696960
Big Foot Beach S.P.	74	C4	42.567330 -88.436790
Blue Mound S.P.	74	A3	43.026990 -89.840740
Brunet Island S.P.	67	F3	45.176220 -91.161610
Buckhorn S.P.	74	A1	43.948280 -90.002130
Copper Culture S.P.	68	C4	44.887440 -87.897940
Copper Falls S.P.	65	D4	46.351710 -90.643670
Council Grounds S.P.	68	A3	45.184840 -89.734290
Devil's Lake S.P.	74	A2	43.429010 -89.734900
Governor Dodge S.P.	74	A3	43.019560 -90.141950
Governor Thompson S.P.	68	C3	45.326309 -88.219205
Harrington Beach S.P.	75	D2	43.499430 -87.811890
Hartman Creek S.P.	74	B1	44.318070 -89.194320
High Cliff S.P.	74	C1	44.166680 -88.291760
Interstate S.P.	67	D3	45.396410 -92.636580
Kinnickinnic S.P.	67	D4	44.837280 -92.733190
Kohler-Andrae S.P.	75	D2	43.672740 -87.719320
Lake Kegonsa S.P.	74	B3	42.978005 -89.230300
Lake Wissota S.P.	67	F4	44.980950 -91.313740
Merrick S.P.	73	E1	44.152740 -91.744120
Mill Bluff S.P.	74	A1	43.961610 -90.317980
Mirror Lake S.P.	74	A2	43.568770 -89.834930
Natural Bridge S.P.	74	A2	43.344930 -89.928290
Nelson Dewey S.P.	73	F4	42.743740 -91.037860
New Glarus Woods S.P.	74	B4	42.786830 -89.631980
Newport S.P.	69	D3	45.241470 -86.998830
Pattison S.P.	64	C4	46.535290 -92.121410
Peninsula S.P.	69	D3	45.133080 -87.213280
Perrot S.P.	73	F1	44.016350 -91.479670
Potawatomi S.P.	69	D4	44.849990 -87.407640
Rib Mtn. S.P.	68	B4	44.915800 -89.669360
Roche-A-Cri S.P.	74	A1	43.996120 -89.812370
Rock Island S.P.	69	E3	45.398990 -86.855970
Rocky Arbor S.P.	74	A2	43.647890 -89.808240
Straight Lake S.P.	67	E2	45.597399 -92.406609
Tower Hill S.P.	74	A3	43.147090 -90.043750
Whitefish Dunes S.P.	69	D4	44.928910 -87.182150
Wildcat Mtn. S.P.	74	A2	43.688870 -90.566800
Willow River S.P.	67	D3	45.017610 -92.672610
Wyalusing S.P.	73	F3	42.978770 -91.118560
Yellowstone Lake S.P.	74	A4	42.777360 -89.993540

WYOMING

WYOMING	PAGE	GRID	LATITUDE LONGITUDE
National Park & Rec. Areas			
Devils Tower Natl. Mon.	25	E3	44.586870 -104.706710
Flaming Gorge N.R.A.	32	A3	41.254860 -109.611400
Fort Laramie N.H.S.	33	E2	42.202530 -104.558590
Fossil Butte Natl. Mon.	31	F2	41.855370 -110.782340
Grand Teton Natl. Park-Granite Canyon Ent.	23	F4	43.597990 -110.801640
Grand Teton Natl. Park-Moose Ent.	23	F4	43.655860 -110.718350
Grand Teton Natl. Park-Moran Ent.	23	F4	43.843640 -110.511950
Medicine Wheel Natl. Hist. Landmark	24	C2	44.826200 -107.921717
Yellowstone Natl. Park-East Ent.	23	F3	44.489540 -110.001560
Yellowstone Natl. Park-North East Ent.	23	F3	45.006120 -109.991550
Yellowstone Natl. Park-North Ent.	23	F3	45.030110 -110.705460
Yellowstone Natl. Park-South Ent.	23	F3	44.134730 -110.666170
Yellowstone Natl. Park-West Ent.	23	F3	44.658720 -111.098970
State Park & Rec. Areas			
Bear River S.P.	31	F3	41.267257 -110.938030
Boysen S.P.	32	C1	43.270160 -108.115260
Buffalo Bill S.P.	24	B3	44.505020 -109.249540
Curt Gowdy S.P.	33	E3	41.175380 -105.243640
Edness K. Wilkins S.P.	33	D1	42.857220 -106.177370
Glendo S.P.	33	E1	42.476060 -104.998910
Guernsey S.P.	33	E2	42.287400 -104.763460
Hot Springs S.P.	24	C4	43.653980 -108.201790
Keyhole S.P.	25	E3	44.356490 -104.825810
Seminoe S.P.	33	D2	42.150350 -106.905870
Sinks Canyon S.P.	32	B1	42.752600 -108.804770
John D. Rockefeller Jr. Mem. Parkway	24	A3	44.108800 -110.685508

CANADA

ALBERTA	PAGE	GRID	LATITUDE LONGITUDE
National Park & Rec. Areas			
Banff Natl. Park-Banff Vis. Ctr.	164	B2	51.177400 -115.570900
Banff Natl. Park-Lake Louise Vis. Ctr.	164	B2	51.425200 -116.178400
Banff Park Mus. N.H.S.	164	B3	51.174300 -115.571100
Bar U Ranch N.H.S.	164	C3	50.420300 -114.244400
Cave and Basin N.H.S.	164	B3	51.168300 -115.591400
Elk Island Natl. Park	159	D4	53.572500 -112.841900
Jasper Natl. Park-Icefield Center	164	A1	52.233500 -117.234800
Jasper Natl. Park-Jasper Information Center	164	A1	52.877300 -118.080900
Rocky Mtn. House N.H.S.	164	C2	52.377590 -114.931237
Waterton Lakes Natl. Park-Waterton Vis. Ctr.	164	C4	49.051400 -113.906300
Wood Buffalo Natl. Park-Fort Chipewyan Vis. Ctr.	155	F2	48.714100 -111.154300
Provincial Park & Rec. Areas			
Aspen Beach Prov. Park	164	C2	52.454530 -113.975750
Beauvais Lake Prov. Park	164	C4	49.409500 -114.117000
Big Hill Springs Prov. Park	164	C3	51.251670 -114.386940
Big Knife Prov. Park	165	D2	52.489720 -112.210560
Birch Mts. Wildland Prov. Park	159	D1	57.509400 -112.957000
Bluerock Wildland Prov. Park	164	C3	50.642300 -114.654000
Bob Creek Wildland Prov. Park	164	C4	49.973700 -114.286000
Bow Valley Prov. Park	164	C3	51.040400 -115.077000
Bow Valley Wildland Prov. Park	164	B3	51.032600 -115.259000
Bragg Creek Prov. Park	164	C3	50.939170 -114.583330
Brown-Lowery Prov. Park	164	C3	50.813900 -114.430600
Calling Lake Prov. Park	159	D3	55.179720 -113.272500
Caribou Mts. Wildland Prov. Park	155	F3	59.205600 -114.897000
Carson-Pegasus Prov. Park	158	C3	54.295800 -115.645000
Chain Lakes Prov. Park	164	C3	50.200000 -114.183330
Chinchaga Wildland Prov. Park	158	B1	57.163400 -119.582000
Cold Lake Prov. Park	159	E3	54.602400 -110.072000
Cold Lake Prov. Park-North Shore	159	E3	54.644800 -110.103600
Crimson Lake Prov. Park	164	C2	52.466900 -115.048000
Cross Lake Prov. Park	159	D3	54.649300 -113.791000
Crow Lake Prov. Park	159	D2	55.800456 -112.152014
Dillberry Lake Prov. Park	165	E1	52.570200 -110.030000
Dinosaur Prov. Park	165	D3	50.770100 -111.480000
Don Getty Wildland Prov. Park	164	B2	50.893000 -114.993000
Dry Island Buffalo Jump Prov. Park	164	C2	51.929500 -112.975000
Dunvegan Prov. Park	158	B2	55.923600 -118.594400
Dunvegan West Wildland Prov. Park	158	B2	56.088900 -119.297000
Elbow Sheep Wildland Prov. Park	164	C3	50.703500 -114.939000
Fort Assiniboine Sandhills Wildland Prov. Park	158	C3	54.387100 -114.608000
Garner Lake Prov. Park	159	D3	54.183420 -111.741000
Gipsy Lake Wildland Prov. Park	159	E2	56.493500 -110.386000
Gooseberry Lake Prov. Park	165	D2	52.116940 -110.759170
Grand Rapids Wildland Prov. Park	159	D1	56.484200 -112.343000
Greene Valley Prov. Park	158	B2	56.140900 -117.242000
Gregoire Lake Prov. Park	159	E1	56.485000 -111.182780
Grizzly Ridge Wildland Prov. Park	158	C3	55.137700 -115.049000
Hay-Zama Lakes Wildland Prov. Park	155	F3	58.774100 -119.016000
Hilliard's Bay Prov. Park	158	C2	55.502900 -116.001000
Hubert Lake Wildland Prov. Park	158	C3	54.554100 -114.244000
Kakwa Wildland Prov. Park	158	A3	54.034600 -119.810000
Kinbrook Island Prov. Park	165	D3	50.437189 -111.910595
La Biche River Wildland Prov. Park	159	D3	54.987000 -112.626000
Lakeland Prov. Park	159	E3	54.759300 -111.557000
Lakeland Prov. Rec. Area	159	E3	54.721800 -111.398000
Lesser Slave Lake Prov. Park	158	C2	55.448000 -114.817000
Lesser Slave Lake Wildland Prov. Park	158	C2	55.497700 -115.567000
Little Bow Prov. Park	164	C3	50.227930 -112.926590
Little Fish Lake Prov. Park	165	D2	51.374246 -112.200944
Long Lake Prov. Park	159	D3	54.439986 -112.763465
Marguerite River Wildland Prov. Park	159	E1	57.638400 -110.266000
Midland Prov. Park	165	D2	51.478295 -112.771085
Miquelon Lake Prov. Park	159	D4	53.246900 -112.874000
Moonshine Lake Prov. Park	158	B2	55.883800 -119.216000
Moose Lake Prov. Park	159	E3	54.272986 -110.931143
Notikewin Prov. Park	158	C1	57.218300 -117.148000
Obed Lake Prov. Park	158	B4	53.558200 -117.101000
O'Brien Prov. Park	158	B3	55.065242 -118.822285
Otter-Orloff Lakes Wildland Prov. Park	159	D2	55.364200 -113.551000
Park Lake Prov. Park	164	C4	49.806621 -112.924681
Peace River Wildland Prov. Park	158	B2	55.983200 -117.765000
Pembina River Prov. Park	158	C4	53.611859 -114.985313
Peter Lougheed Prov. Park	164	B3	50.684100 -115.184000
Pigeon Lake Prov. Park	164	C1	53.029547 -114.150507
Police Outpost Prov. Park	164	C4	49.004503 -113.464980
Queen Elizabeth Prov. Park	158	B2	56.219128 -117.693540
Red Lodge Prov. Park	164	C2	51.947917 -114.243862
Rochon Sands Prov. Park	165	D2	52.461755 -112.892373
Rock Lake Solomon Creek Wildland Prov. Park	158	B4	53.413700 -118.118000
Saskatoon Island Prov. Park	158	B2	55.205201 -119.085401
Sheep River Prov. Park	164	C3	50.647300 -114.660000
Sir Winston Churchill Prov. Park	159	D3	54.832050 -111.976109
Spray Valley Prov. Park	164	B3	50.888700 -115.293000
Stony Mtn. Wildland Prov. Park	159	E2	56.211500 -111.244000
Sundance Prov. Park	158	B4	53.668700 -116.926000
Sylvan Lake Prov. Park	164	C2	52.315760 -114.092272
Thunder Lake Prov. Park	158	C3	54.131941 -114.725882
Tillebrook Prov. Park	165	D3	50.538593 -111.812268
Vermilion Prov. Park	159	E4	53.367679 -110.909771
Wabamun Lake Prov. Park	158	C4	53.565029 -114.441575
Whitehorse Wildland Prov. Park	164	B1	52.957900 -117.395000
Whitemud Falls Wildland Prov. Park	159	E1	56.703400 -110.084000
Whitney Lakes Prov. Park	159	E4	53.847100 -110.537000
William A. Switzer Prov. Park	158	B4	53.492000 -117.804000
Williamson Prov. Park	158	B3	55.081821 -117.560174
Willow Creek Prov. Park	164	C3	50.118067 -113.776021
Winagami Lake Prov. Park	158	C2	55.627500 -116.738000
Winagami Wildland Prov. Park	158	C2	55.611900 -116.635000
Woolford Prov. Park	164	C4	49.178498 -113.190438
Writing-On-Stone Prov. Park	165	D4	49.061400 -111.639000
Wyndham-Carseland Prov. Park	164	C3	50.827750 -113.436542
Young's Point Prov. Park	158	B3	55.148000 -117.572000

BRITISH COLUMBIA	PAGE	GRID	LATITUDE LONGITUDE
National Park & Rec. Areas			
Chilkoot Trail N.H.S.	155	D3	59.756667 -134.960833
Fort Langley N.H.S.	163	D3	49.168056 -122.569167
Fort Saint James N.H.S.	157	D2	54.440278 -124.255556
Glacier Natl. Park-Eastern Welcome Sta.	164	A2	51.511700 -117.442000
Glacier Natl. Park-Rogers Pass Discovery Center	164	A2	51.300600 -117.521500
Gulf Islands Natl. Park Res.	163	D4	48.769400 -123.210000
Gulf of Georgia Cannery N.H.S.	163	D3	49.124722 -123.199722
Gwaii Haanas Natl. Park Res.	156	A3	52.349722 -131.433056
Kitwanga Fort N.H.S.	156	C1	55.119444 -128.018056
Kootenay Natl. Park-Radium Hot Springs Vis. Ctr.	164	B3	50.619500 -116.069800
Kootenay Natl. Park-Vermilion Crossing Vis. Ctr.	164	B3	51.000000 -115.966000
Mount Revelstoke Natl. Park-Western Welcome Sta.	164	A2	51.042000 -117.983900
Pacific Rim Natl. Park Res.-Broken Group Islands	162	B3	48.891100 -125.300800
Pacific Rim Natl. Park Res.-Pacific Rim Vis. Ctr.	162	B3	48.992000 -125.587200
Pacific Rim Natl. Park Res.-West Coast Trail	162	C4	48.704800 -124.866100
Pacific Rim Natl. Park Res.-Wickaninnish Interpretive Center	162	B3	49.012700 -125.674200
Yoho Natl. Park-Field Vis. Ctr.	164	B2	51.397800 -116.492000
Provincial Park & Rec. Areas			
Adams Lake Prov. Park	163	F1	50.983056 -119.733056
Akamina-Kishinena Prov. Park	164	C4	49.032700 -114.178000
Alexandra Bridge Prov. Park	163	E2	49.700000 -121.399722
Alice Lake Prov. Park	163	D2	49.783056 -123.116667
Allison Lake Prov. Park	163	F2	49.683056 -120.599722
Anstey Hunakwa Prov. Park	164	A2	51.140600 -118.924300
Arctic Pacific Lakes Prov. Park	157	E2	54.384400 -121.553000
Arrow Lakes Prov. Park	164	A3	49.883056 -118.065667
Arrowstone Prov. Park	163	E1	50.879900 -121.273000
Atlin Prov. Park	155	E3	59.165400 -133.914000
Babine Lake-Pendleton Bay Marine Prov. Park	157	D2	54.533000 -125.724800
Babine Lake-Smithers Landing Marine Prov. Park	156	C1	55.098400 -126.600000
Babine Mountains Prov. Park	156	C1	54.913100 -126.928000
Babine River Corridor Prov. Park	156	C1	55.577400 -127.032000
Barkerville Prov. Park	157	E3	53.088889 -121.510833
Bear Creek Prov. Park	163	F2	49.930556 -119.520556
Bearhole Lake Prov. Park	158	A3	55.043400 -120.568000
Beatton Prov. Park	158	A1	56.333056 -120.933056
Beaumont Prov. Park	157	D2	54.050000 -124.616667
Beaver Creek Prov. Park	164	A4	49.066667 -117.600000
Big Bar Lake Prov. Park	157	E4	51.316667 -121.816667
Big Bunsby Marine Prov. Park	162	A2	50.120800 -127.504200
Big Creek Prov. Park	157	E4	51.301500 -123.158000
Bijoux Falls Prov. Park	157	E1	55.300000 -122.666667
Birkenhead Lake Prov. Park	163	D1	50.577900 -122.737000
Bishop River Prov. Park	162	C1	50.912500 -124.038000
Blanket Creek Prov. Park	164	A3	50.833056 -118.083056
Bligh Island Marine Prov. Park	162	A2	49.633300 -126.553000
Bowron Lake Prov. Park	157	F3	53.174100 -121.012000
Boya Lake Prov. Park	155	E3	59.380500 -129.090000
Brandywine Falls Prov. Park	163	D2	50.033056 -123.116667
Bridal Veil Falls Prov. Park	163	E3	49.183056 -121.733056
Bridge Lake Prov. Park	157	F4	51.483056 -120.700000
Bromley Rock Prov. Park	163	F3	49.416667 -120.258056
Brooks Peninsula Prov. Park	162	A2	50.180300 -127.657000
Broughton Archipelago Marine Prov. Park	162	A1	50.687100 -126.663000
Bugaboo Prov. Park	164	B3	50.794700 -116.808000
Callaghan Lake Prov. Park	163	D2	50.206900 -123.189000
Bull Canyon Prov. Park	157	E4	52.091667 -123.374722
Canal Flats Prov. Park	164	B3	50.183056 -115.816667
Canim Beach Prov. Park	157	F4	51.816667 -120.872667
Cape Scott Prov. Park	162	A1	50.765900 -128.246000
Cariboo Mts. Prov. Park	157	F3	52.852600 -120.538000
Cariboo River Prov. Park	157	F3	52.873600 -121.222000
Carmanah Walbran Prov. Park	162	C4	48.654500 -124.628000
Carp Lake Prov. Park	157	E2	54.769400 -123.387000
Catala Island Marine Prov. Park	162	A2	49.835833 -127.054167
Cathedral Prov. Park	163	F3	49.069800 -120.174000
Champion Lakes Prov. Park	164	A4	49.184100 -117.624000
Charlie Lake Prov. Park	158	A1	56.316667 -120.999722
Chasm Prov. Park	157	F4	51.178900 -121.438000
Chilliwack Lake Prov. Park	163	E3	49.072200 -121.436000
Clayoquot Arm Prov. Park	162	B3	49.172800 -125.560000
Clayoquot Plateau Prov. Park	162	B3	49.225100 -125.428000
Clendinning Prov. Park	162	C1	50.429700 -123.733000
Codville Lagoon Marine Prov. Park	156	C4	52.060833 -127.855556
Conkle Lake Prov. Park	164	A4	49.166667 -119.100000
Coquihalla Canyon Prov. Park	163	E3	49.371944 -121.366667
Cormorant Channel Marine Prov. Park	162	A1	50.593500 -126.850900
Cowichan River Prov. Park	162	C4	48.780800 -123.920000
Crooked River Prov. Park	157	E2	54.466667 -122.666667
Crowsnest Prov. Park	164	C4	49.649722 -114.699722
Cummins Lakes Prov. Park	164	A2	52.104100 -118.066000
Cypress Prov. Park	163	D3	49.425800 -123.209000
Dahl Lake Prov. Park	157	E2	53.769900 -123.293000
Desolation Sound Marine Prov. Park	162	C2	50.101100 -124.710000
Diana Lake Prov. Park	156	B2	54.216667 -130.166667
Downing Prov. Park	163	E1	51.000000 -121.783056
Dry Gulch Prov. Park	164	B3	50.583056 -116.033056
Duffey Lake Prov. Park	163	D1	50.407500 -122.337000
Dune Za Keyih Prov. Park	155	E3	58.323000 -126.355000
Echo Lake Prov. Park	164	A3	50.199722 -118.700000
Edge Hills Prov. Park	163	E1	51.035900 -121.871000
Elk Falls Prov. Park	162	B2	50.041000 -125.324000
Elk Lakes Prov. Park	164	C3	50.480800 -115.088000
Ellison Prov. Park	164	A3	50.173333 -119.433056
Emory Creek Prov. Park	163	E3	49.516667 -121.416667
Eneas Lakes Prov. Park	163	F2	49.752400 -119.936000
Entiako Prov. Park	157	D3	53.221500 -125.443000
Epper Passage Prov. Park	162	B3	49.219167 -125.949722
Eskers Prov. Park	157	E2	54.081300 -123.205000
Ethel F. Wilson Mem. Prov. Park	157	D2	54.416667 -125.683056
Fillongley Prov. Park	162	C3	49.534100 -124.755200
Finger-Tatuk Prov. Park	157	D2	53.515600 -124.226000
Flat Lake Prov. Park	157	F4	51.499400 -121.521000
Flores Island Prov. Park	162	B3	49.291000 -126.173000
Francois Lake Prov. Park	157	D2	53.966667 -125.166667
French Beach Prov. Park	162	C4	48.383056 -123.933056
Garibaldi Prov. Park	163	D2	49.943200 -122.751000
Gibson Marine Prov. Park	162	B3	49.266667 -126.066667
Gitnadoiks River Prov. Park	156	B2	54.161700 -129.162000
Gladstone Prov. Park	164	A4	49.268900 -118.269000
God's Pocket Marine Prov. Park	162	A1	50.837200 -127.562000
Goldpan Prov. Park	163	E2	50.350000 -121.383056
Gordon Bay Prov. Park	162	C4	48.833056 -124.199722
Graham-Laurier Prov. Park	155	F4	56.594900 -123.466000
Graystokes Prov. Park	164	A3	49.986200 -118.850000
Green Inlet Marine Prov. Park	156	C3	52.918167 -128.485944
Green Lake Prov. Park	157	F4	51.400000 -121.199722
Hamber Prov. Park	164	A2	52.380300 -117.882000
Harmony Islands Marine Prov. Park	162	C2	49.862222 -124.012222
Ha'thayim Marine Prov. Park	162	C2	50.169400 -124.955000
Heather-Dina Lakes Prov. Park	157	E1	55.508300 -123.285000
Height of the Rockies Prov. Park	164	B3	50.488900 -115.228000
Herald Prov. Park	164	A3	50.788056 -119.201000
Hesquiat Lake Prov. Park	162	B3	49.500000 -126.385833
Hitchie Creek Prov. Park	162	C4	48.795556 -124.737500
Horne Lake Caves Prov. Park	162	C3	49.344167 -124.755556
Horsefly Lake Prov. Park	157	F3	52.383056 -121.300000
Inkaneep Prov. Park	163	F3	49.233056 -119.533056
Inland Lake Prov. Park	162	C2	49.953800 -124.481000
Itcha Ilgachuz Prov. Park	157	D3	52.711500 -124.974000
Jackman Flats Prov. Park	164	A1	52.950000 -119.416667
Jedediah Island Marine Prov. Park	162	C3	49.500000 -124.199722
Jewel Lake Prov. Park	164	A4	49.183056 -118.599722
Jimsmith Lake Prov. Park	164	B4	49.483056 -115.833056
Joffre Lakes Prov. Park	163	D2	50.344100 -122.477000
Johnstone Creek Prov. Park	164	A4	49.050000 -119.049722
Juan De Fuca Prov. Park	162	C4	48.489800 -124.290000
Junction Sheep Range Prov. Park	157	E4	51.801000 -122.435000
Juniper Beach Prov. Park	163	E1	50.785833 -121.083056
Kakwa Prov. Park	158	A3	54.057200 -120.296000
Kekuli Bay Prov. Park	164	A3	50.183056 -119.340278
Kentucky-Alleyne Prov. Park	163	F2	49.916667 -120.566667
Kianuko Prov. Park	164	B4	49.421600 -116.456000
Kikomun Creek Prov. Park	164	B4	49.233056 -115.250000
Kilby Prov. Park	163	E3	49.237500 -121.960833
Kinaskan Lake Prov. Park	155	E4	57.496100 -130.234000
Kiskatinaw Prov. Park	158	A2	55.950000 -120.566667
Kleanza Creek Prov. Park	156	C2	54.599722 -128.399722
Klewnuggit Inlet Marine Prov. Park	156	B2	53.688500 -129.697000
Kluskoil Lake Prov. Park	157	D3	53.202900 -123.892000
Kokanee Creek Prov. Park	164	B4	49.605722 -117.133056
Kokanee Glacier Prov. Park	164	B4	49.781800 -117.136000
Kootenay Lake Prov. Park	164	B3	50.085000 -116.931189
Kwadacha Wilderness Prov. Park	155	E3	57.820400 -125.058000

Lac Le Jeune Prov. Park	163	F1	50.483056 -120.483056
Lakelse Lake Prov. Park	156	C2	54.398900 -128.533000
Lawn Point Prov. Park	162	A1	50.333056 -127.966667
Lockhart Beach Prov. Park	164	B4	49.516667 -116.783056
Lockhart Creek Prov. Park	164	B4	49.497300 -116.705000
Loveland Bay Prov. Park	162	B2	50.049722 -125.450000
Lowe Inlet Marine Prov. Park	156	B2	53.555556 -129.580278
MacMillan Prov. Park	162	C3	49.283056 -124.666667
Main Lake Prov. Park	162	B2	50.210000 -125.215000
Mansons Landing Prov. Park	162	C2	50.121500 -124.928300
Maquinna Marine Prov. Park	162	B3	49.390500 -126.342000
Marble River Prov. Park	162	A1	50.544300 -127.526000
Martha Creek Prov. Park	164	A3	51.141667 -118.198122
McConnell Lake Prov. Park	163	F1	50.521944 -120.456667
McDonald Creek Prov. Park	164	A3	50.131056 -117.813667
Mehatl Creek Prov. Park	163	E2	50.036100 -122.054000
Moberly Lake Prov. Park	158	A2	55.800000 -121.700000
Momich Lakes Prov. Park	164	A2	51.327200 -119.353000
Monck Prov. Park	163	F2	50.178667 -120.533056
Moose Valley Prov. Park	157	E4	51.649800 -121.648000
Morton Lake Prov. Park	162	B2	50.116667 -125.483056
Mount Assiniboine Prov. Park	164	B3	50.937400 -115.761000
Mount Blanchet Prov. Park	157	D1	55.275500 -125.863000
Mount Fernie Prov. Park	164	C4	49.483056 -115.099722
Mount Pope Prov. Park	157	D2	54.490700 -124.331000
Mount Robson Prov. Park	164	A1	52.927000 -118.831000
Mount Seymour Prov. Park	163	D3	49.392400 -122.926000
Mount Terry Fox Prov. Park	164	A1	52.940800 -119.254000
Moyie Lake Prov. Park	164	B4	49.373333 -115.837222
Myra-Bellevue Prov. Park	164	A4	49.752100 -119.374000
Nahatlatch Prov. Park	163	E2	49.980200 -121.780000
Naikoon Prov. Park	156	A2	53.863400 -131.889000
Nairn Falls Prov. Park	163	D2	50.283056 -122.833056
Nancy Greene Prov. Park	164	A4	49.250000 -117.933056
Nickel Plate Prov. Park	163	F3	49.399722 -119.949722
Nicolum River Prov. Park	163	E3	49.366667 -121.341667
Nimpkish Lake Prov. Park	162	A2	50.337700 -127.005000
Niskonlith Lake Prov. Park	163	F1	50.795556 -119.777778
Norbury Lake Prov. Park	164	B4	49.533056 -115.483056
Nuchatlitz Prov. Park	162	A2	49.815700 -126.981000
Octopus Island Marine Prov. Park	162	B2	50.278400 -125.242100
Okanagan Lake Prov. Park	163	F2	49.683056 -119.719867
Okanagan Mtn. Prov. Park	163	F2	49.724600 -119.629000
Okeover Arm Prov. Park	162	C2	49.999722 -124.726667
One Island Lake Prov. Park	158	A2	55.300000 -120.266667
Paarens Beach Prov. Park	157	D2	54.416667 -124.399722
Paul Lake Prov. Park	163	F1	50.741667 -120.120556
Pinecone Burke Prov. Park	163	D3	49.526200 -122.721000
Porpoise Bay Prov. Park	162	C3	49.516667 -123.749722
Porteau Cove Prov. Park	163	D3	49.549722 -123.233056
Premier Lake Prov. Park	164	B4	49.900000 -115.650000
Princess Louisa Marine Prov. Park	162	C2	50.203722 -123.766667
Ptarmigan Creek Prov. Park	157	F2	53.487600 -120.880000
Puntchesakut Lake Prov. Park	157	E3	52.983056 -122.933056
Purden Lake Prov. Park	157	E2	53.928000 -121.912000
Quatsino Prov. Park	162	A1	50.491667 -127.816667
Rearguard Falls Prov. Park	157	F3	52.973333 -119.366667
Redfern-Keily Prov. Park	155	F3	57.405600 -123.878000
Roberts Creek Prov. Park	162	C3	49.433056 -123.666667
Rolley Lake Prov. Park	163	D3	49.250000 -122.400000
Rosebery Prov. Park	164	B3	50.033056 -117.400000
Rubyrock Lake Prov. Park	157	D2	54.677100 -125.348000
Ruckle Prov. Park	163	D4	48.766667 -123.383056
Rugged Point Marine Prov. Park	162	A2	49.963889 -127.238889
Saint Mary's Alpine Prov. Park	164	B4	49.877000 -116.348000
Sandy Island Marine Prov. Park	162	C3	49.616667 -124.849722
Schoen Lake Prov. Park	162	B2	50.176500 -126.245000
Schoolhouse Lake Prov. Park	157	F4	51.883600 -120.993000
Seeley Lake Prov. Park	156	C1	55.199722 -127.683056
Seven Sisters Prov. Park	156	C1	54.946900 -128.150000
Silver Beach Prov. Park	164	A2	51.240278 -118.955556
Silver Lake Prov. Park	163	E3	49.316667 -121.399722
Silver Star Prov. Park	164	A3	50.376900 -119.082000
Simson Prov. Park	162	C3	49.479700 -123.962900
Skihist Prov. Park	163	E2	50.249722 -121.500000
Skookumchuck Narrows Prov. Park	162	C2	49.744700 -123.915500
Smelt Bay Prov. Park	162	C2	50.033056 -124.983056
Sowchea Bay Prov. Park	157	D2	54.419167 -124.448333
Sproat Lake Prov. Park	162	C3	49.300000 -124.916667
Squitty Bay Prov. Park	162	C3	49.454167 -124.166667
Stagleap Prov. Park	164	B4	49.058700 -117.048000
Steelhead Prov. Park	163	E1	50.752778 -120.868056
Stemwinder Prov. Park	163	F3	49.366667 -120.133056
Stone Mtn. Prov. Park	155	E3	58.588600 -124.757000
Strathcona Prov. Park	162	B2	49.629300 -125.710000
Stuart Lake Marine Prov. Park	157	D2	54.650000 -125.000000
Sugarbowl Grizzly Den Prov. Park	157	E2	53.801200 -121.589000
Sukunka Falls Prov. Park	157	E1	55.316667 -121.700000
Sulphur Passage Prov. Park	162	B3	49.412000 -126.094000
Summit Lake Prov. Park	164	A3	50.150000 -117.666667
Surge Narrows Prov. Park	162	B2	50.233056 -125.149722
Sutherland River Prov. Park	157	D2	54.338300 -124.818000
Sydney Inlet Prov. Park	162	B3	49.480000 -126.283000
Syringa Prov. Park	164	A4	49.378000 -117.906000
Tahsish-Kwois Prov. Park	162	A2	50.189100 -127.161000
Tatlatui Prov. Park	155	E4	56.996200 -127.386000
Tatshenshini-Alsek Prov. Park	155	D3	59.595900 -137.443000
Taylor Arm Prov. Park	162	B3	49.283056 -125.049722
Ten Mile Lake Prov. Park	157	E3	53.066667 -122.450000
Thurston Bay Marine Prov. Park	162	B2	50.383056 -125.316667
Ts'il-os Prov. Park	157	D4	51.191700 -123.971000
Tudyah Lake Prov. Park	157	E1	55.066667 -123.033056
Tunkwa Prov. Park	163	E1	50.615200 -120.887000
Tyhee Lake Prov. Park	156	C2	54.700000 -127.033056
Union Passage Marine Prov. Park	156	B3	53.410900 -129.436000
Upper Adams River Prov. Park	164	A2	51.682700 -119.228000
Valhalla Prov. Park	164	A4	49.873700 -117.567000
Vargas Island Prov. Park	162	B3	49.174000 -126.031000
Vaseux Lake Prov. Park	164	A4	49.268200 -119.474000
Walsh Cove Prov. Park	162	C2	50.268056 -124.800000
Wasa Lake Prov. Park	164	B4	49.793056 -115.738056
West Arm Prov. Park	164	B4	49.507000 -117.118000
West Lake Prov. Park	157	E2	53.733056 -122.866667
Whiskers Point Prov. Park	157	E1	54.900000 -122.933056
White Pelican Prov. Park	157	E3	52.284000 -123.031000
Whiteswan Lake Prov. Park	164	B3	50.145300 -115.487000
Woss Lake Prov. Park	162	A2	50.060400 -126.626000
Yahk Provincial Park	164	B4	49.083056 -116.083056
Yard Creek Prov. Park	164	A3	50.899722 -118.799722

MANITOBA	PAGE	GRID	LATITUDE LONGITUDE
National Park & Rec. Areas			
Lower Fort Garry N.H.S.	167	E3	50.136850 -96.940569
Riding Mtn. Natl. Park-Deep Lake Ranger Sta.	167	D3	50.860300 -100.836600
Riding Mtn. Natl. Park-Lake Audy Ranger Sta.	167	D3	50.712900 -100.230600
Riding Mtn. Natl. Park-McKinnon Creek Ranger Sta.	167	D3	50.787100 -99.579500
Riding Mtn. Natl. Park-Moon Lake Ranger Sta.	167	D3	50.995900 -100.067200
Riding Mtn. Natl. Park-South Lake Ranger Sta.	167	D3	50.655200 -100.061600
Riding Mtn. Natl. Park-Sugarloaf Ranger Sta.	167	D3	50.985300 -100.742100
Riding Mtn. Natl. Park-Whirlpool Ranger Sta.	167	D3	50.683300 -99.553500
Provincial Park & Rec. Areas			
Asessippi Prov. Park	166	C3	50.966400 -101.379700
Atikaki Prov. Park	167	F2	51.532200 -95.547000
Bakers Narrows Prov. Park	161	D3	54.671100 -101.675000
Beaudry Prov. Park	167	E4	49.853900 -97.473300
Bell Lake Prov. Park	166	C1	52.541700 -101.241400
Birds Hill Prov. Park	167	E3	50.028800 -96.893200
Camp Morton Prov. Park	167	E3	50.710000 -96.990300
Clearwater Lake Prov. Park	161	D3	54.096200 -101.162000
Criddle–Vane Homestead Prov. Park	167	D4	49.707600 -99.596600
Duck Mtn. Prov. Park	167	D2	51.715600 -101.112000
Elk Island Prov. Park	167	E3	50.758300 -96.536500
Grand Beach Prov. Park	167	E3	50.567900 -96.554900
Grass River Prov. Park	161	D3	54.655500 -101.092000
Hecla–Grindstone Prov. Park	167	E2	51.198300 -96.660200
Hnausa Beach Prov. Park	167	E3	50.900300 -96.992200
Kettle Stones Prov. Park	167	D2	52.359200 -100.595300
Lake Saint George Prov. Park	167	E2	51.719703 -97.406772
Lundar Beach Prov. Park	167	E3	50.724000 -98.273000
Manipogo Prov. Park	167	D2	51.517000 -99.550000
Nopiming Prov. Park	167	F3	50.665200 -95.305600
North Steeprock Lake Prov. Park	166	C1	52.611800 -101.380000
Paint Lake Prov. Park	161	E2	55.492100 -98.018000
Patricia Beach Prov. Park	167	E3	50.467300 -96.575300
Pembina Valley Prov. Park	167	E4	49.038500 -98.296400
Pinawa Dam Prov. Park	167	F3	50.145200 -95.945700
Rainbow Beach Prov. Park	167	D3	51.099400 -99.718400
Saint Ambroise Beach Prov. Park	167	E3	50.275500 -98.074300
Saint Malo Prov. Park	167	E4	49.321400 -96.930490
South Atikaki Prov. Park	167	F3	51.041400 -95.417600
Spruce Woods Prov. Park	167	D4	49.703100 -99.141900
Stephenfield Prov. Park	167	E4	49.523400 -98.300500
Turtle Mtn. Prov. Park	167	D4	49.041500 -100.216000
Watchorn Prov. Park	167	E2	51.293100 -98.598500
Whitefish Lake Prov. Park	166	C2	52.333900 -101.587100
Whiteshell Prov. Park	167	F3	50.140900 -95.584400
William Lake Prov. Park	167	D4	49.055000 -100.038800
Winnipeg Beach Prov. Park	167	E3	50.512300 -96.967000

NEW BRUNSWICK	PAGE	GRID	LATITUDE LONGITUDE
National Park & Rec. Areas			
Beaubears Island N.H.S.	179	D3	46.972778 -65.569444
Fort Beauséjour N.H.S.	180	C1	45.865278 -64.290278
Fort Gaspareaux N.H.S.	180	C1	46.040833 -64.072778
Fundy Natl. Park-Vis. Ctr.	180	C1	45.659500 -65.132600
Kouchibouguac Natl. Park-Vis. Ctr.	179	D3	46.773200 -65.004900
Monument Lefebvre N.H.S.	180	C1	45.979167 -64.567222
Roosevelt Campobello International Park	180	A2	44.849722 -66.949722
Saint Andrews Blockhouse N.H.S.	180	A2	45.076389 -67.063889
Saint Croix Island International Hist. Site	180	A2	45.127778 -67.133333
Provincial Park & Rec. Areas			
De la République Prov. Park	178	B3	47.442778 -68.395556
Herring Cove Prov. Park	180	A2	44.866667 -66.933056
Mactaquac Prov. Park	180	A1	45.959025 -66.892556
Mount Carleton Prov. Park	178	C3	47.392300 -66.835500
Murray Beach Prov. Park	180	C1	46.016667 -63.983056
New River Beach Prov. Park	180	A2	45.133056 -66.533056
Oak Bay Prov. Park	180	A2	45.216667 -67.200000
Parlee Beach Prov. Park	180	C1	46.233056 -64.499722
Sugarloaf Prov. Park	178	C2	47.974000 -66.671900
The Anchorage Prov. Park	180	A3	44.649722 -66.800000
Val-Comeau Prov. Park	179	D3	47.466667 -64.866667

NEWFOUNDLAND & LABRADOR	PAGE	GRID	LATITUDE LONGITUDE
National Park & Rec. Areas			
Castle Hill N.H.S.	183	E4	47.251389 -53.971111
Gros Morne Natl. Park-Vis. Ctr.	182	C2	49.571500 -57.877900
Hawthorne Cottage N.H.S.	183	E4	47.543333 -53.210833
L'Anse aux Meadows N.H.S.	183	F1	51.595000 -55.532778
Port au Choix N.H.S.	182	C1	50.712222 -57.375278
Red Bay N.H.S.	183	F1	51.733056 -56.415556
Ryan Premises N.H.S.	183	E3	48.648056 -53.112500
Terra Nova Natl. Park-Information Center	183	E3	48.394900 -54.204000
Terra Nova Natl. Park-Saltons Vis. Ctr.	183	E3	48.580600 -53.958900
Provincial Park & Rec. Areas			
Barachois Pond Prov. Park	182	C3	48.477100 -58.256600
Blow Me Down Prov. Park	182	C2	49.090833 -58.364444
Butter Pot Prov. Park	183	F4	47.390900 -53.071300
Chance Cove Prov. Park	183	F4	46.776900 -53.045400
Codroy Valley Prov. Park	182	C4	47.833333 -59.337778
Deadman's Bay Prov. Park	183	E2	49.331389 -53.692500
Dildo Run Prov. Park	183	E2	49.535556 -54.721667
Dungeon Prov. Park	183	E3	48.666667 -53.083611
Frenchman's Cove Prov. Park	183	D4	47.209444 -55.401667
Gooseberry Cove Prov. Park	183	E4	47.068056 -54.087778
J.T. Cheeseman Prov. Park	182	C4	47.631111 -59.249444
La Manche Prov. Park	183	F4	47.175200 -52.901200
Lockston Path Prov. Park	183	E3	48.437778 -53.379722
Notre Dame Prov. Park	183	E2	49.115833 -55.086389
Pinware River Prov. Park	183	F1	51.631667 -56.704167
Sandbanks Prov. Park	182	C4	47.607222 -57.646944
Sir Richard Squires Mem. Prov. Park	183	D2	49.354000 -57.213400
The Arches Prov. Park	182	C2	50.113333 -57.663056

NORTHWEST TERRITORIES	PAGE	GRID	LATITUDE LONGITUDE
National Park & Rec. Areas			
Nahanni Natl. Park Res.	155	E2	61.083333 -123.600000
Tuktut Nogait Natl. Park	155	E1	69.283333 -123.016667

NOVA SCOTIA	PAGE	GRID	LATITUDE LONGITUDE
National Park & Rec. Areas			
Alexander Graham Bell N.H.S.	181	F1	46.102778 -60.745556
Cape Breton Highlands Natl. Park-East Ent.	182	B4	46.642800 -60.404200
Cape Breton Highlands Natl. Park-West Ent.	182	B4	46.647300 -60.950200
Fort Anne N.H.S.	180	B3	44.741667 -65.519167
Fort Edward N.H.S.	180	C2	44.995556 -64.135278
Fortress of Louisbourg N.H.S.	181	F1	45.900300 -59.995100
Grand-Pré N.H.S.	180	C2	45.108889 -64.311944
Grassy Island N.H.S.	181	F2	45.336667 -60.973611
Kejimkujik Natl. Park (Seaside Adjunct)	180	C4	43.865800 -64.836900
Kejimkujik Natl. Park and N.H.S.	180	B3	44.336700 -65.268200
Marconi N.H.S.	181	F4	46.211111 -59.952778
Port-Royal N.H.S.	180	B3	44.712500 -65.610556
Saint Peters Canal N.H.S.	181	F1	45.655556 -60.870556
York Redoubt N.H.S.	181	D3	44.596583 -63.552439
Provincial Park & Rec. Areas			
Amherst Shore Prov. Park	180	C1	45.961181 -63.879025
Battery Prov. Park	181	F1	45.657022 -60.866764
Beaver Mtn. Prov. Park	181	E2	45.567556 -62.153583
Blomidon Prov. Park	180	C2	45.255869 -64.352056
Boylston Prov. Park	181	E2	45.426839 -61.510603
Cape Chignecto Prov. Park	180	C2	45.375800 -64.891300
Caribou–Munroes Island Prov. Park	181	D1	45.721800 -62.656914
Clam Harbour Beach Prov. Park	181	D3	44.731390 -62.891110
Ellenwood Lake Prov. Park	180	B4	43.929481 -66.005700
Five Islands Prov. Park	180	C2	45.407781 -64.021500
Graves Island Prov. Park	180	C3	44.565550 -64.218642
Laurie Prov. Park	181	D2	44.878175 -63.602194
Martinique Beach Prov. Park	181	D3	44.689911 -63.147567
Mira River Prov. Park	181	F1	46.026006 -60.037433
Porters Prov. Park	181	D3	44.691106 -63.308892
Rissers Beach Prov. Park	180	C3	44.232397 -64.423919
Salsman Prov. Park	181	E2	45.236856 -61.767150
Salt Springs Prov. Park	181	D2	45.545280 -62.878890
Shubenacadie Prov. Wildlife Park	181	D2	45.087222 -63.387500
Smileys Prov. Park	180	C2	45.013925 -63.961247
The Islands Prov. Park	180	B4	43.765503 -65.340347
Thomas Raddall Prov. Park	180	C4	43.844783 -64.919694
Valleyview Prov. Park	180	B2	44.875200 -65.316064
Wentworth Prov. Park	181	D2	45.627222 -63.567222

300 Parks Index with GPS Coordinates
Ontario–Yukon

Whycocomagh Prov. Park	181	F1	45.968094 -61.109908

ONTARIO	PAGE	GRID	LATITUDE LONGITUDE
National Park & Rec. Areas			
Battle of the Windmill N.H.S.	174	B4	44.722778 -75.486944
Bellevue House N.H.S.	173	F1	44.220556 -76.506667
Bruce Peninsula Natl. Park	170	C4	45.189100 -81.485500
Fathom Five Natl. Marine Park	170	C4	45.304800 -81.727600
Fort George N.H.S.	173	D3	43.252778 -79.051111
Fort Henry N.H.S.	173	F1	44.230833 -76.459444
Fort Malden N.H.S.	172	A4	42.108056 -83.113889
Fort Mississauga N.H.S.	173	D3	43.260833 -79.076667
Fort Saint Joseph N.H.S.	170	B3	46.063889 -83.944167
Fort Wellington N.H.S.	174	B4	44.713889 -75.510833
Georgian Bay Islands Natl. Park-Welcome Center	171	D4	44.803900 -79.720400
Glengarry Cairn N.H.S.	174	C3	45.121667 -74.490278
Merrickville Blockhouse N.H.S.	174	B4	44.916667 -75.837500
Peterborough Lift Lock N.H.S.	173	E1	44.308056 -78.300556
Point Clark Lighthouse N.H.S.	172	B2	44.073056 -81.756667
Point Pelee Natl. Park-Park Ent. Kiosk	172	A4	41.987700 -82.549900
Point Pelee Natl. Park-Vis. Ctr.	172	A4	41.931700 -82.513500
Pukaskwa Natl. Park-Information Center	170	A2	48.700400 -86.197200
Queenston Heights N.H.S.	173	D3	43.158056 -79.052778
Saint Lawrence Islands Natl. Park-Vis. Ctr.	174	A4	44.452300 -75.860300
Sault Ste. Marie Canal N.H.S.	170	B3	46.511667 -84.355556
Sir John Johnson House N.H.S.	174	C4	45.144444 -74.580000
Southwold Earthworks N.H.S.	172	B3	42.677778 -81.351389
Trent-Severn Waterway N.H.S.	173	E1	44.137500 -77.590100
Woodside N.H.S.	172	C2	43.466667 -80.499722
Provincial Park & Rec. Areas			
Aaron Prov. Park	168	C3	49.758390 -92.653440
Abitibi-De-Troyes Prov. Park	171	D1	48.786500 -80.066300
Albany River Prov. Park	169	E1	51.358200 -88.134000
Algonquin Prov. Park	171	E4	45.605300 -78.323900
Arrowhead Prov. Park	171	D4	45.391700 -79.197200
Awenda Prov. Park	172	C1	44.854400 -79.989800
Balsam Lake Prov. Park	173	D1	44.642000 -78.864000
Bass Lake Prov. Park	173	D1	44.602000 -79.475000
Batchawana Prov. Park	170	B3	46.941900 -84.587010
Blue Lake Prov. Park	168	B3	49.904200 -93.525600
Bon Echo Prov. Park	171	E4	44.905600 -77.246600
Bonnechere Prov. Park	171	E4	45.658400 -77.570800
Bonnechere River Prov. Park	171	E4	45.674400 -77.661500
Brightsand River Prov. Park	169	D3	49.936700 -90.265400
Bronte Creek Prov. Park	173	D2	43.410490 -79.767830
Caliper Lake Prov. Park	168	B3	49.061670 -93.912780
Carson Lake Prov. Park	171	E4	45.502780 -77.746390
Chapleau-Nemegosenda River Prov. Park	170	B2	48.262300 -83.035300
Charleston Lake Prov. Park	174	A4	44.515400 -76.013600
Chutes Prov. Park	170	C3	46.219510 -82.071480
Craigleith Prov. Park	172	C1	44.535000 -80.367000
Darlington Prov. Park	173	D2	43.875480 -78.778300
Devil's Glen Prov. Park	172	C1	44.361000 -80.207800
Driftwood Prov. Park	171	E3	46.179000 -77.843000
Earl Rowe Prov. Park	172	C1	44.150000 -79.898000
Emily Prov. Park	173	D1	44.340530 -78.532860
Esker Lakes Prov. Park	171	D2	48.290100 -79.906100
Fairbank Prov. Park	170	C3	46.468070 -81.440410
Ferris Prov. Park	173	E1	44.293000 -77.788000
Finlayson Point Prov. Park	171	D3	47.055000 -79.797000
Fitzroy Prov. Park	174	A3	45.482680 -76.209400
French River Prov. Park	171	D3	46.008600 -80.620900
Frontenac Prov. Park	174	A4	44.540500 -76.512700
Fushimi Lake Prov. Park	169	F3	49.824800 -83.913800
Greenwater Prov. Park	170	C1	49.215900 -81.291000
Grundy Lake Prov. Park	171	D4	45.939800 -80.530400
Halfway Lake Prov. Park	170	C3	46.905700 -81.650500
Inverhuron Prov. Park	172	B1	44.298000 -81.580000
Ivanhoe Lake Prov. Park	170	C2	47.957600 -82.742600
John E. Pearce Prov. Park	172	B4	42.617000 -81.444000
Kakabeka Falls Prov. Park	169	D4	48.403290 -89.624130
Kap-Kig-Iwan Prov. Park	171	D2	47.789960 -79.884990
Kettle Lakes Prov. Park	170	C1	48.569400 -80.865400
Killarney Prov. Park	170	C3	46.099400 -81.386900
Killbear Prov. Park	171	D4	45.346200 -80.191200
Kopka River Prov. Park	169	D2	50.006300 -89.493000
Lady Evelyn-Smoothwater Prov. Park	171	D2	47.368500 -80.489300
Lake of the Woods Prov. Park	168	B3	49.221200 -94.606000
Lake on the Mtn. Prov. Park	173	F1	44.039940 -77.056080
Lake Saint Peter Prov. Park	171	E4	45.322000 -78.024000
Lake Superior Prov. Park	170	A2	47.595200 -84.756500
Larder River Prov. Park	171	D2	47.936300 -79.642800
La Verendrye River Prov. Park	169	D4	48.138300 -90.431300
Little Abitibi Prov. Park	170	C1	49.637900 -80.922900
Little Current River Prov. Park	169	E2	50.724100 -86.211000
Long Point Prov. Park	172	C4	42.565000 -80.306000
Lower Madawaska River Prov. Park	171	E4	45.236200 -77.289300
MacGregor Point Prov. Park	172	B1	44.403700 -81.465600
Macleod Prov. Park	169	E3	49.676190 -86.931000
Makobe-Grays River Prov. Park	171	D2	47.617200 -80.376300
Mara Prov. Park	173	D1	44.589000 -79.349000
Mark S. Burnham Prov. Park	173	E1	44.299900 -78.257000
Marten River Prov. Park	171	D3	46.729000 -79.807000
Mattawa River Prov. Park	171	D3	46.315000 -79.108400
McRae Point Prov. Park	173	D1	44.569000 -79.320000
Mikisew Prov. Park	171	D4	45.820000 -79.512000
Missinaibi River Prov. Park	170	B1	49.101400 -83.234700
Mississagi Prov. Park	170	C3	46.596500 -82.682500
Mississagi River Prov. Park	170	C3	47.012600 -82.632700
Murphys Point Prov. Park	174	A4	44.774300 -76.240700
Nagagamisis Prov. Park	169	F3	49.475700 -84.771000
Neys Prov. Park	169	E4	48.750500 -86.591900
North Beach Prov. Park	173	E2	43.951050 -77.522660
Oastler Lake Prov. Park	171	D4	45.309000 -79.964800
Obabika River Prov. Park	171	D3	47.221200 -80.262600
Obatanga Prov. Park	170	A2	48.323000 -85.093700
Ojibway Prov. Park	168	C3	49.990900 -92.144400
Opeongo River Prov. Park	171	E4	45.576256 -77.887363
Otoskwin-Attawapiskat River Prov. Park	169	D1	52.235700 -87.491300
Ottawa River Prov. Park	174	A3	45.741700 -76.779800
Ouimet Canyon Prov. Park	169	D4	48.773350 -88.667400
Oxtongue River-Ragged Falls Prov. Park	171	D4	45.366900 -78.914100
Pakwash Prov. Park	168	B2	50.749800 -93.551400
Pancake Bay Prov. Park	170	B3	46.967200 -84.661100
Petroglyphs Prov. Park	173	E1	44.618300 -78.041700
Pigeon River Prov. Park	169	D4	48.025041 -89.572294
Pipestone River Prov. Park	169	D1	52.244300 -90.313500
Point Farms Prov. Park	172	B2	43.804000 -81.700000
Port Bruce Prov. Park	172	B3	42.664000 -81.027000
Port Burwell Prov. Park	172	C3	42.646000 -80.816000
Potholes Prov. Park	170	B2	47.958700 -84.294020
Presqu'Ile Prov. Park	173	E2	44.007000 -77.735000
Quetico Prov. Park	168	C4	48.404500 -91.498700
Rainbow Falls Prov. Park	169	E4	48.830090 -87.389580
Renè Brunelle Prov. Park	170	C1	49.453700 -82.147900
Restoule Prov. Park	171	D3	46.080400 -79.839800
Rideau River Prov. Park	174	B4	45.060000 -75.672000
Rock Point Prov. Park	173	D3	42.854000 -79.552000
Rondeau Prov. Park	172	B4	42.278200 -81.865100
Rushing River Prov. Park	168	B3	49.681850 -94.234890
Samuel de Champlain Prov. Park	171	D3	46.301900 -78.864100
Sandbanks Prov. Park	173	F2	43.910200 -77.267200
Sandbar Lake Prov. Park	168	C3	49.491000 -91.555700
Sauble Falls Prov. Park	172	B1	44.673170 -81.257350
Selkirk Prov. Park	172	C3	42.824000 -79.961000
Sharbot Lake Prov. Park	174	A4	44.775500 -76.724600
Sibbald Point Prov. Park	173	D1	44.322160 -79.325570
Silent Lake Prov. Park	171	E4	44.907500 -78.047200
Silver Lake Prov. Park	174	A4	44.829770 -76.574680
Sioux Narrows Prov. Park	168	B3	49.429570 -94.037260
Six Mile Lake Prov. Park	171	D4	44.819500 -79.733500
Sleeping Giant Prov. Park	169	D4	48.419300 -88.795500
Solace Prov. Park	170	C3	47.189200 -80.683500
Springwater Prov. Park	173	D1	44.443500 -79.748500
Steel River Prov. Park	169	E3	49.161900 -86.812600
Sturgeon Bay Prov. Park	171	D4	45.623400 -80.414100
Sturgeon River Prov. Park	170	C3	46.949800 -80.523900
The Massasauga Prov. Park	171	D4	45.203400 -80.044300
The Pinery Prov. Park	172	B3	43.257200 -81.834000
The Shoals Prov. Park	170	B2	47.884800 -83.808000
Turkey Point Prov. Park	172	C3	42.694000 -80.333150
Turtle River Prov. Park	168	C3	49.129700 -92.042300
Upper Madawaska River Prov. Park	171	E4	45.513700 -78.078700
Wabakimi Prov. Park	169	D2	50.719100 -89.448500
Wakami Lake Prov. Park	170	C2	47.489700 -82.842000
Wasaga Beach Prov. Park	172	C1	44.494000 -80.027100
Wheatley Prov. Park	172	A4	42.098000 -82.448800
White Lake Prov. Park	170	A1	48.603500 -85.880900
Windy Lake Prov. Park	170	C3	46.619820 -81.455980
Woodland Caribou Prov. Park	168	B2	51.096900 -94.744900

PRINCE EDWARD ISLAND	PAGE	GRID	LATITUDE LONGITUDE
National Park & Rec. Areas			
Port-la-Joye–Fort Amherst N.H.S.	179	E4	46.195278 -63.133611
Prince Edward Island Natl. Park-Brackley Vis. Ctr.	179	E4	46.406200 -63.196600
Prince Edward Island Natl. Park-Cavendish Vis. Ctr.	179	E4	46.492300 -63.379700
Provincial Park & Rec. Areas			
Brudenell River Prov. Park	179	F4	46.209583 -62.588556
Buffaloland Prov. Park	179	F4	46.092500 -62.617778
Cabot Beach Prov. Park	179	E4	46.557250 -63.704250
Cedar Dunes Prov. Park	177	F4	46.622222 -64.381944
Chelton Beach Prov. Park	179	E4	46.303944 -63.747167
Green Park Prov. Park	177	F4	46.590972 -63.890333
Jacques Cartier Prov. Park	177	F4	46.851222 -64.013000
Kings Castle Prov. Park	179	F4	46.019167 -62.567389
Linkletter Prov. Park	179	E4	46.402694 -63.850361
Lord Selkirk Prov. Park	179	F4	46.091889 -62.906000
Mill River Prov. Park	177	F4	46.749722 -64.166667
Northumberland Prov. Park	179	F4	45.966667 -62.716667
Panmure Island Prov. Park	179	F4	46.133056 -62.466667
Red Point Prov. Park	179	F4	46.366667 -62.133056
Wood Islands Prov. Park	181	D1	45.949722 -62.749722

QUÉBEC	PAGE	GRID	LATITUDE LONGITUDE
National Park & Rec. Areas			
Lieu Historique Natl. du Fort-Lennox	175	D4	45.120556 -73.268056
Lieu Historique Natl. du Fort-Témiscamingue	171	D2	47.295000 -79.456667
Parc Natl. de Forillon-North Ent.	179	D1	48.960100 -64.339000
Parc Natl. de Forillon-South Ent.	179	D1	48.854300 -64.396300
Parc Natl. de la Mauricie-East Ent.	175	D1	46.752600 -72.792600
Parc Natl. de la Mauricie-South Ent.	175	D1	46.650000 -72.969200
Réserve de Parc Natl. de l'Archipel-de-Mingan	177	F1	50.237100 -63.606900
Provincial Park & Rec. Areas			
Parc d'Aiguebelle	171	D1	48.510300 -78.745800
Parc d'Anticosti	182	A2	49.463200 -62.819000
Parc de Frontenac	175	E3	45.848600 -71.184600
Parc de la Gaspésie	178	C1	48.941500 -66.214400
Parc de la Gatineau	174	A3	45.566667 -75.949722
Parc de la Jacques-Cartier	175	E1	47.317300 -71.347000
Parc de la Pointe-Taillon	176	C3	48.717300 -71.993600
Parc de la Yamaska	175	D3	45.429400 -72.601800
Parc de l'Île-Bonaventure-et-du-Rocher-Percé	179	E1	48.496389 -64.161944
Parc de Miguasha	178	C2	48.110556 -66.369444
Parc de Plaisance	174	B3	45.597900 -75.123600
Parc de Récréation du Mont-Orford	175	D3	45.344700 -72.212900
Parc des Grands-Jardins	176	C4	47.681300 -70.836900
Parc des Hautes-Gorges-de-la-Rivière-Malbaie	176	C3	47.918700 -70.498700
Parc des Monts-Valin	176	C3	48.598600 -70.825300
Parc du Bic	178	A1	48.355300 -68.797600
Parc du Mont-Mégantic	175	E3	45.450700 -71.167300
Parc du Mont-Saint-Bruno	175	D3	45.555278 -73.309722
Parc du Mont-Tremblant	174	C2	46.443000 -74.344600
Parc du Saguenay	176	C3	48.289900 -70.243400
Parc Marin du Saguenay-Saint-Laurent	178	A2	48.133056 -69.733056
Parc Régional du Massif du Sud	175	F2	46.581389 -70.467778

SASKATCHEWAN	PAGE	GRID	LATITUDE LONGITUDE
National Park & Rec. Areas			
Batoche N.H.S.	165	F1	52.752800 -106.116700
Battle of Fish Creek N.H.S.	165	F1	52.550000 -106.180300
Fort Battleford N.H.S.	165	E1	52.713800 -108.259600
Fort Espèrance N.H.S.	166	C3	50.451400 -101.712800
Fort Livingstone N.H.S.	166	C2	51.903880 -101.960620
Fort Pelly N.H.S.	166	C2	51.795900 -101.951800
Fort Walsh N.H.S.	165	E4	49.559100 -109.901700
Grasslands Natl. Park-East Block Vis. Ctr.	166	A4	49.370800 -106.384800
Grasslands Natl. Park-West Block Vis. Reception Ctr.	166	A4	49.203800 -107.732700
Prince Albert Natl. Park-Waskesiu Vis. Ctr.	160	B3	53.922500 -106.081800
Provincial Park & Rec. Areas			
Blackstrap Prov. Park	166	A2	51.755600 -106.458300
Buffalo Pound Prov. Park	166	B3	50.576200 -105.361000
Candle Lake Prov. Park	160	B4	53.845000 -105.252000
Cannington Manor Prov. Hist. Park	166	C4	49.712900 -102.027300
Clearwater River Prov. Park	159	E1	56.929300 -109.043000
Crooked Lake Prov. Park	166	C3	50.592200 -102.741400
Cumberland House Prov. Hist. Park	160	C4	53.948000 -102.421400
Cypress Hills Interprovincial Park	165	E4	49.632400 -109.809000
Danielson Prov. Park	166	A2	51.252200 -106.866000
Douglas Prov. Park	166	A3	51.025300 -106.480000
Echo Valley Prov. Park	166	B3	50.808500 -103.891900
Fort Carlton Prov. Hist. Park	166	A1	52.867100 -106.542700
Fort Pitt Prov. Hist. Park	165	E1	53.577000 -109.806300
Good Spirit Lake Prov. Park	166	C2	51.543500 -102.707000
Greenwater Lake Prov. Park	166	C1	52.532000 -103.448000
Katepwa Point Prov. Park	166	B3	50.693165 -103.626025
Lac La Ronge Prov. Park	160	C3	55.249200 -104.769000
Last Mtn. House Prov. Hist. Park	166	B3	50.722800 -104.823300
Makwa Lake Prov. Park	159	E3	54.016800 -109.234000
Meadow Lake Prov. Park	159	E3	54.501400 -109.076000
Moose Mtn. Prov. Park	166	C4	49.821300 -102.424000
Narrow Hills Prov. Park	160	C3	54.091300 -104.643000
Pike Lake Prov. Park	166	A2	51.893200 -106.819000
Rowan's Ravine Prov. Park	166	B3	50.995600 -105.179700
Saint Victor Petroglyphs Prov. Hist. Park	166	A4	49.395300 -105.873200
Saskatchewan Landing Prov. Park	165	F3	50.664600 -107.997000
Steele Narrows Prov. Hist. Park	159	E3	54.025900 -109.318400
The Battlefords Prov. Park	165	E1	53.132500 -108.381300
Touchwood Hills Prov. Hist. Park	166	B2	51.306400 -104.014100
Wood Mtn. Post Prov. Hist. Park	166	A4	49.320833 -106.379167

YUKON	PAGE	GRID	LATITUDE LONGITUDE
National Park & Rec. Areas			
Dawson Hist. Complex N.H.S.	155	D2	64.050000 -139.433330
Ivvavik Natl. Park	155	D1	69.519722 -139.525000
Kluane Natl. Park and Res.-North Vis. Ctr.	155	D3	60.991800 -138.520800
Kluane Natl. Park and Res.-South Vis. Ctr.	155	D3	60.752900 -137.510100
Vuntut Natl. Park	155	D1	68.306944 -140.047500
Provincial Park & Rec. Areas			
Herschel Island Territorial Park	155	D1	69.592100 -139.092400

The Latest Wiper Blade Technology!*

All-Season Performance
Frameless design does not
collect snow, ice and debris

Maximum Contact
Contoured flexors distribute
arm pressure evenly along
the entire blade

Longer Blade Life
Advanced rubber technology adds
durability to the wiping element

Fast, Easy Installation
EZ-LOK Connector System™
replaces original equipment and
upgrades/replaces conventional blades

Satisfaction Guaranteed
Superior streak-free wipe

When Was The Last Time You Changed Your Wiper Blades?

Change Your Wiper Blades Today and Help Keep Your Family MICHELIN Safe

A better way forward

Get 25% Off
Plus Free Shipping!

NEW!
NO GUESSWORK
NO SPARKING
NO SHORTING

MICHELIN

SMART
Jumper Cables*

Safer and easier to use than ordinary jumper cables

No guesswork – green indicator lights confirm correct connections

No sparking or shorting when you attach clamps – polarity is adjusted automatically

Built-in surge protector prevents damage to vehicle computer and electronics

1. Go to www.jumperoffer.com
2. Follow the online ordering instructions
3. During checkout, enter the promotion code **OFFER** and receive **25%** off your order, **plus** get free shipping

SMART Jumper Cables™ Help Keep Your Family MICHELIN Safe

This offer is available from 6/01/09 through 12/31/09

* MICHELIN - licensed product

MICHELIN
A better way forward

More miles.
More fuel efficiency.
More than what you pay for.

There are a lot of reasons to choose the
MICHELIN® HydroEdge® Tire. See for yourself:

STOPPING DISTANCE	LONGEVITY	FUEL EFFICIENCY
14' SHORTER[1]	**33,000** MILES LONGER[2]	**#1** IN CATEGORY[3]

We all want more, especially in these times. Good thing the MICHELIN
HydroEdge Tire has great fuel efficiency, and lasts longer[2] than its primary
competitor and is backed with a 90,000 mile warranty.[4] And if that's not
enough, the MICHELIN HydroEdge Tire stops up to a full car length shorter
in wet weather.[1] With a tire that gives you so much more, you have to ask
yourself, why settle for less?

Learn more at **michelinman.com**